The Student's Law-Dictionary: Or, Compleat English Law-Expositor

340.03/STU

Nabu Public Domain Reprints:

You are holding a reproduction of an original work published before 1923 that is in the public domain in the United States of America, and possibly other countries. You may freely copy and distribute this work as no entity (individual or corporate) has a copyright on the body of the work. This book may contain prior copyright references, and library stamps (as most of these works were scanned from library copies). These have been scanned and retained as part of the historical artifact.

This book may have occasional imperfections such as missing or blurred pages, poor pictures, errant marks, etc. that were either part of the original artifact, or were introduced by the scanning process. We believe this work is culturally important, and despite the imperfections, have elected to bring it back into print as part of our continuing commitment to the preservation of printed works worldwide. We appreciate your understanding of the imperfections in the preservation process, and hope you enjoy this valuable book.

THE
Student's Law-Dictionary;
OR
Compleat ENGLISH Law-Expositor;

Containing

An Explanation of every particular Word and Term used in the Law, with an Introduction to the Knowledge of the Law itself, and the present Practice thereof:

Compiled for the Instruction and Benefit of Students, Practitioners in the Law, Justices of the Peace, the Clergy and other Gentlemen.

The Whole collected from the best Dictionaries, and other Authorities hitherto published.

Whereto is added An Alphabetical Table of the most usual *Latin* Contractions that are to be found in our ancient Records, &c.

Originally compiled by an Attorney at Law, and since carefully revised and corrected by a BARRISTER.

In the SAVOY:

Printed by E. and R. NUTT, and R. GOSLING, (Assigns of *Edward Sayer*, Esq;) for JAMES HODGES at the *Looking-Glass* on *London-Bridge*.
MDCCXL.

(*In the Prefs and speedily will be publish'd*)

THE
RULES of PRACTICE
Common-plac'd;
𝕸𝖎𝖙𝖍 𝕽𝖊𝖒𝖆𝖗𝖐𝖘.

PART I. Containing

The present Practice of the Court of *King's Bench.*

PART II. Containing

The present Practice of the Court of *Common Pleas* at *Westminster.*

Exhibited in a View of the *Ancient* and *Modern* RULES and ORDERS of the said COURTS.

By an ATTORNEY at Law.

THE
PREFACE.

TO those who are unacquainted with the ancient Writers of the Law, an Alphabetical Dictionary must needs be useful to explain the Acceptation and different Uses of the Terms, as also their Etymology, whether French, Saxon or Latin of the lower Ages; but without much Nicety of Definition, or tedious Quotations from all the Law-Reports.

WE know, the Old Terms of the Law compiled by J. Rastall in 1527. was esteemed of some Authority before it came to be
en-

The PREFACE.

enlarged *: *Nor have the late Additions mended it in that Respect; so that considering the enormous Bulk and Price of our Law Dictionaries, we hope it may be thought proper to root up all the Weeds, and to preserve what is fittest for the Common Use of Students.*

AS the Records in Latin will be yet of Use for Consultation, though in Practice they are laid aside, we have made a Table of the chief Contractions that are found in our ancient Writings.

---

* *Vide* a MS. Discourse of Sir *Nic. Bacon* on the Succession of the Crown, *temp. Eliz.*

ERRATUM.

Tit. **Cons and Rep**, read **Coter and Rep**, as in some MS. Copies of *Bracton*.

A

A Compleat Law-Dictionary:

OR, THE

New English Law-Expositor.

AB

Abate, is said to be derived from a *French* Word, which signifies to break down or destroy; and, in our Law, *Abate* retains the like Signification; As to *abate a Castle or Fortlet*, which is interpreted to beat it down. See *Old Natura Brev. p. 45. Westm.* 1. c. 17. To *abate a House*, is to ruin or cast it down. *Kitch.* 173. Where a Person enters upon a House or Land, void by the last Possessor, before the Heir takes Possession, such Stranger is said to *abate*, as he that putteth him out, is said to *disseise*. To *abate a Writ*, is to defeat or overthrow it, on account of some Error or Exception. *Britton, c.* 48.

Abatement, is a Derivative from the *French*, and is used for the Act of the *Abator*: As the *Abatement* of the Heir into the Land before he hath agreed with the Lord. *Old Natura Brev.* 91. *Abatement* of a Writ or Plaint, is an Exception in our Law taken and made good, upon an Action brought, either in respect to the Insufficiency of the Matter, or the Uncertainty of what is alledged, or where the Plaintiff, Defendant, or Place is misnamed: An Exception may be likewise made to the Variance between the Writ and Specialty or Record; to the Uncertainty of the Writ, Count or Declaration, on account of the Death of the Plaintiff or Defendant before Judgment had; or where a Woman, being Plaintiff, is married before, or depending the Suit; and for divers other Causes: Upon these and such like Defaults, the Defendant may pray, that the Suit may *abate* or cease for that Time, which being granted, the Plaintiff is at Liberty to bring a new Writ or Plaint. A Party being twice charged for one Debt, is a sufficient Ground of *Abatement*; as where a Plaintiff has another Action depending in the Courts at *Westminster*, for the same Thing: But if such Action be in an inferior Court, that will not answer as a Cause of Abatement, unless Judgment be already given there. 5 *Rep.* 62. A Suit may likewise be abated, on account that the Writ of Debt precedes the Day of Payment. See more on the Head of *Abatement*, under the Titles of *Writ, Misnosmer* and *Variance*, in the *Abridgments*, and the Book called *The Digests of Writs*, where this Matter is fully handled.

Abator, is a Person that *abateth*, or enters upon the Possession of a
B   House

House or Land, void by the Decease of the former Possessor, before his Heir enters upon the same. *Old Nat. Brev.* 115.

Abbrochment, is derived from the *Latin*, and signifies a Forestalling of a Market or Fair, by buying up the Wares, before publickly exposed to Sale, and afterwards retailing them.

Abbuttals, (from a *French* Word signifying to limit or bound) are the Buttings and Boundings of Land, shewing on what other Lands, Rivers, &c. it doth *abut* or *bound*. The Sides on the Breadth of Lands, are properly term'd, *lying* or *bordering*, and the Ends in Length, *abutting* or *bounding*.

Abdicate, from the *Latin*, signifying to renounce or refuse a Thing. *Termes de la Ley*.

Abdication, (from the *Latin*) is a voluntary Act of Renunciation, or refusing of a Thing; a Term, that seems now a-days chiefly adapted to the Case of an unfortunate Prince, not long ago among us.

Abet, (from a *Saxon* Verb) in our Law signifies to encourage or set on. *Abetment*, the Substantive, is used in the like Sense. *Staundf. Pl. Cr.* 105. An *Abettor* is the Instigator or Setter on; that is to say, he that promotes or procures a Crime to be committed. *Old Nat. Brev.* 21. *Abettors* of Murder are such as command, procure, or counsel others to commit it; and in some Cases those *Abettors* will be taken as Principals, tho' in others only as Accessaries, their Presence or Absence at the Time of committing the Fact making the Difference. *Co. Lit.* 475. See *Accessories*. There are also *Abettors* in Treason, but always accounted Principals, there being no *Accessories* in that Crime. See more in *Staunford's Pleas of the Crown*.

Abeyance, is supposed to come from a *French* Word, signifying to gape after, or to expect. It is a fix'd Principle of Law, that there is a Fee-simple of all Land in some Person, or else it is in *Abeyance*; that is to say, tho' at present it appears to be in no Man, yet, in Expectancy, it is belonging to him who is next to enjoy the Land. *Co. Lit.* 341. *c. Discontin.* If a Person makes a Lease for Life, the Remainder to the right Heirs of *A. B.* in that Case the Fee-simple is in *Abeyance* until the Death of *A. B.* when, and not before, his Heir has a good Remainder, and the Fee-simple then ceases to be in Abeyance. *Termes de la Ley* 6. Where a Person is presented by a Patron of a Church, the Fee of the Lands, &c. pertaining to the Rectory is in the Parson: But if he die, and the Church become void, then the Fee of those Lands is in *Abeyance*, until another Parson is presented, admitted and inducted; seeing that the Patron hath not the Fee, but only a Right to present, the Fee being in the Incumbent that is presented. *Termes de la Ley* 6.

Abishering is understood to be quit of Amerciaments. *Termes de la Ley* 7.

Abjuration, (from the *Latin*) is a Forswearing or Renouncing, and signifies a sworn Banishment, or an Oath taken to forsake the Realm for ever. *Staundf. Pl. Cr. lib.* 2. *c.* 40. This Word has also another Signification, extending to the Person of the Pretender, so called in this Kingdom; for by 1 *W. & M.* 13 *W.* 3. 1 *Geo.* 1. &c. all Persons by Oath are to abjure the pretended Prince of *Wales*;

Wales; and such as refuse to take that Oath are liable to divers Penalties and Forfeitures. See *Oaths*.

Abridge, (from the *French*) signifying to contract or make shorter in Words, yet still to retain the Substance: But in the Common Law it is more particularly applied to the making of a Declaration or Count shorter, by substracting or taking away some of the Substance from it. As for Instance, a Man is said to abridge his Plaint in Assise, or a Woman her Demand, in an Action of Dower, if any Land is put into the Plaint or Demand, which is not in the Tenure of the Tenant or Defendant; seeing that, should the Defendant plead Nontenure, Joint-tenancy, &c. in Abatement of the Writ, the Demandant may abridge his Plaint, by leaving out those Lands, and pray that the Tenant may answer to the rest, to which he hath not yet pleaded; and the Cause of this is, for that the Certainty is not set down, but runs in general in such Writs: And tho' the Demandant hath abridg'd his Plaint in part, yet the Writ remains good still as to the rest. *Bro. Abridg. Anno* 21 *H.* 8. *c.* 3.

Abridgment. See **Abridge**.

Abrogate, (from the *Latin*) to disannul or take away; for Example, to abrogate a Law, is to set aside or repeal it. 5 & 6 *Ed.* 6. *c.* 3.

Absque hoc, are Words, which before the late Alteration in the Proceedings in the Law (requiring all Processes and Pleadings to be in *English*) were made Use of in a Traverse; as where the Defendant pleads, that such a Thing was done at C. *Absque hoc*, that is to say, without that, it was done at D. *Mod. Ca.* 103.

Accedas ad curiam, is a Writ where one has received, or fears false Judgment in a Hundred-Court, or Court-Baron. It is issued out of Chancery, and directed to the Sheriff, but returnable in the King's Bench, or Common Pleas, and is near the Nature of the Writ of False Judgment, which lies for him that has received such in the County-Court. This Writ lies as well for Justice delayed, as false Judgment given, and is of the Nature of a *Recordare*, seeing that the Sheriff is obliged to make Record of the Suit in the inferior Court, and certify it into the King's Court. *Reg. Orig.* 9. 56. *F. N. B.* 18. *Dyer* 169.

Accedas ad vicecomitem, is a Writ directed to the Coroner, commanding him to deliver a Writ to the Sheriff, who having a *Pone* delivered, suppresses it. *Reg. Orig.* 83.

Acceptance, is the taking and receiving in good Part, and as it were tacitly agreeing to some Act before done by another, which might have been altogether avoided by the Person accepting, in case the Acceptance had not been: As for Example, If a Husband and Wife seised of Lands in Right of his Wife, join in making a Lease or Feoffment, reserving Rent, and the Husband dies; after which the Widow receives or accepts the Rent: By this the Lease or Feoffment is confirmed, and shall bar her from bringing a *Cui in vita*. *Co. Lit.* 211. If a Tenant for Life grants a Lease for Years, not warranted by the *Statute* 32 *H.* 8. and dies, if the Issue accepts the Rent reserved by that Lease, such Acceptance will bind him. 3 *Leon. Case* 36. If an Infant accepts of Rent at his full Age, it makes the Lease good, and shall bind him. If a Lessor accepts from his Tenant tant or Lessee the last Rent due, and gives him a Discharge for the same, all Rent in Arrear is by Law presumed to be satisfied. *Co. Lit.* 373. *Acceptance* of the Rent that becomes next due after what is in Arrear, bars the Lessor from entring for a Condition broken, on account of Non-payment of the Rent reserved in the Lease, because the Lessor thereby affirms the Lease to have Continuance. *Co. Lit.* 211. A Distress made for Rent likewise affirms the Continuance of the Lease.

Accessory or **Accessary**, at Common Law, is where a Person is guilty of some felonious Offence, tho' not principally concerned, but is a Partaker in the Crime, as by commanding, advising, concealing, &c. A Man may be *accessory* to an Offence two Ways, *viz. before the Fact*, or after it. An *Accessory* before the Fact, is he that commands another to commit Felony, and is not present at the Time it is doing; for his Presence makes him a *Principal*: And therefore there cannot be an *Accessory* before the Fact in *Manslaughter*; for this Reason, that *Manslaughter* is sudden, and not premeditated. *Co. Lit. fol.* 44. An *Accessory* after the Fact, is one that receives, assists, or comforts another, whom he knows to have committed Felony or Murder. He that counsels or commands an Evil, shall be judged *accessory* to all the Consequences that attend it, but not to another distinct Thing: As for Instance, in case a Person commands another to beat a third Person, and the Commanded beats him, so that he dies, the Person commanding shall be *accessory* to the Murder: But it is otherwise in the Case, where a Person orders another to steal a White Horse, and he steals a Black one; or to burn such a House, well known to the Commanded, and he burns another. In these two Cases the Commander shall not be deemed an *Accessory*. Where the *Principal* is pardoned, or has his Clergy, the *Accessory* cannot be arraign'd; it being a Maxim in our Law, that where there is no *Principal*, there can be no *Accessory*: And why? Because it does not appear by the Judgment of Law, that there was a Principal: Yet if the *Principal* after Attainder be pardoned, in that Case the *Accessory* may be arraign'd. 4 *Rep.* 43. By the *Statute* 1 *Ann.* c. 9. where the *Principal* is convicted of Felony, stands mute, or challenges above twenty of the Jury, the *Accessory* is liable to be proceeded against in the same Manner, as if the Principal had been attainted; notwithstanding such *Principal* shall be allowed his Clergy, pardoned, or delivered before Attainder. And by the same Statute, if the *Principal* cannot be taken, the *Accessory* may be prosecuted for a Misdemeanor, and punished by Fine, Imprisonment, &c. See likewise *Stat.* 5 *Ann.* c. 31. In the lowest Offences, such as Riots, forcible Entries, and other the like Transgressions by *Force and Arms*, as well as in the highest, *viz. Treason*, there are no *Accessories*; for all are *Principals*. *Accessory* by Statute, is he that abets, counsels, or conceals the committing, or the having committed of Felony, made so by Act of Parliament; for tho' the Act makes no Mention of Abettors, yet by Interpretation they become included. See *Stuandf. Pl. Cor. lib.* 1. c. 45, 46, 47, 48. There is likewise an *Accessory* of an *Accessory*; that is, to say, he that wittingly receives an Accessory to a Felony: But a Woman with receiving or assisting her Husband, who is an *Accessory*, shall not be deemed one; tho' the Husband in the like Case receiving his Wife, will be deemed *Accessory*. *H. P. Cor.* 218. 3 *Inst.* 108. If a Man counsels a Woman to murder the Child she is pregnant with, and the Woman murders it after it is born, such Man is accessory to that Murder, by his counselling before the Birth of the Infant, and not countermanding it. *Dyer* 186.

Accompt, is a Writ or Action that lies against a Person, who, by Reason of Office or Business undertaken, is to render an *Accompt* to another, but refuses to do it; as a Bailiff or Receiver to a Lord or others. See *Fitz. Nat. Brev. fol.* 116. By the Statute of *Westm.* 2. If an *Accomptant* be found in Arrear, the Auditors assigned are empowered to award him to Prison, there to remain till Agreement be made with the Party: But if the Accomptant be not allowed his reasonable Expences and Costs, or be charged with more Receipts than he ought, he may, by his next Friend, sue out a Writ of *Ex parte talis* (that is to say) *on the Part or Behalf of such a One*, directed to the Sheriff to take four Mainpernors, to bring his Body before the Barons of Exchequer at a certain Day, and to warn the Lord or Master to appear there the same Day. If a Person, tho' neither appointed Bailiff nor Receiver, receives Money for another's Use, an Action of *Accompt* lies against him: Also, where a Man delivers Money to be delivered over to a third Person, the Receiver thereof will be liable to account. The usual Pleas in this Action are, that *he never was Receiver*; that *he hath fully accounted*. This Action is now almost gone into Disuse, there being no Damages given by it; for the Judgment is only that he do *accompt*, on which the Defendant becomes liable to be taken on a *Capias ad computandum*, (that is to say) take to *Accompt*. There are two Judgments on this Writ; as where the Defendant cannot avoid the Suit by Plea, Judgment is first given, *That he do accompt*, which having done before the Auditors, the second Judgment is entered, *viz. That the Plaintiff shall recover of the Defendant so much as is found in Arrears*. 11 Rep. 40. The Process on this Action is, *Summons*, *Pone*, and *Distress*; and upon a *Nihil*, viz. *Nothing* returned, the Plaintiff may proceed to *Outlawry*. The Statute of Limitations, 21 *Jac.* 1. does not debar a Merchant from bringing Action of *Accompt* for Merchandize, at any Time; yet all other Actions of Accompt are within that Statute.

Accord, (from the *French*) is an Agreement between two or more, where any one is injur'd by Trespass, or other Offence committed, to make Satisfaction or Recompence to the Person injured, who after the Accord performed, is entirely barred in Law from any new Action against the Agressor for the same Trespass. *Termes de la Ley* 14. *Accord* executed is pleadable in Bar; but executory is not. 1 *Mod.* 69. In Pleading, it is safest to alledge Satisfaction, and not *Accord* alone; if it be chiefly pleaded by Way of *Accord*, a precise Execution in every Part thereof must be pleaded: But if Satisfaction be pleaded, the Defendant need only to alledge, that he paid the Plaintiff such a Sum, *&c.* in full Satisfaction of the Accord, which he received. 9 *Rep.* 80. When no certain

certain Duty is created by Deed, but the Action is for Wrong or Default, &c. for which Damages are recoverable, there an *Accord* with Satisfaction is a good Plea: But where a Duty accrues by Deed, as by Bill, Bond, or Covenant, for Payment of Money, that Duty arising by Deed, ought to be discharged by Matter of as high a Nature. 6 *Rep.* 43.

Accroche (from the *French*) signifying to fix Hook or Graple unto: In the the Statute 25 *Ed.* 3. c. 8. this Word signifies as much as to encroach, and is there used to that Purpose.

Accusation (from the *Latin*) signifies to charge a Person with some Crime. By *Magna Charta*, viz. 9 *H.* 3. no Man shall be imprisoned or condemned on any *Accusation*, without Trial by his Peers or the Law of the Land. By 25 and 28 *Ed.* 3. None shall be vexed upon any *Accusation*, but according to the Law of the Land: And no Man may be molested by a Petition to the King, unless it be by Indictment or Presentment of lawful Men, or by Process at Common Law. By 38 *Ed.* 3. Promoters of Suggestions are to find Surety to pursue them, and not making the same good, are to satisfy Damages to the *accused* Party, and to pay a Fine to the King. By 5 & 6 *Ed.* 6. there must be two lawful *Accusers* in Treason. None is obliged to answer on Oath to a Matter whereby he may accuse himself of a Crime. 2 *Mod. Rep.* 278.

Acephali, so called in the Laws of *Hen.* 1. they being the Levellers of that Age, and acknowledging no Head or Superior.

Ac etiam, is a short Clause of a Writ, where the Action requires good Bail; and is by 13 *C.* 2, *c.* 2, enjoined to be inserted in Writs where special Bail is required: But it ought not to be inserted, where the Action is against a Peer, or upon a Penal Statute, or against an Executor or Administrator, or for any Debt under 10 *l.* nor in any Action of Account, Covenant, &c. unless the Damages are 10*l.* or more. Nor in Trespass, Battery, Wounding or Imprisonment, except there be an Order of Court for it, or a Warrant under the Hand of one of the Judges of the Court, from whence the Writ is issued. 1 *Lill. Abr.* 13.

Achat (from the *French*) is said to signify a Contract or Bargain, *Brook*, Tit. Contract; from whence it is supposed, that Purveyors in 36 *Ed.* 3. were called *Achators*, because of their frequent making of Bargains.

Acknowledgment Money, is what is paid in some Parts of *England* by Tenants, on the Death of their Lord or Landlord, as an Acknowledgment to the new one; and is paid in such Manner as Money usually is on the Attornment of Tenants.

Acquietantia de Shiris & Hundredis, is to be free from Suits and Services in Shires and Hundreds.

Acquietandis Plegiis, is a Writ of *Justicies* which lies for a Surety against a Creditor, who refuses to acquit the Debtor after the Debt is paid. *Reg. of Writs* 158.

Acquittal (both from the *French* and *Latin*) to free or discharge, signifies in Law, to be free from Entries and Molestations of a superior Lord, on account of Services issuing out of Lands held. In a general Sense it signifies a Deliverance, or setting free from the Suspicion of Guilt; as one that is discharged of Felony, is said to be be *acquitted* thereof; and if he be called in Question again for the same Crime, he may plead, *auter fois acquit*, (that is to say) *that he was heretofore acquitted* of the same Felony, &c. For his Life shall not be put twice in Danger for the same Offence. Acquittal is twofold, viz. either in Law or in Fact. In Law it is where two Persons being indicted, the one as *Principal*, and the other as *Accessory*, the *Principal* being discharged, the Accessory of Consequence becomes *acquitted*. In Fact, it is where a Person, on a Verdict of the Jury, is found not Guilty. 2 *Inst.* 385. See *Staundf. Pl. Cor.* 168. But in Murder, if a Person is *acquitted* an Appeal lies against him. 3 *Inst.* 273. Where a Person is acquitted on a malicious Prosecution, he may sue for Damages, after a Copy of the Indictment and the Judge's Certificate is obtained: Yet it is usual for the Judges of Gaol-Delivery to deny a Copy of an *Acquittal* to the Person, against whom there was a propable Cause for a criminal Prosecution. *Carthew's Rep.* 421.

Acquittance (from the *Latin*) signifies a Release or Discharge in Writing of Money or other Thing due: As where a Person bound for Payment of Money on Bond, or Rent reserved on Lease, &c. and the Party, to whom the Money is due, on Receipt thereof, gives an Acknowledgment in Writing of the Payment: This becomes such a Discharge in Law, that he cannot recover the Money or other thing demanded again, provided the *Acquittance* be produced. *Termes de les Ley* 15 *Dyer* 6, 25, 51. An *Acquittance* is likewise a Discharge and Bar to Actions, &c. As, if one should acknowledge himself to be satisfied by Deed, it may be a good Plea in Bar, whether such Deed be received or not: But an *Acquittance* without Seal, is only an Evidence of Satisfaction, and not pleadable. 1 *Inst.* 52. By 3 & 4 *Ann. c.* 16. Where an Action is brought on a single Bill (that is to say, a Bill without a Penalty) and the Defendant has paid the Money, such Payment may be pleaded in Bar to the Action.

Acre (from the *German*) signifies a Parcel of Land that contains in Length forty Perches, and in Breadth four; and so in Proportion, either as to Breadth or Length. If a Man would erect a new Cottage, he must lay four Acres of Land to it, according to this Measure. 13 *Eliz. c.* 7. *Crompton*, in his *Jurisdiction of Courts, fol.* 222. agrees with this Measure, though he says, that, according to the different Customs of several Countries, the Perch differs, it being in most Places only sixteen Feet and a half, but in *Staffordshire*, twenty-four Feet, as has been formerly adjudged in Exchequer. By the Statute 24 *H.* 8. relating to the sowing of Flax, one Hundred and sixty Perches make an *Acre*, which is forty multiplied by four. With this Account agrees the Ordinance of measuring of Land, made 35 *Ed.* 1.

Action (from the *Latin*) is a legal Demand of a Man's Right, or the Form of a Suit given by Law for the Recovery of a Person's Due. 1 *Inst.* 285. *Bracton* briefly defines it thus, viz. An Action is nothing else than a Right of prosecuting what is due to any one. *Actions* in general may be divided into two Parts, *Criminal* or *Civil*; *Criminal*, to have Judgment of

Death,

Death, as in Appeals of Death, Robbery, &c. or only Judgment for Damage to the Party, Fine to the King and Imprisonment. 1 *Inst.* 284. 2 *Inst.* 40. Under the Head of *Criminal* may be rank'd these following, *viz.*

1. **Actions penal**, which lie for some Penalty or Punishment in the Party sued, whether it be corporal or pecuniary. *Bract.* 2*dly*, *Actions upon the Statute*, brought on Breach of any Statute, by which an Action is given that did not lie before; as where a Person commits Perjury to the Prejudice of another, the injured Party shall have an Action upon the Statute. 3*dly*, *Actions Popular*, given on the Breach of some penal Statute, which every Person has a Right to sue for, on behalf of himself and the Crown, by Information, &c. And the Reason this *Action* is called *Popular* is, that it is not given to one Person in particular, but in general to any that will prosecute for the Penalty or Forfeiture. *Actions Civil*, are divided into *Real*, *Personal* and *Mixt*. *Action Real* is that whereby a Person claims Title to Lands, &c. in Fee, or for Life: And this Action is either Possessory or Auncestrel; Possessory, where the Lands, &c. are of a Person's own Possession and Seisin; Auncestrel, where they were of the Possession and Seisin of his Ancestor. *Action Personal* is what one brings against another, upon a Contract for Money or Goods, or on account of Trespass or other Offence committed; whereby the Debt, Goods, and Chattels, &c. or Damages, is claimed. *Action mixt* lies as well for the Thing demanded, as against him that has it; on which *Action* the Thing becomes recovered, with Damages for the unjust Detention: Yet *Detinue* is held not to be an *Action mixt*, though the Thing demanded and Damages for Detention be recovered; it being only brought for Goods and Chattels, and therefore can be deemed no more than an *Action Personal*. Since the Statute of Limitations, 21 *Jac.* 1. all Actions seem to be temporary, or at least not so perpetual, but that they may by Length of Time be prescribed against: As a *Real Action* may be prescribed against within five Years after a Fine levied, or Recovery suffered. Writs of Formedon for Title to Lands in Being, are to be sued out within twenty Years: *Actions* of Debt, Account, Detinue, Trover and Trespass, are to be brought within six Years; of Assault and Battery within four; and Slander within two: Nevertheless, the Right of Action in these Cases, is saved to Infants, Feme Coverts, Persons beyond the Seas, &c. *See* 21 *Jac.* 1. On a fresh Promise the Time limited may be enlarged; also a filing of a Writ within the Time, is a good bringing of an *Action* to avoid the Statute of Limitations. 1 *Lill.* 19.

Action upon the Case, is a general Action that is given for Redress of Wrongs or Injuries done without Force against another, and which by Law are not provided against: And in these *Actions*, the like Process is to be had as in *Actions* of Debt or Trespass. 19 *H.* 7. *c.* 9. If a Man's Fire by Misfortune burn the Goods of another; for this Injury the Sufferer shall have *Action on the Case* against him: And in Case a Servant puts a lighted Candle or other Fire in any Part of his Master's House, which burns it and a Neighbour's House, *Action upon the Case* lies to the Neighbour against such Master. 1 *Darv.* 10. But see 6 *Ann.* & 10 *Ann. c.* 14. If one delivers Goods to a common Carrier, to be conveyed to a certain Place, and he loseth them, *Action upon the Case* lies against him: It is the same with respect to a common Hoyman or Lighterman, who conveys Goods by Water; but Goods in this Case, may be thrown over Board in a Tempest, to preserve the Passengers Lives in the Lighter, &c. and no *Action* lies for so doing. 2 *Bulstr.* 280. *Action upon the Case* likewise lies for Words spoken to the Injury of another's Reputation; or for Words spoken of a Person, which affect his Life, Office or Trade, or tend to his Loss of Preferment in Marriage or Service, or to his Disinheritance, or which occasion any particular Damage to the Person spoken of.

Action Prejudicial, otherwise *Preparatory* or *Principal*, is what arises from some Doubt in the Principal; as where one sues his younger Brother for Lands descended from the Father, on which it is objected that he is a Bastard: In this Case the Point of Bastardy is to be first tried before the Cause can further proceed: And on this Account it is termed *prejudicial*, because it is first to be judged or determined. *Bract. Lib.* iii. *c.* 4.

Action of a Writ, is where a Person pleads some Matter whereby is shewn, that the Plaintiff had no Cause to have the Writ brought, though perhaps he may be entitled to another Writ for the same Matter. It is likewise called a Plea to the *Action of the Writ*, to distinguish it from a *Plea to the Action*, viz. where the Plaintiff has no Cause of *Action* for the thing demanded. *Termes de la Ley* 17.

Acton Burnel, is the Statute 13 *Ed.* 1. so called from the Place where it was made, *viz. Acton Burnel*, a Castle in *Shropshire*, anciently belonging to the Family of the *Burnels*, but afterwards of the *Lovels*.

Acts Done, may be distinguished into *Acts of God*, *Acts of Law*, and *Acts of Men*. Where the Law prescribes a Means for perfecting or settling an Estate or Right, if by the Act of God this Means in any Circumstance become impossible, no Damage shall accrue to any Party thereby. *Co. Lit.* 123. 1 *Rep.* 97. The *Acts of Law* are esteemed beyond those of Men: And when to the perfecting of a Thing, different Acts are required, the Law has most Regard to the Original *Act*. 8 *Rep.* 78. Whatsoever is contrary to Law is accounted not done. 1 *Inst.* 42. 3 *Rep.* 74. The Law favours Substantial more than Circumstantial *Acts*, and regards *Acts* and Deeds more than Words: It doth not require unnecessary Things. *Plowd.* 10. As to *Acts of Men*; whatsoever one Person does by another, is said to be done by himself: Yet personal Things cannot be done by another. *Co. Lit.* 158. Every Man's Act shall be most strongly construed against himself that does it. *Plowd.* 140.

Acts of Parliament, are positive Laws consisting of two Parts, *viz.* 1. The Words of the *Act*. 2. The Sense and Meaning of them, which joined together make the Law.

Actuary, is the Clerk that registers the Acts and Constitutions of the Convocation.

Addition, in our Law signifies a Title given to a Person besides his Christian and Surname, shewing his Estate, Degree, Trade, Place of Abode, &c. *Additions* of Estate are *Yeoman, Gentleman, Esquire*, &c. Additions of Degree are *Knight, Baronet, Earl, Marquess, Duke*. *Additions* of Trade are *Merchant, Grocer, Smith*, or other Occupation whereby a Person gets his Living: *Addition* of Place, as *London, Bristol, Winchester*, &c. These *Additions* were ordained, to prevent one Man's being grieved or molested in the Room of another; and that every Person might be certainly known, so as to bear his own Burden. An Earl of *Ireland* is no *Addition* of Honour here in *England*; and therefore such Person must be written by his Christian and Surname, with the *Addition* of *Esquire* only. The *Addition* to the Christian and Surname of an *English* Nobleman, tho' he has the Title of Nobility given him in respect to his Family, is that of *Esquire*; as such a one *Esquire, commonly called Lord A.* &c. 2 *Inst.* 596, 666. By 1 *H.* 5. *c.* 5. it is ordained, that in Suits or Actions where Process of Outlawry lies, *Additions* shall be made to the Name of the Defendant, to shew his Estate, &c. And that Writs without such Additions shall abate, if the Defendant take Exceptions thereto. By pleading to Issue the Defendant passes by the Advantage of Exception for Want of *Addition*; since by the Common Law it is good without *Addition*. Cro. *Jac.* 610. 1 *Roll.* 780. If a City or Town be a County of itself, and has several Parishes in it, the bare *Addition* of such City, &c. as of *London*, is sufficient. But in the *Addition* of a Parish, not in a City, &c. the County must be mentioned, otherwise it will not be good. 1 *Dan.* 237.

Ad Inquirendum, is a *Judicial* Writ, commanding Enquiry to be made of any Thing relating to a Cause depending in the King's Courts for the better Execution of Justice; of which you may see a great Diversity in *Reg. Judic.*

Adjournment, (both from the *Latin* and *French*) signifies a putting off until another Day, or to another Place. So *Adjournment in Eyre*, by 25 *Ed.* 3. signifies an Appointment of a Day, when the Justices in *Eyre* will sit again. A Court of Law, the Parliament, and Writs, &c. may be *adjourned*. The Substance of *Adjournment* of Courts, is to give License to all Parties, having any Thing to do before the Court, to forbear their Attendance, until a certain Time. The last Day of every Term, and every Eve of a Day in Term, that is not *Dies Juridicus*, viz. a Law-Day, the Courts are *adjourned*; and that is usually done two several Times, sitting the Courts. 2 *Inst.* 26. The Term may be also *adjourned* to another Place, and there the Courts at *Westminster* be held. The King's Proclamation for the *Adjournment* of a Term, is a sufficient Warrant to the Keeper of the Great Seal to make out Writs accordingly; and Proclamation must be made, appointing all Persons to keep their Time and Place, to which &c. 1 *And.* 279. 1 *Lev.* 176. If the Judges of the *King's Bench*, &c. are divided in Opinion two against two, upon a Demurrer or special Verdict, the Cause must be adjourned into the *Exchequer Chamber*, there to be determined by all the Judges of *England*. 3 *Mod.* 156. 5 *Mod.* 335.

Adjudication, is the pronouncing by Judgment a Sentence or Decree. See 16 & 17 *Car.* 2. *c.* 10.

Adjure

Adjurn Regis, is a Writ brought by the King's Clerk, who is presented to a Living, against such as endeavour to eject him, to the Prejudice of the King's Title. *Reg. of Writs* 61.

Adlegiance, (from the *French*) is to purge one's Self by Oath of a Crime. This Word is to be found in the Laws of King *Alfred*, in *Brompt. Chron. cap.* 4.

Admeasurement, (from the *Latin*) is a Writ brought against such as usurp more than their Share, in order to bring them to Reason. This Writ lies in two Cases; and the one is termed *Admeasurement of Dower;* which is, where a Man's Widow after his Death holds from the Heir more Land, &c. as her Dower, than of Right belongs to her: And the other is *Admeasurement of Pasture* (that is to say) that which lies between those that have Common of Pasture appendant to their Freehold, or Common by Vicinage, where one or more of them surcharge the Common. *Reg. Orig.* 156, 171. In the first of these Cases, the Heir shall have this Writ against the Widow, whereby she shall be *admeasured*, and the Heir restored to the Overplus; and in the last of these, it may be brought against all the other Commoners, as well as him that surcharged; for all the Commoners shall be *admeasured. Termes de la Ley* 23. If the Widow after Assignment of Dower improves the Land, so as to make it better than it was at the Time of the Assignment made, an *Admeasurement* of that Improvement does not lie. *Nat. Brev.* 332. In case the Lord surcharge the Common, his Tenant cannot have this Writ against him, but an Assise of Common lies against the Lord for such Surcharge. 18 *Ed.* 2.

c. 20. As this Writ does not lie against the Lord, so neither does it for the Lord; yet the Lord may distrain such Cattle of the Tenant as are Surplusage.

Adminicle, signifies Aid, Help or Support, and is used to that Purpose in the *Statute, Ed.* 4. *c.* 1.

Administrator, (a *Latin* Word, is he who has the Goods of a Man dying *intestate* committed to his Charge, for which he is to be accountable when required. The Bishop of the Diocese where the Intestate dies is regularly to grant *Administration:* But when the Intestate has Goods in several Dioceses, which are *Bona notabilia*, *Administration* must be granted by the Archbishop in the Prerogative Court, otherwise it will be void. 1 *Plowd.* 281. Where a Person dies without Issue or Kindred, Administration may be granted by Letters Patent; but, in that Case, the *Administrator* ought to be admitted by the Ordinary. 1 *Salk.* 37. To whom *Administration* is grantable, see *Wood's Inst.* 333. By *Stat.* 22 & 23 *Car.* 2. *c.* 10. on granting *Administrations*, Bonds with Sureties are to be taken for the Administrator to make and exhibit an Inventory of the Deceas'd's Goods, render a just Account thereof, and, after Debts paid, to make a Distribution of the Surplusage according to Law, &c. Distribution of a personal Estate, is to be equally made between the whole Blood and Half Blood. 2 *Lev.* 173. If an Infant is intitled to Administration, the Administration may be granted to another *durante minori ætate*, till he arrives to the Age of 21 Years: But if an Infant is made Executor, such Administration granted *during his Minority* ceases at his coming to the Age of 17. 1 *Salk.* 39.

An *Administrator durante minori ætate* cannot sell the Deceased's Goods, unless upon the Necessity of Payment of Debts, or where the Goods are perishable. 5 *Rep.* 29.

Administration cum Testamento annexo, is where an Executor refuses to prove a Will or Testament; and on that Account *Administration with the Will annexed* to it is granted to the next of Kin, &c. And if an Executor dies before Probate of the Will, *Administration* is to be granted with the *Will annexed*; and the Testator, in that Case, is look'd upon in Law to die intestate. 1 *Inst.* 113.

Administratrix, (*Latin*) is she that has the Goods and Chattels of the Intestate committed to her Charge in the like Manner as an *Administrator*.

Admiral, (from the *Latin*) signifies a high Officer or Magistrate, who has the Government of the King's Navy, and the determining of all Causes, both civil and criminal, belonging to the Sea. Of late Years this high Office has been generally executed by Commissioners, who, by 2 *W. & M. c.* 2. are empowered to use and execute the like Authorities as Lord *Admiral*. The *Admiralty* holds Cognizance of the Death or Maim of a Person committed in any Ship or Vessel riding in great Rivers, beneath the Bridges thereof, next the Sea: Yet by the Common Law, if one be killed upon an Arm of the Sea, where Land can be seen on both Sides, the Coroner is to make Enquiry into it, and not the *Admiral*, seeing that the County may take Cognizance of it; and where a County may inquire, the Lord Admiral can have no Jurisdiction. 3 *Rep.* 107. All Ports and Havens are within the Body of the County, so that the Admiral cannot have Jurisdiction of any Thing done in them. Between the high and low Water Mark, the Common Law and Admiral have Jurisdiction by Turns; the one upon the Water, and the other on the Land. 3 *Inst.* 113 Admiralty Process issues in the Name of the *Admiral*; and the usual Proceedings are according to the Civil Law, and the Maritime Laws of *Oleron*, and other Maritime Laws. But by 28 *H.* 8. Murder, Robbery, &c. by Sea, may be tried by special Commission to the Lord *Admiral*, &c. according to the Laws of *England*. See 11 & 12 *W.* 3. *c.* 7. The *Admiralty* has Jurisdiction where the Common Law can afford no Remedy; and all Maritime Causes, or such as arise wholly upon the Sea, that Court has Cognizance of. 6 *Rep.* It likewise has Jurisdiction in Matters of Freight, Mariners Wages, or Breach of Charter-parties, tho' made within the Kingdom, provided the Penalty be not demanded: As also in the Case of Building, Mending, Saving, and Victualling of Ships, &c. so as the Suit be against the Ship, and not solely against the Parties. 2 *Cro.* 216.

Admission, (from the *Latin*) is where a Patron of a Church having presented a Clerk to it, the Bishop upon Examination admits him as able, by saying, *Admitto te habilem*; tho' it is properly the Ordinary's Declaration that he approves of the Person presented, to serve the Cure of the Church to which he is presented. *Co. Litt.* 344.

Admittendo Clerico, is a Writ granted to the Person that has recovered his Right of Presentation against the Bishop in the Common Pleas.

Pleas. See *Fitz. Nat. Brev.* 38. and *Regist. Orig.* 33.

Admittendo in Socium, is a Writ for associating certain Persons to Justices of Assize appointed. *Reg. Orig.* 206.

Adnichiled, (from an old *Latin* Word) signifies annulled, cancelled, made void, or brought to nothing. See *Stat.* 28 *H.* 8. *c.* 7.

Ad quod damnum, is a Writ that ought to be issued before the King grants certain Liberties, as a Fair, Market, or the like, which by being granted, may be prejudicial to others; and therefore it seems convenient, that, before such Grant be made, it be enquired into by the Country, what Prejudice it is like to work either to the Grantor or others. See *Fitz. Nat. Brev.* 121. The Writ of *Ad quod damnum* also lies for the turning and changing of Highways, which must not be done without the King's License by this Writ obtained, on Inquisition returned, that such Change will not be detrimental to the Publick. *Vaugh. Rep.* 341. But see the *Stat.* 8 & 9 *W.* 3. *c.* 16. for enlarging of Highways by Order of Justices of the Peace, &c.

Adrectare, signifies to do Right, satisfy or make Amends. *Gerv. Dorobern. Anno* 1170.

Ad Terminum qui præteriit, is a Writ that lies for the Lessor and his Heirs, where a Lease has been made for a Term of Years, or Life; and after the Expiration of the Term, the Lands, &c. leased are withheld from the Lessor or his Heir, by the Tenant or other Occupier thereof. *Fitz. Nat. Brev.* 201.

Advent, (from the *Latin*) is a Time that contains about a Month preceding the Feast of the Nativity of our Saviour, commonly called *Christmas*. Great Reverence and Devotion was paid to this Time by our Ancestors, in regard to the Approach of that solemn Festival: For in *Advent* it was held, that no Assise ought to be taken. *Int. Placit. de Temp. Regis Johann. Ebor.* 126. But by *Stat. Westm.* 1. *c.* 48. it is ordained, that notwithstanding the said usual Solemnity, it should be lawful, in respect of Justice and Charity, which ought at all Times to be regarded, to take Assises of Novel Disseisin, &c. at the Time of *Advent, Septuagesima*, and *Lent*.

Ad ventrem inspiciendum, is a Writ mentioned in the *Statute* 12 *Ed.* 2. by which a Woman is to be searched whether she be with Child to a former Husband, on her withholding of Lands from the Heir. See *Ventre inspiciendo*.

Adventure, is a Thing sent by a Person to Sea, the *Adventure* of which the Sender stands to out and Home. *Lex Mercat.* See *Aventure*.

Advltery, *Anno* 1 *H.* 7. *c.* 4. and in other Authors termed *Advowtry*, is the Sin of Incontinence between two married Persons; tho' if but one of the Persons offending be married, it is still Adultery: But in this last Case it is called *single Adultery*, to distinguish it from the other. This Crime was in former Times severely punished both by the Laws of God and Man: But at this Time, in most Countries, the Punishment is Fine, and sometimes Banishment. In *England* it is punished by Fine, Penance, &c.

Advocate, is he who is a Patron of a Cause, assisting his Client not only with Advice, but on Occasion pleading for him. Both by the Civil and Ecclesiastical Laws it is the same as a Counsellor by the Common Law. *Advocati* were such as

we

we now call Patrons of Churches, and who reserved a Liberty to them and their Heirs to present a Person on any Avoidance. *Blount.*

Advocatione Decimarum, is a Writ that lies for the fourth Part or upwards of Tithes belonging to any Church. *Reg. Orig.* 29.

Advow or **Avow,** (from the *French*) signifies to justify or maintain some Act before done; as where one takes a Distress for Rent, and the Person distrained sues a Replevin, in which Case the Distrainer, justifying or maintaining the Act, is said to *advow* or *avow*: Hence comes Advowant and Avowry. *Old Nat. Brev.* 43.

Advowee, or **Avowee,** is used for the Person that has a Right to present to a Benefice. 25 *Ed.* 3. *Stat.* 5. where we find *Advowee Paramount,* taken for the highest Patron, *viz.* the King.

Advowson, is where a Person has Right to present a Clerk to a Church or Benefice. He that has the Right to present, is stiled *Patron*; because such as originally obtained the Right of Presentation of any Church, were Maintainers or Benefactors to that Church. *Advowsons* are either Appendant, or in Gross: Appendant is a Right of Presentation dependant upon a Manor, Lands, *&c.* and passes with the Manor, *&c.* as incident thereto: *Advowson in Gross,* is a Right of Presentation subsisting by itself, belonging to a Person, and not to a Manor, *&c.* Wherefore when an *Advowson* appendant is once severed by Grant or Deed from the corporeal Inheritance, to which before it was appendant, then it becomes an *Advowson* in Gross. 1 *Inst.* 121, 122.

Affeerers, (from the *French*) signifies to affirm. They are such Persons as in Court-Leets, upon Oath, settle and moderate the Fines and Amerciaments imposed on those that have committed Faults arbitrarily punishable; that is to say, such as have no express Penalty appointed by Statute against them. *Affeerers* are also appointed in Courts-Baron, for moderating of Amerciaments. Those that are nominated to this Office, are to affirm on Oath what Penalty they think ought to be inflicted on Offenders. This Word we find used *Stat.* 25 *Ed.* 3. *c.* 7. See the Form of the Oath in *Kitchin* 46.

Affiance (from the *Latin*) is the Plighting of Troth between a Man and a Woman on Agreement of Marriage. *Litt. Sect.* 39.

Affidavit, generally speaking, is an Oath taken in Writing, and sworn before some Person authorized to take the same. In an *Affidavit,* the Time, Place of Habitation, and Addition of the Person who makes it, are to be inserted. 1 *Lill. Abr.* 44, 46. *Affidavits* are chiefly used for certifying the serving of Process, or other Matters concerning the Proceedings in a Cause.

Affirm, (from the *Latin*) signifies to ratify or confirm some former Law or Judgment: And in the same Sense the Substantive *Affirmance* is used in the *Stat.* 8 *H.* 6. *c.* 12.

Affirmation, is an Indulgence by Law allowed to the People called *Quakers,* who, where an Oath is required from others, are allowed to make a solemn Affirmation, that what they say is true: And if they make a false one, they are subject to the Penalties of Perjury: But this Indulgence only relates to Oaths to the Government, and on publick Occasions; for Quakers cannot give Testimony in any criminal

Afforciament, a Fortress, strong Hold, or other Fortification. *Pryn. Animad.* on *Coke* 184.

Afforciare, to add, increase, or make strong. *Bract. lib.* 4. *c.* 19.

Afforest, is to turn Ground into Forest. *Charta de Forest, cap.* 1, & 30. *Anno* 9 *H.* 3. See *Forest*.

Affray, (from the *French*) formerly signified no more than to *affright*; as where Persons appeared with unusual Armour or Weapons, to the Terror of others. 2 *Ed.* 3. *c.* 3. But it now signifies a Skirmish or Fighting between two or more; and there must be a Stroke given or offered, or some Weapon drawn, or else it cannot be an Affray. 3 *Inst.* 158. It differs from Assault; for that it is a Wrong to the Public; whilst Assault is of a private Nature. *Lamb. lib.* 2.

Afreightment, signifies the Freight of a Ship. See *Charter-Party*.

Afri or **Afra**, signifies Bullocks, Horses, or Beasts of the Plough. *Westm.* 2. *c.* 18. The People in the County of *Northumberland* do to this Day call a dull, or slow Horse, a false *Aver*, or *Afer*. *Spelm. Gloss.*

Age, (from the *French*) in the Law is used for those particular Times wherein Persons of both Sexes are enabled to do certain Acts, which before, for Want of Years and Judgment, they are prohibited to do: As for Instance, a Man at twelve Years of *Age* ought to take the Oath of Allegiance in a Leet; at fourteen he may consent to Marriage, and chuse his Guardian; and at twenty-one he may alien his Lands, Goods, and Chattels. A Woman at nine is Dowable; at twelve may consent to Marriage; at fourteen she may chuse a Guardian; and at one and twenty may alienate her Lands, &c. 1 *Inst.* 78. The Age of twenty-one is the full Age that enables Man or Woman to contract and manage for themselves, either in respect to their Estates or otherwise, before which Time they cannot act with Security to such as deal with them, their Acts in most Cases being either void or voidable. *Perk.* Yet a Person under the Age of one and twenty may contract for Necessaries suitable to his Quality, and he shall be thereby bound: Likewise one under Age may be Executor of a Will. 1 *Inst.* 171.

Age-Prier, is where an Action being brought against a Person under Age for Lands descended to him, he, by Motion or Petition, shews the Matter to the Court, praying the Action may be staid till his full Age, which is generally agreed to by the Court: But a Minor or Infant shall not have his *Age-Prier*; nor shall have it in a Writ of Assize, nor in a Writ of Dower, nor of Partition. 3 *Ed.* 1. 38 *Ed.* 3. *Hob.* 342.

Agenhine, signifies a Guest at an Inn after three Nights, when he becomes accounted one of the Family. See *Hogenhine*.

Agent and Patient, is where a Person is the Doer of a Thing, as well as the Party to whom it is done: As in Case a Woman should endow herself of the best Part of her Husband's Possessions, she by this sole Act of her own becomes *Agent* and *Patient*: Likewise one being indebted to another, afterwards makes his Creditor Executor, and dies; the Executor may retain so much of the Goods of the deceased Testator, as may be sufficient to satisfy his Debt; and by this means he becomes *Agent* and *Patient*, *viz.* the Party to whom

whom the Debt is due, and the Person who pays it. Nevertheless, a Man shall not be Judge in his own Cause. 8 *Rep.* 138.

Agist, (from the *French*) in the Common Law signifies to take in and feed the Cattle of Strangers in the King's Forests, and gather in the Money due for the same. *Chart. de Forest.* 9 *H.* 3. *c.* 9. The Officers appointed for this End are called *Agisters*, or *Gist-Takers*, and are created by Letters Patent: And there are Four of them in all Forests where the King has any Pawnage. The Feed or Herbage of the Cattle is called *Agistment*, which, in a large Signification, extends to all Manner of Common, or Herbage of any Kind of Ground, Land or Woods, or to the Money due or received for the same, as well within Forests, as without them. See *Manw. Forest Laws* 80.

Agitatio animalium in Foresta, signifies the Drift of Beasts in a Forest. *Leg. Forest.*

Agnus Dei, is a Piece of white Wax of a flat Oval Form, stamped with the Figure of the Lamb, and consecrated by the Pope. *Agnus Dei, Crosses,* &c. are, by 13 *El. c.* 2. upon Pain of *Præmunire*, prohibited to be brought here into *England*.

Agreement. In *Plowd.* 17. it is made to signify the joining together of two or more Minds, in any Thing done or to be done. This *Agreement* consists of three Kinds; *First,* An Agreement already executed at the Beginning, as when Money is paid, or other Satisfaction made for the Thing agreed or bought. *Secondly,* An *Agreement* after an Act done by another, is where one Person does a Thing, and another *agrees* or assents to it afterwards, which is also executed. And, *Thirdly*, An *Agreement* executory, *viz.* to be executed or performed in Time to come; for which see 26 *H.* 8. *c.* 3. This last Sort of Agreement may be divided into two Parts; the one certain at the Beginning; and the other, where, without the Certainty appearing at first, the Parties agree, that that Uncertainty shall be performed upon the Certainty known: As where one sells to another all his Wheat lying in such a Part of his Barn unthreshed, at the Rate of 3 *s.* a Bushel, when it is threshed clean and measured. Every Agreement should be perfect, full and compleat, it being the mutual Consent of the Parties, and ought to be executed with a Recompence, or so certain, as to afford an Action or other Remedy thereon. *Plowd.* 5. Whatsoever Instrument is in Writing under Hand and Seal, and importing an Agreement, will amount to a Covenant; but it does not so, if put in Writing only by way of *Memorandum* or Remembrance: A *Proviso*, by way of *Agreement*, likewise amounts to a Covenant; and Action may be acordingly brought. 1 *Lev.* 155. See *Hob.* 79. By Stat. 29 *Car.* 2. *c.* 1. of *Frauds and Perjuries*, certain *Agreements* must be reduced into Writing, otherwise void. The Forms of Articles and Memorandums of *Agreement*, you may see in the *Young Clerk's Magazine*, and other Books of Precedents in Conveyancing.

Aid, (from the *French*) in general, is taken to signify a Subsidy granted to the Crown. By 34 *Ed.* 1. it is ordained, that the King shall levy no Aid or Tax without his Parliament.

Aid Prier, signifies to pray or crave Assistance; and is a Word used

used in Pleading, for a Petition to call in Help from another Person that has Interest in Land or other Thing contested: It gives Strength to him that prays in *Aid*, and to the other likewise, who thereby has an Opportunity given of avoiding a Prejudice, which might otherwise accrue to his own Right: As when a Tenant for Life, by Courtesy, in Dower, for Term of Years, &c. is impleaded, such may pray Aid of the Person in Reversion; that is to say, desire the Court that he may be called by Writ, to alledge what he thinks proper in Maintenance of the Right of the Person calling him, and that of his own. *Fitz. Nat. Brev.* 50. *Aid* is to be granted to the Defendant *in Ejectione firmæ*, in case the Title of the Land is in question: Likewise a Lessee for Years, and Tenants at Will shall have Aid in Trespass; but Tenant in Tail shall not have *Aid* of the Person in Remainder in Fee, seeing that he himself hath Inheritance. *Dan. Abridg.* 292.

Aid of the King, is where the King's Tenant prays *Aid of the King*, on account of Rent demanded by others. The *Aid of the King* may be prayed by a City or Borough that holds a Fee-farm of the King, where any Thing is demanded of them that belongs thereto: The King's Bailiffs, Receivers and Accountants may likewise pray in *Aid of the King*: In all which Cases the Proceedings are stopped till the King's Counsel are heard what they have to offer, for avoiding the King's Prejudice.

Aiel, (from the *French*, signifying a Grandfather) is a Writ that lies, where a Person's Grandfather or Great Grandfather (by our Common Lawyers called *Besaiel*) being seised of Lands, &c. in Fee-simple the Day that he died, and a Stranger abates or enters the same Day, and dispossesses the Heir of his Inheritance. *Fitz. Nat. Brev.* 222.

Aisiamenta, includes any Liberty of Passage, open Way, Water-Course, or other Customary Benefit, for the Ease and Accommodation of the Owners or Tenants of a House or Land: And hence a House of Office is called an *Easement*, that is to say, a House of Ease. See *Kitch*.

Aler sans jour, (from the *French*, signifying to go without Day) in the Law signifies, to be finally dismissed the Court, there being no further Day assigned for Appearance. *Kitch.* 146.

Ale-Silver, is an annual Rent or Tribute paid to the Lord Mayor of *London*, by Persons that retail Ale within the City. *Antiq. Purvey.* 183.

Ale-Taster, is an Officer that is appointed in every Court-Leet, and sworn to look after the Assize and Goodness of Ale and Beer, &c. within the Precincts of the Lordship: But in *London* Officers of this kind are called *Ale-Conners*.

Alias, is a second or further Writ that issues from the Courts at *Westminster*, after a first hath been sued out without Effect. *Pract. Attorn.* Edit. 1. See *Capias*.

Alias Dict', in *English*, *otherwise the said*, is where one particularly ascertains the Name and Additions of a Defendant, in a Declaration for Debt on Bond, &c. See *Misnomer*.

Alien, (from the *Latin*) signifies one Born in a strange Country, not within the Allegiance of the King: It is taken to be quite contrary to what we call a Denizen or natural Subject. A Person born out of the Land, provided it be within the Limits of the King's Obedience beyond Sea, is not an *Alien*. *Stat.* 25. *Ed.* 3. *c.* 2. And if a Man born out of the King's Obedience, come and reside in *England*, and has Children begotten and born here, they are not *Aliens*, but *Denizens*. 7 *Rep.* All that are the King's natural-born Subjects, may inherit, as Heirs to their Ancestors, notwithstanding such Ancestors were *Aliens*. If an *English* Merchant that lives beyond Sea, marries there, and has a Child by his Wife, and afterwards dies, this Child is born a Denizen, and shall inherit, notwithstanding the Wife was an *Alien*. *Cro. Car.* 605. *March* 91. An Alien cannot hold Lands by Descent or Purchase, or be Tenant by the Curtesy, or in Dower. 5 *Rep.* 502. He (being a Merchant) may purchase a House for Years, for Habitation during his Residency; but Lands he cannot. If an Alien that is a Merchant leaves the Kingdom, the King shall have the Lease; and in case he dies here possessed thereof, neither his Executors nor Administrators shall have it, but the King. If an *Alien* who is not a Merchant shall leave the Kingdom, the King shall have his Lease for Years, tho' it were intended for his Habitation. 7 *Rep.* 18. 1 *Inst.* 2, 129. 2 *Inst.* 741. Likewise where an Alien purchases Land, the King shall have it. 1 *Inst.* 2. An *Alien* Enemy cannot maintain any Action, nor lawfully get any Thing within the Realm. *Termes de la Ley* 36. See 1 *Lev.* 59. *Danv. Abr.* 322.

Alienation, signifies the transferring of the Property of any Thing from one Person to another; and it chiefly relates to Lands or Tenements; as to alien Lands, &c. in Fee, is to sell or convey the Fee-simple thereof. To *alien* in Mortmain, is to convey or make over Lands, &c. to a religious House, or Body politick; for which the King's License must be obtained, otherwise the Lands aliened in Mortmain be forfeited. 15 *R.* 2. *c.* 5. Generally, all Persons having Right to Lands, &c. may alien them; yet some Alienations are forbidden; as those by particular Tenants, such as Tenants for Life, &c. which Alienations incur a Forfeiture of the Estate *aliened*. 1 *Inst.* 118. For if Tenant for Life, Tenant in Dower, Tenant for Years, &c. *aliens* a greater Estate than he can lawfully make, it is a Forfeiture. 1 *Inst.* 223, 251.

Alimony, (from the *Latin* signifying Nourishment or Maintenance) in the Law, is taken for that Allowance which a married Woman sues for, and is intitled to, upon any occasional Separation from her Husband; as where a Wife is divorced from her Husband's Table and Bed, she may in her own Name sue him for *Alimony* out of his Estate during the Separation, either in the Chancery, or spiritual Court, where it will be allowed, except in Cases of Elopement or Adultery. 1 *Inst.* 235. But the spiritual Court is proper to sue in for *Alimony*. It was antiently expressed by the Name of *Rationabile estoverium*; that is to say, Reasonable Maintenance. *Rot.* 7 *Hen.* 3.

Allay, (from the *French*) is used for the Temper or Mixture of baser Metals with Silver or Gold, so as to increase the Weight, and thereby defray the King's Charge of Coinage. See 9 *H.* 5. What Allay a Pound Weight of Silver or Gold consists of, you'll find by looking into *Lownd*'s *Essay upon Coins,*

Coins, pag. 19. The Worth of Gold or Silver, with or without *Alloy*, may be known, by perusing the *Mod. Inst.* Tit. *Coin*, pag. 120.

Allegiance, (formerly called Ligeance) is the natural and sworn Allegiance, or legal Obedience every Subject owes to his Prince. This *Allegiance* cannot be confin'd to any particular Kingdom, but follows the Subject wherever he goes. Whence the Subjects are called *Liege People*, and by their *Allegiance* are bound to go with the King in his Wars, as well at home as abroad. 1 *Inst.* 2, 329. 2 *Inst.* 741. Justices of the Peace may summons Persons above the Age of 18 Years to take the Oaths of Allegiance, &c. 1 *El.* 1 *W. & M.* &c.

Allocation, in the Sense of the Law signifies an Allowance made on Account in the Exchequer, or rather a Placing or Adding to a Thing.

Allocatione facienda, is a Writ for allowing to an Accountant such Money as he has lawfully expended in his Office; and is directed to the Lord Treasurer, and Barons of the Exchequer, upon Complaint made. *Reg. Orig.* 206.

Allodial, is where an Inheritance is held, without any Acknowledgment to a Lord or Superior, and therefore in its Nature differs from what is called *Feodal*: For *Allodian Lands* are free Lands, which a Person enjoys, without paying any Fine, Rent, or Service to another.

Almanack, is a Part of the *English* Law, which the Courts must take Notice of in the Returns of Writs, &c. And the *Almanack* in this Case to go by, is that which is annexed to the *Book of Common Prayer*. *Mod. Caf.* 41, 81.

Almner or **Almoner**, is an Officer of the King's House, whose Office or Business is to distribute the King's *Alms* every Day; especially on Holidays; and to do several other charitable Duties; for which Purpose he has the Forfeitures of *Deodands*, and the Goods of *Felo's de se*, allowed him by the King. See *Fleta*; lib. 2. c. 22.

Almoine. See **Almone**, and **Franckalmoyne**.

Alnage, (from the *French*) signifies a Measure, and particularly the measuring with an Ell. 17 *Ed.* 4. c. 5.

Alnager, is a publick sworn Officer of the King, whose Business is to examine into the Assise of all Woollen Cloth made throughout the Kingdom, and to fix Seals upon them, &c. This Officer was appointed by 25 *Ed.* 3. and other antient Statutes: But now there are three Officers appointed for the Regulation of Clothing, who bear distinct Names, viz. *Searcher*, *Measurer*, and *Alnager*, all which were formerly comprised in one. 4 *Inst.* 31.

Alodium, signifies a Manor, and *Alodarii*, the Lords of a Manor. *Domesday*, Tit. *Rent.* 1 *Inst.* 1, 5.

Altarage, signifies the Offerings made upon the Altar, and the Profit arising to the Priest therefrom. See 2 *Cro.* 516.

Alto & Basso, or *in Alto & Basso*, whereby is meant, the absolute Submission of all Differences. *Anno* 2 *H.* 5.

Ambassador, is a Servant to the State, and represents the King in a foreign Country, to take Care of the publick Affairs. By our Statute Law, no Ambassador or other publick Foreign Minister, nor his Domestick Servant, that are registred in a Secretary of State's Office, are to be arrested in Person,

Goods, &c. If they are, the Process not only becomes void, but the Parties suing out and executing it, are liable to such Penalties and corporal Punishment, as the Lord Chancellor, or either of the Chief Justices shall think fit to inflict. 7 *Ann. c.* 12.

Ambidexter, (*Latin*) properly denotes a Person that can use his Left-hand as well as his Right; or one that plays on both Sides: But in a legal Sense, it signifies a Juror or Embracer, who takes Money of both Parties for the giving of his Verdict; for which Offence he forfeits *Decies Tantum*, that is to say, ten times as much as he takes. 38 *Ed.* 3. 12. *Cromp. Justice* 156.

Amenable, (from the *French*) signifies tractable, one that may be led or governed: And in our Law Books it is commonly applied to a Woman who is governable by her Husband. *Cow. Interp.*

Amendment, signifies the Correction of an Error committed in a Process, which may be amended after Judgment; But if there be Error in giving the Judgment, it is not amendable, but the Party is driven to his Writ of Error: Yet where the Fault appears to be in the Clerk that wrote the Record, it may be amended. See *Termes de les Ley,* Tit. *Error and Admendment.*

Amerciament, or **Amercement,** (from the *French*) signifies the Pecuniary Punishment of an Offender against the King, or other Superior in his Court, who is found to have offended, and therefore to stand at the *Mercy* of the King or Lord. *Amerciaments* differ from Fines; *Kitch.* 214. For Fines are said to be certain Punishments that grow expresly from some Statute; but *Amerciaments* are such as are arbitrarily imposed. *Kitch.* 78. Besides, Fines are assessed by the Court, but *Amerciaments* by the Country: And no Court can impose a Fine, but a Court of Record; all other Courts can only amerce. 8 *Rep.* 39, 41. Sheriffs are *amerceable* for the Faults of their Officers; and Clerks of the Peace may be *amerced* in the King's Bench for gross Faults in Indictments removed to that Court. *Hill.* 21 *Car.* The *Amerciament* of a Sheriff, Coroner, or other Officer of the King, is called *Amercement Royal. Termes de les Ley.* A Town is amerceable for the Escape of a Murderer in the Day-time; and if it be walled, it is said to be subject to *Amercement,* whether the Escape be by Day or Night. 3 *Inst.* 53.

Amittere Legem Terræ, (*Latin*) in a legal Sense is taken to signify to lose, or be deprived of the Liberty of swearing in any Court: As to become infamous, renders the Person incapable of being an Evidence. See *Glanvil, lib.* 2. 5 *Eliz. c.* 9.

Amnesty, signifies an Act of Pardon or *Oblivion,* such as was granted by King *Charles* II. upon his Restoration.

Amortization, signifies an Alienation of Lands or Tenements in Mortmain, viz. to a Corporation or Fraternity and their Successors, &c. The Right of *Amortization* is a Privilege or Licence of taking in Mortmain. The *French Amortisement,* from whence this Word is derived, is used in 27 *Ed.* 1. *Stat. de Libertatibus perquirendis.*

Amortize or **Amortise,** signifies to alien Lands in Mortmain. See **Amortization.** See also **Mortmain.**

Ampliation, in a legal Sense denotes a Referring of Judgment till the

the Cause is further examined.

Amy (from the *French*) signifies a Friend; as *Prochein Amy* denotes the next Friend to be entrusted for an Infant or Orphan. And an *Alien Amy* is a Foreigner here that is Subject to some Power abroad in Friendship with us.

An Jour and Waste, (*French*, signifying Year, Day and Waste) is a Forfeiture of Lands to the King, in case of Petit Treason or Felony committed; for which Offence the Offender's Lands are to be seised for the King, and remain in his Hands for a Year and a Day next after the Attainder.

Ancestor, is of the like Signification with that of *Predecessor*, or one who has gone before in a Family: Yet the Law makes a Difference between what is commonly called an *Ancestor* and *Predecessor*; the first being applied to a natural Person and his *Ancestors*, and the last to a Body Politick and their *Predecessors*. *Co. Lit.* A Prepossessor of an Estate may be called *Ancestor*.

Ancestrel, signifies any Thing that relates to what has been done by one's Ancestors; as *Homage Ancestrel*, &c.

Anchorage, is a Duty taken of Ships for the Haven where they cast Anchor. *MS. Ar. Trevor, Ar.* No Person can let an Anchor fall on the King's Ground in a Port or Haven, without paying the King's Officer for it.

Ancients, is a Word referred to Gentlemen of the Inns of Court. In *Gray's* Inn the Society consists of Benchers, Ancients, Barristers and Students under the Bar. In the *Middle Temple*, those that have past their Readings, are called *Ancients*. *Ancient Demesne*, is a certain Tenure, whereby all the Manors belonging to the Crown in the Days of St. *Edward*, and *William* the *Conqueror* were held.

Ancienty, (from the *French*) is used in the Statute of *Ireland*, 14 *Hen.* 3. for Seniority or Eldership.

Aniens, or **Aniente**, (from the *French*) signifies to be void, or of no Force. *Fitz. Nat. Brev.*

Annales, denotes Yearlings, or Cattle of the first Year.

Annats, or **Annates**, carries with it the same Meaning with that of *First-Fruits*, Anno 25 *Hen.* 8. *c.* 20. And the Reason of it is, because the Rate of First-Fruits paid for spiritual Livings, is accounted after the Value of one Year's Profit. See *Pol. Virg. de Invent. rer. lib.* 8. *c.* 2.

Aniented, (from the *French*) signifies frustrated, abrogated, or reduced to Nothing. *Litt. c.* 3. *sect.* 741.

Anni nubiles, signifies the marriageable Age of a Woman, *viz.* when she is of 12 Years of Age. 2 *Co. Inst.* 434.

Anno Domini, denotes the Computation of Time from our Saviour's Incarnation; and before the late Alteration by Parliament, ordained to be made in the Proceedings in the Law, it was generally inserted in the Dates of all Deeds and Writings, with or without the Addition of the Year of the King's Reign. Instead of *Anno Domini*, the *English* thereof are now inserted in all publick Writings; as *In the Year of our Lord*.

Annoisance, **Annoyance**, or **Noisance**, has a double Signification, it being used as well for any Hurt done to a Highway, Bridge, or common River, as to a private Place, as by laying any Thing therein, which may breed Infection, by encroaching on some Person's Right, or other such like Means. The Word *Annoisance* is mentioned

mentioned in the *Stat.* 22 *H.* 8. *c.* 5. See **Nusance**.

Annua Pensione, is a Writ anciently used for providing a King's Chaplain, who was unpreferred, with a Pension out of what was annually due to the King from an Abbot or Prior. *Reg. Orig.* 165, 307. *Fitz. Nat. Brev.* 231.

Annuity, signifies a yearly Sum payable for Life, a Term of Years, or in Fee; and is used for a Writ that lies against a Person for Recovery of such annual Sum. *Reg. Orig.* 158. There are several Differences between an *Annuity* and Rent, *viz.* every Rent is issuing out of Lands; but Annuity charges the Person only, as the Grantor and his Heirs, who have Assets by Descent: Also no Action lies for an *Annuity*, but only a Writ of Annuity; but for the Recovery of Rent, the same Action lies as for Lands: Besides, an Annuity is never taken for Assets, it being no Freehold in Law; and therefore shall not be put in Execution upon a Statute Merchant, Staple, or *Elegit*. *Doct. & Stud. c.* 3. *Dyer* 345. 2 *Rep.* 144. An Annuity cannot be severed. *Co. lib.* 8. 52.

Antejuramentum, or **Præjuramentum**, of old was called *Juramentum Calumniæ*, wherein both the Accuser and Accused were, before any Trial or Purgation, respectively to make the following Oath, *viz.* The Accuser to swear that he would prosecute the Criminal; and the Accused to make Oath on the very Day he was to undergo the Ordeal, that he was innocent of the Crime charged against him. *Leg. Athelstan apud Lambard.* 23.

Apostata Capiendo, is a Writ now in Disuse, that formerly lay against a Person, who having entered into, and professed some religious Order, broke out again, and wandered up and down the Country, contrary to the Rules of this Order. *Reg. Orig.* 71, 267.

Apparator, or **Apparitor**, is a Messenger that serves a Process of the Spiritual Court; whose Duty it is to cite Offenders to appear, to arrest them, and to execute the Sentence or Decree of the Judge of that Court. See 21 *H.* 8. *c.* 5.

Apparator Comitatus, was formerly an Officer distinguished by that Name: But that Office is now altered. See *Hale of Sheriffs Account* 164.

Aparlement, (from the *French*) signifies a Resemblance or Likelihood; as *Aparlement* of War. 2 *R.* 2. *Stat.* 1. *c.* 6.

Aparatura, was anciently used to signify Furniture, *Apparel*, Tackle or Implements. See 14 *Hen.* 7.

Appeal, (from the *French*) is generally taken for the Accusation of a Murderer, by the Person that had Interest in the Party killed; or of a Felon by one of his Accomplices: But in a particular Sense it is used for the Removal of a Cause from an inferior Court or Judge to a superior. 1 *Inst.* 287. An *Appeal* or Accusation is commenced two Ways, either by Writ or Bill: By Writ, where a Writ is purchased out of the Court of Chancery by one Person against another, commanding him to appeal a Third of some Felony committed by him, and to find Pledges for doing it with Effect. By Bill, is where a Person of himself gives in the Accusation in Writing, offering to undergo the Burden of *appealing* the Person therein named. *Bracton.* In an *Appeal* of Death, &c. the King cannot pardon the Defendant, it being the *Appellant's* private Action or Suit; and not, as in an Indictment, the Suit of the King. 3 *Inst.* 237. If a Peer be indicted for Murder, he shall be tried by his Peers: But on an *Appeal* of Murder he shall be tried by a common Jury. 3 *Hen.* 7. An Appeal of Murder must be brought within a Year and Day after the Death of the Person murdered. See 2 *Inst.* 665. The Party who brings the *Appeal* is called the *Appellant*; and the Person against whom it is brought, the *Appellee*. Appeals of *Maihem, Rape* and *Robbery*, are now much in Disuse; but the *Appeal* of Murder still continues, and is frequently brought.

Appearance, in Law signifies the Defendant's filing special or common Bail, or any Process issuing out of the Courts at *Westminster*. There are four Ways for Defendants to make their Appearance to Actions, *viz.* in Person, by Attorney, by Persons of full Age, and by Guardians, or a next Friend. *Show.* 165. By 12 *Geo.* 2. *c.* 29. where a Defendant is serv'd with a Copy of a Process in Debt, &c. under 10 *l.* a common Appearance may be entered; that is to say, common Bail may be filed by the Plaintiff, in case the Defendant does not appear within eight Days after the Return of the Writ or Process, an Affidavit being first made of the Service of the same. See also 5 *Geo.* 2. *c.* 17.

Appendant, is any Thing that is inheritable, belonging to some Inheritance more worthy; as an Advowson, Commons, Courts, &c. may be appendant to a Manor; Common of Fishing to a Freehold, Land to an Office, &c.

Appenditia, signifies the Appendages or Appurtenances of an Estate. *Kennet's Paroch. Antiq.* 110.

Apportionment, signifies the dividing of a Rent into Parts, in the like Manner as the Land out of which it issues, is divided among two or more: As if a Man has a Rent-Service growing out of Land, and he purchases Part of that Land, the Rent shall be apportioned according to the Value of the Land. *Termes de les Ley* 47. Where a Person lets Lands for Years, reserving Rent, and afterwards a Stranger recovers Part of the Land, the Rent shall be *apportioned*, and the Lessee shall pay, he having Regard to the Value of what is recovered, and what remains in his Hands. Where the Lessor recovers Part of the Land let, or enters for Forfeiture on Part of it, the Rent shall be apportioned accordingly. 1 *Inst.* 144. But Rent-Charge cannot be apportioned; neither can Things that are entire be apportioned: As if one holds Lands by Service, to pay yearly at a certain Feast, a Horse, a Hawk, a Rose, or the like. 1 *Inst.* 149. Yet in some Cases a Rent-Charge may be apportioned: As where Part of the Land, out of which the Rent-Charge issues, descends to the Grantee of the Rent; in which Case that Rent shall be apportioned. *Dawv.* 507. If a Person purchases Part of the Land wherein he has Common Appendant, the Common shall be apportioned: But, in this Case, Common Appurtenant, and not Appendant, becomes extinct by such Purchase. *Co. Lit. lib.* 8, 79. See 8 *Rep.* 79.

Appofal of Sheriffs, signifies the charging them with Money received upon their Accounts in the Exchequer. See 22 & 23 *Car.* 2.

Appraisers, are such as are sworn to make a true Appraisement of Goods; and if they value them too high, they are obliged to take them at the appraised Price. 13 *Ed.* 1.

Apprentice, (from a *French* Word signifying to learn) signifies a young Person that is bound by Indenture to some Tradesman or Artificer, in Order to be instructed in the Master's Mystery or Trade. *Apprentices* are said to be a kind of Bondsmen, differing only in this, *viz.* that they are Servants by Covenant, and for a certain Term, usually seven Years. See *Smith's Rep. Angl. lib.* 3. *c.* 8. Seven Years Service is required to intitle a Person to use any Trade, Craft or Mystery: But this does not extend to such as get a Livelihood by mere Labour, where there is no Craft or Mystery. 1 *Roll. Rep.* 10. See more in the Statutes 2 *P. & M. c.* 11. 5 *Eliz. c.* 4. The Form of an Indenture of Apprenticeship you may see in the *Young Clerk's Magazine* and other Collections of Precedents in Conveyancing.

Appropriation, (from the *French*) signifies the Annexing of a Benefice to the proper and perpetual Use of some religious House, Bishoprick, College, or spiritual Person: And when once *Appropriation* is made, the Patron is perpetual Parson, the *Appropriation* alone being a sufficient Admission, &c. *Plowd.* 499. In order to make an *Appropriation*, the King's License in Chancery, the Consent of the Ordinary, Patron, and Incumbent (where the Church is full) but if the Benefice be void, then that of the Diocesan and Patron, must be obtained. *Plowd.* 496. 15 *R.* 2. *c.* 6. An Appropriation may be made by the King alone, where he himself is Patron; as when by Letters Patent he grants the Advowson that he is seised of, in Right of his Crown, to a Dean and Chapter, &c. *Plowd.* 499. Altho' *Appropriations* cannot be made to any but spiritual Persons and their Successors; yet by 31 *Hen.* 8. The King's Patentees (though Laymen) are made capable of Parsonages; but these are generally called *Impropriations*: And *Appropriations* themselves have been judged to be an Abuse or Robbery of the Church and Parish Priests. See *Kennet's Paroch. Antiq.* 433.

Appropriare ad Honorem, signifies to bring a Manor within the Liberty of a certain Honour. *Paroch. Antiq.* 336.

Appropriare Communiam, is to discommon, that is to say, to inclose any Parcel of Land that before was open Common. *Paroch. Antiq.* 336.

Approve, signifies to increase or augment a Thing to the utmost: As to approve Land, is to make the greatest Benefit of it, by increasing the Rent, &c. 2 *Inst.* 474.

Approvement, in general is taken to be the same with Improvement; but is more particularly used for the inclosing a Part of a Common by the Lord of the Manor, having nevertheless sufficient Common, with Egress and Regress, for the Commoners. *Reg. Jud.* 8, 9.

Approver or **Prover,** (from the *French*) is one that, confessing a Felony he has committed, appeals or accuses others to be guilty of the same Crime. He is called *Approver*, because he must prove his Allegation; and that Proof was in former Ages by Battle, or the Country, at the Election of him that was appealed. See *Bracton, lib.* 3. *Staundf. Pl. Cor.* 52. *Cromp. Just.* 250. If a Person has once pleaded not guilty, he cannot

AP

cannot be an Approver. 3 *Inst.* 129. As it is in the Discretion of the Court to suffer an *Approver*, the admitting such has of late been seldom practised: Yet in Cases of Burglaries and Robberies, we have what seems to amount to pretty near the same; it being by 5 *Ann. c.* 31. ordained, that where a Person, out of Prison and charged with such Crimes, discovers two others concerned in the same Crime, such Discoverer shall be pardoned, &c.

Approvers, Bailiffs of Lords in their Franchises are called so by *Stat.* 9 *H.* 6. But by 2 *Ed.* 3. *c.* 12. *Approvers* are those that are sent into Countries to increase the Farms of Hundreds, &c. held by Sheriffs. Persons who have the letting of the King's Demesnes in small Manors, are called *Approvers* of the King. 51 *H.* 3. And in 1 *Ed.* 3. *c.* 8. Sheriffs are called the King's *Approvers*.

Appurtenances, (from the *French*) signifies Things, both Corporeal and Incorporeal, that appertain or belong to another Thing as Principal: As Hamlets to a Manor; Common of Fishery, Common of Pasture, &c. *Brit. c.* 39. Common *Appurtenant* may be to a House, Pasture, &c. Outhouses, Yards, Orchards, and Gardens, are *Appurtenant* to a Messuage; but Lands cannot properly be said to be so. 1 *Lill. Abr.* 91. The Word *Appurtenant* or *Appertaining*, may be taken in the Sense of usually letten or occupied with the House. *Plowd.* 170.

Aquage, signifies a Water-Course. See *Ordin. Marisc. de Romney*, fact. *Temp. Hen.* 3. & *Ed.* 1.

Arace, (in *English* to rase) signifies to scratch or pull out.

E

AR

Aratrum Terrae, is as much Land as can be tilled with one Plough. *Thorn. Anno* 1616.

Arbitrator, (*Latin*) signifies a private and extraordinary Judge chosen by the mutual Consent of contending Parties, to determine Controversies between them. *West. Sym. Sect.* 21. Arbitrators are so called, because they are invested with an *arbitrary* Power of determining; for if they observe the Submission, and keep within due Bounds, their Sentence becomes definitive, so that no Appeal can lie from it. 1 *Roll. Abr.* 251. Sometimes Matters in Dispute are referred by the Judges at the Assises to the three Foremen of the Jury, as *Arbitrators*; after whose Award or Sentence, the Plaintiff may have an Attachment, &c. to oblige Performance. 1 *Salk.* 84. Where there is but one Arbitrator, which generally happens where the Matters in Controversy are referred to two, who cannot agree, but leave the whole to be determined by a third Person, in the Law called an *Umpire*. 8 *Rep.* 98.

Arbitrement, is the Award or Determination pronounced and published by the *Arbitrators*, after they have heard all Parties: And it is either general or special; General of all Actions, Quarrels and Demands, &c. Special, of some certain Matters in Controversy. 8 *Rep.* 98. There are five Things incident to an *Arbitrament*, viz. 1. Matter of Controversy. 2. Submission. 3. Parties to the Submission. 4. Arbitrators. 5. Giving up the Arbitrament. *Hardr.* 44. Submissions are usually by Bond, and the Parties binding themselves thereto, are obliged to stand to the Award or *Arbitrament*, at their Peril: But Matters relating to a Freehold, Debts due

on

on Bond or other certain Contract, are not to be arbitrated; neither are Offences Criminal. *Danv. Abr.* 513. 9 *Rep.* 78. 1 *Roll. Abr.* 342, 244. See **Award**.

Archery, signifies the Service of keeping a Bow for the Use of the Lord, for the Defence of his Castle. *Co. Lit. Sect.* 157.

Arches or **Court of Arches**, is the chief and most ancient consistory Court, which belongs to the Archbishop of *Canterbury* for the debating of spiritual Causes: And it is so called from the *Arches* of the Church where this Court was formerly held, *viz.* St. *Mary le Bow, London,* commonly called *Bow Church.* The Judge of this Court is termed the Dean of the *Arches,* or Official of the Arches Court. Of his Jurisdiction, see 4 *Inst.* 337.

Archives, signifies the Rolls, or any Place where ancient Records, &c. are kept: Also the Chancery, Exchequer Office, &c.

Arериесment, signifies Surprise, or Affrightment. See *Rot. Parl.* 21 *Ed.* 3.

Argentum Dei, God's Money, that is to say, Money given in Earnest upon the making of a Bargain: And hence comes *Arles,* and *Arles Penny* the same as Earnest, much used in *Yorkshire,* where Servants Vails are likewise called Arles. *Cowel.*

Armour or **Arms**, in a legal Sense is extended to any Thing that a Person wears for his own Defence, takes into his Hands, or uses in Anger to strike or throw at another. *Cromp. Just.* 65. Arms are also what we call Ensigns of Honour.

Arraiatio Peditum, signifies the Arraying of Foot Soldiers. *Pat.* 1. *Ed.* 2.

Arraign, (from the *French*) signifying to set a Thing in Order, or in its proper Place, has the same Signification in our Law: For a Person is said to arraign a Writ of *Novel Disseisin,* who prepares and fits it for Trial before the Justices of the Circuit. *Old Nat. Brev.* 109. *Littleton* 78. *Arraign* is likewise taken in an other Sense, wherein it is said to be derived from a *French* Word, signifying to call a Person to answer in Form of Law; as where a Criminal is indicted and brought to Trial, he is said to be arraigned: And the *Arraignment* of a Criminal is to take Care that he appear to be tried, and hold up his Hand to the Bar, to discover the Certainty of the Person; and that he plead a sufficient Plea to the Indictment. 1 *Inst.* 262. See more 3 *Inst.* 217.

Array, (from an old *French* Word) signifying the Ranking or setting forth of a Jury of Men impanelled upon a Cause. 18 *Hen.* 6. c. 14. To *array* a Panel, is to set forth the Persons impanelled one by another. *Fitz. Nat. Brev.* 157. To challenge the *Array* of the Panel, is at once to except against such as are arrayed or impanelled, on Account of Partiality, &c. 1 *Inst.* 156. *Array* does also in particular relate to Military Order. See 14 *Car.* 2. *c.* 3.

Arrerages, (from the *French*) is taken for Money that is unpaid at the due Time, as Rent behind, the Remainder due on an Account, or Money remaining in the Hands of an Accomptant.

Arrectatus, is one that is suspected of any Crime. *Offic. Coronat. Spelm. Gloss.*

Arrenatus, is one that is arraigned or accused. *Rot. Parl.* 21 *Ed.* 1.

Arrentation, (from the *Spanish*) signifies the licensing of an Owner of of Lands in a Forest, to enclose them with a low Hedge and a small Ditch according to the Assize of the Forest, under an Annual Rent. *Saving the Arrentations* is a Power reserved of granting such Licences. *Ordin. Forestæ*, 34 *Ed.* 1.

Arrest, (from the *French*) signifies a Stop, Stay, or Restraint of a Person, in order to oblige him to be obedient to the Law: It is likewise defined to be the Execution of the Command of some Court of Record, or Officer of Justice. None shall be arrested for Debt, Trespass, Detinue, or other Cause of Action, but by Virtue of a Precept out of some Court; except in Cases of Treason, Felony, or Breach of the Peace, where any Man may arrest without Warrant or Precept. *Termes de les Ley* 54. A Person is said to be *arrested*, where apprehended for Debt, &c. And in Writs *Arrest* is expressed by two several Words, *viz.* to take and catch hold of a Person; for an Officer must actually lay hold of the Defendant in the Writ, besides saying he arrests him; otherwise it will not be a lawful *Arrest.*

Arrest of Judgment, signifies *to move in Arrest of Judgment*, that is to say, to shew Cause why Judgment should be staid after a Verdict given. The chief Causes for *Arrest of Judgment*, are 1. for Want of Notice of Trial; 2. where the Plaintiff before Trial treats the Jury; 3. where the Record differs from the Deed pleaded; 4. for material Defect in pleading; 5. where Persons are misnamed; 6. where more is given by the Verdict than is laid in the Declaration; 7. or where the Declaration doth not set forth the Thing with Certainty:

In all which Cases all Matters of Fact are to be made out by proper Affidavits. See *Comp. Attorn.* 329, &c. Four Days are allowed the Defendant to move in Arrest of Judgment, though he has all the Term, wherein the Verdict was given, to do it in, if the Plaintiff has neglected to give his four Day Rule, and sign Judgment; after which Time the Defendant is driven to his Writ of Error. 2 *Lill.* 93.

Arrestandis Bonis ne dissipentur, is a Writ that lies for a Person, whose Cattle or Goods are taken by another, which second Person during the Contest does or is likely to take them away, without being in Ability to make Satisfaction. *Reg. Orig.* 126.

Arresto facto super bonis Mercatorum, is a Writ that lies for a Denizen against the Goods of *Aliens* found within this Realm, in Recompence of Goods taken from him in a Foreign Country, to which such Alien belonged, after the Denizen has been denied Restitution there. *Reg. Orig.* 129.

Arretted, is said to be where a Person is convened before a Judge and charged with a Crime. *Staundf. Pl. Cor.* 45. It is by *Littleton*, c. *Remitter*, used for imputed or laid unto.

Arson, signifies House-burning, which is Felony at Common Law. 3 *Inst.* 66. The Crime must be maliciously and voluntarily committed, and an actual Burning. It must likewise be the Burning of another Man's House, and not that of his own; for if a Person burns his own House only, tho' with an Intent to burn another's, it is not Felony, but a great Misdemeanor. See more 2 *Inst.* 188. *H. P. C.* 85. 3 *Inst.* 67.

AS

Arfor in le Maine, (*French*) signifying Burning in the Hand, is the Punishment of Criminals that are allowed the Benefit of the Clergy.

Art and Part, is used in *North Britain*, and likewise in the North of *England*, for a Person that is charged with a Crime, in the committing whereof he was both a Contriver of and acted his Part in it.

Articuli Cleri, that is to say, *Articles of the Clergy*, are Statutes that contain certain Articles relating to the Church and Clergy, &c. 19 *Ed.* 2. 14 *Ed.* 3.

Artificers, are taken for those whose Employment chiefly consists of bodily Labour: And if such conspire not to work under certain Prices, they are liable to certain Penalties. 2 & 3 *Ed.* 6. *c.* 15. See likewise 5 *Geo.* 1. *c.* 27. for preventing certain Artificers from going out of the Land.

Asach or **Asath,** was a Custom of Purgation anciently used in *Wales*, whereby the Party accused did clear himself by the Oaths of 300 Men. 1 *H.* 5.

Assart, in *Manwood's Forest Laws*, is called an Offence committed in the Forest, by pulling up the Woods by the Roots, that are Thickets and Coverts for the Deer, and making the Ground as plain as arable Land. This Offence is esteemed the greatest that can be done in the Forest to Vert or Venison, it containing in it Waste and more; for Waste of the Forest is nothing but the felling and cutting down the Coverts, which may grow up again, whilst Assart is the plucking them up by the Roots, so that they never grow again: Yet by a Writ of *Ad quod Damnum* a Person may sue out a Licence to *assart* Ground in the Forest, and make it several for Tillage. *Reg. Orig.* 253.

Assault, is a violent Injury offered to a Man's Person, and is of a higher Nature than Battery; seeing that it may be committed by offering a Blow, or by a terrifying Speech. *Lamb. Eiren. lib.* 1. *c.* 3. As to threaten a Collector with harsh Words, so that out of Fear he dares not execute his Office, has been deemed an Assault: And to strike at a Man, tho' he be neither hurt nor hit, has been adjudged the like. 22 *Lib. Ass. Pl.* 60. For Assault does not always imply a Blow or Striking; because in Trespass for *Assault* and Battery, a Person may be found guilty of the *Assault*, and excused of the Battery. 25 *Ed.* 3. *c.* 24.

Assay of Weights and Measures, signifies the Examination of Weights and Measures by Clerks of Markets, &c. *Reg. Orig.* 279.

Assayer of the King, is an Officer of the Mint indifferently appointed between the Master thereof and the Merchants, for the Trial of Silver brought thither for Exchange. 2 *H.* 6. *c.* 12. By the Statutes 28 *Ed.* 1. *c.* 20. and 18 *Car.* 2. *c.* 5. Vessels of Gold are ordained to be *assayed*.

Assembly unlawful, (from the *French*) is the Meeting of three or more together to do an unlawful Act, although they commit it not; as to assault or beat a Person, enter into Houses or Lands, &c. *West. Symb. Part* 2. *Sect.* 65. It is their meeting and abiding together makes the Crime, even though their Intentions are not executed: In some Cases where their Intention is put in Execution, it is adjudged Treason. See 3 *Inst.* 9. See likewise the Riot Act, 1 *Geo.* 1. *c.* 6.

Assent,

Assent, is the same with Consent.

Assessors, are such as *assess* publick Taxes; as two Inhabitants of every Parish were formerly *Assessors* for the Royal Aid, that is to say, rated every Person according to the Proportion of his Estate. *Anno* 16 & 17 *Car.* 2.

Assets, (from the *French*) signifies Goods or Effects sufficient to discharge that Burden which is cast upon the Executor, Administrator or Heir, in satisfying the Debts and Legacies of the Testator or Ancestor whom he represents. *Bro. Tit. Assets*. *Assets* are either real or personal; as where a Person dies seised in Fee-Simple of Lands, &c. which descend to the Heir, those are called *Assets* Real; and where the deceased dies possessed of a personal Estate, that is to say, Goods or Chattels, which come to the Executors, or Administrators, they are called *Assets* Personal. *Assets* are likewise divided into two Parts, viz. *Assets per Discent*, and *Assets inter Maines*.

Assets per Descent, is where a Person is bound in an Obligation, and dies seised of Lands in Fee, which descend to the Heir, the Land in that Case being Assets, the Heir shall be charged so far as the Land descended to him will extend: *Assets inter Maines*, is when a Person indebted makes Executors and dies, leaving them sufficient to pay his Debts; or where some Commodity or Profit arises to them in Right of the Testator, which in *English* are called Assets in their Hands. *Termes de les Ley* 56, 77. Goods and Chattels which belonged to the Testator at his Death, and that come to the Hands of the Executor are *Assets* to make such Executor chargeable. 6 *Rep.* 47. See *Chattels*.

Assign, in a general Sense, signifies to set over a Right to another or appoint a Deputy, &c. And in a special Sense, to set forth or point at; as to assign Error, assign false Judgment, Waste, &c. In assigning of Error, it must be shewed where the Error is committed; in false Judgment, wherein the Judgment is unjust; in Waste, wherein in particular the Waste is committed. *Fitz. Nat. Brev.* 19. 113. *Reg. Orig.* 72. Justices are likewise said to be assigned to take the Assizes. 11 *H.* 6. *c.* 2.

Assignee, is a Person appointed by another to do an Act, transact a Business, or enjoy some particular Commodity. *Assignees* may be by Deed or Law: By Deed, where a Lessee of a Term, &c. assigns the same to another: By Law, where the Law makes an *Assignee*, without any Appointment of the Person entitled to make him; as an Executor is an *Assignee* in Law to the Testator. *Dyer* 6. So an Administrator to the Intestate. An Assignee is one that possesses or enjoys a Thing in his own Right; but *Deputy* is he that does it in the Right of another. *Perkins*, Tit. *Grants*.

Assignment, is the transferring the Interest of any Thing from one to another. *Assignments* may be made of Lands in Fee, for Life of Years; of an Annuity, Rent-Charge, Judgment, Statute, &c. but as to Lands, they are usually made of Leases and Estates for Years, &c. No Freehold Estate, or Term of Years shall be assigned but by Deed in Writing, signed by the Parties; except by Operation of Law. 29 *Car.* 2. *c.* 3. A Deed of *Assignment* chiefly consists of the following Parts, viz. 1. The Names and Additions of the *Assignor* and *Assignee*, that is to to say, the Party assigning, and the Party to whom the Assignment is made. 2. A Recital of the Thing to be *assigned*, and the Interest the Assignor has therein. 3. The granting or assigning Part. 4. The *Habendum* or explanatory Clause, shewing what Interest in the Thing assigned is intended to be granted to the *Assignee*. The usual Covenants to be inserted in an Assignment, particularly in that of a Lease for Years, are that the *Assignor* hath good Right to *assign*; that the Assignee shall quietly enjoy the Thing assigned; and that the *Assignor*, upon Request, shall make such further Assurance in the Law, as the *Assignee* or his Counsel shall reasonably require. Where there is an *Assignment* of a Bond or Judgment, it is necessary to insert a Clause, in the Nature of a Letter of Attorney, with a Covenant, that the *Assignor* hath not received nor will receive the Money due thereon, nor release or otherwise discharge such Bond, &c. The Forms of *Assignments* in divers Cases you may see in *The young Clerk's Magazine* and other Collections of Instruments in Conveyancing.

Assisa cadere, is the same with what we call to be nonsuited; as where there is such a plain and legal Insufficiency, that the Plaintiff can proceed no further in his Suit or Complaint. *Fleta, lib. 4. c. 15. Bract. lib. 2. c. 7.*

Assisa cadit in juratam, signifies, that the Thing in Controversy being so doubtful, it must necessarily be tried by a Jury. *Fleta, lib. 4. c. 15.*

Assisa continuanda, is a Writ directed to the Justices of Assise for the Continuation of a Cause, where certain Records alledged cannot be produced by the Party who wants to use them. *Reg. Orig. 217.*

Assisa prorogaranda, is a Writ directed to the Justices of *Assise*, to stay Proceedings, on Account of the Party's being employed in the King's Business. *Reg. Orig. 208.*

Assise, in *Custum. Normand. c. 24.* is defined to be an Assembly of Knights and other substantial Men, with the Justice in a certain Place, and at a certain Time appointed. This Word is properly derived from a *Latin* Verb, signifying *to sit together*; and is also taken for the Court, Place or Time, when and where the Writs and Processes of Assise are handled or taken; in which Signification Assise is general; as when the Justices go their respective Circuits with Commission to take all Assises: Or special; as where a special Commission is granted to particular Persons (formerly much in Use) for taking an Assise upon one or two Disseisins only. *Bract. lib. 3.* As to the general *Assise*, all the Counties of *England* are divided into six Circuits, and two Judges are assigned by Commission to every Circuit, who hold the *Assises* twice a Year in every County, except *Middlesex* (where the Courts of Records do sit) and some few other Counties in the North of *England*, where the Assises are only held once a Year: And these Judges have five several Commissions. 1. Of *Oyer and Terminer*, whereby they are impowered to try Treasons, Felonies, &c. 2. Of *Gaol-Delivery*, which empowers them to try every Prisoner committed in Gaol for any Offence whatsoever; so that one Way or other the Gaol is rid by them of all the Prisoners in it. 3. Of *Assise*, which empowers them to take *Assises* and do Right upon Writs of *Assise* brought by Persons wrongfully thrust out of their Lands and Possessions; but that Method of proceeding is now in Disuse, Possessions being sooner recovered by Ejectments, &c. 4. Of *Nisi Prius*, by which civil Causes come to Issue in the Courts above, are tried in the Vacation by a Jury of twelve Men of the County where the Cause of Action arises, on the Return of whose Verdict to the Court, the Judges there give Judgment. 5. A *Commission of the Peace*, in every County where the Circuits run, and all Justices of the Peace of such County are bound to be present at the *Assises*, where Sheriffs are likewise to give their Attendance on the Judges, otherwise shall be fined. *Bacon's Elem*. 15, 16, &c. *Assise* is also used for a Jury, where Assises of *Novel Disseisin* are tried. *Assise* is likewise taken for a Writ, for Recovery of the Possession of Things unmoveable, whereof a Person and his Ancestors have been disseised. In another Sense it signifies an Ordinance or Statute. *Reg. Orig*. 279.

Assise of Novel Disseisin, is a Writ that lies where Tenant in Fee, Tail, or for Life, is put out and disseised of his Lands, Tenements, Rents, Common of Pasture, Common Way, &c. *Glanv. lib*. 10. *Reg. Orig*. 197. See likewise *Bract. lib*. 4. *Britton, c*. 70. &c. An Assise may be brought for an Office held for Life, provided it be an Office of Profit, not of Charge only: It likewise lies for the Toll of a Mill or Market. 8 *Rep*. 46, 47. For the Method of proceeding on this Writ, see 1 *Lill. Abr*. 105, 106. *Plowd*. 411, 412. In Cities and Corporations an *Assise of fresh Force* lies for the Recovery of Possession of Lands, &c. within forty Days after the *Disseisin*, as the ordinary *Assise* in the County. *Fitz. Nat. Brev*. 7.

Assise of Mort d' Ancestor, is a Writ that lies where a Person's Father, Mother, Brother, Sister, &c. died seized of Lands, &c. in Fee, and after the Deceased's Death a Stranger abateh. *Reg. Orig*. 223. It is good not only against the Abator, but also any other Person in Possession of the Lands: Yet it does not lie against Brothers or Sisters, &c. where there is Privity of Blood between the Parties contending. *Co. Lit*. 242. If a Person be barred in *Assise* of *Novel Disseisin*, upon shewing a Discent or other special Matter, he may have *Mort d' Ancestor* or Writ of Entry *sur Disseisin*, &c. 4 *Rep*. 43.

Assise of Darrein Presentment, is a Writ which lies where a Person and his Ancestors have presented a Clerk to a Church, and afterwards, the Church becoming void, a Stranger presents his Clerk to the same Church, whereby the Person having Right is disturbed. *Reg. Orig*. 30. A Person may have an Assise of Darrein Presentment, tho' neither he nor his Ancestors did present to the last Avoidance; as where Tenant for Life or Years, in Dower, or by the Courtesy, suffers an Usurpation into a Church, &c. and dies; the Person in Reversion who is Heir to the Deceased shall have this Writ. Where a *Darrein Presentment* will not lie, but instead thereof a Writ of *Right*, see 10 *Ed*. 3. See more *New Nat. Brev*. 74.

Assise de Utrum, is a Writ that lies for a Parson against a Layman, or a Layman against a Parson, for Lands or Tenements doubtful whether they be Lay-Fee or Free-Alms appertain-

appertaining to the Church. *Bract. lib.* 4. This Writ is of the highest Nature a Parson can have; for if a Parson, Prebendary, &c. lose by Default in a real Action, he may have this Writ, it being his Writ of *Right*. 6 *Rep.* 8. This and the three preceding Writs of *Assise*, in Respect to the Grand *Assise*, are called *Petit Assises*; for this Reason, *viz.* that the Law of Fees is grounded upon two Rights, the one of Possession, and the other of Property; and as the grand *Assise* serves for the Right of Property, so the *Petit Assise* serves to settle the Right of Possession. *Horn's Mirr.*

Assise of the Forest, is a Statute or Condition concerning Orders to be observed in the King's Forest. *Manw.* 35. *The Assise of the King* is called View of Frank-Pledge. *Assise of Bread and Ale* is so called. *Anno* 51 *Hen.* 3. There is likewise an *Assise* of Nusance, which is where a Person makes a Nusance to the Freehold of another, the Injured may bring that Writ to redress the same. See more on the Head of *Assises. Bract. lib.* 4. *Fitz. Nat. Brev.* 105.

Assisus, signifies rented or farmed out for such a certain assessed Rent in Money or Provisions.

Association, is a Writ or Patent sent by the King, either of his own Motion, or at the Suit of a Party Plaintiff, to the Justices of Assise or of Oyer and Terminer, to have others associated to them to take the Assise. This is usually done, where a Justice of Assise dies; upon which a Writ is issued to the Justices alive to admit the Person associated. This is likewise practised where a Justice is disabled. *Fitz. Nat. Brev.* 185. *Reg. Orig.* 201, 206, 223.

Assoile, signifies to deliver or discharge from Excommunication. *Staundf. Pl. Cor.*

Assumpsit, is taken for a voluntary Promise, whereby a Person assumes or takes upon him to perform or pay any Thing to another. This Word comprehends in it any verbal Promise made upon Consideration. When a Person becomes legally indebted to another for Goods sold, the Law implies a Promise that the Buyer will pay this Debt; and if he do not pay it, an *Indebitatus Assumpsit* lies against him. 1 *Danv. Abr.* 26. An *Indebitatus Assumpsit* likewise lies for Goods sold and delivered to a third Person at the Request of the Defendant. *Ibid.* 27. But on an *Assumpsit* for Goods sold, the Price agreed on must be proved, otherwise that Action will not lie; yet this is helped by adding to the *Indebitatus Assumpsit* a *Quantum valebant*, or (in Case of Business done) a *Quantum meruit*, wherein if you fail in the Proof of the Price agreed on, you may recover according to the Value of the Goods sold, or the Desert of the Business performed. *Wood's Inst.* 536.

Assurance. See *Insurance*.

Atia, is a Writ of Enquiry whether a Person be committed to Prison on just Cause of Suspicion. See *Odio & Atia*.

Attach, (from the *French*) signifies to apprehend a Person by Virtue of a Writ or Precept. *Lamb. Eyren. lib.* 1. *c.* 16. *Attachment* according to the common Use of the Word, is an Apprehending a Man by his Body, in order to bring him to answer the Action of the Plaintiff: And an Attachment may be had of Course in Chancery upon Affidavit that the Defendant was duly served with a Process of
Subpœna

Subpœna issuing out of that Court, in Case the Defendant does not appear according to the Return of the *Subpœna*: It may likewise be had upon Non-performance of any Order or Decree made by the said Court: And upon a Return made of this *Attachment*, that the Defendant *is not to be found*, Attachment with Proclamation issues out against him. See *West. Symb.* Generally *Attachment* lies for any Thing done in Contempt of the Courts at *Westminster*. It also lies against Attornies for Injustice to their Clients, as well as for Contempts of Court. 2 *Hawk.* 144. It likewise lies against Sheriffs for false Returns of Writs, and against Bailiffs for Frauds in Arrests, and for exceeding the Bounds of their Power, &c. In Contempts of an extraordinary Kind, *Attachments* may be issued against Peers. 2 *Hawk.* 152, 153. *Attachment* lies against a Defendant's Goods only; as in a Court-Baron for Debt. *Kitch.* 79. Besides the Attachments already mentioned and divers others, there is an *Attachment* of the Forest, the Nature of which you may see in *Manwood* 90, 93. *Foreign Attachment* is used to *attach* the Goods of Foreigners found within a City or Liberty, for a Debt due to the Party himself: And by the Custom of some Places, particularly that of *London*, a Person may attach the Debtor's Goods or Money, that are in the Hands of a Stranger: As if *A*. owe to *B*. 10 *l*. and *C*. has any of *A*.'s Goods in his Hands, or owes *A*. Money, *B*. may attach the Goods or Money in *C*.'s Hands, to satisfy himself in part or of all, according as the Debt is.

Attachment of Privilege, is used where a Person by Virtue of his Privilege calls another in an Action, in that Court whereunto he himself belongs, in respect whereof he is privileged. *New Book of Entries* 431.

Attaint, is a Writ which lies against a Jury that have given a false Verdict in any Court of Record, in a real or Personal Action, where the Debt or Damages amount to above 40 *s*. For the Form and Use of this Writ, see *Fitz. Nat. Brev.* 105. and the *New Book of Entries* 84. It seems to derive this Name of Attaint from the Party's endeavouring thereby to *taint* or stain the Credit of the Jury, by whose Verdict he is grieved.

Attainted, is particularly used for such Persons as are found guilty of some Crime, more especially Treason or Felony. A Man is attainted by two Means, *viz*. By Appearance, or by Process. Attainder by Appearance, is by Confession, or Verdict: Confession, when the Prisoner being upon his Indictment asked whether *Guilty*, or *Not Guilty?* answers, *Guilty*, without putting himself upon his Country. Verdict when the Prisoner at the Bar pleads Not guilty, and is found guilty by the Verdict of the Jury. *Attainder* by Process, otherwise called *Attainder* by Default or Outlawry, is when the Criminal flieth, and is not found, until he has been five Times publickly called or proclaimed in the County; on the last of which, upon his Default, he is pronounced outlawed. *Staundf. Pl. Cor.* 44, 122, 182. *Attainder* is said to be larger than *Conviction*, *Conviction* being only by the Jury, or the Confession of the Criminal, who cannot be attainted, till after the Judgment has passed upon him. 1 *Inst.* 390. Likewise Persons may be attainted by by Act of Parliament. A Person attainted of High Treason, forfeits all his Lands, Tenements and Hereditaments; his Blood is corrupted, and likewise his Posterity are rendered base; and this Corruption cannot be taken off, but by Act of Parliament. *Co. Lit.* 391.

Attainder, is where a Man has committed Felony or Treason, and after Conviction Sentence passes on him; or where a Person is attainted of Treason, and condemned by Parliament, on a Bill brought into the House for that Purpose.

Attendant, denotes one that owes a Service or Duty to another, or in some Manner depends on another. Where the Wife is endowed by the Guardian, she shall be attendant to the Guardian, and to the Heir at his full Age. *Cowel*. See also *Kitch*. 109.

Attermining, (from the *French*, signifying a Fine granted for Payment of a Debt.) In the *Stat. Westm. c.* 24. it seems to signify the purchasing or gaining a longer Time.

Attornare Rem, signifies to *attorn*; that is to say, to assign over Money or Goods to some particular Use.

Attornato faciendo vel recipiendo, is a Writ, which a Person owing Suit to a County or other Court may have directed to the Sheriff, &c. commanding him to admit an Attorney to appear for the Person that owes Suit to the Court. *Fitz. Nat. Brev.* 156.

Attorney, is a Person appointed by another to do something in his Stead. *West*, in his *Symb*. defines him thus, That he is such a Person, as by the Consent or Request of another looks after, and takes upon him the Charge of other Men's Business in their Absence. What was the Practice in ancient Times, as to the Admitting of Attornies, you may see in *Cowel*, and also in *Termes de la Ley*. In what Cases a Person at this Day may have an Attorney, and in what not, see *Fitz. Nat. Brev.* 25. *Attorney* is either general or special: *General*, is a Great Officer of the King, created by Letters Patent, whose Office it is to exhibit Informations, and prosecute for the Crown in Criminal Causes, and to exhibit Bills, or Informations in the Exchequer, for any Matter concerning the Crown in Profits or Inheritance: *Special*, is he who is imployed in one or more Things, which he is particularly authorized to act; as to prosecute a Suit, defend an Action brought, or to demand and receive Rent, &c. There is also an *Attorney of the Court of the Dutchy of* Lancaster, who is the second Officer in that Court, and seems, on account of his Skill in Law, to be there placed as Assessor to the Chancellor thereof, to act between the King and his Tenants. *Cowel*.

Attornment, is where a Person is Tenant for Life, and he in Reversion or Remainder, grants his Right or Estate to another; in which Case it behoves the Tenant for Life to agree thereto, and such Agreement is called *Attornment*: For if he in Reversion grants his Right to another, and the Tenant for Life does not attorn, nothing passes by the Grant, unless it be granted by Fine in a Court of Record; in which Case he must attorn. *Termes de la Ley* 65. *Attornment* may be made by Words or Act, or by Payment of a Penny Rent, or other Acknowledgment. See *Littleton*

AU

Littleton, lib. 3. *c.* 18. Where *Attornment* is not now altogether neceſſary, ſee 4 & 5 *Annæ.*

Audience Court, is a Court belonging to the ...

... up a ge...
...book, whereby the Difference between their Receipts and Charge, and their Allowances, is ſhewn; as the Auditors of the Exchequer take the Accounts of ſuch Receivers as collect the Revenues, as

AV

likewiſe of the Sheriffs, Eſcheitors, Collectors and Cuſtomers. *Cowel.* See alſo 33 *H.* 8. *c.* 33. & 4 *Inſt.* 106.

... the Receipts, is an Officer ... Exchequer, who files ... Bills, and makes En... and alſo weekly ... Lord Treaſurer of the ... ceived the preceding ... likewiſe makes De... ch Teller, before they ... ney, and takes their ... more 4 *Inſt.* 167.

... Impreſt, are thoſe ... he Exchequer who ... up the great Ac... King's Cuſtoms, ... *Excheq.* 83.

... Miſchance cauſing ... Perſon, without

... to have ſignified ... ich the Tenant ... y Horſe or Car... ow more com... ontribution that ... rs proportion... the Loſſes of ... ir Goods caſt ... Safeguard of ... other Goods, ... as are on ... And in this ... age, becauſe ... the Rate of ... or Goods ... 14 *Car.*

... ſignifies a ... rchants as ... in ... on's Ship, ... for his Care, ... ver and above the Freight; as in the Bills of Lading it is uſually wrote, —— *Paying ſo much Freight for the ſaid Goods, and Primage and Average accuſtomed. Cowel.*

Averiis Captis in Withernam, is a Writ for taking Cattle to his Uſe, who has his Cattle unlawful-

F 2 ly

ly taken by another, and driven out of the County where they were taken, so that they cannot be replevied. *Reg. Orig.* 82.

Averment, (from the *French*) signifies an Offer to make good an Exception pleaded in Abatement or Bar of the Plaintiff's Action, as well as the actual doing it. It is either *General* or *Particular*; a General *Averment*, which concludes every Plea, &c. or that is in Bar of a Replication, or other Pleadings, containing Matters that are affirmative, ought to be averred with these Words, *viz. And this he is ready to prove*, &c. A particular *Averment*, is when the Life of a Tenant for Life, or Tenant in Tail is *averred*. See *Lit. Co.* 362.

Augmentation, was the Name of a Court erected 27 *Hen.* 8. and the Office still remains, wherein there are many Records of great Use and Importance. *Cowel.*

Avisamentum, Advice, or Counsel.

Aumone. See **Frank almoigne**.

Avoidance, has two Significations; the one when a Benefice becomes void of an Incumbent; the other, when in Chancery it is said in Pleading, confessed or avoided, &c. *Cowel*.

Avowee. See **Advowee**.

Avowry, is where a Person takes a Distress for Rent or other Thing, and the Person grieved sues out a Replevin; in which Case the Distrainer shall justify his Plea, for what Cause he took it: And if it were in his own Right, he ought to shew it, and justify the Taking; and this is called his *Avowry*: But if he took it in the Right of another, in that Case, after he has shewn the Cause, he must make Cognizance of the Taking, either as Bailiff, or Servant to him, in whose Right he did it. *Termes de la Ley* 79.

Auterfoits acquit, is a Plea by a Criminal, that he has already been acquitted of the same Crime wherewith he stands charged. See 3 *Inst.* 213. *H. P. C.* 244.

Authority, signifies a Power given by Word or in Writing, to a second Person to act something.

Award, (from the *French*) signifies the Judgment and Arbitration of one or more Persons, indifferently chosen by two Parties that are at Variance, for the determining of the Matter in Dispute. An *Award* in Writing consists, 1*st*, Of a general Recital of the Differences that have arisen between the contending Parties. 2*dly*, Of the Arbitration Bonds entered into by them, for submitting all Matters in Dispute to the Arbitrators. 3*dly*, The Arbitrators Decision or Determination, which generally concludes with ordaining the contending Parties to execute general Releases to each other. The Form of an Award you may see in the *Young Clerk's Magazine*, and other Treatises on the Subject of Instruments in Conveyancing.

B.

Badger, (from the *French*) signifies one that is licensed to buy Corn in one Place, and carry it to another to sell: Such a Person is exempted by 5 & 6 *Ed.* 6.

Bail, (from the *French*) is, where a Person being arrested or imprisoned upon any Action, either civil or criminal, is freed or set at Liberty, on Sureties given for his Appearance at a certain Day and Place. See *Bract. lib.* 3. And it is called *Bail*, because, by this means, the Party restrained of his Liberty, is delivered into the Hands of his Sureties for his

Forth-

Forthcoming. There is both *Common* and *Special Bail*: *Common* is in Actions of small Concern; and is called so, because any Sureties are taken: But upon Causes of greater Weight, *Special Bail*, or Sureties must be taken. By 12 *Geo.* 1. *c.* 29. none shall be held to Bail on Process out of a Superior Court for any Sum under 10 *l.* which must be sworn to before the Writ issues; and the Sum sworn to must likewise be indorsed on the Back of the Writ; otherwise the Defendant's Body shall not be arrested. For the Difference between Bail and Mainprize, see *Manwood* 167.

Bailiff, is sometimes taken for a Magistrate of some Town, and sometimes for inferior Officers; such as *Bailiffs of Liberties*, and *Bailiffs errant*. *Bailiffs of Liberties*, are such as are appointed by Lords of Manors, within his Liberty to do such Offices as the Sheriff's Officer does abroad in the County. *Bailiffs errant*, are those that the Sheriff appoints to go about the County to execute Writs, to summon the County Sessions, Assises, and the like.

Bailiwick, generally signifies that Liberty which is exempted from Sheriffs of the County, over which Liberty the Lord thereof appoints his own Bailiff, with the like Powers within his Precinct, as the Under-Sheriff exercises under the Sheriff of the County: But, in a particular Sense, *Bailiwick* is taken for the County.

Bailment, signifies a Delivery of any Thing to another; sometimes to be delivered back to the *Bailor*, the Person that delivered them, sometimes to the Use of the *Bailee*, the Person to whom delivered; and sometimes to a third Person: And this Delivery is called a *Bail-ment*, which may be either simple, or conditional: Simple, where the Thing delivered is to be kept for the *Bailor*'s Use: Conditional, where it is to be returned upon Payment of Money, &c.

Baliva, by *Co. Lit.* 105. is said to signify Jurisdiction.

Balivo amovendo, is a Writ for removing a Bailiff from his Office, for Want of his having sufficient Land in his Bailiwick. *Reg. Orig.* 73.

Bank, in the Common Law, is usually taken for a Seat of Judgment, as the King's Bench, or Common Bench, generally called the *Common Pleas. Kitchin* 102.

Bankrupt, in general, is taken for any Person, that, getting his Livelihood by buying and selling, has got into his or her Hands any Goods, and absconds from his Creditors in order to defraud them. By the *Statute* 1 *Jac.* 1. *c.* 15. a Bankrupt is thus described, *viz.* All and every Person and Persons that shall use the Trade of Merchandize, by way of Bargaining, Exchange, Bartery, Chevisance, or otherwise in Gross, or by seeking his, her or their Trade of Living by buying and selling, and being a Subject born within the Realm, or any of the King's Dominions, or Denizen, who shall depart the Realm, or begin to keep his, her or their House or Houses, or otherwise absent him or herself, or take Sanctuary, or suffer him or herself willingly to be arrested for any Debt or other Thing not grown or due, for Money delivered, Wares sold, or any other just or lawful Cause, or good Consideration or Purpose, or hath, or will suffer him or herself to be outlawed, or yield him or herself to Prison; or willingly or fraudulently hath or shall procure him or herself to be arrested

arrested, or his or her Goods, Money or Chattels to be attached or sequestred, or depart from his or her Dwelling-house, or make, or cause to be made, any fraudulent Grant or Conveyance of his, her or their Lands, Tenements, Goods, or Chattels, to the Intent or whereby his, her or their Creditors, being Subjects born, shall or may be defeated or delayed for the Recovery of their just Debts; or being arrested for Debt, shall after his or her Arrest lie in Prison six Months or more, upon that Arrest or Detention in Prison, such Person shall be accounted and adjudged a Bankrupt.

Bargain and Sale, is properly defin'd to be a Contract made of Manors, Lands, Tenements, &c. whereby the Property is transferred from the Bargainor to the Bargainee. It is where a Recompence is given to both the Parties to the Bargain; as if one *bargain* and sell to another for Money, the Money in this Case is a Recompence to the other for the Land. A Bargain and Sale of Lands, &c. in Fee, must be in Writing indented and inrolled, either in the County where they lie, or in one of the Courts at *Westminster*; which Inrollment must be made within six Months after the Date of the Deed. See 27 H. 8. c. 16. But this does not extend to *Bargains* and *Sales* for a Term of Years, &c. they being good, tho' neither indented nor inrolled. A Deed of Bargain and Sale in Fee, consists of the following Principal Parts, *viz.* 1*st*, The Names of the Parties, their Places of Abode, and their Additions. 2*dly*, The Consideration and granting Part, with the Particulars of what is granted. 3*dly*, The *Habendum*, or explanatory Clause, shewing what Interest is granted, to whom, and for whose Use. 4*thly*, A Clause of Warranty: And *Lastly*, Covenants, that the Bargainor is seised in Fee, hath good Right to grant; that the Premisses are free from Incumbrances, and that he will make a further Assurance to the Bargainee of the Lands granted. See the Forms of *Bargains* and *Sales*, in the *Young Clerk's Magazine*, and other Treatises on Conveyances.

Baron, has different Significations; For, 1*st*, It is taken for a certain Degree of Nobility. 2*dly*, For an Officer; as the *Barons* of Exchequer, the Principal of whom is called the *Lord Chief Baron*, the other three being his Assistants, in Causes of Justice between the Crown and the Subjects, touching Affairs appertaining to the Exchequer and the King's Revenues. The Chief Baron alone in Term-Time sits upon *Nisi Prius*, which comes out of the Remembrancer's Office, or out of the Office of the Clerk of the Pleas. He takes Recognizances for the King's Debts, for Appearances and observing of Orders. There are several other Branches of the *Lord Chief Baron*, for which see *Cowel*. 3*dly*, *Baron*, in another Signification is used for the Husband, in relation to his Wife, who, in our Law is called *Feme*; and they are deemed but one Person; so that a Wife cannot be a Witness either for or against her Husband, nor he against or for her, (except in the Case of High Treason.

Bar, signifies a peremptory Exception to a Demand or Plaint, and is said to be such a Plea, as is sufficient for ever to destroy the Plaintiff's Action. *Cowel*. It is divided into a *Bar to common Intendment*, *Bar Special*, *Bar Temporary*,

rary, and *Bar Perpetual*. *Bar to common Intendment* is a General *Bar*, which commonly disables the Plaintiff's Declaration or Plea. *Bar Special*, is what is more than common, and falls out in the Case in Question, upon some particular Circumstance of the Fact; as where an Executor is sued for his Testator's Debt, pleads, that he had no Goods in his Hands at the Day of the Writ sued out: This is a good Bar to common Intendment, or at first View; but yet it may so happen, that more Goods might come into his Hands since that Time, which if the Plaintiff, by Way of Replication, can shew, then, unless the Defendant has a more special Plea or Bar to be alledged, he must be condemned in the Action. See *Plowd*. 26, 28. *Bar Temporary*, is a good Bar for the present, yet may afterwards fail, as *Plene administravit*; that is to say, *fully administred*, until it appears, that more Goods came to the Hands of the Executors, &c. afterwards. *Bar Perpetual*, is that which overthrows the Plaintiff's Action for ever.

Barraster, or **Barrister**, are Counsellors at Law admitted to plead at the Bar on Behalf of their Clients.

Barrator, or **Barretor**, in our Law signifies a common Mover or Maintainer of Suits and Quarrels, either in Courts, or elsewhere in the Country, and is one that is never quiet himself, but is continually at Variance with one or another. None can be deemed a *Barrator* on the Account of one Act only; for the Indictment must charge the Defendant with being a common *Barrater*.

Barter, in our Books signifies to exchange Wares for Wares. 1 R. 3. c. 9. And in the same Sense the Substantive *Bartry* is used. 13 *Eliz*. c. 7.

Base Fee, is to hold in Fee at the Will of the Lord.

Bastard, is one that is born of an unmarried Woman, whose Father is not known by Order of Law; and therefore such a one is reputed the Child of the People. If a Man marries a Woman that is big with Child by another that was not her Husband, and the Child is born within the Espousals, then it shall be deemed the Child of the Husband, tho' it were born but one Day after the Solemnization of the Marriage. *New Termes de la Ley*.

Bastardy, signifies Defect of Birth in one begotten out of Wedlock. *Bract. lib*. 5. c. 19. *Bastardy* is either General or Special: General, is a Certificate from the Bishop of the Diocese to the King's Justices, after just Enquiry made, whether the Party is a *Bastard* or not, upon some Question of Inheritance. *Bastardy Special* is a Suit commenced in the King's Courts against a Person that calls another *Bastard*; and it is called so, because Bastardy is the principal Point in Trial, and no Inheritance contended for. Whence it appears, that *Bastardy* is rather taken for Examination or Trial, whether a Person's Birth be legitimate or not, than for Bastardy itself.

Baston, by some old Statutes, signifies one of the Servants to the Warden of the Fleet, that attends the King's Court with a painted Staff, for the taking into Custody such as are committed by the Court. 1 R. 2. c. 12. 5 *Eliz*. c. 23. See **Tipstaff**.

Batable Ground, was the Land that heretofore lay between *England* and *Scotland* (when the Kingdoms were distinct) and in question to whom it belonged. 23 H. 8. c. 6.

c. 6. 32 *H*. 8. *c*. 6. According to the Opinion of *Skene*, the Word seems to mean as much as if one should say *Debateable Ground*. *Lamb. Brit. Tit. Cumberland*.

Battel, in the Common Law, signifies a Trial by Combat, the Manner of which, because of its Length, being full of Ceremonies, and now totally in Disuse, we think proper to refer you to *Glanv. lib.* 14. *Bract. lib.* 3. *Brit. c.* 22. *Smith de Rep. Angl. lib.* 2. See **Combat**.

Battery, (from the *French*) is a violent Beating or Striking of a Person; for which Offence, as it tends to the Breach of the Peace, the Party injured may either indict the other, who thereupon shall be fined to the King; or have his Action of Trespass, Assault and Battery against him, and recover such Damages as the Jury shall give him. This Action will lie as well before, as after the Indictment: But if the Plaintiff made the first Assault, the Defendant shall be quit, and the Plaintiff shall be amerced to the King for his false Suit. Here it will be proper to observe, That the Record of the Conviction of the Defendant on an Indictment, may serve for Evidence in the Action of Trespass. Yet in some Cases a Person may justify the moderate Beating of another; as a Parent his Child, the Master his Servant or Apprentice, the Gaoler, or his Servant, the unruly Prisoners, the Officer him that is arrested, and cannot otherwise be made to obey. A Man may likewise justify the Beating another in Defence of his own Person, or the Person of his Wife, Father, Mother, or Master. One may likewise justify the Beating of another, in Defence of one's Goods, or in Maintenance of Justice: But here it is to be observed, that a Person cannot justify the Deed, unless he be constrained to it by a necessary Cause.

Bawdy-House, is a House of ill Repute, to which lewd Persons of both Sexes frequently resort, and there commerce together. Keeping a Bawdy-House is a common Nusance, not only on account that it endangers the Publick Peace, by drawing together debauched and idle Persons, and creating Quarrels, but likewise for its Tendency towards the Corruption of the Manners of the Commonalty. Persons convicted of keeping Bawdy-Houses, are punishable by Fine and Imprisonment; and also are liable to be set in the Pillory, and suffer such other infamous Punishments, as the Court shall at their Discretion inflict.

Beacon, signifies a Signal that is well known, such as Fires maintained on the Coasts of the Sea, to prevent Shipwrecks and Invasions. And *Beaconnage* signifies the Money paid towards the Maintenance of a *Beacon*.

Bearors, is taken to be the same as Maintainers. By *Stat.* 4 *Ed.* 3. *c.* 11. Justices of Assise shall enquire, hear, and determine of Maintenors, *Bearors* and Conspirators, and of those that commit Champarty, *&c.*

Beau-Pleader, is a Writ upon the Statute of *Marlbridge*, 52 *H*. 3. *c*. 11. whereby it is ordained, That neither in the Circuit of Justices, nor in Counties, Hundreds, or Court-Barons, any Fine shall be taken of any Person for *Fair Pleading*; that is to say, for pleading fairly, or to the Purpose; upon which Statute this Writ was ordained against such as violate the Law herein. See *Fitz. Nat. Brev.* 270. who defines it to this Effect, *viz.* The Writ for not Fair Pleading

ing lies, where the Sheriff, or Bailiff, in his Court, will take Fine of the Party, either Plaintiff or Defendant, for that he pleaded not fairly: And *Beau-Pleader* was as well in respect to the vicious Pleadings, as of the fair Pleadings. 2 *Inst.* 122.

Bedel, is a Messenger or Apparitor of a Court, who cites Persons to appear and answer. It also signifies an Inferior Officer of a Parish or Liberty, such as are well known in *London* and the Suburbs. *Manwood* says, a Bedle is an Officer of the Forest, who makes all Manner of Garnishments for the Courts of the Forest, and all Proclamations as well within the Courts of the Forest, as without; and also executes the Process of the Forest, like unto a Bailiff Errant of a Sheriff in his County.

Bedelary, is the same to a *Bedel*, as Bailiwick to a Bailiff. *Lit. lib.* 3. *c.* 5.

Bederepe, is a customary Service, whereby Tenants were anciently bound to reap their Landlord's Corn in Harvest-time; in Imitation whereof, some are to this Day tied to give them one, two, or more Days Work.

Benefice, is generally taken for an Ecclesiastical Living, whether a Dignity, or other: And by 13 *R.* 2. *Stat.* 2. *c.* 8. are divided into Elective, and of Gift; and in the same Sense it is used in the Canon Law. *Duarenius de Beneficiis.* The Portions of Lands and other immoveable Things granted by the Lords to their Followers, for their Maintenance, were at first called *Munera*, Gifts, while they were revocable at the Lord's Pleasure: But afterwards, while *Temporary*, or held for some limited Time, they were called *Beneficia*: And when by Degrees these Tenures became perpetual and hereditary, then they left their former Name of *Beneficia* or *Benefice* to the Clergy, and retained to themselves the Name of *Feuds.* See *Spelm. of Feuds, c.* 2.

Beneficio primo Ecclesiastico habendo, is a Writ directed from the King to the Lord Keeper, to bestow the first Benefice that shall fall in the King's Gift, above or under such a Value, upon this or that Person. *Reg. Orig.* 307.

Benevolentia Regis habenda, is the Form of purchasing the King's Pardon in ancient Times, and Submissions, in order to be restored to Estate, Title or Place. *Cowel.*

Besaile, signifies the Father of a Grandfather; and, in our Law, is a Writ that lies where the Great Grandfather was seised in Fee of any Lands, &c. at the Time of his Death; and after his Decease a Stranger enters the same Day upon him, and keeps out the Heir. See *Fitz. Nat. Brev.* 221.

Bigamus, is any Man that hath married two or more Wives, successively after each other's Death, or a Widow. 18 *Ed.* 3. *c.* 2. 1 *Ed.* 6. *c.* 12. 2 *Inst.* 273.

Bigamy, denotes a double Marriage; it is used in the Common Law for an Impediment to be a Clerk, on account he has been twice married. 4 *Ed.* 1. *c.* 5. The 1 *Jac.* 1. *c.* 11. calls that *Bigamy*, where a Person marries a second Wife, &c. the first being living, which is made Felony: But *Bigamy* is improperly so called, that Crime being rather *Polygamy*; for *Bigamy* is not where a Man has two Wives at a Time, but where he has two Wives one after another.

Bilanciis deferendis, is a Writ directed to a Corporation, for carrying tying Weights to such a Haven, there to weigh the Wool. Persons were formerly licensed to transport Wool. *Reg. Orig.* 170.

Bilinguis, in a general Sense denotes a double-tongued Man; but in a legal one is used for a Jury that passes in any Case between an *Englishman* and a Foreigner; of which Jury, Part ought to be *English*, and Part Strangers. This is vulgarly called a Party-Jury; but more properly a Jury *de Medietate Linguæ*. See 28 *Ed.* 3. *c.* 13.

Bill, has divers Significations in Law. First, it is all one with what we call a Bond or Obligation, only that it has not a Condition as a Bond has, and it is frequently made without a Penalty, in which Case it is called a *single Bill*; but if with a Penalty, then a *Penal Bill*. The Forms of these Bills you may see in the *Young Clerk's Magazine* and other Treatises on Conveyancing. Secondly, a Bill is a Declaration in Writing, wherein is expressed either the Wrong the Complainant has suffered by the Defendant, or else some Fault that the Party complained of has committed against some Law or Statute of the Realm. This kind of Bill is sometimes exhibited to Justices *Itinerant*, at the general Assises, by Way of Indictment or Information; but more especially is addressed to the Lord Chancellor, for unconscionable Wrongs done. It is sometimes referred to others having Jurisdiction, according as the Law directs. It contains the Fact complained of, the Damages thereby suffered, and Petition and Process against the Defendant for Redress. *Cowel*. *Billa Vera*, or a *true Bill*, is two Words indorsed by the Grand Inquest upon a Presentment or Indictment, thereby signifying that the Prosecutor has Presentment or Indictment with probable Evidence, and that on that Account it is worthy of further Consideration: Whereupon the Defendant is said to stand indicted; and if the Crime touch the Life of him that is indicted, it is still referred to another Inquest, called the Jury of Life and Death, by whom, if found guilty, then he stands convicted of the Crime, and is by the Judge to receive Sentence. See *Ignoramus*. See also *Indictment*.

Bill of Exchange, is a Security entred into among Merchants, which on the Credit of the Drawer gnerally passes as Money: These *Bills* are made payable either at Sight, or at so many Days, Weeks or Months after Date. The Space of a Month after the Date of a Bill is called *Usance*, and if two or three Months after, double or treble Usance.

Bill of Store, is a Sort of a Licence granted at the *Custom-house* to Merchants, to carry such Stores and Provisions as are necessary for their Voyage, Custom free. *Cowel*.

Bill of Sufferance, is a Licence granted at the Custom-house to a Merchant, suffering him to trade from one *English* Port to another, without paying Custom. 14 *Car.* 2. *c.* 11.

Bissextile, is vulgarly called Leap-Year, because the sixth Day before the Calends of March is twice reckoned, *viz.* on the 24th and 25th of *February*; on which Account the *Bissextile* Year has one Day more than other Years, and happens every fourth Year. This Intercalation of a Day was first invented by *Julius Cæsar*, in order to make the Year agree with the Course of the Sun. To prevent

vent all Doubt that might arife thereupon, by a Statute 21 *H.* 3. it is ordained, that the Day increafing the Leap-Year, and the Day next before, fhall be accounted but one Day.

Blackmail, in the Counties of *Cumberland, Northumberland,* and fome other Northern Counties, denotes a certain Rate of Money, Corn, *&c.* formerly paid to fome inhabiting near the Borders, being Men of Name and Power, and who were allied with certain great Robbers within thofe Counties; to the End that they might be protected by them againft fuch Robbers. 43 *Eliz. c.* 23. Thefe Robbers were called Mofs-Troopers, and feveral Statutes made againft them. *Black-Mail* is the fame with Black Rents, fignifying the Rents that were formerly paid in Corn and Flefh.

Blacks of Waltham, were a Set of defperate Deer-Stealers, againft whom a Law was made in the Reign of *Geo.* 1. See *Waltham Blacks.*

Black Rod. The Gentleman Ufher of the *Black Rod*, takes his Name from the *Black Rod* he carries in his Hand, and is the chief Gentleman Ufher to the King. He has alfo the keeping of the Chapter-houfe Door, when a Chapter is fitting; and in Time of Parliament attends on the Houfe of Peers. He has the like Habit with that of the *Regifter* of the Order and Garter King at Arms, which he wears on the Feaft of *St. George,* and all Chapters. He has great Power; for all Peers called in Queftion for any Crime, are committed to his Cuftody.

Blanch-Firmes. The Crown Rents were in ancient Times referved in *Liberis albis*, or *Blanch-Firmes,* in which Cafe the Buyer was holden *Dealbare firmam*; that is to fay, his bafe Money or Coin was to be melted down in the Exchequer, and reduced to the Finenefs of Standard Silver; or inftead of that he paid to the King 12*d.* in the Pound by Way of Addition.

Blank-Bar, is the fame with what is called a *Common Bar,* and fignifies a Plea in *Bar,* which in an Action of Trefpafs is put in to compel the Plaintiff to affign the certain Place where the Trefpafs was committed: It is moftly in Practice in the *Common Pleas*; for in the *King's Bench* the Place is commonly afcertained in the Declaration. 9 *Cro.* 594.

Blank-Farm, fignifies a white Farm, that is to fay, where the Rent is paid in Silver, and not in Cattle.

Blafarius, denotes an *Incendiary.* See **Blount.**

Blafphemy, is a great Indignity or Injury offered to the *Almighty,* by denying what is his Due and of Right belonging to him, or attributing to the *Creator* that which is not agreeable to his Nature. *Blafphemers* of God, fuch as thofe who deny his Being, or Providence, and all contumelious *Reproachers* of *Jefus Chrift* are Offences at the Common Law, and punifhable by Fine, *&c.* See 1 *Hawk. P. C.* 87. By 9 & 10 *W.* 3. *c.* 32. If any Perfon by Writing or Speaking, *&c.* fhall deny any of the Perfons in the Trinity, *&c.* he fhall be incapable of Office, *&c.*

Bloodwit, is often ufed in ancient Charters, for an Amercement for *Bloodfhed.* By *Skene* it is wrote *Bloodweit,* that is to fay (as the *Scotchmen* call it) an Unlaw for Wrong or Injury, fuch as the Effufion of Blood is: For he that hath

hath Bloodwit granted him, has free Liberty to take all Amercements of Courts for shedding of *Blood*. *Bloodwit* is likewise said to be a Customary Fine, paid as a Composition or Attonement for the Shedding or Drawing of Blood, for which the Place was answerable, if the Offender was not discovered: Wherefore a Privilege or Exemption from this Penalty was granted by the King, or Supreme Lord, as a special Favour. See *Paroch. Antiq. p.* 114.

Bloody-hand, signifies the Apprehending of a Trespasser in a Forest, upon the Circumstance of his Hands or other Parts being bloody, though he be not found chasing or hunting the Deer. See *Manwood*.

Bockland, in the *Saxons* Time is what we now call Freehold Lands or Land held by Charter; by which Name it was distinguished from *Folkland* or Copyhold Land. *New Termes de la Ley* 88.

Bodies Politick. See **Corporation**.

Bolting, is a Term of Art used among the Gentlemen of our Inns of Court, thereby intending a private Arguing of Cases. The Manner of it, as we are told, is this, *viz.* An Ancient and two Barristers sit as Judges, and three Students bring each a Case, out of which the Judges chuse one to be argued; which done, the Students first begin to argue, and after them the Barristers. It is inferior to *Mooting*. In *Lincoln's Inn* in the Vacation, *Mondays* and *Wednesdays* are the *Bolting* Days; *Tuesdays* and *Thursdays* the *Mooting* Days. *Cowel*.

Bona Fide, is as much as to say such a Thing was really done without either Fraud or Deceit.

Bona Notabilia, are such Goods as a Party dying has in another Diocese, than that in which he dies, amounting to the Value of 5 *l.* at least; in which Case the Will of the Deceased must be proved, or Administration granted, in the Court of the Archbishop of the Province; unless by Composition or Custom other Dioceses are authorised to do it. How *Bona Notabilia* are rated, see Book of Canons 92, 93. *Perk. Sect.* 489.

Bona Patria, is an Assise of Countrymen or good Neighbours: Sometimes called *Assisa bonæ Patriæ*, when twelve or more are chosen out of the Country to pass upon an *Assise*: And they are likewise called *Juratores*, because they swear judicially in the Presence of the Party. *Skene.* See **Assisors**.

Bona peritura, denotes perishable Goods. See 13 *Ed.* 1. *c.* 4.

Bond, is an obligatory Instrument or Deed in Writing, whereby one binds himself to another to pay a certain Sum of Money, or to perform some other Act; as that the Obligor shall re-deliver to the Obligee a Box of Writings and Papers intrusted in his Hands by the Obligee; shall execute a sufficient Conveyance of his Estate; shall perform the Covenants of a Deed, *&c.* A Bond contains a preremptory Obligation, with a Penalty; and usually under it is written a Condition expressly mentioning the Sum that is to be paid, or other Thing to be performed, to whom, and at what limited Time. The Condition of a Bond must be to do a Lawful Act, and likewise what there is a Possibility of doing; otherwise it is void: It must also have at the End of it these Words, *viz. Then this Obligation to be void*; for if they are omitted, the Condition becomes void;

void; but not the Obligation. The Forms of Bonds and Conditions you may see in the *Young Clerk's Magazine*, and other Collections of Instruments in Conveyancing.

Bonis non Amovendis, is a Writ directed to the Sheriffs of *London*, &c. charging them, that one against whom Judgment is obtained, and prosecuting a Writ of Error, be not suffered to remove his Goods, until the Error be tried. *Reg. Orig.* 131.

Bordagium, is the Tenure of *Bordlands*.

Bordhalfpeny, is said to be paid in Fairs and Markets, for setting up Tables, *Boards*, and Stalls for Sale of Wares.

Bordlands, are the *Demesnes* which Lords keep in their own Hands for the Maintenance of their Board or Table. *Bract. lib.* 4. *tract.* 3. *c.* 9.

Bordlode, was an ancient Service required of Tenants to carry Timber out of the Woods of the Lord to his House: It is likewise said to signify the Quantity of Food or Provision, which the *Bordarii* or Boardmen paid for their Bord-Lands.

Bord-Service, is said to be a Tenure of *Bord-Lands*, whereby some Lands in certain Places are said to be held of the Bishop of *London*, and that the Tenants do now pay Six-Pence an Acre in Lieu of finding Provisions, as anciently for the Lord's Board or Table.

Borough, is a Corporate Town, that is not a City, and such a Town as sends Burgesses to Parliament. *Skene* tells us, that *Burg* or *Burgh*, whence we derive our *Borough*, does in a metaphorical Sense signify a Town having a Wall or some Kind of Inclosure about it. In *Lit. Sect.* 164. We are told, that all Places, that in Old Time had among our Ancestors the Name of *Borough*, were one Way or other fenced or fortified.

Borough-English, is a customary Descent of Lands or Tenements, whereby in some Places, Lands, &c. descend to the youngest Son; or if the Owner of the Land have no Issue, then to his younger Brother; as in *Edmonton*, &c. *Kitch.* 102.

Borough-Head, see *Headborough*, *Borough Goods*, before 11 *Ed.* 1. seem not to have been deviseable.

Boscage, signifies that Food which Wood and Trees yield to Cattle as Mast: Yet *Manwood* says to be quit of *Boscage*, is to be discharged of paying any Duty of Windfall Wood in the Forest. *Cowel*.

Bote, is an old Word signifying Recompence or Amends.

Bothagium, signifies *Boothage*, or customary Dues paid to the Lord of the Manor or Soil, for the Pitching and Standing of Booths in Fairs or Markets. 19 *H.* 6.

Bottomry, is by some defined to be, where a Master of a Ship borrows Money upon the Keel or Bottom of his Ship, and binds the Ship itself, that if the Money be not paid by the Day limited, the Creditor shall have her: But by others *Bottomry* is defined to be, where a Person lends Money to a Merchant, who wants it to traffick with, and is to be paid a greater Sum at the Return of the Ship, standing to the Hazard of the Voyage; on which Account though the Profit be greater than the common Interest, yet it is not Usury, by Reason that the Money is furnished at the Hazard of the Lender; for if the Ship perishes, he shares in the Loss. Where a Master of a Ship, is in a strange Country, where none of the Owners are, nor any Goods of theirs, nor of his own; and for Want of Money he cannot perform his Voyage; in that Case he may take up Money upon *Bottomry*, and all the Owners will be chargeable therewith. The Form of a Bill of Bottomry you may see in the *Scrivener's Guide*.

Bow-bearer, is an Under-Officer of the Forest, whose Duty it is to oversee, and make true Inquisition, as well of sworn Men as unsworn, in every Bailiwick of the Forest; and of all Trespasses done, either to Vert or Venison; and to cause them to be attached, in the next Court of Attachment, there to be presented without any Concealment. *Crompt. Jurisd.* 201.

Brandy, is a Spirit or strong Water, chiefly made in *France* from the Lees of Wine or Cyder; and is mentioned in the Statute 20 *Car.* 2. *c.* 1. In 1688. Upon an Argument in the Exchequer, whether *Brandy* were a *Strong-Water*, or *Spirit*, it was resolved to be a *Spirit*. But in 1669. by a grand Committee of the whole *House of Commons*, it was voted to be a *Strong-Water* perfectly made. See 22 *Car.* 2. *c.* 4.

Brasium, signifies Malt; and in the ancient Statutes *Brasiator* is taken for a Brewer, and also at this Time for a Malster.

Breach, is said to be where a Person breaks through the Performance of the Condition of a Bond, Covenant, &c. that he entered into; on an Action upon which a *Breach* must be assigned: And this Assignment of *Breach* must not be general, but particular.

Brecca, signifies a Breach, Decay, or other Want of Repair, and in that Sense it is used. *Pat.* 16 *Ric.* 2.

Bredwite, was a Fine or Amercement formerly imposed for Defaults in the Assise of Bread; to be exempted from which, was a special Privilege granted to the Tenants of the Honour of *Wallingford* by King *Hen.* 2. See *Paroch. Antiq.* 114.

Brehon. In *Ireland* their Judges were anciently called *Brehones*, and consequently from thence their Law might be termed *Brehon Law*.

Breve, which is said to be so called from the Brevity of it, is a Writ directed to the Chancellor, Judges, Sheriffs or other Officers, where a Person is summoned or attached to answer in the King's Courts, &c. A Variety of Forms of Writs you may see in the Register. See more under Tit. *Writ*.

Breve Perquirere, denotes a Purchasing of a Writ or Licence for Trial in the King's Courts: Whence comes the present Usage of paying 6 *s.* 8 *d.* Fine to the King, where the Debt is 40 *l.* and of 10 *s.* where it is 100 *l.* &c. in Suits for Money due upon Bond.

Breve de Recto, is a Writ of Right, or Licence for a Person ejected, to sue for the Possession of the Estate detained from him. *Cowel*. See **Recto**.

Brevibus & Rotulis liberandis, is a Writ or Command to a Sheriff to deliver to his Successor the County, with the Appurtenances, together with the Rolls, Writs and other Things belonging to that Office. *Reg. Orig.* 295.

Bribery, (from a *French* Word, signifying to devour or eat) is a high Offence; as where a Person in a judicial Place takes any Fee, Pension, Gift or Reward of any Person, save the King only, for doing his Duty: But in a larger Sense it is taken for the Receiving or Offering

BR

Offering any undue Reward, to or by any Man concerned in the Administration of publick Justice, to act contrary to his Office.

Bribour, is taken to denote a Person that pilfers another Man's Goods. 28 *Ed.* 2. *c.* 1.

Brief, is a *Compendium* or Abrigment of a Client's, wrote out for the Instruction of Counsel, on a Cause depending, in which Care must be taken, that the Client's Case be briefly, yet fully stated; the Proofs be orderly laid down, with the Objections that may be apprehended will arise in the Cause from the opposite Side; together likewise with Answers to those Objections.

Brief for Loss by Fire, see 4 & 5 *Ann. c.* 14.

Brigbote, denotes to be freed from the Reparation of Bridges.

Brocage, by some termed *Brokerage*, is taken for the Wages or Hire of a Broker.

Brodehalfpeny, or **Broadhalfpeny**. See **Bordhalfpeny**.

Brokers, are of two Sorts, *viz.* An *Exchange-Broker* and *Pawn-Broker*. An Exchange-Broker is he that deals in Matters of Money and Merchandise between Merchants and Tradesmen, for which they have a Fee or Reward allowed them. These *Exchange Brokers* are to be licensed in *London*, by the Lord Mayor, who administers them an Oath, and takes Security for the faithful Discharge of their Offices; and for Want of such Licence they are liable to a Penalty, as well as the Persons that employ them. A *Pawn-Broker* is one who commonly keeps a Shop, and lends out Money to Persons in Want of it upon a Pledge or Pawn, and usually at an exorbitant Interest.

Brothel-Houses, Lewd Places

BU

were so called, by a Proclamation *Anno* 37 *H.* 8. See 3 *Inst.* 205. See **Bawdy-House**.

Brockbote or **Brugbote**. See **Brigbote**.

Buggery, in *Co.* 12. *Rep.* 36. is defin'd to be a carnal Copulation against Nature, and this either by the Confusion of Species; that is to say, a Man or a Woman with a Brute Beast; or Sexes; as a Man with a Man, or a Woman with a Woman. We are told that this Sin against God, Nature, &c. was first brought into *England* by the *Lombards*. *Rot. Parl.* 50 *Ed.* 3. *Numb.* 58. This abominable Crime has for many Years past been much practised in this Kingdom, without any exemplary Punishment of the Offender, (tho' by *Statute* it is made without Clergy) until 12 *Geo.* 1. when a Number of Wretches being convicted of these detestable Practices, some of them were put to Death.

Bull, signifies a Brief or Mandate of the Pope, which by 28 *Hen.* 8. are declared to be void. See also 13 & 23 *Eliz.*

Bullion, signifies Gold or Silver in Mass or Billet, 9 *Ed.* 3. *Stat.* 2. *c.* 2. It likewise signifies the King's Exchange, or Place to which Gold in the Lump is brought to be tried, or exchanged. See 27 *Ed.* 3. *Stat.* 2. *c.* 14.

Burgage, denotes an ancient Tenure, whereby the Inhabitants by Custom held their Lands, &c. of the King, or other Superior of the Borough, at a certain annual Rent. See **Borough**.

Burgagium liberum, was where the Tenants had paid their yearly Rent to the Superior Lord, they were free from all other Services. *Cowel.*

Burgbote, signifies a Contribution towards the Building or Repairing

of

of Castles, or Walls of Defence of a City or *Borough*.

Burg-English. See **Borough-English**.

Burgesses, properly signifies Men of Trade, or the Inhabitants of a Borough or walled Town; but this Name is usually applied to the Magistrates of such a Town; as the Bailiff and Burgesses of *Morpeth*, &c. We also call those Burgesses, who serve in Parliament for a Borough or Corporation.

Burgh-breche, is a Fine imposed on the Community of a Town for a Breach of the Peace. *Leg. Canuti* 55.

Burgheriste, signifies a Breach of the Peace in a Town. *Blount*.

Burgware, denotes a Citizen or Burgess.

Burglary, is a felonious Breaking and entering into another Person's Dwelling in the Night-time, with an Intent to commit some Felony, whether he executes the same or not: Yet, in the natural Signification, *Burglary* signifies no more than the robbing of a House; but our Lawyers restrain it to robbing a House, or breaking into by Night, in order to rob, or execute some other felonious Act. The like Offence committed by Day is called *House-breaking*, to distinguish it from *Burglary*. The Offence of *Burglary* is excluded the Benefit of Clergy, and may be committed several Ways. For which see *Cromp. Just.* 28, 29, 30. 3 *Inst.* 363.

Burning of Houses, &c. See *Arson*.

Butlerage, signifies an old Duty imposed upon Wine imported, which the King's Butler might take of every Ship, *viz.* 2 *s.* a Ton of all Strangers.

Bye, or **Bee** (from the *Saxon*) signifies a Dwelling-place or Habitation.

By-Laws, are Laws made by the *By*, as those that are made by Consent in Courts-Leet, or Courts-Baron; Orders of Corporations, for the governing of their Members; Gilds and Fraternities of Trades, who by Letters Patent of Incorporation, may likewise make By-Laws, for the better Regulation of Trade among themselves, &c. But *By-Laws* must be reasonable, and ought to be for the common Benefit, and not to the private Interest of any particular Person; and likewise must be agreeable to the publick Laws in Being. How By-Laws are to be approved, see 19 *Hen.* 7. *c.* 7.

C.

Cabal, signifies a private Meeting.

Cablish, according to the Writers of the Forest-Laws, signifies Brushwood; but *Spelman* thinks it more properly to denote Windfall-Wood.

Cachepolus, signifies a *Catchpole* or inferior Bailiff.

Cade, of Herrings, is 500, of Sprats 1000. But it is said, that anciently 600 made the Cade of Herrings, six Score to the Hundred, which is called *Magnum Centum*. *Cowel*.

Caep Gildum, signifies the restoring Goods or Cattle.

Calangium, or **Calangia**, denotes a Challenge, Claim or Dispute.

Calcagium, was a Contribution formerly paid by the neighbouring Inhabitants towards the Making and Repairing of Causeys or common Highways, from which Burden some Persons were exempted by Royal Charter. *Kennet's Glos.*

Calefagium, signifies a Right to take Fuel yearly. *Blount*.

Callis, by some of our ancient Authors,

Campartum, signifies any Part or Portion of a larger Field or Ground. *Cowel.*

Campus Martii or **Maii**, was an Assembly of the People yearly on *May-Day*, where they confederated to defend the Kingdom against all Enemies. *Leg. Ed. Confess. c.* 35.

Candlemas-Day, or the Feast of the *Purification* of the Blessed Virgin *Mary*, being the second Day of *February*, is held in *Hillary Term*, by all the Inns of Court, as a grand Day: And this Festival is no Day in any of the Courts at *Westminster*; wherefore the Judges do not sit that Day.

Canfara, signifies a Trial by hot Irons, which was formerly used in this Kingdom. See *Ordeal*.

Canon, denotes a Law of the Church, which Law partly consists of certain Rules taken out of the Scripture; partly of the Writings of the Fathers of the Church, partly of the Ordinances of general Councils, and partly of Decrees of the Popes in former Ages.

Cantel, by *Blount*, is said to signify that which is added above Measure, tho' it rather seems to signify what we now call Lump; as to buy by Measure, or by the Lump.

Cantred, in *Wales*, signifies a Hundred; for there they divide their Counties into *Cantreds*, as we do ours into Hundreds.

Capacity, in general, signifies an Ability or Fitness to contain or receive: And in Law, is where a Person or Body Politick is able to give or take Lands, or other Things, or to sue Actions: As an Alien has a sufficient Capacity to sue in a personal Action, but in a real he has not. The King has two Capacities, a *Natural* and a *Politick*; in the first of which he may purchase to him and his Heirs; in the latter to him and his Successors. Persons attainted of Treason or Felony, Ideots, Lunaticks, Infants, Feme Coverts without their Husbands, &c. are not, unless in some special Cases, capable to grant or convey: But Persons void of those Impediments, are capable to grant, sue and be sued, at the Age of twenty-one Years; and at fourteen, which is their Age of Discretion, they are by Law capable to marry, be a Witness, &c.

Cape, is a judicial Writ, concerning Plea of Lands or Tenements; and is so termed, as most Writs that have that Word in it, which carries the chief End of it. This Writ is divided into *Cape Magnum*, and *Cape Parvum*, both which affect Things immoveable. *Cape Magnum*, or the *Grand Cape*, lies before Appearance, to summons the Tenant to answer the Default, and also over to the Demandant. The *Cape Parvum* summons the Tenant to answer the Default only; and therefore is frequently called *Petit Cape*, not by Reason it is of small Force, but for that it consists of few Words. *Cape Magnum*, in *Old Nat. Brev.* is defin'd to be where a Person has brought a *Præcipe quod reddat* of a Thing that touches a Plea of Land, and the Tenant makes Default at the Day given to him in the original Writ; then this Writ shall go for the King, to take the Land into his Hands; and if he comes not at the Day given him, he loses his Land, &c.

Cape ad Valenciam, is of the same Species of *Cape Magnum*, and is where I am impleaded of Lands, and vouch to warrant another, against whom the Summons *Ad warrantizandum* has been awarded, and he comes not at the Day given; then if the Demandant recover against me, I shall have this Writ against the Vouchee, and recover so much in Value of the Land of the Vouchee, in case he has so much; and if not, I shall have Execution of such Lands and Tenements as shall descend to him in Fee; or if he purchases afterwards, I shall have a Resummons, &c. against him. *Note;* This Writ lies before Appearance. See *Old Nat. Brev.* 161.

Capias, is a Writ of two Sorts, one before Judgment and the other after. That before *Judgment* is called *Capias ad respondendum*; and those after Judgment are called *Capias ad satisfaciendum, Capias pro fine*, &c. Where the Defendant is not taken upon the *Capias ad satisficiendum*, there may be an *Alias*, and a *Pluries Capias* issued. See *Pract. Solic.* 290.

Capias ad satisfaciendum, is a Writ of Execution that issues after Judgment is obtained, and lies where a Person recovers in a personal Action; as for Debt, Damages, or Detinue in any of the King's Courts, and the Defendant has not Lands or other Effects to be levied upon: And in this Case, he that recovers, shall have this Writ directed to the Sheriffs, commanding him that he take the Defendant's Body, and he shall be imprisoned till Satisfaction be made for the Debt, &c. recovered against him.

Capias pro fine, is a Writ that lies where a Person is fined to the King for some Offence committed against a Statute, and the Defendant neglects to discharge the Fine according to the Judgment; his Body is therefore to be taken by this Writ, and committed to Gaol till the Fine be paid. *Co. lib.* 3. 12.

Capias Utlagatum, is a Writ which lies against one that is outlawed upon an Action personal or criminal, by Virtue of which the Sheriff apprehends the Party outlawed, for not appearing upon the *Exigent*, and keeps him in safe Custody until the Day of Return, and then presents him to the Court, to be there further ordered for his Contempt; and the Defendant in such Case, in the *Common Pleas*, was in former Times to be committed to the *Fleet*, there to remain, until he had sued out the King's Pardon, and appeared to the Action. Upon a special *Capias Utlagatum* in the same Writ, the Sheriff is commanded, and may seise all the Defendant's Lands, Goods and Chattels, for the Contempt to the King; and the Plaintiff, after Inquisition taken thereon, and returned into the Exchequer, may have the Lands, &c. extended, and a Grant of the Goods, &c. thereby to compel the Defendant to appear; which, when he shall do so, and reverse the Outlawry, are to be restored to him. See *Old Nat. Brev.* 154. Upon a *Capias Utlagatum*, the Defendant is required to give an Attorney's Engagement to appear for him, where special Bail is not required; and his Bond, with Sureties, to appear where it is required. See 4 & 5 *W. & M. c.* 18.

Capias in Withernam, is a Writ which lies for Cattle in *Withernam*, that is to say, where a Distress taken is driven out of the Country, so that the Sheriff cannot make Deliverance upon a Replevin; on which Account this Writ issues, commanding the Sheriff

riff to take as many Beasts of the Distrainer, &c. *Reg. Orig.* 82, 83.

Capite is an ancient Tenure, which was held immediately of the King, as of his Crown, whether it were by Knight's Service, or in Socage, and not of any Honour, Castle or Manor; and for this Reason it is called a Tenure, holding only of the King. In *Dier* 44. it is otherwise called, Tenure holding of the Person of the King. A Person may hold of the King, and not *in Capite*; that is to say, not immediately of the Crown in gross, but by Reason of some Honour, Castle or Manor belonging to the Crown. See *Kitch.* 129. This Tenure is now abolished; and by 12 *Car.* 2. *c.* 24. all Tenures are turned into free and common Socage. The ancient Tenure *in Capite* was of two Sorts; the one *Principal* and *General*, and the other *Special* and *Subaltern*: The *Principal* and *General* was of the King, the Fountain from whence all Feuds and Tenures have their main Original. The *Special* and *Subaltern* was of a particular Subject, as *Caput Feudi, seu terræ illius,* so termed, from his being the first that created the Feud or Land in such Manner of Tenure; and hence he was called *Capitalis Dominus, & Caput terræ illius.* See *Spelm. of Feuds, c.* 4.

Capituli Agri, is said to signify the Head-Lands, such as lie at the Head or upper End of the Lands or Furrows.

Capitula Ruralia, are Clerical Assemblies, or Chapters held by the Rural Dean and Parochial Clergy within the Precinct of every distinct Deanry; at first every three Weeks, then once a Month, but more solemnly once a Quarter. See *Cowel.*

Caption, in Law is so called, when a Commission is executed, the Commissioners subscribe their Names to a Certificate, declaring when and where the Commission was executed. These *Captions* chiefly relate to three Kinds of Business, that is to say, to Commissions, to take Answers and Depositions of Witnesses in Equity, and to take Fines of Lands, &c.

Capture, in general, signifies the taking of a Prey or Seizure; but more particularly denotes Prizes taken by Privateers in Time of War, or by Way of Reprisals for Injuries done.

Caput Baroniæ, is the Castle or chief Seat of a Nobleman, which, if there be no Son, must descend to the eldest Daughter.

Caput Jejunii is used in our Records for *Ash-Wednesday,* the first Day in *Lent.*

Caputagium, by some is said to signify Head or Poll-Money, or the Payment of it; tho' it seems rather to be the same with *Chevagium.* See **Chevage.**

Carcatus, signifies *Loaden*; as a Ship with her Freight. *Pat.* 10. *R.* 2.

Carke, signifies a certain Quantity of Wool, thirty of which make a Sarpler. 27 *H.* 6. *c.* 2.

Curno, has been used for an Immunity or Privilege. See *Cromp. Jur.* 191.

Carrat or **Carract,** was formerly used for any Weight or Burden, but is now applied to the Weight of four Grains in Diamonds.

Carrick or **Carrack,** (from the *Italian*) denotes a Ship of great Burden.

Carucage, signifies a Tribute imposed on Ploughs for the publick Service.

Carucate or **Carve of Land,** denotes a certain Quantity of Land, by which

which the Subjects have been heretofore taxed; whence the Tribute so levied is called *Carucage. Bract. lib.* 2. *c.* 26. *Skene* says, that it contains as great a Portion of Land as may be tilled in a Year and a Day with one Plough, which is also called *Hilda* or *Hida Terræ. Rastal*, in his Exposition of Words, informs us, that Carvage is to be quit, if the King shall tax all Men by *Carves*; that is to say, a Privilege by which one is freed from Carvage.

Carucatarius, is he that held Land in *Carvage*, or Plough Tenure. *Paroch. Antiq.* 354.

Castel, or **Castle**, signifies a Fortress in a Town, or the principal Mansion-House of a Nobleman, &c. In King *Hen.* the Second's Time there were 1115 Castles in *England*, and each Castle contain'd a Manor; so that the Constable of a Castle was the Constable of a Manor. 2 *Inst.* 31.

Castellain, is taken for the Lord or Owner of a Castle, and sometimes for the Captain or Constable of it, or some fortified House. *Bract. lib.* 2. *c.* 16. 3 *Ed.* 1. *c.* 7. It has been sometimes taken for him that had the Custody of one of the King's Mansion-Houses, tho' no *Castle*, or Place of Defence. 2 *Inst.* 31. *Manwood* says there was an Officer of the Forest called so.

Castellarium, or **Castellarii**, signifies the Precinct or Jurisdiction of a Castle.

Castellorum Operatio, signifies Castle-Work, or Labour, or Service done by inferior Tenants, for the Building and Upholding of Castles, and other publick Places of Defence, towards which some gave their personal Assistance, and others paid Contribution. This was one of the three necessary Burdens, to which all Lands among our *Saxon* Ancestors were subject. *Cowel*.

Castlegard or **Castleward**, was an Imposition laid on such as dwelt within a certain Compass of any Castle, towards the Maintenance of such as watched and warded it. *Magna Charta*, *c*. 20. See also 32 *Hen.* 8. *c*. 48. It is sometimes used for the Circuit itself, which is inhabited by such as are subject to this Service. *Termes de la Ley* 102.

Casu Consimili, is a Writ of Entry granted where a Tenant by Curtesy, for Term of Life, or for the Life of another, aliens in Fee, in Tail, or for the Term of another's Life. This Writ is brought by him in Reversion against the Person to whom such Tenant does so alien to the Prejudice of the Reversioner, in the Tenant's Lifetime. This Writ takes its Name from this, *viz.* That the Clerks of the Chancery did, by their common Assent, frame it to the Likeness of the Writ called *in Casu Proviso*, according to the Authority granted them by the *Stat. Westm.* 2. *c.* 24. which Law, as often as there happens a new Case in Chancery something like a former, and not specially suited to any Writ, authorizes them to frame a new Form answerable to the new Case, and as like the former as they can. 7 *Rep.* 4. For the Form and Effect of this Writ, see *Fitz. Nat. Brev.* 206.

Casu Proviso, is a Writ of Entry founded on the Statute of *Gloucester*, *c.* 7. where a Tenant in Dower aliens in Fee, or for Life, or in Tail, the Land which she holds in Dower; and lies for the Party in Reversion against the Alienee, or the Person that has the Freehold of the Land; and that during the Life of the Tenant in Dower. *Fitz. Nat. Brev.* 205.

Catals. See **Chattels**.

Catallis

Catallis captis nomine Districtionis, is a Writ which lies, where a House is within a Borough, for Rent issuing out of the same; and it warrants the Taking of Doors, Windows or Gates, by Way of Distress for the Rent. See *Old. Nat. Brev.* 66.

Catallis reddendis, is a Writ that lies where Goods, being delivered to a Person to keep until a certain Day, are not upon Demand delivered at the Time. This Writ may otherwise be called a Writ of *Detinue*. See *Reg. Orig.* 139. *Old Nat. Brev.* 63.

Catch-land, is said to signify certain Grounds in *Norfolk*, where it is not known to what Parish they certainly belong; so that the Minister who first seises the Tithes, does by that Right of Pre-occupation enjoy them for that one Year: Wherefore the Land of this dubious Nature is called *Catch-land*. *Cowel*.

Catchpol, was anciently used, without Reproach, for what we now call *Serjeants of the Mace*, Bailiffs, or others that use to arrest Persons upon any Action.

Cauda Terræ, signifies the Land's End, or the Bottom or extreme Part of a Ridge or Furrow in arable Land. *Cowel*.

Caveat, is in the Nature of a Process, to stop the Probate of a Will, the granting of Letters of Administration, &c.

Cavers, are Offenders in respect to the Mines in *Derbyshire*, and are punishable in the *Berghmote*, or Miners Court.

Causa Matrimonii prælocuti, is a Writ that lies where a Woman gives Lands to a Man in Fee, to the Intent he shall marry her, and he refuses to do it in a reasonable Time, being thereunto required by the Woman. The Form and Use thereof you may see in *Reg. Orig.* 333. and *Fitz. Nat. Brev.* 205.

Causam nobis significes, is a Writ directed to a Mayor of a Corporation, &c. who having, by the King's Writ, been commanded to give Seisin of Lands, &c. to the King's Grantee, delays so doing; wherefore this Writ requires him to shew Cause why he makes such Delay in the Performance of his Duty. *Co. lib.* 4.

Cautione admittenda, is a Writ which lies against a Bishop, holding an excommunicated Person in Prison for Contempt, after that he has offered sufficient Caution or Sureties to obey the Commandments and Orders of *Holy Church*. See *Reg. Orig.* 66.

Cenegild, is an Expiatory Mulct that was formerly paid by one who killed another to the Deceased's Kindred.

Ceuninga, is a Notice that was formerly given by the Buyer to the Seller, that the Thing sold was claimed by another, in order that he might appear and justify the Sale.

Censure, which is expounded to be a Kind of Personal Money paid for every Poll, in divers Manors in *Cornwal* and *Devon*, signifies the calling of all Residents therein, above the Age of sixteen, to swear Fealty to the Lord, to pay 11 *d.* per Poll, and 1 *d.* yearly ever after: And the Persons thus sworn, are called *Censers*.

Cepi Corpus, is a Return made by the Sheriff, that upon a *Capias*, *Exigent*, or other Process, he has taken the Defendant's Body. *Fitz. Nat. Brev.* 26.

Certificando de Recognitione Staputlæ, is a Writ directed to the Mayor of the *Staple*, commanding him to certify to the Lord

Lord Chancellor a *Statute Staple* taken before him, where the Party himself detains it, and refuses to bring it in. *Reg. Orig.* 152. A Writ of the like Kind lies for certifying a *Statute Merchant*, &c.

Certificate, signifies a Writing made in any Court, to give Notice to another Court of any Thing done therein; as a Certificate of the Cause of *Attaint*, is a Transcript briefly drawn up by the Clerks of the Crown, Clerk of the Peace, or Clerk of Assise, to the Court of King's Bench; wherein is contained the Tenor and Effect of every Indictment, Outlawry or Conviction, and Clerk attainted, made or declared in any other Court. 34 *Hen.* 8. 14.

Certification of Assise of Novel Disseisin, is a Writ that issues for the Re-examining of a Matter passed by Assise before Justices. This Writ is used, where a Person appearing by his Bailiff to an *Assise* brought by another, has lost the Day, and having something more to plead, as a Release, &c. which the Bailiff either did not, or might not plead for him, desires a further Examination of the Cause, either before the same Justices or others, and obtains Letters Patent to them for that End; which being done he brings a Writ directed to the Sheriff to call both the Party for whom the *Assise* passed, and the Jury that was impanell'd thereon, before the said Justices at a certain Day and Place. It is called a Petition, because Mention is therein made to the Sheriff, that upon the Party's Complaint of the defective Examination, or Doubts still remaining upon the Assise passed, the King has directed his Letters Patent to the Justices, for the better certifying of themselves whether all Points of the said Assise were duly examined. *Reg. Orig.* 200. *Fitz. Nat. Brev.* 181.

Certiorari, is a Writ which issues out of the Court of Chancery, directed to an inferior Court, to call up the Records of a Cause depending there, in order that Justice may be done therein: And this Writ is obtained upon Complaint that the Party who seeks it has received hard Usage, or is likely to be a Sufferer by a Trial in the inferior Court. See *Fitz. Nat. Brev.* 242. This Writ is made returnable, either in the *King's Bench*, *Common Pleas*, or in *Chancery*. A *Certiorari* not only issues out of *Chancery*, but likewise out of the *King's Bench*, in which last mentioned Court it lies where the King would be certified of a Record. See further, *Fitz. Nat. Brev.* 245. Indictments from inferior Courts, and Proceedings of the Quarter-Sessions of the Peace, &c. may be also removed into the *King's Bench*.

Cert-Money, signifies Head-Money, or a certain Fine, annually paid by the Resiants of several Manors, to the Lords of the same, for the certain keeping of the Leet; and sometimes to the Hundred.

Cervisarii, signifies a Duty, that was in the Time of the *Saxons* called *Drinclean*.

Cessavit, is a Writ which lies in several Cases, upon this general Ground, that the Person, against whom it is brought, has for two Years neglected the performing Service, or to pay such Rent as he is by his Tenure tied to, and has not upon his Lands, &c. sufficient Goods or Chattels to be distrained. See *Fleta, lib.* 5. *c.* 34. *Fitz. Nat. Brev.* 280. Where a Tenant for Years of Land, at a Rent certain, suffers it to be behind two Years, and there is not sufficient

Distress

CE

Distress to be had on the Land, in such Case the Landlord shall recover the Land; yet if the Tenant come into Court before Judgment given, and tender the Arrearages and Damages, and at the same Time find Security, that he shall not any more cease in Payment of the Rent, then the Tenant shall not lose his Land. *Termes de la Ley* 107. But the Heir cannot maintain this Writ for Cessure made in the Time of his Ancestor. *Ibid.*

Cessavit de Cantaria, is a Writ which lies where a Person gives Land to a religious House, &c. to say Divine Service, feed the Poor, or perform other Alms; then if the said Services be not done in two Years, the Donor or his Heirs shall have this Writ against the Person that holds the Land thus given, after such Cessure. *Westm.* 2. *c.* 41.

Cession, signifies a Ceasing, Yielding up, or giving over, and is where an Ecclesiastical Person is created a Bishop, or when a Parson of a Parish takes another Benefice without Dispensation, or otherwise not qualified, &c. In both which Cases their Benefices become void, and are said to become void by *Cession*: And to those Benefices, that the Person had who was created Bishop, the King may present for that Time, whosoever is Patron of them; and in the other Case the Patron may present.

Cessor, is used for one that ceases or neglects so long to perform a Duty, as he thereby incurs the Danger of the Law, and may have the Writ *Cessavit* brought against him. *Old Nat. Brev.* 136.

Cessure, or **Cesser**, is taken to signify a Giving over, Giving of Place. *Westm.* 2. *c.* 41.

Cestui que vie, signifies the Person

CH

for whose Life any Lands, &c. are granted. *Perk.* 97.

Cestui que use, denotes him to whose Use any other is enfeoffed in Lands or Tenements. See the *New Book of Entries*, Tit. *Uses*.

Cestui que Trust, is the Person that has a Trust in Lands or Tenements committed to him, for the Benefit of another. 12 *Car.* 2. *c.* 30.

Chafewax, is an Officer in Chancery, who fits the Wax for sealing of Writs, and other Instruments as are there issued out.

Chaffers, seem to signify Wares or Merchandizes; and we still use Chaffering for Buying and Selling. But see 3 *Ed.* 4. 4.

Chaldron or **Chalder of Coals**, contains 36 Bushels of Coals heaped up, according to the sealed Bushel kept at *Guild-hall, London*. 16, 17 *Car.* 2. *c.* 2.

Chalking, signifies divers Impositions that the Merchants of the Staple required to be eased of; such as *Chalking*, Ironage, Wharfage, &c. *Rot. Parl.* 50 *Ed.* 3.

Challenge, in a legal Sense, signifies an Exception to Persons or Things: Persons; as in *Assize*, to the Jurors, or any one or more of them: Things; as in the Case of *Felony*, where the Prisoner at the Bar excepts against the Indictment. See *Old Nat. Brev.* 76. *Challenge* is either to the *Array*, or to the *Polls*: To the *Array*, is where an Exception is taken to the whole Number of Jurors impanelled: To the *Polls* is, where an Exception is taken to one or more of the Jurors as not indifferent. *Challenge to the Jurors* is also divided into Challenge *Principal* or *Peremptory*, and Challenge *for Cause*, that is to say, upon Cause or Reason: *Challenge Principal* is, what the Law allows, without any Cause alledged

CH

alledged or Examination; as a Prisoner at the Bar arraigned for Felony, may challenge peremptorily the Number allowed him by Law, viz. 20. one after another, without alledging any Cause at all, but his own Dislike; and the Jurors so challenged shall be put off, and new ones taken in their Places. In the Case of *Treason* or *Petit Treason*, the Number of 35 Jurors may be peremptorily *challenged*, without shewing any Cause: And more both in Treason and Felony may be *challenged*, shewing Cause. *Challenge upon Cause or Reason*, is when the Party alledges some such Exception against one or more of the Jurors, as is not forthwith sufficient, upon Acknowledgment of the Truth thereof, but rather arbitrable and considerable by the rest of the Jurors; as, if the Son of a Juror has married or espoused the adverse Party. *Termes de la Ley* 110. This Challenge for Cause seems to be termed by *Kitch.* 92. *Challenge for Favour*; or rather *Challenge for Favour* is there said to be a *Species* of *Challenge* for Cause; and there you may also read what Challenges are commonly accounted for *Principal*, and what not. A Difference may be observed between *Challenge Principal*, and *Challenge Peremptory*; Peremptory being only used in Matters Criminal, and alledged without other Cause than barely the Prisoner's Fancy. *Staundf. Pl. Cor.* 124. But *Principal*, in Civil Actions, for the most part, and with assigning some such Cause of Exception, as being found true, the Law allows: For Example, if either Party say, that one of the Jurors is the Son, Brother, Cousin, or Tenant to the other, or espoused his Daughter; this Exception, if true, is strong enough without

CH

any further Examination. How far the *Challenge* of Kindred reaches, you may see in *Plowden* 425. For the Ground of this Challenge, you may see *Fleta, lib.* 4. *c.* 8.

Chamberdekins, or **Chamberdakins**, were *Irish* Beggars, who by 1 *H.* 5. *c.* 8. were at a limited Time ordained to avoid this *Realm*.

Chamberlain, is used in different Senses; as Lord Great *Chamberlain* of *England*, Lord *Chamberlain* of the King's House, and the King's *Chamberlain*. See 13 *Ed.* 1. *c.* 41. 17 *Ric.* 2. *c.* 16. See likewise 7 *Ed.* 6. *c.* 1. There are also *Chamberlains* of the Exchequer, of whose Office you may read in the *Stat.* 51 *H.* 3. *c.* 15. You may see Mention anciently made of two Officers of the Name of *Chamberlains* of the Exchequer in 34 & 35 *Hen.* 8. *c.* 16. To this Name of *Chamberlain* may be added that of *Chamberlain* of the City of *London*, who is commonly the Receiver of all Rents and Revenues belonging to that City, viz. such as are payable into the Chamber of *London*: And he has likewise a great Power in determining Rights of Freemen, concerning Apprentices, Orphans, &c.

Chambers of the King, anciently signified the Havens or Ports of the Kingdom. See *Mare Claus.* 242.

Champerty, signifies a Contract made with either the Plaintiff or Defendant in any Suit at Law, for the giving Part of the Land or other Thing sued for to the Party that undertakes to carry on or maintain the Charges of the Suit, provided he succeeds therein. This seems to have been an ancient Grievance in this Nation; for notwithstanding the *Statutes* 3 *Ed.* 1. *c.* 25. 13 *Ed.* 1. *c.* 49. 28 *Ed.* 1. *c.* 11. &c. and a Form of a

Writ

Writ framed to answer the Ends of those Statutes; yet by the 4 *Ed. 3. c. 11.* it was enacted, That whereas former Statutes provided Redress for this Grievance in the King's Bench only, (which at that Time followed the Court) from thenceforth it should be lawful for the Justices of the Common Pleas likewise, and Justices of Assise in their Circuits, to enquire, hear, and determine this and such like Cases, as well at the Suit of the King, as of the Party. You may see how far this Writ extends, and the Form thereof, in *Fitz. Nat. Brev.* 171. *Reg. Orig.* 183. Every Act of *Champerty* implies Maintenance; but every Maintenance is not *Champerty*; for *Champerty* is only a Species of Maintenance. *Cromp. Jur.* 39. See also *Cromp. Just.* 155. *2 Inst.* 208. This Word is said to be significantly derived from *Campus*, a Field, and *Partitio*, a Dividing; because the Parties in *Champerty* agree to divide the Thing in Dispute.

Champertors, are those that move, or cause to be moved, Pleas or Suits, by their own, or the Procurement of others, and sue them at their own proper Costs, in order to have Part of the Lands or Gains in Dispute. By 33 *H.* 1. & 37 *H.* 8. *c.* 7. Justices of the Peace at their Quarter-Sessions, are authorised, as well by the Oaths of twelve Men, as by the Information of any other Person, to enquire of the Offenders and Offences against the Laws made touching *Champerty, Maintenance*, &c. *Cowel*.

Champion, has anciently been taken in divers Senses; but now in this Kingdom is applied to the Person termed the King's Champion, whose Office it is, at the Coronation of our Kings, to ride into *Westminster-Hall*, armed, at the Time the King is at Dinner there, and throw down his Gauntlet by Way of Challenge proclaimed by a *Herald*, to this Effect, *viz. That if any Man shall deny the King's Title to the Crown, he is there ready to defend it in single Combat*, &c. Which being done, the King drinks to him, and sends him a gilt Cup with a Cover, full of Wine, which the *Champion* drinks, and has the Cup for his Fee. This Office, ever since the Coronation of King *Richard* the Second, when *Baldwin Freville* exhibited his Petition for it, was adjudged from him to Sir *John Dymocke*, his *Competitor*, (both claiming from *Marmion*) and has ever since continued in the worthy Family of the *Dymockes*, who hold the Manor of *Scrivelsbury* in *Lincolnshire*, hereditary from the *Marmions* by grand Serjeanty, to wit, that the Lord thereof shall be the King's *Champion*: And accordingly Sir *Edward Dymocke* performed this Office at the Coronation of King *Charles* the Second. *Cowel*.

Chancellor, is an Officer that of late Times has been greatly advanced, he being no less than the chief Administrator of Justice next to the Sovereign. All other Justices in this Kingdom are tied to the Law, but the *Chancellor* is invested with the King's absolute Power to moderate the written Law, governing his Judgment purely by the Law of Nature and Conscience, and ordering all Things according to *Equity* and *Justice*. On which Account *Standf.* says the *Chancellor* has two Powers; one absolute, the other ordinary; (that is to say) that altho' by his ordinary Power, in some Cases, he must observe the Form of Proceedings as other inferior Judges,

I yet

yet as to his absolute Power he is not limited by the written Law, but by Conscience and Equity, according to the Circumstances of Things. He that bears this Office of Magistracy is called the *Lord High Chancellor of Great Britain* (which is the highest Honour of the long Robe) he being so made by the Delivery of the Great Seal to him by the King. By 5 *El. c.* 18. the *Lord Chancellor* and *Keeper* have one and the same Power; for which Reason there cannot, since that Statute, be a *Lord Chancellor* and *Lord Keeper* at one and the same Time.

Chancellor of the Dutchy of Lancaster, is an Officer appointed in that Court, chiefly to hear and determine Controversies between the King and his Tenants of the Dutchy Land, and otherwise to direct all the King's Affairs belonging to that Court.

Chancellor of the Exchequer, is a great Officer, whose Office 'tis thought was originally created for the qualifying of Extremities in the Exchequer: He sits in the Exchequer Court and Exchequer Chamber, and among the rest of the Judges there, to order Things to the King's best Benefit. By 33 *H.* 8. *c.* 39. he is impowered with others to compound with others upon Penal Statutes, Bonds, and Recognizances entered into to the King. He has likewise great Power in the Management of the Revenues of the Crown, which, indeed of late seems to be his principal Business and Care, he being commonly the first Commissioner of the Treasury. When there happens to be a Lord Treasurer, the Chancellor of the Exchequer is called *Under-Treasurer*.

Chancemedley, is where a Person, without any evil Intent, acts a lawful Thing, or what is not prohibited by Law, and yet another is slain by such Act, or comes to his Death thereby; as when a Person in the Fields, or other open Place throws a Stone, which hits another, who afterwards dies of the Blow received; or it is when a Person shoots an Arrow, and another passing by is thereby killed, or the like. It is also called *Manslaughter by Misadventure*, for which the Offender shall have his Pardon of Course. See *Stat.* 6 *E.* 1. *c.* 9. In the Case of *Chancemedley* it is to be considered, whether he that committed the Manslaughter by Misadventure, was doing a lawful Thing at the Time of committing it: For if the Act was unlawful, as in the Case where two are fighting together, and a third Person comes to part them, and is killed by one of the two, without any Malice forethought, or evil Intent in the Person that killed him; yet this is Murder in the Person that killed, and not Manslaughter by *Chancemedley*; for this Reason, that the two that fought together were doing an unlawful Act: And if these two were met with Malice prepensed, *viz.* the one intending to kill the other, then it is Murder in them both.

Chancery, is the highest Court of Judicature in this Realm, except that of the Parliament, and is a Court of Equity and Conscience, moderating the Rigour of other Courts, that are strictly tied to the Letter of the Law, of which Court the *Lord High Chancellor*, or *Keeper of the Great Seal*, is the Chief Judge. This Court's Jurisdiction is of two Kinds, ordinary, or legal: The ordinary, in which the Lord Chancellor, in his Proceedings, is bound to observe the Method of the Common Law; in which

which Case the Proceedings were formerly in *Latin*, but are now in *English*, and filed or inrolled in the Petty-Bag Office. His extraordinary Jurisdiction, is that in which the Lord Chancellor has an unlimited Power to exercise in Cases of Equity, wherein Relief is to be had by Way of Bill and Answer. The Officers belonging to this Court are the *Lord Chancellor*, or *Lord Keeper of the Great Seal*, the *Master of the Rolls*, who, in the *Lord Chancellor's* Absence, hears Causes, and gives Orders: There are also twelve Masters in Chancery, who by Turns sit on the Bench, as Assistants. The next are the six Clerks, each of whom has about fifteen Clerks under him, in the Nature of Attornies in the Court: There are likewise two chief Examiners, who have five or six Clerks apiece: To which may be added several other Officers of no small Note or Distinction; For which see 4 *Inst.* 82. The Forms of Bills, Answers, and other Proceedings in Chancery, you may see in *Prax. Alm. Cur.* and other Treatises of that Kind.

Changer or **Chaungor**, is an Officer belonging to the King's Mint, whose Business was chiefly to exchange Coin for Bullion brought in by Merchants or others. See 2 *Hen.* 6. *c.* 12.

Chapelry, is the same Thing to a *Chapel* as a Parish to a Church. See 14 *Car.* 2. *c.* 9.

Chapiters, in our Law, formerly signified a Summary or Content of such Matters as were enquired of or presented before Justices in Eyre, Justices of Assise, or of the Peace in their Sessions. See 3 *Ed.* 1. *c.* 27. But at this Time it is said to signify such certain Articles as are delivered by the Mouth of the Justice in his Charge to the Inquest; whereas *Bracton* and *Britton* say, that they were, after an Exhortation given by the Justice for the good Observance of the Laws and the King's Peace, first read in open Court distinctly, and then delivered in Writing to the Grand Inquest, who were to answer upon their Oaths to all the Articles so delivered to them, and by that Means save the Judges the Trouble of making long and learned Charges, frequently to little or no Purpose, for Want of the Grand Jury's retaining the same in their Memories, they thinking their Duty sufficiently performed, if they only present those few of many Misdemeanors that are brought before them in the Way of Indictment. What those *Chapiters*, or Articles were wont to contain, is expressed by *Horn* in his *Mirror of Justices*, lib. 3. See likewise the *Book of Assises* 138.

Chaplain, is one that performs Divine Service in a *Chapel*, and therefore is commonly taken for him that is depending upon the King or other Person of Worth, for the Instruction of him and his Family, by praying and preaching, in his private House, where there commonly is a *Chapel* kept for that Purpose. See 21 *Hen.* 8. *c.* 13. wherein is set down what Persons may retain, or privilege one or more Chaplains to discontinue from their Benefices. Unless a Chaplain be retained by Letters Testimonial, under Hand and Seal, he is no legal *Chaplain*; whence it is evident, that it is not sufficient for a Clergyman to be by Word only retained a *Chaplain*, by a Person that can qualify him by the Statute to hold Livings, &c. even tho' he continue to serve as

Chaplain in the Family: And where a Nobleman has once retained, and by his Letters Testimonial qualified his Number of *Chaplains*, if he, even upon Displeasure dismisses them from their Attendance, after as before preferred, they are still his Chaplains at large, and may hold their Livings during their Lives; and in such Case the Nobleman, tho' he should retain further Chaplains in his Family, meerly as such, cannot qualify others to hold Pluralities whilst the first are living.

Charge, in general, is taken to be any Thing done that bindeth the Person doing it, or his Representatives or Posterity to the Performance thereof; As Land may be charged several Ways, as by Grant of Rent out of it, properly called a Rent-Charge, by Statutes, Recognizances, Judgments, &c. *Charge* of Judges, &c. see **Chapiters**.

Charitable Corporation, is a Term of a late standing, when a Society or certain Number of Persons obtained a Law to empower them to lend Money to poor industrious People, at the Rate of 5 *l. per Cent.* Interest, over and above the like Sum for Warehouse-Room, &c. on Pledges or Pawns, in order to save them from falling a Prey to the Pawn-brokers; and on that Account this Society was called the *Charitable Corporation*, for the Relief of the Sufferers wherein, several Statutes were afterwards made, particularly that of the 5 *Geo.* 2. *c.* 31, 32. and 7 *Geo.* 2. *c.* 11.

Charre, is a Quantity of Lead that consists of 30 Pigs, each Pig containing 6 Stone, wanting two Pounds, and every Stone being twelve Pounds.

Charta, is a Word used not only for a *Charter*, for holding an Estate, but also is made Use of to signify a particular Statute, *viz. Magna Charta.*

Chartel, was used to signify a Letter of Defiance or Challenge formerly in Use, when Combats to decide difficult Controversies at Law were in Practice.

Charter, is used for a written Instrument or Evidence of Things acted between one Person and another. The King's Charter is, where the King makes a Grant to any private Person, or Body Politick.

Charter-land, is such Land as one holds by *Charter*; that is to say, by Evidence in Writing, otherwise termed *Freehold*.

Charter-party, is a Deed or Instrument in Writing, which is generally made between Merchants and Sea-faring Men, concerning their Merchandise and maritime Affairs. A *Charter-party* of Affreightment settles the Agreement in relation to the Freight of the Ship and Cargo, between the Merchant and Commander or Master of the Vessel. The Form of a *Charter-party* of Affreightment, you may see in the *Young Clerk's Magazine*, and other Treatises of Instruments in conveyancing.

Chartis Reddendis, is a Writ that lies against a Person, who has Charters of Feoffment delivered to him to keep, and afterwards refuses to redeliver them. *Old Nat. Br.* 66. *Reg. Orig.* 159.

Chase, in our Law, has two different Significations, the one signifying a Driving of Cattle to or from any Place; as to chase a Distress to a Castle or Fortlet. *Old Nat. Brev.* 45. The other denoting a Place of Reception for Deer and wild Beasts, and is of a middle Nature between a Forest and a Park,

Park; it being commonly less than a Forest, and not having so many Liberties; and yet perhaps of a larger Compass, and stored with great Diversity, both of Keepers and wild Beasts, or Game, than a Park. *Crompton* says, That a Forest cannot be in the Hands of a Subject, but whenever it is so, it loses its Name, and takes that of a *Chase*. Whence a *Chase* differs from a Forest in this, *viz.* because it may be in the Hands of a Subject, which a Forest, in its true Nature, cannot; and it likewise differs from a Park, in that it is not inclosed, and has not only a larger Compass, and a greater Store of Game, but of Keepers and other Officers. See *Cromp. Jur.* 148. See likewise *Manwood*.

Chattels, comprehend all Things moveable and immoveable, except what are in the Nature of Freehold, or Part or Parcel of it. An Estate of Inheritance, in our Law, cannot be termed Goods or Chattels, neither can a Freehold for Life be deemed so; yet a Lease for Years may pass as such. Chattels are either *Personal* or *Real*: *Personal*; as Gold, Silver, Plate, Jewels, Furniture, &c. *Real*, are such as do not immediately appertain to the Person, but have a Dependency on some other Thing; as a Box or Chest of Writings of Land, &c. the Body of a Ward, the Apples upon a Tree, or the Tree itself growing upon the Ground. See *Cromp.* 33. or else what are issuing out of something immoveable to the Person; as a Lease or Rent for a Term of Years.

Check-Roll, signifies a *Roll*, or Book, wherein is contained the Names of such as are Attendants, and in Pay to the King, or other great Persons, as their Houshold Servants. See 19 *Car.* 2, c. 1.

Chevage, is taken for a Tribute, or a certain Sum formerly paid by such as held Lands in Villenage, or otherwise, to their Lords by Way of Acknowledgment, and was a Kind of Poll or Head-Money. See *Bracton, lib.* 1. c. 10.

Chevantia, signifies a Loan of Money upon Credit. *Cowel.*

Chevisance, Denotes an Agreement or Composition made; as an End or Order set down between a Creditor and his Debtor; and is sometimes taken for an indirect Contract or Booty; but, in our Statutes, is most commonly used for an unlawful Bargain or Contract. See 37 *H.* 8. c. 9. 13 *Eliz.* c. 5 & 8. and 12 *Car.* 2. c. 13.

Childwit, denotes a Power to take a Fine of a Bond-Woman, unlawfully begotten with Child. Within the Manor of *Writtel* in the County of *Essex*, every reputed Father of a base Child pays to the Lord for a Fine, 3 s. 4 d. where it seems to extend as well to Free as Bond-Women; and this Custom is there still called *Child-wit*.

Chimin, in Law, denotes a Way, and is divided into two Sorts, *viz.* The King's Highway, and a private Way: The King's Highway is that by which the King's Subjects, and all under his Protection, have free Liberty to pass, tho' the Property of the Soil on both Sides of such Way may perhaps belong to some private Person. A private Way is that through which one or more may pass, either by Prescription or Charter through another's Ground. *Kitchin* tells us, that this is divided into *Chimin in Gross*, and *Chimin Appendant*. *Chimin in Gross*, is a Way a Person holds principally and solely in itself: *Chimin Appendant*, is what one has appurtenant or adjoining to some other Thing: As if he hire

CH

hire a Close or Pasture, and covenant for Ingress and Regress to and from the said Close, &c. through some Ground, by which he could not otherwise pass.

Chiminage, signifies a Toll for Wayfrage through a Forest.

Chimney-Money, that is to say, *Hearth-Money*, was a certain Tax imposed by 14 *Car.* 2. *c.* 12. on every *Fire-Hearth, Stove,* &c. (except of those Persons who paid not to the Church and Poor.) This Tax has been since taken away, and instead of it another Tax imposed, not less grievous than the former, *viz.* the Window-Sess.

Chirograph, did in the Time of the *Saxons*, signify any publick Instrument of Gift or Conveyance, attested by the Subscription of the present Witnesses. Formerly when they made a *Chirograph*, or Deed, which required a Counter, as we commonly call it, they engrossed it twice upon one Piece of Parchment contrariwise, leaving a Space between, in which they in great Letters wrote the Word *Chirograph*, and then cut the Parchment in two, sometimes even, and sometimes Indenture-wise. This Manner of engrossing of Fines, and cutting the Parchment in two Pieces, is still observed in the *Chirographer's* Office.

Chirographer of Fines, in the Common Law signifies that Officer who ingrosses Fines in that Court, acknowledged into a perpetual Record, after they are acknowledged and fully passed by the proper Officers, by whom they were formerly examined; and who writes and delivers the Indentures of them to the Party. This Officer also makes two Indentures, one for the Buyer, and the other for the Seller, and makes another indented Piece, which contains also the Effect of the Fine, which he delivers to the *Custos Brevium*; and that is called the Foot of the Fine. The *Chirographer* likewise, or his Deputy, proclaims all the Fines in the Court every Term, according to the Statute, and then repairing to the Office of the *Custos Brevium*, there indorses the Proclamations upon the Back-side of the Foot thereof; and he always keeps the Writ of Covenant, as also the Note of the Fine.

Chivalry, in our Law, denotes a Tenure of Land by Knight's Service: For the better Understanding of which it is to be observed, that there is no Land, but what is mediately or immediately held of the Crown by some Service; and on that Account all Freeholds are called Fees, as proceeding from the King's Bounty, for some small yearly Rent, and the Performances of such Services as were originally laid upon the Land, at the giving of the same: For as the King gave to his Nobles, his immediate Tenants, large Possessions for ever, to hold the same of him for such a Service or Rent; so they afterwards in Time parcelled out to others their Lands so received of the King's Bounty, for such Rents or Services as they thought fit. And these Services are divided by *Littleton* into two Sorts, *Chivalry* and *Socage*; the first of which was *Martial* and *Military*, and the other *Clownish* and *Rustical:* Wherefore Chivalry is a Tenure of Service, whereby the Tenant is bound to perform some noble or military Office to his Lord; and is of two Kinds, either *Regal*, that is to say, such as may be held only of the King; or such as may be also held of a common Person as well as the King: That which may be held only of the King, is properly called

called *Sergeanty*, which is also divided into *Grand* and *Petit Sergeanty*. Grand Sergeanty is where a Person holds Lands of the King by Service, which he ought to do in his own Person; as to carry the King's Banner or Spear, to lead his Army, or to find a Man at Arms to fight, &c. *Petit Sergeanty* is, where one holds Land of the King, to yield him yearly some small Thing towards his Wars, as a Sword, Dagger, Bow, &c. See *Littl.* Tit. *Petit Sergeanty*. *Chivalry* that may be held of a common Person, is termed *Escuage*, that is to say, Service of the Shield; and this is either uncertain or certain. *Escuage* uncertain is likewise of two Kinds; *First*, Where the Tenant is bound by his Tenure to follow his Lord, going in Person to the King's Wars, against his Enemies, either himself, or to send a sufficient Man in his Place, there to be maintained at his Costs so many Days as were agreed upon between the Lord and his Tenant at the granting of the Fee: The Days of which Service seem to have been rated by the Quantity of the Land so held: As, if it extended to a whole Knight's Fee, then the Tenant was bound to follow his Lord 40 Days; and a Knight's Fee was so much Land as in those Days was accounted a sufficient Living for a Knight, *viz.* 680 Acres, as some held, or 800, as others think, or 15 *l. per Annum*. See *Camd. Brit.* 110. If the Land extended only to the Moiety of a Knight's Fee, then the Tenant was bound to follow his Lord but 20 Days; if to a 4th Part then only 10 Days. *Fitz. Nat. Brev.* 83, &c. The other Kind of *Escuage* uncertain was called *Castleward*, which is where the Tenant by his Tenure was bound, either by himself, or some other, to defend a Castle, as often as it should come to his Turn; and the Reason why this Tenure is called uncertain, is because of the Uncertainty how often a Man should be called to follow his Lord to the Wars, or to defend a Castle, or what Charge would attend doing the same. *Escuage* certain, is where the Tenant is assessed to a certain Sum, to be paid instead of uncertain Service; as that he pay yearly for a Knight's Fee 20 *s.* for a Half Fee 10 *s.* or any other the like Rate: And this Service being drawn to a certain Rent, becomes of a mixt Nature, not meerly *Socage*; and yet it is Socage in Effect, being now neither personal Service nor uncertain. *Littleton*. The Tenure of *Chivalry* had divers other Conditions annexed to it, until the great Alterations made in those Things by the *Stat.* 12 *Car.* 2. *c.* 24. whereby it is ordained, that Tenures by *Knight's Service of the King*, or any other Person *in Capite*, &c. and the Fruits and Consequences thereof happened, or which shall or may happen or arise thereupon, or thereby be taken away and discharged; and that all Tenures be construed and adjudged to be free and common *Socage*, &c.

Chop-Church, is used in 9 *H.* 6. *c.* 65. in the Sense of a Kind of Trade: But *Brook*, in his *Abridgment*, calls it not an Occupation, but a Thing permissable by Law. It is likewise said to be a Nick-name given to such as changed Benefices; and the Person that made such Changes, was called *Church-Chopper*.

Chose, is a *French* Word, and is used in our Law with divers Epithets; as *Chose Local*, signifies any Thing that is annexed to a Place,

Place, such as a Mill, or the like: *Chose Transitory*, is said to signify something that is moveable, and can be taken away, or carried from Place to Place. *Chose in Action* is an incorporeal Thing, and only a Right, as an Annuity, Bond for Debt, a Covenant, Voucher by Warranty, and generally all Causes of Suit, of what Nature soever, are accounted *Choses in Action*, and may well be called *Choses in Suspence*, because they have not any real Existence or Being, nor can properly be said to be in our Possession.

Chrismatis Denarii, in *English*, *Chrisom-Pence*, denotes Money that was paid to the *Diocesan*, or his *Suffragan*, by the Parochial Clergy for the *Chrism*; that is to say, the Confection of Oil and Balsam consecrated by them about *Easter*, for the holy Uses of the ensuing Year. As this customary Payment was made in *Lent*, near *Easter*, it was therefore in some Places called *Quadragesimals*, and in others *Paschals*, or *Easter-Pence*. The Bishop's Exaction of this Payment was condemned by one of the ancient Popes for Simony and Extortion, and on that Account the Custom was released by some of our *English* Bishops. *Cowel*.

Christianitatis Curia, signifies the Ecclesiastical Judicature. See *Court Christian*.

Church, is a Place or Edifice consecrated to God and Religion, or is where People assemble together for religious Worship; and in case it holds Administration of the Sacraments and Burial, it is in Law adjudged a Church.

Church-wardens, are such Officers as are elected annually in *Easter* Week, by the Minister and Parishioners of every Parish, to look after the *Church*, Church-yard, and such Things as belong to both; and also to observe the Behaviours of the Parishioners, as to such Faults as appertain to the Censure or Jurisdiction of the Ecclesiastical Court. *Church-wardens* are a Kind of Corporation, being by Law enabled to sue and be sued for the Goods belonging to the Church, or Poor of their Parish. See *Lamb. Duty of Church-wardens*.

Churcheset, is said to signify a certain Measure of Wheat, which, in former Times, every Person on St. *Martin*'s Day gave to the Holy Church, as well in the Times of the *Britains* as of the *English*: But many great Persons, after the coming of the *Romans*, gave that Contribution according to the ancient Law of *Moses*, in the Name of *First-Fruits*. This Word *Churcheset* has been anciently called *Churchsed*, or *Churchseed*. *Seld. Hist. Tithes* 216.

Church-scot or **Churfot**, signified Customary Oblations made to a Parish-Priest; from which the Religious sometimes purchased an Exemption for themselves and Tenants.

Churle, **Ceorle** or **Carl**, in the Time of the *Saxons*, was used for a Tenant at Will, of free Condition, who held some Land of the *Thane*, on Condition of Rent and Service. These *Ceorles* were of two Sorts, *viz.* the one that hired the Lord's Out-land or Tenementary Land, like one of our Farmers; the other, that tilled and manured the Demesnes, yielding Work and no Rent; and on that Account were called *Sockmen* or *Ploughmen*. See *Spelman*.

Cinque Ports, are particular Havens that lie towards *France*, such as *Dover, Sandwich, Rumney, Winchelsea*, and *Rye*; to which may

may be added *Hythe* and *Hastings*, which two last are reckoned as Members of the *Cinque Ports*. There is an especial Governor, called *Lord Warden* of the *Cinque Ports* appointed, who has not only the Authority of an Admiral among them, but that of sending out Writs in his own Name. There are likewise several particular Privileges or Franchises which the Inhabitants of those *Ports* enjoy; for the King's Writs, except in some particular Cases, do not run there.

Circada, signifies a Tribute that was anciently paid to the Bishop or Archdeacon for visiting the Churches. *Du Fresne.*

Circuity of Action, denotes a longer Course taken in proceeding for the Recovery of a Thing sued for than is necessary; as where a Person grants a Rent-Charge of 5 *l.* a Year out of his Manor of *C.* and afterwards the Grantee disseises the Grantor, who thereupon brings an Assise, and recovers the Land and 10 *l.* Damages; which being paid, the Grantee brings his Action for 5 *l.* of the Rent due during the Time of the Disseisin, which the Grantee must have had, if there had never been any Disseisin. This is termed *Circuity of Action*, because as the Grantor was to receive 10 *l.* Damages, and pay 5 *l.* Rent, he might but have received the 5 *l.* only for the Damages, and the Grantee might have cut off and retained in his Hands the other 5 *l.* by way of Retainer for his Rent, and by that means saved his Action.

Circumspecte Agatis, is the Title of a Law made 13 *Ed.* 1. prescribing some Cases to the Judges, wherein the King's Prohibition does not lie.

Circumstantibus, is a Word of Art, signifying the Supplying, or making up the Number of Jurors, where any of those that are impanelled do not appear, or upon Appearance are challenged by either Party; which is done by adding to them so many of such Persons as are present, standing by, and qualified, as will serve the Turn. See 35 *Hen.* 8. *c.* 6. See likewise *Tales.*

Citation, is a Summons to appear, and is peculiarly applied to a Process issuing out of the *Spiritual Court*, the Proceedings of which are according to the Course of the Civil and Canon Laws, by *Citation*, *Libel*, &c.

Citatio ad Instantiam Partis, is used 22 & 23 *Car.* 2. for laying Impositions on Proceedings at Law.

City, is generally taken for such a Town corporate as has a Bishop and Cathedral Church. The same Place in *Latin* is called *Urbs, Civitas* and *Oppidum*; *Civitas*, in regard it is governed in Justice and Order of Magistracy; *Oppidum*, on account that there are great Plenty of Inhabitants therein; and *Urbs*, because it is in due Form begirt about with Walls: Yet that Place which has a Bishop is commonly called *Civitas*; but *Crompton*, in his Jurisdictions, reckons up all the Cities, and leaves out *Ely*, tho' it has a Bishop, as likewise a Cathedral Church, and takes in *Westminster*, tho' at present it has no Bishop: But it appears by 35 *Hen.* 8. *c.* 10. That there was formerly a Bishop of *Westminster*, since which Time, by 27 *Eliz. c.* 5. it is called a *City* or *Borough*.

Civil Law, is taken for that Law which every particular Nation, Common-wealth, &c. has peculiarly established for itself: But in a stricter Sense denotes that Law which the old *Romans* made Use of of, and were compiled from the Laws of Nature and Nations.

Clack, is particularly applied to Wool, as to *clack, force*, or *bard*, otherwise beard Wool. To *clack* Wool, is to cut off the Mark of the Sheep, in order to make it weigh less, and consequently to yield the less Custom to the Crown: To *force* it, is to clip the upper and most hairy Part of it; and to *bard* or *beard* Wool, is to cut the Head and Neck from the other Part of the Fleece.

Claim, is the Challenge by any Person of the Property or Interest in any Thing which is unlawfully withheld from him by another; as *Claim* by Charter, Discent, &c. *Claim* may be either verbal; as where one makes a *Claim* or Challenge by Word of Mouth, or by Action; as where one sues for the Thing withheld: And it is sometimes for Lands, and sometimes for Goods and Chattels. The Party that makes this Claim frequently reaps great Advantage therefrom; since by it he may avoid a Discent of Lands, and likewise thereby save his Title, which without it would be lost; as if a Person be disseised of Lands, &c. and the Disseisee makes a continual Claim, that is to say, if he claims the Lands, &c. whereof he is disseised within a Year and a Day before the Decease of the Disseisor; then he may enter, notwithstanding the Discent. If a Fine be levied of another's Lands, then the Person that has Right thereto, ought to make his Claim within five Years after the Proclamation made or certified: But one that has no Right cannot of his own Head enter or make Claim in the Name of the Person who has Right, to avoid the Fine, within the five Years, without Authority precedent, or Assent subsequent; yet a Guardian for Education, or in Socage, may enter and make Claim in the Name of the Infant that has Right to enter or claim; by which Means the Estate of the Infant will be helped. *Termes de la Ley*.

Claim of Liberty, is a Petition or Suit to the King in the Court of *Exchequer*, to have Liberties and Franchises confirmed there by the King's Attorney General. See *Co. Ent*. 93.

Claimea admittenda in itinere per Attornatum, is a Writ whereby the Justices in *Eyre* are commanded to admit by Attorney the Claim of a Person who is imployed in the King's Service, and cannot personally appear. *Reg. Orig.* 19.

Claves Insulæ, is a Term used in the *Isle of Man*, where all weighty and ambiguous Cases are referred to twelve, who are called *Claves Insulæ*, viz. the Keys of the Island.

Clause Rolls, are preserved in the Tower, and contain such Matters as were committed to close Writs.

Clausum Fregit, denotes as much as an Action of Trespass, and is so called, because in the Writ the Defendant is summoned to answer *Quare Clausum fregit*, that is to say, *Why he broke such a Clause*, or did such a Trespass.

Clergy, has divers Significations, being sometimes taken for the whole Number of those who are *de Clero Domini*, viz. of our Lord's Lot or Share, as the Tribe of *Levi* was in *Judea*: It is likewise taken for a Plea to an Indictment of Felony, &c. it having been an ancient Privilege of the Church, where a Priest or other Person in Orders is arraign'd of Felony before a secular Judge, he may pray his *Clergy*, which is as much as to say

say, he prayed to be delivered to his Ordinary, to purge himself of the Offence objected against him. See *Staundf. Pl. Cor. lib. 2. c. 41.* The ancient Law in this Point is much altered; for, by 18 *El. c.* 7. Clerks are no more delivered to their Ordinaries to be purged, but since 18 *El. c.* 7. every Person to whom this Benefit is granted, tho' not in Orders, is put to read at the Bar, after he is found guilty and convicted of Felony, and so burnt in the Hand, and set free for the first Time, provided the Ordinary, his Commissioner or Deputy, standing by, do say, *he reads as a Clerk,* otherwise he suffers Death. But reading at last, as well as Purgation, is now entirely laid aside. See 5 *Ann. c.* 6.

Clerico admittendo, is a Writ directed to the Bishop, for the admitting of a Clerk to a Benefice, upon a *Ne admittas* tried and found for the Party that sued out the Writ. *Reg. Orig.* 31.

Clerico capto per Statutum Mercatorum, &c. is a Writ for the Delivery of a Clerk out of Prison, who is in Custody upon the Breach of a *Statute Merchant. Reg. Orig.* 147.

Clerico convicto commisso Gaolæ in defectu Ordinarii deliberando, &c. is a Writ that formerly lay for the Delivery of a Clerk to his Ordinary, who before had been convicted of Felony, for that his Ordinary did not challenge him according to the then Privileges of Clerks. See *Reg. Orig.* 69.

Clerico infra Sacros ordines constituto non eligendo in officium, is a Writ that is directed to the Bailiffs, &c. who have thrust a Bailiwick or other Office upon one in Holy Orders, charging them to release him from such Office. *Reg. Orig.* 143.

Clerk, according to the most general Acceptation of the Word, signifies one that belongs to the Holy Ministry of the Church; that is to say, in these Times, either Minister or Deacon, or of what other Degree or Dignity soever; for this Word comprehends all Sorts of Priests, Deacons, and others in Holy Orders, either secular or regular, tho' more properly a Priest. The other Signification of this Word is particularly applied to such as by their Course of Life practise their Pens in any Court or Office, as the Clerk of the Rolls of Parliament, Clerks of the Chancery, or the like.

Clerk of the Acts, is an Officer appointed in the Navy-Office, for receiving and recording all Orders, Contracts, Bills, Warrants, &c. transacted by the Lord Admiral and Commissioner of the Navy. See 16 *Car.* 2. *c.* 5. and 22 & 23 *Car.* 2.

Clerk of the Affidavits, is an Officer belonging to the Court of Chancery, whose Business is to file all Affidavits made use of in that Court.

Clerk of the Assise, is the Person who writes all Things judicially done by the Justices of *Assise* in their Circuits. See *Cromp. Jurisd.* 227.

Clerk of the Bails, is a particular Office belonging to the Court of *King's Bench,* who files all Bail-Pieces taken in that Court, and attends for that very End.

Clerk of the Check, is an Officer belonging to the King's Court, and is so called because he has the Check and Controllment of the Yeomen of the Guard, and all other ordinary Yeomen that belong either to the King, Queen, or Prince, he either giving Leave, or allowing their Absence in Attendance,

dance, or lessening their Wages for Defaults that Way. He likewise by himself or Deputy takes a View of such as are to watch in the Court, and sets the said Watch. See 33 H. 8. c. 12. There is also an Officer of the same Name in the King's Navy, for which see 19 Car. 2. c. 1.

Clerk of the Crown, is an Officer in the *King's Bench*, whose Office is to frame, read and record all Indictments against Offenders arraigned or indicted there of any publick Crime. He is likewise termed Clerk of the *Crown Office*, in which Capacity he exhibits Informations, by the Order of the Court for divers Offences.

Clerk of the Crown in Chancery, is an Officer belonging to that Court, whose Business is constantly to attend the Lord Chancellor, or Lord Keeper in Person, or by his Deputy, and to write and prepare for the Great Seal, special Matters of State by Commission, either immediately from his Majesty, or by the Order of his Council, both ordinary and extraordinary, *viz.* Commissions of Lieutenancy, of Justices of Assise, *Oyer* and *Terminer*, of Gaol-Delivery, and of the Peace, together with their Writs of Association, &c. Also all general Pardons upon Grants of them on a Coronation, or in Parliament, where he sits in the House of Lords in Time of Parliament: And into this Officer's Office the Writs of Parliament issued by the Clerks of the Petty-Bag, with the Names of the Knights and Burgesses elected thereon, are to be returned and filed. His Office is likewise to make out all special Pardons and Writs of Execution on Bonds of Statute-Staple forfeited, which Function was annexed to his Office, in Consideration of his chargeable Attendance.

Clerk of the Declarations, is he that files all Declarations in Causes depending in the Court of King's Bench, after they are ingrossed, &c.

Clerk of the Deliveries, is an Officer of the Tower, whose Function it is to take Indentures for all Stores issued thereout.

Clerk of the Errors, is an Officer in the Court of *Common Pleas*, who transcribes and certifies into the *King's Bench* the Tenor of the Record, upon which the Writ of *Error* made out by the Cursitor is brought, there to be judged and determined. The Clerk of the Errors in the *King's Bench*, transcribes and certifies the Records of Causes in that Court into the Exchequer, in case the Cause of Action were by *Bill*; but if by *Original*, the Lord Chief Justice certifies the Record into the House of Peers in Parliament, by taking the Transcript from the *Clerk of the Errors*, and delivering it to the *Lord Chancellor*, or *Lord Keeper*, there to be determined, pursuant to 27 *El. c.* 8. and 31 *El. c.* 1. The Business of the Clerk of the Errors in the Exchequer, is to transcribe the Records transferred thither out of the *King's Bench*, and to prepare them for Judgment in the *Exchequer* Chamber, there to be given by the Judges of the Common Pleas, and the Barons. See 16 *Car.* 2. *c.* 2. and 20 *Car.* 2. *c.* 4.

Clerk of the Essoins, is he that in the *Common Pleas*, keeps the *Essoin Rolls*, and has the Providing of Parchment, and cutting it out into Rolls, making the Numbers upon them, and delivering out of all the Rolls to each Officer of the Court, and likewise the receiving of them again

again when they are written, and also the making up and binding the whole Bundles of every Term; which Function he performs as Servant to the Chief Justice of the *Common Pleas*, who is at the Charge of the Parchment of all the Rolls, for which he is allowed, as the Chief Justice of the *King's Bench* is, over and above the Penny for the Seal, of every Writ of Privilege and Outlawry, the seventh Penny taken for the Seal of every Writ in Court under the Green Wax, or Petit Seal, in the Court of *King's Bench*, and *Common Pleas*, respectively, on account that the Chief Justices have annexed to their respective Offices the Custody of the said Seals which belong to each Court.

Clerk of the Estreats, is an Officer belonging to the *Exchequer*, who every Term receives the *Estreats* out of the Lord Treasurer's Remembrancer's Office, and writes them out, in order to be levied for the Crown: He likewise makes Schedules of such Sums *estreated*, as are to be discharged.

Clerk of the Hamper, or **Hanoper**, is an Officer belonging to the *Chancery*, whose Function it is to receive all the Money due to the King for the Seals of Charters, Letters Patent, Commissions and Writs; as likewise the Fees due to the Officers for enrolling and examining the same. He is bound to daily Attendance on the *Lord Chancellor*, or *Lord Keeper*, during Term-Time, and at all Times of Sealing, bearing with him Leather Bags, in which are put all Charters, &c. after sealed; which Bags are then sealed up with the Lord Chancellor's private Seal, and afterwards delivered to the Comptroller of the *Hamper*.

Clerk of the Inrollments, is an Officer of the Court of *Common Pleas*, whose Office is to enroll and exemplify Fines and Recoveries, and Returns of Writs of Entry, &c.

Clerk of the Juries, is an Officer belonging to the Court of *Common Pleas*, who makes up the Writs called *Habeas Corpora* and *Distringas*, for the Appearance of *Juries*, either in Court, or at the Assises, after the *Jury* or Panel is returned upon the *Venire facias*: His Business is likewise to enter into the Rolls, the awarding of these Writs, and to make all the Continuances from the issuing out of the *Habeas Corpora*, until the Verdict be given.

Clerk Comptroller of the King's House, is an Officer belonging to the King's Court, who is authorised to allow or disallow the Charges and Demands of Pursuivants, Messengers of the *Green-Cloth*, &c. He has likewise the Authority of inspecting and comptrolling all Defects and Miscarriages of any of the inferior Officers, and to sit in the *Counting-house* with the superior Officers, to wit, the Lord Steward, Mr. Treasurer, Comptroller, and Cofferer, for the regulating Matters out of Order. See 33 *H.* 8. *c.* 12.

Clerk Marshal of the King's House, is an Officer that attends the *Marshal* in his Court, and records all his Proceedings there. See 33 *H.* 8. *c.* 12.

Clerk of the King's Silver, is an Officer of the Court of Common Pleas, to whom every Fine is brought, after it has been with the *Custos Brevium*; and it is he by whom the Effect of every Writ of Covenant is entered into a Paper-Book, according to which all the Fines of that Term are recorded in the Rolls of the Court, after

after a particular Form, which being done, and the King's Silver entered, it is accounted a Fine in Law, but not before.

Clerk of the King's Great Wardrobe, is an Officer belonging to the King's House, whose Business is to keep an Account or Inventory of all the Things belonging to the *King's Wardrobe*.

Clerk of the Market, is an Officer belonging to the King's House, to whom is given the Charge of the King's Measures, and the Keeping of the Standards of them, which are the Guides for all Measures throughout *England*; as likewise of Weights: His Office is also to see that all Weights and Measures in every Place be answerable to such Standard. See *Fleta, lib.* 8, 9, &c.

Clerk of the Nichils, or Nihils, is an Officer of the Exchequer, who makes a Roll of such Sums as are *nihiled* by the Sheriffs upon their Estreats of Green Wax, and delivers the said Roll into the Remembrancer's Office, in order to have Execution done for the King thereon. The *Nihils* themselves, from whence this Officer takes his Name, are Issues by Way of Fine or Amercement. See 5 R. 2. c. 13.

Clerk of the Ordinance, is an Officer of the Tower, who registers all Orders concerning the King's Ordnance.

Clerk of the Outlawries, is an Officer of the Common Pleas, and is as Servant or Deputy to the King's Attorney General, for making out all Writs of *Capias utlagatum*, after Outlawry; the Name of the King's Attorney General being to those Writs.

Clerk of the Paper-Office, is an Officer belonging to the *King's Bench*, whose Business is to make up the Paper-books of special Pleadings and Demurrers in that Court.

Clerk of the Papers, is an Officer of the Court of *Common Pleas*, who has the Custody of the Papers of the Warden of the *Fleet*, enters the Commitments and Discharges of Prisoners, delivers out Day-Rules, &c.

Clerk of the Parliament-Rolls, is an Officer that records all Transactions in the High Court of Parliament, and ingrosses them in Parchment Rolls for their better Preservation to Posterity: There are two of these Officers, one in the House of Lords, and the other in the House of Commons.

Clerk of the Patents, that is to say, of the Letters Patent under the Great Seal, is an Office erected 18 *Jac.* 1.

Clerk of the Peace, is an Officer belonging to the Sessions of the Peace, whose Duty is to read Indictments, inroll the Acts and other Proceedings, and to draw the Process. His Business is likewise to certify unto the *King's Bench* Transcripts of Indictments, Outlawries, Attainders and Convictions had before the Justices of the Peace within the Time limited by Law, under a certain Penalty. See *Lamb. Eiren. lib.* 4. c. 3. This Office is in the Gift of the *Custos Rotulorum* of the County, and may be executed by Deputy. See 37 H. 8. c. 1.

Clerk of the Pell, is an Officer that belongs to the Exchequer, whose Business is to enter every Toller's Bill into a Parchment Roll, called *Pellis Receptorum;* and also to make another Roll of Payments, termed *Pellis Exituum*, in which he sets down by what Warrant the Money was paid.

Clerk

Clerk of the Petty-Bag, is an Officer of the Court of Chancery, of which Sort there are three, of whom the Master of the Rolls is the Chief. Their Business is to record the Return of Inquisitions out of every Shire; to make out Patents of Customers, Gaugers, Comptrollers, &c. As likewise, *Congé d' Eslires* for Bishops; all *Liberates* upon Extents of Statutes Staple; the Recovery of Recognizances forfeited, and all *Elegits* upon them: They also have the Making out the Summons of the Nobility, Clergy, and Burgesses to Parliament; Commissions directed to the Knights, and others of every Shire, for assessing Subsidies.

Clerk of the Pipe, is an Officer belonging to the Exchequer, who having the Accounts of all Debts due to the King delivered and drawn out of the Remembrancer's Office, charges them down in the Great Roll, and is called *Clerk of the Pipe*, purely from the Shape of that Roll, which is folded up together in the Shape of a *Pipe*: He likewise writes out Warrants to Sheriffs to levy the said Debts upon the Goods and Chattels of the Debtors; and in case they have no Goods, &c. to be levied upon, then he draws them down to the Lord Remembrancer, to write Estreats against their Lands. The ancient Revenue of the Crown remains in Charge to the *Clerk of the Pipe*, who sees the same answered by the Farmers and Sheriffs: He also makes a Charge to all Sheriffs of their Summons of the *Pipe* and Green Wax, and his Business is to take Care, that the same be answered on their Accounts: Finally, He has the Drawing and Ingrossing of all Leases of the King's Land, having proper Officers under him for that Purpose.

Clerk of the Pleas, is an Officer belonging to the Exchequer, in whose Office all the Officers of the Court (upon special Privilege belonging to them) ought to sue, or be sued in any Action, &c. Actions at Law are likewise prosecuted by Persons that are not Officers, as well as those that are; yet, in Strictness, the Plaintiff ought to be Tenant or Debtor to the King, or some Way accountant to him; for which Reason it is, that in all Suits commenced at Law, the Plaintiff, in the Declaration, is set forth to be a Debtor to the Crown, whether he be really so or not; which Formality to this Day is held to be absolutely necessary to be observed in all Declarations for Debt, Trespass, &c. commenced in this Office.

Clerk of the Privy Seal. There are four of these Officers, who attend the Lord *Privy Seal*; or if there be no Lord *Privy Seal*, the Principal Secretary of State, writing and making out all Things that are sent by Warrant from the Signet to the *Privy Seal*, and which are to pass the *Great Seal*: They also make out *Privy Seals*, upon a special Occasion of the *Sovereign's* Affairs; as for Loan of Money, or the like.

Clerk of the Rolls, is an Officer of the Court of Chancery, whose Business is to make Searches after and Copies of Deeds, Offices, &c.

Clerk of the Rules, is an Officer of the *King's Bench*, whose Province it is to draw up and enter all the Rules and Orders made in Court, and to give Rules of Course on divers Writs.

Clerk of the Sewers, is an Officer belonging to the Commissioners of *Sewers*, who writes and records

CL

records their Proceedings, transacted by Virtue of their Commissions, and the Authority given them by Law. See 13 *Eliz. c.* 9.

Clerk of the Signet, is an Officer who continually attends on the King's principal Secretary, who has the Custody of the *Privy Signet*, as well for sealing the King's private Letters, as also all such Grants as pass the King's Hand by Bill signed. There are four of these Officers that attend in their Course, and have their Diet at the Secretary's Table.

Clerk of the Supersedeas, is an Officer of the *Common Pleas*, who makes out Writs of *Supersedeas*, upon the Defendant's appearing to the Exigent on an Outlawry; by which the Sheriff is forbidden to return the Exigent.

Clerk of the Treasury, is an Officer belonging to the *Common Pleas*, who has the Charge of keeping the Records of the Court, and makes out all the Records of *Nisi Prius*; and also all Exemplifications of Records being in the *Treasury*. By his Office, he has all the Fees due for all Searches; and is said to be a Servant of the Chief Justice's, and removeable at Pleasure, which other Officers are not, they having their Offices for Term of Life. This Officer is allowed an Assistant, called a Secondary or Under-Clerk of the *Treasury*: There is likewise belonging to this Office an Under-Keeper, who always keeps one Key of the *Treasury-Door*, and the chief Clerk of the *Secondary* another; so that the one may not go in without the other.

Clerk of the Warrants, is an Officer of the *Common Pleas*, whose Business is to enter all Warrants of Attorney for Plaintiffs and Defendants in Suits, and to inroll all

CO

Deeds of Bargain and Sale, that are acknowledged in Court, or before a Judge out of Court: His Office is likewise to estreat into the Exchequer all Issues, Fines and Amerciaments, that grow due to the Crown in that Court.

Closh, was an unlawful Game, forbidden by 17 *Ed.* 4. *c.* 3. It is said to have been the same with our Nine Pins. See more 33 *H.* 8. where it is more properly called *Clash*.

Clove, is the two and thirtieth Part of a Weigh of Cheese, *viz.* eight Pounds. See 9 *H.* 6. *c.* 8.

Coadjutor, signifies Assistant, and is particularly applied to a Person appointed to assist a Bishop, when grown so old and infirm, as not to be able to perform his Duty.

Cocket, is a Seal belonging to the King's Custom-house, or it may be rather said to be a Scroll of Parchment sealed and delivered by the Officers of the Custom-house to Merchants, as a Warrant that their Wares or Merchandizes are customed.

Codicil, is a certain Writing made by Way of Supplement to a Will, where any Thing is omitted which the Testator would have added, explained, altered or recalled. This *Codicil* is of the same Nature with a Will or Testament, only that it is made without an Executor; besides one can leave behind but one Will, yet as many *Codicils* as he will. *Codicils* are always taken as Part of the Testament, and ought to be annexed to the same; and the Executor is bound to see those *Codicils* performed.

Cofferer of the King's Houshold, is a Principal Officer belonging to the King's House, next under the *Comptroller*, who in the Counting House, and elsewhere, has the special Charge of other Officers of the

the Houshold, to all whom he pays their Wages; and he passes his Accounts in the Exchequer.

Cognisance, has divers Significations in our Law; sometimes denoting an Acknowledgment of a *Fine*; or Confession of something done; sometimes the Hearing of a Matter judicially, as to take Cognisance of a Cause; and sometimes a particular Jurisdiction; as Cognisance of Pleas, is an Authority to call a Cause or Plea out of another Court, which no Person can do but the King, except he can shew Charters for it; seeing that such *Cognisance* does not lie in Prescription.

Cognisor and Cognisee, are two Persons in different Respects concerned in a Fine: The *Cognisor*, is the Person that acknowledges it; and the *Cognisee* is the Person to whom it is acknowledged. See 32 *H.* 8. *c.* 5.

Cognitionibus mittendis, is a Writ directed to one of the Justices of the *Common Pleas*, or other Person that has Power to take a Fine, who having taken Acknowledgment thereof defers to certify it; wherefore he is, by this Writ, commanded to certify the same. *Reg. Orig.* 68.

Cognovit actionem, denotes the Case where a Defendant acknowledges the Plaintiff's Cause against him to be true, and, after Issue join'd, suffers Judgment to be entered up against him without a Trial.

Coif, appertains to a Title given to Serjeants at Law, who are otherwise called *Serjeants of the Coif*; from the *Lawn Coif* they wear under their Caps, when they are created.

Coin, is a collective Word, containing in it all Manner of the several Stamps and Species in any Nation. It is one of the Royal Prerogatives belonging to a Prince, that he in his own Dominions may order and dispose the Quantity, Value and Fashion of his Coin; yet the Coin of one King is not commonly current in the Dominions of another, unless at great Loss. If a Person binds himself to pay 100 *l.* of lawful Money of *Great Britain* to another, and the Obligor at the Time limited pays the Money due, in *French, Spanish*, or other Foreign Coin, made current in this Kingdom by Act of Parliament, or the King's Proclamation; the Obligation is said to be well performed.

Coinage, in general denotes the making and stamping of Money by the King's Authority. It likewise signifies a Duty imposed on Wine, Beer, and Brandy imported, called the *Coinage-Duty*, taking its Name from its being granted for the Expence of the King's *Coinage*.

Collateral, in a legal Sense, is taken for any Thing that hangeth by the Side of another whereto it relates; as a *Collateral Assurance* is that Instrument which is made over and above the Deed itself: For Example, If a Man by Deed covenants with another to perform some particular Act, &c. and at the same Time enters into a Bond for the Performance of his Covenant, the Bond is termed a Collateral Assurance; for that it is external, and without the Nature and Essence of the Covenant. Where a Person has Liberty to pitch Booths or Standings for a Fair or Market in another's Grounds, such Liberty is *collateral* to the Ground. The private Woods of a common Person, within a Forest, may not be cut without the King's Licence, it being a Prero-

Prerogative collateral to the Soil; as to be subject to the Feeding of the King's Deer is *collateral* to the Soil of a Forest.

Collateral Discent and Warranty. See **Discent and Warranty.**

Collation of a Benefice, denotes the bestowing of a *Benefice* by a Bishop, who has Right of Patronage: It differs from Institution in this, that Institution is performed by the Bishop upon the Presentation of another, whilst *Collation* is the Bishop's sole Act of Presentation: Yet Collation may supply the Place of Presentation and Institution, and amounts to the same as Institution, where the Bishop is both Patron and Ordinary.

Collatione facta uni post mortem alterius, is a Writ to the Justices of the *Common Pleas*, commanding them to issue their Writ to the Bishop for the Admission of a Clerk in the Place of another presented by the King, such Clerk, during the Suit between the King and the Bishop's Clerk, being dead: And it is grounded upon this, that Judgment once passed for the King's Clerk, who dying before Admittance, the King may bestow his Presentation on another. *Reg. Orig.* 31.

Collatione Hermitagii, was a Writ whereby the King conferred upon a Clerk the keeping of an *Hermitage*. *Reg. Orig.* 303, 308.

Collegiate Church, is a Church erected and endowed for a Society or Body corporate, consisting of a Dean or other President, and secular Priests, such as Canons or Prebendaries in the said Church. Before the Reformation there were many of these Societies, and some are still established, as *Westminster, Windsor, Rippon, Wolverhampton, Southwell, Manchester,* &c.

Colloquium, signifies a Talking together, or Affirming of some particular Fact, and is commonly laid in Declarations for Words in Action of Slander, &c.

Collusion, denotes a deceitful Contract or Agreement between two or more, for the one to bring an Action against the other, to some evil Purpose; as to defraud a Person of his Right, &c. It may be either apparent, as where it shews itself on the very first Appearance of the Act; or it may be done under-hand and in the Dark, and covered over with the Shew of Honesty. The Law abhors *Collusion* in all Respects, and on that Account, when discovered, it makes void every Thing that depends thereon, tho' otherwise in themselves never so good.

Colonus, denotes a Husbandman, or Villager, who was formerly bound to pay an annual Tribute, or at certain Times to plough some Part of the Lord's Land: Whence comes the Word *Clown*.

Colour, according to the legal Acceptation of the Word, denotes some probable Plea of a Defendant to an Action brought, which in Fact is false; and it has this End in it, *viz.* to draw the Trial of the Cause from the Jury to the Judges; as where *A.* brings an Assise of Land against *B.* who says he himself did let the same Land to one *C.* for Term of Life, and afterwards granted the Reversion to *A.* the Demandant; and that *C.* the Tenant for Life died, after whose Decease, *A.* the Demandant, claiming the Reversion by Force of the Grant (to which *C.* the Tenant, did never attorn) entered, and upon him *B.* entered, against whom *A.* for that Entry brings this Assise, &c. This is a good Colour, because, according to the

vulgar

vulgar Notion, the Land will pass by the Grant without Attornment, where in Fact it will not pass. In an Action of Trespass *Colour* must be given, whereof there are an infinite Number; as for Instance, an Action of Trespass being brought for taking away the Plaintiff's Beasts, the Defendant says, that before the Plaintiff had any Property in them, he himself was possessed of them, as of his own proper Goods, and delivered them to *A. B.* to deliver to him again, when, &c. and that *A.* delivered them to the Plaintiff, and that the Plaintiff supposing the Property to be in *A.* at the Time of the Gift, took them, and the Defendant took them from the Plaintiff, whereupon the Plaintiff brings his Action. This is a good *Colour*, and consequently a good Plea. *Cowel.* See more of this Subject in *Doctor and Student, lib.* 2. *c.* 13.

Colour of Office, is always taken in the worst Sense, and signifies an Act illegally done by the Countenance of an Office, or what is more generally called, under Colour of Authority, the Office being no more than a Shadow or Vail to the Falshood.

Combarones, formerly signified the Fellow Barons, or Commonalty of the Cinque Ports: But the Title of Barons of those Ports, is now given to the Representatives in Parliament; and the Word *Combaro* is used for a Fellow-Member, as the *Baron* and his *Combarons.*

Combat, in our ancient Law denoted a formal Trial of a doubtful Case or Quarrel by the Swords or Batoons of two Champions. The last Trial by *Combat* in *England*, was in the sixth Year of King *Charles* the first, between *Donald* Lord *Rey*, Appellant, and *David Ramsay*, Esq; Defendant, who were both *Scotchmen*: But after many Formalities, the Matter was referred to the King's Pleasure.

Combinations. See **Confederacy**.

Combustio Pecuniæ, was the ancient Way of trying Money, by melting it down upon Payment into the *Exchequer.*

Comitatus, signifies a County: And *Ingulphus* tells us, that *England* was first divided into Counties by King *Alfred*, and Counties into Hundreds, and those again into Tithings.

Comitatu commisso, is a Writ whereby the Sheriff is authorised to take upon him the Charge of the County. *Reg. Orig.* 295.

Comitatu & Castro commisso, is a Writ by which, not only the Charge of a County, but likewise that of a Castle, is committed to the Sheriff. *Reg. Orig.* 295.

Commandment, has divers Significations in our Law: Sometimes it is taken for the *Commandment* of the King; as where, upon his own Motion, and from his own Mouth he orders a Person to Prison: Sometimes it is taken for the Commandment of the Justices, which is either *absolute*, or *ordinary*: *Absolute*, when upon their own Authority they commit a Person to Prison for Contempt, &c. as a Punishment: *Ordinary*, where they commit one rather for safe Custody, than for any Punishment, and the Person thus committed by *ordinary Commandment* is bailable. See *Staundf. Pl. Cor.* 73. *Commandment* is likewise used for a Person that orders another to do some unlawful Act; as Theft, Murder, or the like.

Commandry, signified a Manor or chief Messuage, with Lands and Tenements appertaining thereto, and which anciently belonged to the Priory of St. *John* of *Jerusalem*, until they were given to King *Henry* the Eighth. He who had the Government of any such Manor or House, was called the *Commander*, who could not dispose of it otherwise than to the Use of the Priory, and at the same Time only taking thence for his own Sustenance according to his Degree, which was usually that of a Brother of the same Priory.

Commendam, signifies the holding of a Benefice, which, being void, is commended to the Care of some sufficient Clerk, in order to be supplied, until it may be conveniently provided with a Pastor. The Person to whom the Church is commended has the Fruits and Profits thereof only for a certain Time, and the Nature of a Church is not thereby changed, but it is deposited in the Hands of him to whom it is commended, who has no more Interest in it than the bare Custody thereof, which may be revoked. When a Parson is created a Bishop, there is, by his Promotion, a Cession of the Benefice; yet if the King gives him a Power to retain his Benefice, he shall still continue Parson, and is said to hold the Benefice *in commendam*.

Commendatary, is a Parson who has a Church-Living *in commendam*.

Commendatory Letters, are such as are wrote by one Bishop to another, in Behalf of any of the Clergy, or others belonging to his Diocese, who are travelling thither, in order that they may be received among the Faithful, or that the Clerk may be promoted, or Necessaries administred to both.

Commendati Homines, were Persons who by voluntary Homage put themselves under the Protection of a superior Lord; and hence the singular *Commendatus* denotes one that lives under the Protection of some great Personage. *Commendati dimidii*, were Persons that had Dependance on two several Lords, and were to pay one Half of their Homage to *this*, and the other to *that*. *Sub-Commendati*, were those that, like Under-Tenants, were under the Command of such as were themselves depending on some superior Lord: There were likewise *Dimidii Sub-commendati*, who bore a double Relation to such depending Lords.

Commissary, is an Ecclesiastical Title, which appertains to him that exercises spiritual Jurisdiction in Places of the Diocese, so far distant from the chief City, that the Chancellor cannot call the Subjects to the Bishop's principal Consistory, without too great Inconvenience to them. This Officer is, by the Canonists, termed *Commissary*, or *Officialis foraneus*, and is appointed for the special End, that he should supply the Office and Jurisdiction of the Bishop in the Out-places of the Diocese, or in such Parishes as are peculiar to the Bishop, and exempted from the Archdeacon's Jurisdiction; for where an Archdeacon, either by Prescription or Composition has Jurisdiction, as in most Places they have, there this *Commissary* is superfluous, and rather tends to the Prejudice, than Good of the People.

Commission, signifies the Warrant, or Letters Patent, which all Persons exercising Jurisdiction, either ordinary or extraordinary, have to empower them to hear or determine

mine any Cause or Suit. This Word is sometimes further extended than to Matters of Judgment; as the *Commission* of *Purveyance*, &c.

Commission of Anticipation, was a Commission under the Great Seal, to collect a Subsidy before the Day. See 15 *H*. 8.

Commission of Association, is mentioned in the 18 *Eliz. c.* 9. and denotes a Commission under the Great Seal, to associate two or more learned Persons with the Justices in the several Circuits and Counties of *Wales*.

Commission of Bankrupts, is a Commission that issues from the Lord Chancellor, directed to certain Commissioners appointed to examine into and secure the *Bankrupt's* Lands and Effects for the Satisfaction of his Creditors. See *Bankrupt*.

Commission of charitable Uses, issues out of the Court of Chancery, and is directed to the Bishop and others of the Diocese, where any Lands given to charitable Uses are misapplied, or there is any Fraud or Disputes concerning them, in order to enquire into and redress the Abuse, &c.

Commission of Delegates, issues under the Great Seal, directed to certain Persons, usually two or three temporal Lords, as many Bishops, and two Judges of the Law, authorising them to sit upon an Appeal to the King in the Court of Chancery, from a Sentence given in any Ecclesiastical Cause by the Archbishop.

Commission of Lunacy, issues out of the Court of Chancery, and authorises the Commissioners thereby appointed to enquire, whether a Person, represented to be a Lunatick, be so or not; so that, if *Lunatick* the King may have the Care of his Estate.

Commission of Rebellion, which is now generally termed a Writ of *Rebellion*, issues, where a Person (after Proclamation made by the Sheriff, upon a Process out of the Chancery or Exchequer, upon Pain of his Allegiance, to present himself to the Court by a Day assigned) neglects to appear. This Commission is directed by Way of Command to certain Persons, to the Intent that they three, two, or one of them, do apprehend, or cause to be apprehended, the Party as a Rebel, and Contemner of the King's Laws, in whatsoever Place he can be found within the Kingdom, and bring, or cause him to be brought to the Court, on a Day therein assigned. *Note*; This Commission does not issue till after a *Non est inventus* is returned on an Attachment granted.

Commission of Sewers, is a Commission directed to certain Persons, authorising them to inspect and see Drains and Ditches well kept in the Marshy and Fenny Parts of *England*, for the better conveying of the Water into the Sea, and preserving the Grass upon the Land.

Commissioner, is he that is authorised by Commission, Letters Patent, or other lawful Warrant, to execute any publick Office.

Committee, is one, or more, to whom the Consideration or ordering of a Matter is referred, either by the Consent of some Court, or by the Consent of Parties to whom it belongs: As in Parliament, a Bill being read, is either consented to and pass'd, or denied, or neither, but referred to the Consideration of certain Persons appointed by the House for a further Examination

amination of the Matter, who are thereupon called a *Committee*. In *Kitchin* 160. this Word is used in a quite different Sense, *viz.* the Widow of the King's Tenant is called the *Committee* of the King, that is to say, one committed by the ancient Law of the Land to the King's Protection and Care.

Commitment, denotes the sending of a Person to a Gaol or Prison, by Warrant or Order, on account of some Crime charged or committed. This *Commitment* may be made by the King and Council, by the Judges of the Law, the Justices of the Peace, or other Magistrates, who are authorised by the Laws so to do, which Laws must be exactly pursued. Every *Commitment* in general ought to be made by Warrant under the Hand and Seal of the Party committing; and the Cause of *Commitment* should at the same Time be expressed in the Warrant, &c.

Commonalty, is generally taken for the middle Sort of the King's Subjects, *viz.* such of the Commons as are raised above the ordinary Sort, and coming to have the Management of Offices, and, on that Account, are only one Degree below Burgesses, who are superior to them in Order and Authority.

Common, denotes that Soil or Water, whereof the Use is *common* to this or that Town or Lordship; as *Common of Pasture, Common of Fishing, Common of Estovers, Common of Turbary,* &c. *Common of Pasture* is divided into *Common in Gross, Common Appendant, Common Appurtenant,* and *Common because of Neighbourhood. Common in Gross,* is, where a Person by Deed grants to another to have Common alone, without any Lands, &c. in the Grantor's Land. *Common Appendant,* and *Common Appurtenant,* as appears by *Fitz. Nat. Brev.* are in a great Measure confounded, and are defined to be a Liberty of *Common* appertaining to, or depending on some particular Freehold; which Common must be taken with Beasts *commonable*, as Horses, Oxen, Kine and Sheep, and not with Goats, Hogs and Geese: Yet some make this Difference, *viz.* that *Common Appurtenant* may be severed from the Land whereto it belongs; but not *Common Appendant. Common because of Neighbourhood,* is a Liberty that the Tenants of one Lord in one Town have to common with the Tenants of another Lord in another Town. Those that challenge this Kind of Common, (which in our ancient Law-Books is called *Common pur Cause de Vicinage,* usually called *Intercommoning*) may not put their Cattle in the Common of the other Lord; for if they do, they are distrainable; but turning them into their own Grounds, if they stray into the *Neighbour Common*, they must be suffered.

Common of Estovers, denotes a Right of taking Wood out of another Person's Woods, for House-bote, Plough-bote, and Hay-bote.

Common of Piscary, signifies a Liberty of Fishing in another's Water.

Common of Turbary, signifies a Licence to dig Turf upon the Ground of another, or in the the Lord's Waste. This *Common* is appendant or appurtenant to a House, but not to Lands; for Turfs are to be burnt in the House.

Common Bench, is the Name that was anciently given to the Court of *Common Pleas*; and in Law-Books and References, the *Court of Common Pleas* is frequently wrote

wrote C. B. from *Communi Banco*, the *Common Bench*: And in our Records the Justices of that Court are filed *Justiciarii de Banco*. See **Common Pleas**.

Common Day in Plea of Land, denotes an ordinary Day in Court, as in *eight Days of Hillary*, from the Day of *Easter* in fifteen Days.

Common Fine, denotes a certain Fine which the Resiants within the Liberty of some Lords pay to the Lord of the same, and is called in divers Places *Head-Silver* or *Head-Pence*, in others *Cert Money*. This Fine was first granted to the Lord, towards the Charge of his Purchase of the Court-Leet, whereby the Resiants have the Ease to do their Suit within their own Manors, and are not compellable to go to the *Sheriff's Turn*. For this *Common Fine* the Lord cannot, without Prescription, distrain.

Commons House of Parliament, is so called, on Account that the *Commons* of the Kingdom, viz. the Knights, Citizens and Burgesses, who represent the whole Body of the Commons do sit there.

Common Intendment, is as much as to say common Meaning or Understanding, according to the subject Matter, without being strained to any extraordinary Sense: Hence *Bar to Common Intendment*, is a general Bar, which commonly disables the Plaintiff's Declaration.

Common Law, is taken for the Law of *England* simply, without any other Laws whatsoever; that is to say, for such Laws as were generally holden, before any Statute was enacted in Parliament to alter them. The *Common Law* is grounded upon the general Custom of the Realm, including in it the Law of Nature, the Law of God, and the Principles of Law: It is likewise founded upon Reason, and is said to be the Perfection of *Reason*, to be acquired by long Study, Observation and Experience, and refined by the Learned in all Ages. It may likewise be well said to be the common Birth-right that the Subject has for the Safe-guard and Defence of his Liberties and Properties, viz. not only of his Goods, Lands and Revenues, but also of his Wife and Children, Body, Fame and Life.

Common Pleas, is one of the King's Courts now held in *Westminster-Hall*, but in former Times was moveable. *Gwyn*, in his Preface to his *Reading*, says, That until the Time of the granting of the Great Charter by King *Henry* the Third, there were but two Courts in all, that were called the King's Courts; one of which was the *Exchequer*, the other called the *King's Bench*, which was then called *Curia Domini Regis*, and *Aula Regia*, because it followed the King and Court; and that upon the Grant of that Charter, the Court of *Common Pleas* was erected and settled in a certain Place, viz. *Westminster-Hall*; after which Time all the Writs ran, *Quod sit coram Justiciariis nostris, apud Westmonasterium*; whereas before they ran *Coram me, vel Justiciariis meis*, without any Addition of Place. All Civil Causes, as well real as personal, are, or were in former Times, tried in this Court, according to the strict Law of the Land: And by *Fortescue*, c. 50. it seems to have been the only Court for real Causes. The chief Judge of this Court is called the *Lord Chief Justice of the Common Pleas*, who is assisted by three other Judges, or Associates, who are all created by Letters Patent from the King. The other Officers of the Court are, the

the *Custos Brevium*, three *Prothonotaries*, and their *Secondaries*, the Clerk of the *Warrants*, Clerk of the *Essoins*, fourteen *Philazers*, four *Exigenters*, the Clerk of the *Juries*, the *Chirographer*, the Clerk of the *King's Silver*, Clerk of the *Treasury*, Clerk of the *Seal*, Clerk of the *Outlawries*, the Clerk of the Inrollment of *Fines* and *Recoveries*, and Clerk of the *Errors*, &c.

Common Weal, in our Law, denotes a common Good, for which many Things are tolerated by Law to be done, which otherwise might not be done: On which Account it is, that all Monopolies, Bonds and Covenants to restrain free Trade or the like, are adjudged void in Law.

Commorancy, denotes an Abiding, Inhabiting, or Continuing in any Place; as the Inhabitant of a House in a Village, &c. Where *Commorancy* for a certain Time may make a Settlement in a Parish, see *Dalt.* under Title *Poor*.

Commote, in *Wales*, anciently signified Half a *Cantred* or Hundred; with us it signifies a great Seigniory, including one or divers Manors. *Co. Lit.* 5.

Communance, as *Cowel* says, did formerly signify the Commoners Tenants, or Inhabitants, who had the Right of *Common*, or Commoning in open Fields, &c.

Commune Concilium Regni Angliæ, is taken for the Common Council of the King and People assembled in Parliament.

Communia Placita non tenenda in Scaccario, is a Writ anciently directed to the Treasurer and Barons of the Exchequer, forbidding them to hold Plea between common Persons in that Court, neither of whom belonged to the same. See *Reg. Orig.* 187.

Communi Custodia, is a Writ that anciently lay for the Lord, whose Tenant holding by Knight's Service died, and left his eldest Son under Age, against a Stranger who entred the Land, and obtained the Ward of the Body. *Old Nat. Brev.* 89. This Writ since Wardships were taken away by 12 *Car.* 2. *c.* 24. is become obsolete.

Community. See **Commonalty**.

Companion of the Garter, is taken for one of the Knights of that most Honourable Order. See 24 *Hen.* 8. *c.* 13.

Computorium, in the Civil Law, signifies a Judicial Inquest made by Delegates, or Commissioners, to search out and relate the Truth of a Cause.

Composition, in general, signifies a Contract between a Parson, Patron, or Ordinary, or all of them jointly, to accept of Money, or other Things, in Lieu of Tithes. This Word is likewise applied to the compounding of Debts with Creditors; as where a Debtor thro' Losses, &c. becomes insolvent, and upon Application to his Creditors prevails with them to accept of some small Part of the Money due to them, in full Satisfaction of the Whole; such as five Shillings, more or less, in the Pound for every 20 s. due.

Comprint, in a proper Sense, signifies to print together; but according to the general Acceptation of the Word among Booksellers, it denotes a surreptitious Printing of another's Copy, in order to make Gain thereby, which is expresly contrary to the Statute 14 *Car.* 2. *c.* 33. and other Laws in Force.

Compromise, usually denotes a mutual Promise of two or more Parties in Difference, to refer the

Decision

Decision of their Controversies to the Determination of one or more Arbitrators. *West*, in his *Symb.* defines it thus, *viz.* That it is the Faculty or Power of pronouncing Sentence between Persons at Variance, given to Arbitrators by the Parties mutual Consent. Hence Matters *compromised* denote Matters in Law referred, or made an End of.

Comptroller. See **Controller.**

Compurgator, denotes a Person that by Oath justifies another. See **Oath.**

Computation, in our Law, denotes the true Construction of Time, to the End, that neither Party to an Agreement, &c. may do Wrong to the other, nor the Determination of Time be referred at large; but it is to be computed according to the just Censure of the Law; as where a Lease is dated the 1st Day of *May*, 1738. to hold for three Years from henceforth, and the Lease is not executed until the 2d Day of *May* in the said Year; in which Case, the Words, *From henceforth*, shall be accounted from the Delivery of the Deed, and not by any Computation from the Date: And if the Lease be delivered at Four of the Clock in the Afternoon of the said second Day, this Lease shall end the 1st Day of *May* in the third Year; the Law, in this Computation entirely rejecting all Fractions, or Divisions of the Day.

Computo, is a Writ that compels a Bailiff, Receiver, or Accountant, to yield up his Accounts. It also lies against Guardians. See *Reg. Orig.* 135.

Concealers, are those Persons that find out concealed Lands, that is to say, such as are privily kept from the King by common Persons, who have nothing to shew for their Estate or Title therein. See 39 *Eliz. c.* 22. and 21 *Jac. c.* 2. There are likewise *Concealers of Crimes*, and *Concealers of Treason*, &c. for which see *Misprision*.

Concessi, *I have granted*, has been frequently used in Conveyances, a Covenant in Law being thereby created; so *Dedi*, *I have given*, amounts to a Warranty. *Co. Lit.* 384.

Concionator, denotes a Common-Council Man, or Freeman, called to the Hall or Assembly, as most worthy.

Conclusion, is where a Person, by his own Act upon Record, has charged himself with a Duty, or Thing, or confessed some Matter, whereby he shall be concluded; as where a Sheriff returns upon a *Capias*, that he has taken the Body, and yet has it not in Court at the Day of the Return of the Writ; the Sheriff by this Return becomes concluded from a Plea of Escape. This Word is likewise taken in another Sense, as for the Ending or latter Part of a Declaration, Plea or Replication, &c. As where to the Bar there ought to be a Replication, the Conclusion of the Plea must be, *And this he is ready to affirm*. The Conclusion of other Pleas runs thus, *viz. And upon this he puts himself upon his Country*. See *Kitch.* 219, 220.

Concord, has a peculiar Signification in the Common Law, as to denote the very Agreement between Parties, who intend to levy a Fine of Lands, &c. one to another, how, and in what Manner the Lands, &c. shall pass: In short, it is the Substance and Foundation of the Fine, which is taken and acknowledged before one of the Judges of the Common Pleas, or before Commissioners appointed for that Purpose in the Country. Concord is likewise taken for an Agreement made between two or more, upon a Trespass committed, and is divided into *Concord executory*, and *Concord executed*: And according to some Opinions, the one does not bind, as being imperfect; but the other being absolute ties the Party; yet by the Opinions of others, Agreements *executory* are perfect, and not less binding than *Concords executed*.

Concubinage, according to the general Acceptation of the Word, denotes the Keeping of a Whore or *Concubine*: But in a legal Sense is taken as an Exception against a Widow that sues for her Dower, whereby it is alledged, that she was not a Wife lawfully married to the Party in whose Lands she seeks to be endowed, but only his *Concubine*.

Conders, are Persons that stand upon high Places near the Sea-Coasts, at the Time of Herring-Fishing, in order to make Signs with Boughs, &c. to the Fishermen at Sea, which Way the Shole of Herrings passes, which may be better discovered by those that stand upon a high Cliff on the Shore, than such as are in the Ships or Boats for Fishing. These *Conders* are otherwise called *Huers* and *Balkers*, *Directors* and *Guiders*. See 1 *Jac. c.* 23.

Condition, is a Restraint or Bridle annexed to a Thing, so that by the Non-performance, the Party thereto shall receive Prejudice and Loss, and by the Performance, Profit and Advantage. There are different Kinds of Conditions, *viz*. *Conditions* in *Deed*, *Conditions* in *Law*, *conditions precedent*, and *subsequent*, *Conditions inherent*, and *collateral*, *affirmative*, and *negative*, &c. *Condition in Deed*, is what is joined by express Words to a Feoffment, Lease, or other Grant; as where a Person grants a Lease of a House to another, reserving a certain yearly Rent to be paid at such and such Feasts, upon Condition that if the Lessee fail in Payment, at any of the Days limited, then it may be lawful for the Lessor to re-enter. A *Condition* in *Law*, is where a Person grants an Office to another, as that of a Keeper of a Park, &c. for Term of Life, in which Case, tho' there be no Condition expressed in the Grant, yet the Law makes one, *viz*. if the Grantee does not duly execute his Office, then the Grantor may re-enter, and discharge him from the same: And these Conditions are likewise distinguished by the Names of *Condition expressed*, and *Condition implied*. *Condition precedent* does gain the Thing or Estate made upon Condition, by the Performance of it; as where an Estate is granted to one for Life upon Condition, that if the Lessee pay to the Lessor a certain Sum on such a Day, then the Lessee shall have a Fee-simple in that Estate: In which Case the Condition preceeds the Estate in Fee, and on Performance thereof the Fee-simple is gained. *Condition subsequent*, keeps the Thing made upon Condition, by the Performance of it; as where a Person grants to another certain Lands, &c. in Fee, upon Condition that the Grantee pay to him at such a Day 50 *l*. otherwise that his Estate shall cease; here the *Condition* is subsequent, and following the Estate, and upon the Performance of it, preserves the same. An *Inherent Condition*, is that which descends to the Heir with the Land granted, &c. And a *Collateral Condition* is that which is annexed to any collateral Act. A Condition *affirmative* consists of doing; and *negative*, consists of not doing.

Cone and Key. In ancient Times a Woman might, at the Age of 14 or 15. take the Charge of her House, and receive *Cone* and *Key*, she being then held to be of competent Years to keep the *Accounts* and *Keys* of the House.

Confederacy, is where two or more combine together to do some Injury to another, or to commit any unlawful Act: And tho' a Writ of Conspiracy does not lie, if the Party be not indicted, and in a lawful Manner acquitted; yet false Confederacy shall be punished, tho' nothing be put in Execution: But this Confederacy punishable before it is executed, ought to have these Incidents, *viz.* 1*st*, It must be declared by some Matter of Prosecution, as entring into Bonds or Promises the one to the other. 2*dly*, It should be malicious. 3*dly*, It ought to be false against an innocent Person. And, *Lastly*, It is to be out of Court, voluntarily.

Confession, is where a Prisoner being indicted of Treason or Felony, and brought to the Bar to be arraign'd, and after his Indictment is read to him, the Court demands what he can say thereto; where he either *confesses* the Offence, and the Indictment to be true, pleads *Not guilty*, or gives an indirect Answer, which in Effect is standing mute. Confession may be made two several Ways, and to two several Ends: The one is, that the Prisoner may confess the Offence whereof he is indicted openly in the Court before the Judge, and submit himself to the Censure of the Law; which Kind of Confession is the most certain Answer, and greatest Satisfaction that can be given to a Judge for the Condemnation of the Offender, provided such Confession proceeds freely of the Prisoner's own Accord, without any Threats or Extremity used; For if the Confession proceeds from any of these Causes, it ought not to be recorded; as in the Case of a Woman that was indicted for the felonious taking of Bread to the Value of 2 *s.* and being thereof arraigned confessed the Felony, and said she did it by the Commandment of her Husband, yet the Judges in Compassion would not record her Confession, but caused her to plead *Not guilty* to the Felony charged: Whereupon the Jury found that she committed the Fact by the Compulsion of her Husband against her Will, for which Reason she was acquitted. 27 *Assis. Pl.* 50. The other Kind of Confession is, when a Prisoner confesses the Indictment to be true, and that he has committed the Offence of which he is indicted, and then becomes an Approver or Accuser of others that have committed the same Offence whereof he is indicted, or other Offences with him; after which he prays the Judge to have a Coroner assigned him, to whom he may relate those Offences, and the full Circumstances thereof. There was anciently a third Kind of Confession made by an Offender in Felony, not in Court before a Judge, as the other two are, but before a Coroner in a Church, or other privileged Place; upon which the Offender was by the Law of the Land to abjure the Realm.

Confirmation, is a Conveyance of an Estate or Right in Being, whereby a voidable Estate is made sure and unavoidable, or by which a particular Estate is increased, or a Title confirmed and made perfect;

fect; as where a Bishop grants his Chancellorship by Patent, for the Life of the Patentee; this Grant is not void, but voidable by the Bishop's Death, unless it be strengthened by the Dean and Chapter's *Confirmation*. Every *Confirmation* is either *perfecting, increasing,* or *diminishing*. *Perfecting,* as if a Feoffee upon Condition make a Feoffment, and the Feoffor confirm the Estate to the second Feoffee. *Increasing,* enlarges the Estate of a Tenant; as Tenant at Will, to hold for Years; or Tenant for Years, to hold for Life. *Diminishing,* as when the Lord of whom the Land is holden confirms the Tenant's Estate, to hold by a less Rent.

Confiscate, is said to be derived from the *Latin* Word *Fiscus*, originally signifying a Hamper or Basket, and metonymically applied to the Emperor's Treasure. As the *Romans* have called such Goods, as were forfeited to the Emperor's *Treasury* for any Offence, *Bona Confiscata*; so we say of such Goods as are forfeited to the King's Exchequer, the Title to which is by Law given to the King, for Want of being claimed by some other; as where a Person is indicted for stealing the Goods of another, when in Fact they are the proper Goods of the indicted Party; and the Goods being produced in Court against him, and he asked what he has to say to them, disclaims the same, he, by such Disclaimer, shall lose the Goods, tho' afterwards he be acquitted of the Felony, and the King in such Case shall have them as *confiscated*. The same Law holds where Goods are found in the Felon's Possession, which he disavows, and afterwards is attainted of other Goods, and not of them; in which Case the Goods he disclaimed become confiscated to the King: But had he been attainted of the same Goods, they would have been said to be *forfeited,* and not *confiscated*.

Congeable, (from the *French,* signifying Leave or Permission) in our Law, denotes as much as lawful, or lawfully done, or acted with Leave or Permission. See *Lit.* Sect. 410.

Conge d' Accorder, signifies Leave to accord or agree. See the *Statute of Fines,* 18 *Ed.* 3. where these Words are mentioned.

Conge d' Eslire, (*French,* signifying Leave to chuse) in our Law denotes the King's Royal Licence to a Dean and Chapter to chuse a Bishop; or to an Abbey or Priory of his own Foundation, to chuse an Abbot or Prior. *Fitz. Nat. Brev.* 169, *&c.* But an Election by *Conge d' Eslire,* as now used, seems to be little more than meer Form.

Conjuration, in a general Sense, signifies a Compact made by Persons combining by Oath or solemn Promise to do any publick Harm: But in our Law it is more particularly used for the having a Conference with the Devil or some evil Spirit, in order to know any Secret, or to effect any Purpose. See 5 *Eliz. c.* 16. The Difference between *Conjuration* and *Witchcraft* is thought to be this, *viz*. That the Person that practises the one, endeavours by fervent Prayers and Invocations, to compel the Devil to say or do what he commands him; the other rather deals by a friendly and voluntary Conference or Agreement with the Devil or Familiar, to have his or her Desires served, in Lieu of Blood or other Gift offered. Both of these differ from *Enchantment* or *Sorcery,* they being personal Conferences

with

with the Devil, as already observed; but *Enchantment* or *Sorcery*, denotes no more than certain Medecines and ceremonial Forms of Words, usually called *Charms*, without any Apparition.

Consanguinity, denotes a Kindred by Blood or Birth; as Affinity signifies a Kindred by Marriage.

Conservator, signifies a Preserver or Maintainer; or a delegated Umpire, or standing Arbitrator, chosen and appointed to compose Differences between contending Parties.

Conservator of the Peace, is a Person who hath an especial Charge to see the King's Peace kept; which Peace is defined in Effect to be a Withholding or Abstinence from that injurious Force and Violence that boisterous and unruly Men are naturally prone to use towards others, were they not restrained by Laws, and the Dread of Punishment. Of these Conservators, *Lambard* says, That before King *Edward* the Third's Time, who was the first that erected the Office of *Justices of the Peace*, there were divers Persons, who by the Common Law had Interest in keeping the Peace; of whom some had that Charge as incident to their Offices which they bore, and so included within the same; and nevertheless were called by the Names of their Offices only: Others again had it simply, as of itself, and on that Account were termed *Custodes Pacis*, that is to say, Wardens or Conservators of the Peace.

Conservator of the Truce and Safe Conducts, was an Officer formerly appointed in every Sea-Port by the King's Letters Patent, whose annual Salary was 40 *l.* at least. His Office was to make Enquiry of all Offences committed against the King's *Truce and Safe Conducts* upon the main Sea, without the Liberties of the Cinque Ports, as the Admirals were accustomed to do, and such other Things as are declared in 2 *Hen.* 5. *c.* 6. See likewise 4 *Hen.* 5. *c.* 7.

Consideratio Curiæ, denotes the Judgment of a Court, and is often mentioned in Law Pleadings; as *ideo consideratum est per Curiam*, that is to say, it is therefore adjudged by the Court.

Consideration, denotes the material Cause or Grounds of a Contract, without which the contracting Party could not be bound. This Consideration is either expressed, as where a Person agrees to pay 40 *s.* for a Horse; or implied, as when the Law itself forces a Consideration, as in the Case of a Person's coming to a common Inn, and there staying some Time, takes Meat, Lodging, or other Necessaries for himself and Horse, the Law here presumes he intends to pay for both, notwithstanding nothing further be covenanted between the Guest and his Host: Wherefore if he discharge not the House, the Host may stay his Horse. There is also a *Consideration* of Nature and Blood, as also what is called a valuable *Consideration* in Deeds and Conveyances. Where a Person is indebted to divers others, and in Consideration of Natural Love and Affection gives all his Goods, &c. to his Son or other Relation, this Gift shall be construed a fraudulent one, in respect to the Creditors. See 13 *Eliz. c.* 5. which intends a *valuable Consideration*.

Consign, is a Term used by Merchants, where Goods are assigned or entrusted to a Factor, &c. to dispose of.

Consilium is used for a speedy Day appointed by the Judges of a Court

for

for the arguing of a Demurrer, which is granted by the Court after Demurrer joined, on reading the Record of the Cause.

Consistory, denotes as much as a *Tribunal*, and is commonly used for a Council-House of Ecclesiastical Persons on the Place of Justice in the Ecclesiastical Court; as also for an Assembly or Session of Prelates. Every Archbishop and Bishop has a *consistory* Court held by his Chancellor or Commissary in his Cathedral Church, or other convenient Place of his Diocese, for the Decision of Ecclesiastical Causes.

Consolidation, is used for the Uniting of two Benefices into one. This Word is taken from the Civil Law, where it properly denotes Uniting of the Possession or Profit with the Property. *Cowel*.

Conspiracy, denotes an Agreement between two or more falsly to indict, or procure to be indicted an innocent Person of Felony, who, after being acquitted, is entitled to a Writ of Conspiracy against his malicious Accusers. This Writ likewise lies for one that is indicted of a Trespass, and afterwards acquitted, notwithstanding no Felony is charged, as also for a Riot, and in divers other Cases. The Punishment of a Conspiracy, upon an Indictment of Felony, at the King's Suit, is, that the attainted Party loses his *Frank Law*, whereby he becomes disabled to be upon any *Juries*, or to give Evidence in Court, &c. and his Lands, Goods, and Chattels are to be seised into the Hands of the Crown, and his Body committed to Prison.

Conspirators, are by the *Stat.* 33 *Ed.* 1. defined to be such as bind themselves by Oath, Covenant, or other Alliance to assist one another falsly and maliciously to indict Persons, or falsly to move or maintain Pleas, &c. Likewise such as retain Men in the Country with Liveries or Fees, in order to support their malicious Enterprises; which extends as well to the Takers as the Givers, and to Stewards and Bailiffs of Lords, who by their Office or otherwise take upon them to maintain Quarrels, or Pleas, which concern other Parties than such as relate to the Estate of their Lords or themselves.

Conspiratione, is a Writ that lies against *Conspirators*. See *Reg. Orig.* 134.

Constable, is a Word that in our Law is used divers Ways; 1*st*, For the *Lord Constable* of *England*, whose Authority was anciently so vastly extensive, that that Office has been since thought too great for any Subject, and therefore entirely laid aside, except upon particular Occasions, such as the Coronation of a King. The Jurisdiction of the *Lord High Constable* was formerly the same with that of the *Earl Marshal*, and he sat as Judge in the Marshal's Court, having Precedence of the *Earl Marshal* there: Yet the *Constable* of *England* is in some Books also called *Marshal*; whose Office is to take Cognisance of all Matters of War and Arms; and originally the *Marshal* had several Courts under him, tho' now only the *Marshalsea*; and his Office is in Force both in Time of Peace and War: And tho' the *Lord Constable* had the Precedence, yet the Court held by him was called the *Marshal's Court*. From this high Office of *Constable* of *England*, were drawn those inferior *Constables*, whom we call *Constables of Hundreds* and

Fran-

Franchises, and who were first ordained by the Statute of *Ed.* 1. which appoints, for the Conservation of the Peace, and View of Armour, two Constables in every Hundred and Franchise, who are now called *High Constables*, on Account that the Increase of People and Offences made it necessary to appoint others under these in every Town, &c. called *Petty Constables*, who are of the like Nature, tho' of inferior Authority to the other. There are, besides these, Officers of particular Places, called by the Name of *Constables*; such as, *Constable of the* Tower, *Constable of the Exchequer*, *Constable of* Dover *Castle*, and other Castles, who are more properly called *Castellanes*.

Constat, is a Certificate that the Clerk of the Pipe and Auditors of the Exchequer grant at the Request of any Person that intends to plead or move in that Court, for the Discharge of any Thing. The Effect of this *Constat*, is a certifying what does *constare* or stand upon Record touching the Matter in Question. The Exemplification under the Great Seal of the Inrollment of any Letters Patent is likewise called a *Constat*.

Consuetudinibus & Serviciis, is a Writ of Right Close that lies against the Tenant, who deforces his Lord of the Rent or Service due. See *Fitz. Nat. Brev.* 151. and *Reg. Orig.* 159.

Consultation, is a Writ by which a Cause being removed by Prohibition from the Spiritual Court to the King's Court, is returned thither again; and the Reason of this is, that if the Judges of the King's Court, on comparing the Libel with the Suggestion of the Party, find the Suggestion false or not proved, and on that Account the Cause to be wrongfully called from the Ecclesiastical Court, then upon this *Consultation* or Deliberation they decree it to be returned: Whence the Writ thus obtained is called a *Consultation*.

Contempt, denotes a Disobedience to the Rules and Orders of a Court, which has Authority to punish such Offence. Attachment lies against a Person for Contempt of Court. If a Sheriff being required to return a Writ to him directed, does not return the same, it is a Contempt. See **Attachment**.

Contingent Use, is a Use limited in a Devise or Conveyance of Lands, &c. that may, or may not happen to vest, according to the *Contingency* mentioned in the Limitation of the *Use*. A *contingent Remainder* is where an Estate is limited to take Place at a Time to come, upon an uncertain Event; as where a particular Estate that supports a Remainder, may or may not determine before the Remainder may commence.

Continual Claim, denotes a Claim that is made from Time to Time within every Year and a Day, to Lands, &c. which in some Respects one cannot attain without Danger; as where a Person is disseised of his Lands, &c. into which, tho' he has a Right to enter, he dares not enter, for Fear of Death or Beating; in which Case it behoves the disseised Party to hold on his Right of Entry at his best Opportunity, by approaching as near the Land as he can once every Year as long as he lives, and there make Claim thereof, by which means he saves to his Heir the Right of Entry. This Claim must always be made within the Year and Day before the Death of the Tenant; otherwise if such Tenant

Tenant do not die seised within a Year and a Day after such Claim made, and yet his Heir or Person that has the Right, dare not enter, then it behoves him that has the Right to make another Claim within the Year and Day after the first Claim, and after such second Claim, to make a third Claim in case he would be certain to save his Entry. *Termes de la Ley*. See more of this in *Lit. lib.* 3. *c.* 7.

Continuance, signifies the Continuing of a Cause in Court, by an Entry thereof made for that Purpose upon the Records there; as the *Continuance* of a Writ or Action is from one Term to another, where the Sheriff has not returned a former Writ, issued out in the same Action.

Continuando, is a Word, that when the Proceedings in Law were allowed to be wrote in *Latin*, was used in a special Declaration of Trespass, where the Plaintiff intended to recover Damages for several Trespasses in one and the same Action; and, in order to avoid Multiplicity of Suits, a Person may in one Action of Trespass recover Damages for many Trespasses committed, he laying the same to be done with a *Continuando*, that is to say, a *Continuing*.

Contraband Goods, are such as are prohibited by Act of Parliament, or the King's Proclamation, to be imported into, or exported out of this into any other Nation.

Contract, denotes an Agreement between two or more Persons, where one Thing is given or exchanged for another, which is commonly called *Quid pro quo*; as where a Person sells or exchanges a Horse for a Sum of Money, or other Thing, to or with another, or covenants in Consideration of a certain Sum, or annual Rent to be paid, to grant a Lease, of a Messuage, &c. These are deemed good Contracts in Law, because there is one Thing for another: But if a Person does promise to give or pay another 20 s. which afterwards, on being demanded, he refuses to pay, no Action lies for the 20 s. because such Promise will not amount to a Contract, it being no more than a bare or naked Promise, in Law termed *Nudum Pactum*; yet if any Thing was given as the Consideration of such Promise, were it even so small a Trifle, as a Penny, or its Value, the Promise shall be looked upon as a good Contract, and consequently will be binding. An *Usurious Contract* is a Contract or Agreement to pay more Interest for Money than the Law allows of.

Contra Formam Collationis, is a Writ that formerly lay, where a Person had given Lands in perpetual Alms to any late Houses of Religion, as to an Abbot and Convent, or to the Warden or Master of an Hospital, to supply certain poor Men with Necessaries, and do Divine Service. And if they aliened the Lands, then the Donor and his Heirs had this Writ to recover the same back.

Contra Formam Feoffamenti, is a Writ that lies for the Heir of a Person enfeoffed of certain Lands or Tenements by Charter of *Feoffment* from a Lord, to make certain Services to his Court, and such Heir is afterwards distrained for more than is contained in the Charter. See *Reg. Orig.* 176. *Old Nat. Brev.* 162.

Contra Formam Statuti, against the Form of the *Statute*, is the usual Conclusion of every Indictment or Information laid for any Offence created by *Statute*.

Contra

Contramandatio Placiti, seems to have signified a Respiting, or giving a Defendant further Time to answer, or a Countermand of what was formerly ordered.

Contramandatum, denotes a lawful Excuse which the Defendant by his Attorney alledges for himself, in order to shew that the Plaintiff has no Cause to complain.

Contrarients, was a Word brought in Use in King *Edward* the Second's Time, when *Thomas* Earl of *Lancaster*, taking Part with the Barons against that King, it was not thought proper, in Regard of their Power, to call them Rebels or Traitors, but *Contrarients*.

Contribules, denotes Kindred or Cousins. See *Lamb.* 75.

Contribution, is used where Persons pay their Share, or *contribute* a Part to any Thing.

Contributione Facienda, is a Writ which lies where two or more are bound to one Thing, and yet one is put to the whole Burden; as if Joint-Tenants, or Tenants in common hold a Mill, *pro indiviso*, undivided, and equally take the Profits thereof; if the Mill falls to Decay, and one or more of the Persons interested therein, refuses to contribute towards the Reparation of the same, the rest shall have this Writ to compel them thereto. If there be three Coparceners of Land, who owe Suit to the Lord's Court, and the eldest perform the Whole, she may then have this Writ to compel the other two to a *Contribution* towards the Charge. See *Reg. Orig.* 176. *Fitz. Nat. Brev.* 162.

Controller, denotes an Overseer or Officer relating to publick Accounts, of which Name there are divers Officers; as *Controller* of the *King's Houshold*, of the *Navy*, of the *Customs*, of the *Excise*, &c. The Office of *Controller of the Houshold*, is to control the Accounts of the Green Cloth. The *Controller of the Navy*, is he that controls the Payments of Wages, examines and audits Accounts, and also inquires into the Rates of Stores for Shipping, &c. *Controllers of the Customs and Excise*, are appointed for *controlling* the Accounts of those respective Revenues. The *Controller of the Mint*, is he who controls the Payment of the Wages and Accounts relating thereto. *Controller of the Hamper*, attends the Lord Chancellor, or Lord Keeper, daily in Term-Time, and upon Seal-Days; and his Office is to take all Things sealed from the Clerk of the Hamper, inclosed in Leathern Bags, and to mark the Number and Effect of every Thing so received, and make an Entry thereof in a Book, with all the Duties belonging to the Crown, and other Officers for the same. The *Controller of the Pipe*, is an Officer of the Exchequer, whose Office is to make out a Summons twice every Year to the Sheriffs, to levy the Farms and Debts of the Pipe; and his Function is also to keep the Controlment of the Pipe, &c. *Controller of the Pell*, is likewise an Officer in the Exchequer, of which Kind there are two, who are the Chamberlain's Clerks, and they do, or ought to keep a Controlment of the Pell, of Receipts and Goings-out. It is said that this Officer was originally such a one as took Notes of other Officers Accounts or Receipts, to the Intent to discover if they dealt amiss, and was appointed for the Prince's better Security. See *Fleta*, lib. 1. c. 18. and 12 *Ed.* 3. c. 3.

Controver, denotes a Person that devises or invents false News.

Conventicle, signifies a private Meeting or Assembly of Persons for the Exercise of Religion, which at first was attributed in Disgrace to the Meetings of *Wickliff*, about 200 Years ago, and has been since applied to the illegal Meetings of the *Nonconformists*.

Conventio, is a Word that has been used in our Law Pleadings for an Agreement or Covenant.

Conventione, is a Writ which lies for the Breach of any Covenant in Writing, whether it be real or personal. *Fitzherbert*, in his *Nat. Brev.* 145. calls it a *Writ of Covenant*.

Convention, in general, signifies an Assembly or Meeting of People, and in our Law is applied to the Case where a Parliament is assembled, and no Act passed, or Bill signed. See **Parliament.** The Assembly of the remaining Part of the Members of a former Parliament, summoned by the Prince of *Orange*, were declared a Parliament, and as such, in the Year 1688, placed him on the Throne. See *Stat.* 1 *W. & M.* This Word has of late received an additional Signification, denoting an imperfect Treaty, or a Meeting in order to Agreement, as that of the Commissioners for the late *Spanish* Depredations.

Conveyance, is a Deed or Instrument that passes Land, &c. from one to another.

Convict, denotes a Person that is found guilty of an Offence by Verdict of a Jury. *Staundf. Pl. Cor.* Yet *Crompton* says, that *Conviction* is either when one is outlawed, appears and confesses, or is found guilty by the Inquest. See *Cromp. Just.* 9. In our Books, Conviction and Attainder are often confounded.

A Recusant convict, denotes a Person that has been legally presented, indicted and convicted for refusing to attend the Church, to hear the Common Prayer, according to the several Statutes injoining the same. This Term is most generally applied to Papists, tho' any other Person refusing to attend the Church in like Manner, are as properly called by that Name. See more of this under *Tit.* **Recusants.**

Convocation, is an Assembly of the Clergy, to consult of Ecclesiastical Matters in the Time of Parliament. There are two Houses of Convocation; the one called the *Higher* or *Upper House*, consisting of Archbishops and Bishops, who severally sit by themselves; and the other the *Lower House of Convocation*, where all the rest of the Clergy sit, *viz.* All the Deans and Archdeacons, one Proctor for every Chapter, and two Proctors for each Diocese, in all making up the Number of 166 Persons. Each House of *Convocation* has a Prolocutor, chosen among themselves respectively; and that of the *Lower House* is presented to the Bishops, &c. The Archbishop of Canterbury presides in the *Convocation*, and as Occasion serves prorogues or dissolves it, by Virtue of the King's Mandate. By 25 *Hen.* 8. the Convocation is authorised in making of Canons, with the Assent of the King: This *Convocation* has also the Examining and Censuring of Heretical and Schismatical Books and Persons, &c. yet Appeal lies to the King in Chancery, or to his Delegate from their Censure.

Conusance of Pleas, denotes a Privilege which a City or Town has to hold Pleas. See **Cognisance.**

Conusant, signifies a Knowing or Understanding; as where the Son is *conusant*, and agrees to the *Feoffment*.

Coparce-

Coparceners, who are otherwise called *Parceners*, denote such Persons as have an equal Portion in the Inheritance of an Ancestor: And *Parceners* by Law are the Issue Female, which in Default of Heirs Male, come in Equality to the Lands of their deceased Ancestor. See *Parceners*.

Copartnership, is a Deed or Instrument in Writing, containing Covenants between two or more, for carrying on a joint Trade in Merchandize, &c.

Copia Libelli Deliberanda, is a Writ which lies where a Person cannot get the Copy of a Libel from a Judge of the Spiritual Court, in order to get the same from him. See *Reg. Orig.* 151.

Copy, in our Law, signifies the Transcript of any original Writing; as the *Copy* of a *Patent, Charter, Deed*, &c.

Copyhold, is a Tenure for which the Tenant has nothing to shew but the Copy of the Rolls made by the Steward of the Lord's Court, on such Tenants being admitted to any Part of the Lands and Tenements belonging to the Manor: For the Steward, as he enrolls and makes Remembrances of other Things acted in the Lord's Court, so he does also of such Tenants as are admitted in the Court to any Parcel of Land, &c. appertaining to the Manor; and the Transcript of this is called the *Copy of the Court-Roll*, which is all the Tenant receives from him, and keeps as his only Evidence. *Copyhold* is called a *Base Tenure*, because the Tenant holds it at the Will of his Lord. *Fitzherbert*, in his *Nat. Brev.* 12. says that it was anciently called *Tenure in Villenage*, and that that of Copyhold is but a modern Name; yet it is not simply held at the Will of the Lord, but according to the Custom of the Manor; wherefore if a Copyholder do not break the Custom of the Manor, and thereby forfeit his Tenure, he cannot be said to stand so much at his Lord's Courtesy for his Right, as that he may be displaced at Pleasure. Some Copyholds are fineable at Will, and others *certain:* That which is fineable at Will, the Lord takes at his Pleasure; tho' if it exceed two Years Revenue, the Court of *Chancery, King's Bench, Common Pleas,* or *Exchequer,* may reduce the Lord to Reason: That which is *certain,* is a Sort of Inheritance, and in several Places called *Customary,* because the Tenant dying, and the Tenure thereby becoming void, the next of Blood, paying the *customary Fine,* cannot be denied his Admission. Some *Copyholders* have likewise by *Custom* the Wood growing upon their own Land, which the Law would not allow them. Other *Copyholders* again hold by the *Verge* in ancient Demesne, and tho' they actually hold by Copy, yet they are accounted a Kind of *Freeholders*. Some others there are that hold by *common Tenure,* called *Meer Copyhold. West,* in his *Symb.* Part 1. *lib.* 2. *Sect.* 646. briefly defines a Copyholder thus, viz. *Tenant by Copy of Court-Roll, is he who is admitted Tenant of any Lands or Tenements within a Manor, which Time out of Mind, by Use and Custom of the Manor, have been demisable, and demised to such as will take the same in Fee-simple, or Fee-Tail, for Life, Years, or at Will, according to the Custom of the Manor, by Copy of Court-Roll.*

Corsage, is said to denote an extraordinary Imposition, growing upon some unusual Occasion, and

CO

seems to be of certain Measures of Corn, *Corus tritici* denoting a Measure of Wheat. See *Bract. lib. 2. c. 16. Numb. 6.*

Coram non Judice, is a Term used where a Cause is brought and determined in a Court, of which the Judges there have no Jurisdiction; in which Case such Cause is said to be *Coram non Judice*, and void.

Cord of Wood, is a Quantity of Wood, which, according to the *Statute*, ought to be eight Foot long, four Foot broad, and four Foot high.

Cordiner or **Cordwainer**, (from the *French*) denotes a Shoe-maker, and is much used in several of our Statutes, particularly in the 1 *Jac. c. 22.*

Corium Forisfacere, denotes one condemned to be whipt; which was the ancient Punishment of a Servant.

Cornage, (from the *Latin Cornu*, a Horn) was a Kind of Tenure in *Grand Serjeanty*: The Service required by which Tenure was to blow a Horn, when any Invasion from the *Scots* was perceived: And by this Tenure many formerly held their Lands Northward, about the Wall commonly called *The Picts Wall*.

Corody, anciently signified a Sum of Money, or Allowance of Meat, Drink and Cloathing, due to the King from an Abbey or other House of Religion, of which he is the Founder, towards the Sustenance of such a one of his Servants as he thought proper to bestow it upon: And the Difference between a *Corody* and a *Pension* is, that a *Corody* is allowed to any of the King's Servants that live in an Abbey, but a Pension is given to one of the King's Chaplains for his better Maintenance,

CO

till he can be provided of a Benefice.

Corodio habendo, was a Writ in Use for exacting a Corody of an Abbey, or religious House. See *Reg. Orig. 164.*

Corona Mala, or **Mala Corona**, is a Name that was formerly given to such of the Clergy as abused their Character.

Coronatore eligendo, is a Writ that lies on the Death or Discharge of a *Coroner*, and is directed to the Sheriff out of the Court of *Chancery*, commanding him to call together the Freeholders of the County, for the *Election* of a new *Coroner*; and to certify into the said Court, both the Election, and the Name of the Party chosen, and to give the Elected his Oath. See *Fitz. Nat. Brev.* 163. and *Reg. Orig.* 177.

Coronatore exonerando, is a Writ that is for the Discharge of a *Coroner*, on Account of Negligence, or Insufficiency in the Discharge of his Duty. *Coroners* may likewise by this Writ be discharged, where they are so far engaged in any other publick Business that they cannot attend the Office, or are disabled by old Age or Disease to execute the same.

Coroner, is an ancient Officer of Trust, and is so called, because he deals wholly for the *King* and *Crown*. A *Coroner*, by the *Statute of Westminster*, c. 10. ought to be a sufficient Person, that is to say, the wisest and discreetest Knight, that best might, and would attend upon such an Office. By looking into the *Regist.* 177. you may find a Writ termed *Nisi sit Miles*, whence it may appear, that it was a sufficient Cause to remove a *Coroner*, chosen, for Want of his being a Knight, or not having 100 Shillings yearly Rent of Freehold.

Freehold. The Lord Chief Justice of the *King's Bench* is the Sovereign *Coroner* of the whole Realm wheresoever he is in Person. The Office of *Coroners* more especially concerns the Pleas of the Crown, who are Conservators of the Peace in the County where elected. They are invested with *Judicial* and *Ministerial* Authority; *Judicial*, in the Case where a Person comes to a violent Death, is killed, *&c.* And by such their *Judicial* Authority, they can take Appeals of Murder, pronounce Judgment upon Outlawries, *&c.* Their *Ministerial* Power, is where they execute the King's Writs, on Exception taken to the Sheriff, as being Party to a Suit, of Kin to either of the contending Parties, or on Default of the Sheriff, *&c.* There are likewise certain special *Coroners* of divers Liberties, as well as those ordinary ones already mentioned; as the *Coroner of the Verge*, which is a certain Compass about the King's Palace or Court, who is by *Crompt.* called the *Coroner of the King's House*: And some Colleges and Corporations are impowered to appoint their Coroner within their own Precincts. See *Coke's Rep. lib.* 4. 46. and 4 *Inst.* 271.

Corporal Oath. See **Oath.**

Corporation, denotes a Body *Politick*, or a Body *incorporate*, and is so called, because the Persons or Members are made into a Body, and are of Capacity to take and grant, *&c.* Or it may be defined to be an Assembly, and a Joining and Knitting together of many Persons into one Brotherhood, Fellowship and Mind, whereof one is Chief or Head, and the rest are the Body; and this Head and Body so knit together, make the *Corporation*. It is also made up of several Members, like unto the natural Body, and fram'd by *Fiction* of Law to continue in perpetual Succession. Some *Corporations* are *Sole*, some *Aggregate*; *Sole*, in the Case of one single Person, as the King, Bishop, Dean, *&c.* *Aggregate*, which is most common, consists of many Persons, as *Mayor* and *Commonalty*, *Dean* and *Chapter*, &c. There are also *Corporations Spiritual*, or *Temporal*: *Spiritual*, of Bishops, Deans, Archdeacons, Vicars, *&c.* *Temporal*, as Mayors, Commonalty, Bailiffs, and Burgesses, *&c.* Besides, some *Corporations* are of a *mixt Nature*, being composed of both spiritual and temporal Members, as the Heads of Colleges, Hospitals, *&c.*

Corporeal Inheritance. See **Inheritance.**

Corpus cum Causa, is a Writ that issues out of the Chancery, for removing both the Body and Record, relating to the Cause of a Person lying in Execution upon a Judgment for Debt, into the *King's Bench*, &c. there to lie till he has satisfied the Judgment. See **Habeas Corpus.**

Corrector of the Staple, is a Clerk belonging to the Staple, whose Business is to write down and record the Bargains of Merchants made there.

Corruption of Blood, is an Infection arising to the State of a Man attainted of Felony or Treason, whose Blood, on that Account in Law, becomes corrupted, so that neither his Children, nor any of his Blood, can be Heirs to him or any other Ancestor. If the Person attainted be of Nobility, or a Gentleman, both he and all his Posterity are rendered base and ignoble; yet by the King's Pardon of the Offender, the Corruption of the Childrens Blood, who are born after

ter the Pardon, is cleansed, and they may inherit the Land of their Ancestor purchased at the Time of the Pardon or afterwards; but those that are born before the Pardon cannot do so. There are likewise divers Limitations even in Treason, made by Statutes, that save *Corruption of Blood*, tho' a Person be attainted.

Corseprefent, (from the *French*) signifies a Mortuary.

Corsned Bread, was a certain superstitious Trial made Use of among the *Saxons*, by a Piece of Barley Bread, first accursed by the Priest, and afterwards offered to the suspected Criminal, to be swallowed by him in the Way of Purgation; it being in those Days believed, that a Person guilty could never swallow a Morsel so accursed; and if he did, it would *choak* or prove *Poison* to him. The Form of the Execration was thus, *viz. We beseech thee, O Lord, that he who is guilty of this Theft, when exorcised Bread is offered to him, in order to discover the Truth, that his Jaws may be shut, his Throat so narrow, and that he may cast it out of his Mouth, and not eat it.* Tho' this rude and barbarous Way of Purgation was often condemned, and by Degrees entirely abolished, yet it is too truly observed that we have still some Rembrance of that horrid Custom in some of our modern Phrases of Adjuration; as, *I will take the Sacrament upon it.* ——— *May this Bread or Drink be my Poison.* ——— *May this Bit be my last.*

Cosenage, is a Writ that lies where the *Tresail*, *viz.* the Father of the *Besail*, or Great Grandfather, being seised of Lands and Tenements in Fee at his Death, and a Stranger enters upon the Heir and abates; then shall the Heir have this Writ of *Cosenage*; the Form of which you may see in *Fitz Nat. Brev.* 221. See also *Brit. c.* 89.

Cosening, denotes an Offence, tho' not properly termed by any special Name whereby any Thing is acted guilefully, or with Deceit, in Contracts, or otherwise.

Costs, is a Word that denotes the Expences of a Suit, recovered by the Plaintiff, together with Damages: And if the Plaintiff become nonsuit or cast on Trial, the Defendant's Expences or Costs in defending the Suit are to be allowed. See 4 *Jac.* 1. *c.* 3. Costs are likewise allowed on the putting off of Trials, or insufficient Pleas, on their Amendments, &c. Yet Costs are not to be paid for barely putting off a Trial, when Fault was in the Party against whom it was moved; for Costs are only paid by such as have occasioned the other Party to be at extraordinary Charges; and Costs are not to be allowed for uncommon Motions, but only such as the Party was necessarily put to.

Cottage, denotes a little House or Habitation, without Land belonging to it: And the Inhabitants of these *Cottages* are called *Cottagers*: Yet by 31 *Eliz. c.* 7. it is ordained, that no Person shall build a *Cottage*, unless he lay four Acres of Land to it; except it be in Market-Towns or Cities, or within a Mile of the Sea, or for the Habitation of Labourers in Mines, Sailors, Foresters, Shepherds, &c.

Coucher, according to the general Acceptation of the Word, was a Factor that continued in some Place or Country for Traffick. See 37 *Ed.* 3. *c.* 16. It was likewise used for the General Book, in which any religious House or Corporation, &c. did register their particular Acts.

Covenable,

Covenable, comes from the *French*, and signifies convenient or agreeable. See *Plowd.* 472.

Covenant, is the Consent or Contract of two or more by Deed, to perform or not to perform some Act or Thing agreed on between them. *Covenant* is either in *Fact* or in *Law*; in *Fact*, where the Thing agreed on between the Parties is expresly inserted in the Deed: In *Law*, it is that *Covenant* which the Law implies, tho' it be not expressed in Words; as where a Person grants a Lease of a House, &c. for a certain Term, the Law will intend a Covenant on the Lessor's Part, that the Lessee shall quietly enjoy the Premisses during the whole Term, against all Incumbrances. Under this Head of *Covenant* may be also included a *Covenant real*, and *Covenant Personal*. A *Real Covenant* is that whereby a Person binds himself to pass some real Thing, as Lands or Tenements; or to levy a Fine of Lands, &c. And *Covenant Personal* is where the same is altogether personal; as where a Person by Deed covenants with another to build him a House, or to do him some other Service, &c. *Covenant* is likewise the Name of a Writ. See **Convention**. All Covenants must be to do what is lawful, otherwise they will not be binding. If the Thing to be performed be impossible, the Covenant is void; yet if a Person covenants to do a Thing by such a Day, and by the Act of God it becomes impossible, this shall not excuse the Person covenanting, for that he has precisely bound himself to do it. So likewise, if one covenants to repair a House, which afterwards by Accident is burnt, yet he must repair it; since it was in his Power to have provided against it by his Contract. *Covenant* to stand seised to Uses, is when a Man who has a Wife, Children, Brother, Sister, or other Kindred, does by *Covenant* in Writing, under Hand and Seal promise and agree, that for their Provision or Preferment, he and his Heirs should stand seised of Land, &c. either in Fee-simple, Fee-Tail, or for Life. The usual Consideration of these Deeds of Covenant, are natural Affection, Marriage, &c.

Covert Baron, is a married Woman.

Coverture, in our Law, is applied to the State and Condition of a married Woman, who is under the Power of her Husband; and therefore is disabled to contract with any Person to the Detriment either of herself or Husband, without his Privity or Consent, Allowance, or Confirmation of the same. A married Woman is called a *Feme Covert*; and whatever is acted concerning her, during the Marriage, is said to be done during the Coverture. Every Thing that is the Wife's is the Husband's; neither has the Wife Power over herself, but only the Husband.

Covin, denotes a deceitful Agreement between two or more to deceive or prejudice another Person. *Covin* is generally used in and about conveyancing of Land by Fine, Feoffment, Recovery, &c. wherein it tends to defeat Purchasers of the Land they purchase, and Creditors of their just Debts; and it is likewise so used in Deeds of Gift of Goods: It is sometimes also made Use of in the Suits of Law, and Judgments therein had.

Counsellor, is a Person that is retained by his Client to plead his Cause in a publick Court of Judicature. He has a Privilege to enforce any Thing whereof he has

Infor-

Information by his Client, in case the same be pertinent to the Matter in Hand, and is not obliged to examine whether it be true or false, it being at the Peril of the Person that informs him. A Counsellor must not set his Hand to a frivolous Plea, to delay a Trial, which doubtless argues either Ignorance or foul Practice: And tho' *Counsellors* have a special Privilege to practise the Law, yet are they punishable by Attachment, &c. for Misbehaviour. No Counsel is allowed to a Prisoner upon a general Issue on Indictment of Felony, &c. unless some Point of Law do arise; for the Court is the Prisoner's only *Counsel*. In Appeals, and upon special Pleas, &c. the Prisoner shall have Counsel assigned him by the Court; yet the *Counsel* is not to prompt the Prisoner in Matters of Fact.

Count, denotes the original Declaration of Complaint in a real Action. Count may be distinguished from *Declaration* thus, viz. *Declaration* is applied to personal, but *Count* only to real Causes; yet these two Words are frequently confounded, being made to signify the same Thing.

Countermand, is where a Thing before executed, is afterwards by some Act made void by the Party that did it. A Countermand may be either *actual* or *implied*: *Actual*, where a Power to execute any Authority, is by a formal Writing or Deed for that very Purpose put off for a Time, or made void: *Implied*, where a Person makes his last Will and Testament, whereby he devises his Land, &c. to A. B. and afterwards conveys the same Land, &c. to another; this Conveyance is, as to that Devise, a Countermand of the Will, without any express Words to make it so. Should a Woman seised of Land, &c. make a Will, and thereby devise the same to A. B. and his Heirs, in case he survive her; and she afterwards is married to the said A. B. here, by taking him to Husband and Coverture, at the Time of her Death the Will becomes countermanded. *Termes de la Ley* 198. But where a Woman makes a Lease at Will, and then marries, this Marriage is a *Countermand* of the Lease, without some express Matter acted by the Husband after the Marriage to determine the Will. *Ibid.* Any Person may countermand his Licence or Authority granted, before the Thing is done; and if the Person authorising die, it will likewise become *countermanded*. Notice of Trial, &c. in Law Proceedings may also be *countermanded*.

Counterplea, is when the Tenant in any real Action, Tenant by the Courtesy, or in Dower, in his Answer and Plea vouches any one to warrant his Title, or prays in Aid of another who has a greater Estate; as of him in Reversion; or it is, where one that is a Stranger to the Action, to save his Estate, comes and prays to be received, then whatsoever the Demandant alledges against such Prayer is called a *Counterplea*. So that, in short, *Counterplea* is nothing else than a Replication to *Aid Prier*, and is called a *Counterplea to the Voucher*: But when the Voucher is allowed, and the Vouchee comes in and demands what Cause the Tenant has to vouch him, and the Tenant shews his Cause, upon which the Vouchee pleads any Thing to avoid the Warranty; that is called a *Counterplea of the Warranty*. *Termes de la Ley* 199.

Counter-Rolls, are such *Rolls* as Sheriffs have with the *Coroners* of their Proceedings, as well of Appeals, as of Inquests, &c.

Counters, are said to signify such *Serjeants* at Law, as a Person retains to defend his Cause, and speak for him in a publick Court for their Fees; as in the Court of *Common Pleas*, none but Serjeants at Law may plead. They were anciently called *Serjeant-Countors*.

County, is the same with **Shire**, the one coming from the *French*, and the other the *Saxons*, each of which contain a Circuit or Portion of the Realm, into which the whole Land is divided, for the better Government thereof, and the more easy Administration of Justice: Insomuch, that there is no Part of this Nation but what lies within some County, and each County is governed by a yearly Officer, called the *Sheriff*, whose Office is ministerial; and he, among the other Duties appertaining to his Office, puts in Execution all the Commandments and Judgments of the King's Courts, that are to be executed within his Circuit. Of these Counties four are more remarkable than the others, and therefore termed *Counties Palatine*; as *Lancaster*, *Chester*, *Durham* and *Ely*. The Chief Governors of those *Counties Palatine*, did formerly issue out all Writs in their own Names, and acted all Things relating to Justice as absolutely as the Prince himself in other *Counties*, only that they acknowledged him as their Superior and Sovereign. But by 27 *Hen.* 8. this Power is greatly abridged. Over and above these Counties of both Sorts, there are also annexed unto some Cities, some Territory, Lands, or Jurisdiction; as the County of *Middlesex* to *London*, by King *Henry* the First, the *County* of the City of *York, Ann.* 32 *Hen.* 8. the *County* of the City of *Chester, Ann.* 45 *Eliz.* the *County* of the City of *Bristol, Norwich, Worcester*, &c. the *County* of the Town of *Kingston* upon *Hull*, and the *County* of the Town of *Newcastle* upon *Tyne*, &c. See *Lamb. Eiren. lib.* 1. and *Cromp. Just.* 59. There are reckoned in all to be forty *Counties* in *England*, besides twelve in *Wales*. *County* is also used in another Signification, as that of the *County-Court*, held every Month by the Sheriff within his Charge, or by his Deputy. See more of this under *Tit.* **Comitatus**.

County-Court, is by *Lamb.* divided into two Sorts; the one retaining the general Name, as the *County-Court* held monthly by the Sheriff or his Deputy; and the other called the *Turn*, which is held twice a Year, *viz.* within a Month after *Easter* and *Michaelmas*. See *Cromp. Jurisd.* 241. Before the Courts at *Westminster* were erected, the *County-Courts* were the chief Courts of this Realm; and in ancient Times had the Cognition of great Matters, as appears by *Glanv. lib.* 1. *c.* 2. and others: However, it still retains the Determination of certain Trespasses, and Debts under 40 *s.* but cannot hold Plea of Debt or Damage to the Value of 40 *s.* or above, tho' of Debt and other personal Actions above the Value of that Sum, the Sheriff may hold Plea, by Virtue of a Writ of *Justicies*, it being in the Nature of a Commission to him to do it. In this Court the Practice is, for the Plaintiff to take out a Summons, to which if the Defendant does not appear, an *Attachment* or *Distringas* is made out against him; but if he does appear, the Plaintiff must file his Declaration,

Information by h[...]
the same be pert[...]
ter in Hand, an[...]
examine wheth[...]
false, it being [...]
Person that info[...]
sellor must not [...]
frivolous Plea [...]
which doubtle[...]
norance or fo[...]
Counsellors h[...]
to practise t[...]
punishable b[...]
Misbehavio[...]
ed to a Pris[...]
on Indictm[...]
some Poin[...]
Court is t[...]
sel. In [...]
cial Pleas [...]
have Co[...]
Court ; [...]
prompt [...]
Fact. [...]
Count, [...]
ration [...]
tion. [...]
from [...]
clara[...]
Coun. [...]
two [...]
foun[...]
sam[...]
Coun[...]
bef[...]
for[...]
th[...]
b[...]

[...] is taken divers Ways; sometimes for the King's House or Palace, but more commonly for the Place where Justice is judicially administred. The Superior Courts are those of *Westminster*. Some *Courts* are of Record; and some not, which are therefore accounted *Base Courts*, in respect to the others: A *Court* of *Record* is a Court that has Power to hold Plea according to the due Course of the Common Law, that is to say, of real, personal and mixed Actions, where the Debt or Damage is 40 *s*. or above; such are the Courts of *King's Bench, Common Pleas, &c*. A Court not of Record is where it cannot hold Plea of Debts or Damage amounting to 40 *s*. or where the Proceedings are not according to the Course of the Common Law, nor inrolled; such are the *County-Court, Hundred-Court, Court-Baron*, &c. The Rolls of the Superior *Courts of Record* are of the greatest Authority, so as not to admit of any Proof against them, they being only triable by themselves: But the *County-Courts, Courts-Baron*, &c. not being *Courts* of Record, the Proceedings there may be joined, and tried by a Jury: Besides, upon their Judgment, a Writ of Error does not lie, but a Writ of false Judgment.

Court of Admiralty, is generally held to have been erected by King *Edward* the Third, for deciding of Maritime Causes. This *Court* is not allowed to be a Court of Record, because it proceeds according to the *Civil Law*, and the Judge thereof has no Power to take such Recognizance, as a Court of Record may. The Process and Proceedings of this Court are in the Name of the Lord *Admiral*, and by Libel; and both the Plaintiff and Defendant give Bail for Appearance, and to abide the Sentence. This Court has Jurisdiction to determine all Causes arising wholly upon the Sea, out of the Jurisdiction of a County, the Judgment of a Thing done upon Land being entirely out of their Jurisdiction, and of Course void. Where the *Court* of *Admiralty* holds Plea of an Agreement made at Sea, which was reduced into Writing, and sealed in Foreign Parts, a *Prohibition* will lie; but it is said not,

not, if only a bare Memorandum or Remembrance was made of it at Land.

Court-Baron, is a Court that every Lord of a Manor has within his own Precincts: It must be held by Prescription, seeing that it cannot be created at this Day. A *Court-Baron* is of two Natures, viz. by *Common Law*, which is the *Barons* or *Freeholders Court*, of which the Freeholders, being Suitors, are the Judges: By *Custom*, which is called the *Customary Court*, and concerns the Customary Tenants and Copyholders, of which the Lord or his Steward is Judge. As there can be no Court-Baron without Freeholders; so there cannot be any customary Court without Copyholders or Customary Tenants. The *Freeholders Court*, the Jurisdiction whereof consists in trying of Debt, Trespass, &c. under 40 s. may be held every three Weeks, and is much like the *County-Court*, as to the Method of Proceeding, with this particular Difference, that on a Recovery of a Debt they have not Power to make Execution, but must distrain the Defendant's Goods, and retain them till Satisfaction is made. The Customary Court, which is for taking and passing of Estates, Surrenders, Admittances, &c. is usually held but once or twice a Year along with the Court-Leet, unless it be purely for granting an Estate, in which Case it is held as often as requisite. In the Customary Court the *Homage Jury* are to inquire that their Lords lose not their Services, Duties or Customs; but that their Tenants make their Suits of Court, &c.

Court of Chivalry, or the *Marshal-Court*, is said to be the Fountain of the *Marshal Law*: The Judges of it are the Lord *Constable* of *England*, and the *Earl Marshal*, who has both a *Judicial* and *Ministerial Power*; he being not only one of the Judges, but is to see Execution done.

Court Christian, is so called, because, as in secular *Courts*, the King's Laws are to sway and decide Causes; so in Ecclesiastical *Courts*, the Laws of *Christ* should be the Guide; and on this Account the Judges of this Court are Divines, as Archbishops, Bishops, Archdeacons, &c.

Court of Delegates, is said to be the highest *Court* for Civil Affairs that concern the Church; and the Jurisdiction of it was established by 25 *Hen.* 8. *c.* 19. It is called *Delegates*, from the Judges being delegated, and sit by Force of the King's Commission, under the Great Seal, upon Appeals to the King from the Sentence of an Archbishop, &c. From this Court there lies no Appeal. *Cowel.*

Courts Ecclesiastical, are such Courts as are held by the King's Authority, as Supreme Governor of the Church, for Matters chiefly relating to Religion.

Court of Hustings, is the highest Court of Record that is held at *Guildhall* for the City of *London*, before the Lord Mayor and Aldermen, the Sheriffs and Recorder, where all Pleas real, personal and mixt are determined; and where all Lands, Tenements and Hereditaments, &c. within the said City or its Bounds, are pleadable in two *Hustings*, the one called the *Hustings of Plea of Lands*, and the other the *Hustings of Common Pleas.*

Court-Leet, is said to be the most ancient Court of Record in the Kingdom, and was ordained for the Punishment of Offences against the Crown. It inquires of all Offences

fences under High Treason; but such as are punishable with Loss of Life or Member, are only inquirable and presentable in this Court, and to be certified over to the Justices of Assise. This Court is likewise called the View of *Frank-Pledge*, on Account that the King is to be there certified by the View of the Steward, how many Persons are within every Leet, &c. And every Person of the Age of twelve, who has remained within the Leet for a Year and a Day, may be sworn to be faithful to the King. Every one from the Age of twelve to sixty, is obliged to do Suit in this Court; except Peers, Clergymen, &c. unless that they be liable to answer the *Sheriff's Turn*.

Court of Marshalsea, is a Court of Record, the ancient Jurisdiction of which was, to hear and determine Causes between the King's Domestick Servants, and others, within the Verge of the Court; and had Jurisdiction of all Matters within such Verge, and also of all Pleas of Trespass, where either Party is of the King's Family; and all other personal Actions, wherein both Parties were the King's Servants, belonged to the original Jurisdiction of the Court of Marshalsea: But since King *Charles* the First's Time, when his said Majesty, by Letters Patent, created it a Court of Record, by the Name of *Curia Palatii*; it has had Power to try all Personal Actions between Party and Party; and the Jurisdiction of this Court now extends twelve Miles about *Whitehall*. The Judges about this Court are the Steward of the King's *Houshold*, the Knight Marshal, and the Steward of the Court or his Deputy, being always a Lawyer: This Court is held once a Week in *Southwark*, and before the late wholesome Act, for the preventing of *vexatious Suits*, abounded with Numbers of Causes that constantly were depending therein. The Proceedings in this Court are either by *Capias* or *Attachment*, and in all other Respects is the same with those of the *Common Law Courts*.

Court Martial, is a Court for the Punishment of Offences of Officers and Soldiers in Time of War; for in Time of Peace, if any Person in Commission put any Man to Death by the *Martial* Law, it is said to be against *Magna Charta*, and to be Murder: But in late Reigns, by several *Temporary* Acts of Parliament our Kings have been enabled to hold Courts Martial in Time of Peace, &c. See 4 & 5 W. & M. c. 13. An Acquittal or Conviction in a Court *Martial* is a good Bar to an Indictment. See *Ann. c. 4.* 1 Geo. 1. c. 9. and 9 Geo. 1. c. 6.

Court of Piepowders, or **Curia Pedis Pulverisati**, is a Court held in Fairs for doing Justice to Buyers and Sellers, and for Redress of Disorders there committed: It is so called, because they are most usually held in the Summer Season, when the Suitors to the Court have Dusty Feet; and from the Expedition in hearing Causes proper to that Court before the Dust goes off the Feet of the Plaintiffs and Defendants. By *Doct.* and *Stud.* it is defined to be a Court of Record incident to every Fair, and it is only to be held during the Time the Fair is kept.

Court of Requests, was a Court of Equity of the same Nature with that of the *Chancery*, yet in many Respects inferior to it: It was chiefly instituted for the Relief of such Petitioners, as in conscionable Cases

CO

Cafes addreſſed themſelves by Petition to the King. This Court was intirely taken away by 16 & 17 Car. 2. c. 10.

Court of the Lord Steward of the King's Houſe, is a Court where the *Lord Steward*, or in his Abſence the Treaſurer and Controller of the King's Houſe, and Steward of the Marſhalſea, may inquire of, hear and determine in this Court, all Treaſons, Murders, Manſlaughters, Bloodſheds, and other malicious Beatings, whereby Blood may be ſhed, in any of the Palaces or Houſes of the King, or in any other Houſe where the King ſhall take up his Abode.

Court of Star-Chamber, is a Court that was erected *Ann.* 3 H. 7. in which the Lord Chancellor, Treaſurer, and Lord Privy Seal, calling a Biſhop, and a Lord of the King's Council, and the two Chief Juſtices to their Aſſiſtance, on Bill or Information might iſſue out Proceſs againſt Maintainors, Rioters, Perſons unlawfully aſſembling, and for other Miſdemeanors; and might puniſh them, as if the Offenders had been convicted at Law by a Jury. By 17 Car. 2. c. 10. the Act that conſtituted this Court was repealed, and the ſaid Court from that Time became diſſolved.

Courts of the Univerſities, The *Courts of the Univerſities of* Oxford *and* Cambridge are called the *Chancellor's Courts*, and are held by the Vice-Chancellors of the Univerſities. The Juriſdiction of theſe Courts extends to all Cauſes Eccleſiaſtical and Civil (except in the Caſe of Maihem, Felony, or any Thing that relates to Freehold) where a Scholar, Miniſter or Servant of the Univerſities is one of the Parties to the Suit. See more of *Courts of Univerſities* in *Wood's Inſt.*

Courts of Wales, Beſides, County-Courts, Hundred-Courts, Courts-Leet, &c. in *Wales*, it is by 34 & 35 Hen. 8. c. 26. ordained, that there ſhall be a Court of Grand Seſſions held twice in every Year, in every of the twelve Counties of *Wales*; the Juſtices of which Courts may hold Pleas of the Crown in as large a Manner as the Court of *King's Bench*: And alſo Pleas of Aſſiſes, and other Pleas and Actions, both real and perſonal, as fully as the *Common Pleas* can or may do. The Proceedings in theſe Courts are according to the Laws of *England*; and the King's Writs ought not to go into *Wales*: Yet a *Quo minus* out of the *Exchequer* is often ſent thither.

Court-Lands, are Lands kept in the Lord's Hands, to ſerve his Family. See *Curtiles Terræ*.

Couſenage. See **Coſenage**.

Couthutlaugh, (from the *Saxons*) denotes a Perſon that wittingly receives, or cheriſhes one *outlawed*; in which Caſe the Perſon ſo offending was in ancient Times liable to the ſame Puniſhment as the *Outlaw* himſelf was.

Cranage, denotes a Liberty of uſing a *Crane*, for the hoiſting up of Goods and other Things out of Ships or Veſſels, at a Wharf or other Place on Land, made Uſe of for the unlading of Ships, &c. This Word likewiſe ſignifies the Money paid, and taken for ſuch Liberty.

Craſtino Sancti Vincentii, or the Morrow after the Feaſt of St. *Vincent* the Martyr, *viz.* 22d of *January*, is the Date of the *Statutes* made at *Merton, Ann.* 20 Hen. 3. Before all Proceedings in the Law were ordained to be wrote in *Engliſh,*

CR

English, there were certain Returns of Writs which began with *Crastino*; as *Crastino Purificationis beatæ Mariæ Virginis*, in Hillary Term; *Crastino Ascensionis Domini*, in *Easter* Term; *Crastino Sanctæ Trinitatis*, in *Trinity* Term; and *Crastino Animarum*, in *Michaelmas* Term.

Cravare, in *Leg. Hen.* 1. *c.* 30. this Word is made to signify *to impeach*.

Creamer, properly denotes a Foreign Merchant; tho' it is generally taken for one that keeps a Stall in a Fair or Market.

Creansor, has been used to denote the same as *Creditor*. See **Creditor**.

Creditor, signifies one who trusts another with Money or other Debt, be it in Goods, Wares, &c.

Creek, denotes a Part of a Haven, where any Thing is landed from the Sea; and by some it is said to be a Shore or Bank on which the Water beats, running in a small Channel from any Part of the Sea.

Croft, denotes a little Close adjoining to a Dwelling-house, and inclosed for Pasture or Arable, or other particular Use, at the Owner's Pleasure. It is thought to be derived from the old *English* Word *Creaft*, which signified *Handy-Craft*, because such Sort of Land is usually manured and well drest by the Hand and according to the best Skill of the Owner.

Crown, signifies the Dignity of a King or Queen of any Kingdom; as the *Crown* of *England*, *France*, &c. originally the Crown of *England* was hereditary; but sometimes our Kings have thought fit to bestow it on whom they pleased to appoint their Successors. The Parliament have likewise for some political Reasons taken upon them to intermeddle in settling the Succession of the Crown; and by 1 *Ann. c.* 2. it is declared, *That if any Person affirm by Writing, &c. that the King or Queen of England cannot by the Authority of Parliament make Laws to bind the Crown, such Person shall be deemed guilty of Treason*. Note; There is no *Inter-regnum* in this Kingdom; for the Minute the Crown descends to the right Heir, he becomes King before *Coronation*; for this Reason, *viz*. That there must always be a King in whose Name the Laws may be maintained and executed; and on this Account we say the King never *dies*, but instead thereof *demises*.

CU

Crown-Office, is an Office belonging to the Court of *King's Bench*, in which the Attorney General, and Clerk of the Crown severally exhibit Informations for Crimes and Misdemeanors; the first does it *ex officio*, and the other generally by Order of the Court. In this Office Informations may be exhibited for Offences and Misdemeanors, either at Common Law, or on Statute Law; at Common Law, as in the Case of *Batteries, Conspiracies, Libelling, Nusances,* &c. On Statute Law, as for the *Breach of any particular Statute*.

Cucking Stool, is an Engine that was invented for the Punishment of Scolds and unquiet Women, by ducking them; and in ancient Time it was called a *Tumbrel*: It was likewise anciently a Punishment that was inflicted on Bakers and Brewers, upon their transgressing the Laws, in respect to their respective Trades, who, on offending, were to be ducked in such a Chair, in some muddy Pond or standing Water.

Cui ante divortium, is a Writ which a Woman being divorced from her Husband, has to recover her

her Lands or Tenements, which before her Coverture she held in Fee, in Tail, or for Life, from the Person to whom the Husband had alienated them during the Marriage, when she had it not in her Power to gainsay it.

Cui in vita, is a Writ of Entry which a Widow may have against the Person to whom her Husband in his Life-time did alienate her Lands or Tenements, without her Consent first had. In this Writ the Title of the Woman must be shewn, whether it be of her Purchase or Inheritance; and if the Husband alien the Right of his Wife, and afterwards both he and she die, the Heir to the Wife may have a Writ of *sur cui in vita* against the Person to whom the Right of the Wife was so aliened.

Culprit, is a formal Reply of a proper Officer in Court in Behalf of the King, whereby, after a Criminal has pleaded Not guilty, he affirms him to be guilty. This Word is compounded of a Contraction of the *Latin* Word *Culpabilis*, and the *French*, *Prit*, signifying as much, as that *he is ready to prove the Criminal guilty.*

Cuntey Cuntey, is taken for a Kind of Trial, which *Cowel* is of Opinion was that by an *ordinary Jury*.

Curia advisari vult, denotes a Deliberation which a Court of Justice sometimes takes upon any Point of Difficulty that arises in a Cause before they give Judgment.

Curia cursus Aquæ, is mentioned in 2 *Geo.* 2. c. 26. and signifies a Court held by the Lord of the Manor of *Gravesend*, for the better Management of Barges and Boats that use the Passage between that Place and *London*, &c.

Curia claudenda, is a Writ that lies for compelling another to make a Fence or Wall, which he ought to make between his Land and that of the Plaintiff.

Curia Domini, denotes the Lord's House, or Court, where the Tenants attend at the Time of holding Courts.

Curia Penticiarum, is a Court held by the Sheriff of *Chester*, in a certain Place there called the *Pendice* or *Pentice*.

Currier, is a Person that dresses Leather, and is mentioned by that Name in the 1 *Jac.* 1. and other Statutes.

Curstors, are Clerks that belong to the Chancery, whose Business is to make out original Writs. In the Oath appointed by 18 *Ed.* 3. these Clerks are called *Clerks of Course*, and are twenty-four in Number; to each of whom are allotted certain different Shires, into which they issue out the Original Writs required: And these Clerks together make a Corporation of themselves.

Curtesy of England, is where a Man takes a Wife seised in Fee, or in Tail general, or as Heiress in special Tail, by whom he has Issue born alive, the Husband, if the Wife dies, whether the Issue be living or not, shall hold the Lands during his Life: And the Husband in this Case is called Tenant by the *Curtesy* of England, because such Privilege is not granted in any other Nation except *Scotland* now united to this Kingdom. Tho' the Child be born alive, yet it must be such a one, as by Possibility may come to inherit; for should Lands or Tenements be given to a Woman and the Heirs Male of her Body lawfully to be begotten, and she afterwards marries and has Issue a Daughter, and dies, the Husband in this Case shall not be Tenant by the *Curtesy*, because his

Issue,

CU

Iſſue, the Daughter, cannot poſſibly inherit.

Curteyn. The Name of King *Edward* the Confeſſor's Sword, was the firſt Sword carried before the Kings of *England* at their Coronation; and we are told the Point of it is broken, as an Emblem of Mercy.

Curtilage, denotes a Piece of Ground adjoining to a Dwelling-houſe, ſuch as a Court, Yard, Backſide, or the like; but it is thought it differs from a Garden.

Curtiles Terræ. The Lands which were anciently appropriated to the Uſe of the Court, or Houſe of the Lord, were anciently called ſo.

Cuſtantia, was formerly uſed to ſignify Coſts.

Cuſtode admittendo, and **Cuſtode amovendo,** are Writs for the admitting or removing of a Guardian. See *Reg. Orig.*

Cuſtodes Libertatis Angliæ Authoritate Parliamenti, was the Stile in which the Writs and all other judicial Proceſs did run, during the moſt unnatural Rebellion, from the Murder of King *Charles* the Firſt, till the traiterous Uſurpation of *Oliver Cromwell*.

Cuſtom, is defined to be a Law, or Right not written, which being eſtabliſhed by long Uſage, has been, and daily continues to be practiſed. As no Law can oblige a People without their Conſent; ſo wherever ſuch Conſent is had, and a certain Rule uſed as a Law, ſuch Rule gives it the Force of a Law; and if ſuch Rule is once become univerſal, then it is Common Law; but if reſtrained to this or that particular Place, then it is *Cuſtom*: *Cuſtom* differs from Preſcription, becauſe *Cuſtom* is common to many, but Preſcription, according to ſome Opinions, is particular to this or that Man:

CU

Beſides Preſcription may be for a ſhorter Time than Cuſtom, *viz.* for five Years or leſs; as in the Caſe of a Fine duly levied of Lands, *&c.* if the ſame be not gainſaid within five Years, excludes all future Claim: Again, if a Perſon omits his continual Claim for Year and Day, then the Tenant in Poſſeſſion may preſcribe an Immunity againſt the Entry of the Demandant and his Heir: In a Word, Preſcription is an Exception founded on ſo long a Time paſt as the Law limits it for the Purſuit of any Action or Proſecution; as in the 1 *H.* 8. *c.* 4. it is enacted, that in all Actions popular Information ſhall be made within three Years after the Offence committed, otherwiſe the ſame is not to be in Force. Cuſtom is alſo uſed for the Tribute Merchants pay to the Crown on the Importation or Exportation of Wares or Merchandizes. In which Signification it is in *Latin* called *Cuſtuma.* See *Reg. Orig. Laſtly,* It is uſed for ſuch Services as Tenants of a Manor owe to their Lord.

Cuſtomary Tenants, are ſuch as hold Land, *&c.* by the Cuſtom of the Manor as their only Evidence.

Cuſtom-Houſe, is a Houſe in maritime Cities or Port-Towns, where the King's Cuſtoms or Duties on Importation or Exportation are received, and other Buſineſs relating thereto is tranſacted.

Cuſtoms and Services, is a Writ of *Right Cloſe,* which iſſues againſt a Tenant, who deforces his Lord of the Rent or Service due to him. *Termes de la Ley.*

Cuſtos Brevium, is the principal Clerk that belongs to the Court of *Common Pleas,* whoſe Buſineſs is to receive and keep all the Writs made returnable in that Court, and

and to file the same, every Return by itself, and at the End of every Term to receive of the *Prothonotaries*, all the Records of *Nisi Prius*, called the *Postea's*, which are first brought in by the Clerks of Assise of every Circuit to the Prothonotary that entered the Issue in the Cause, in order for him to enter the Judgment; and after the Prothonotary has entered the Verdict and Judgment thereon into the Rolls of the Court, he delivers them over to the *Custos Brevium*, who binds them into a Bundle. The *Custos Brevium* likewise makes Entries of all Writs of Covenant, and the Concord upon each Fine; as also makes out Exemplifications and Copies of all Writs and Records in his Office, and of all Fines levied; which Fines, after they are ingrossed, are divided between the *Custos Brevium* and the *Chirographer*, which last always keeps the Writ of Covenant and the Note, and the *Custos Brevium* the Concord and Foot of the Fine, whereon the *Chirographer* causes the Proclamations to be indorsed, after they have been all proclaimed. There is also a *Custos Brevium* and *Rotulorum* in the King's Bench, whose Business is to file all Writs that are used to be filed in that Court, and likewise all Warrants of Attorney, and makes out the Records, &c.

Custos Placitorum Coronæ, was an Officer, who, it is thought, was the same with him that we now call *Custos Rotulorum*.

Custos Rotulorum, is an Officer that has the Custody of the Rolls and Records of the Sessions of the Peace, as also, as some believe, of the Commission of the Peace itself. He is constantly a Justice of the Peace and *Quorum* in the County where his Office is kept: And he is rather deemed a Minister than a Judge. This Officer is appointed by a Writing under the King's *Sign Manual*, which is a Warrant to the Lord Chancellor to put him in Commission: And he is at Liberty to execute his Office by Deputy, and likewise impowered to appoint the Clerk of the Peace.

Custos of the Spiritualties, is an Officer that exercises Spiritual Jurisdiction of any Diocese during the Vacancy of the See.

Custos Temporalium, was the Person to whose Custody a vacant See or Abbey was committed by the King as Supreme Lord: His Office was, as Steward of the Goods and Profits, to give Account to the *Escheator*, who was to do the like into the *Exchequer*.

Cutter of the Tallies, is an Officer of the Exchequer, whose Office is to provide Wood for the *Tallies*, and to cut or notch the Sum paid upon them.

D.

Damage, in the Common Law, denotes Part of what the *Jurors* in a Cause are to inquire of, in giving their Verdict for the Plaintiff in any real or personal Action: For after they have given their Verdict, in Relation to the principal Cause, they are asked touching Costs and Damages, wherein is comprehended a Recompence for what the Plaintiff has suffered by Means of the Wrong done him by the Defendant. This Word in the Law is taken in two different Senses, the one *Properly* and *Generally*, and the other *Strictly* and *Relatively*; *Properly*, as in Cases where Damages are founded upon 2 *Hen.* 4. *c.* 1. and 8 *Hen.* 6. *c.* 9. wherein Costs are included

included in the Word Damages, and taken as such: But when the Plaintiff declares for the Wrong done him, to the Damage of a certain Sum, they must be taken *relatively* for the Wrong done before the Suit commenced, and is assessed on Account of the Trespass foregoing, and can never extend to Costs of Suit, which are future, and quite of another Nature.

Damage-cleer, was a Fee formerly assessed by the tenth Part in the *Common Pleas*, and twentieth in the *King's Bench* and *Exchequer*, out of all Damages exceeding five Marks, recovered either by Verdict, Confession or Judgment of the Court in Actions upon the Case, Covenants, Trespass, and all others, wherein the Damages are uncertain, which the Plaintiff was obliged to pay to the *Prothonotary*, or other chief Officer of that Court wherein the Damages were recovered, before he could have Execution for them. By the *Stat.* 17 *Car.* 2. *c.* 6. this *Damage-cleer* is taken away, and a Penalty enacted on any Officer that is guilty of taking *Damage-cleer*.

Damage-feasant, denotes the doing of some Hurt or Damage, as where a Stranger's Beasts get into another Man's Grounds, without the License of the Owner or Occupier thereof, and there feed, tread down, or otherwise spoil the Corn, Grass, Woods, &c. In this Case, the Person to whom the Damage is done, may distrain, take and impound them, either by the Night, or in the Day-Time, which cannot be done in other Cases, as for Rent and Services, &c. which was only to be done in the Day-Time.

Danegelt or **Danegeld**, denotes to be freed from a certain Tribute which the *Danes* levied in *England*; which Tribute itself bore that Name.

Danger, denotes a Payment in Money, made by Forest-Tenants to the Lord for Liberty to plough and sow in Time of *Pannage*, or Mast-feeding.

Darrein, seems to be a Corruption of a *French* Word, signifying *the last*; and in this Sense it is used in our Law, as *Darrein Continuance*, &c.

Darrein Presentment. An Assise thereof lies where a Person, or his Ancestors have presented a Clerk to a Church, and afterwards, the Church becoming void by the Death of such Clerk, or otherwise, a Stranger presents his Clerk to the same Church, in Disturbance of the first Presentor. If a Husband and Wife present to an Advowson, the Right of the Wife, that is appendant to the Wife's Manor, and afterwards the Husband sells an Acre or Parcel of the Manor, with the Advowson in Fee, to a Stranger, and dies; after which the Stranger presents, and then aliens the Parcel purchased by him to another in Fee, reserving the Advowson to himself, and at Length the Church becomes void, then the Widow of the Deceased shall present, and if she be disturbed, she shall have an Assise of *Darrein Presentment*, because the Advowson was severed from the Acre: But if the Advowson had been appendant thereto, then she ought to recover the Acre before she presents to the Advowson. *Termes de la Ley.*

Date, is a Description of the Time, to wit, the Day, Month, Year of the Reign of the King or Queen upon the Throne, and the Year of our Lord, in which a Deed or other Writing was made; yet anciently Deeds had no Dates, other than

than that of the Month and Year. A Deed is said to be good, tho' it has no Date of the Day, or if the same be mistaken, or tho' it contains an impossible Date, as the 30th of *February*, &c. But then he that pleads such a Deed, must set forth the Time when it was delivered.

Dative or **Datif**, signifies any Thing that may be disposed of at Pleasure.

Day, denotes a certain Space of Time, which contains 24 Hours, which is called a natural Day, it containing both a *Solar Day* and Night, to distinguish it from an *Artificial Day*, which begins from the Rising of the Sun, and ends when it sets. Day, in a legal Sense, relates to the *Day of Appearance* of the contending Parties, or the Continuance of a Suit, where a *Day* is given.

Day-light. Before Sun-rising and after Sun-setting, is in our Law accounted Part of the Day; as in the Case of *Robberies* in the Day-Time, when the Hundred is liable.

Days-man. In some Parts in the North, an Arbitrator, or the Person that is chosen to determine an Affair in Dispute, is frequently called a *Dies-man*, or *Days-man*.

Daywere of Land, is said to have denoted as much arable Land as could be ploughed up in one Day's Work, or as the Farmers call it, one *Journey*. Hence it is conjectured, that a Person who assists a Workman in *daily Labour*, is called a *Journeyman*.

Deadly Feud, was formerly used to denote a Profession of an irreconcilable Hatred, till a Person is revenged by the Death of his Adversary, which Enmity was allowed in the old *Saxon* Laws; seeing that where any Person was killed, if a pecuniary Satisfaction was not made to the Kindred of the slain Party, it was lawful for them by Arms to revenge themselves upon the Murderer. See **Feud**.

Dead-Pledge. See **Mortgage**.

Dean, (from a *Greek* Word signifying *Ten*) is an Ecclesiastical Magistrate, and is so called, on Account that he presides over Ten Canons or Prebendaries at the least. He is called a *Dean*, that is, next under the Bishop, and Chief of the Chapter, usually in a Cathedral Church; and the rest of the Society we term the *Chapter*. As there are two Foundations of Cathedral Churches in *England*, the old and the new (the new being those that King Henry the Eighth, upon the Suppression of Abbots, transformed from an Abbot, a Prior and a Convent, to Dean and Chapter) so likewise are there two Means of creating those Deans; they of the old Foundation being raised to their Dignity much like Bishops, the King first sending his *Conge d' Eslire* to the Chapter, after which the Chapter chusing, the King granting his Royal Assent, and the Bishop confirming the Person chosen, and giving his Mandate to install him: But those of the new Foundation are installed by a much shorter Course, by Virtue of the King's Letters Patent, without either Election or Confirmation. This Word is also applied to several who are the Chief of certain peculiar Churches or Chapels, as the *Dean of the King's Chapel*, the *Dean of the Arches*, the *Dean of St. George's Chapel* at *Windsor*, &c. *Termes de la Ley*.

Death. There is in Law both a natural Death of a Person, and a civil Death: *Natural* is where Nature

ture itself expires or extinguishes; *Civil*, where a Person is not actually dead, but is adjudged so by Law, as where he or she enters into religious Orders, &c.

De bene esse, are but common *Latin* Words, whose Meaning nevertheless is somewhat dark; as to take or do a Thing *de bene esse*, is to allow a Thing at present to be well done, till it comes to be more fully examined, and then to stand or fall by it; as in the Court of *Chancery*, upon a Motion for one of the Defendants to be examined, the Court frequently orders it to be done *de bene esse*, that is to say, that his Deposition, at the Hearing of the Cause may be allowed or suppressed, as the Court shall think proper.

Debenture. That of Soldiers is in the Nature of a Bond or Bill, whereby the Government is charged with the Payment of the *Soldier-Creditor*, or his Assigns, the Money due on the auditing the Account of his Arrears. Soldiers Debentures were first ordained by a Law made during the Usurpation of *Oliver Cromwell*. *Debentures* are likewise used in the *Exchequer*, and are given to the King's Servants for the Payment of their Wages, Board Wages, &c. There are also *Custom-house Debentures*, &c. for the Draw-back of the Duties on the Exportation of divers Commodities.

Debet & Detinet, are *Latin* Words, till of late used in the bringing of Actions. An Action must always be in *Debet* and *Detinet*; that is to say, he *owes and detains*, where the Person that contracts or lends Money to another, or he to whom a Bond is made, brings an Action against the Person bound, or Party to the Contract, or to the lending of the Money. See more of this in *New Nat. Brev.* and *Reg. Orig.*

Debet & Solet, have been frequently used by the Writers of the Common Law, particularly in the *Old Nat. Brev.* 69 and 98. See likewise *Reg. Orig.* 140.

Debt, is an Action that lies against a Person who owes another Money on Bond, or Contract for any Thing sold; which the Debtor omits to pay on the Day agreed, then the Creditor may have Action of Debt against him for the same.

Debt to the King. This Word comprehends in it all Rents, Issues, Amerciaments, and other Things due to the King, who is to have Preference in all Suits.

Deceit, denotes a subtile Trick, or Shift, whereunto may be added all Manner of Craft, Subtilty, Collusion, or any underhand Practice made Use of, in order to deceive or defraud another Person, in any Respect whatsoever. *Deceit* is an Offence both at Common Law and by Statute Law. All Practices of Fraud, or endeavouring to defraud another of his Right, are punishable. For any that receives Damage or Injury from another that acts deceitfully in the Name of another, the Writ *Deceptione*, or *Deceit*, lies, which Writ is either *Original* or *Judicial*. See *Old Nat. Brev.* 50.

Decem Tales, is a Term used where a full Jury does not appear on a Trial at Bar; then a Writ thus called issues, directed to the Sheriff, whereby he is commanded to make a Supply of Jury-men, in order to proceed on the Trial.

Decies Tantum, is a Writ which lies against a Juror, for having taken Money of either Party on Account of giving his Verdict; and it takes its Name from the Effect, *viz.*

viz. Because it is to recover of the Defendant ten Times as much as he took. Any Person, tho' not a Party in the Suit, may bring this Writ in the Name of the King and himself, and recover the like, one Half to the Crown, and the other to the Informer or Prosecutor. If the King upon Recovery in this Action were even to release by Pardon to such a Juror, yet that can be no Bar against the Person that brings the Action, who is intitled to one Moiety of the Sum recovered, provided the Action be commenced before the Pardon: And the same Law holds in Respect to all other popular Actions; that is to say, where one Part is given to the Crown, and the other to the Party that sues for the same. This Writ likewise lies against *Embracers*, who procure such an Inquest; and they are to be further punished by Imprisonment. See *Fitz. Nat. Brev.* 171. *Reg. Orig.* 188. and 38 *Ed.* 3. *c.* 1.

Decimation, properly signifies the punishing every tenth Soldier by Lot, but it likewise is said to signify *Tithing*, or paying the tenth Part. *Cowel* justly observes there was another Kind of *Decimation* in the Times of *Cromwell*'s Usurpation, which too many Loyalists have had sad Cause to remember.

Decimis solvendis pro Possessionibus Alienigenarum, was a Writ or Letters Patent, which lay against such as had farmed the *Priors Aliens* Lands of the King, for the Rector of the Parish, for the Recovery of his Title to them. *Cowel.*

Deciners, Decenniers, or **Dozeiners**, anciently signified such as were wont to have the Oversight of ten Free Burghs for the Maintenance of the King's Peace; the Limits of whose Jurisdiction was called *Decenna*. These are thought to have had large Authority in the Time of the *Saxons*, taking Cognisance of Causes within their Circuit, and redressing Wrongs by Way of Judgment: For which see the Laws of King *Edward*, in *Lbam. Numb.* 32. Of late Times *Decennier* is not used for the chief Man of a *Dozen*, but one that is sworn to the King's Peace; besides, there are now no other *Dozeins*, but *Leets*.

Declaration, is a formal shewing in Writing, the Ground of Complaint of the Plaintiff on an Action against the Defendant, wherein the Plaintiff is supposed to have received some Wrong or Injury: And this *Declaration* ought to be plain and certain, for this Reason, that it impeaches the Defendant, and obliges him to answer thereto. It must set forth both the Names of the Plaintiff and Defendant, the Nature and Cause of the Action, *&c.* and the Damage charged to be received. In an Action real a *Declaration* is termed a *Count*. A *Count* or *Declaration* ought to contain *Demonstration, Declaration,* and *Conclusion*: In *Demonstration* are included three Things, *viz. The Person who complains, against whom, and for what Matter*: And in the *Declaration* there ought to be comprised, *how the Action between the Parties arose, when, and what Day, Year and Place,* and *to whom the Action shall be given*: And lastly, in the Conclusion, the Plaintiff ought to *aver*, and *offer to prove the Suit and Damage sustained*. To which may be added, that a *Declaration* is an Exposition of the Writ or Process, with the Addition of Time, Circumstances, *&c.* and ought to be true as well as clear, since the Court will not take Things in it by Implication.

The

The Forms of common Declarations in *English*, you may see in the *Young Clerk's Magazine*, and other small Collections of Precedents in Common Law, &c.

Dedi, *I have given*, amounts to a Warranty in Law.

Dedimus Potestatem, is a Commission given to one or more, for the forwarding and dispatching some Act appertaining to a Judge or some Court; and it is granted in some Cases, such as the taking Answers in the Country in Chancery, Depositions of Witnesses in a Cause depending in that Court, to levy a Fine in the *Common Pleas*, &c.

Dedimus Potestatem de Attornato faciendo. Anciently the Judges would not suffer the Parties to make Attornies in any Suit without this Writ, which is now entirely gone into Disuse, since by late Statutes, the Plaintiff or Defendant may make Attornies, without any such Writ.

Deed, is an Instrument written on Parchment or Paper, purporting some Contract, Bargain, or Agreement between Party and Party, in Relation to the Matters therein specified: To which three principal Points belong, *viz.* *Writing*, *Sealing* and *Delivery*; *Writing*, to express the Contents thereof, whereby the Intention of the Parties may be known; *Sealing*, to show the Consent of the Parties; and the *Delivery* to confirm and bind the Whole. There are two Kinds of Deeds, *viz.* *Deeds indented*, and *Deeds Poll*, the respective Names of which chiefly arise from the Shape of them, the one being cut in and out at Top, which is termed *indented*; and the other being plain. A *Deed indented*, consists of two or more Parts; as there are *Deeds Tripartite*, of three Parts, *Qua-dripartite*, of four, *Quinquepartite*, of five Parts, and *Sextipartite*, of six, &c. and so on: In which respective Deeds it is expressed, that the Parties thereunto have interchangeably set their Hands and Seals; and the Reason of indenting these Deeds is, that as they contain more Parts than one, each Part of them is indented, or cut one into the other, whereby it may appear they belong to one and the same Business. A *Deed Poll*, is a *Deed* that only consists of one Part, and is without indenting: It is used where a Grantor in a Bill of Sale, &c. only seals; and there is no Need of a Counter-part; the Nature of the Contract being such, as that it requires no Covenant in Return from the Grantee. The several Parts of Deeds by Indenture, are such as appertain to the *Feoffor*, *Grantor*, or *Lessor*, &c. of the one Part; and the *Feoffee*, *Grantee*, or *Lessee*, of another Part; and some other Persons, as Trustees, &c. of a third Part, &c. All the Parts of an indented *Deed* in Law are judged to make up but one *Deed*; so that each Part is of as great Force as all the Parts together, they being esteemed the mutual Acts of either Party, that is bound by either Part of the same, and therefore the Words of the Indenture are the Words of each of the Parties thereto. But a *Deed Poll* is not so, it being look'd upon as the sole Deed of him that makes it, and the Words thereof shall be deemed to be his own Words, and bind him only.

Deemsters, denotes Judges or Umpires, and we are told there are a Kind of those in the *Isle of Man*, who, without Process or Charge to the contending Parties, decide all Controversies in that Island; and these

these are chosen among themselves.

De Essendo quietum de Tolonio, is a Writ which lies for those who are by Privilege free from the Payment of Toll, whenever they are molested therein.

De Expensis Militum, is a Writ commanding the Sheriff to levy 4 s. *per Diem* for the Expences of a Knight of the Shire for his Attendance in Parliament. There is another of the like Nature, called *Expensis Civium & Burgensium,* for levying 2 s. *per Diem* for the Expences of every Citizen and Burgess of Parliament.

De facto, denotes a Thing that is actually and *bona fide* done. A King *de facto,* is a Person who is in actual Possession of a Crown, yet has no legal Right to the same; and in this Sense it is opposed to a King *de jure,* who has just Right to a Crown, but is out of Possession thereof.

Default, is generally taken for Non-Appearance in Court at a Day assigned; yet it does also extend to any Omission of that which we ought to do; as the Omission of Payment of Money secured on Bond, &c.

Defamation, is where a Person speaks slanderous Words of another, of a Court of Justice, Magistracy, or Title of Land; for which the Slanderer is punishable according to the Nature of his Offence, either by Action upon the Case at the Common Law, or by Statute, or in the Ecclesiastical Court. But as to *Defamation* determinable in a Spiritual Court, it ought to have three Incidents. 1*st,* It should concern Matters meerly Spiritual, and determinable in an Ecclesiastical Court; as for calling a Person Heretick, Schismatick, Adulterer, Fornicator, or the like. 2*dly,* That it be Spiritual Matter only; for if the Defamation concerns any Thing that may be determined at the Common Law, the Ecclesiastical Judges cannot have Conusance of it. 3*dly,* Tho' the Defamation be merely spiritual, yet the Person defamed cannot sue in that Court for Damages; for the Suit ought to be only for Punishment of the Fault, for the Soul's Health, of the offending Party. As to the Slander of a Title to Land, if *A.* says that *B.* has Right to the Lands of *C.* by which *C.* becomes damnified, he may have an Action against *A.* for this Defamation of his Title, notwithstanding that *B.* may have a colourable Title; yet *A.* shall be punished, on Account that he hath taken upon him the Knowledge of the Law, and interfered in a Matter that did not concern him: But if a Person says that he himself has Right to the Land of another, in this Case no Action for Slander lies, even tho' he knows his Title to be false. *Coke, lib.* 4. *Fol.* 18.

Defeasance, (from a *French* Word, signifying to *undo* or *make void* what is done) in our Law denotes a Condition that relates to some certain Deed, which, when once performed, the Deed becomes defeated and rendered void, as if it had never been in Force. The Difference between a Defeasance and a common Condition is this, *viz.* That the Condition is inserted in the Deed; but a Defeasance is a Deed by itself, which has Relation to some separate Deed. The Requisites for making a good Defeasance are these; 1*st,* It must be by Deed, since there can be no Defeasance of a Deed without a Deed. 2*dly,* It must recite the

most

most material Part of the Deed it relates to. 3*dly*, It must be made between the same Parties that were to the former Deed. 4*thly*, It must be made at the Time, or after the making of the first Deed, but not before. 5*thly*, It must be made of a Thing voidable. The Form of a Defeasance you may see in the *Young Clerk's Magazine*, and other Collections of Precedents of Conveyances.

Defence, in our Law, signifies a Plea, or what the Defendant ought to make immediately after the Plaintiff's Count or Declaration, that is to say, that he defends all the *Wrong, Force* and *Damage*, &c. where, and when he ought, *&c.* Thus by defending the Force and Wrong, he excuses himself of the Wrong surmised against him, and thereby makes himself Party to the Plea; and by his defending the Damage, he affirms that the Plaintiff is able to be answered unto. As for the Residue of the Defence, he accepts of the Power of the Court to hear and determine their Pleas: For if the Defendant would plead to the Jurisdiction, he ought in his Defence to omit the Words, *where and when he ought*, &c. and if he would shew any Disability in the Plaintiff, and demand Judgment if the Plaintiff shall be answered unto, he ought to omit the Defence of the Damage. *Termes de la Ley*. In personal Actions there is usually a full Defence, which is where the Plea begins thus, he comes and defends the *Force and Wrong, when,* &c. In real Actions the Plea generally begins thus, *viz. He comes and says*, &c.

Defend, in our ancient Laws, signified to forbid; as in divers Parts of *England, Blount* tells us, that they commonly say *God defend*, instead of *God forbid*.

Defendant, denotes a Person that is sued in a *Personal* Action; as *Tenant* is he who is sued in a *Real* Action. *Cowel.*

Defendemus, is a Word formerly used in Feoffments and Grants, and has this Validity, that it binds the *Feoffor* or *Grantor*, and his Heirs, to defend the *Grantee*, and his Heirs, against the Persons claiming Right to the Land, &c. granted, other than as contained in the Grant. The *English* of this Word, *Defend*, you may see under the Tit. **Warranty**.

Defender of the Faith, is a peculiar Title belonging to the King of *England*, as that of *Catholick* to the King of *Spain*, *Christian* to the King of *France*, &c. This Title of *Defender of the Faith* was first given to King *Henry* the Eighth, by Pope *Leo* the Tenth, for writing against *Martin Luther:* But the Pope afterwards, at the Time of the *Reformation*, deprived that Prince both of his Title and Crown, which the Parliament in the 35th Year of his Reign confirmed; so that that Title has ever since continued to be used by all our succeeding Kings.

Defendere se per Corpus suum, anciently signified *to offer Duel* or *Combat*, in Place of a legal Trial and Appeal.

Defendere unica Manu, was used to denote *to wage Law*, or a Denial of the Accusation upon Oath.

Defensiva, is a Title that was formerly bestowed on the Lords or Earls of the Marshes, who were the Warders or Defenders of their Country.

Deforcement, signifies a With-holding of Lands or Tenements by Force from the right Owner.

Defor-

Deforceor, is a Person that overcomes and casts out another by Force; and it differs from a *Disseisor*, on Account, 1*st*, That a Man may be disseised without Force; which is called *Simple Disseisin*; and, *next*, because one may deforce another that never was in Possession; as where many have a Right to Lands, as common Heirs, and one of them enters and keeps out the rest, in which Case the Law says he *deforces* them, tho' he never disseised them. A *Deforceor* likewise differs from an *Intruder*, for this Reason, that a Person is made an *Intruder* by a wrongful Entry only into Land, &c. void of a Possessor, whilst a *Deforceor* is he that holds out against the right Heir. Because Force and Violence are entirely opposite to the Peace and Justice of the Land, and a Dishonour of the Crown, as well as a Discredit to the Law, that any one should presume to enter forcibly into the Possession of another before the Law has given a Decision of his Title therein; several Statutes have been made, in order to restrain and reform these Abuses. See *Forcible Entry*.

Deforciant. See **Deforceor**.

Deforciatio, in *Paroch. Antiq.* 293. is used as a Distress or Seizure of Goods for the Satisfaction of a lawful Debt.

Degrading or **Disgrading**, is where a Person having taken upon him a spiritual or temporal Dignity, becomes afterwards deprived thereof. By the Canon Law there are two Sorts of Degradings; the one summary, by Word only, and the other solemn, by devesting the *degraded Party* of those Ornaments and Rites that are the Ensigns of his Order or Dignity.

Degradation. See **Degrading**.

De Injuria sua propria, are Words, the *English* of which are now used in Replications, in Actions of Trespass, or on the Case: And *de injuria sua propria* is a good Plea where it is brought in Excuse of some Injury alledged to be done to the Plaintiff's Person, or where the Defendant justifies in Defence of his Possession, in Case the Title does not come in Question. See more under *Tit. Son Tort Demesne*.

Dei Judicium, was an old *Saxon* Trial, so called, because they judged it an Appeal to God for their Justice of a Cause, and believed that the Decision was agreeable to the Will and Pleasure of Divine Providence.

Delatura, (from the *Saxons*) signifies an Accusation, and has some Times been taken for the Reward of an Informer.

Delegates, are certain Commissioners deputed by the King, to hear and determine Appeals from the Ecclesiastical Court.

Deliverance, is a Word used by the Clerk in Court, when a Criminal being arraigned and asked whether he is *Guilty* or *Not Guilty*, he answers, *Not guilty*, and puts himself upon God and his Country; whereupon the Clerk wishes him a good *Deliverance*.

Delivery of Deeds. See **Deed**.

Demains, or **Demesnes**, in a general Sense are taken for all the Parts of any Manor, not in the Hands of Freeholders, tho' held by Copyholders, &c. *Demesnes*, is sometimes used in a more special Sense, being set opposite to Frank-fee; as such Lands, as were in the Possession of *Edward* the Confessor, are called *Ancient Demesne*, and all others *Frank-fee*: No private Person has any *Demesnes*, according to the simple Acceptation of the Word, because there

there is no Land but what depends mediately or immediately upon the Crown, that is to say, of some Honour or other belonging to the Crown, and not granted in Fee to any inferior Person; wherefore, when a Person in Pleading will signify his Land to be his own, he says, that he is, or was seised thereof in his *Demesne* as of Fee; where it appears, that tho' his Land be to him and his Heirs for ever, yet it is not true *Demesne*, but depending upon a superior Lord. *Demesnes*, according to common Speech, are only understood to be the Lord's chief Manor-Place or Mansion-House, which he and his Ancestors have Time out of Mind kept in their own Hands, with all the Buildings, Houses, Meadows, Pastures, Woods, Arable Lands, &c. occupied therewith. *Termes de la Ley.*

Demand, signifies the Calling upon a Person for any Thing that is due. There are two Kinds of Demands, the one in *Deed*, and the other in *Law:* In Deed, as in every *Præcipe* there is an express Demand, and on that Account the Plaintiff in all real Actions is called *Demandant*. In Law, as every Entry on Land, Distress for Rent, Taking of Goods, &c. all which may be done without Words, are Demands in Law; the one, as already observed, being in Writing without speaking, as in the *Præcipe*; one without Writing, being a verbal Demand of the Person by whom something is to be done or performed; and another made without either Speaking or Writing, which is termed a Demand in Law, as in Cases of Entries on Lands, &c. Now, as an Entry on Land, and taking a Distress, are a Demand in Law of the Land and Rent; so the Bringing an Action of Debt for Money due on Bond, &c. is a Demand in Law of the Debt.

Demandant. See **Demand.**

Demise, is applied to an Estate, either in Fee, for Term of Life, or for Years, tho' most usually the latter. The Word *Demise* in a Lease for Years, amounts to a Warranty to the Lessee and his Assigns; and upon this Word an Action of Covenant lies. The Death of the King of this Kingdom is in Law termed a *Demise* of the King to his Royal Successor to his Crown and Dignity.

Demise and Redemise, is where there are mutual *Leases* from one to another of one and the same Land, or at least something out of it.

Demurrer, denotes a Delay or Stop put to any Action, upon some Point of Difficulty, which is only determinable by the Court, before any further Proceedings can be had in the Suit; since in every Action the Controversy consists either in Fact, or in Law; when it is in Fact, it must be tried by a Jury; if in Law, the Court proceeds to Judgment, and whatever is there concluded, stands firm, without admitting of any Appeal. This Word in *Latin* is called *Moratur in Lege.* Where an Action is brought, and the Defendant says, that the Plaintiff's Declaration is not sufficient for him to answer unto; or when the Defendant pleads, and the Plaintiff says it is not a sufficient Plea in Law, after which the Defendant says it is a good Plea; upon which both Parties submit to the Judgment of the Court: This is called a *Moratur in Lege*, that is to say a *Demurrer*, so that, in short a *Demurrer* is an Issue joined entirely upon Matter of Law, which

which is only determinable by the Judges. A *Demurrer* may be also either to the Writ, Count or Declaration, or to any Part of the Pleadings: It may be likewise to a *Demurrer*; as where a *Demurrer* is double, and the Person that demurs assigns one Error in Fact, and another in Law, which is always judged ill, and may be demurred to on the other Side. Whereupon a Demurrer the Point in Law is difficult and doubtful, then a Stop is made, to consider further thereon by the Judges, in order to agree, if they can, or otherwise, for all the Justices to meet together in the *Exchequer Chamber*; and upon hearing of what the Serjeants can say upon both Parts, to determine what is Law in the Case. There is also a Demurrer to an Evidence given to a Jury upon Trial of an Issue, which is where a Question of Law arises thereon, as when the Plaintiff produces in Evidence any Records, Deeds, Writings, &c. upon which a Question in Law arises, and the Defendant offers to demur upon it, after which the Plaintiff joins in *Demurrer*, or waves his Evidence.

Demurrer to Indictments, is where a Criminal joins Issue upon a Point of Law in an Indictment or Appeal, allowing the Fact, as laid, to be true; this is a Demurrer in Law: And if the Indictment or Appeal prove good, in the Opinion of the Judges, they proceed to Judgment and Execution, as if the Party had been convicted by Confession or Verdict.

Demy Sangue, signifies the Half Blood; as where a Man marries a Woman, by whom he has Issue a Son, and the Wife afterwards dying, he marries another, by whom he has also a Son; in this Case these two Sons, tho' called *Brothers*, are but *Brothers of the Half Blood*, because they had different Mothers, and therefore by Law they cannot be Heirs one to the other; since he that claims by Discent, must be of the whole Blood to him from whom he claims.

Den and Strond, did anciently signify a Liberty for Ships to run or come on Shore.

Denarii de Caritate, were customary Oblations made to *Cathedral Churches* at a certain Time in the Year.

Denarius Dei, is the same as what we call *God's Penny*, or Earnest Money given and taken by Parties to Contracts, &c.

Denarius Sancti Petri, was an annual Payment made by every Family to the *Pope* on St. *Peter*'s Day.

Denizen, is an Alien created a Subject by the King's Letters Patent, and is otherwise called *Donaison*, because his Ligitimation proceeds *ex donatione Regis*, from the King's Gift. A *Denizen*, in several Respects is enabled to act as the King's natural Subjects do, *viz.* to purchase and possess Lands, &c. enjoy any Office or Dignity; and he is no sooner thus enfranchised, than he is said to be under the King's Protection, before which Time he cannot possess any Thing in *England*: Yet it is short of *Naturalization*; for a Stranger, when once naturalized, may inherit Lands by Discent, which a *Denizen* cannot do. A *Denizen* may purchase Lands, and his Issue that are born afterwards may inherit them, but those he had before shall not: But tho' a *Denizen* may purchase, yet he cannot inherit the Lands of his Ancestors: As a Purchaser he may enjoy them, and likewise may take Lands by Devise.

De non Decimando, denotes to be discharged of Tithes. See *Modus Decimandi*.

De non Residentia Clerici Regis, is a Writ that was anciently used where a Person is employed in the King's Service, &c. in order to excuse and Discharge him of *Non-Residence*.

Deodand, is compounded of *Deo* and *Dandum*, and denotes a Thing given as it were to God, to appease his Wrath, where a Person is killed by Mischance, not by any reasonable Creature, and is forfeited to the King; as if a Man in driving a Cart falls so that one of the Cart Wheels runs over him, and kills him, the Wheel that was the immediate Cause of his Death, becomes forfeited to the King, to be sold, and the Produce distributed to the Poor by the King's *Almoner*, for an Expiation of that dreadful Event, the Spilling of Human Blood: So likewise, if in the Felling of a Tree Warning is given to Company standing by, when it is near falling, and one of them happen to be slain; nevertheless the Tree is a *Deodand*, and becomes forfeited, as in the other Case.

De onerando pro Rata Portionis, is a Writ which lies where a Person is distrained for Rent, which ought to be paid by others proportionably with him; as if one holds five or more Ox-gangs of Lands by Fealty at a certain Rent, and aliens one Ox-gang to one, and another to another, one of the Alienees shall not be distrained for the whole Rent, but for the Value of what he purchased; and if he be distrained for more, he then shall have this Writ.

Departure, in our Law denotes a Parting or going from a Plea given in Bar of an Action; as where a Person pleaded in Bar, and afterwards having his Plea replied unto, does in his Rejoinder shew some fresh Matter contrary to, or not pursuing his first Plea, which is termed a Departure from his first Plea. *Departure* is likewise where a Plaintiff in his Declaration sets forth one Thing, and after the Defendant has pleaded, he in his Replication not pursuing his Declaration, shews new Matter. If one plead a general Agreement in Bar, and in his Rejoinder alledges a special one, this Will be adjudged a *Departure*: Also, where an Action is brought at Common Law, and the Plaintiff afterwards by his Replication endeavours to maintain it by Custom, is a *Departure*.

Departure in Despight of the Court, is where a Tenant or Defendant appears to an Action and has a Day given him in the same Term, or is called after, without having a Day given, so that it be in the same Term; if he does not appear, it is a *Departure in Despight of the Court*. See more under Tit. *Default*.

Depopulation, denotes a Desolation or unpeopling of any Place.

Depopulatores Agrorum, were great Offenders by the ancient Common Law, and were so called from their ruining the Habitations of the King's People, they having as it were depopulated Towns and Villages, and even leaving them without Inhabitants.

Deposition, denotes the Testimony of a Witness reduced into Writing by Way of Answer to Interrogatories, exhibited for that Purpose, in *Chancery*, &c. And the Person thus giving his Testimony is called a *Deponent*. Proof in the Court of Chancery is by Depositions of Witnesses, Copies of which being regularly taken and published, are read

read as Evidence at the Hearing, instead of having the Witnesses examined *Viva voce*, as is used in the Common Law Courts.

Deprivation, is a Bereaving or Taking away, as when a Bishop, Parson, Vicar or Prebend is deprived or deposed from his Preferment for any Matter in Fact or in Law, such as when a Schismatick or meer Layman is presented, admitted and inducted, there is good Cause of *Deprivation*. If an Incumbent have Plurality of Benefices, or subscribe not to the Articles of Religion, according to 13 *Eliz. c.* 12. he is liable to *Deprivation*. See other Causes of *Deprivation*, 21 *Hen.* 8. *c.* 13. There are two Sorts of Deprivations, *Deprivation from a Benefice*, and *Deprivation from an Office*: A *Deprivation from a Benefice*, is when a Minister for some great Crime, &c. is for ever deprived of his Living. *Deprivation from an Office* is, when a Minister is for ever deprived of his Orders, which is also called *Deposition* or *Degradation*, and is usually for some heinous Crime meriting Death, and is performed by the Bishop in a most solemn Manner.

Deputy, is a Person that exercises either Office or other Thing, in another's Right: And the Forfeiture or Misdemeanor of such Deputy shall cause the Person whom he represents to lose his Office. A Person cannot in all Cases appoint a Deputy, except his Grant will justify him in so doing; neither can a Deputy authorise another Person under him; for the Common Law never takes Notice of Under-Deputies. If the Office of Parkership be granted to one, he cannot grant it over, or depute another, because it is an Office of Trust, and shall not be forfeited.

It is to be observed that there is a great Difference between a Deputy and an Assignee of an Office, the Assignee having an Interest in the Office itself, and transacting all Things in his own Name, for whom his Grantor is not answerable, unless in special Cases: But a Deputy has no Interest in the Office, he being only a Shadow of the Officer by whom he was deputed. Where an Officer can make Assigns, he may make *Deputies*. *Cowel*.

De quibus sur Disseisin, is a Writ of *Entry*. See *Fitz. Nat. Brev.*

Deraign, or **Dereine**, is said to come from a *French* Word, signifying to confound or put out of Order, in our Common Law it is used different Ways; but usually to prove any Thing; as to *deraign* that Right, *deraign* the Warranty. By some this Word is applied to a Summons that may be challenged as defective, or not lawfully made; whilst others again confound it with our Waging of Law.

Derelict, denotes a Thing that is forsaken, or cast away. Derelict Lands left by the Sea are the King's.

Descent. See **Discent**.

De son tort Demesn, are formal Words used in an Action of Trespass, by Way of Reply to the Defendant's Plea; as if *A.* sues *B.* in Action of Trespass; to which *B.* in his Plea says, that he did what is alledged against him by the Order of his Master; whereto *A.* by Way of Replication, says, that *B.* did it *De son tort demesne, sans ceo que C. luy Command, modo & forma, &c.* that is to say, that *B.* did it of his own Wrong, without that, that *C.* commanded him, in such Form, *&c.*

Detachiare, denotes, by Writ of Detachment or other Course of Law,

Law, to seize or take into Custody another's Goods or Person. *Cowel.*

Detinet. See **Debet** and **Detinet.**

Detinue, is a Writ that lies against one that has got Goods or other Thing delivered to him to keep, and afterwards refuses to redeliver them: In which Action the Thing detained is generally to be recovered, and not Damages; yet if one cannot recover the Thing itself, he may recover Damages for the Thing, and also for the Detainer.

Devastavit, or **Devastaverunt Bona Testatoris,** is a Writ which lies against Executors or Administrators for paying Debts upon simple Contracts, before Debts on Bonds and other Specialties; in which Case they become as liable to Action as if they had squandered away the Deceased's Effects, or converted them to their own Use, and therefore are compellable to pay such Debts on Specialty out of their own Goods, to the Value of what they so paid without Compulsion; for such voluntary and illegal Payments are in Law accounted a Wasting of the Testator's Goods, as much as if they had given them away without Cause, or sold them, and converted the Produce thereof to their own Use. A *Devastavit* likewise lies where an Executor or Administrator pays Legacies or Debts, so as not to have Sufficient to pay both: And in these and all other Cases of *Waste,* the Executor, *&c.* is chargeable for so much *de bonis propriis,* out of his own Goods. See more of this in the *Office of Executors.*

Devenerunt, is a Writ that was formerly directed to the King's Escheator, on the Death of the Heir of the King's Tenant, commanding the *Escheator,* that by the Oaths of good and lawful Men, he inquire what Lands or Tenements came to the King on the Death of the Tenant: But this Writ is now entirely gone into Disuse; yet a new Use of it is prescribed by 14 *Car.* 2. *c.* 11.

Devest, signifies the taking away of the Possession of any Thing from another.

Devise, is properly applied in the Common Law to him, that by his last Will and Testament in Writing gives away any Lands or Tenements to another. The Person so giving away, is called the *Devisor,* and he to whom the Lands are given, the *Devisee.*

Devoires of Calais, was an ancient Custom due to the King for Merchandize brought into, or carried out of *Calais,* when our Staple continued there.

Dicker, or **Dicker of Leather,** is a certain Quantity of Leather, consisting of ten Hides, by which Leather is bought and sold: Iron is likewise sold by the *Dicker,* which consists of ten Bars.

Dictores and **Dictum.** The first signifies an Arbitrator, and the other an Arbitrament.

Dictum de Kenelworth, was an Award between King *Henry* III. and those Barons and others who had been in Arms against him; and it was so called, on Account of its being made at *Kenelworth Castle* in *Warwickshire, Ann.* 51. *Hen.* 3. wherein was contained a Composition of those who had forfeited their Estates in that Rebellion.

Diem clausit extremum, was a Writ that issued out of the Court of Chancery, directed to the Escheator of the County, upon the Death of any of the King's Tenants, to inquire by a Jury of what Lands he died seised, of what Value,

and

and who was the next Heir to him.

Dies, a Day, of which there are several Sorts, *viz. Natural, Artificial* and *Legal. Sunday*, as to legal Proceedings and Contracts, is no Day in Law. See **Day**.

Dies Datus, is a Day or Time of Respite allowed to the Defendant in a Cause, by the Court.

Dieu & Mon Droit, *God and my Right*, is a *Motto* of the *Royal Arms*, first given King *Richard* I. whereby is intimated, that the King of *England* holds his Crown of none but God.

Dieu son Act, are Words anciently used in our Law; and to this Day it is a Maxim in Law, that the *Act of God* shall prejudice no Man, and therefore if a House be blown or beaten down by Tempest or other *Act of God*, the Lessee or Tenant for Life or Years shall not only be quit of an Action of Waste, but by the Law is allowed Liberty to take Timber to rebuild the House for his Habitation. So, where the Condition of an Obligation consists of two Parts in the Disjunctive, both which at the Time of the Obligation made are possible, and one of them afterwards by the *Act of God* becomes impossible to be performed; the Obligor in this Case is not bound to perform the other Part, for that the Condition shall be taken beneficially for him.

Diffactio, (from the Verb *Diffacere*, to destroy) denotes a Maiming a Person.

Dignitaries, are such as are advanced to any Ecclesiastical Dignity or Preferment; as a Bishop, Dean, Archdeacon, &c.

Dilapidation, is when an Incumbent suffers the Parsonage House, or Outhouses, to fall down, or be in Decay, for Want of necessary Reparation. It, likewise denotes the pulling down or destroying any of the Houses or Buildings belonging to a Spiritual Living, or destroying of the Woods, Trees, &c. that appertain thereto; it being said to extend to the Committing or Suffering any wilful Waste upon the Inheritance of the Church.

Diligiatus, denotes outlawed, that is to say, *de lege ejectus*, cast out of Law.

Dilligrout. There was an ancient Tenure in Serjeanty, by which Lands where held of the King, by the Service of furnishing *Dilligrout*, the Pottage formerly made for the *King's Table*, on his *Coronation-Day*.

Dimidietas, denotes the Moiety or one Half.

Diminution, is where the Plaintiff or Defendant in a Writ of Error alledges to the Court, that Part of the Record remains in the inferior Court not certified, and therefore prays that it may be certified by *Certiorari*. *Diminution* cannot be alledged of what is fully certified, but of something that is wanting; as the Want of an Original, &c.

Dimissory Letters, are those that are used, where a Candidate for Holy Orders having a Title in one Diocese, and being to be ordained in another, the proper Diocesan gives those Letters to some other ordaining Bishop, giving Leave that the Bearer may be ordained to such a Cure within his District.

Diocese, signifies the Circuit of each Bishop's Jurisdiction; for this Realm has two Sorts of Divisions; the one into Shires or Counties, in Respect to the Temporal State; and the other into *Dioceses*, in Respect to the Ecclesiastical, of which *Dioceses* are reckoned twenty-two in *England*, and four in *Wales*.

Disability, is where a Person is rendered incapable to inherit Lands, or take a Benefit, which otherwise he might have done:

And

And this may happen four Ways; by the Act of the Ancestor, the Act of the Party, by the Act of God, or by the Act of the Law. *Disability* by the Act of the Ancestor, is where a Man is attainted of Treason or Felony, by which Means, of Course, his Blood becomes corrupt, and his Children are thereby disabled to inherit: *Disability* by the Act of the Party, is where one binds himself by Obligation, that upon the Surrender of a Lease, he will grant a new Estate in the same Premisses to the Lessee, and afterwards he grants over the Reversion, whereby he becomes disabled to perform his Obligation. *Disability* by the Act of God, is where a Person is *non sanæ Memoriæ*, not of sound Memory, which incapacitates him to make any Grant, &c. which so far disables him, that in all Cases where he gives or passes any Thing or Estate from him, after his Death, it may be disannulled and made void: And it is a Maxim in our Law, that a Man of full Age shall never be received to disable his own Person: Lastly, *Disability* by Act in Law, is where one by the sole Act of the Law, without any Thing by him done, is rendered incapable of receiving the Benefit of the Law, as an Alien born, &c. There are also by the Common Law other Disabilities, in respect to Grants, &c. such as Ideocy, Infancy, and Coverture.

Disagreement, will cause a Nullity of a Thing that had a Being before. See **Agreement**.

Disceit. See **Deceit**.

Discent, denotes an Order or Means, whereby Lands or Tenements are derived unto any Man from his Ancestors. It is either by the *Common Law*, *Custom*, or *Statute*: By the Common Law, as where one has Lands of Inheritance in Fee, and dies without having made any Disposal thereof; and therefore the Land *descends* or goes in Course to the eldest Son and Heir, it being thrown upon him by Law: *Discent* by Custom is, that sometimes the Land descends to all the Sons, or to all the Brothers, where one Brother dies without Issue, as in *Gavelkind*; sometimes to the youngest Son, as in *Borough English*; and sometimes to the eldest or youngest Daughter, according to the particular Customs of different Places: And *Discent* by Statute, is a *Discent* in Fee-Tail, as directed by the Nature and Manner of the Limitation or Settlement, pursuant to *Stat. Westm.* 2. and 13 *Ed.* 1. c. 1. *Discent* at Common Law, is either *Lineal* or *Collateral*; Lineal, is that which descends or goes down in a right Line, from the Grandfather to the Father, the Father to the Son, Son to the Grandson, &c. so that the *Lineal Heir* shall always first inherit: *Collateral Discent*, is that which springs from the Side of the whole Blood, as another Branch of it, such as the Grandfather's Brother, the Father's Brother, and so downwards; and therefore if a Man purchases in Fee, and dies without Issue, here, for Want of the right Line, he that is next of Kin in the *collateral* Line of the whole Blood, tho' never so remote, shall come in by Discent as Heir to the deceased Purchaser; there being, as *Littleton* observes, not only a next of Kin by Right of Representation, but likewise by Propinquity or Nearness of Blood. *Discent of Crown-Lands* differs from that Inheritance; for those that the King is seised of *in jure Coronæ*, must attend and follow the Crown; insomuch, as to whomsoever the Crown

Crown descends, those Lands descend also. *Discent* of Dignities likewise differ from that of common Inheritances, and does in no Respect go according to the Rules of the Common Law; for it descends to the Half Blood, and there is no Coparcenership in it, but the eldest takes the Whole: Yet the Dignity of Peerage is personal, annexed to the Blood, and so inseparable, that it cannot be transferred to any Person; for it can only move downward to Posterity; so that nothing but Corruption of Blood can hinder the *Discent* to the right Heir.

Discharge, in our Law has divers Significations; 1*st*, On Writs and Process, *&c.* where a Person confined by some legal Authority, does that which by Law he is required to do, he becomes released from the Matter for which he was confined.

Disclaimer, is a Plea, wherein is contained an express Denial or *disclaiming* of a Thing; as where, upon the Distress of the Lord, a Tenant sues a Replevin, and the Lord avows the Taking, by alledging the Tenant holds of him as of his Lord, and that he distrained for the Rent unpaid, or Service not performed; in which Case if the Tenant deny that he holds of him, this is called a *Disclaimer*, and on that Account, if the Lord prove the Tenant to hold of him, the Tenant, on a Writ of Right, shall lose his Land. If a Writ of *Præcipe* be brought against two for Land, and one of them being Tenant, says he is not Tenant, nor claims any Thing in the Land; in which Case the other shall have the whole Land: Yet a verbal *Disclaimer* will not take Place against a Deed made of Land. After a Tenant upon an Action hath disclaimed, he shall not have a Writ of Error against his own *Disclaimer*, and so consequently cannot have Restitution on such Writ brought; for the Form of the Disclaimer is this, *viz. He hath nothing, neither claims he to have in the Land, neither at the Day of bringing the original Writ aforesaid,* &c. *had or claimed, but any Thing in the same Land to have he disavows and disclaims. Termes de la Ley.* A Person in his Plea denying himself to be of the Blood or Kindred of another, is said to disclaim his Blood. There is also a *Disclaimer* of Goods; as where one being arraigned of Felony, *disclaims* the Goods charged against him; in which Case, tho' acquitted, he loses them. In the Court of Chancery, if the Defendant in his Answer denies his having any Interest in the Thing in Question, this is likewise a *Disclaimer*. To these may be added a *Disclaimer* in Deed; as the Renouncing of an Executorship of a Will, or the Renouncing the Right to an Administration, *&c.*

Discontinuance, denotes an Interruption or Breaking off; and is of two Sorts, *Discontinuance of Possession,* and *Discontinuance of Process*: *Discontinuance of Possession,* is that a Person may not enter upon his own Lands, *&c.* alienated, whatever his Right be thereto, of his own Authority, but must bring his Writ, and thereon seek to recover Possession by Law; as where a Person seised in Right of his Wife, or a Tenant in Tail makes a Feoffment, or a Lease, *&c.* not warranted by the *Stat.* 32 *H.* 8. such an Alienation is called a *Discontinuance,* which in Fact is an Impediment to an Entry, the Owner being left only to his Action. *Discontinu-*

ance of Process or Plea, in general, is where the Instant is lost, and cannot be regained, without a new Writ to begin the Suit afresh; for, as *Cowel* says, to be *discontinued*, and to be put *sine die, without a Day*, is one and the same Thing as to be finally dismissed the Court: For every Suit or Prosecution, whether Civil or Criminal, and all Processes thereon, ought to be continued from Day to Day from the Commencement thereof to the Conclusion of the same; any Default wherein is in our Law called a *Discontinuance*; and the Continuance of a Suit by improper Process, or by giving the Party an illegal Day is called a *Miscontinuance*. For Want of entring of *Continuances* from one Term to another, in a Suit, there will become a *Discontinuance*; whereupon a Writ of Error lies.

Discovert, denotes a Widow, or Woman unmarried.

Discretion, is a Word frequently made Use of in last Wills and Testaments; as where any Thing is by the Testator ordained to be done at the Discretion of the Executor, &c. In which Case the Law always intends, that such Thing shall be done with *sound Discretion*, and according to Law. In many Cases, for Crimes not capital, the Judges have a Discretionary Power to inflict a Corporal Punishment on an Offender. Infants under the Age of Discretion, are not punishable for Crimes by them committed; and Want of Discretion is a good Exception against a Witness.

Disfranchise, signifies to take away one's Privilege or Freedom, and is quite reverse to the Word *Enfranchise*. Corporations are impowered to *disfranchise* Members thereof, for acting any Thing contrary to their Oaths; but for Contempts cannot do so.

Disherison, denotes the same as *Disheriting*.

Disheritor, anciently was used to signify one that puts another out of his Inheritance.

Dismes, denotes Tithes, or the *tenth* Part of all the Fruits of the Earth, or of Beasts, or Labour, due to the Clergy. It likewise signifies the Tenths of all *Spiritual Livings*, given to the Prince, which is termed a *perpetual Dism*. See *Tithes*.

Disparagement, in the Sense of our Law denotes a Matching an Heir in Marriage under his or her Degree, or against Decency.

Dispauper, denotes a Person that by Reason of his Poverty sworn to, of not being worth 5 *l.* all Debts paid, is admitted to sue *in forma pauperis*, and if afterwards, before the Suit is ended, the same Person have Lands or other Estate fallen to him, or if he act any Thing whereby he becomes liable to have this Privilege taken from him, he is said to be dispaupered. See *Forma Pauperis*.

Dispensation. The Archbishop of *Canterbury*, by Statute has Power of dispensing in any Case, wherein Dispensations were formerly grantable by the See of *Rome*: And during the Vacancy of the Diocese of *Canterbury*, the Guardian of the Spiritualties may grant *Dispensations*. See 25 *Hen*. 8. *c.* 21. Every Bishop of common Right has the Power of Institution into Benefices, and of *dispensing* in common Cases, &c. A *Dispensation* of the King makes a Thing prohibited, lawful to be done by the Person that has it; yet *Malum in se*, a Thing evil in itself, will not admit of a *Dispensation*. Nevertheless, where the Subject has

an

an immediate Interest in an Act of Parliament, the King cannot *dispense* with it, which he may do, if the Suit be only the King's for the Breach of a Penal Law, that is not to the Damage of a third Person. There is likewise a *Dispensation* by *Non obstante*, which is where a Statute tends to restrain any particular Prerogative incident to the Person of the King, such as the Right of pardoning or commanding the Service of the Subject for the Benefit of the Publick, &c. each of which Prerogatives are inseparable from the King. To prevent the dispensing Power from being carried too high, it is enacted, that no Dispensation by *Non obstante* of any Statute, or Part thereof, shall be allowed, but that the same shall be of no Effect, except the *Dispensation* be allowed in the Statute itself. See 1 *W. & M. c.* 2.

Dispersonare, denotes to scandalize or disparage.

Disseisin, denotes an unlawful dispossessing a Person of his Lands or Tenements; as where one enters into Lands, &c. not having a lawful Right of Entry, and keeps the Person that has a Right to the Estate out of the Possession thereof. It is of two Kinds, either single *Disseisin*, which is committed without Force of Arms; or *Disseisin by Force*, tho' more properly termed *Deforcement*.

Disseisor, is he that illegally puts another out of Possession of his Lands or Tenements; and *Disseisee* is the Person so put out.

Disseisoress, is she that disseiseth another of Lands, &c.

Dissenters, denotes Non-Conformists, or Separatists from the Church and the Service and Worship thereof.

Distress, in general, is taken for any Thing that is seised or distrained for Rent in Arrear, and unpaid, or other Duty unperformed, even tho' the Property of the Thing *distrained* belongs to a Stranger; yet if they are Beasts belonging to a Stranger, it is necessary, that they were Levant and Couchant upon the same Ground: that is to say, that the Beasts continued upon the Ground for a certain Space, and that they have rested themselves well there; otherwise they are not distrainable, either for Rent or Service. The Effect of a *Distress* is to compel the Party either to replevy the Things distrained, and contest the Taking, by Action of Trespass against the Distrainer, or rather to oblige him to compound, or pay the Debt or Duty for which he was distrained. There are likewise compulsory Distresses in Actions, to cause a Person to appear in Court; of which Sorts there is a *Distress Personal*, of a Person's moveable Goods, and the Profits of his Lands, &c. for Contempt in not appearing after summoned; and a *Distress Real*, of one's immoveable Goods. *Distress* may be either *Finite*, or *Infinite*: *Finite*, is that which is limited by Law; here often it is to be made, in order to bring the Party to Trial of the Action: And *Infinite*, is without any Limitation, till the Party appears; as against a Jury, which refuses to appear upon a Certificate of Assise, the Process is *Venire facias, Habeas Corpora*, and *Distress Infinite*. It is likewise divided into a *Grand Distress*, and an *Ordinary Distress*, of which the former extends to all the Goods and Chattels that the Party has within the County. See *Old Nat. Brev.* 43, 113. *Brit. c.* 26. *fol.* 52.

District, signifies a Place of Jurisdiction, such as the Territory or Circuit in which a Person may be compelled to appear: It likewise denotes the Place wherein one has the Power of distraining.

Distringas, is a Writ directed to the Sheriff or other Officer, whereby he is commanded to distrain a Person for a Debt to the King, &c. or for his Appearance at a certain Day. This Writ was formerly called *Constringas*. See *Fitz. Nat. Brev.*

Distringas Juratores, is a Writ directed to the Sheriff, commanding him to distrain upon a Jury to appear, and to return Issues on their Lands, &c. for Non-appearance.

Dividend in the Exchequer, is said to signify *one Part of an Indenture*.

Dividend in the University, denotes that Share, which every one of the Fellows do equally *divide* among themselves of their annual Stipend.

Dividend in Law Proceedings, is taken for dividing of Fees and Perquisites between Officers of the Court, and which arise from Writs, &c.

Divisa, has divers Significations, it being sometimes used for a *Device, Award* or *Decree*; sometimes for a Devise of a Portion or Parcel of Land, &c. by Will; and sometimes for the Bounds of a Parish, or Farm.

Divise, See **Devise**.

Divorce, denotes a Separation of two who are actually married together, made by Law: And as it is a *Judgment Spiritual*, if there be Occasion, it ought to be reversed in the Ecclesiastical Court. The usual Divorces are of two Sorts, viz. *a Mensa & Thoro*, from Bed and Board; and *a Vinculo Matrimonii*, from the Bond or Tie of Marriage. That of *a Mensa & Thoro*, does not dissolve the Marriage, since the Cause of it is subsequent to the Marriage, and at the same Time supposes the Marriage to be lawful: And this *Divorce* may be on Account of Adultery in either of the Parties, for Cruelty of the Husband, &c. Now as it does not dissolve the Marriage, so it does not debar the Woman of her Dower; neither does it bastardize the Issue, nor render void any Estate for the Life of Husband and Wife, &c. The Woman upon this Divorce must sue by her next Friend; and she may also sue her Husband for Alimony. A Divorce *a Vinculo Matrimonii*, intirely dissolves the Marriage and renders it void from the Beginning, the Causes thereof being precedent to the Marriage; a *Præcontract* with some other Person, Consanguinity or Affinity within the *Levitical* Degrees, Impotency, Impuberty, &c. The Consequences attending this last Divorce is, that Dower is thereby gone, and the Children begotten between the *divorced Parties* become Bastards.

Diurnalis, is taken to be as much Land as can be ploughed in a Day by one Ox. This Word by some is wrote *Diuturna*.

Docket, or **Dogget** signifies a Brief in Writing made on a small Piece of Paper or Parchment, containing the Purport of a larger Writing. See *Practis. Attorn.*

Dog-draw, is an apparent Deprehension of an Offender against Venison in a *Forest*, where he is found drawing after a Deer by the Scent of a Hound led in his Hand: Or it is, where a Person has wounded a Deer or wild Beast, by shooting at him, or otherwise, and is caught with a Dog drawing after

DO

after him in order to receive it. See *Marwood*.

Do Law, denotes the same as make Law.

Dombec, is conjectured to have been a Book of Statutes of the *English Saxons*, wherein the Laws of the ancient *Saxon* Kings were contained.

Dome, or **Doom**, in general signifies a Judgment, Sentence or Decree.

Domesday, is a very ancient Record made in the Time of *William* the *Conqueror*, which now remains in the *Exchequer*, and consists of two Volumes, a greater and a less; the greater containing a Survey of the greatest Part of the Lands of *England*. Questions, whether Lands are *Ancient Demesne* or not, are to be decided by this Book, from whence no Appeal lies, it being a Book of that Authority, that even the *Conqueror* himself submitted thereto in some Cases wherein he was concerned.

Domes-men, are Persons appointed to hear and determine Suits and Controversies between Party and Party. See **Days-man**.

Domina, is a Title that was anciently given to Honourable Women, who in their own Right held a Barony.

Domo Reparando, is a Writ that lies for a Person against his Neighbour, by the Fall of whose House he is apprehensive Damage may be done to his own.

Donative, is a Benefice purely given and celebrated by the Patron, to a Man, without either Presentation, Institution by the Ordinary, or Induction by his Order. Anciently the King might found a Church or Chapel, and exempt it from the Jurisdiction of the Ordinary: He may likewise by his

DO

Letters Patent grant Licence to a common Person to found such a Church or Chapel, and to ordain it to be made **Donative**, and not Presentable; and that the Chaplain shall be deprivable by the Founder or his Heirs, and not by the Bishop, which seems to be the Original of Donatives in *England*. *Termes de la Ley*.

Donor, is he who gives Lands or Tenements to another in Fee, Tail, &c. And the Person to whom such Lands, &c. are given, is called the **Donee**.

Dote Assignanda, is a Writ that formerly lay for a Widow, where it was found by Office, that the King's Tenant was seised in Fee, or Tail at the Time of his Death, and that he held of the King in Chief, &c. In which Case the Widow was to come into the Court of *Chancery*, and there make an Oath that she would not marry without the King's Leave; upon which she was to have this Writ to the Escheator to assign her Dower, &c. Yet it was more usual to make the Assignment of the Donor in *Chancery*, and then to award a Writ to the Escheator, to deliver the Lands assigned to her.

Dote unde nihil habet, is a Writ of Dower, which the Widow may have against the Person that bought Land of her Husband in his Life, whereof he was seised in Fee, Tail, or of which she is endowable.

Dotis Admensuratione, or Admeasurement of Dower, is where the Widow holds more than her Share of her deceased Husband's Estate. See **Admeasurement**.

Double Plea, is where a Defendant alledges two several Matters in Bar of the Plaintiff's Action, where one is sufficient, which will not be allowed; as where a Person pleads several

ral Things, the one having no Dependance upon the other, on which Account such his Plea is accounted *double*, and will not be admitted; but where the Things pleaded have a mutual Dependance on each other, and the Party cannot leave the last Plea without the first, there the Whole will be received. If a *double Plea* be wrong, and the Plaintiff reply thereto, and take Issue of one Matter pleaded, and that be found against him, he cannot afterwards plead in Arrest of Judgment, he having by his Replication allowed the whole Plea to be good.

Double Quarrel, is a Complaint made by any Clerk, or other to the Archbishop of the Province, against an inferior Ordinary, for delaying Justice in any Spiritual Cause; as to give Sentence, institute a Clerk or the like; the Effect whereof is, that the Archbishop taking Notice of the Delay, directs his Letters, under his Authentical Seal, to all Clerks of his Province, commanding them to admonish the said Ordinary within a certain Time limited, to do the Justice required, or otherwise to appear before him or his Official, there to alledge the Cause of his Delay; and, *lastly*, To signify to the Ordinary, that if he neither perform the Thing enjoined, nor appear to shew Cause against it, he himself in his *Court of Audience* will forthwith proceed to act the Justice required. This is termed *Double Quarrel*, because the Complaint is usually made both against the Judge, and the Party at whose Suit Justice is delayed.

Dow, comes from the *Latin* Word *Do*, signifying to give or bestow.

Dowager, is a Title that is applied to the Widows of Princes, Dukes, and other great Personages.

Dower, denotes that Portion the Law allows a Widow out of the Lands of her deceased Husband. *Dower*, by the Common Law is a third Part of such Lands or Tenements, as the Husband was solely seised of in Fee, or Tail, during the Coverture; and this the Widow is intitled to enjoy during her Life. There is likewise *Dower by Custom*, which is that Part of the Husband's Estate whereto the Widow is intitled after her Husband's Decease, by the Custom of some Manor or Place, so long as she shall live sole and chaste; which is frequently more than a third Part; for in some Places she shall have Half the Land, and in others the Whole during Life; and this is called her *Free Bench*. There was formerly another Kind of Dower, called *Dower ad Ostium Ecclesiæ*, which was made by the Husband immediately after the Marriage, who expresly named such particular Lands, whereof his Wife should be endowed: And as the Certainty of the Land was openly declared, the Wife after her Husband's Decease might enter upon the Land of which she was endowed, without any other Assignment. There was also *Dower ex Assensu Patris*, which was likewise of Lands named by a Son, being then Husband, with the Consent of his Father; and this was always reduced into Writing as soon as the Son was married. To these we may add another Kind of Dower anciently in Use, *viz. Dower de la pluis Belle*, which was where the Wife was endowed with the fairest Part of her Husband's Estate: However the two first of these Writs are only now in Use: Yet, as in great Estates *Jointures* in

Lieu

Lieu thereof are usually made, these Actions of *Dower* are not so frequently brought as formerly.

Dowry, was in ancient Time applied to what the Wife brought with her in Marriage, commonly called *Maritagium*, or *Marriage Goods*, which are more properly termed Goods given in Marriage.

Drift of the Forest, denotes nothing more than a View or Examination of what Cattle are in the Forest, in order to know whether it be surcharged or not; and whose Beasts are there, and whether such are commonable, in order to discover whether any Cattle of Strangers be there, which ought not to common. See *Manwood*.

Droit, (from the *French*, signifying Right) is deemed to be the highest Writ of all other real Writs, and takes its Name of a *Writ of Right*, from the greatest Respect, and most assured and final Judgment being shewn to it. There are several Sorts of those Writs used in our Law, such as, *Droit de Advowson, Droit de Dower, Droit de Garde, Droit Patent, Droit Rationabili Parte, Droit sur Disclaimer*. See **Retto**.

Dry Exchange, is a Term formerly invented for the disguising of *Usury*, in which something was pretended to pass on both Sides, when in Fact nothing passed but on one Side, and on that Account that Practice was called *Dry*.

Dry Rent, denotes a Rent that is reserved without a Clause of Distress. See **Rent Seck**.

Duces tecum, is a Writ commanding a Person to appear at a certain Day in the Court of *Chancery*, and to bring with him certain Writings, Evidences or other Things, which the Court is minded to view.

Duces tecum licet languidus, is a Writ directed to the Sheriff, upon a Return that he is not able to bring his Prisoner without Danger of Death, he being *adeo languidus*; upon which the Court will grant a *Habeas Corpus* in Nature of a *Duces tecum licet languidus*.

Duel, in our Law did anciently denote a Fight or Combat between Persons in a doubtful Case for the Trial of the Truth; which Kind of Duel is now entirely in Disuse, and what we now term a *Duel*, is a Fighting between two upon some Quarrel precedent, in which if a Person be killed, both the Principal and Seconds are guilty of Murder, whether the Seconds engage or not. *H. P. C.*

Dum fuit infra ætatem, is a Writ which an Infant who has aliened his Lands, may have when he arrives to full Age, for the Recovery of what he so aliened.

Dum non fuit Compos Mentis, is a Writ which a Person that is not of sound Memory, having aliened his Lands or Tenements, shall have against the Alienee, on which he must alledge, that he was not of *Sane Memorie*, but being visited with Infirmity, lost his Discretion for a Time, so as not to be capable of making a Grant, &c.

Duodena, denotes a Jury of twelve Men.

Duodena Manu, are twelve Witnesses called to purge a Criminal of an Offence.

Duplex Querela, or **Double Quarrel**, is an Ecclesiastical Process.

Duplicate, is taken for the second Letters Patent granted by the Lord Chancellor in a Case wherein he had before granted one, tho' it is more commonly used for a Copy or Transcript of any Deed or Writing, Account, &c. It is likewise taken for a second Letter, written and sent to the same Party and Purpose, as a former, for Fear of Miscarriage of the first.

Duress, is where a Person is wrongfully imprisoned or restrained of his Liberty contrary to Law, till he executes a Bond or other Writing to another; or is threatned to be killed, wounded or beaten, if he does not do it: On which Account the Deed or other Writing so obtained becomes void in Law. *Duress* by some is joined together with *Manus*, that is to say, Hardship and Threatning; as if a Person under a just Dread of being imprisoned, killed, &c. enters into a Bond, &c. to the Person that threatens, it is *Duress per Minas*, and may be pleaded for the avoiding the Bond, yet it must be a Threatning of a Life or Member, or of Imprisonment, and not of a Battery alone, or the threatning to take away Goods, &c.

Dutchy Court, is a Court of the *Dutchy Chamber of Lancaster*, held at *Westminster* before the Chancellor of the same, for Matters concerning the Lands and Franchises of the Dutchy: The Proceedings in which Court are by *English* Bill, as in *Chancery*.

Duty, is any Thing that is known to be due by Law, and on that Account recoverable; for till recovered it is a *Duty*.

E.

Alderman, among the *Saxons*, denoted as much as Earl among the *Danes*: And now we call those *Aldermen*, who are Associates to the Mayor or Chief Officer in the Common Council of a City or Borrough Town. See **Alderman**.

Earl, is said to have been a great Title among the *Saxons*, and is the most ancient of the *English* Peerage, since there is no Title of Honour used by our present Nobility that was likewise in Use among the *Saxons*, except this of *Earl*.

Easement, is a Privilege or Convenience, which one Neighbour has of another, by Writing or Prescription, without Profit; such as a Way through his Land, a Sink, or the like.

Eberemorth, or **Eberemors**, was to signify bare or downright Murder; whence came the Word *Eberemurder*, bearing the like Signification.

Ecclesia, according to *Fitzherbert*, in our Law Proceedings is a Word intended for a Parsonage.

Ecclesiastical Jurisdiction. The Doctors of the Civil Law, tho' Laymen, are by *Stat.* 37 *H.* 8. *c.* 7. enabled to exercise Ecclesiastical Jurisdiction.

Edict, denotes an Ordinance, Command, or Statute.

Effractores, denotes Breakers, and is applied to *Burglars*, those that break open Houses to steal.

Effusio Sanguinis, denotes the Mulct, Fine, or Penalty anciently imposed for the Shedding of Blood.

Egyptians, vulgarly called *Gypsies*, are a counterfeit Kind of Rogues, who disguised themselves both in Speech and Apparel, and wander up and down the Country, pretending to tell Fortunes, cure Diseases, &c. whereby they abuse the ignorant common People, by stealing and pilfering from them every Thing that is portable, and which they may carry off undiscovered.

Ejecta, signifies a Woman deflowered, or cast forth from the Virtuous: So *Ejectus* denotes a *Whoremonger*.

Ejections

Ejectione Custodiæ, or **Ejectment de Gard**, is a Writ that lies against the Person that casts out the *Guardian* from any Land during the Minority of the Heir. There are two other Writs of the like Nature with this, the one called *Ravishment de Gard*, and the other *Droit de Gard*.

Ejectione Firmæ, or *Ejectment*, is a Writ or Action that lies for the Lessee for Years, on his being *ejected* before the Expiration of his Term, whether it be by the Lessor or a Stranger. It may be also brought by a Lessor against the Lessee, for Rent in Arrear, or holding over his Term, &c. Ejectment of late Years is become an Action in the Place of many real Actions, as *Writs of Right, Formedon*, &c. which had been very difficult, as well as tedious and expensive: And this is now become the common Action for Trial of Tithes, and recovering of Lands, &c. illegally held from the right Owner: Yet all Titles cannot be tried by this Action, as where Entry is taken away by *Discents, Fines* and *Recoveries, Disseisins*, &c. in which Cases an Ejectment shall not be brought.

Eire, or **Eyre**, denotes the Court of Justices *Itinerant*. These Justices anciently were sent with a general Commission into several Counties to hear such Causes as were termed *Pleas of the Crown*; which was done for the Ease of the People, who otherwise must have been hurried up to the Court of *King's Bench*, if the Cause were above the Jurisdiction of the County-Court.

Election, is where one is left to his own Free-Will, to take or do one Thing or another, as he pleases; as if *A.* covenants to pay *B.* a Pound of Coffee or Tea before *Easter*, it is at the Election of *A.* at all Times before *Easter*, which of them he will pay; but should he not pay it before the said Feast, then afterwards it is at the *Election* of *B.* to demand and recover which he pleases. So if a Man give to another one of his Horses in his Stable, in that Case the Donee shall have the *Election*, and be the first Agent, by taking or seizing of one of them. Likewise if a Justice of the Peace direct his Warrant to a Constable to bring the Party, when apprehended, before him or some other Justice of the Peace, it is in the *Election* of the Constable to carry the Person apprehended before what Justice he pleases.

Election of a Clerk of Statutes-Merchant, is a Writ that lies for a Clerk assigned to take *Statutes-Merchant*; and issues out of the Court of *Chancery*, upon Suggestion that the Clerk formerly assigned is gone to dwell at another Place, or is under some Impediment to attend the Duty of his Office, or has not Lands sufficient to answer Transgressions, in Case he should act amiss in his Office.

Election of a Verderer of the Forest, is a Writ which lies for the Choice of a Verderer, upon the Death or Removal of any such Officer of the Forest. This Writ is directed to the Sheriff, and the Verderer is to be *elected* by the Free-holders of the County.

Election of Members of Parliament. See **Parliament**.

Eleemosyna, signifies Alms, whence *Frank-almoigne* which denotes perpetual Alms; as Lands that were commonly given in ancient Times to religious Uses.

Eleemosyna Regis, otherwise **Eleemosyna Aratri**, is a Penny which King *Ethelred* ordered to be paid for every Plough throughout the Kingdom, towards the Support of the *Poor*.

Eleemosynarius, an Almoner. See **Almoner**.

Elegit, is a Writ of Execution which lies for the Person that has recovered Debt or Damages, or upon a Recognizance in a Court, against a Defendant that is not able to satisfie the same in Goods; and it is directed to the Sheriff, commanding him to make a Delivery of a Moiety of the Party's Lands and all his Goods, Oxen and Beasts of the Plough excepted: And the Creditor by Virtue thereof shall hold the said Moiety, until his whole Debt and Damages are paid and satisfied; and during that Time he is *Tenant by Elegit*: But this Writ ought to be sued out within a Year and a Day after the Judgment obtained. If such Tenant be put out within the Time, he shall have an Assise of *Novel Disseisin*, and afterwards a *Redisseisin* if Occasion require. If he commits Waste, the Defendant may have against him a Writ of *Venire facias ad computandum*, &c. by which it shall be inquired, whether he has levied all the Money, or only Part thereof; and in Case he has not levied the Money, then it must be inquired to how much the Waste amounts; and if the Waste amounts only to Parcel, then as much of the Money, as the Waste amounts to shall be deducted from the Sum that was to be levied: And if he has committed more Waste than the Amount of the Money to be levied, the other shall immediately be discharged of the said Money, recover the Land, and Damages for the Superfluity of the Waste made above that Money. There is another Kind of *Elegit* upon adjudging Execution against Tertenants, on which only one Moiety of the Lands, against which Execution is awarded, is extended by the Sheriff, and nothing is therein mentioned of any Goods or Chattels as in the other *Elegit*. *Termes de la Ley*.

Elisors. See **Elisors**.

Eloine, (from the *French*) signifies to remove or send away, and is used in 13 *Ed*. 1. *c*. 15. which enacts, that if such as be within Age be *eloined*, so that they cannot sue personally, the next Friends shall be admitted to sue for them.

Elongata, is a Return made by the Sheriff on a Replevin, that Cattle are not to be found or removed, so that he cannot make Deliverance, &c.

Elopement, is where a married Woman departs from her Husband, and cohabits with an Adulterer. A Woman thus forsaking her Husband is said to *elope*, and in that Case her Husband is not obliged to allow her any *Alimony*, or to be chargeable for Necessaries for her in any Kind. Where this *Elopement* is notorious, whoever gives her Credit, does it at his Peril. On an *Elopement*, the bare putting a Wife in the Gazette, or other Publick Papers, is not a legal Notice to Persons in general not to give her Credit; yet a Personal Notice given to particular Persons by the Husband, will be good. If the Wife departs from the Husband and continues with the Adulterer, without voluntarily returning, and being reconciled to her Husband, she forfeits her Dower.

Embargo, is a Prohibition upon Shipping, to prevent Vessels going out

out of any Port, and generally happens on the Breaking out of a War.

Emblements, are properly the Profits of Land sown; but it is sometimes taken for the Products that naturally arise from the Ground, as Grass, Fruit, Hemp, &c. In some Cases he that sowed the Grain shall have the *Emblements*, and in some not: As if Tenant for Life sow the Land, and afterwards die, his Executor shall have the *Emblements*, and not he in Reversion: But where Tenant for Years sows the Land, and before he has reaped, his Term expires, there the Lessor, or he in Reversion shall have the *Emblements*. If a Lessee at Will sows the Land, he shall have the *Emblements*; yet if he determine the Will himself he shall not have them, but the Lessor. Again, if the Lessee at Will sow the Ground, and the Lessor before Severance of the Corn enters, the Lessee in this Case shall have the *Emblements*.

Embraceor, is a Person that when a Cause is on Trial between Party and Party, comes to the Bar with one of the Parties, having received a Reward so to do, and speaks in the Case, or privily labours the Jury, or stands there to survey or overlook them, in order to awe them, or put them in Fear, or Doubt of the Matter; the Penalty of which Offence, by 19 *Hen.* 7. c. 13. is 20 l. and Imprisonment at the Discretion of the Justices: But Lawyers, Attornies, &c. may speak in the Cause for their Clients, without being deemed *Embraceors*. If a Party himself instruct a Juror, or promise any Reward for his Appearance, he in this Case is likewise an *Embraceor*: And a Juror may be also the same, where he by indirect Practices, gets himself sworn on the *Tales*, in order to serve on one Side. This Offence of *Embracery* is punishable upon Indictment at Common Law, as well as by Action on the Statute.

Embracery, is the Act or Offence of *Embraceors*. See **Embraceor**.

Emendals, is an old Word, but still used in the Accounts of the *Inner Temple,* where so much in *Emendals* at the Foot of an Account, denotes so much Money in the Bank or Stock of the House, for the Supply of Emergencies, &c.

Emendare, signifies to make Satisfaction or Amends for any Crime or Trespass committed. Hence a Capital Crime not to be atoned for, was said to be *inemendable.* Cowel.

Emendatio, was formerly used for the Power of *amending* and correcting Abuses to particular stated Rules, such as the Power of Inspecting into the Assise of Cloth, &c.

Empanel a Jury. See **Impanel**.

Encheson, is a *French* Word, and used in our old Law Books, &c. in the Sense of *on Occasion,* Cause or Reason wherefore any Thing is done.

Endeavour. If a Person, who has the Use of Reason, attempts or endeavours to commit a Felony, &c. he is punishable, tho' not to that Degree, as if he had actually committed it: As where one assaults another on the Highway, with an Intent to rob him, but takes nothing from him; this is not punishable as Felony, because the Felony was not accomplished, tho' as a Misdemeanor, it is liable to a Fine and Imprisonment. See 7 *Geo.* 2. c. 21. See **Intendment**.

Endowment, denotes the Bestowing or Assuring of a Dower to a Woman.

Woman. See **Dower**. This Word by a Metaphor is sometimes used for the settling a Provision on a Parson on the Building of a Church or Chapel, as well as the severing of a sufficient Portion of Tithes, &c. for a Vicar, towards his perpetual Maintenance, when the Benefice is apropriated. *Cowel*.

Enemy, according to its proper Signification, is an Alien or Foreigner, who in a publick and hostile Manner invades a Kingdom, or Country; and if such Aliens come to this Realm by themselves, or in Company with *English* Traitors, they are not punishable as Traitors, but are to be dealt with by Marshal Law: Yet where a Subject of a Foreign Nation comes into this Realm, and lives here under the King's Protection, and afterwards takes up Arms, &c. against the Government, in such Case he is punishable as a Traitor, and not as an Alien Enemy. See **Treason**.

Enfranchise, denotes to make free, or incorporate a Person into a Society, &c. It is likewise used where a Person is made a free *Denizen*, that being a Kind of Incorporation into the Common-wealth.

Enfranchisement, denotes a Person's being incorporated into a Society or Body Politick, as also the Act of incorporating. So he that is created a *Denizen*, is said to be *enfranchised*, he being thereby let into the Liberties in common with the Subjects of the Kingdom. Likewise a Person who is made a Citizen of *Bristol*, or other City, or a Burgess of any corporate Town, whereby he becomes a Partaker of those Liberties which appertain to such City or Corporation, is, according to the general Sense of the Word, an *enfranchised Person*. Where a Person is once enfranchised into the Freedom of a City or Corporation, he is said to have a Freehold in such Freedom during Life, and cannot forfeit the same, unless by endeavouring any Thing to the Prejudice of the Corporation. A Villein was anciently *enfranchised*, by being made free by his Lord, whereby he was rendered capable of the Benefits appertaining to Freemen.

Englecery, Englechery, Englechire, or **Engleshery**, is an ancient Word, denoting no more than that of being an *Englishman*: As where a Person was privily killed, such a one was deemed *Francigena*, which anciently was taken to comprehend every Alien, until *Englecery* was proved, that is to say, until it was made out that he was an *Englishman*. The Manner of proving the slain Party to be an *Englishman* was before the Coroner, by two Men that knew the Father, and two Women that knew the Mother. *Cowel*.

Ensient, signifies a Woman's being pregnant, or with Child.

Entail, signifies *Fee-Tail*, or *Fee* entailed, *viz.* abridged, and limited to certain Conditions, at the Will of the Grantor. See **Fee**. See **Tail**.

Entendment, in the Sense of our Law, signifies as much as the true Meaning or Signification of a certain Word or Sentence. Where a Point is in Doubt, it is sometimes made out by *Entendment*; as where an Inquisition is found before a Coroner, that a Person was murdered at *A.* which is a Liberty, and it is not in the Inquisition said at *A.* within the Liberty of *A.* yet this shall be good by *Entendment*, for this Reason, *viz.* that perhaps the Liberty may extend beyond the Town.

Enterpleader, denotes the Discussing or Trial of a Point incidentally falling

falling out, before the principal Cause can be determined; as anciently two several Persons being found Heirs to Land, the King was brought in Doubt, to which of them Livery ought to be made, on which Account they first were obliged to enterplead, that is to say, formally try between themselves which of them was the right Heir. At this Time, if one bring's Detinue against a Defendant upon Bailment of Goods, and another against the same Person upon a *Trover*, in such Case there shall be an *Enterpleader*, to ascertain which of the Persons has Right to the Action: And the Reason of this is plain, *viz*. That the *Enterpleader* is given purely for the Defendant's Security, that he may not be twice charged for one and the same Thing.

Entiertia, that is to say *Entireness*, is an express Contradiction to what we call a Moiety, it always denoting the whole of a Thing: As a Bond, Damages, &c. are said to be entire, when they cannot be divided or separated.

Entire Tenancy, is directly contrary to *several Tenancy*, it signifying a sole Possession in one Person, whilst the other denotes a joint or common Possession in two or more.

Entry, according to its proper Signification, denotes the taking Possession of Lands or Tenements, where a Person has Right of Entry thereon. It is also taken for a Writ of Possession. *Littelton* tells us, that an *Entry* into Lands, is where any Person enters into or takes Possession of any Lands, &c. in his own Person; and it is an actual Entry when made by the Person's Self, or an Attorney daily authorized by him that has the Right; or it is an *Entry in Law*, a *continual Claim* being an Entry implied by Law, and carrying the same Force with it. Writs of *Entry* relate to the Right of Property, and are of divers Sorts, they being distinguished into four Degrees, suitable to which those Writs are varied. The first is a Writ of *Entry sur Disseisin*, which lies for the Disseisee against the Disseisor, upon a Disseisin committed by himself. The second is a Writ of *Entry sur Disseisin in le per*, which lies for the Heir by Discent, who is termed to be in the *Per*, for that he comes in by his Ancestor. The third is a Writ of *Entry sur Disseisin in le per & cui*, which lies where the Feoffee of the Disseisor makes a Feoffment to another, in which Case the Disseisee shall have this Writ of *Entry sur Disseisin in le per & cui* of the Lands in which the other had no Right of *Entry*, but *by* the Feoffee of the Disseisor, to whom the Disseisor demised the same. The fourth is a Writ of *Entry sur Disseisin en le post*, which lies, when after a Disseisin the Land is removed from one Hand to another. There are five Things which put the Writ of *Entry* out of the Degrees, *viz*. 1. *Intrusion*, which is where the Disseisor dies seised, and a Stranger abates. 2. *Succession*, that is to say, when the Disseised is a Person of Religion, and dies, or is deposed, and his Successor *enters*. 3. *Disseisin* upon *Disseisin*, viz. when the Disseisor is disseised by another. 4. *Judgment*, When a Person recovers against the Disseisor. 5. *Escheat*, which is where the Disseisor dies without Heir, or commits Felony, &c. on which Account the Lord enters. In all these Cases a Disseisee or his Heir shall not have a Writ of Entry within the Degrees of the *Per*, but

but in the *Post*; for that they are not in by Discent, nor Purchase.

Entry ad communem Legem, is a Writ of Entry, that lies where a Termor for Life, Tenant for the Term of another's Life, Tenant by the Curtesy, or Tenant in Dower aliens, and dies, in which Case he in Reversion shall have this Writ against whomsoever is in Possession.

Entry ad terminum qui præteriit, is a Writ that lies against a Tenant for Years, who holds over his Term, and thereby keeps out the Lessor.

Entry in casu proviso, is a Writ which lies where a Tenant in Dower aliens in Fee for Term of Life, or for that of another's Life, tho' the Tenant in Dower be living, he in Reversion shall have this Writ. See *Stat. Glouc. c.* 7.

Entry in casu consimili, is a Writ provided by the *Stat. Westm.* 2. *c.* 24. and lies where Tenant for Life, or Tenant by the Curtesy aliens in Fee, in which Case he in Reversion shall have this Writ.

Entry sine assensu capitali, is a Writ which lies where a Bishop, Abbot or Prior, aliens Lands, &c. of Right belonging to the Church, without the Consent of the *Convent* or *Chapter*.

Entry causa matrimonii prælocuti, is a Writ that lies where Lands or Tenements are given to a Man upon Condition, that he take the Donor to his Wife within a limited Time, and he does not marry her within the Time limited, or espouses another, or otherwise disables himself from being capable to perform the Condition; then the Donor and her Heirs may have this Writ against him, or against any other Person that is in Possession of the Land.

Enboyce. See **Inboyce.**

Enure, signifies to take Effect, or to avail; as a Release made to a Tenant for Life shall enure to him in the Reversion.

Eodorbrice, in King *Alfred's* Days was used for Hedge-breaking.

Eorle. See **Earl.**

Episcopalia, were Synodals, Pentecostals, or other customary Payments from the Clergy to their Diocesan Bishop, and were formerly collected by the Rural Deans, and by them transmitted to the Bishops. *Cowel.*

Episcopus Puerorum. We are told it was a Custom in former Times for some Lay Person, about the Feast of the *Epiphany*, to plait his Hair, and take on the Garments of a Bishop, and therein to exercise *Episcopal* Jurisdiction, and to perform several ludicrous Actions; whence he was called *Episcopus Puerorum*, the Bishop of the Boys. See *Mon.* 3. *Tom.* 169.

Equity, is of two Kinds; the one abridges and takes from the Letter of the Law, whilst the other enlarges and adds thereto. The first is defined to be *the Correction of the Law generally made in that Part in which it fails*: As where an Act of Parliament is made, that whosoever commits such a Thing, shall be deemed a Felon, and suffer Death; yet if a Madman, or an Infant that has no Discretion commit the same, they shall not be deemed Felons, nor suffer Death for it. The breaking of Prison is made Felony in the Prisoner himself; yet if the Prison be on Fire, and those that are within break Prison to save their Lives, this will be excused by the Law of Reason. The like would be, where a Person, to save his Life, kills another that assaults him. The other *Equity* is defined to be an *Extension of the Words of the Law* *to Cases unexpressed*, yet having the same Reason: As the Statute which ordains, that in an Action of Debt against Executors, he that appears by Distress shall answer by Equity, extends to Administrators; for such of them as appears first by Distress shall by Equity of the said Act answer, *because they are of the like Kind. Termes de la Ley.* Likewise the Statute of *Glouc.* gives Action of Waste against the Person that holds Land for Life or Years; and by the Equity thereof a Man may have an Action of Waste against him that only holds for one Year, or Half a Year, notwithstanding that this is without the Words of the Statute, but within the Meaning of the same; and the Words that enact the one, *by Equity enact the other. Ibid.*

Equity of Redemption, is applied to Mortgages; as where Money being due on a Mortgage, the Mortgagee is desirous to bar the Mortgagor's Equity of Redemption, that is to say, his Right to redeem the Mortgage; the Mortgagee in this Case may oblige the Mortgagor either to pay the Money, or to be foreclosed, or cut off from his Equity of Redemption, which is a Thing frequently done in the Court of *Chancery*, where in Order to foreclose the Equity of Redemption, the Practice is to exhibit a Bill, to which an Answer being put in, and a Decree obtained, a Master of that Court certifies what is due for Principal, Interest and Costs, to be paid within the Time limited by the Decree; which being done, the Estate mortgaged is to be reconveyed to the Mortgagor; otherwise, for Default of Payment, the Mortgagor is decreed to be foreclosed from all Equity of Redemption, and absolutely to convey the mortgaged Premisses to the Mortgagee. If a Person has once mortgaged Lands, &c. and mortgages the same a second Time, without discovering the first Mortgage, for so doing he forfeits his *Equity of Redemption*, and the second Mortgagee in that Case may redeem, &c.

Equivalent, denotes a certain annual Sum payable to *Scotland* since the Union. See 1 *Geo.* 1. c. 27. 5 *Geo.* 1. See likewise **Scotland.**

Errant, or **Itinerant,** is a Title that is applied to Justices that go the Circuit, and likewise to Bailiffs at large. See **Eyre.**

Erraticum, denotes an *erring* or wandring Beast, such as a Waif or Stray.

Error, denotes some Mistake in the Process, or Pleading, on which the Writ that is brought for Remedy is called a *Writ of Error*. This Writ issues out of *Chancery*, and lies where a Person is grieved by the Proceedings and Judgment in any Court of Record that has Power to hold Plea of Debt, or Trespass, above the Value of 40 s. and it is returnable in the *King's Bench*, where if upon the Transcript of the Record it appears that there is *Error* in the Record or Process, the Judgment shall be reversed; otherwise it will be affirmed with double Costs. On what different Accounts this Writ lies, see 27 *Eliz.* c. 9. *Reg. Original*, and *Reg. Jud.* where a Writ of *Error* is brought in the *King's Bench* upon a Judgment obtained in the *Common Pleas*, and the Judgment is reversed or affirmed there, the Party grieved may have a Writ of *Error* returnable in Parliament. See 31 *Eliz.* c. 1.

Erthmiotum, was anciently used for a Meeting of the Neighbourhood, in order to compromise Differences, which was a customary Thing in former Days.

Escaldare, that is to say, to scald, was one of our ancient Tenures in *Serjeanty.*

Escambio, signifies a Licence that was formerly granted to assign over a Bill of *Exchange* to another beyond Sea. See *Reg. Orig.* 194. See likewise **Exchange.**

Escape, in a legal Sense, is a violent or privy Evasion out of some lawful Restraint; as where a Person being arrested or imprisoned, by Violence or otherwise, gets away before he is delivered by due Course of Law. There are two Sorts of Escapes, the one *voluntary,* and the other *negligent: Voluntary,* is when a Person arrests another for Felony or other Crime, and afterwards freely lets him go; in which Case the Party that permits such *Escape* is deemed guilty of the Crime committed, and consequently must answer for it: *Negligent Escape,* is where one is arrested, and afterwards *escapes* against the Will of the Person that arrested, or had him in Custody; and is not pursued by fresh Suit, and retaken before the Party pursuing has lost Sight of him. The Gaoler, &c. is fineable for *negligent Escapes;* and the Sheriff is not answerable for the Gaoler, only in Civil Cases. There may be an *Escape* without an Arrest; as where Murder is committed in the Day-Time, and the Murderer gets away untaken, for which the Town where the Murder was done shall be amerced. It is to be observed, that a Person may be said to *escape,* notwithstanding he always continues in Prison: As where one is in Prison upon two Executions at the Suit of two several Persons, and the old Sheriff delivers him over by Indenture to the new Sheriff, according to the usual Course, and in that Indenture no Mention is made of one of those two Executions; this Omission in Law shall be deemed an *Escape,* for which the old Sheriff shall answer, notwithstanding the Execution was Matter of Record, of which the new Sheriff might have taken Notice: Yet it is otherwise where an old Sheriff dies, in which Case it behoves the new Sheriff at his Peril to take Notice of all the Executions, that are of any that he finds in the Gaol: But even in the Case where the old Sheriff dies, and a Prisoner under Execution breaks the Gaol, and afterwards goes at large, this is no *Escape;* for this Reason, that upon the Death of a Sheriff all the Prisoners are in the Custody of the Law, until a new one be made.

Escape Warrant, is a Process that issues out against any Person committed or charged in Custody in the *King's Bench* or *Fleet Prison,* in Execution, or on mesne Process, &c. who afterwards, without being duly discharged from the same, takes upon him to go at large: And this Warrant is obtained on Oath made thereof before a Judge of the Court in which the Action was brought, and is directed to all Sheriffs, &c. throughout *England,* commanding them to retake the Prisoner, and to commit him to the County-Gaol next to the Place where taken, there to remain till the Debt is fully satisfied. Upon this Warrant a Person may be apprehended on a *Sunday.* See 1 *Ann. c.* 6. See also 5 *Ann. c.* 9. which empowers the Judges of the respective Courts just mentioned, to issue Escape Warrants, on Oath made before Persons

sons by them commissioned to take Affidavits in the Country, the same being first filed.

Escapio quietus, relates to an *Escape* of Beasts in a Forest; wherefore to be by Charter *Quietus de escapio*, is to be delivered from that Punishment which by the Forest Laws lies upon those Persons whose Beasts are found within the Land forbidden.

Escheat, denotes any Lands, Tenements or other Things that casually fall to a Lord within his Manor, by Way of Forfeiture, or by the Death of his Tenant having no Heir general or special. This Word is also sometimes used for the Place or Circuit, in which the King or other Lord has *Escheats* of his Tenants. It is also used for a Writ that lies where a Tenant having an Estate in Fee, Lands or Tenements holden of a superior Lord, dies without any Heir, in which Case the Lord may have this Writ against the Person in Possession of the Lands, &c. after the Tenant's Death, and shall thereby recover the same in lieu of his Services.

Escheator, was an Officer anciently appointed by the *Lord Treasurer* in every County, to observe the Escheats due to the King; and his Office was to certify the same into the *Chancery* or *Exchequer*, and to find Offices after the Death of the King's Tenants that held by Knights Service. As this Office had its chief Dependance on the Court of Wards, it is now entirely laid aside. *Cowel*.

Escheccum, was formerly used for a Jury or Inquisition.

Eschequer. See **Exchequer**.

Escrow, denotes a Deed delivered to a third Person, to be the Deed of the Party making it, upon a future Condition, that, when a certain Thing is perform'd, it is to be delivered to the Party to whom it was made.

Escuage, was a Kind of Knight's Service, termed *Service of the Shield*, by which the Tenant at his own Charge was bound to follow his Lord into the Wars. It has likewise been taken for that Duty which such as held Lands under that Tenure were bound to make to their Lord, when they neither went to the Wars, nor provided any other in their Place; and this was performed in Lieu of all Services. This Word has also been used to signify a reasonable Aid, demanded and levied by the Lord of his Tenants that held by Knight's Service. See *Chivalry*.

Esingæ. The Kings of *Kent* were so called from the first King *Ochta*, whose Surname was *Ess*.

Esketores, was used to signify Robbers, or Destroyers of other Mens Lands, &c.

Eskippeson, is said to have anciently signified Shipping, or Passage by Sea.

Esnecy, denotes a private Prerogative allowed to the eldest *Coparcener*, where an Estate has descended to Daughters for Want of an Heir Male, to chuse first after the Estate of Inheritance is divided.

Esplees, signifies the Profit or Commodity which is to arise or be taken from a Thing: As of a Common, the taking of Grass by the Mouths of the Beasts that common there; of an Advowson, the taking of gross Tithes by the Parson; of Wood, the selling of Wood; of an Orchard, the selling of Apples or other Fruit growing there; of a Mill, the Taking of Toll, &c. In a Writ of Right of Land, Advowson, &c. the Demandant ought to alledge in his Count, that he or his Ancestors took

took the *Esplees* of the Thing demanded, otherwise the Pleading will not be good. *Termes de la Ley*.

Espousals, denotes a Contract or Promise made between a Man and a Woman to marry each other; and in all Cases where Marriages may be consummated, Espousals go before. Marriage is termed to be an *Espousal de præsenti*, and a joining together of a Man and Woman in a constant Society.

Esquire, was anciently the Person that attended a Knight in Time of War, and carried his Shield; whence he was in *French* called *Escuier*, and in *Latin*, *Armiger*, that is, to say, *Armour-Bearer*. Those, to whom this Title is now of Right due, are Noblemens younger Sons; and the eldest Sons of such younger Sons; the eldest Sons of Knights, and their eldest Sons; the Officers of the King's Courts, and of his Houshold; Counsellors at Law, Justices of the Peace: Yet these latter are only *Esquires* in Reputation. A Justice of the Peace holds this Title no longer than during the Time he is in Commission, in case he be not otherwise qualified to bear it; but a Sheriff of a County being a superior Officer, holds the Title of *Esquire*, during Life, in regard to the great Trust reposed in him.

Esquires of the King, are such as have that Title by *Creation*, the Formality of which you may read in *Camd*.

Essendi quietum de Tolonio, is a Writ that lies for the Citizens or Burgesses of any City or Corporation, that by Charter or Prescription ought to be exempted from *Toll*, in case the same is exacted of them.

Essiors, are Persons nominated by a Court of Law, to whom, on a Challenge made to the Sheriff and Coroners, a Writ of *Venire facias* is directed to impanel a Jury; which Writ the *Essisors* return in their own Names, with a Panel of those of the Jurors.

Essoine, denotes an *Excuse* for the Person that is summoned to appear and answer to an Action, &c. by Reason of Sickness, or other just Cause of Absence: And it is of the Nature of an *Imparlance*, a Craving of a longer Time that lies in Real, Personal and Mix'd Actions. There are divers Causes that serve to *Essoin*, the chief of which are these, *viz.* 1. *Essoin de ultra Mare*, when the Defendant is beyond Sea, which will entitle the Defendant to have Forty Days granted him. 2. *De Terra Sancta*, when the Defendant was on an Expedition to the *Holy Land*, where he will have a Year and a Day. 3. *De Malo veniendi*, when the Defendant, being infirm, is not able to come, which is termed the *Common Essoin*. 4. *De malo Lecti*, when the Defendant is sick in Bed; on which the Defendant may be viewed by four Knights. 5. *De Servitio Regis*, which lies in all Actions, except in Assise *de Novel Disseisin*, Writ of *Dower*, *Darrein Presentment*, and in Appeal of Murder. The *Essoin* Days in Court is regularly the first Day of every Term; yet the fourth Day after is allowed by Way of Indulgence.

Essoin de malo Ville, is where a Defendant appears in Court the first Day, but is gone away without Pleading; and afterwards by being surprized by Sickness, &c. cannot attend, and therefore sends two *Essoiners* to declare in open Court, that he is detained by Sickness in such a *Village*, and on that Account he cannot attend, which will be admitted, it lying on the Plain-

Plaintiff to prove, whether the *Essoin* is true or not.

Essoins and Proffers. See **Proffer.**

Establishment of Dower, signifies the Assurance of Dower made to the Wife by the Husband, or some Friend acting on his Behalf, on Marriage: And Assignment thereof denotes the Setting out of such *Dower* by the Heir afterwards, pursuant to the Establishment.

Estandard. See **Standard.**

Estate, denotes that Title or Interest that a Person has in Lands, &c. As *Estate-simple*, otherwise termed *Fee simple*; and *Estate conditional*, which, as *Littleton* says, is either upon *Condition in Deed*, or upon *Condition in Law*. *Estate upon Condition in Deed*, is where a Person by Deed enfeoffs another in Fee, reserving to him and his Heirs a certain annual Rent to be paid at limited Times, upon Condition, that if the Rent be behind, it shall be lawful for the Feoffor and his Heirs to re-enter upon the Lands, &c. granted. *Estate upon Condition in Law* is such as carries a Consideration in Law annexed to it, not specified in the Writing; as where one by Deed grants to another the Office of a Parkership for Life; here it is implied by Law, that the Grantee shall enjoy this Office for Life, on Condition that he shall so long well and truly keep the Grantor's Park. *Estates* are either *Real* or *Personal*, otherwise distinguished into *Freeholds*, which descend to the Heirs; or *Chattels*, which go to the Executors or Administrators.

Estoppel, is an Impediment or Bar to an Action, which arises from a Person's own Fact, who otherwise might have had the Action: As where a Tenant by Collusion aliens to another, and the Lord afterwards accepts the Service of the Alienee; the Lord by so doing debars himself of the Wardship of his Tenant's Heir. This Word by *Co. lib.* 2. 4. is defined to be a Bar or Hindrance to one to plead the Truth; and he does not restrain this Bar to the Impediment given to a Person by his own Act only, but likewise by another's.

Estovers, (from the *French*) signifies to supply with Necessaries, and is in Law most generally taken for certain Allowances of Wood made to Tenants, such as *House-bote*, *Hedge-bote*, and *Plough-bote*; as if one has in his Grant these general Words, viz. *Reasonable Estovers in the Woods*, &c. he may thereby claim all those three. *Termes de la Ley*.

Estray, denotes any Beast that is not wild, which is found in a Lordship, and not owned by any Person; in which Case it being cried, according to Law, in the two next Market-Towns adjacent, and not claimed by the Owner within a Year and a Day, it becomes the Property of the Lord of the Soil or Liberty. If the Beast proclaimed stray to another Lordship within the Year, the first Lord may not retake it, for this Reason, that until the Expiration of the Year and Day he has no Property therein. In Case the *Estray* was not duly proclaimed, the Owner may take it again at any Time; and where it is legally proclaimed, if the Owner claims it within a Year and a Day, he shall have it again, upon paying the Lord for the Keeping thereof.

Estreat, denotes a true Copy, Duplicate or Note of an original Writing or Record, especially Fines, Amercements, Penalties, &c. set down in the Rolls of a Court,

Court, to be levied by the Bailiff or other Officer. Estreats likewise relate to Fines for Crimes and Offences, Defaults and Omissions of Persons concerned in Suits, and also to Officers; Non-appearance of Defendants and Jurors, &c. Before Process issues to levy Forfeitures on Recognizances to the King's Use, the Recognizances must be first *estreated* into the *Exchequer*, by Sheriffs of Counties.

Estrepement, denotes any Spoil made by Tenant for Life, upon any Lands, &c. to the Prejudice of the Reversioner; and it is also taken to signify the making Land barren by continual Ploughing, and thereby drawing out the Heart of the Ground, without manuring or other good Husbandry, by which Means it becomes impaired. It may likewise be applied to the Cutting down of Trees, or lopping them further than the Law allows. This Word is also made Use of for a Writ that lies in two Cases, viz. The one is where a Person having an Action depending, as a *Formedon*, a *Writ of Right*, &c. sues to prohibit the Tenant from committing Waste, during the Suit: The other is for the Demandant, who is adjudged to recover Seisin of the Land, and before Execution sued out by the Writ *Habere facias Seisinam*, in order to prevent Waste being made before he can get into Possession.

Etheling, or **Ætheling**, was, among the *English Saxons*, the Title of the King's eldest Son.

Evasion, is a cunning Endeavouring to evade or set aside, or to escape the Punishment of the Law, which is not to be endured; as where one declares to another that he will not strike him, but will give him a Shilling to strike first; and accordingly the Person spoke to does strike, the Returning the Stroke in this Case is not justifiable; and were the Person that first struck to be killed, it would be Murder; since no Person is to evade the Justice of the Law by any such Pretence to screen his Malice; neither can any be allowed to plead Ignorance of the Law, in order to evade it.

Eves-droppers, are those that stand under the *Eves*, *Walls* or *Windows* of a House, by Day or Night to listen after News, and convey it to others, and by that Means raise Strife and Contention in the Neighbourhood; and therefore are termed *Evil Members of the Common-wealth*; and by Stat. *Westm.* 1. c. 33. they are upon a Presentment punishable in a Court Leet, or on an Indictment at the Quarter-Sessions.

Eviction, denotes a Recovery of Lands or Tenements by Law. When Lands, &c. are evicted before the Rent reserved on a Lease becomes due, the Lessee shall not be liable to pay any Rent. Likewise, if on an Exchange of Lands, &c. either of the Parties is evicted of the Lands, &c. passed in Exchange, the Party evicted may in such Case re-enter on his own Lands.

Evidence, in general denotes any Proof, whether it be the Testimony of Persons, Records or Writings. The Reason that it takes this Name of *Evidence* is, that the Point at Issue in a Cause depending, is thereby to be made *evident* to the Jury; for Proofs ought to be evident and clear. See *Co. Lit.* 283. As to *Evidence*, Witnesses cannot testify a Negative; and no certain Number of Witnesses are required by the Common Law, tho' in some Cases by Statute it is. The Testimony of a single *Evidence*

EX

dence is allowed as sufficient for the Crown in all Causes, except Treason, where there must be two. *Evidence* by Records or Writings, is where Acts of Parliament, Statutes, Judgments, Fines and Recoveries, Proceedings of Courts, and Deeds, &c. are admitted as *Evidence*. And here it is to be observed, that the printed Statute Book is good Evidence upon a general Act of Parliament, which need not be pleaded; but in the Case of a private Act it is otherwise; for there it must be pleaded, and examined by the Records of Parliament before it can be admitted in *Evidence*.

Evagium, or **Evvage**, is the same with Aquage, and denotes a Toll formerly paid for the Passage of Water.

Evvbrice, (from the *Saxons*) denotes *Adultery*.

Ewe, (from the *Germans*) was used by the *English Saxons*, and signifies a Law.

Exaction, is a Wrong done by an Officer, or any Person in pretended Authority, in taking a Reward or Fee that is not countenanced or allowed of by Law. Most of our *English* Expositors seem to confound the Sense of this Word with that of *Extortion*; wherefore see *Extortion*.

Exactor Regis, has been sometimes taken for the Sheriff, tho' generally any one that exacts or collects the publick Monies, &c. who is properly called the *King's Exactor*, or *Collector*.

Examination, denotes an Enquiry into Facts charged against Felons by a Civil Magistrate, who is authorised to *examine* the Felons apprehended, and Witnesses before the Felon is committed; and upon the Committing such Offender, the Magistrate must bind the Ac-

EX

cusers over to appear and give Evidence at the *Old Baily*, the next Assises, &c. to which the Examinations are to be certified. See 2 & 3 *Ph. & M.*

Examiners in Chancery, are two Officers of that Court, who upon Oath examine Witnesses produced by either the Complainant or Defendant in a Cause depending there (in Case such Witnesses live in *London*, or near it) upon such Interrogatories as the Parties in any Suit exhibit for that Purpose. Sometimes the Parties themselves are, by particular Order, also *examined*. In the Country, above twenty Miles from *London*, Witnesses, instead of being examined by an *Examiner*, are on the Parties joining in Commission, *examined* by Commissioners, who are usually Counsellors or Attornies not concerned in the Cause.

Exannual Roll, was a *Roll* wherein, according to the old Way of exhibiting *Sheriff's Accounts*, the illeviable Fines and desperate Debts were transcribed: And this Roll was yearly read over to the Sheriffs, to see what might be gotten.

Excambiators, was anciently used to denote Exchangers of Land; and it is supposed they were such as we now call *Brokers*, who transact Business upon the Exchange between Merchants.

Exception, is a Term used in our Law, denoting a Stop or Stay to an Action, &c. It is divided into *Dilatory* and *Peremptory*; in Proceedings at Common Law: But in *Chancery*, it is what is alledged against the Sufficiency of an Answer, &c. And *Exception* in its Nature is no more than a Denial of what is taken to be good by the other Party, either in Point of Law or Pleading.

Exception in Deeds and Writings, is a saving a particular Thing out of a general one granted by Deed; as a Shop, Cellar, or Room out of a House, a Field or Close out of Land, &c.

Exchange, in our Law, is peculiarly used for that Compensation which the Warrantor must make to the Warrantee, Value for Value, in Case the Land warranted be taken from the Warrantee: And where a Person is seised of certain Lands or Tenements, and another is seised of other Lands, &c. those two Persons may exchange their Lands, &c. so that each of them shall have the other's Lands to him so exchanged, in Fee, Tail, or for Term of Life: But it must be observed, that, in *Exchange*, the Estates limited must be equal, seeing that, should one have an Estate in Fee in his Land, and the other an Estate in the other Land only for Term of Life, or in Tail, such *Exchange* is void on account of the Inequality; but if the Estates be equal; as an Estate in Fee for another in Fee, Tail for Tail, &c. this *Exchange* is good, tho' the Lands *exchanged* be not of equal Value. The Form of a Deed of Exchange of Lands, you may see in the *Young Clerk's Magazine*. There is likewise *Exchange* among Merchants, which is a Commerce of Money, that is to say, a *Bartering* or *Exchanging* of the Money out of one City or Country for that of another. There is also *Exchange* of Church-Livings, which is now but seldom used; yet if two Parsons by an Instrument in Writing agree to *exchange* their Benefices, and in Order thereto, resign them into the Hands of the Ordinary, the Exchange in such Case being executed by both Parties, is good; and therefore each may enjoy the other's Living, provided the Patrons present them again to each Living; for if they refuse to do that, or in Case the Ordinary will not admit them respectively, the Exchange is not executed; and in that Case either of the Persons may return to his former Living, even tho' one of them were admitted to the Benefice of the other.

Exchangers, are such as return Money by Bills of *Exchange*.

Exchequer, is one of our ancient Courts of Record, in which all Causes concerning the Revenues and Rights of the Crown are heard and determined, and where the Crown Revenues are received. It took this Name from the Cloth that covered the Table of the Court, which was partly coloured or chequered. In the *Exchequer*, by some, there are reckoned to be seven Courts, *viz.* the *Court of Pleas*, the *Court of Accounts*, the *Court of Receipts*, the *Court of the Exchequer Chamber*, (which is the Assembly of all the Judges on difficult Matters in Law) the *Court of Exchequer Chamber for Errors in the Exchequer, for Errors in the King's Bench*, and the *Court of Equity in the Exchequer Chamber*: But the *Exchequer* for Dispatch of Business is usually divided into two Parts, of which the one is chiefly conversant in the judicial Hearing and deciding of all Causes relating to the King's Coffers, formerly termed *Scaccarium Computorum*, the *Exchequer of Accounts*; the other is called the *Receipt of the Exchequer*, which is principally employed in the Receiving and Payment of Money. The judicial Part of the *Exchequer* is a Court both of Law and Equity: The Court of Law is held in the Office of Pleas, according

according to the Course of the Common Law, before the Barons; and in this Court the Plaintiff ought to be a Debtor or Accountant to the King; and the leading Process here is a Writ, of *Subpœna*, or *Quo Minus*, which last frequently goes into *Wales*, where no Process out of our Courts of Law ought to run, except a *Capias Utlagatum*. The Court of Equity is held in the *Exchequer Chamber* before the Treasurer, Chancellor, and Barons, tho' generally before the Barons only; the Proceedings in this Part of the Exchequer, are by *English* Bill and Answer, according to the Practice of the Court of *Chancery*, with this Difference, that the Plaintiff here must be careful to set forth, that he is Debtor to the King, whether he be so or not; and this he must do to keep up to the ancient Form of Proceeding here. In this Court of Equity the Clergy usually exhibit Bills for the Recovery of their Tithes, &c. The King's Attorney General does here exhibit Bills for any Matters concerning the Crown; and a Bill may be exhibited against him by any Person grieved in any Cause prosecuted against him on Behalf of the King; in which Case the Practice is for the Plaintiff to attend on the Attorney General with a Copy of the Bill, and procure him to give in an Answer thereto; in which Case the Attorney General may call in any Person interested in the Cause, or any Officer, or others, to instruct him in making his Answer, which is to be put in without Oath.

Excise, denotes a certain Duty imposed upon Beer, Ale, Cyder, and other Liquors, which had its Rise in King *Charles* the Second's Time. See 12 *Car*. 2. *c*. 23. since which Time there have been other Statutes made, whereby several additional Duties of *Excise* have been granted.

Excommengement, is the same with *Excommunication* in *English*.

Excommunication, is where a Person, by the Censure or Judgment of an Ecclesiastical Court, is excluded from the Communion of the Church, and from the Society of the Faithful; on which Account he becomes disabled to sue any Action in the King's Court: And if he remain *excommunicate* Forty Days, and will not be justified by his Ordinary, then the Bishop shall send his Letters Patent to the Chancellor to certify such *Excommunication*; whereupon the Sheriff shall be commanded to take the Body of the Person *excommunicated*, by a Writ termed *De Excommunicato Capiendo*, until he has made Satisfaction to the Church for the Contempt and Wrong done: And after that he is justified, the Bishop sends his Letters to the King, certifying the same; upon which the Sheriff shall be commanded by a Writ called *Excommunicato Deliberando*, to discharge him.

Excommunicato Capiendo. See **Excommunication**.

Excommunicato Deliberando. See **Excommunication**.

Excommunicato Recipiendo, is a Writ by which excommunicated Persons for their Obstinacy being committed to Prison, and afterwards illegally delivered, before they have given *Caution* (or *Bail*) to obey the Authority of the Church, are commanded to be retaken and imprisoned again.

Execution, is the compleating or finishing of some Act; as of a Judgment, Deed, &c. *Coke*, in his 6 *Rep*. 87. makes two Sorts of Executions, the one *final*, and the other

other with a *Quousque*, that tends to an End; An *Execution final*, is that which procures Money of the Defendant's Goods, or extends his Lands, and delivers them to the Plaintiff, who accepts the same in Satisfaction; and this is the End of the Suit, and the whole the King's Writ requires to be done. The *Execution* with a *Quousque*, tho' it tends to an End, yet is not *final*, as in the Case of a *Capias ad Satisfaciendum*, which is not *final*: seeing that the Defendant's Body is to be taken, in order that the Plaintiff may be satisfied his Debt, &c. and his Imprisonment is not absolute, it being only until the Plaintiff's Demands be satisfied. Where the Person taken in Execution dies, it is no Satisfaction in Law of the Debt, &c. and therefore the Plaintiff may have a *Fieri facias* against the Deceased's Goods, or an *Elegit* against his Lands. When once the Defendant's Body is charged in Execution on a *Capias ad satisfaciendum*, the Plaintiff cannot have another Execution, either against his Goods, or Lands, except where the Defendant escapes, is privileged, or dies.

Executione facienda, is a Writ that issues for the Execution of a Judgment, and is used several Ways. See *Reg. Orig.*

Executione facienda in Withernam, is a Writ that lies for taking the Person's Cattle, who has conveyed the Cattle of another out of the County, by which Means the Sheriff is not able to replevy them. See *Reg. Orig.*

Executione Judicii, is a Writ that issues and is directed to the Judge of an inferior Court, commanding him to do Justice therein, or to return reasonable Cause why he delays the Execution. If on this first Writ Execution be not done, or reasonable Cause shewn why it is delayed, an *Alias* shall issue, and afterwards a *Pluries*. And if upon this last Writ Execution be not done, or reasonable Cause returned for its not being so, the Party shall have an Attachment against him that delays the same; and this Attachment is made returnable in the *King's Bench* or *Common Pleas*.

Executor, denotes the Person that is appointed by another's last Will and Testament, to have the Execution of the same after his Decease, as well as the Disposing of the Testator's Goods and Effects, according to the Intent of the Will. An *Executor* is either *Particular*, or *Universal*: *Particular*, where only this or that Thing is committed to his Charge: *Universal*, where all is committed to his Charge. The Law accounts an Executor one Person with the Party whose Executor he is, he having all the Advantage of Action against others that he had, and at the same Time being subject to another's Action as he himself was.

Executor de son Tort, that is to say, *Executor of his own Wrong*, is the Person that takes upon him the Office of an Executor by Intrusion, he not being constituted so by the *Testator*, nor for Want thereof appointed by the Ordinary to administer. *Cowel*. Where an *Executor* of his own Wrong takes upon himself the Office of an Executor, without any lawful Authority for so doing, he becomes chargeable to the rightful Executor, as also to all the Testator's Creditors, and likewise to the Legatees, so far as the Goods or Effects amount to which he wrongfully possessed. An Executor of this Kind is created by some Act of Acquisition, transferring or making

making himself Master of any of the Personal Estate, Goods or Effects of the Deceased: But this does not extend to Acts of Necessity, Piety, or Charity. If a Person gets an Intestate's Goods into his Hands, he becomes chargeable for them as *Executor de son Tort*, until he makes Satisfaction for them to the Administrator.

Executory, is when an Estate in Fee that is made by Deed or Fine, is to be executed afterwards by Entry, Livery, &c. Leases for Years, Annuities, Conditions, &c. are termed *Inheritances executory*. See *Wood's Inst.* 293. But Estates executed are such as pass immediately to the Grantee without any After-Act required. *Executory Devise*, is where a Fee by Devise is vested in any Person, and is to be vested in another upon Contingency.

Exemplificatione, is a Writ that is granted for the Exemplification of an Original Record. See *Reg. Orig.* 290.

Exemplification of Letters Patent, is a Transcript or Duplicate of Letters Patent, made from the Inrollment thereof, and sealed with the Great Seal: And these *Exemplifications* are as effectual, and may be shewn or pleaded, as the *Letters Patent* themselves. It is held that nothing but Matter of Record ought to be exemplified. See 3 *Inst.* 173.

Exemption, denotes a Privilege to be free from Service or Appearance; as a Baron and Baroness, on Account of their Dignity, are *exempted* from being sworn upon Inquests: Also Knights, Clergymen, and others are exempted from appearing at the Sheriff's Turn, and Peers from being put upon Inquests. Persons of 70 Years of Age, Apothecaries, &c. are likewise exempted from serving on Juries: And Justices of the Peace, Attornies, &c. from Parish-Offices.

Exfrediare, is a Word anciently used to denote to break the Peace, or to commit some open Violence.

Ex gravi Querela, is a Writ which lies for the Person to whom any Lands or Tenements in Fee are devised by Will, and the Heir of the Devisor enters thereon, and detains them from the Devisee.

Exhibit, denotes a Deed or other Writing produced in a Chancery Suit to be proved by Witnesses, after the Examination of whom, the Examiner writes on the Back of the Deed or Writing exhibited, that the same was shewn to the Witness, at the Time of his Examination, and by him sworn to.

Exigendaries of the Common Pleas. See *Exigenters*.

Exigent, is a Writ that lies where the Defendant in a personal Action cannot be found, nor any Effects of his, within the County, whereby he may be attached or distrained: And this Writ is directed to the Sheriff, to proclaim and call the Defendant five County-Court Days successively, and charging him to appear under the Pain of *Outlawry*. It seems to take its Name from that of its exacting the Party, whose Appearance is required to answer the Law; for if he comes not at the last Day's Proclamation, he is said to be *Quinquies exactus*, five Times exacted, and then is outlawed.

Exigenter, is an Officer belonging to the *Common Pleas*, of which Kind there are four in Number; and their Office is to make out all Exigents and Proclamations in Actions, where Process of Outlawry lies; as also Writs of *Supersedeas*, as well as the *Prothonotaries*, upon such Exigents as were made in their Offices

Offices; yet *Jacob* tells us, that the Issuing out of *Supersedeas* is taken from these Officers by an Officer in the same Court, constituted by Letters Patent granted by King *James* the First.

Exilium, in a legal Sense, denotes a Destruction or Spoiling. It likewise seems to signify to be done to Tenants, by altering their Tenure, ejecting them, &c. See *Fleta*.

Exitus, denotes Issue or Offspring, and in our Law is applied to the Issues or annual Rents and Profits of Lands or Tenements.

Exlegalitus, is the Person that is prosecuted as an *Outlaw*.

Ex mero motu, are Words formerly used in the King's Charters and Letters Patent, to signify that he does what is contained therein, *of his own Will and Motion*; the End and Effect of which Words are to bar all Exceptions that might be taken to the Instrument, wherein they are contained, by alledging, that the King in granting that Charter, &c. was abused by false Suggestions.

Ex officio, takes its Name from the Power a Person has by Virtue of his Office to do certain Acts without being applied to: As a Justice of the Peace may *ex officio*, at his Discretion, demand and take Surety of the Peace, without any Complaint or Request made by any Person whatsoever.

Exoneratione sectæ, is a Writ that formerly lay for the King's Ward, to be freed or disburdened of all Suits to the County-Court, Hundred Court, &c. There is likewise a Writ of the same Nature, called *Exoneratione sectæ ad Curiam Baron'*, sued out by the Guardian of the King's Ward, and directed to the Sheriff or Steward of the Court, that they do not distrain him for not doing Suit at Court.

Ex parte, of the one Part, is a Term used in the Court of *Chancery*, where a Commission is taken out and executed by one Side or Party only, upon the other Party's neglecting or refusing to join. When both Parties proceed together, it is called a joint Commission.

Ex parte talis, is a Writ that lies where a Bailiff or Receiver, who after having Auditors assigned for passing his Accounts, cannot procure from them reasonable Allowance, but is cast into Prison; the Practice in which Case is, to sue this Writ out of the Court of *Chancery*, directed to the Sheriff, to take the four *Mainpernors* to bring his Body before the *Barons* of the *Exchequer*, at a certain Day, and to warn the Lord to appear at the same Time. *Cowel*.

Expectant, is in our Law used with the Word *Fee*; as *Fee-expectant*. Where Land is given to a Man and his Wife, and to their Heirs, they have a *Fee-simple*; but if it be given to them, and the Heirs of their Bodies begotten, they have in this Case a *Fee-tail*, and a *Fee-expectant*.

Expeditate, is a Word that is used in the Forest-Laws, signifying to cut out the Balls of great Dogs Feet for the Preservation of the King's Game; yet the Ball of the Foot of Mastives is not to be cut out, but only the three Claws of the Fore-foot to the Skin: And one of the Articles relating to the Forest is, to make Enquiry, whether all the Dogs or Mastives of Persons living near the Forest be expeditated according to the Laws of the Forest. Every Person that keeps any great Dog that is not *expeditated*,

EX

Expeditated, forfeits 3 *s*. 4 *d*. to the King.

Expenditors, denotes the Persons that disburse or *expend* the Money collected by the Tax for the Repairs of Sewers, after the same is paid into their Hands by the Collectors. The Steward or Officer that supervises the Repair of the Banks and Water-Courses in *Romney Marsh*, is called the *Expenditor*.

Expensis militum levandis, is a Writ that was anciently used, and was directed to the Sheriff for levying the Allowance for Knights of the Shire.

Expensæ Litis, Costs of Suit. See **Costs**.

Expensis militum non levandis, &c. is a Writ to hinder the Sheriff from levying any Allowance for the Knights of the Shire, upon such as held in Ancient *Demesne*.

Explees. See **Esplees**.

Exportation, denotes the Shipping and carrying out of this Realm Wares or Commodities to Foreign Countries. See **Importation**.

Ex post facto, in our Law, signifies something that is done after another that was committed before.

Extend, in a legal Sense, signifies to value the Lands or Tenements of a Person bound by Statute, who has forfeited the same, at such an indifferent Rate, as that by the yearly Rent the Creditor in Time may be paid his Debt. See *Fitz. Nat. Brev.*

Extendi facias, is a Writ generally called an *Extent*, whereby the Value of Lands or Tenements are commanded to be made and levied. See *Reg. Orig.*

Extent, bears two Significations, it sometimes signifying a Writ or Commission to the Sheriff, for the Valuing of Lands or Tenements; and sometimes the Act of the Sheriff or other Commissioner upon this Writ: And it has been more frequently taken to be an Estimate or Valuation of Lands, &c. which when performed to the utmost Value, is said to be the full Extent; and hence come our Extended Rents or Rack-Rents. If a Person be bound to the King by Specialty, or to answer by Statute, &c. and forfeits it; insomuch as by the yearly Rent of the Debtor's Lands, the Creditor is to be paid his Debt, the Creditor in this Case may sue out this Writ, directed to the Sheriff to deliver him the Lands and Goods to the Value of the Debt; and this is term'd a *Liberate*.

Extinguishment, in a legal Sense, denotes the Effect of Consolidation or Union; as where a Person has due to him a yearly Rent out of Lands, and afterwards purchases the Lands out of which the Rent arises. In this Case both the Property and Rent becoming united in one Possessor, the Rent is therefore said to be extinguished. So it is likewise where a Person has a Lease for Years, and afterwards buys the Property of what is leased; this by such Purchase becomes a Consolidation of the Property and the Fruits, and consequently is an *Extinguishment* of the Lease. In like Manner it is, if one have a Highway appendant, and afterwards purchase the Land in which the Highway is; then the Way is *extinct*: And so it likewise is of a Common Appendant. It is otherwise where a Person has an Estate in Land only for Life or Years, and his Fee-simple in the Rent, in which Case the Rent is not *extinguished*, but in Suspence for the Time: And if there be Lord, Mesne and Tenant, and the Lord purchase the Tenancy; then the Mesnalty

Mesnalty becomes *extinct*; yet the Mesne shall have the Surplusage of the Rent, if there be any, as Rent-Seck. *Cowel*.

Extirpation, is a judicial Writ, that lies either before or after Judgment, against a Person, who after a Verdict found against him for Land, &c. maliciously overthrows a House, or extirpates Trees upon it. See *Reg. Jud.* 13. 56, 58.

Extortion, denotes an unlawful taking or wresting from a Person Money, or other valuable Thing, under Colour of Office or Authority, either before the Time it is due, more than is due, or where nothing at all is due; and in an extensive Sense *Extortion* is taken for any Oppression by Power or Pretence of Right. In a Word, *Extortion* has been deemed more odious than Robbery, as it carries with it an Appearance of Truth and Justice.

Extracta Curiæ, denotes the Issues and Profits of holding a Court, arising from the Customary Dues, Fees and Amercements. *Cowel*.

Extracts. See **Estreats**.

Extrajudicial, is where Judgment is given in a Cause not depending in the Court where the same passed, or wherein the Judge has no Jurisdiction.

Extra-Parochial, signifies to be without the Bounds or Limits of a Parish; or where any Thing is exempt from the Duties of a Parish.

F.

Fabrick Lands, were such as were formerly given towards the Rebuilding or Repairing of Cathedrals or Churches; and anciently few or none but gave more or less to the Fabrick of the Cathedral or Parish Church where he dwelt.

Facto, denotes any Thing that is actually done.

Factor, is an Agent for Merchants who resides beyond the Seas, or in remote Parts, and is constituted by a Letter of Attorney or other Instrument to act for the Merchant that authorises him: And he may be concerned for several at a Time, who shall all run a Risque of his Actions. Where the Principal gives his Factor a general Commission to act for the best, he may in that Case do as he thinks fit, but otherwise he shall not. See *Lex Mercat.* 151.

Factorage, is the Allowance made to a Factor by the Merchant; and the Gain thereof is certain, be the Success what it will to the Merchant. See *Lex Mercat.* 155.

Factum, denotes a Person's own Act or Deed.

Faculty, is taken for a Privilege granted to a Person by Favour and Indulgence to do what by Law he ought not to do. For the granting of such there is a Court under the Archbishop of *Canterbury*, called the *Court of the Faculties*, the chief Officer whereof is stiled the Master of the Faculties, who is empowered to grant Dispensations; as to marry Persons without Banns first published, to eat Flesh on Days prohibited, to ordain a Deacon under Age, for a Son to succeed the Father in his Benefice, a Clerk to hold two or more Ecclesiastical Livings.

Fasting Men. See **Festing Men**.

Failure of Record, is where an Action is brought against a Person that alledges in his Plea Matter of Record in Bar of the Action, and avers to prove it by the *Record*;

Faint Action, to which the Plaintiff replies, *Nul tiel Record*, there is no such Record; whereupon the Defendant has a Day given him by the Court to bring it in; which if he fails to do, he is then said to *fail of his Record*, and the Plaintiff on that Account shall have Judgment.

Faint Action, that is to say a feigned Action, is such as that altho' the Words of the Writ are true, yet for some certain Causes the Plaintiff is not entitled to recover thereby: But a *False Action* is where the Words of the Writ are actually false. *Termes de la Ley.*

Faint Pleader, is a covinous, false and collusory Manner of Pleading to the Deceit of a third Party, against which, among other Things, it is thought the Statute 3 E. 1. c. 29. was made. *Termes de la Ley.*

Fair Pleader. See *Beaupleader*.

Fair, is a solemn or greater Kind of Market, granted to a Town by Privilege, for the more speedy and commodious providing of such Things as the Commonalty stands in Need of. It is incident to a *Fair*, that Persons there shall be privileged from being molested or arrested in it, for any other Debt or Contract, than what was at first contracted in the same, or at least promised to be paid there. *Termes de la Ley.*

Fait, a Deed. See *Deed*.

Faitours, denotes evil Doers, or idle Livers; and in the Statute 7 R. 2. c. 5. it seems to be synonymous with Vagabonds. *Termes de la Ley.*

Falcatura, was anciently used to signify one Day's mowing of Grass, which was a customary Service to the Lord by his inferior Tenants: Whence *Falcata* denoted the Grass fresh mowed, and laid in Swathes; and *Falcator* the servile Tenant performing the Labour.

Faldage, is a Privilege, of old reserved to Lords, of setting up Folds for Sheep in any Fields within their Manors, for the better Manurance thereof: And this was usually done as well with their Tenants Sheep, as their own.

Faldsey or **Fald-fee**, is a Rent or Acknowledgment paid by some customary Tenants for Liberty to fold their own Sheep on their own Land.

False Claim, is a Term used in the Forest Laws, and is where one claims more than his Due.

False Imprisonment, is a violent Trespass committed against a Person, by arresting or imprisoning him contrary to Law; or it is where a Person is detained in Prison without legal Process. This Word is likewise used for a Writ brought for this Trespass, for which considerable Damages are recoverable upon Actions brought.

False Judgment, is a Writ which lies where false Judgment is given in the County-Court, Court-Baron, or other Courts not of Record, whether the Plea be Real or Personal.

Falso retorno brevium, is a Writ that lies against the Sheriff for *false returning of Writs*.

Fanaticks, are Persons that pretend to Inspiration; as *Quakers*, *Anabaptists*, and other Sectaries, including *Dissenters* from the Church of *England*.

Fardel of Land, according to some Authors, denotes the fourth Part of a Yard-Land; but *Noy*, in his *Compleat Lawyer*, takes it to be only an eighth Part, saying, that two *Fardels* make a *Nook*, and four *Nooks* a *Yard-Land*.

FE

Farding-deal, denotes the fourth Part of an Acre.

Fare, signifies the Money paid for a Voyage or Passage by Water; and in *London* and other Cities, it denotes what is paid by a Person for being conveyed from one Part of the Town to another in a Coach or Chair.

Farley, or **Farleu**, is Money paid by the Tenants in the West of *England*, in Lieu of *Heriot*.

Farm, or **Ferm**, denotes the chief Messuage, in a Village or Town, whereto belongs great Demeans of all Sorts, such as Meadow, Pasture, Wood, Common, &c. and which has been used to be let for Term of Life, Years, or at Will, under a certain yearly Rent payable by the Tenant for the same.

Farmer, is he that tenants or occupies a *Farm*, or is Lessee thereof: And every Lessee for Life or Years is generally called a *Farmer*, tho' he occupies only a small House with a Parcel of Land.

Fat or **Vate**, is a Wooden Vessel made Use of by Malsters and Brewers for measuring of Malt with, the Contents of which are set down in 1 *Hen.* 5. c. 10. and 4 *Hen.* 6. c. 8. It has also the Name of a leaden Vessel or Pan, used by Brewers to run their Wort into.

Fatua Mulier, denotes a Whore.

Fautors, are such as are Favourers of others, as Abettors of Crimes, &c.

Feal, is a Word used in the Oath formerly taken by Tenants by Knights Service, who swore to their Lord to be *feal* and *leal*, that is to say, faithful and loyal.

Fealty, (from the *French*) denotes an Oath taken at the Admittance of each Tenant, to be true to the Lord of whom he holds his Land: And he that holds Lands by this Oath, holds in the freest Manner; for this Reason, that all that have Fee, hold *per Fidem & Fiduciam*, that is to say, by *Fealty* at the least. See *Smith de Repub. Angl. lib.* 3. c. 8.

Fee, in our Law has divers Significations: And, *first*, It is said to be that Estate which we hold by the Benefit of another, and for which we do Service, or pay Rent or other Acknowledgment to the chief Lord. Those that have written on this Subject divide all Lands and Tenements wherein a Person has a perpetual Estate to him and his Heirs, into *Allodium* and *Feudum*: *Allodium* is defined to be every one's own Land, &c. which he enjoys merely in his own Right, without making Acknowledgment of any Service, or Payment of any Rent to another; which indeed is a Property in the highest Degree: But *Feudum* is what we hold by the Benefit of another, and for which we owe Service, pay Rent, or perhaps both, to a Superior Lord. All the Land in *England*, except the Crown Lands which are in the King's own Hands, in Right of his Crown, is in the Nature of *Feudum* or *Fee*; seeing that, tho' many have Lands by Descent from their Ancestors, and others have at a high Rate purchased Land, yet such Land cannot come to any, either by Descent or Purchase, without the Burden that was imposed upon the Person that had *Novel Fee*, or that at first received it from his Lord; whence it is obvious, that no Person has *Directum Dominium*, that is to say the very Property or Demain, except it be the Prince himself in Right of his Crown: And yet, tho' he that has a *Fee*, has *jus perpetuum, & utile Dominium*, still he owes a Duty for it, and

and therefore it cannot be said to be simply his own; for he that can say the most of his Estate, says thus, *viz. I am seised of this or that Land or Tenement in my Demain, as of Fee*; which is as much as to say, it is my Demain or proper Land to me and my Heirs for ever; but still I hold it in Nature of a Benefit from another. *Cowel.* This Word *Fee* is sometimes used for the Bounds or Circuit of a Lordship or Manor; as the Lord of the *Fee*; that is to say, the Lord of the Manor. *Fee* is generally divided into *Fee absolute*, otherwise termed *Fee-simple*; and *Fee conditional*, otherwise called *Fee-Tail*. *Fee-simple* is where a Person is seised of Lands or Tenements to hold to him and his Heirs for ever. *Fee-Tail* is where a Person is seised of Lands, &c. with a Limitation to him and the Heirs of his Body, &c. See *Litt. lib.* 1. *c.* 2.

Fee-Expectant. See **Expectant**.

Fee-Farm, is where a Tenant holds of his Lord in *Fee*, paying annually the Value, at least of a fourth Part of the Land; without Homage, Fealty, or other Services to be done, more than are especially comprised in the Feoffment. The Nature of this Tenure is, that if the Rent be behind, and unpaid for two Years successively, then the Feoffor and his Heirs may bring an Action for the Recovery of the Lands, &c.

Felo de se, or **Suicide,** is where a Person lays violent Hands upon himself, and is the Occasion of his own untimely Death; as where one with Deliberation purposely kills himself, by Shooting, Hanging, Drowning, Stabbing, &c. But here it is to be observed, that the Person that commits this Felony, must be of the Age of Discretion, and *Compos Mentis*; for if an Infant under Fourteen Years of Age, an Ideot, a Lunatick during his Lunacy, or one distracted by a Disease, kill himself, it is not *Felony*. After a Verdict of *Felo de se* brought in before the Coroner, the Offender forfeits all his Goods and Chattels both Real and Personal.

Felony, is a Word that comprehends divers heinous Offences, for which the Offenders ought to suffer Death, and lose their Goods, &c. and every Offence that is in Degree next Petit Treason, is accounted Felony; as Murder, Theft, Suicide, Sodomy, Rape, wilful Burning of Houses, and the like. Felony differs from lighter Offences in this, that the Punishment thereof is Death, but not in all Cases; for *Petit Larceny*, which is the Stealing of any Thing under the Value of 12 *d.* is Felony; and the Reason it is accounted so is, because the Indictment against such an Offender must have these Words, *Feloniously took*, notwithstanding this Offence is not punished by Death, tho' the Offender forfeits his Goods, &c. There are reckoned two Sorts of Felonies, the one lighter, that is to say, such as for the first Offence may be allowed the Benefit of the Clergy; but the other, the heavier, may not: And these you may learn from the Statutes; for Clergy is always allowed, where it is not expresly taken away by a Statute. The Goods of Felons and Fugitives are by 17 *Ed.* 2. *c.* 1. granted to the Crown. Where the King grants to a Person and his Heirs the Goods of Felons, the Grantee, by 32 *Hen.* 8. cannot devise them, &c. they not being of an annual Value; yet where a Man is seised of a Manor, whereto they are appendant,

pendant, it is otherwise, seeing that they will pass as appurtenant.

Feme Covert, denotes a married Woman, who is also termed a *Covert Baron*.

Fence, is a Hedge or other Inclosure of Land, made for the greater Preservation and Improvement thereof. For not upholding and repairing of Fences, whereby Cattle get into the Ground of another, and do Damage, Action upon the Case lies.

Fence-Month, denotes a Month in which the Female Deer in Forests usually *fawn*, and on that Account it is made unlawful to hunt in Forests during that Time, which commences 15 Days before *Midsummer*, and ends 15 Days after it. See *Manwood*. This Month, by ancient Foresters, is called the *Defence Month*, for that the Deer are then to be defended from being disturbed: And there are also *Defence Months* for Fish, especially Salmon, for which see Stat. *Westm.* 2. c. 47, &c.

Feod, or **Feud,** is a Right which a Vassal has in Lands, or other immoveable Thing of his Lord's, to make Use of the same, and take the Profits thereof hereditarily; rendring to the Lord such *Feodal* Duties and Services as belong to Military Tenure, &c. the Property of the Soil itself always remaining to the Lord. *Cowel.*

Feodal, denotes any Thing belonging to the Fee.

Feodality, or **Fealty,** is what was paid to the Lord by his *feodal Tenant.*

Feodary, or **Feudary,** was an ancient Officer in the *Court of Wards*, who was appointed by the Master of that Court, to be present with the *Escheator* in every County at the finding of Offices of Lands; and to give in Evidence for the Crown as well for the Value as the Tenure: And his Office was also to survey the Lands of the Ward after the Office found, and to rate the Value thereof into Court; and likewise to assign Dower to the King's Widow, and to receive the Rents of Wards Lands within his Circuit, for which he was answerable to the Receiver of the Courts. By 12 *Car.* 2. *c.* 24. this Office seems to be entirely taken away.

Feodatory, denotes the Tenant that anciently held his Estate by *Feodal Service*: These Grantees to whom Lands in Feud or Fee were granted from a Superior Lord, were generally called *Homagers*; and in some Writings they are termed *Vassals*, *Feuds*, and *Feudataries*.

Feodum Militis or **Militare,** denotes a Knight's Fee, containing a certain Quantity of Land, for which was usually paid to the King or other Lord 100 Shillings.

Feodum Laicum, signifies a Lay-Fee, that is to say, Land held in Fee of a Lay Lord by the common Services whereto Military Tenure was subjected. See *Kennet's Gloss.*

Feoffment, in our Law, denotes a Gift or Grant of any Manors, Messuages, Lands or Tenements to another in Fee, that is to say, to the Grantee and his Heirs for ever, by delivering Seisin and Possession of the Estate granted. The Grantor in every Feoffment is called the *Feoffor*; and the Grantee is termed the *Feoffee*. *Littleton* makes a Distinction between *Feoffer* and *Donor*, *viz.* that the one grants in *Fee-simple*, the other in *Fee-Tail*. A Deed of *Feoffment* is our most ancient Conveyance of Lands; and it is said in a great Measure to exceed the Conveyance by Fine and Recovery, because it clears all Disseisins, Abatements, Intrusions, and other

other the like wrongful Estates, which neither Fine, Recovery, nor Bargain and Sale by Deed indented and inrolled does. A *Feoffment* must not be made of such Things whereof Livery and Seisin may not be made, seeing that no Deed of *Feoffment* is good to pass an Estate without Livery of Seisin; so that if either of the Parties die before Livery, the Feoffment becomes void. A Deed of Feoffment must be applied to some corporal and immoveable Thing, and is made up of the general Words, have *granted, bargained, sold, enfeoffed and confirmed*. A Deed of Feoffment usually consists of the following Parts, *viz*. The Names and Additions of the Parties, the Consideration, the granting Part, the Thing granted, the *Habendum* or explanatory Clause for what End or Use it is granted; a Covenant that the Feoffor is seised in Fee, and has good Right in Law to grant, and that the Premisses are free from Incumbrances; and lastly, a Covenant for quiet Enjoyment. The Form of this Deed, with that of the Memorandum of Livery and Seisin proper to be indorsed thereon, you may see in the *Young Clerk's Magazine*, and other Treatises on Conveyancing.

Feoffor and **Feoffee**. See **Feoffment**.

Feræ Naturæ, denotes Beasts and Birds that are wild; and is used in Opposition to such as are tame; as Foxes, Hares, Wild Ducks, &c. in which no Person can claim a Property.

Ferdwit, did formerly denote the being quit of Manslaughter, committed in the Army; yet it is said to be rather a Fine imposed on Persons for not going forth in a Military Expedition, which Duty every one that holds Lands was obliged to; so that upon a Neglect or Omission of this common Service to the Public, the Party was punished with a pecuniary Mulct of 120 s. called the *Ferdwite*.

Ferm. See **Farm**.

Ferry, is a Liberty by Prescription, or the King's Grant, to have a Boat for Passage on a River, for conveying of Horses, &c. over the same for reasonable Toll. It has been held, that the not keeping up a Ferry is indictable.

Festing-Men, (from the *Saxons*) signifies a Surety or Pledge.

Festing-Penny, was formerly used to signify Earnest given to Servants when hired into Services.

Feud, (from the *Germans*) signifies an implacable Hatred, which is not to be satisfied but with the Death of the Enemy; such was that among the People of *Scotland*, when there was a Combination of all the Kindred to revenge the Death of any of the Blood upon the Slayer and all his Race. *Termes de la Ley*.

Feudbote, denotes a Recompence for engaging in a Feud.

Feuds, denotes Lands that are hereditary, and signifies the same as Fee-simple.

Fiat, denotes a short Order or Warrant made by some Judge for making out and allowing certain Processes, &c.

Fiat Justitia, is where the King, on a Petition to him for his Warrant to bring a Writ of Error in Parliament, writes on the Top, *Fiat Justitia*, Let Justice be done; upon which the Writ of Error is made out, &c.

Fiction of Law, is what is allowed in many Cases; as the Seisin of the Conusee in a Fine, which is only an invented Form of Conveyance; a common Recovery, which is no more than a formal Device

Device by Consent, for the docking of an Estate-tail, &c.

Fidem mentiri, did formerly signify the Tenant's not keeping that Fealty which he had sworn to his Lord.

Fief, is what we call *Fee*.

Fieri facias, is a Writ that lies where a Person has removed Judgment for Debt or Damages in any of the King's Courts; which Writ is directed to the Sheriff, commanding him to levy the Debt and Damages on the Defendant's Goods and Chattels. This Process must be sued out within a Year and a Day after the Judgment obtained; otherwise the Judgment must be revived by a Writ of *Scire facias*: But where a Man recovers Judgment against a single Woman, who marries within the Year and Day; then the Plaintiff must take out a *Scire facias* against the Husband. Upon a *Fieri facias* the Sheriff is to use his best Endeavours to levy the Money on the Defendant's Goods and Chattels. A *Testatum fieri facias* may go out into another County, if the Defendant has not Goods sufficient in the County where the Action is laid to satisfy the Execution. Where a Person recovers Judgment for Debt or Damages, and levies only Part of it by *Fieri facias*, upon a Return made of this Writ, he may take the Defendant's Body in Execution for the rest of the Debt, by Virtue of a *Capias ad satisfaciendum*.

Fightwite, denotes a Fine for fighting or creating a Quarrel.

Filacer, or **Filazer,** is an Officer of the Common Pleas, who is so called, on Account that he files those Writs whereon he makes out Process. There are fourteen of these Officers, who are severally allotted to particular Divisions and Counties, and make out all Writs and Processes upon original Writs issuing out of the Court of Chancery, returnable in that Court. They enter all Appearances and special Bails, upon any Process issued by them, and make out the first *Scire facias* on special Bails, Writs of *Habeas Corpus*, *Distringas super vicecomitem, vel Ballivum*, and all Writs of *Supersedeas* upon special Bail.

File, signifies a Thread, String, or Wire, whereon Writs and other Exhibits in Courts are put or *filed*, for their greater Safety in keeping, and the more ready turning to the same: And as a *File* is a Record of the Court, so the *filing* of a Process of a Court, makes it a Record of it.

Field-Ale, or **Filstale,** was a Kind of Drinking anciently used in the *Field* by Bailiffs of Hundreds; to support which they collected Money of the Inhabitants of the Hundred whereto they belonged: But this Custom hath long ago been prohibited.

Finders, is a Word mentioned in several ancient Statutes, and seems to signify such Persons as we now distinguish by the Name of *Searchers*; who are imployed for the Discovery of Goods imported or exported, without paying the Duties or Custom thereon imposed.

Fine, in our Law has divers Significations; it being sometimes taken for a Sum advanced and paid for the Income of Lands, &c. It is likewise used in another Sense; and that is, where a Sum of Money is paid as an Amends, or by Way of Punishment for an Offence committed: And lastly, a *Fine* is taken for a *final* Agreement or Conveyance upon Record, for the settling and confirming of Lands or Tenements, and is acknowledged in the King's Court by the *Cognisor*, to be the Right of the *Cognisee*, the Person to whom the Acknowledgment is made. This *final* Agreement is briefly defined thus, *viz.* That it is a Covenant made before Justices, and entered upon Record, for Conveyance of Lands or other inheritable Thing, in order to cut off all Controversies. This last mentioned *Fine* was anciently a Determination of a real Controversy, but at present it is generally a feigned Action upon a Writ of Covenant, &c. and supposes an Action, when in Fact there is none; and this is done in order to secure the Title which a Person has in his Estate against all others; or to cut off *Intails*; so that the Title to Lands, &c. may with the greater Certainty be conveyed, either in Fee, Tail, for Life or Years. As this Fine is a Concord acknowledged before a competent Judge, concerning Lands, Tenements, Hereditaments, or other immoveable Things; and for its better Credit is supposed to be made in the King's Presence, on Account of its being levied in his Court; it therefore binds Women Covert, who are Parties, and others whom the Law generally disables to act; and for this Reason, because all Presumption of Deceit is excluded, where the King and his Court of Justice are supposed to be privy to the Matter transacted. These Fines, on Account of their Solemnity, are now acknowledged in the Court of *Common Pleas* at *Westminster*: They may be likewise acknowledged before the Lord Chief Justice of the *Common Pleas*, as well in, as out of Court; and two of the Justices of that Court may take them in open Court. Justices of Assise may also take *Fines*, by Virtue of the general Words of their Commission, tho' they seldom certify them without a special *Dedimus Potestatem*; by Virtue of which Writ *Fines* may also be taken in the Country by Commissioners. In every one of those Fines there are five Parts; 1*st*, An original Writ, usually termed a *Writ of Covenant*. 2. The *Licentia Concordandi*, or the King's Licence, for which a Fine, called the *King's Silver*, is paid. 3. The Concord, which contains the Agreement between the Parties, in what Manner the Land, &c. shall pass. 4. The Note of the Fine; that is to say, the Abstract of the original Contract. 5. The Foot of the Fine, wherein all is included, and in which is set forth the Day, Year, and Place, and before what Justices the Concord was made, &c. Of the different Sorts and Forms of Fines, you may read in the *Young Clerk's Magazine*, and other Collections of Precedents in Conveyancing.

Fine adnullando levato de Tenemento quod fuit de antiquo Dominico, is a Writ directed to the Justices of the *Common Pleas*, to disanul a Fine levied of Lands held in Ancient *Demesne* to the Prejudice of the Lord.

Fine capiendo pro Terris, &c. is a Writ which lies where a Person upon Conviction of an Offence by a Jury, having his Lands and Goods taken into the King's Hands, and his Body committed to Prison, for a Sum of Money, &c. obtains the Favour to be remitted his Imprisonment, and his Lands and Goods to be restored to him. *Cowel.*

Fine Force, is when a Person is forced to do that which he can no Way avoid.

Fine levando de Tenementis de Rege, is a Writ that was formerly in Use, and directed to the Justices of the *Common Pleas*, enabling them to admit of a Fine for Sale of Lands held *in Capite*.

Finem facere, signifies to compound, or make some Satisfaction for a Crime.

Fine non capiendo pro pulchre placitando, is a Writ for hindring Officers of Courts from taking Fines for fair Pleading.

Fines for Alienation, were Fines formerly paid to the King by his Tenants in Chief, for a Licence to alien their Lands. But by the 12 *Car.* 2. *c.* 24. these Fines are taken away.

Fine pro Redisseisina capienda, is a Writ that lies for the Release of a Person imprisoned for *Redisseisin* upon a reasonable Fine.

Finite. See **Finem facere**.

Firebote, denotes Fuel or Firing by Law allowed to Tenants out of the Lands granted to them. See **Estovers**.

Firma Alba, denotes Rent of Land farmed, paid in Silver, and not in Provision for the Lord's House.

Firma Noctis, was a Custom or Tribute anciently paid towards the Entertainment of the King for one Night, or at least the Value of it.

First-Fruits, are the Profits of any spiritual Living for the first Year.

Fledwite, or **Flightwite**, in our ancient Law signifies a Person's being discharged from Amercements, who having been a Fugitive of his own Accord, or with Licence, comes to the Peace of the King.

Fleet, is a famous Prison in *London*, to which Persons are most usually committed for Contempt of the King and his Laws, particularly of his Courts of Justice; or for Debt, where a Person will not, or is unable to pay his Creditors.

Flem, or **Fleth**, was anciently used to denote an Outlaw. *Cowel.*

Flemenesfrinth, or **Flymenesfrynthe**, denotes the Receiving or Relieving of a Fugitive or Outlaw.

Flight. See **Fugitives**.

Flood-Mark, or **High-Water Mark**, is that Mark which the Sea makes on the Shore, at Flowing Water and the highest Tide.

Flotson, or **Flotzam**, denotes any Goods that by Shipwreck are lost, and are floating on the Top of the Water, which, with *Jetson* and *Lagan*, are generally given to the Lord Admiral by his Letters Patent. Here it is to be observed, that *Jetson* signifies any Thing that is thrown out of a Ship being in Danger, and afterwards is beaten to the Shore by the Water, or cast on Shore by the Mariners: And *Lagan* is where heavy Goods are thrown overboard before the Ship becomes a Wreck, and sinks to the Bottom of the Sea.

Focage. See **Housebote**, or **Firebote**.

Focal, denotes a Right of taking Wood for Firing. *Cowel.*

Foiterors. See **Faitours**.

Folclands, were Copyhold Lands so called in the Time of the *Saxons*. *Folcland* was likewise termed *Terra vulgi*, the Land of the vulgar People, who had no Estate therein, but held it under the accustomed Rents and Services at the Will only of their Lord the Thane.

Folcmote or **Folkmote**, denotes two Kinds of Courts, the one called the *County-Court*, and the other the *Sheriffs-Turn*: And we are told that this Word is still in Use in the City of *London*, where it denotes, *Celebrem ex Civitate Conventum*. See *Stow's Survey*.

Footgeld, denotes an *Amerciament* for not cutting out the Balls of great Dogs Feet in the Forest: And

And to be quit of *Footgeld*, signifies a Privilege to keep Dogs within the Forest unlawed, without Punishment. *Termes de la Ley.* See **Expeditate**.

Force, in our Law, is generally taken in an evil Sense, and denotes any unlawful Violence offered. By some it is defined to be an Offence whereby Violence is used to Things or Persons: And it may be divided into *Simple* and *Compound*; Simple Force is what is so committed, as that it has no other Crime attending it; as where a Person by Force enters upon another's Possession, without committing any other unlawful Act: *Compound Force* is where some other Violence is committed over and above such an Act; which of itself is criminal; as where one enters by Force into another's Possession, and there kills a Person, or ravishes a Girl, &c. There is likewise a *Force* implied in Law; such as a Trespass, Rescous, or Disseisin. Any Person may lawfully enter a Tavern, Inn or victualling House, so may a Landlord enter a Tenant's House to view Repairs, &c. But if in any of these Cases the Person that enters commits any Violence or Force, the Law will intend that he entered for that very Purpose.

Forcible Entry, is a violent and actual Entry into Houses or Lands: And, on the other Hand, *forcible Detainer* is, where one by Violence withholds the Possession of Land, &c. so that the Person who has Right of Entry, is barr'd or hinder'd therefrom. If a Person be seised of a Freehold, and by Force be put out thereof; or if he be disseised peaceably without any Force or Violence acted, and the Disseisor afterwards detains and holds the same from him by Force, the Disseisee, in either of these Cases, may have a Writ of *Forcible Entry* against the Disseisor. There are forcible Entries punishable by Law; as where one or more arm'd with unusal Weapons violently enter into the House or Land of another; or where they do not enter by Violence, in case they put another Person out of his Possession; and in the like Manner it is, where a Person enters another's House without his Consent, even tho' the Door be open.

Foreclosed, that is to say, shut out or excluded, denotes the being barr'd the Equity of Redemption on Mortgages, &c.

Foregoers, was a Name anciently given to the King's Purveyors, from their *going before* to provide for the King's Houshold.

Foreign, in our Law, is used adjectively, and is frequently joined with Substantives of different Significations.

Foreign Matter, denotes a Matter that is triable in another County, or Matter acted in another County.

Foreign Attachment, denotes an Attachment of the Goods of *Foreigners*, found within a City or Liberty, for the Satisfaction of the Citizen to whom the *Foreigner* is indebted; or it signifies an Attachment of a Foreigner's Money in the Hands of another. See **Attachment**.

Foreign bought and sold, denotes an ancient Custom within the City of *London*, which being found prejudicial to the Sellers of Cattle in *Smithfield*, it was by 22 & 23 *Car.* 2. enacted, That as well Foreigners, as Freemen, may buy and sell any Cattle there.

Foreign Kingdom, denotes a Kingdom under the Dominion of a *Foreign Prince*.

Foreign Opposer, or Opposer. See *Exchequer*.

Foreign Plea, denotes an Objection to the Judge of a Court, by refusing him, as incompetent, because the Matter in Question is not within his Jurisdiction.

Foreign Service, is that *Service* whereby a mean Lord holds of another without the Compass of his own Fee; or it is that which the Tenant performs either to his own Lord, or to the Lord Paramount out of his Fee. *Cowel.*

Foreigners, according to the general Acceptation of the Word, denote such as are the natural-born Subjects of some *foreign Prince;* who, tho' made *Denizens,* or naturalized here, are disabled to bear Office in the Government, to be of the Privy Council, or Members of Parliament, &c. See the Acts of Settlement of the Crown, 12 *W.* 3. *c.* 2. 1 *Geo.* 1. *c.* 4. Persons that are not Freemen of a City or Corporation, are also called *Foreigners,* to distinguish them from the Members of the same.

Forejudger, signifies a Judgment by which one is deprived of, or put by the Thing in Question. To be *forejudged the Court,* is where an Officer or an Attorney of any Court is expelled the same, for male Practice, or for not appearing to an Action on a Bill filed against him, &c. And after an Attorney is forejudged, but not before, he becomes liable to be arrested as another Person.

Foreschoke, signifies as much as *forsaken;* and in one of our old Statutes it is used for Lands or Tenements seised by the Lord, for Want of Services performed by the Tenant, and by that Means quietly held by such Lord above a Year and a Day: Now, as the Tenant who sees his Lands, &c. taken into the Hands of his Lord, and by him possessed so long, without any due Course of Law taken by him the Tenant to recover it, does in Presumption of Law disavow or *forsake* all the Right he has thereto; for which Reason those Lands shall be called *Foreschoke.* See 10 *Ed.* 2. *c.* 1.

Forest, in general, is defined to be a Place privileged by Royal Authority or by Prescription, for the peaceable abiding of the Beasts, or Birds of the *Forest,* for the Sport of the King. *Termes de la Ley.* But *Manwood* gives a Forest this particular Definition, *viz. That it is a certain Territory of Woody Grounds and Pastures, fixed in its Bounds, and privileged for wild Beasts and Fowls of Forest, Chase, and Warren, to rest and abide under the safe Protection of the King, for his Princely Delight and Pleasure; which Territory of Ground is meted and bounded with unremoveable Marks and Boundaries, which are either known by Matter of Record, or else by Prescription; and it is also replenished with wild Beasts of Venary or Chase, and with great Coverts of Vert, for the Succour of the said wild Beasts to have their Abode in; for the Preservation and Continuance of which said Place, together with the Vert and Venison, there are particular Laws, Privileges and Officers belonging only to the same.* The same Author tells us, That the Manner of creating Forests is thus, *viz.* The King issues out a Commission under the Great Seal, directed to certain discreet Persons for the View, Perambulation, Meting and bounding of the Place, the King is aminded to be a Forest; which Commission being returned into the Court of *Chancery.* Proclamation is made throughout the whole

whole Shire, where the Ground lies, that none shall hurt or chase any Manner of wild Beasts in that Precinct, without the King's Licence; after which is done, the King appoints Ordinances, Laws and Officers fit for the Preservation of the Vert and Venison; and then it becomes a Forest by Matter of Record. See *Manwood*.

Faustagium, is thought to signify some Duty payable to the King's Forester, as *Chiminage*, or the like. *Cowel*.

Forester, is a sworn Officer of the Forest, who is appointed by the King's Letters Patent, to walk the Forest at all Hours, watching both the Vert and Venison, and attaching and presenting Trespasses committed against them within their own Walk or Precinct.

Forestal, in a legal Sense denotes to buy or bargain for any Corn, Cattle, Sheep, Eggs, or other Merchandise, in the Way as they come to Fairs or Markets to be sold, before they get thither, with an Intent to sell the same again at a higher Price. Any buying or contracting for any Merchandise, Victuals, or other Thing whatsoever in the Way, as they are carrying to Market, either by Water or Land, to any Fair or Market, or to any Port, &c. to be sold, or procuring the same to be bought, or dissuading Persons by Word, Letter or otherwise, from bringing such Goods to Market, or to advance the Price thereof after they are brought thither, the Person acting in any such Manner is guilty of *Forestalling*; for which Offence, upon Conviction at the Quarter-sessions by two or more Witnesses, the Offender becomes liable to pecuniary Forfeitures, as well as a corporal Punishment. 5 & 9 *Ed*. 6. *c*. 14.

Forestaller, denotes a Person guilty of *Forestalling*, which see.

Forfang, or **Forefang**, (from the *Saxons*) anciently denoted the Taking of Provision from any Persons in Fairs or Markets, before the King's Purveyors were served with Necessaries for the King.

Forfeiture, properly denotes the Effect of the transgressing of some *Penal Law*; and it extends to Lands or Goods: It differs from *Confiscation*, in that Forfeiture is more general, whilst *Confiscation* is particularly applied to such Things as become forfeited to the King's *Exchequer*; and Goods that are confiscated, are said to be such as no Body claims. There is likewise *Plena Forisfactura*, or *Plena Wita*, *a full Forfeiture*, which signifies a Forfeiture of Life and Member, together with all that a Person has. There is also a Forfeiture in *Civil* Cases; as where one has an Estate for Life or Years, he may forfeit it divers Ways as well by *Treason*, *Felony*, &c. as by granting a greater Estate than is vested in him, &c.

Forfeiture of Marriage, is a Writ that formerly lay against a Person, who holding by Knight's Service, and being under Age, and *unmarried*, refused her that the Lord offered him without his Disparagement, and *married* another.

Forgabel, denotes a small Rent anciently reserved in Money or Quit-Rent.

Forgery, in a legal Sense, is when a Person fraudulently makes and publishes false Writings to another's Prejudice, in his Right or Interest; or it signifies the Writ that lies against him that offends that Way. *Forgery* is either at Common Law, or by Statute, and is an Offence punishable by Indictment, Information, &c. yet there cannot be be any *Forgery*, where none is prejudiced thereby besides the Person that does it.

Forinsecum Manerium, did anciently signify that Part of a Manor which lay without the Town, and not included within the Liberties thereof.

Forinsecum Servitium, was formerly the Payment of some extraordinary Aid, opposed to *Intrinsecum Servitium*, which denoted the common ordinary Duties within the Lord's Court.

Forisfamiliari, is where a Son accepts of his Father's Part of Lands, &c. in the Life-time of the Father, and rests contented with it; so that he cannot claim any more, and on that Account he is called *Forisfamiliari*.

Forma pauperis, is where a Person has just Cause of Suit, but is so poor, that he cannot defray the usual Expences of suing at Law or in Equity; in which Case, on making Oath, that he is not worth 5 l. in the World (all his just Debts being paid) and producing a Certificate from some Lawyer, that he has good Cause of Suit, the Judge will admit him to sue *in Forma Pauperis*, that is to say, without paying any Fees to Counsellors, Attornies or Clerk; the *Stat.* 11 *Hen.* 7. having ordained, that Counsel, Attornies, &c. shall be assigned them *gratis*.

Formedon, is a Writ that lies for a Person that has Right to Lands or Tenements, by Virtue of an *Intail*, arising from the Statute of *Westm.* 2. c. 2. This Writ lies three Ways, viz. in *Descender*, *Remainder* and *Reverter*. *Formedon in Descender* lies where Tenant in Tail enfeoffs a Stranger, or is disseised and dies; after which the Heir brings this Writ: *Formedon in Remainder* lies where a Man gives Lands, &c. in Tail, and for Default of Issue of his Body, the Remainder to another in Tail; in this Case, if the Tenant in Tail die without Issue, and a Stranger abates and enters into the Land, he in Remainder may have this Writ. *Formedon in Reverter*, lies where Lands are intailed on certain Persons and their Issue, with Remainder over for Want of Issue, which Remainder ceasing, then to revert to the Donor, and his Heirs: In this Case, if the Tenant in Tail dies without Issue, as also he in Remainder, the Donor and his Heirs to whom the Reversion returns may have this Writ for the Recovery of the Estate, even tho' it has been aliened.

Fornagium, denotes a certain Fee or Acknowledgment formerly taken by a Lord of his Tenants who were bound to bake in his common Oven.

Fornication, denotes the Act of Incontinency between single Persons; for where either of the Parties is married, such Act is called Adultery. The Spiritual Court now has the sole Cognisance of this Offence, which anciently was cognisable in other Courts.

Forprise, denotes an Exception or Reservation, and is frequently used in Leases and Conveyances, wherein any Exception is inserted. In another Sense it is taken for any Exaction.

Forspeaker, denotes an Attorney or Advocate in a Cause.

Fortiori, is a Word often used by *Littleton*, by Way of Argument, to this Purpose, viz. if it be so in such a Point, much more is it so in another mentioned.

Fossa, anciently was used to signify a Ditch full of Water, wherein Women that committed Felony were

were drowned, but Men hanged for that Crime. *Cowel.*

Fossatorum Operatio, denotes Fosse-Work, or the Service of Labouring, performed by Inhabitants and adjoining Tenants, for Repair and Maintainance of the Ditches round a City or Town; the Contribution towards which was called *Fossagium*.

Foundation, denotes the Founding and Building of a College or Hospital.

Fourcher, signifies a Delaying or Putting off an Action; and by *Cowel* it is compared to stammering, whereby the Speech is drawn out to more than ordinary Length of Time, as by *Fourching* the Suit is prolonged, which otherwise might be brought to a Determination in a shorter Space. In *Fourching*, the Device usually made Use of is, when an Action is commenced against two Persons, who being jointly concerned, are not to answer till they both appear; and the *Essoin* of one will excuse the other's Default; and they agree between themselves, that one shall appear or be essoined one Day, and for Want of the other's Appearance, have a Day over to make his Appearance with the other Party; on which Day allowed he does appear; but he that appeared before does not, with an Intent to gain another Day of the Party, who then made his Appearance. *Termes de la Ley.*

Frampole Fences, are those *Fences* that any Tenant in the Manor of *Writtle* in *Essex* sets up against the Lord's Demeans; and such Tenant is entitled to the Wood growing on these Fences, and as many Trees or Poles as they can reach from the Top of the Ditch with an Ax's Helve, towards the Repair of his Fence. *Cowel.* Why those *Fences* are called *Frampole,* Authors are still at a Loss to determine.

Franchise, denotes a Privilege or Exemption from ordinary Jurisdiction, as for a Corporation to hold Pleas among themselves to such a Value, or the like. This Word likewise signifies an Immunity from Tribute, in which Sense it is either personal or real, that is to say, belonging to a Person immediately; or else by Means of this or that Place or Court of Immunity, of which he is Chief, or a Member.

Franchise Royal, is thought to be that where the King's Writ does not run; but in *Termes de la Ley* we are told, that a *Franchise Royal* is where the King grants to one and his Heirs, that they shall be quit of Toll, &c.

Francigenæ, is a general Appellation formerly given to all Foreigners. See **Englicery**.

Frankalmoign, denotes a Tenure by spiritual Service, where Lands or Tenements are held by an Ecclesiastical Corporation, sole or aggregate, to them and their Successors of some Lord and his Heirs in free and perpetual Alms, which implies as much as a Fee-simple; and yet it may pass without the Word *Successors*. When Lands, &c. are granted in *Frankalmoign*, no Mention must be made of any Kind of Service, it being always *free* from any temporal Service, and being likewise a Tenure of the highest Nature, as it is a Tenure by spiritual Service. Where an Ecclesiastical Tenure is held by certain Services to be performed, as to read Prayers on particular Days, &c. this is not called *Frankalmoign*, but *Tenure by Divine Service*; since it cannot be called *Frankalmoign*, or free Alms, where

Y

where any certain Service is required.

Frank-Bank. See *Free-Bench*.

Frank-Chase, is defined to be Liberty of *Free-Chase*, whereby any Person that has Lands within the Compass of the same are prohibited to cut down any Wood, &c. without the View of the Forester, even in their own Demesnes.

Frank-Fee, denotes as much as to hold Lands or Tenements in Fee-simple, and which is pleadable at Common Law, and not in Ancient Demesne. *Termes de la Ley*.

Frank-Ferm, was anciently used to signify Lands or Tenements, changed in the Nature of the Fee, by Feoffment, &c. out of Knight's Service for peculiar yearly Service.

Frank-Law, is a Word generally applied to the Free and Common Law of the Land.

Frank-Marriage, is where a Person seised in Fee of Lands or Tenements, gives them to another, with his Daughter, Sister, or otherwise of Kin to the Donor in *Free-Marriage*; by Virtue of which Words, the Husband and Wife have an Estate in special Tail, and shall hold the Land of the Donor discharged of all Services, except Fealty, until the fourth Degree be past. Gifts in *Frank-Marriage* were anciently common, but are now gone into Disuse.

Frank-Pledge, denotes a *Pledge* or Surety for Freemen, according to the ancient Custom of Freemen of *England*, for the Preservation of the publick Peace: And this Custom anciently was, that every Free-born Man at the Age of Fourteen, (except Religious Persons, Clerks, Knights, and their eldest Sons) should find Surety for his Truth towards the King and his Subjects, or otherwise to be imprisoned; upon which a certain Number of Neighbours ordinarily became bound one for another, to see each Person they became bound for, forthcoming at all Times, or to answer the Transgression of any of their *Pledges* that were gone away: Wherefore, whosoever offended, it was forthwith inquired in what *Pledge* he was, and then those that were bound, either produced the Defendant in thirty-one Days, or made Satisfaction for his Offence. This, *Cowel* says, was called *Frank-Pledge*, and the Circuit thereof *Decenna*, on Account that it commonly consisted of ten Housholds, and each Person mutually bound as Surety, was called *Decennier*, because he was of one *Decenna* or another. He further says, that this Custom was so kept up, that the Sheriffs in every County did, from Time to Time, take the Oaths of Youths as they attained the Age of Fourteen, and see that they were comprized in some Dozen; whereupon this Branch of the Sheriff's Authority was termed *Visus Franci Plegii*, that is to say, View of *Frank-Pledge*.

Frank-Tenement. See *Freehold*.

Fratriagium, anciently denoted a younger Brother's Inheritance, or that Part of the Estate which comes to him from his Father; wherefore whatever the younger Sons possess of the Estate of the Father, they are said to enjoy it *ratione fratriagii*, and were to do Homage to the elder Brother for the same, he being bound to do Homage to the Superior Lord for the Whole.

Fraud, signifies a Deceit in a Grant or Conveyance of Lands, &c. Bargains and Sales of Goods, &c. to the Damage of another Person. *Fraudulent* Conveyances of Lands, or Goods, to deceive Creditors, as

FR

to Creditors, are void in Law. See 50 *Ed.* 3. *c.* 6. 13 *Eliz. c.* 5. *Fraudulent* Conveyances in order to defraud Purchasers, are also to such Purchasers void, and the Persons putting off such Grants as good, shall forfeit the Year's Value of the Lands, and the full Value of the Goods and Chattels; and moreover, shall be imprisoned.

Fraus Legis, is a Term used by *Raym. fol.* 276. where he says, That if a Person who has no Manner of Title to Houses, procure an Affidavit of the Service of a Declaration in Ejectment, and thereon obtains Judgment; and by Virtue of a Writ of *Habere facias Possessionem* turns the Owner out of Possession of the House, and seises and converts the Goods within the same to his own Use, he may for such an Offence be punished as a Felon for that he used the Process of the Law with a felonious Purpose *in fraudem Legis*.

Fredum, was a Composition anciently made by a Criminal, in order to be freed from Prosecution, a third Part of which Composition was paid in to the *Exchequer*.

Free-Bench, denotes that Estate in Copyhold Lands, which the Wife, being espoused a Virgin, has after her Husband's Decease, for her Dower, according to the Custom of the Manor. As to this *Free-Bench*, several Manors have several Customs; as in particular, the Manors of *East* and *West Enborne*, in the County of *Berks*, and in other Parts of *England*, there is a Custom, that when a Copyhold Tenant dies, the Widow shall have her *Free-Bench*, in all the deceased Husband's Lands, *dum sola & casta fuerit*, whilst she lives single and chaste; but if she commits *Incontinency*, she forfeits the Estate:

Nevertheless upon her coming into the Court of the Manor, riding on a *Black Ram*, and having his Tail in her Hand, and at the same time uttering these Words following, the Steward is obliged by the Custom to re-admit her to her *Free-Bench*: The Words are these, *viz.*

Here I am,
Riding upon a Black Ram,
Like a Whore as I am;
And for my Crincum Crancum,
Have lost my Binkum Bankum,
And for my Tail's Game,
Have done this worldly Shame,
Therefore I pray you Mr. Steward,
Let me have my Land again.

Freebord, denotes Ground claimed in some Places, more or less, beyond or without the Fence. In *Mon. Angl.* 2 *Par. Pag.* 241. it is said to contain two Foot and a Half.

Free Chapel, according to the Opinion of some, is a Chapel founded within a Parish for the Service of God, by the Liberality of some good Person, over and above the Mother-Church, to which it was *free* for the Parishioners to come or not, and endowed with Maintenance by the Founder, and therefore called *Free*: Others again more properly call those Chapels *Free Chapels*, that are of the King's Foundation, and by the Prince exempted from the Ordinary's Visitation or Jurisdiction.

Freehold, denotes Lands or Tenements held in Fee-simple, Fee-tail, or for Term of Life. *Freehold* is thus divided, *viz. Freehold in Deed*, and *Freehold in Law*; the first of which signifies the real Possession of Lands, *&c.* in Fee or for Life: And the other denotes the Right that a Person has to such

Lands or Tenements, before his Entry or Seisure. This Word has also been extended to Offices that one holds either in Fee, or during Life. It has likewise been defined much to this Purpose, *viz*. That *Frank-Tenement* is a Possession of the Soil, or Services issuing out therefrom, which a Freeman holds in Fee to him and his Heirs in Fee simple, Fee-Tail, for Term of Life, in Dower, or by the Courtesy, under which there is no *Freehold*; for he that has an Estate for Years or at Will, has no Freehold, such Estates being only called *Chattels*. A Lease for 99 Years, &c. determinable on the Decease of the Lessee, &c. is not such a Lease for Life as to create a Freehold, it being no more than a Lease for Years, determinable as above.

Freeholders, are such as hold any Freehold Estate.

Freeman, denotes a Person that is born, or made *free*.

Freight, signifies the Money paid for Goods carried by Sea; and in a more extensive Sense, it is taken for the whole Cargo or Burden of the Ship. Vessels are generally freighted by the Ton, or by the Great; and wherever a Ship freighted by the Great is cast away, the Freight in that Case is lost; but where the Merchant, &c. agrees by the Ton, or after such a Rate for every Piece of the Commodities on Board, it is there said she ought to be answered her *Freight*, according to the Rate.

Frenchman, was formerly wont to be used for every outlandish Man. See **Francigenæ**. See also **Englescery**.

Friendless Man, is an old *Saxon* Term, denoting a Person that we call an *Outlaw*.

Frendwite, is by some thought to denote a Mulct exacted of a Person, who harboured his outlawed Friend.

Fresh Disseisin, signifies such a *Disseisin* as a Person may seek to defeat of himself, and by his own Power, without the Help of the King or Judges; as where it is of a short Continuance, *viz*. not above fifteen Days. *Cowel*.

Fresh Fine, denotes a Fine that was levied within a Year past.

Fresh Force, signifies a *Force* that is newly done; as where a Person is disseised of any Lands or Tenements within any City or Borough, or deforced from them after the Death of his Ancestor, &c. the Person having Right may, within Forty Days after the Force committed or Title to him accrued, bring his Assise or Bill of *fresh Force*. See *Fitz. Nat. Brev. fol.* 7. and *Old Nat. Brev. fol.* 4.

Fresh Suit, denotes such a present and close following of an Offender, as never ceases from the Time of the Offence committed or discovered, until the Offender is apprehended. The Benefit and Effect of this in Respect to the *Pursuit* of a Felon, is, that the Party pursuing shall have his Goods again, which otherwise would be the King's. A Person may be said to have made fresh Suit, tho' he does not take the Thief presently, but that it be some Time after the Robbery committed, provided he did his utmost of his Endeavour to take the Offender; yea tho' the Criminal were taken by a Person not interested in Things carried away, yet in this Case the Party robbed shall be deemed to have made fresh Suit. *Termes de la Ley*. Fresh Suit is likewise, where the Lord comes to distrain for

Rent or Service, and the Owners of the Goods distrained makes Rescous, and drives them into another's Ground not holden of the Lord; whereupon the Lord immediately follows and retakes them.

Friburgh, or **Frithburgh**, is said to denote the same with *Pledge* or *Frank-Pledge*.

Friar, or **Frier**, is the Name of an Order of religious Persons, of which Kind there are reckoned four principal Branches, that is to say, 1. *Minors, Grey-Friers*, or *Franciscans*. 2. *Augustins*. 3. *Dominicans*, or *Black-Friers*. 4. *White-Friers*, or *Carmelites*; from which the other Orders descend.

Frier-observant, is a particular Branch of the *Franciscan Friers*, who are Minors, as well the *Observants* as the *Conventuals* and *Capuchines*. The Reason that they are called *Observants* is, because they are not combined together in any Cloister, Convent or Corporation, as the Conventuals are; but are only tied to observe the Rules of their Order more strictly than the *Conventuals* do, and for their Singularity of Zeal separate themselves from them, betaking themselves to certain Places and Companies of their own chusing. *Cowel*.

Fripeter, is taken for a Person that scours and furbishes up old Cloaths in order to sell again.

Frith, denotes a Plain between two Woods. *Termes de la Ley*.

Frithgild, denotes the same as what we now stile a *Guild-Hall*, or a Company or Fraternity. *Cowel*.

Frithsoke, or **Frithsoken**, denotes a Surety of Defence.

Frodmortel, denotes a Freedom or Immunity for committing Manslaughter. *Cowel*.

Frumgyld, anciently signified the first Payment made to the Kindred of a Person slain, by Way of Recompence for his Murder.

Frumstol, anciently denoted the chief Seat or Mansion-house.

Frussura, signifies a Demolishing, and also a Ploughing and Breaking up: And *Frussura Domorum*, signifies House-breaking; and *Frussura Terræ*, new broke Land, or Land lately ploughed up.

Frustrum Terræ, denotes a small Piece of Land.

Fryth. See **Frith**.

Fuage, or **Focage**, denotes a certain Imposition laid upon the Subjects in the Dukedom of *Acquitaine* in King *Edward* the Third's Time, *viz.* 12 d. for every Fire.

Fuer, (from a *French* Verb, signifying to fly) is in our Law used substantively, and is taken two Ways, *viz. To fly in Fact*, as where a Person does apparently and corporally fly; and *fly in Law*, that is to say, when being called in the County, he does not appear until he is outlawed; which the Law implies to be a *Flight*.

Fugam fecit, is used, when it is found by Inquisition, that a Person *fled* for Felony, &c. If Flight and Felony be found on an Indictment for Felony, or before the Coroner, where a Murder is committed; the Offender shall forfeit all his Goods, and the Issues of his Lands till he is acquitted or pardoned.

Fugitives Goods, signifies the proper *Goods* of the Person that flies upon Felony by him committed; which Goods lawfully found after the Flight, do belong to the King.

Fumage, by some, is taken for Dung, or a Manuring therewith; yet anciently this Word was taken for *Smoke-money*, which was a customary Payment for every House that had a Chimney.

Fu-

Furcam & Flagellum, formerly denoted the meanest of all Servile Tenures, when the Bondman was at the Lord's Disposal for Life and Limb.

Furigeldum, denotes a Mulct anciently paid for Theft.

Furlong, denotes a certain Quantity of Land, containing, for the most part Forty Poles or Perches in Length, each Pole being sixteen Foot and an Half long; and eight of these Furlongs make a Mile.

Fyrderinga, denotes a going out upon some military Expedition at the King's Command, refusing to do which, was anciently punished by Fine at the Discretion of the King.

G.

Gabel, is an old Word, which is to be found in ancient Records, and signifies Rent, Duty, Custom or Service yielded to the King or other Lord.

Gabulus Denariorum, according to *Selden,* denotes Rent paid in Money.

Gafold-gild or **Gaful-land,** (from the *Saxons*) denotes the Payment or rendring of Custom or Tribute, and is sometimes taken for Usury.

Gage, is the same with Pawn or Pledge. There is also *Gage-Deliverance,* which is where a Person has taken a Distress, being sued, not having delivered the Cattle, &c. that were distrained, in which Case he shall not only avow the Distress, but *gager Deliverance, viz.* put in Surety or Pledges that he will deliver them; yet in some Cases he shall not be tied to Surety; as if the Cattle distrained died in the Pound, or if he claim a Property in the Cattle seised.

Gainge, denotes the Gain or Crop of tilled or planted Grounds, as also the Draught-Oxen, Horses, Wain, Plough and Furniture for carrying on the Work of Tillage by the lower or baser Sort of *Sokemen* and *Villeins.* We are told, that anciently the *Villein,* when amerced, had his *Wainage* free, to the Intent the Plough might not stand still; and indeed the Law, for the same Reason does still allow a like Privilege to the Husbandman, that his Draught, Horses and Oxen are not in many Cases distrainable. *Cowel.*

Gainery, denotes Tillage or Ploughing, or the Profit arising therefrom, or from the Beasts used therein.

Gallihalpence, was a particular Coin imported into this Realm in Galleys, and prohibited by 3 *Hen.* 5. *c.* 1.

Game, signifies the Catching or Destroying of Birds or Prey by Fowling or Hunting: And there are divers Statutes against such Practices, committed by Persons by Law not qualified to take or destroy the Game, or to have Nets, Guns, or other Instruments that may be applied to that Use.

Game-keepers, are those that have the Care of preserving of the Game, and are appointed to that Office by Lords of Manors, &c. who not being under the Degree of an *Esquire,* may, by writing under their Hand and Seal, authorize one or more *Game-keepers,* who, by Virtue of their Office, may seise Guns, Dogs, Nets, or other Engines used by unqualified Persons for destroying the Game. A Lord of a Manor, &c. may authorise their *Game-keepers* within his Royalties, to kill Hare, Pheasant, Partridges,

tridges, &c. for his own Use; yet if a Game-keer, so authorized, under Colour of such his Authority, kill *Game*, and afterwards sell it without the Consent of the Person that impowers him, in such Case, on Conviction, he becomes liable to a corporal Punishment. See 5 *Ann. c.* 14. & 9 *Ann.* See likewise 3 *Geo.* 1. *c.* 11.

Gaming, or **unlawful Games**, such as playing at Cards, Dice, &c. have been anciently looked upon as a Thing of pernicious Consequence to the Common-wealth: And we find in King *Edward* the Third's Time, that Prince enjoined the Exercise of Shooting, and of Artillery, to take Place, and in the Room of the Diversions of casting the Bar, the Hand and Foot-Balls, Cock-fighting, and other vain Diversions, which were expresly forbid by that Prince: But no desired Effect having attended that Prohibition, King *Hen.* 8. in the 28th Year of his Reign, issued out a Proclamation against all unlawful Games, whereupon we are told, that throughout the Realm, Tables, Dice, Cards, and Bowls were burnt by the Order of Commissioners appointed for the due Execution of that Proclamation; since which Time divers other Statutes have been made, and are still in Force against *Gaming*.

Gaol, (from a *French* Word, signifying a Cage,) is in our Law Metaphorically used for a Prison; and thence the Keeper of the Prison is called *Gaoler*. It is a strong Place for confining of Debtors and Offenders in.

Gaol-Delivery. *Justices of Assise* and *Gaol-Delivery* are appointed by a Commission or Patent from the King, in the Nature of a Letter from him to certain Persons, who are thereby appointed his Justices, or two or three of them, and authorising them to deliver his *Gaol* at such a Place, of the Prisoners that are therein; and for that End it commands them to meet at such a Place and Time, &c.

Garble, denotes to chuse or pick the Good from the Bad; as the *Garbling* of Spice is nothing but the Purifying of it from the Dross and Dust that is mixed therewith; and by 21 *Jac.* 1. *c.* 19. all Drugs must be garbled before sold.

Garbler of Spices, is an ancient Officer within the City of *London*, who is authorised to enter into Shops, Warehouses, &c. there to view and search Drugs, Spices, &c. and to garble the same.

Gard or **Gardian**. See **Guard** and **Guardian**.

Garnish, signifies to warn; as to *garnish* the Heir. See 27 *Eliz. c.* 3.

Garnishment, in our Law, denotes a Warning given to a Person for his Appearance, for the better furnishing of the Cause and Court; as where one is sued for the Detaining of Charters or Writings delivered him by the Plaintiff and another upon some certain Condition: and therefore the Plaintiff prays that that other may be warned to plead with him whether the Conditions be performed or not, which is interpreted to be either a Warning of that other, or else Furnishing the Court with Parties sufficient to determine the Cause; because, until he appears and joins, the Defendant may be supposed to be out of Court, the Court not being provided with all the Parties to the Action. This Word *Garnishment* is further used as a Warning; as *Garnister le Court*, signifies to warn the Court; and *reasonable Garnishment* is where

GA

where a Person has reasonable Warning

Garnishee, is used for the Party in whose Hands Money is attached within the Liberties of the City of *London*, in the Sheriff's Court there, and he is so called, because he has had Garnishment or Warning not to pay the Money; but to appear and answer to the Plaintiff-Creditor's Suit. *Cowel.*

Garranty. See **Warranty.**

Garth, in the North of *England*, denotes a little Close or Backside: And it also signifies a Dam or Wear in a River, for catching Fish, which is vulgarly called a *Fishgarth.*

Garthman, was anciently used to denote a Fisher. See 17 *R.* 2. *c.* 9.

Gavel, denotes Tribute, Toll, Custom, or yearly Revenue, of which we had in ancient Times; as Gavel-Corn, Gavel-Malt, &c.

Gavelet, is an ancient and peculiar *Cessavit* used in *Kent*, where the Custom of *Gavel-kind* continues, by which the Tenant forfeits his Lands and Tenements to his Lord, in Case he withdrew from him his Rent and Services due. The Method in Respect to this *Gavelet* was, that the Lord was to seek by Award of his Court from three Weeks to three Weeks, to find Distress upon the Lands or Tenements, until the fourth Court; and if in that Time he could find no Distress on the Premisses, whereby he might obtain Justice of his Tenant, then at the fourth Court it was awarded, that he should take the Lands, &c. into his Hands in the Name of a Distress, and the Lord to keep it a Year and a Day in his Hands, without manuring; in which Space of Time, if the Tenant did not come and pay his Arrearages,

GA

and make the Lord a reasonable Amends, then the Lord was to re-enjoy the Lands, &c. But if the Tenant came within the Time, then the Lord was to go to the next County-Court with his Witnesses of his own Court, and pronounce there the Process to have further Witnesses; after which, by the Award of his Court, he became intitled to enter and manure those Lands, &c. And if the Tenant wanted to re-enjoy his Lands, &c. as he did before, he was then obliged to make Agreement with the Lord for the same. There is also a Writ used in the *Hustings* of *London*, that goes by the Name of *Gavelet.*

Gavelgeld has been applied to the Payment of Tribute or Toll.

Gavelkind, denotes a Tenure or Custom belonging to Lands in *Kent*, by which the Lands of the Father are at his Death equally divided among all his Sons; or the Land of the Deceased Brother among all the Brethren, in Case he leaves no Issue of his own. This Custom came from the *Saxons*, and we are told, that the Reason why it was retained in *Kent*, is, because the *Kentishmen* were not conquered by the *Normans.* In *Gavelkind*, tho' the Father suffer Death, the Son shall inherit; for their Custom is, the Father to the Bough, the Son to the Plough. See *Doctor and Student, cap.* 10. *Co. Litt. lib.* 2. *c.* 10.

Gavelman, denotes a Tenant that is liable to Tribute.

Gavelmed, denotes the Duty of mowing Grass, or cutting of Meadow Land, required by the Lord of his customary Tenant. *Cowel.*

Gavelcester, was a certain Measure of Rent-Ale. This by some goes under the Name of *Tolcester*, in Lieu of which Duty the Abbot of

Abbingdon

Abingdon is said to have received the Penny mentioned by *Selden* in his Dissertation annexed to *Fleta*.

Gabel-weak, was a Duty to be performed, either by the Hands of the Tenant, or by his Carts or Carriages.

Gauger, is a King's Officer, who is appointed to examine all Tuns, Pipes, Hogsheads, Barrels, and Tertia's of Wine, Beer, Ale, Oil, Honey, Butter, &c. and to give them a Mark of Allowance before they be allowed to be sold in any Place. See **Excise**.

Gauge-penny, is thought to be the *Gauger's* Fee.

Geld, among the *Saxons*, denoted Money or Tribute, also a Compensation for some Crime committed; and hence in our ancient Laws *Wergeld* was used for the Value of a Man slain; and *Orfgeld* of a Beast.

General Issue, is a Plea to the Fact charged, whereby it becomes referred to the Jury to bring in their Verdict whether the Defendant has acted any such Thing as the Plaintiff lays to his Charge.

Gentleman, properly is one whose Blood and Race makes him noble and known: But under this Name are comprised all above Yeomen; on which Account Noblemen are truly called *Gentlemen*. In a more general Sense Gentleman is defined to be one, who, without any Title, bears a *Coat of Arms*, or whose Ancestors have been Freemen.

Gestu & Fama, is an ancient Writ now out of Use, which lay where a Person's good Behaviour was impeached.

Gift, in a legal Sense, is a Conveyance, whereby either Lands or Goods are passed. It is said to be of a larger Extent than a *Grant*, it being applied to Things moveable and immoveable. A *Gift* may be by Deed, by Word, or in Law; as all a Person's Goods and personal Chattels, except in some particular Cases, may be given without Deed; and where such *Gift* is not made to defraud Creditors, the same is good without any Consideration: Yet a general Gift of all a Man's Goods, is liable to Suspicion of being fraudulent, and made with an Intent to deceive Creditors; for by giving all one's Goods to another, there seems to be a secret Trust and Confidence implied, *viz.* that the Donee shall deal favourably with the Donor: Wherefore, whenever a *Gift* is made in Satisfaction of a Debt, it is proper to be done in a publick Manner, before Witnesses of Credit; and that the Goods and Chattels at the same Time be appraised to the full Value, and that the Gift be expresly made in full Satisfaction of the Debt. The Forms of Deeds of Gift you may see in the *Young Clerk's Magazine*, and other Books of Conveyancing.

Gild. See **Guild**.

Gift of Action, denotes the Cause for which an Action lies, that is to say the Ground and Foundation of it, without which it cannot be maintained.

Glassmen, by some ancient Statutes, are included in the Number of wandring Rogues and Vagrants.

Glebe, denotes Church-Land, and is commonly taken for the Land belonging to a Parish-Church, beside the Tithes. In the *New Nat. Brev.* 386, &c. we are told, that if a Person is distrained in his Glebe-Lands by a Sheriff, or other Officer, a Writ grounded on the Statute *Articuli Cleri*, c. 6. lies against such Officer.

Glomerels, were certain Commissaries formerly appointed to determine

mine Differences between Scholars of a *School* or *University*.

Glove-Silver, denotes Money anciently by Custom given to some Servants to buy them Gloves, as a Reward or Encouragement of their Labours. *Cowel*.

Go, in our Law is sometimes used in a special Signification; as to go without Day, (usually termed *sine Die*) is to be dismissed the Court.

God-bote, (from the *Saxons*) denotes an Ecclesiastical Fine imposed for Offences against God.

God-gild, signifies any Thing that is offered to God or his Service.

Goldwith or **Goldwitch**, is taken for a Golden Mulct.

Good Abearing, denotes an exact Carriage and Behaviour to the King and his People, whereto Persons on Misbehaviour are sometimes bound. One that is thus bound, is said to be more strictly bound, than when bound to the Peace; seeing that the Peace is not broken without an Affray; but this Surety *de bono gestu*, of good Behaviour, may be forfeited by the Number of a Man's Company, or by his or their Weapons.

Good Behaviour, differs very little from *good Abearing*, and Surety for the *good Behaviour* denotes Surety for the Peace. A Justice of the Peace, by Virtue of his Office, may, at the Request of another, or where he himself sees Cause, demand Surety for the good Behaviour; and to that End the Justice may issue out his Warrant against any Person whatsoever, who is under the Degree of Nobility, against whom a particular Complaint must be made in the Court of *Chancery* or *King's Bench*, where such Nobleman may be bound to keep the Peace. Infants, Feme Coverts, who ought to find Surety by their Friends, may be bound over to the good Behaviour; as likewise a Lunatick, who has sometimes lucid Intervals, and in short all other Persons suspected to break the Peace, or who break it by Affrays, Assaults, Battery, Wounding, Fighting, Quarrelling, Threatning, Rioters, &c. may be bound. A Person may be also bound over to his good Behaviour for a scandalous Way of Living, Keeping or haunting Bawdy-Houses, Gaming-Houses, &c. and so may common Drunkards, Whoremongers, and common Whores Night Walkers, and those that live idly, Cheats, Libellers, &c.

Goods. See **Chattels**.

Gore, denotes a narrow Slip of Ground.

Governors of the Chest at Chatham, are certain Officers deputed to take Care and relieve the Poor and Maimed Seamen belonging to the Royal Navy.

Grace, is a Term in our Law used to denote some Act of Clemency; as Acts of Parliament for a general and free Pardon, are called Acts of *Grace*.

Graffer, denotes a Notary or Scrivener.

Graffium, signifies a Writing-Book, Register or Cartulary of Deeds and Evidences. *Cowel*.

Graile, denotes a Book that contains some of the Offices of the *Romish* Church; and it is sometimes taken for a *Mass-Book*.

Grain, denotes the 24th Part of a Penny Weight.

Grand Assise. See **Magna Assisa**.

Grand Cape, is a Writ that lies on a Plea of Land, where the Tenant makes Default in Appearance at the Day given, for the King to take the Land into his Hands, &c. See **Cape Magnum**.

Grand Days, are certain Days in the Terms, which are solemnly kept

GR

kept in the Inns of Court and Chancery, *viz. Candlemas Day* in *Hillary* Term, *Ascension Day* in *Easter* Term, St. *John the Baptist* in *Trinity* Term, and *All Saints Day* in *Hillary* Term: All which Days, as well as *Sunday*, are called *Dies non Juridici*, no Days of the Law.

Grand Distress, is a Writ that lies in two Cases, either when the Tenant or Defendant is attached, and does not appear, but makes Default; or where, after he has appeared, afterwards makes Default; in either of which Cases this Process lies instead of a *Petit Cape*: And thereby all the Goods and Chattels of the Defendant may be distrained within the County; and therefore this is called a *Grand Distress*.

Grand Serjeanty. See **Chivalry**.

Grange, is a House or Farm, where Corn is laid up in Barns, *&c.* and which is provided with Stables for Horses, Stalls for Oxen, Sties for Hogs, with other Things necessary towards Husbandry.

Grangiarius or **Grangerus**, denotes the Person that has Care of a *Grange*, for Corn and Husbandry: And anciently religious Houses had a *Granger*, or *Grange-Keeper*, who look'd after their *Granges* or *Farms* that were in their own Hands.

Grant, in a legal Sense, denotes a Conveyance in Writing of what cannot be properly passed or conveyed by Word only; as Rent, a Reversion, Services, *Advowsons* in gross, Tithes, *&c.* and they are made by Persons who cannot give but by Deed; as the King and all Bodies Politick; which Differences are often confounded in Speech, and on that Account *Grant* is generally by Mistake taken for every Gift made of any Thing by any Person whatsoever; in which Case he that granteth is called the *Grantor*, and the Person to whom it is granted the *Grantee*. *Cowel.* A Grant tending to a Monopoly cannot be made by the King, to the Detriment of the Interest and Liberty of the Subject; neither can the King make a *Grant non obstante* any Statute made, or to be made; for if he does, any subsequent Statute prohibiting what is *granted*, will be a Revocation of the Grant: Yet a *Non obstante* may be good to a former *Grant* made by the King, where he has been deceived in such *Grant*, as when it contains more than was intended to be granted, or where there is any Deceit in the Consideration, *&c.* by which the first Grant will be rendered void.

Grass-hearth, denotes the Grasing or Turning up of the Earth with a Plough; and hence the ancient customary Service for the inferior Tenants of the Manor of *Amersden* in *Oxfordshire*, to bring their Ploughs, and do one Day's Work for their Lord, was called *Grass-hearth* and *Grass-hurt*.

Gravare and **Gravatio**, anciently denoted an Accusation or Impeachment.

Great Men, are understood to denote some Persons of Note or Distinction; as the Temporal Lords of Parliament, the Members of the House of Commons, *&c.*

Great Seal of Great Britain. See **Keeper of the Great Seal**.

Gree, (from a *French* Word, signifying Liking or Allowance) in a legal Sense denotes Satisfaction or Contentment; as in 25 *Ed.* 3. c. 19. it is said, that Judgment shall be put in Dispense till *Gree* be made to the King of his Debt, where this Word is taken for Satisfaction: So to make *Gree* with the Parties, is as much as to say, to agree and satisfy them for some Offence done.

Green Cloth, is a Court of Justice composed of the *Lord Steward*, Treasurer of the King's Houshold, Comptroller, and other Officers, to whom is committed the Government of the King's Court, and and the Keeping of the Peace within the Verge of the same, &c. and it takes this Name of *Green Cloth* from the *Green Cloth* that covers the Table of that Court.

Greenhew or **Greenhue**, is the same with **Vert**.

Green-silver, is an ancient Custom within the Manor of *Writtel* in the County of *Essex*, for every Tenant, whose Fore-door opens to *Greenbury*, to pay a Halfpenny yearly to the Lord, by the Name of *Green silver*. *Cowel*.

Green Wax, denotes the Estreats of Fines, Issues and Amerciaments in the *Exchequer*, under the Seal of that Court, which is made in *Green Wax*, to be levied in the County.

Greve, denotes Power or Authority, and signifies as much as *Comes*, or *Vicecomes*, a Sheriff.

Grith, (from the *Saxons*) denotes Peace.

Grithbreche, from the *Saxons*) signifies a Breach of the Peace.

Grocers, were anciently such Persons as engrossed all Merchandise that was vendible; but now they are incorporated into a Company in the City of *London*, and have a grand Hall, stiled after them *Grocers Hall*.

Groom, in a general Sense is the Name of a Servant in an inferior Place: But it is more particularly applied to the two superior Officers belonging to the King's Court; as *Groom of the Chamber*, *Groom of the Stole*, &c. the last of which is a great Officer of the King's Houshold, whose Province is to be in the King's Bed-chamber, where the Lord Chamberlain has no Business. *Jacob* observes, that the Stole signifies a Robe of Honour, and not a *Close-stool*, as vulgarly apprehended.

Groom Porter, is an Officer of the King, and is *Superintendant* over the King's Gaming-Tables.

Gross, signifies absolute or independent; as a Villein in *Gross* was anciently such a servile Person as was not appendant, or annexed to the Lord of the Manor, and to go along with the Tenure, as an Appurtenance of it; and therefore was like the other personal Goods and Chattels of the Lord, at his Pleasure and Disposal. *Cowel*.

Gross-bois, is taken to be such Wood as by the Common Law or Custom is deemed Timber.

Groundage, denotes a Custom or Tribute paid for the Ground whereon a Ship stands in a Port.

Growth-Halfpenny, is a Rate paid in some Parts for the Tithes of every fat Beast, or other unfruitful Cattle.

Gruarii, (from the *French*) in general, denotes the principal Officers of the Forest.

Guard or **Gard**, in our Law, is particularly used for a Writ concerning *Wardship*; as *Droit de Gard*, *Ejectment de Gard*, and *Ravishment de Gard*.

Guardian, signifies a Person that has the Charge of any Person or Thing, but most generally one who has the Custody and Education of such Persons as are not of sufficient Discretion to take Care of themselves and their own Affairs; as Children and Ideots.

Guardian d' Eglis, are Church-Wardens, Officers that are chosen in every Parish to look after and take the Care and Custody of the Church Goods.

Guardians of the Peace, are those Persons that have the Keeping of the Peace, and may be termed Wardens or Conservators of the same.

Guardian of the Cinque Ports, denotes a Magistrate thereof, having the Jurisdiction of the Ports or Havens that are commonly distinguished by the Names of the *Cinque Ports*, who there has the Authority and Jurisdiction the Admiral of *England* has in Places not exempt.

Guardian of the Spiritualties, denotes the Person to whom the *Spiritual Jurisdiction* of any *Diocese* is committed during the Time the See is vacant.

Guest, denotes a Lodger or Stranger in an Inn, &c. An Action lies against an Innkeeper refusing a Guest Lodging.

Guidage, is an old Word in the Law, signifying what is given for safe Conduct thro' a strange Road or Land in an unknown Country.

Guild, denotes a Fraternity or Company, for this Reason, *viz*. that every one was to pay something towards the Charge and Support of the Company; and hence *Guild-Halls* are said to come, that is to say, the Halls of the Society or Fraternity, where the Companies meet, and make Laws and Orders among themselves. The Original of these Guilds or Companies, was thus, *viz*. it was a Law among the *Saxons*, that every Freeman of Fourteen Years of Age should find Sureties to keep the Peace, or be committed; whereupon certain Neighbours entered into an Association, and became bound for each other to produce the Person that committed an Offence, or to make Satisfaction to the injured Party; in order the better to do which, they raised a Sum among themselves, which they put into a common Stock, and thereout on Occasion made a *pecuniary* Compensation according to the Quality of the Offence committed; and hence came our Fraternities and Guilds, and they were in Use long before any formal Licences were granted for them: But now they are a Company joined together with Laws and Orders made by themselves, by the Licence of the Prince.

Guild-Hall, is the Chief Hall of the City of *London*, for the Meeting of the Lord Mayor and Commonalty of the City, in order for the making of Laws and Ordinances for the Welfare and Regulation of the City, and for holding of Courts there, &c.

Guildhalda Teutonicorum, was a Term formerly used for the Fraternity of *Easterling* Merchants in *London*, called the *Still-yard*.

Guild-Rents, are *Rents* payable to the Crown by any Guild or Fraternity; or those Rents that formerly belonged to religious Houses, and fell into the Hands of the Crown at the general Dissolution of Monasteries, when ordered to be sold, by 22 *Car*. 2. *c*. 6.

Gule of August, is the first Day of *August*, commonly called the Feast of Saint *Peter ad Vincula*; and it is said to have got this Name of the *Gule of August*, from *Gula*, a Throat, for this Reason, *viz*. That one *Quirinus*, a *Tribune*, having a Daughter diseased in her Throat, went to *Alexander*, then Pope of *Rome*, who is said to have been the sixth from St. *Peter*, and requested of him to see the Chains that St. *Peter* was chained with under *Nero*; which Petition being granted, the Daughter by kissing the Chains, was immediately cured of her Disease; and *Quirinus* with his Family was thereupon baptized:

tized: Whereupon this Day, that before had been only called *the Calends of August*, indifferently acquired the Name of either the Instrument that was supposed to have wrought the Miracle, and so called St. *Peter's Day ad Vincula*, or of that Part of the Girl whereon the Miracle was wrought, and therefore termed the *Gule of August*. See *Durand's Rationale Divinorum*, Lib. 7.

Guns. See **Game.**

H.

Habeas Corpora, is a Writ that issues for the Bringing in of a Jury, or such of them as refuse to appear upon the *Venire facias*, for the Trial of a Cause brought to Issue.

Habeas Corpus, is a Writ of two Kinds, the one being no less than the great Writ of the *English-Liberty*, which lies where a Person is indicted for any Crime or Trespass before Justices of the Peace, or in a Court of a Franchise, and being on that Account imprisoned, has offered sufficient Bail, which is refused in a Case that is bailable; then he may have this Writ out of the Court of *King's Bench*, to remove himself thither, in order to answer the Cause there. See *Fitz. Nat. Brev.* The Practice in a Case of this Kind is first to procure a *Certiorari* out of the Court of *Chancery*, directed to the Justices for removing the Indictment into the *King's Bench*, and thereupon to procure this Writ directed to the Sheriff, for causing the Body to be brought at a certain Day. See *Reg. Jud.* The other Kind of *Habeas Corpus* is used for bringing the Body of a Person into Court, who is committed into Gaol or Prison, either in Criminal or Civil Causes; which said Writ will remove a Person and Cause from one Court to another. The *Habeas Corpus* Act, 31 *Car.* 2. *c.* 2. by which the *English Liberty* was doubtless intended to be secured, or at least strengthned, has ordained, that a Person may have a *Habeas Corpus* from any Judge, on Complaint made, and View of the Copy of the Warrant of Commitment (except it be where a Person is committed for Treason or Felony expressed in the Warrant, or some other Offence that is not bailable) which *Habeas Corpus* must be made returnable *immediate*, immediately; and upon producing a Certificate of the Cause of Commitment, the Prisoner is to be discharged on Bail to appear in the Court of *King's Bench* the next Term, or at the next Assises, &c. where Cognisance can be had of the Offence. Even Persons committed for Treason or Felony, expresly mentioned in the Warrant, on Motion in open Court the first Week of the Term, or Day of Sessions, &c. after Commitment, are to be brought to Trial; and in Case they are not indicted the next Term or Sessions, &c. after Commitment, upon Motion the last Day of that Term, they shall be let out upon Bail, except it shall appear upon Oath, that the King's Witnesses are not ready; and if they are not indicted or tried the second Term after Commitment, they shall be discharged. This Law has further ordained, that no Person who has been delivered upon a *Habeas Corpus*, shall be committed again for the same Offence, unless it be by the legal Order of the Court, where they shall be bound to appear, on Pain of 500 *l.* And further, That if any Person be in Prison or in an Officer's Custody

stody for a Criminal Matter, such Person shall not be removed into the Custody of any other Officer, but by *Habeas Corpus*, under the Penalty of 100 *l.* for the first Offence, and 200 *l.* for the second, and at the same Time to be disabled to execute his Office: And no Person shall be sent Prisoner to *Scotland*, or *Ireland*, or any Place beyond Sea in the Dominions of the King, and if they are, it shall be deemed false Imprisonment, on which the Prisoner shall recover treble Costs, and no less than 500 *l.* Damages, and the Party committing or detaining him, shall be subject to the Penalty of a *Præmunire*: And also it is enacted that Judges denying a *Habeas Corpus*, shall forfeit 500 *l.* and if an Officer refuse to obey it, or to deliver a true Copy of the Commitment-Warrant he, in that Case forfeits 100 *l.* for the first Offence, *&c.* This *Habeas Corpus* Act, wholesome as it is, has in late Reigns been too frequently dispensed with, so that in a great Measure it may be said, on some particular Occasions to have been looked upon as a dead Letter, and indeed treated as such.

Habeas Corpus ad prosequendum, is a Writ for the Removal of a Person, in order to Prosecution and Trial in the proper Place.

Habeas Corpus ad faciendum & recipiendum, is a Writ that issues out of the Court of *Common Pleas*, on Behalf of Defendants who are sued in inferior Courts, in order to remove their Causes into the said Court.

Habeas Corpus ad respondendum, is a Writ which lies where a Person is imprisoned on a Process at another's Suit, in any Prison, except that of the *King's Bench*; and a third Person would sue the Prisoner in the *Common Pleas*, in which Case this Writ will remove the Prisoner from the Prison where he was, into the *King's Bench*, to answer the Action in that Court.

Habeas Corpus ad satisfaciendum, is a Writ that lies against a Person in the *Fleet* Prison, *&c.* to charge the Defendant in Execution; and the Delivery of this Writ to the Warden is sufficient.

Habendum, is a particular Part or Form contained in a Deed or Conveyance, each of which consists of two principal Parts, *viz.* the *Premisses*, and the *Habendum*. The Office of the Premisses is to express the Names of the Grantor and Grantee, with their Additions, and the Thing granted. The Office of the *Habendum* is to shew what Property, Interest or Estate the Grantee is to have in that which is granted, or to what Use, Intent or Purpose the same is granted: But *Cowel* says the Office of the *Habendum* is to limit the Estate, so that the general Implication of the Estate, which by Construction of Law passes in the *Premisses*, is by the *Habendum* controlled and qualified; as in a Lease to two Persons, *Habendum*, to have and to hold, to the one for Life, and the Remainder to the other for Life; this alters the general Implication of the Joint-Tenancy in the Freehold, which would pass by the Premisses, were it not for the *Habendum*.

Habere facias Possessionem, is a Writ which lies where one has recovered a Term for Years on an Action of *Ejectione firmæ*, in order to put him into Possession: The Sheriff upon this Writ cannot return that another is Tenant of the Land by Right, but must execute the Writ.

Habere facias Seisinam, is a Writ that lies where a Person has recovered

vered Land in the King's Court; and it is directed to the Sheriff, commanding him to give *Seisin* of the Land recovered. This Writ sometimes issues out of the Records of a *Fine Executory*, directed to the Sheriff, and requiring him to give the Cognisee, or his Heirs, *Seisin* of the Land, of which the *Fine* is levied; and this Writ lies within the Year after the Fine or Judgment upon a *Scire facias* brought. There is also a Writ called *Habere facias Seisinam, ubi Rex habuit Annum, Diem & Vastum*, which lies for the Delivery of Lands to the Lord of the Fee after the King has taken his Due of the Lands of one convicted of Felony. *Cowel.*

Habere facias visum, is a Writ that lies in several Cases in Actions real; as in *Dower, Formedon, &c.* where a View is necessary to be taken of the Lands or Tenements in Question.

Hærede abducto, is defined to be a Writ that anciently lay for the Lord, who having by Right the Wardship of his Tenant under Age, could not come by his Body, it being carried away by another Person. See *Old Nat. Brev.*

Hærede deliberando alii, qui habet Custodiam Terræ, is a Writ directed to the Sheriff, requiring him to command one, that has the Ward of another, to deliver him to the Person whose Ward he was by Reason of his Land: But this Writ is now in Disuse.

Hærede rapto. See **Ravishment of Guard or Gard.**

Hæredipeta, formerly was used for the next Heir to Lands.

Hæretico comburendo, is a Writ which formerly lay against a Heretick, who having been once convicted of *Heresy* by his Bishop, and afterwards abjured it, did at Length fall into the same again, or at least into some other, and thereupon was committed into the Hands of the secular Power: And by Virtue of this Writ, upon a Certificate of the Conviction, *Hereticks* were burnt.

Half Blood, is where a Man marries a second Wife, the first being dead; and by his first *Venter* has Issue a Son, and by his second *Venter* has likewise another Son, in which Case the two Brothers are but of Half Blood, they being Issue by different Venters; and therefore Lands in Fee cannot descend from the one to the other; except in the Case of Crown Lands, Dignities, or of Estates-Tail: But *Half Blood* is no Impediment to an Administration being granted to that as well as the Whole Blood, of the Effects of an Intestate; and the *Half Blood* shall come in for a Share of his personal Estate, equally with the *Whole Blood*, the Brothers by different *Venters* being next of Kin in equal Degree.

Halfendeal, denotes a Moiety, or one Half Part of a Thing.

Half-mark, in *Fitz. Nat. Brev.* is defined to be a *Noble, viz.* 6 s. 8 d. in Money. That Author says, that in Case a Writ of Right be brought, and the Seisin of a Demandant, or his Ancestor, be alledged, the Seisin is not traversable by the Defendant, but he must tender the *Half-mark* for the Enquiry of this Seisin, which is as much as to say, that the Defendant shall not be admitted to deny, that the Demandant or his Ancestors, was seised of the Lands in Controversy, and to prove his Denial; but he may be allowed to render *Half a Mark* in Money to have an Enquiry made whether the Demandant, *&c.* were so seised or not: Yet in a Writ of Advowson brought

HA

brought by the King, the Defendant shall not be obliged to tender the *Half Mark*, for this Reason, because in the King's Case, the Defendant shall be permitted to traverse the Seisin by Licence obtained of the King's Serjeant. See *Fitz. Nat. Brev.* 31.

Half-Seal, is used in the *Chancery* for the Sealing of Commissions to *Delegates*, upon any Appeal, either in Ecclesiastical or Marine Causes. *Cowel*.

Half-Tongue. See *Medietas Linguæ*.

Hall, anciently denoted a chief Mansion-House or Habitation; and it is a Word that we retain to this Day, in many of our Counties, especially in the County Palatine of *Chester*, where every Gentleman of Quality's Seat is called a *Hall*.

Hallege, denotes a Fee due for Cloaths brought for Sale to *Blackwell Hall* in *London*. It also denotes the Toll due to the Lord of a Fair or Market, for such Commodities as are vended in the common *Hall* of the Place.

Hallamass, is otherwise called the Day of *All Hallows*, or *All Saints*, viz. *Nov.* 1.

Hallmote or **Halimote**, was a Court anciently used among the *Saxons*, which we now call a Court-Baron; and the Etymology of the Word is the Meeting together of the Tenants of one *Hall* or Manor. *Cowel* tells us, that it is sometimes taken for a Convention of Citizens in their publick Hall, in which they held their Courts, and this was also called *Falkmote* and *Halmote*: Tho' the Word *Halimote* rather denotes the Lord's Court that is held for the Manor, wherein the Differences between the Tenants were determined.

Halymote, is defined by *Cowel* to signify a Holy or Ecclesiastical Court; and there was a Court formerly held in *London* by that Name, before the Lord Mayor and Sheriffs, for regulating the Bakers; and this Court was anciently held on *Sunday* next before St. *Thomas*'s Day; and thence called the *Halymote* or *Holy Court*.

Halywercfolk or **Holyworkfolk**, did anciently signify such Persons of the Diocese of the County Palatine of *Durham*, as held their Lands to defend the Corps of St. *Cuthbert*, and therefore claimed the Privilege of not being forced to go out of the Bishoprick, either by King or Bishop.

Hamlet, **Hamel** or **Hampsell**, signifies a small Village, House, Cottage, or Parish. *Hamlet*, which is only now used, seems to signify the Seat of a Freeholder.

Hamfare, by *Brompton*, is said to be a Breach of the Peace in a House.

Hamsoken, denotes the Liberty or Privilege in a Man's House; and in *Scotland* it is used for the Crime of him that violently, and contrary to the Peace, assaults a Person in his own House, which, as *Skene* says, is punishable equally with the Crime of ravishing a Woman or Girl. This Word likewise is said to denote a Franchise granted to Lords of Manors, whereby they hold Pleas, and take Cognisance of the Breach of that Immunity.

Hand-borow, denotes a Surety or manuel Pledge, that is to say, an inferior Undertaker; whilst *Headborow* signifies a superior or chief Instrument.

Hand-habend, is taken for a Thief caught in the very Fact, having the Goods stolen found in his Hands.

HA

Hand in and out, is the Name of an ancient Game prohibited by 17 *Ed.* 4. *c.* 2.

Hand-grith, signifies Peace or Protection given by the King under his own Hand.

Hand-gun, is an Instrument or Engine for destroying Game; and which is prohibited to be used or carried about, by 33 *Hen.* 8.

Hangwite, otherwise **Hangwite**, as *Rastal* tells us, denotes a Liberty granted to a Person to be quit of a Felon or Thief hanged without Judgment, or escaped out of Custody; and it is read to be without *legal Trial*.

Hanse, signifies a Society of *Merchants* for the good Usage and safe Passage of Merchandize from one Kingdom to another. This Society was, and in Part still is, endowed with many large Privileges of Princes within their respective Territories.

Hantelode, denotes an Arrest, from a *German* Word signifying a Hand or Load; as an Arrest is made by laying Hands or Hold on the Debtor, &c.

Hap, in a legal Sense, denotes the same as to *hap* the Rent, where Partition is made by two Parceners, and more Land is allowed to one than the other, and she that has most of the Land changes it to the other, who haps the Rent.

Haque, is one of those little Hand-Guns, about three Quarters of a Yard long, that are prohibited by 33 *Hen.* 8. *c.* 6. and 2 & 3 *Ed.* 6. *c.* 14.

Haquebut, is said to be a bigger Sort of Hand-Gun from the *Haque*, and is otherwise called *Harquebuss*, and vulgarly a *Hagbut*.

Harbinger. See **Herbinger**.

Harro or **Harron**, anciently was used to denote an *Outcry* after Felons, the Original of which Words came from the *Normans*.

Harriers, denotes small Hounds for hunting the Hare; and anciently divers Persons held Lands of the King by the Tenure and Service of keeping Packs of *Beagles* and *Harriers*.

Hawkers, anciently denoted those deceitful Fellows that wandered from Place to Place, buying and selling Brass, Pewter, and other Things, which ought to be uttered in open Market. *Hawkers* and *Pedlars* that travel from Town to Town with Goods, &c. are to be licensed by particular Commissioners authorised for that Purpose, or otherwise to be liable to certain Penalties; and a *Hawker* is liable to be seised by any Person, till he produces a Licence. See 3 & 4 *Ann.* 4. and 4 *Geo.* 1. in which Acts, Traders in the Linen and Woollen Manufactures, who sell their Goods in Markets or Fairs by Wholesale, are excepted: And to those we may add Makers of any Goods, who sell those of their own Making; as also the Makers and Sellers of *English* Bone-Lace, who go from House to House. Such Persons as go to and fro in the Streets of *London*, crying of News-Books and Papers, and selling them by Retail, are likewise called *Hawkers*; but the Persons that sell them by Wholesale from the Press, are called *Mercuries*.

Haybote, denotes a Liberty to take Thorns, &c. to make and repair Hedges, Gates, Fences, &c. by Tenant for Life or Years: And this Word is likewise taken for Wood for the making of Rakes and Forks, wherewith Men in Harvest Time make Hay.

Hay-market, is a particular Place in the Suburbs of *London*, where

Hay is sold, where for all Carts of *Hay* that are to be sold there, 3 *d. per* Load is to be paid towards the Paving and Amending of the Street. After Three o'Clock in the Afternoon, Carts are not to stand there loaden with Hay, under a certain Penalty. *Hay* that is sold in *London*, &c. between the first of *June*, and the last of *August*, being new, is to weigh sixty Pounds a Truss; and old Hay the other Part of the Year is to weigh fifty-six Pounds, under the Penalty of 2 *s.* 6 *d.* for every Truss that is offered to Sale under that Weight.

Hayward, denotes the Person who keeps the common Herd or Cattle of a Town; one Part of whose Office is to see that the Cattle neither break nor crop the Hedges of inclosed Grounds, by which Means he keeps the Grass from being hurt and destroyed: And this Officer is appointed in the Lord's Court, and is to look to the Fields, and impound Cattle that commit Trespass therein; and likewise to inspect that no Pound-breaches be made, and if any be, to present them at the Leet.

Hazard, denotes a certain unlawful Game at Dice called by that Name, the Players at which are called *Hazarders*.

Headborow, denotes the Person that is Head of the Frank-pledge in *Boroughs*, and signifies the Person who formerly had the Government within his own Pledge. This Person was likewise stiled *Borowhead, Bursholder, Thirdborow, Tithingman*, &c. These *Headborows*, we are told, were the Chief of the ten Pledges, and that the other nine were stiled *Handborows*, or inferior Pledges. *Headborows* at this Time are only a Kind of Constables.

Headland, is taken to signify the upper Part of Ground left for the Turning of the Plough; and hence comes the Word *Headway*.

Head-pence, was a certain Sum anciently exacted by the Sheriff of *Northumberland* of the Inhabitants of that County, without any Account thereof to be given to the King; which Exaction is now utterly abolished.

Head-silver, was a certain Fine anciently paid to Lords of Leets.

Halfang or **Haisfang**, (from the *Saxons*) denotes the Punishment of Hanging by the Neck; and it is sometimes taken for a pecuniary Mulct paid, by Way of Composition for standing in the Pillory, to the King or chief Lord.

Hearth-money. See **Chimney-money.**

Hebbermen, is said to denote Fishermen or Pochers below *London Bridge*, that fish for Whitings, &c. commonly at the Time of Ebb.

Hebbing-wears, denotes certain *Wears* or Engines that are made or laid at the Time of Ebb.

Hebdomadius, signifies the Week's Man, Canon, or Prebendary belonging to a Cathedral Church, and who has the Care of the Choir, and those that belong to it for his own Week.

Heccagium, is taken to denote Rent formerly paid to the Lord of the Fee, for Liberty for the Use of certain Engines called *Hecks*.

Hedagium, signifies Toll or Customary Duties paid at a *Hith* or *Wharf*, for Landing of Goods, &c.

Hedge-bote, denotes Stuff that is necessary for the Making of Hedges, and which a Lessee for Years, &c. may of common Right take in the Ground that he holds.

HE HE

Hedge-breakers, are Persons that break down or destroy Hedges, who by 43 *Eliz. c.* 7. are to pay Damages at the Discretion of a Justice of the Peace; and if not able to pay the same, they are to be committed to the Hands of a Constable, in order to be whipp'd. Peace-Officers and others may apprehend Persons suspected of *Hedge-stealing*, and carry them before a Justice of the Peace, when not giving a reasonable Account how they came by Wood, &c. they are both to make such Recompence as the Justice of the Peace shall adjudge, and likewise pay a Sum not exceeding 10 s. to be applied to the Use of the Poor; or otherwise to be sent to the House of Correction. See 15 *Car.* 2. *c.* 2.

Heir, denotes the Person that succeeds another by Descent to Lands, &c. being an Estate of Inheritance, that is to say, an Estate in *Fee*, because nothing passes by Right of Inheritance, but *Fee*; so that at Common Law a Person cannot be Heir to Goods and Chattels. *Heir* is by some briefly defined to be the Person to whom Lands or Tenements do by the Act of God and Right of Blood descend; as the eldest Son after the Death of his Father becomes his Heir: And if there be a Grandfather, Father and Son, and the Father die before the Grandfather, who afterwards dies seised in Fee; the Land in that Case shall go to the Grandson or Grandaughter, and not to any other Children of the Grandfather. This Heir in our Law is termed *Hæres jure repræsentationis*, on Account of his representing the Person of his Father. Where the Father dies without Issue, the next eldest Brother shall have the Lands, &c. as *Heir*; and for Want of a Brother they descend to the Sisters of the Father. The Word *Heir* is a collective Name, and extends unto all *Heirs*, under which the Heirs of Heirs are comprehended, *in infinitum*; as where Lands are given to one and his Heirs, all his Heirs are thereby totally vested in the Donee, so that he may dispose of the same when and to whom he pleases. Not only Land, but Rent not in Arrear of the Ancestor, the Lessor, shall go to the Heir; so Corn sown by a Tenant for Years, in Case his Term expires before the Corn is ripe. An *Heir* has this Advantage, that he can enforce the Administrator to pay Debts out of the personal Estate of the Intestate, to preserve the Inheritance free; and likewise where an Executor has Assets, the *Heir* may in Equity compel him to redeem a Mortgage; and in the like Manner he is obliged to act, where the Heir is charged in Debt. Where an Heir is sued for his Ancestor's Debt, and pays the same, he shall be reimbursed by the Executor or Administrator of such Ancestor, who has Assets in his Hands. A Creditor may sue either *Heir*, Executor or Administrator, each of whom are chargeable. Whether an *Heir* has Lands by Descent or not, is triable by a Jury, who are to ascertain the Value of the Lands descended, if any, in order to make the Heir answerable. Where an Ancestor has bound himself and his Heirs for the Payment of Money, or Performance of some other Act, the Heir, tho' never so much Land comes to him from such Ancestor by Gift in Tail or other Conveyance of the Father, and not by Descent, he is in no Respect chargeable; and it is likewise

wise so in all other Estates, except *Fee-simple*.

Heir apparent, is a Person so called in the Life-time of his Ancestor.

Heiress, is a Female Heir to one who has an Estate of Inheritance; and where there are two or more of such, they are called *Co-heirs* or *Coheiresses*. The Consequence of stealing an *Heiress*, and marrying her against her Will, is by the *Stat.* 3 *Hen.* 7. *c.* 2. declared Felony.

Heir-loome, is a Word that comprehends in it divers Implements of Houshold-stuff or Furniture; as a Marble Hearth, the first best Bed, and other Things which by the Custom of some Places have belonged to a House for certain Descents, and are such as are never inventoried after the Death of the Owner, as Chattels, and therefore never go to the Executor or Administrator, but to the Heir along with the House itself by Custom, and not by the Common Law.

Hencpenny, was a customary Payment of Money, instead of Hens at *Christmas*.

Herald, **Heralt** or **Harold**, denotes an Officer at Arms. The Duty of these, as at this Time exercised in this Kingdom, is to denounce War, proclaim Peace, and further to be imployed by the King in Martial Messages. These Officers are also Examiners of Gentlemens *Coats of Arms*, and their *Genealogies*; and they marshal the Solemnities at the Coronations, and Funerals of Princes, and other great Men.

Herbage, signifies a Green Pasture and Fruit of the Earth, by Nature provided for the Food of Cattle. This Word is likewise used for a Liberty which a Person has to feed his Cattle in the Ground of another Person, or in the Forest, &c.

Herbagium anterius, was anciently used to denote the first Crop of Hay or Grass, in Contradistinction to the second Cutting, or After-Math.

Herbinger or **Harbinger**, signifies an Officer belonging to the King's Houshold, who goes before, and allots the Noblemen, and other Attendants on the King, their Lodgings.

Hereditaments, denotes all immoveable Things, either corporeal or incorporeal, which a Person has to him and his Heirs; and which, if not otherwise devised or conveyed, descend to him that is next Heir, and not to the Executor or Administrator, as Chattels do. In short, it comprehends whatever is inheritable, or may descend to an *Heir*. In Conveyances by the Grant of *Hereditaments*, both Manors, Houses, Lands, &c. will pass.

Heresy, denotes some Opinion contrary to the sound Principles of Religion, and among us of the Reformed Religion is taken for a false Opinion that is repugnant to some essential Point of Doctrine of the Christian Faith revealed in Scripture, perversely maintained and persisted in by Professors of the Name of Christ.

Heretick, denotes a Person convicted of Heresy, or who maintains Opinions or Principles contrary to the Christian Religion.

Hergripa, signifies the Offence of pulling one by the Hair, which was punishable by the Laws of *Hen.* 1.

Heriot, anciently signified a Tribute given to a Lord of a Manor, for his better Preparation for War; but it is now taken for the best Beast, either Horse, Ox, or Cow, that the Tenant dies possessed of, and

H I

and which is due to the Lord; and in some Manors, the best Goods, Piece of Plate, &c. are all called *Heriots*. There are likewise Heriot-Service, and Heriot-Custom: Heriot-Service is payable on the Death of a Tenant in Fee; and Heriot-Custom on the Death of a Tenant for Life. *Co. Lit.* 185. says, that when a Tenant holds by Service to pay a Heriot at his Decease, which is expresly reserved in the Deed of Feoffment, this is *Heriot-Service*: And where *Heriots* have been customarily paid Time out of Mind, after the Death of a Tenant for Life, this is termed *Heriot-Custom*.

Herischild, anciently denoted a military Service or Knight's Fee.

Hermaphrodite, denotes a Person that is both Man and Woman. *Hermaphrodites*, as they partake of both Sexes, are capable of granting Lands, &c. or inheriting as Heirs to their Ancestors, and shall inherit according to the prevailing Sex.

Herring-Silver, is thought to be a Composition in Money, for the Custom of paying such a Number of Herrings towards the Provision of a religious House.

Hidage, was an extraordinary Tax anciently paid to the King for every *Hide* of Land. This Word has likewise sometimes been used for the being quit of that Tax; which likewise was *Hidegild*, a Ransom paid to save one's Skin or Hide from beating.

Hide of Land, denotes such a Quantity of Land as might be ploughed with one Plough in a Year, or so much as would maintain a Family.

High Treason. See **Treason**.

Highway, is a free Passage for the King's Subjects, and on that Account is called the King's Highway; tho' the Freehold of the Soil be in the Lord of the Manor, or Owner of the Land. For the Repairing of Highways, it is by 2 & 3 *P. & M. c.* 8. enacted, That Constables and Churchwardens of Parishes, calling the Parishioners together, shall annually elect two honest Persons to be Surveyors of the *Highways*, who are thereby authorised to order and direct the Persons and Carriages that are to be employed for the Amending of the *Highways*; and the Persons thus chosen shall take upon them the Execution of the Office, on Pain of forfeiting 20 s.

Highwaymen. See **Robbery**.

His Testibus, are *Latin* Words anciently used in Deeds, after the *In cujus rei Testimonium*; when the Witnesses were first called, then the Deed read to them, and their Names were entered down: But this Part of a Clause in Deeds is now entirely gone into Disuse.

Hindeni Homines, (from the *Saxons*) denotes a Society of Men. In the Time of our Ancestors, the *Saxons*, all Men were ranked into three Classes, the *Lowest*, the *Middle*, and the *Highest*, and were rated according to the Class they were in; that is to say, if any Injury was committed, Satisfaction was to be made according to the Value of the Person to whom it was done. The *Lowest* were those that were worth 200 Shillings, and they were called *Viri ducenteni*, or *Twybindemen*, and their Wives were termed *Twibinda's*: The *Middle* were valued at 600 Shillings, and were filed *Sixhindemen*, and their Wives *Sixhinda's*: And the *Highest* were valued at 1200 Shillings, and were *Twelfhindemen*, and their Wives *Twelfhinda's*.

Hine,

HO

Hine, is properly taken for a Servant at Husbandry; and the *Master-Hine* for the Person that oversees the rest.

Hiriscunda, anciently denoted the Division of an Inheritance among the Heirs.

Hireman, is thought properly to signify a Person that serves in the King's Hall, as a Guard to him.

Hith or **Hyth**, denotes a Port, Wharf, or small Haven, to embark or land Wares at; as *Queenhith*, &c.

Hlaforcus, (from the *Saxons*) denotes the Benefit of the Law.

Hloth, formerly denoted an unlawful Assembly, from the Number of seven to thirty-five.

Hoastmen, are an ancient Fraternity incorporated in *Newcastle upon Tyne*, who deal in Sea-Coal.

Hoblers or **Hobilers**, were anciently Light Horsemen, or certain Tenants, who by their Tenure were bound to maintain for certifying any Invasion, or the like Danger towards the Sea-side.

Hockettor, or **Hocqueteur**, was anciently used for a Knight of the Post; as also a decayed Man, or a Basket-Carrier.

Hock-Tuesday Money, was a Duty anciently paid to the Landlord, for giving Leave to his Tenants and Bondmen to solemnize that Day whereon the *English* conquered the *Danes*, being the second *Tuesday* after *Easter-Week*. *Cowel.*

Hogenhine, (*Saxon*) denotes one that comes as a Guest to an Inn, and continues there the third Night, from which Time he is accounted of that Family, so that if he offend the King's Peace, his *Host* must be answerable for him. *Cowel.*

Hoke-day or **Hock-Tuesday**, was a Day very remarkable in ancient Times, so that Rents were usually reserved payable thereon.

Holde, is thought to denote a Bailif of a City or Town.

Homage, has its Derivation from *Homo*, a Man, because when a Tenant did his Service to the Lord, he said, *I become your Man*. In the ancient Grants of Lands or Tenements in Fee, the Lord not only obliged his Tenants to certain Services, but also took a Submission with Promise or Oath, that they would be true to him, as their Lord and Benefactor; and this Kind of Submission, which is said to have been the most honourable, as it was from a Freehold Tenant, was called *Homage*.

Homage Auncestrel, is where a Person and his Ancestors, Time out of Mind, held Lands of the Lord and his *Ancestors* by *Homage*.

Homage Jury, denotes a *Jury* in a *Court Baron*, which consists of Tenants that do *Homage* to the Lord of the Fee: And this Jury makes Enquiry into, as well as Presentments of Defaults and Deaths of Tenants, Admittances and Surrenders in the Lord's Court.

Homager, signifies any Person that is bound to do *Homage* to another.

Homagio respectuando, is a Writ directed to the Escheator, whereby he is commanded to deliver Lands to the Heir of the King's Tenant, who is of full Age, notwithstanding his Homage be not done.

Homagium reddere, has been used to denote, *to renounce Homage*; as where the Tenant or Vassal made a solemn Declaration of disowning his Lord: For which we are told there was a set Form prescribed by the *Feudatory* Laws.

Homesoken, is a particular Privilege that every Person has in his own House, which is generally called

called his Castle: And he that invades such Freedom or Privilege is said *facere Homesoken*, to do or commit *Homesoken*; which *Cowel* takes to be what we now call *Burglary*, a Crime of the highest Nature, as it is not only a Breach of the King's Peace; but likewise a Breach of that Liberty which every Person has, or ought to have, in his own House, and therefore ought not to be invaded.

Homicide, denotes the Killing or Slaying of a Person; and it is divided into *Voluntary* and *Casual*: *Voluntary*, is that which is done with Deliberation, and committed with a full Purpose to kill: *Casual Homicide*, is where the Death of a Person happens by Chance, without any Intention to kill: The former of these, if done out of Malice prepensed, is *Murder*; and the latter may be *Manslaughter*, *Chancemedley*, &c.

Homine eligendo ad custodiendam peciam sigilli pro Mercatoribus editi, is a Writ directed to a Corporation, for the Choice of a new Person to keep one Part of the Seal appointed for *Statutes Merchant*, when the former Person is dead.

Homine replegiando, is a Writ used for the Bailing of a Person out of Prison, and lies where a Person is in Prison without the Commandment of the King or his Judges, or for any Cause that is repleviable; and this Writ is directed to the Sheriff, commanding him to *replevy* the Prisoner.

Homine capto in Withernamium, is a Writ for the apprehending of any Person that has taken any other, and conveyed him or her out of the County, so that they cannot be replevied by Law.

Homines, were a Sort of *Feudatory* Tenants, who claimed a Privilege of having their Causes and Persons tried only in their Lord's Court; and *Cowel* gives us an Instance of this Kind, where *Gerard de Camvil*, in the fifth Year of *Richard* the First, was charged with Treason, and other high Misdemeanors, he pleaded that he was *Homo Comitis Johannis*, and therefore would stand to the Law or Custom of his Court.

Homiplagium, was formerly used to signify the Maiming of a Person.

Homo, is a *Latin* Word, and includes in it both Man and Woman.

Hond-habend, denotes some Circumstance of manifest Theft; as where a Person is apprehended with the Things stolen in his Hand. It also signifies the Right the Lord has of determining this Offence in his Court.

Honour, is particularly used to denote a more noble *Seigniory* or *Lordship*, on which inferior Manors or Lordships depend, by Performance of Customs and Services: And originally no Lordships were *Honours*, but such as belonged to the King; but afterwards they were given in Fee to Noblemen.

Honour-Courts, are Courts held within particular *Honours*, mentioned in the 33 *H*. 8. *c*. 37. We are told there is likewise a *Court of Honour* of the *Earl Marshal of England*, wherein Disputes touching Precedents and Points of Honour are examined.

Honourary Services, were such Services as were made out to the Tenure of Grand Serjeanty, and commonly annexed to some *Honour*.

Horn with Horn, or **Horn under Horn**, denotes the promiscuous Feeding of Bulls and Cows, or all horned Beasts, which are allowed to run together upon the

same

same Common: And *Cowel* tells us that the Commoning of Cattle *Horn* with *Horn*, was properly where the Inhabitants of different Parishes let their common Herds run upon the same open Common; and therefore that there might be no Dispute about the Right of Tithes, the Bishop ordained that the Cows should answer all Profit to the Minister of the Parish where the Owner lived.

Horngeld, denotes a Tax within the Forest, payable for *horned* Beasts.

Hors de son Fee, denotes an Exception to avoid an Action brought for Rent or Services that issue out of Land, by the Person that pretends to be the Lord; in which Case if the Defendant can prove the Land to be *Hors de son Fee*, that is to say, *without his Fee*, the Action drops.

Hostilers, has been used for *Innkeepers*; and *Hosters* was anciently taken in the same Sense.

Hospitalers, were the Knights of a certain religious Order; and were so called, because they built an *Hospital* at *Jerusalem*, in which Pilgrims were received. We are told that the Institution of this Order was first allowed by Pope *Gelasius* the Second, in the Year 1118. and was afterwards confirmed here by Parliament; which said Order had many Privileges granted them, as Immunities from Payment of Tithes, &c. And that the chief Place of their Abode is at present at *Malta*, an Island that was given them by the Emperor *Charles* the Fifth, after they were driven from *Rhodes* by *Solyman* the Magnificent, Emperor of the Turks; and for this Account that Order is now called *Knights of Malta*. *Cowel*.

Hospital, denotes some charitable Foundation laid for the Sustenance and Relief of the Poor, to continue for ever: And any Person seised of an Estate in *Fee*, may by Deed inrolled in *Chancery*, erect and found an *Hospital*, and nominate such Heads or Governors therein as he shall think fit: And this charitable Foundation shall be incorporated and subject to the Inspection and Guidance of the Heads nominated. As few of our Precedent Books contain the Form of a Deed for Erecting and Founding of an Hospital, we think proper here to insert one, which take as follows:

THIS INDENTURE, made the —— Day of —— in the —— Year of the Reign of our Sovereign Lord —— by the Grace of God of Great Britain, France *and* Ireland *King, Defender of the Faith*, &c. *and in the Year of our Lord* - *Between* A. B. *of* —— *in the County of* —— *Gentleman, of the one Part, and* C. D. E. F. *and* G. H. *of*, &c. *of the other Part. Whereas the said* A. B. *is seised in Fee-simple, or other Estate of Inheritance, of and in a certain Messuage and Lands of the yearly Value of* —— *lawful Money of* Great Britain, *situate, lying and being in* —— *and now in the Possession and Occupation of him the said* A. B. *And whereas the said* A. B. *of his charitable Affection and Disposition has erected and founded several Edifices and Buildings upon the said Land adjoining to the aforesaid Messuage, to be an Hospital for the Sustenance and Relief of poor and impotent Persons, to have Continuance for ever. Now this Indenture witnesseth, that the said* A B *doth in and by these Presents found, erect and establish all and singular the said Edifices and Buildings so* erected

erected and founded as aforesaid, for an Hospital of poor and impotent People for ever, and according to the Power given to the said A. B. by the Statute in that Case made and provided. And the said A. B. by these Presents covenants and grants to and with the said C. D. E. F. and G. H. their Heirs, Executors and Administrators, and every of them, and doth hereby limit and appoint, that the said Hospital, and the poor and impotent Persons therein at present, placed by the said A. B. that is to say, J. K. L. M. N. O. &c. together with the said C. D. E. F. and G. H. and their Successors, shall for ever hereafter be incorporated by the Name of the Master and Brethren of the Hospital of ―― in the County aforesaid. And further, the said A. B. doth by these Presents nominate and appoint the said C. D. to be the present Master of the said Hospital, and the said E. F. G. H. J. K. L. M. N. O. &c. to be the present Brethren of the same; and by by the Name of Master and Brethren they shall have full Power and lawful Capacity and Ability to purchase, take, hold, receive and enjoy, and to have to them and their Successors for ever as well Goods and Chattels, as Lands, Tenements, Goods and Hereditaments, being Freehold of any Person or Persons whatsoever, according to the Form and Effect of the Statutes in that Behalf made: And that the said Hospital, and the Persons being so incorporated, founded and named, shall have full Power and lawful Authority by the said Name of Master and Brethren of ―― to sue and be sued, implead and be impleaded, to answer and to be answered unto in all Manner of Courts and Pleas, as well Spiritual as Temporal, in all Manner of Suits whatsoever, and of what Kind or Nature soever such Suits or Actions may or shall be. And the said A. B. doth by these Presents also covenant, grant and appoint, that the said Master and Brethren, and their Successors, shall at all Times, and for ever hereafter, have a common Seal, with ―― engraven thereon, by which the said Master and Brethren, and their Successors, shall or may seal any Instrument or Writing touching or concerning the said Corporation, and the Lands, Tenements and Hereditaments, Goods, or other Things thereto belonging, or in anywise appertaining. And that it shall and may be lawful to and for the said A. B. during the Term of his natural Life, upon the Death or Removal of the said Master, or any of the said Brethren, to nominate, place or appoint one other Person in the Room or Place of him that so dieth or is removed; and after the Death or Decease of the said A. B. it shall and may be lawful for the Rector or Parson of the Parish of ―― aforesaid, and the Churchwardens of the said Parish for the Time being, for ever after the Decease of the said A. B. upon the Death or Removal of the Master, or any other of the Brethren of the said Hospital, to place one other Person in the Room of him that dies, or is removed, successively for ever. And the said A. B. doth by these Presents further declare and appoint, that it shall and may be lawful for him the said A. B. during his Life, and also for the Rector or Parson of the said Parish of ―― for the Time being, after the Decease of the said A. B. to visit the said Hospital, and inspect into the Government and State of the same. And lastly, that the Rents and Profits of the said Messuage and Lands

Lands before-mentioned, shall on the Feast Day of ——, for ever be paid to the Master of the said Hospital, and his Successors, and be applied towards the Maintenance of the —— Brethren and poor impotent Persons aforesaid, and their Successors; and to and for no other Use, Intent or Purpose whatsoever. In Witness whereof, the said Parties to these Presents have hereunto interchangeably set their Hands and Seals the Day and Year first above-written.

Commission by 32 *Eliz. c.* 6. and 43 *Eliz. c.* 4. may be awarded to particular Persons, to make an Inquiry of Lands or Goods given to Hospitals; and the *Lord Chancellor*, or *Lord Keeper of the Great Seal*, is impowered to issue out Commissions to Persons for inquiring by a Jury after all Grants and Abuses of a Trust, &c. of Lands granted to charitable Uses; and these Commissioners may make Orders and Decrees relating to the same, and the due Application of the Produce of the Lands or Goods granted, and may likewise decree that Recompence be made for Frauds and Breaches of Trust, &c. Provided that their Orders and Decrees be certified into the Court of *Chancery*: And the *Lord Chancellor* is to take Notice for the Execution of the said Order and Decrees, and after a Certificate produced, may examine into, annul or alter them agreeable to Equity, on Complaint justly made: However this does not extend to Lands, &c. granted to any College or Hall in either of the Universities, or to an *Hospital*, over which special Governors are appointed by the Founder; neither shall it be prejudicial to the Jurisdiction of the Bishop or Ordinary, in respect to his Power of inquiring into, and reforming of Abuses of *Hospitals*. Commissioners thus appointed may order Houses to be repaired by the Persons who receive the Rents, and likewise see that the Lands be let at the utmost Rent; and if any Tenant commit Waste, by cutting down and Sale of Timber, they may order Satisfaction to be made, and may likewise decree that the Lease shall be void. These Commissioners have also Power, where Money is kept back and unpaid, or paid where it should not, to order Payment thereof to the right Use.

Hostelagium, was anciently used to signify a Right to have Lodging and Entertainment, and was reserved by Lords in the Houses of their Tenants.

Hotchpot, (from the *French*) properly denotes a confused Mingling of Things together, and by a Metaphor in our Law is used for a Mixing of Lands given in Marriage, with other Lands in *Fee*, which fall by Descent; as where a Man seized of thirty Acres of Land in *Fee*, has Issue only two Daughters, and he gives with one of them 10 Acres in Marriage, and afterwards dies seized of the other 20; in this Case, she that was thus married, in order to gain her Share of the rest of the Land, must quit her Part granted in Marriage in *Hotchpot*, that is to say, she must refuse to receive the sole Profits of the same, and cause her Land to be mixed with the other, whereby an equal Division may be made of the whole between her and her Sister, as if none had been given to her that was married; and by this Means, for her 10 Acres, she shall have 15, otherwise her Sister would have had the 20, of which her Father died seized. This may be said

said to be little else than waving of a Provision made for a Child in the Life-time of the Father after his Death; but it greatly depending on *Frankmarriage* and Gifts or Grants that Way, it is almost now in Disuse.

House, denotes a Habitation or dwelling Place, to which four Things are necessary; 1. The Habitation of a Man. 2. The Pleasure of the Inhabitant. 3. The Necessity of Light. 4. The Wholesomness of the Air. For any Prejudice to the first, third and fourth of these, Action lies; and the House of every Person is to him as his Castle, not only for his Defence against Violence, but likewise for his safe Repose. Every Person has Right to Air and Light in his own Habitation; wherefore if any Thing of an infectious Smell be laid near the *House* of another, or the Lights of the Inhabitant be stopt up or darkened by Buildings, &c. such Facts are deemed Nusances, and are punishable by our Laws; yet no Action will lye for a Prospect being stopt, that being only a Matter of Delight, as was before observed. A *House* being a Man's Castle, if Thieves or others come there to rob or kill him, and the Owner, or his Servant, kills the Aggressor in defending himself, or the *House*, this is not *Felony*, neither shall the Person slaying in this Case forfeit his Goods, &c. A Person must be careful to use his own *House* in such a Manner, as not to damnify his Neighbour's; and in several Cases, by a Writ *de domo reparanda*, one may compel another to repair his *House*. Plowd. tells us, that Doors of a *House* may not be broke open, unless in Cases of *Treason, Felony, Outlawry, Escape*, &c.

House of Correction, is a Place built at the Charge of every County, with proper Conveniencies for the setting People to Work; and the Justices at the Sessions, are required to appoint Governors or Masters of those *Houses*, whose Salaries are to be paid quarterly by the Treasurer out of the County's Stock: And the Office of the Governors or Masters is to set the Persons committed to their Charge to Work, and to give them moderate Correction, by whipping, &c. and to render a true Account every Quarter-Sessions of Persons committed into their Custodies; and where any of their Prisoners escape, they are fineable by the Justices. This *House* is appointed chiefly for the Punishment of idle and disorderly Persons, such as Parents of Bastard Children, Beggars, Servants running from their Masters, loose and disorderly Women, Trespassers, Gamesters, Rogues, Vagabonds, &c. Poor Persons refusing to work, are there to be whipp'd and set to Work; and Persons living extravagantly, having no visible Way to support themselves, may be likewise sent there to Work, and shall be continued in the Place, until they give the Justices Satisfaction in Respect to their Way of Living. The *House of Correction* in *London* is called *Bridewell*.

House-bote, signifies an Allowance of Timber out of the Lord's Woods, &c. for the Repairing and upholding of a *House*. There is *Estoverium ædificandi*, and *Estoverium Ardendi*. See **Common of Estovers**.

Hue and Cry, denotes the Pursuit of a Person who has committed a Robbery on the Highway; as where the Party robbed, or any that

that was in Company with the Party murdered or robbed, goes to a Constable of the next Town, and requires him to raise *Hue and Cry*, or to pursue the Offender, having described him, and giving an Account, as near as he can, what Course he steered; the Constable must forthwith call upon the Parish for Aid in seeking after the Felon; and if he cannot be found within the Bounds of that Parish, then he must give the next Constable Warning, and he the next, and so on, until the Offender be apprehended, or otherwise pursued to the Sea-side. *Hue and Cry* may be thus generally defined, *viz.* That it is a Pursuit of an Offender from Town to Town, till he is taken, which all Persons present at the committing of a Felony, or where a dangerous Wound is given, are by the Common Law bound to do. Where the Inhabitants of any Hundred, after *Hue and Cry* is made, neglect to pursue the same, they shall answer one Half of the Damages recoverable against the Hundred where a Robbery is committed. In case a Robbery is committed on the Highway in the Day-Time of any Day, except *Sunday*, the Hundred in which the Robbery was acted is answerable for the same, provided Notice be given thereof with all convenient Speed, to some of the Inhabitants of the next Village, to the Intent, that they may make *Hue and Cry* for the apprehending of the Offender; in the making of which, diligent Search must be made in all suspected Houses and Places, and not only Officers but also all private Persons that pursue the *Hue and Cry*, may arrest the Bodies of such Persons as in their Pursuit they shall find suspicious, and carry them before a Justice of the Peace of the County where taken, to be examined and give an Account of themselves. If the Offender is taken within 40 Days after the Robbery was committed, and convicted, the Hundred in that Case will be excused; but if not, the 40 Days being past, the Party robbed may make Oath before a Justice of the Peace of the County, in which the Robbery was done, of the Time and Place of the Robbery, and of what Money he was robbed, and that he was not acquainted with any of the *Robbers*; and afterwards in 20 Days the Person that was robbed may bring his Action against the Hundred by an original Writ, which must be sued out within a Year after the Robbery. Justices of the Peace at their Sessions may make a Rate upon the whole Hundred to pay and reimburse the Money levied on the Lands of any of the Hundred, recovered against the Hundred by a Person robbed. The Party that is robbed is not bound to pursue the Offender himself, or to lend his Horse for that End; yet still has his Remedy against the Hundred, in Case the Offender is not taken: But if the Offender is taken within 40 Days after the Robbery, or before the Plaintiff recovers against the Hundred, in either of these Cases the Hundred is discharged. If a Quaker, or his Servant being a Quaker, be robbed, and either of them refuse to take the Oath of the Robbery, and that he did not know any of the Robbers, the Hundred in such Case is not answerable. In Case of a Carrier's being robbed of another Person's Goods, either he or the Owner thereof may sue the Hundred. In Actions brought against a Hundred, poor Persons and Servants are allowed as good Wit-

Witnesses for the Hundred, which Householders who are worth any Thing are not; and the Plaintiff is allowed to be a Witness in his own Cause.

Hundred, signifies a particular Part of a County, and is so called, because it used to contain ten Tithings and a *Hundred* Families, or for that it found a Hundred able Men for the King's Wars. After the Division of this Land into Counties, and the Government of each County was given to a Sheriff, those Counties were subdivided into *Hundreds*, of which the Constable was the chief Officer.

Hundredors, denotes Persons dwelling within a *Hundred*, who are fit to be impanell'd on Juries for Trials. *Hundredor* is likewise taken for him that has the Jurisdiction of the *Hundred*, and in some Places is applied to the Bailiff of a *Hundred*.

Hundred-lagh, was anciently taken for the *Hundred Court*.

Hundred Setena, was anciently taken for the Inhabitants of a *Hundred*.

Hurrers, is a Name the Cappers and Hatters of *London* formerly went by.

Husband. See *Baron and Feme*.

Husbrece, formerly denoted that Offence which we now call *Burglary*.

Husfastne, (from the *Saxons*) denotes a Person that holds Lands or Tenements.

Husgable, anciently signified some Tax or Tribute imposed upon a House, as House-Rent.

Hustings (from the *Saxons*) is a Court held before the Lord Mayor and Aldermen of *London*, and is reckoned to be the Supreme Court of the City.

Hybernagium, was anciently taken for the Season for sowing Winter Corn, *viz.* between *Michaelmas* and *Christmas*; as *Tremagium* formerly denoted the Season for sowing the Summer Corn in the Spring; And these Words have likewise been taken for the different Seasons of the Year; as also, for the different Lands on which the different Grains were sown; and sometimes this Word has been taken for the different Sorts of Corn; as *Hybernagium* has been used to signify Wheat and Rye, which with us are still all termed *Winter Corn*.

Hypothecate, was formerly used to signify as much as to pawn a Ship for Necessaries.

Hyth. See *Hith*.

I.

Jactivus, denotes a Person that loses by some Default.

Jampnum, is a Word anciently used in Fines of Lands, &c. and is thought to be derived from a *French* Word, signifying Yellow; and on that Account *Jampnum* is taken to signify Gorsy Ground, the Blossoms of *Furze* or *Gorse* are of a yellow Colour.

Jannum or **Jaun**, is taken to denote Whins or Furze, which no Person is allowed to cut down in a Forest without a License first had.

Ich Dien (from the *Germans*) is the *Motto* of the *Prince of Wales*'s Arms, in *English* denoting *I serve*.

Ictus Orbus, is said to signify a Maim, Bruise, or other Hurt, without breaking the Skin, or occasioning the shedding of Blood.

Identitate Nominis, is a Process which issues where a Person is taken and arrested in any Personal Action and committed to Prison, instead of another of the same Name; in which Case he may have this

this Writ directed to the Sheriff, who, as a Commissioner thereby appointed, is to make Inquiry whether the Prisoner be the same Person against whom the Action was brought or not; and if not, then the Sheriff is empowered to discharge him: Yet where there are two Persons of one Name, and one is sued without any Name of Place or Addition to distinguish the Defendant, this Writ will not lie; and in the like Manner it is where there is Father and Son, both of the same Name, in Case there be no Addition of *Junior*, the Person sued will always be looked upon as *Senior*; and if the younger in this Case be arrested for the Father, he may have an Action for false Imprisonment. This Writ likewise lies for wrongfully seising Goods or Lands of a Person outlawed, for Want of a sufficient Declaration of his Surname.

Ideot, with us denotes a Person that is born a *natural Fool*. The King has a Right to the Custody of an *Ideot's* Lands, and to receive the Profits of the same during his Life, without Commitment of Waste, and finding him and his Family (if any) Necessaries; and after his Decease the Lands are to be returned to the Heir at Law, not being an *Ideot*. The King has likewise a Right to the Custody of the Body, Goods and Chattels of an *Ideot*, after Office found. The Custody indeed of the Lands is granted to the King by the Statute *de Prærogativa Regis*, viz. 17 *Ed.* 2. *c.* 9. And the Use of them is by that Statute lodged in the King; and yet the Freehold is in the *Ideot*. So likewise the Custody of the Body and Goods are the King's by the Common Law. Where an *Ideot* shall alien his Lands, the King, upon an Inquisition found, that he is an *Ideot*, may have a *Scire facias* against the *Alienee*, and make a Reseisin of the same into his Hands; but still the Inheritance, as before observed, is in the *Ideot*. *Staundford* tells us, that if a Person has had once Understanding, and afterwards by Chance or Misfortune becomes a Fool, the King cannot have the Custody of him: And we are likewise told, that if a Man have so much Knowledge as to measure a Yard or two of Cloth, tell or number Twenty-pence in small Money, or regularly to name the Days of the Week, or to beget a Child, by which it may appear he retains some Light of Reason, he may not by our Laws be accounted an *Ideot*. *Ideots*, *Lunaticks*, or Persons *non compos mentis*, are incapable of making Wills or Testaments; and all Deeds, Grants or Conveyances, by them made are voidable; yet what they act concerning Lands or Tenements, in a Court of Record, as Fines, Recoveries, Judgments, Statutes, &c. shall be binding to them, and all others that claim under them; tho' it is the Opinion of some, that the Judges ought not to suffer an *Ideot* to do any such Act. However, by a late Statute, viz. 4 *Geo.* 2. *c.* 10. Persons that are *Ideots*, *Lunaticks*, or *non compos mentis*, and are seised of Estates in *Fee*, for Term of Life, or for Years, either in Trust or by Way of Mortgage, are rendered capable to make Conveyances or Assignments of such their Estates, in such Manner as the *Lord Chancellor* shall direct, upon the Hearing of the Parties for whom such *Ideots*, or Lunaticks shall be seised in Fee, &c. and those Conveyances shall be good in Law; and *Ideots* may in the like Manner be compelled to convey such

such Estates as other Persons may. *Ideots* may not appear by Attorney, but whenever they sue or defend an Action, they must appear in proper Person, and the Suit carried on in their Names, tho' followed by others.

Ideota inquirendo vel examinando, is a Writ that lies to examine, whether an *Ideot* be one or not. The Method of suing out this Writ, is briefly this, *viz.* As the King has the Protection of his Subjects, and the Government of the Lands of such as are naturally defective in their Understanding, this Writ issues, directed to the Sheriff, whereby he is commanded to call before him the Person suspected of *Ideocy*, and to examine him, and inquire by the Oaths of a Jury of twelve Men, whether any of the Parties is an *Ideot* or not; and after such Inquisition is taken, the same is to be certified into the Court of *Chancery*; which being done, the Party may afterwards be examined by the *Lord Chancellor*, &c.

Idoneum se facere, was anciently used to signify to purge one's Self of an Oath, whereof the Person is accused.

Jeofaile, (from the *French*) denotes some Oversight in Pleading, or other Proceedings in Law: And it is where the Parties to a Suit have proceeded so far, that they have joined Issue, so that the Cause is triable, or tried by a Jury or Inquest, and it happened that this Pleading or Issue is so ill pleaded or joined, that it will be Error if the Parties proved further; for which Reason either of the Parties may shew it to the Court, either after Verdict given, and before Judgment, or before the Jury are charged. The Shewing of these Defects in Law Proceedings, was anciently thus done by the Counsel, *viz.* When the Jury came into Court in order to try the Issue, they often said to the Jury, *this Inquest you ought not to take*; and after Verdict would say to the Court, *this Judgment you ought not to go, or pass*. As for *Example*; if a Defendant in an *Assumpsit* pleads Not guilty, and thereon Issue is joined, and found for the Plaintiff, he in this Case may have Judgment, tho' the Issue in this Action is improper; for this Reason, that as there is a Deceit alledged, the Plea of *Not guilty* is an Answer thereto, and it can be only said to be an Issue misjoined, which is added by the Statute of *Jeofails*; for an ill Plea and Issue are aidable by that Statute, after a Verdict. Where a Verdict is once given in a Court of Record, the Judgment is not to be stopped or reversed for Variance in Form between the original Writ or Bill and the Declaration, &c. Or for Want of Averment of the Party's being living, so as the Party is proved to be alive; or for that the *Venire facias* is in Part misawarded, nor for Misnomer of Jurors, provided they be proved to be the Jurors returned, &c. See 21 *Jac.* 1. c. 13.

Jetsen, Jetson, or Jetsom, (from the *French*) denotes any Thing thrown out of a Ship or Vessel that is in Danger of being a Wreck, and which by the Waves is driven ashore. See **Flotsam**.

Jesuits, are Persons of a particular *Romish* Order, against whom several Statutes are made in this Kingdom; as where any Person born within the King's Dominions, and ordained by the pretended Jurisdiction of *Rome*, remaining in *England*, or coming from beyond Sea into this Realm, and not submitting

mitting to some Justice of the Peace within three Days, and taking the Oaths, are guilty of High Treason. See 27 *Eliz. c.* 2. whereby the Receivers, Aiders and Harbourers of such Persons are made guilty of Felony. See likewise 22 *Car.* 2.

Ignis Judicium, denotes a Purgation by Fire, or the ancient judicial fiery Trial.

Ignoramus, that is to say, We are ignorant, is a Term used in our Law where the *Grand Jury* or *Inquest* impanell'd on the Inquisition of Criminal Causes, reject the Evidence as too weak or defective to induce them to approve of the Presentment or Indictment brought against a Person, so as to bring him upon his Trial by a *Petty Jury*; and in this Case they indorse this Word on the Back of the Bill, of the Presentment or Indictment; the Effect of which is, that all further Inquiry and Proceedings against the Party accused, is thereby stopped, and the supposed Offender becomes thereby delivered without further Answer: But in some Cases, such as Assaults, Libels, and other Breaches of the Peace, there have been frequent Instances, especially in late Reigns, of Persons being prosecuted on the Crown Side of the *King's Bench*, upon Informations exhibited there, even after an Indictment or Presentment has been rejected and thrown out by the Grand Inquest.

Ignorance, in a legal Sense denotes the Want of Knowledge of the Law, which will not excuse any Person from the Penalty of it; for every Person is at his Peril bound to take Notice what the Law of the Land is; and *Ignorance* thereof, tho' it may appear to be visible, shall not excuse him. Even an Infant that is arrived to the Age, of Discretion is punishable for Crimes, and yet may well be supposed to be ignorant of the Law; but at the same Time Infants under the Age of Discretion have *Ignorance* by Nature, and therefore shall be excused: And in like Manner Persons that are *non compos mentis* shall be excused. *Ignorance* of a Fact will excuse, tho' *Ignorance* in Law will not.

Illeviable, denotes any Debt or Duty that cannot, or ought not to be levied; as *Nihil* set or returned upon a Debt is a Mark to signify, that it is *illeviable*.

Illiterature, denotes a Want of Skill in Letters or Learning; so that if a Person who is *illiterate* be to seal any Deed, or Instrument in Writing, he is not bound to do it, in Case none be present to read it to him, if required; and the Reading of a Deed, *&c.* false renders the same void. In Case a Time be limited for a Person to seal a Writing in, there *Illiterature* can be no Excuse, seeing that he might have provided a skilful Person to instruct him: Yet it is otherwise where he is obliged to seal on Request.

Imbargo, signifies an Arrest upon Ships, Vessels, or Merchandize by publick Authority; which is generally acted upon Ships, *&c.* of Foreigners in Time of War, or Difference with the Nations to which those Ships do belong. In Time of Danger the King may grant an *Imbargo* on Ships, or employ those of his Subjects, for the Service of the Nation; tho' a Warrant to stop a Ship on a private Account, is by no Means a legal *Imbargo*.

Imbezle, denotes to steal, pilfer or purloin; and it also signifies to waste or diminish Goods, *&c.* entrusted to a Person's Charge or Care.

Cafe. By 12 *Ann. c.* 7. where a Servant imbezles, or purloins Goods of the Master to the Value of 40 *s.* he becomes guilty of Felony without the Benefit of the Clergy.

Immunities, signifies to be free from certain Burdens; as an *Immunity* from Tolls, &c. denotes to be exempted from the Payment thereof.

Imparlare, was anciently used to signify to *impound*, or put in a *Pound*.

Impanel, signifies to write down and enter into a Parchment List or Schedule, the Names of a Jury by the Sheriff, summoned to appear for such Services as Juries are usually employed in.

Imparlance, in our Law, is taken for a Defendant's Petition in Court for a Day to consider or advise what Answer he shall make to the Plaintiff's Action; and it is the Continuance of the Cause till another Day, or for a further Time given by the Court. *Imparlance* is either *General* or *Special*: *General*, is when it is entered in general Terms, without any special Clauses, as thus, *viz. And now at this Day, to wit, on ―― Day next after ―― in this same Term, until which Day the said* E. D. *the Defendant had Licence to imparl to the Bill aforesaid,* &c. *Special Imparlance*, is where the Defendant desires a further Day to answer, and it is thus set down and entered, *viz. Saving all Advantages, as well to the Jurisdiction of the Court, as to the Writ and Declaration,* &c. *Imparlance* in general is to the next Term after Process sued out; and in Case the Plaintiff amends his Declaration after the same is delivered or filed, the Defendant in Course may *imparl* to the next Term afterwards, unless the Plaintiff pays Costs. In like Manner it is, where the Plaintiff having declared, he does not proceed in three Terms after; in which Case the Defendant may imparl to the next succeeding Term. If a Defendant's Case require a special Plea, the Matter to be pleaded being difficult, he will, upon Motion to the Court, be granted an *Imparlance*, or longer Time to put in his Plea, than by the Rules of Court could otherwise be allowed. An *Imparlance* may be likewise granted, where a Plaintiff keeps up a Deed or other Writing from the Defendant, by which he ought to make his Defence. Where a Person is sued by an Attorney or other privileged Person of the Court, the Defendant cannot have an *Imparlance*, but on the contrary must plead presently. After an *Imparlance* taken, a Defendant cannot plead in Abatement; and if he does, and the Plaintiff tenders to him an Issue, whereto the Defendant demurs, and the Plaintiff joins with him in Demurrer, in such Case we are told, the Plea is not peremptory; seeing that the Plaintiff ought not to have joined in Demurrer, but to have mov'd the Court, that the Defendant might be compelled to plead in chief. After an *Imparlance* a Defendant in a common Case cannot have *Oyer* of a Deed. It has lately been held as an Order or Rule of Court, that where a Defendant is arrested by Process out of the *Common Pleas*, wherein the Cause of Action is specially expressed; or where the Copy of the Process is delivered, and the Plaintiff has declared; the Defendant may not have an *Imparlance* without Leave first granted, but must plead within the Time allowed to a Defendant

dant sued by original Writ. Upon Writs returnable the first or second Return of a Term, the Declaration may be delivered with Notice to plead in eight Days after the Delivery of the same, in Case the Defendant does not live above twenty Miles from *London*, &c. and if the Defendant does not plead within that Time, Judgment may be signed.

Imparsonee. See **Parson**.

Impeachment, denotes an Accusation or Prosecution of a Person for Treason or other Crimes and Misdemeanors. Any Member of the Lower House may impeach any one belonging to that Body; so likewise may any Lord of the Higher House: And the Method is to exhibit Articles on Behalf of the Commons, by whom Managers are appointed to make good their Charge.

Impeachment of Waste, denotes a Prohibition or Restraint from committing of Waste upon Lands or Tenements; as also a Demand of Satisfaction or Recompence for Waste committed by a Tenant who has only a particular Estate or Interest in the Land granted: Yet a Person that holds Lands on Lease containing this Clause, viz. *To hold without Impeachment of Waste*, has thereby such an Interest in the Lands held, that he may commit *Waste* without being *impeached* or questioned for it.

Impediments in Law, denotes Stop or Stay to a Person's seeking for his Right in Law; and Persons under such Impediments are those that are within Age, under Coverture, *Non Compos Mentis*, in Prison, beyond Sea, &c. who by a saving Clause, 21 *Jac*. 1. are allowed Time to claim or prosecute their Rights, after the Impediments are removed, even in Case of Fines levied.

Impescatus, was anciently used to signify impeached or accused.

Impetration, was anciently used to denote an obtaining any Thing by Request or Prayer; but in our old Laws denotes a Pre-obtaining of Church-Benefices in this *Realm* from the Court of *Rome*, which lie in the Disposition of the King, and other Lay Patrons of this Land.

Impierment, denotes an Impairing or Diminution; as to prejudice or impair a Person's good Name.

Implead, signifies to sue or prosecute by Course of Law.

Implements, not only signifies to furnish Things of necessary Use in a Trade or Mystery, without which the Work cannot be carried on; but also the Furniture of a House, as Houshold Goods, comprehending Tables, Cupboards, Presses, and other Moveables.

Implication, is where the Law implies something which is not declared between the Parties concerned, in their Contracts, Deeds, or Agreements; as where a Husband by Will devises all the Goods in his House to his Wife, and that after her Decease, his Son shall have them and his House; here, tho' the House is not expresly devised to the Wife, yet in Law these Words seem to imply, that the Widow has an Estate for Life in the House; seeing that no other Person could then have it, the Son by the Will not being mentioned to have any Thing till after the Decease of the Mother: But otherwise it is, where a Person devises Part of his Lands to his Wife for Life, and that the Part so devised, together with all the rest of his Lands, shall remain to the youngest Son, and his Heirs,

IM

after the Wife's Decease; in which Case, as there is no Devise of the rest of the Lands to the Wife, she cannot have them by *Implication*, for this Reason, that the eldest Son and Heir is not by the Will excluded, and therefore shall have them during his Mother's Life, till the Devise to the youngest Son takes Effect. See **Intendment** and **Use**.

Importation, denotes a Bringing in of Goods or Merchandise from other Nations.

Impost, in general denotes a Tribute or Custom, but more particularly that Tax which the Crown receives for the Importation of Merchandises into any Port or Haven: And some indeed distinguish *Impost* from *Customs*, which last are said to be rather the Profits arising to the Crown from Goods exported.

Impossibility. Whatever is *impossible* in Law, is equally the same Thing with what is *impossible* in Nature; and on this Account it is, that where any Impossibility is by a Bond or Deed required to be performed, such Bond, &c. becomes void.

Imprest-Money, is what is paid at the Inlisting of Soldiers.

Imprisii, denotes those Persons that side with, or take the Part of another, either in defending, or otherwise.

Imprisonment, signifies a Confinement or Restraint of a Person's Liberty under the Custody of another; and is where a Person is held in a Gaol, House, Stocks in the Street, or in any other Manner, in all which Cases the Party restrained is said to be a Prisoner, so long as he continues deprived of his Liberty of freely going about his Business as before his being held. No Person by Law is to be impri-

IN

soned, but either by the Command or Order of a Court of Record, or by lawful Warrant, or the King's Process. Where the Law authorises to imprison, in such Case it becomes justifiable, provided he that does it in Pursuance of a Statute, does exactly pursue the Statute in the Manner of doing it; otherwise it will be deemed *False Imprisonment*; and of Consequence it is unjustifiable. Every Warrant of Commitment ought to run, *Till delivered by due Course of Law*, and not *until further Order*, which is held ill: And so it is, where a Person is committed on a Warrant, not mentioning any Cause. See **Bail**, and **Habeas Corpus**.

Impropriation, according to its proper Signification, is when a Spiritual Benefice is in the Hands of a Layman; but when in the Hands of a Bishop, College, or Religious House, it is termed *Appropriation*.

In auter Droit, is as much as to say in another's Right; as when Executors or Administrators sue for a Debt, &c. in Right of the Testator or Intestate.

In casu consimili & proviso, is a Writ. See **Casu consimili**, &c.

Incertainty, is a Word opposed to *Certainty*, and is where any Thing is set or wrote down in such ambiguous Terms, as that a Person cannot comprehend it: And this may be well said to be the *Mother of Contention*. On *Incertainty*, Questions in Law sometimes arise on Matter of Record; such as Writs, Counts, Pleas, Verdicts, &c. and sometimes on Deeds, Writings or Contracts, &c. which in the Proceedings of the Law renders them void; and *the Reason is plain, because all Proceedings at Law must be certain as well as affirmative, so that the Defendant*

dant may be at a Certainty as to what he shall answer.

Inchanter, denotes a Person that by Verses or Charms conjures the Devil.

Inchantress, denotes a Woman that makes Use of Charms and Incantations. *Cowel.* See **Conjuration**.

Inchartare, denotes to grant a Thing by some Instrument in Writing.

Inch of Candle, denotes a particular Manner of selling or disposing of Goods by Merchants, &c. which is performed thus, *viz.* After Notice has been once given upon the *Exchange*, or other publick Place, of the Place and Time of Sale, between the Publishing of which and the Day of Sale, the Goods to be sold are divided into Lots, whereof printed Papers, as well as of the Conditions of Sale are directly published: All which being done, a small Piece of Wax Candle, near an Inch long, is lighted, and the last Bidder when the Candle goes out, becomes intitled to the Lot or Parcel exposed to Sale. In order impartially to do Justice to each Bidder, if any Difference arises in judging to whom a Lot belongs, where several Persons bid together, the Lot in that Case is put up again; and then the last Bidder is obliged to take the Lot, whether it be good or bad. Here it is to be observed, that the Parcels to be vended are always set up at such and such a Price.

Incident, is any Thing that necessarily depends on, or appertains to another, which is principal or more worthy; as a Court-Baron is inseparably *incident* to a Manor; so a Court of Piepowder to a Fair: And these two are so far incident to their Principals, that by the Grant of one, the other becomes likewise granted; and they cannot, except in special Cases, be separated or made extinct. *Fealty is incident* to Tenures; Distress to Rent or Amercement; Rent to a Reversion; Timber-Trees to a Freehold; Deeds, Charters, and a Way to Lands.

Inclausa, signifies some small Inclosure near a House.

Incompatible, is used where Benefices cannot stand one with another, in case they be with Cure, and of such a Value in the King's Books.

Incontinency, denotes a Crime that may be committed several Ways, and of which there are divers Degrees; as in the Case of *Fornication, Polygamy, Adultery, Rapes* of Women, *Sodomy,* or *Buggery.*

Incrementum, signifies Increase or Improvement.

Incroachment, (from the *French* Word signifying the Grasping of a Thing) denotes an unlawful Stealing or Gaining upon the Estate or Possession of another: As for Example, where a Person sets his Wall or Hedge too far into the Ground of his Neighbour, he is said to incroach, or make an *Incroachment* upon him. Rent may be likewise said to be incroached, where the Lord compels his Tenant to pay more than he owes. This Word may likewise properly be applied to Power or Authority; as where any Officer deputed by the King assumes to himself a greater Power or Jurisdiction than the Law intends them.

Incumbent, denotes a Clerk or Parson who is resident on his Benefice with Cure, and he is called Incumbent of that Church or Benefice, because he does, or at least ought to bend his whole Study to discharge his Cure.

Incurramentum, denotes an Incurring or being subject to a Penalty, Fine, or Amercement.

Indebitatus assumpsit, is a Term used in the Proceedings at Common Law, where one is indebted to another; and an Action thereupon lies. See **Action upon the Case**.

Indecimable, denotes that which is not chargeable with Tithe.

Indefeasible, is any Thing that cannot be defeated or made void; such as an *indefeasible* Estate of Inheritance, &c.

Indefensus, signifies a Person who being impleaded, refuses to answer.

Indenture, is a Deed or Instrument in Writing, wherein is contained some Article, Covenant, Contract or Conveyance made between two or more, and is indented or tallied at the Top thereof answerable to another Part of the same Deed, &c. and contains the same Contents. Altho' a Deed or other Writing begins thus, *viz. This Indenture*, &c. and yet is not indented, it is no *Indenture*, but a *Deed Poll*, and will only work as such: And, on the other Hand, if the Deed be actually *indented*, but wants those Words, *This Indenture*, that Deed nevertheless is an *Indenture* in Law: To which may be added, that Words in *Indentures*, tho' one Party only, are binding to both.

Indicavit, is a Writ or Prohibition which lies for a *Patron* of a Church, whose Clerk is sued in a spiritual Court by another Clerk for Tithes, amounting to a fourth Part of the Profits of the Advowson; in which Case the Suit lies in the King's Courts; and on that Account the *Patron* of the Defendant, being likely to be prejudiced in his Church and Advowson, should the Plaintiff recover in the Spiritual Court, has the Means of this Writ left to remove the other Suit into the King's Courts. The Clerk sued is likewise entitled to this Writ, which is directed as well to the Judges of the spiritual Court, as to the Plaintiff there: But this Process is not to be had before the Defendant is libelled against in the Ecclesiastical Court, and Copy thereof ought to be produced in the *Court of Chancery* before this Writ be granted: It must likewise be brought before Judgment passes in the Spiritual Court; for otherwise the *Indicavit* will be void.

Indiction, was anciently the Space of 15 Years, by which Computation all publick Charters and Writings were dated at *Rome*, and likewise in *England*.

Indictment, is a formal Bill or Declaration of Complaint that is drawn up and exhibited for some Criminal or Penal Offence, and preferred to the Grand Jury or Inquest of the County; upon whose Oaths (taken before proper Judges having Power to punish or certify the Offence) are to find whether the Complaint in the Indictment is true or not. And *Indictment* is otherwise defined to be an Accusation at the King's Suit, by the Oaths of twelve Men of the same County in which the Offence was committed, who are returned to inquire of all Offences in general that are committed within the County. When any Complaint or Accusation is found by a grand Jury without any Bill or Indictment exhibited, but afterwards is reduced to a formed Indictment, the same then is called a *Presentment*; and when Jurors are returned in order to inquire of any particular Offence only, such Enquiry is called an *Inquisition*. An *Indictment* may also be briefly defined to be an Inquisition taken by twelve

twelve Men, at the least, who are thereunto sworn, by which they find or present, that a certain Person of such a Place, in such a County, and of such a Degree, has committed Treason, Felony, Trespass, Assault, or any other Offence against the Peace of the King, his Crown and Dignity. An *Indictment* differs from a bare Accusation in this, *viz.* That the Preferrer of the Bill is not tied to the Proof thereof, under any Penalty, except in Case there appear a *Conspiracy*: And tho' an *Indictment* should be preferred to a Grand Jury upon Oath, they are not to be obliged to find the Bill, where they see Cause to the contrary; and they may not find specially a Part of a Bill, but must find the Whole, or otherwise reject it. Every one of the Grand Inquest ought to be of the same County, and returned by the Sheriff, or other proper Officer. Any one that is under Prosecution for a Crime, may, before he is indicted, challenge any of the Persons returned on the Grand Jury, who is either outlawed, returned at the Instance of the Prosecutor, or not returned by the proper Officer, &c. If a Person who is not returned on the Grand Jury, procures his Name among those of others actually returned, and by that Means becomes sworn of the Jury; for which he becomes indictable, and also finable, and the Indictment at the same Time so found shall be rendered void. *Indictments* found at the Sessions may be removed by *Certiorari* into the Court of *King's Bench*; yet Indictments that are removed may, where there is Cause for it, be sent back again into the County or Place whence the same was removed. An *Indictment* being the King's Suit, the Prosecutor is a good Witness to prove the Fact therein complained of; so that no Damages can be given to the Party grieved thereby, unless particularly grounded on some Statute; yet the Court of *King's Bench*, by virtue of the King's Privy Seal, may give a Prosecutor a third Part of the Fine imposed for any Offence; and in like Manner the Fine to the King may be mitigated, when the Defendant makes Satisfaction to the Prosecutor for the Costs of Prosecution, as well as the Damages by the Injury received. As *Indictments* are purely for the Good and Quiet of the Common-wealth, they are only to be preferred for Criminal, not Civil Matters. They are used in Cases of High Treason, Petit Treason, Felony, and Trespasses of all Kinds, and, in short, in all Sorts of Pleas of the Crown; tho' they cannot be used so for Injuries of a private Nature, they neither concerning the King nor the Publick. *Indictments* ought to be brought for Offences that are committed against the Common Law, or against Statutes, but not for every slight Misdemeanour. They will not lie for a private Nusance, on which Action on the Case only lies for a private Nusance, and not an *Indictment*. Where in an Action upon the Case the Defendant justifies for scandalous Words spoken, such as the Calling the Plaintiff Traitor, Thief, &c. if on the Trial a Verdict pass for the Defendant, an Indictment may forthwith be brought to try the Plaintiff for the Felony. A Clerk or Clergyman may be indicted for preaching against the Government of the Church, for that the Civil and Ecclesiastical Government are so incorporated, that one cannot subsist

subsist without the other, and both of them centring in the King. *Indictments* must be certain in every Point, charge some particular Offence, and not an Offender in General, neither must Goods, &c. which are stolen be set down, without particularly expressing the Things stolen: Therein must be also set forth the Christian Name, Surname and Addition of the Offender, the Certainty of the Time of committing the Offence, as the Day, Year, &c. and the Place where it was committed; as also, the Nature of the Offence; and lastly, the Value of the Thing whereby it was committed. In an *Indictment* for Murder, the Length and Depth, or other Demensions of the Wound must be expressed, that it may be judged whether it was mortal or not: And in Felony, the Value of the Goods, &c. stolen, is to be particularly mentioned, in order that it may appear whether the Offender has been guilty of *Grand* or *Petit* Larceny. A Mistake in Spelling the Defendant's Surname, is not a sufficient Cause for abating the Indictment, provided it sounds like it. An Offender may be indicted for a Felony committed against a Person unknown; notwithstanding which, upon the Trial a Property must be proved in some Body, otherwise it will be presumed to be in the Prisoner, he having pleaded *Not Guilty*. Indictments for Facts committed must be laid in the County where they were done; and the particular Place or Parish wherein they were committed must be set forth; otherwise upon pleading the General Issue, *Not Guilty*, if it appear that the Offence was committed in a different County or Place from that laid in the Indictment, the Defendant shall be acquitted. It has been held by some, that in case a Person steals Goods, &c. in one County, and afterwards conveys them into another, he may be indicted in the other County: And if a Person steals Goods from another who had stolen them before, he may be indicted as having stolen them from the true and original Owner, because in Judgment of Law, the Possession or Property of the Things stolen still continued in such Owner. We are told, that if an Offence does wholly arise from any joint Act that is criminal of several Defendants, they may be all charged in one Indictment, jointly and severally, or only jointly; and that in either Case some of the Defendants may be convicted, and others acquitted; for this Reason, that the Law looks upon the Charge as several against each Defendant, notwithstanding the Words do purport a joint Charge against all. Where an Indictment is founded upon a Statute, if a private one, it ought to pursue the Words of that Statute; but it is otherwise on a general Statute; for there it is sufficient to conclude generally thus, *viz. Against the Form of the Statute in that Case made and provided*. If a Word of Substance be omitted in an Indictment, it renders the Whole naught; but it is not so where a Word of Form is omitted, or where there is an Omission of a synonymous Word, where the Sense appears to be the same. *Indictments*, except in Criminal Prosecutions, are amendable the same Term they are brought into Court, but not afterwards. No more than 2 s. is to be taken for the Drawing of an Indictment against a Felon, &c. See 10 & 11 *W*. 3. *c*. 23. Where one Part of an Indictment is inconsistent with another Part thereof, the whole is rendered void; but where the Sense appears plain, the Court may dispense with a small Inconsistency. A Person that is indicted for Felony, may have Counsel allowed to speak for him, as to Matter of Law only. Such as are indicted for High Treason, must have a Copy of their Indictment before Trial, in order to advise with Counsel; and all such *Indictments* must be found within three Years after the Offence committed, unless the Treason be directly against the King's Person.

Indictor, denotes the Prosecutor or Person that indicteth another for some Offence; and the *Indictee* is the Defendant or Person who is *indicted*.

Indistanter, anciently signified without Delay.

Indivisum, denotes that which two Persons hold in Common without Partition, in which Case it is said, that he holds *pro indiviso*.

Indorsement, denotes any Thing that is written on the Back-side of a Deed; such as Receipts for Consideration Money paid, &c. There is likewise an Indorsement, by Way of an Assignment, on Bills or Notes, which is performed by a Person's only writing his Name on the Back-side thereof; which Notes passing one to another in Trade or otherwise, all the Indorsors become liable to the Payment of the Money specified in those Bills or Notes, as well as the Drawer of the same. See 3 & 4 *Ann. c.* 9.

Indowment. See **Endowment**.

Inducement, denotes any Thing that may be alledged as a Motive against a Thing; and in our Law it is specially used in divers Cases; as there is *Inducement* to Actions, to a Traverse in Pleading, to an Offence committed, &c. In *Inducements* to Actions, it is not necessary to have so much Certainty as in other Cases. We are told, that a general *Indebitatus* is insufficient, where it is the Ground of the Action; but where it is only the *Inducement* to it, as in Consideration of forbearing such a Debt till a certain Day, which being a collateral Promise, is good, without shewing how the Debt arose due: It is likewise said, that a Person ought to *induce* his Traverse, when he denies the Title of another; for this Reason, because he should not deny it, until he shew some colourable Title in himself; seeing that, if the Title traversed should be found naught, and no Colour of Right appear for him who traversed, in that Case no Judgment can be given. The Reason an *Inducement* cannot be traversed, is, that that would be a Traverse after a Traverse, and quitting a Man's own Pretence of Right, and falling upon another.

Induction, signifies the giving a Clerk or Parson Possession of his Church, which is done thus, *viz*. After the Bishop has granted an Institution, he issues out his Mandate to the Archdeacon to induct the Clerk, that is to say, to put him into the Possession of his Church, and he thereupon, either does it personally, or otherwise commissions some neighbouring Clergyman to do it; and this may well be compared to Livery and Seisin, it being a Placing the Minister in actual Possession of the Church, together with the Glebe-Lands, which are termed the Temporalities thereof. The Form of performing an Induction, is this, The Arch-deacon, or one of the Commissioners, takes the Clerk intended to be inducted by the Hand, lays it on the Key of the Church, and speaks to the following Effect, *viz. By Virtue of this Mandate* (in case the Induction be performed by the Archdeacon); *or by Virtue of this Commission*, (if otherwise) *I induct you into the real and actual Possession of the Rectory of ——— in the County of ——— and Diocese of ——— with all its Appurtenances*: And having spoken these Words, the *Inductor* opens the Church-Door, and puts the Parson into Possession thereof, when it is usual for the *Inducted* to toll a Bell, &c. thereby to shew and give Notice to the People, that he has taken corporal Possession of the Church. We are told in the *Count. Pars. Compan.* That an *Induction* may be made by Delivery of a Clod of Turf. An *Induction* made by the Patron of the Church is void. The Dean and Chapter of Cathedral Churches, are proper Persons for inducting Prebends; yet it has been held, that a Bishop may by the Common Law *induct* a Prebend. Where the King grants one of his free Chapels, the Parson to whom the same is granted, must be put into Possession by the Sheriff of the County, and not by the Bishop: And it is held, that no *Induction* is necessary, where the Patron by Donation in Writing puts the Parson into Possession without Presentation. If an Archdeacon upon a Mandate refuse to *induct* a Parson, or to grant a Commission to others to do it, Action upon the Case lies against him, and thereon Damages shall be recovered; and in the Spiritual Court, by Sentence he may be likewise compelled to induct the Clerk, and for Want of doing it, shall answer the Contempt. It is *Induction* alone that makes the Parson compleat Incumbent, and fixes the Freehold in him.

In esse, denotes any Thing that is in Being; and by some a Distinction is made between Things *in esse*, and Things *in posse*; as any Thing that is not, but which may be, is said to be *in posse*; whilst, on the other Hand, what is apparent and visible, is said to be *in esse*, that is to say, in actual Being; but the other is casual, and nothing but mere Possibility: As for Example, a Child before he is born may be said to be a Thing *in posse*; but after he is born, he is said to be *in esse*.

Infalistatio, was used to denote an ancient Punishment of Felons, by throwing them among the Rocks and Sands, a Thing customarily used in Port-Towns; and it is the Opinion of some, that *Infalistatio* did imply a certain capital Punishment, by fixing the Malefactor upon the Sands, until the next Tide carried him away.

Infamy, is a Word which extends itself to *Forgery, Perjury, Gross Cheats*, &c. and a Person is thereby disabled to be a Witness or Juror, provided he be not restored by the Pardon of his Crime.

Infangthef, or **Infangenethcof**, (from the *Saxons*) denotes a Privilege granted to Lords of certain Manors, to judge or condemn any Thief within their Fee.

Infant, in a legal Sense, denotes a Person under the Age of One and twenty, the Acts of whom are in many Cases void, or voidable, as when an Infant within Age executes a Deed, and even tho' afterwards he delivers it again at full Age, yet this second Delivery, as well as the first, and likewise the Deed itself are void, since the Deed must take Effect from the first Delivery: And if an *Infant* bargain

bargain and sell Lands by Deed indented and inrolled, he may avoid the same. If one within Age who is seized in Fee, makes a Feoffment, and dies, his Heir may enter; but if such *Infant* be seized in Right of his Wife, makes a Feoffment, and dies, his Heir in that Case cannot enter and avoid it, for this Reason, that no Right descends to the Heir; for the Husband, had he lived, could have entered only in Right of his Wife. If Baron and Feme are both within Age, and join in a Feoffment, after which the Husband dies, the Wife may enter and avoid the Deed, or have a Writ of *Dum fuit infra Ætatem*. Where an *Infant* demises for a Term of Years, he may, at his full Age, either confirm the Lease, or bring Trespass against the Lessee for the Occupation: And if an *Infant* grants a Lease under a certain reserved Rent, and after his coming to Age accepts the Rent, the Lease that otherwise would have been voidable, becomes valid. An *Infant* may purchase where it is intended for his Benefit, tho' at his full Age he may either avoid or confirm such Purchase, be it by Agreement or otherwise; and should he when at Age disagree thereto, his Heirs that succeed him may disagree to the same. It is to be observed, that an *Infant's* Acts on Record, as his Fine levied, Recovery suffered, or Statute acknowledged, cannot be avoided but by Matter of Record, *viz.* by Writ of Error, or an *Audita Querela*, during his Infancy. An Infant may sue by *Prochein Amy*, the next of Kin, or by his Guardian, but must always defend by his Guardian. Where the Defendant in an Action is within Age, the Plaintiff has six Years to commence his Action in after the Defendant's Arrival at Age; so likewise the Plaintiff that is an Infant, has six Years after his coming of Age to sue. All Acts of Necessity are said to bind Infants; as in the Case of Presentations to Benefices, Admittances and Grants of Copyhold Estates, assenting to Legacies, &c. By 7 *Ann. c.* 19. where Infants are seised of Estates in Fee, in Trust, or in Mortgage, on Petition to the Court of Chancery of the Person for whom the Infant is seised in Trust, or of the Mortgagor, &c. he may by Order of the said Court make Conveyances of such Estates, in like Manner as Trustees of Mortgages at full Age may. An Infant may bind himself Apprentice, and in Case he serve seven Years, have the Benefit of exercising his Trade; and if he be guilty of Misbehaviour, the Master may give him gentle Correction, or complain to a Justice of the Peace, and have him punished; he may likewise bind himself for the Payment of Necessaries, such as Meat, Drink, Washing, Apparel and Learning, yet not by Bond with Penalty, tho' a Bill or Note without a Penalty given for Necessaries will bind him. Infants are said not to be obliged to pay for Cloaths, unless it be averred they were for their own Wearing, and convenient and necessary for them to wear, according to their particular Degree and Estate; and likewise that an Infant may buy Necessaries, but cannot borrow Money for them, for the Law will not trust him with Money, except it be at the Peril of the Lender, who must either see it thus laid out, or take Care to lay it out himself in those Necessaries; and even where Money is lent to an Infant,

Infant, by whom it is employed in buying of Necessaries, yet he is not liable, for this Reason, that the Foundation of the Contract is the Lending. *Wood* in his Institutes tells us, That if an Infant enters into a Bond, pretending to be of full Age, tho' he may avoid it by pleading his *Infancy*, yet he may be indicted for a Cheat. The King cannot by the Common Law be an Infant, and his Grants, &c. cannot be avoided on Account of *Infancy*.

Infidels or **Heathens**, are such as do believe neither the Old nor New Testament to be the Word of God, on one of which Oaths being to be taken, those Persons by our Law cannot be Witnesses.

In forma Pauperis. See **Forma Pauperis**.

Information, in the Crown-Office, is pretty near the same Thing as what in our common Law Courts, we call a *Declaration*; and it is sometimes directly brought by the King, or his Attorney General, or the Clerk of the Crown-Office; and frequently an Information is brought by a private Person, who informs or sues as well for the King as himself, upon the Breach of some popular Statute; that is to say, a Statute wherein a Penalty is given to the Party that will sue for the same. It differs from an Indictment, which must be found by the Oaths of twelve Men at least; whereas an *Information* is only the Allegation of the Officer or other Party that brings it. Informations are either exhibited solely at the King's Suit, or otherwise at the Suit of both the King and Party; which last is called an *Information qui tam*, for this Reason, because the Informer sues as well for the King as himself. In all Cases where a Matter concerns the publick Government an *Information* will lie. An *Information* likewise lies for Offences of the Common Law; as Batteries, Conspiracies, Nusances, Contempts, Libels, Seditious Words, &c. and also in sundry Cases by Statute, wherein the Offender is render'd liable to a Fine or other Penalty. *Information* does likewise lie against the Inhabitants of a Town, for not repairing of Highways, for going armed in an Affray of the Peace, &c. and in general for any Offence against the Quiet of the Community, or against the Principles of Justice. Where an Information that is only vexatious is brought, the Defendant, by 18 *Eliz.* c. 5. may bring an *Information* against such vexatious Informer. All *Informations* upon Penal Statutes, must be sued in one of the superior Courts at *Westminster*, and not in an inferior Court, seeing that the Attorney General cannot be there to acknowledge or deny, as he can in a superiour Court: And all Informations that are brought on Penal Statutes by an Informer, where a certain Sum is allowed him, the same must be brought in the proper County where the Offence was committed, and within a Year after Committing the same; tho' a Party grieved, not being a common Informer, is not obliged to bring his Information in the proper County, but may lay the same in what County he pleases. See 31 *Eliz.* c. 3. There are two or three Years allowed to the King for exhibiting an Information. Informers by 18 *Eliz.* c. 5. are ordained to exhibit their Suit in proper Person, by Information, or original Action;
and

and in Case *Informers* discontinue their Suit, or become Nonsuit, the Court are to assign Costs to the Defendant, provided the *Information* be not brought by an Officer, or grounded on the Statutes of Maintenance, Champerty, &c. Where any *Information* is exhibited for Trespass, Battery, &c. to which the Defendant appears and pleads to Issue, and the Prosecutor does not bring on the Trial within a Year after Issue joined; or in Case a Verdict pass for the Defendant, the Court is to award Costs to the Defendant, unless it be certified that there was reasonable Cause for the *Information*. In all Cases where the Attorney General exhibits an Information, he is said to do it *ex officio*; but the Clerk of the Crown generally does by Order of Court. Upon a popular Statute, where a Penalty is divided between the King and the *Informer*, if the King prefer his Information first, he shall have the whole Penalty; but if the *Informer* prefers his first, then he shall have his full Share of the Penalty, which the King cannot deprive him of. Where an *Informer* dies, the Attorney General may proceed on the Information for the King, against whom a Nonsuit of an Informer is no Bar; and on the other Hand, a *Noli prosequi* entered by the Attorney General is no Bar to the *Informer*. It has been held, that if two *Informations* are preferred on the very same Day, for one and the same Offence, they mutually abate each other; for this Reason, *viz.* because there is no Priority to attach the Right of Suit in one *Informer*, more than in the other. After a Plea is put into an Information for an Offence, the Defendant may be so far indulged by the Court, as to appear by Attorney; and before Plea pleaded, the Defendant's Appearance may be dispensed with, except in Cases where a Personal Appearance is expresly required by some Statute. *Hawkins* tells us, that a Replication to an *Information qui tam*, on a special Plea in the Courts at *Westminster* must be made by the Attorney General; but if it lies before the Justices of Assise, then it must be made by the Clerk of Assise; yet, as the same Author observes, the Replication to a general Issue on an *Information qui tam* in the Courts at *Westminster* must be made by the Attorney General only; but that in Actions *qui tam*, most of the Precedents are for the Replication to be made by the Plaintiff and a Demurrer may be made to an *Information qui tam*, without the Attorney General.

Informer, denotes a Person that *informs* against, or prosecutes another upon any Penal Statute.

Ingenuitas Regni, was anciently used to denote the Commonalty of the Realm; and we are told, that this Title was likewise given to the Barons and Lords of the King's Council.

Ingress, Egress and Regress, are general Words frequently used in Leases of Lands or Tenements; and they comprehend in them a free Entry into, a Going out of, and Returning from one Part of the Premisses leased to another.

Ingressu, denotes a Writ of Entry, by which one seeks an Entry into Lands, &c. And this Process is likewise termed a *Præcipe quod reddat*. See **Entry**.

Ingressus, was anciently used to signify the Relief which the Heir at full Age paid to the Lord, for entering

entering upon the Fee defcended to him by the Death or Forfeiture of the Tenant.

In Grofs. See **Grofs.**

Ingroffer, denotes a Perfon that buys and fells Things by Wholefale; and if fuch a one by Buying, Contract or Promife, other than upon Demife or Grant of Lands, get into his Hands, Corn or Grain, Butter, Cheefe, Fifh, or other Victuals, within the Kingdom, with an Intent to fell the fame again, he fhall be deemed an unlawful Ingroffer. See 5 & 6 Ed. 6. c. 14. But it is here to be obferved, that the Buying of Corn for the making of Starch, in order to fell again, is not intended in this Statute; for this Reafon, that it is not bought for Sale again in the fame Nature it was bought, but to be firft altered in the Way of Manufacture; and for the like Reafon the Buying of Corn to be manufactured into Meal, is faid not to be included in this Act. Foreign Corn and Victuals, except Fifh and Salt, are likewife exempted; fo are licenfed Badgers, Fifhmongers, Butchers, Poulterers, &c. who buy in their own Ways of Dealing, provided they are not guilty of Forestalling and felling the fame again at unreafonable Prices by Retail: But a Merchant, either a Subject or Foreigner, who imports Victuals or other Merchandizes into the Kingdom, may difpofe of the fame in Grofs; tho' the Perfon that purchafes them of him may not do fo; fince by that Means the Price would of Courfe be enhanfed, by paffing thro' more Hands than one: Befides, if this were allowed, a money'd Man might eafily ingrofs into his Hands a whole Commodity, and afterwards fell it at what Price he thought proper, which being of very evil Confequence, the *Ingroffing* of a whole Commodity, only with an Intent to fell it again at an unreafonable *Price*, is no lefs than an Offence *indictable* at Common Law, whether the Ingroffer fells any Part of it or not, and the Offender is liable to a *Pecuniary Penalty*, as alfo to a *Corporal Punifhment*. See **Foreftaller.**

Ingroffer of Deeds, properly denotes any Perfon that writes Records, Deeds, or other Inftruments of Law, on Skins of Parchment, or even on Paper, after the Draft thereof is firft fettled.

Ingroffing of a Fine, denotes the making the Indentures of a *Fine* by the *Chirographer*, and alfo the Delivery of the fame to him to whom the *Fine* is levied.

Inhabitant, denotes one that has a *Dwelling* or *Habitation* in any Place.

Inheritance, denotes the having a perpetual Right or Intereft in Lands or Tenements, to a Perfon and his Heirs; and it is ufed not only where one has Lands or Tenements by Defcent of *Heritage*; but likewife where a Perfon becomes feifed in Fee-fimple, or Fee-tail by Purchafe. *Inheritances* are either *Corporeal* or *Incorporeal*: Thofe that are *Corporeal*, relate to Lands, Tenements, &c. which may be touched or handled; and *Incorporeal* relate to fuch Rights as iffue out of, are annexed to, or attend upon *Corporeal Inheritances*; as *Advowfons, Tithes, Annuities,* &c. There is another *Inheritance* that is termed *Several*; and that is, where two or more hold Lands or Tenements feverally; as where two Perfons hold to them and the Heirs of their two Bodies, in which Cafe thefe two have a joint Eftate during their Lives,

Lives, but their Heirs have *several Inheritances*. None can inherit but he that is of full Blood; on which Account it is, that the Person who has the whole Blood, shall *inherit* before another that has only Part of the Blood of his Ancestor. According to the Law of Inheritance the first Child is always preferred, the Male before the Female. It is held, that if a Person purchase in Fee, and dies without Issue, the Heirs of the Blood on the Father's Side, in Case there be any, shall inherit; and for Default thereof, the Lands, &c. shall go to the Heirs of the Mother's Side: Yet where it descends to the Son, or other Heir of the Father, the Heirs of the Mother cannot inherit it.

Inhibition, is in the Nature of a Writ of *Prohibition*, and is to forbid a Judge to proceed in a Cause before him. This Process generally issues out of a higher *Court Christian*, directed to an *Inferior*, upon an Appeal lodged.

Injunction, is a Writ of the same Nature of that of a Prohibition, and is granted in divers Cases; tho' it is for the most part grounded upon some Interlocutory Order or Decree made in the Court of *Chancery* or *Exchequer*, for staying of Proceedings in Courts of Law, or in the Ecclesiastical Courts. It sometimes issues to give the Complainant or Plaintiff Possession of Lands, &c. for Want of the Defendant's Appearance; and it is likewise granted for the Quieting of Possession, or to stay Waste, &c. An *Injunction* is obtained sundry Ways, either for Contempt in not appearing and putting in an Answer in due Time upon Equity confessed in the Answer, or upon some Matter appearing on Record, or by Deed or other Writing or Evidence shewn in Court, whereby it may appear that there is a Probability that the Complainant ought to be relieved in Equity. An Injunction may be set aside on Account of a Delay in Proceedings for a considerable Time; yet the same may be afterwards revived on sufficient Cause shewn. Where this Writ issues to stay Waste, there must be an Affidavit first made of Waste committed in Lands, &c. belonging to the Complainant: And if it be for staying of Suits in other Courts, it is grantable upon the Suggestion of some Matter whereby the Complainant is rendered incapable to make his Defence there, either for Want of Witnesses, or that he is sued for that which in common Justice he ought not to pay, or for that the Court where he is sued, acts erroneously, or denies him the Benefit the Law allows him, &c. If an *Attorney* after having been served with an Injunction, presumes to proceed against the Party that obtained it, the Court whereout the same issued will commit him to the *Fleet* for Contempt. This Writ is directed not only to the Party Proceeding, but also to all and singular his Counsellors, Attornies, and Solicitors, &c.

Injury, denotes a Wrong acted upon a Man's Person or Goods.

Inlagation, signifies the Restoring of an outlawed Person to the Protection of the Law.

Inlagh, anciently denoted a Person that belonged to some *Frank-Pledge*, and who was not outlawed.

Inland Trade, denotes any Trade that is intirely managed at Home in one Nation: In like Manner,

Inland Duties are such Duties or Impositions as are imposed upon certain Goods manufactured within our own Kingdom; and these Duties

Duties are generally under the Management of the Commissioners of Excise.

Inmates, are by *Kitchin* defined to be such Persons as lodge or dwell in another's House, and are unable to maintain themselves: And *Inmates* are generally said to be idle Persons that are harboured in Cottages, in which it has been usual for Families to dwell, whereby the Poor of Parishes have been increased. See 31 *Eliz. c.* 7. Where a Person has a single Room in a House, and is of Ability, he is not an *Inmate*.

Innotescimus, is a Word that denotes *Letters Patent*.

Innovations, signifies a Change or Breaking in upon Proceedings or Customs anciently in Use, which our Judges have ever been careful to suppress.

Inns, denotes Places appointed for the Entertainment and Relief of Travellers; and formerly by the Common Law any Person might set up and keep an *Inn* or *Alehouse* to accommodate Travellers; but at this Time they are to be licensed and regulated by Justices of the Peace, who take Recognizances from the Person licensed, for keeping good Orders. A Person that keeps a common Inn is not to refuse to receive a Traveller as a Guest into his House, or to find him Victuals or Lodging, he tendring a reasonable Price for the same, upon Pain of being liable to an Action of Damages; and he may likewise for offending in that Respect be liable to be indicted and fined at the King's Suit. An *Innkeeper* is said to be compellable by the Constable of the Town or Division to receive and entertain a Traveller as his Guest, whether he keeps any Sign or not, provided the *Innkeeper* make it his common Business to entertain Travellers. An *Innkeeper* is indictable and finable for harbouring of Thieves or Persons of a scandalous Character, or for suffering Disorders in his House, or for setting up a new Inn, where there is no Need of one, to the Hindrance of well governed Inns before standing. An Inn-keeper may justify the Stopping of a Horse or other Thing of his Guest for his Reckoning, and may detain the same till paid. Action upon the Case lies against an Inn-keeper, if any Theft be committed on his Guest, by a Servant of the Inn, or other Person not belonging to the Guest; but it is not so where the Guest is not a Traveller, but only one of the same Village or Town, in which Case the *Innkeeper* is not chargeable; neither is the Master of a private Tavern answerable for a Robbery committed upon his Guest. An *Innkeeper* is not answerable for any Thing that is out of his Inn, but only for such Things as are within it; tho' should he of his own Accord put the Guest's Horse to Grass, and the Horse be stolen, he will in that Case be answerable, he not having had the Guest's Orders for putting such Horse to Grass. By the Custom of the Land, if a Person lie in an *Inn* one Night, the Keeper of the *Inn* may detain his Horses until such Time as he is paid for the Expences. It is said that in Case a Person brings his Horse to an *Inn*, and leaves him in the Stable there, the *Innkeeper* may detain him till the Owner pay for the Keeping; and the Master of such Inn, after a reasonable Appraisement made, may sell the Horse and pay himself: But should a Guest bring several Horses to an Inn, and afterwards take them all away, except one;

one; this Horse so left may not be sold for Payment of the Debt for the others, seeing that every Horse is to be sold towards Satisfaction of what is due for his own Meat. It is likewise said, that should a Guest not even deliver his Goods, &c. to the Innkeeper to keep, &c. if they be stolen, the Innkeeper notwithstanding is liable.

Inns of Court, are Places wherein the Students there not only study the Laws of this Kingdom to render them capable of practising in the Courts of Law at *Westminster*, but likewise apply themselves to such other Studies as may enable them to be more serviceable in the King's Courts. The four most noted *Inns of Court*, are the *Inner Temple, Middle Temple, Lincoln's Inn*, and *Gray's Inn*; and the other Inns are these, viz. the two *Serjeants Inns*, and eight *Inns of Chancery*, called *Clifford's Inn, Symond's Inn, Clement's Inn, Lion's Inn, Furnival's Inn, Staple's Inn, Bernard's Inn*, and *Thavie's Inn*; and to these may be added *New Inn*. These Inns of Court, which are justly fam'd for their Production of Men of Learning, are governed by Masters, Principals, Benchers, Stewards and other Officers, and have publick Halls for Exercises, Readings and Arguments, which the Students are obliged to attend and perform for a certain Number of Years, before they can be admitted to plead at the Bar.

Innuendo, is a Word that was frequently used in Informations, Indictments, and Declarations of Slander, when the Proceedings at Common Law were in *Latin*; but now, instead thereof, we write, *Meaning so and so*: And indeed the Doctrine of Stretching *Innuendo's* or *Meanings* has of late Years, on the Crown-side of the *King's Bench*, too much prevailed among us, particularly in the Affairs of Printing and publishing; tho' at the same Time it has been held, that an *Innuendo* cannot make that certain, which was uncertain before; it being said that the Law will not allow Words to be enlarged by an *Innuendo*, so as to support an Action on the Case for uttering the same: And in Slander it is held, that both the Person and Words should be certain, and not want an *Innuendo* to make them out.

Inoperatio, anciently denoted one of the legal Excuses allowed to exempt a Person from appearing in Court.

Inordinatus, is said anciently to have denoted a Person that died *intestate*.

Inpeny and Outpeny, anciently signified the Money that was paid by the Custom of some Manors, upon the Alienation of Tenants, &c.

Inquest, in general, denotes an Inquiry made by Jurors in Civil or Criminal Causes on Proof made of a Fact on either Side, upon a Trial referred to them, who are impanelled by the Sheriff for that Purpose. There is likewise *Inquest of Office*, which is to make *Inquiry* whether a Criminal be a Lunatick or not; upon which Inquest, if it be found that the Criminal only feigns himself to be a Lunatick, and at the same Time he refuses to plead, he may be dealt with in Law as one standing mute. Where a Person is attainted of Felony and escapes, and afterwards being retaken, denies that he is the same Man, Inquest must be made thereof before he can be executed.

Inquirendo, denotes an Authority formerly given to one or more, to inquire into something for the Advantage of the King.

Inquisition, denotes a certain Manner of Proceeding, in the Nature of a Search or Examination, and which is used on the Behalf of the King, in Causes and Profits that are Temporal. An Inquisition is frequently used upon an Outlawry found; as also in Cases of Treason and Felony committed; and likewise upon a *Felo de se*, &c. in order to intitle the Crown to the Forfeitures of Lands and Goods. It is said that there is no great Nicety required in an Inquisition, because it is only to inform the Court how Process may issue for the King, the Title of whom arises from the Attainder, and not from the Inquisition. We are also told, that there are two Kinds of Inquisitions, the one to inform the King, and the other to secure an Interest in him. There is moreover a judicial Writ called *Ad inquirendum*, which is to inquire by a Jury into any Thing concerning a Cause that depends in a Court; and also an Inquisition is had upon Extents of Lands, &c. and Writs of *Elegit*, where Judgment is had by Default, and Damages and Costs are recovered.

Inquisitors, denotes Sheriffs, Coroners, upon the View of the Body, or the like, that are authorised by their Office to make Inquiry in certain Cases.

Inrollment, signifies the Returning in the Rolls of *Chancery*, *King's Bench, Common Pleas*, or at the Quarter-sessions, of any lawful Act, such as a Statute or Recognizance acknowledged, a Deed of Bargain and Sale, &c. Inrollments of Deeds must be ingrossed in Parchment, and recorded in Court, for the Sake of Perpetuity: Yet it is said that the Inrolling of a Deed does not make it a Record, tho' by inrolling it becomes recorded; for that a Record is an Entry in Parchment of judicial Matters that are controverted in a Court of Record, and of which the Court is to take Notice; whereas an *Inrollment* of a Deed is no more than a private Act of the Parties thereto, whereof the Court takes no Cognizance at the Time of acting the same, tho' the Court accedes to it. The Manner of inrolling a Deed is, that it be acknowledged before a Master of the Court of *Chancery*, or a Judge of the Court where it was inrolled; which being the Officer's Warrant for the Inrollment of the same, such Inrollment becomes a sufficient Proof of the Deed itself. A Deed may be inrolled without the Examination of the Grantor, it being sufficient that Oath be made of the Execution thereof. If Livery and Seisin be made before the Inrollment of a Deed, the Party shall be in thereby, as a more worthy Ceremony to pass Estates by, than that of inrolling a Deed. As to the Inrollment of Deeds, see 27 H. 8. c. 16. 34 & 35 H. 8. c. 22. 4 & 5 W. & M. c. 22. 3 Geo. 1. c. 18.

Inscriptiones, was anciently used to denote any Instrument in Writing, whereby any Thing was granted.

Insestator, in old Times denoted a Prosecutor, or other Adversary at Law.

Insiliarius, is an evil Counsellor.

Insilium, denotes evil Counsel.

Insimul computassent, that is to say, they accounted together, are Terms used in Declarations, wherein it is set forth, that the Plaintiff and Defendant such a Day and Year *accounted together concerning divers Sums of Money by him* (naming the Defendant to the same, naming

naming the Plaintiff) *before that Time due and unpaid*, &c.

Insimul tenuit. See **Formedon.**

Insinuation, in the Common Law denotes a clandestine creeping into Mind or Favour: But among the Civilians, it bears a different Signification; as the Insinuation of a Will denotes the first Production of it, that is to say, the Leaving it in the Hands of the Register, in order for the procuring a Probate of it.

Insolvent, denotes a Person that is unable to pay his Debts.

Inspeximus, is a Word formerly used in Letters Patent, and is the same with *Exemplification*.

Installment, signifies the Establishing or Placing a Person in some particular Dignity or Order.

Instant, is a Word, that tho' it cannot be actually divided, yet by the Intention of the Law, it may in divers Cases; as he who commits *Suicide*, lays violent Hands upon himself, is not guilty of Felony until he is dead, at which Time he is not in Being, and on that Account is not to be termed a Felon; but is adjudged to be so at the very Instant of Time the Fact was done: And *Plowden* tells us, that there are divers other Cases in our Law, where the Instant of Time that is not in Nature to be divided, is in the Consideration of the Mind dividable.

Instaurum, was anciently used in Deeds to denote a Stock of Cattle; and it was likewise frequently applied to the Books, Vestments, and other Utensils belonging to a Church.

Institution, denotes the particular Form of a Bishop's fixing a Parson presented to the Living of a Church: And it likewise signifies a Faculty made by the Ordinary, by which a Clerk is approved to be inducted to a Rectory or Parsonage. Where a Bishop approves of a Parson presented, as capable of the Benefice, he of Course admits and institutes him. An Institution may be granted sundry Ways, either by the Bishop under his Episcopal Seal; or by his Vicar General, Chancellor or Commissary. The Letters Testimonial of Institution may be granted by the Bishop, even when out of his Diocese. By Institution the Cure of Souls is transferred to the Parson instituted; and if the Bishop refuse to grant Institution, the Party may have his Remedy in the *Court of Audience* of the Archbishop by a *Duplex Querela*, Institution being properly cognizable in the Spiritual Court. It is said, that where Institution has been granted, and suspected to be void, for Want of Title in the Patron, a Super-institution has been granted, in order to try by Ejectment the Title of the Incumbent. Upon a Clerk's being instituted, he has Right to enter on the Parsonage-House and Glebe-Lands, and to take the Tithes; yet he cannot grant or do any Act to charge them, until such Time as he is inducted into the Living; for this Reason, *viz.* tho' he be compleat Parson as to the Spiritualty, by Means of the Institution, he is not so as to the Temporalty; for by the Institution he is only admitted to the Office to pray and to preach, and in no wise intitled to the Benefice before a formal Induction. After a Bishop has given Institution to a Clerk, he is to issue his Mandate for Induction; and in Case the Archbishop shall *inhibit* the Archdeacon to induct the instituted Clerk, he may, notwithstanding such *Inhibition* do it.

Insuper, that is to say, *over and above*, is a Term used by Auditors in their Accounts in the *Exchequer*; as where a certain Sum is charged upon a Person as due on his Account, they say so much remains *insuper* to the Accountant.

Insurance, is where a Person for a certain Sum paid by a Merchant, or other Person, obliges himself to answer for the Loss of a Ship, Houses or Goods, in Proportion to the Value of the *Premium* advanced. Insurance is either publick or private; the one done at the publick Office of Assurance, and the other contracted between Merchant and Merchant in a private Way. Some Insurances are to certain Places, and others general, and in trading Voyages; that is to say, where Ships deliver their Goods at one Port, and take in a fresh Cargo at another, and afterwards proceed to other Ports; the *Premium* in such a Case generally runs higher. Should a Ship be insured from the Port of *London* to any Foreign Place, and before she breaks Ground she chances to take Fire, and is thereby consumed, the Insurers are not bound to answer, unless the Words of the Insurance are, *At and from the Port of* London; seeing that the Adventure did not commence until the Ship's Departure from that Port; wherefore if the Ship had broken Ground, and after that had been driven back to the same Port, and then taken Fire, the Insurers in such Case must answer. The Form of a Policy of Insurance is as follows, *viz.*

Know all Men *by these Presents, that A. B. of ——— Merchant, as well in his own Name, as for and in the Name and Names of all and every other Person and Persons, to whom the same shall, or may belong or appertain, doth make Assurance, and hereby cause himself and them, and every of them, to be insured, lost or not lost, at and from the Port of* London, *to ——— in the Kingdom of ——— and at and from thence back to* London *again, upon the Body, Tackle, Apparel, Ordnance, Munition Artillery, and other Furniture of and in the good Ship the ——— Burden ——— or thereabouts, whereof* C. D. *is Master; and likewise upon all Kinds of Goods and Merchandises shipped on Board of the said Ship; commencing and beginning the Adventure upon the said Ship and Goods, from and immediately after the Day of the Date hereof, and so to continue and endure, until the said Ship with her Tackle and Apparel shall be arrived back, and returned to* London *aforesaid, and hath there moored at Anchor twenty-four Hours. And it shall and may be lawful to and for the said Ship in this Voyage to proceed, sail to, touch, and stay at any Ports or Places whatsoever, especially at ——— aforesaid, without Prejudice to this Insurance: And the said Ship and Goods,* &c. *for so much as concerns the Insured, is and shall be rated and valued at ——— of lawful Money of* Great Britain, *without further Account to be given by the Assureds for the same. And touching the Adventures and Perils which we the Insurers are content to bear, and do take upon us, they are of the Seas, Men of War, Fire, Enemies, Pirates, Rovers, Thieves, Letters of Mart, and Reprisals at Sea, Arrests, Restraints and Detainments of all Kings, Princes and People of what Kingdom, Nation, People, Condition or Quality soever, Barratry of the Master and Mariners, and all other Losses and Misfortunes that shall come to the Hurt or Damage of the said Ship, Goods, &c. or any Part thereof. And in Case of any Misfortune, it shall and may be lawful to and for the Insured, their Factors, Servants and Assigns, to sue, labour, and travel for, in and about the Defence, Safeguard and Recovery of the said Ship, &c. or any Part thereof, without Prejudice to this Insurance; to the Charges whereof we the Insurers will contribute each of us according to the Rate and Quantity of his Sum herein assured. And so we the Insurers are contented, and do hereby promise and bind ourselves, each for his own Part, our Heirs, Executors and Administrators, Goods and Chattels, to the Insured, their Executors, Administrators and Assigns, for the true Performance of the Premisses, confessing ourselves paid the Consideration due to us for this Insurance, by ———— at and after the Rate of ———— per Cent. and in Case of Loss to abate, &c. and to pay without further Proof, &c. more than this present Policy; any Usage or Custom to the contrary notwithstanding. In Witness, &c.*

Intendment, in a legal Sense, denotes the Understanding, Intention and true Meaning of a Thing; and in our Law it frequently supplies what is not fully expressed or apparent; so that in some Cases where a Thing is doubtful, *Intendment* will make it out; yet it is said that *Intendment* cannot supply the Want of Certainty in a Charge laid in an Indictment. A Thing may be necessarily intended by something that goes before or follows it; and if an indifferent Construction may bear two Intendments, the Rule in Law is, to take it strongly against the Plaintiff: Yet it is otherwise where the Plaintiff declares that the Defendant is bound by Obligation, in which Case it is intended that the Bond was sealed and delivered again; if a Person be bound to another, and it is not expressed in the Bond to whom the Money shall be paid, or even if said to the Obligor, the Law will intend it to be payable to the Obligee; and should no Time of Payment be limited, the Law will intend that the Money shall be paid presently. Tho' the Intent of Parties in Deeds and Contracts is much regarded by the Law, yet it cannot take Place against the Rules of Law. If a Person enter a House in the Night-time, with an Intent to commit Burglary, it is Felony; and so it is likewise made by 23 *Car*. 2. *c*. 1. where a Person maliciously cuts off or disables a Limb or Member, with an Intent to disfigure. If an Intention be only to beat, and Murder ensues, the Person thus offending is punishable for the Crime acted.

Intension, is a Writ that issues against one who enters into Lands after the Death of a Tenant in Dower, for Life, &c. and keeps out the Person in Reversion or Remainder.

Inter Canem & Lupum, were Words which were anciently used in Appeals, to denote some Crime to have been committed in the *Twilight*, or *betwixt Hawk and Buzard*, as termed by some.

Intercommoning, is in Case the Commons belonging to two Manors lie contiguous, and the Inhabitants of both have been accustomed to depasture their Cattle in each of them.

Interdict, denotes a spiritual Censure, whereby a Person is prohibited to hear Divine Service, or to to partake of the Sacraments, &c. An Interdict may likewise be of Place, as where Divine Service is prohibited to be had in such a Church; and this *Interdict* has only a Regard to the Church or Place, and hath no Regard to the People or Congregation: But an *Interdict* of Persons pursues them wherever they go. Sometimes an Interdict has been nothing less than a general Excommunication of a whole Kingdom or Country: But such a severe Church-Censure has been for a long Time disused. *Interdicted of Fire and Water*, which *Livy* calls *Legitimum Exilium*, anciently denoted such Persons as were banished for some particular Offence; by which Judgment it was ordered, That no Person should receive them, or allow them *Fire* or *Water*; and this doubtless amounted as it were to a Civil Death, the Offender being wholly deprived of the two necessary Elements of Life.

Interest, is generally taken for a real Chattel, such as a Lease for Years, &c. but more for a future Term. An Estate in Lands, &c. is much better than a bare Right or Interest in them; yet according to the Sense of the Law, an Interest extends to Estates and Titles which a Person has in or out of Lands, &c. so as is observed in *Co. Lit.* by a Grant of a Man's whole Interest in particular Lands, &c. a Reversion therein as well as Possession in Fee thereby passes. There is likewise Interest of Money, of which you may read under *Tit.* **Usurp.**

Interlocutory Order, is an Order that does not decide the whole Cause, but only some Matter incident thereto, which happens between the Beginning and End of the Cause; as where the Plaintiff in *Chancery*, or the *Exchequer*, obtains an Order for an Injunction till the Hearing of the Cause; which Order not being *final*, is called *Interlocutory*.

Interlopers, is a Word among Merchants, to denote such Persons as intercept the Trade of a Company of Merchants.

Interpleader. See **Enterpleader**.

Interrogatories, are certain Questions reduced into Writing, and to be demanded of Witnesses produced in a Cause, more especially in the Court of *Chancery*, and that of the *Exchequer*. These *Interrogatories* must be only to Points necessary, and they must be either drawn up or perused by Counsel, and by him signed: But Care must be taken, that Interrogatories be not leading, that is to say, calculated to lead a Witness, by putting, as it were, Words in his Mouth; as, *Did you not act or see such a Thing? &c.* For Depositions taken upon such *Interrogatories* as these will be suppressed; seeing that they ought not to lean to one Side more than another, and therefore should be drawn up after this Manner, *viz. Did you see, or did you not see? &c.* The Examiners, as also the Commissioners, who examine the Witnesses on *Interrogatories*, must examine to one Interrogatory only at a Time.

Intertiate, anciently signified to sequester, or put a Thing into the Hands of a third Person.

Intestate, denotes a Person who dies without making his Will; in which Case a Distribution is to be made of the Intestate's Personal Estate, after the Debts and Funeral Charges are fully paid, among the Wife and Children of the Deceased;

ceased; or for Want of such, then among the next of Kin, &c. See 22 & 23 *Car.* 2. *c.* 10. which Statute does immediately upon the Death of the *Intestate*, vest an Interest in the Persons intitled, insomuch that if one dies before Distribution, his Share shall go to his Executors or Administrators, and not to the Survivors of the next of Kin to the Intestate. See **Administrators**.

Intrusion, is taken to be where an Ancestor dies seised of an Estate of Inheritance; which is expectant upon an Estate for Life, after which the Tenant for Life dies; whereupon a Stranger enters before the Heir, and on that Account such Stranger is said to *intrude*. In short, *Intrusion* denotes any unlawful Entry upon Lands, &c. by a Person who has no Right to the same, in Prejudice of the Person to whom they are legally descended. We are told by *Fitzherbert*, in his *Nat. Brev.* that the Difference between an *Intruder* and an *Abator* is this, *viz.* that an *Abator* enters into Lands, &c. void by the Death of Tenant in Fee; whilst an *Intruder* on Lands void by the Death of a Tenant for Life or Years. An *Intruder* upon the King's Lands is punishable, as well as he that intrudes upon the Lands of a private Person. On Informations of Intrusion exhibited on Behalf of the King, the Defendant may plead the general Issue.

Intrusion de Gard, was a Writ formerly in Use, where the Infant within Age entered upon his Lands, and kept out his Lord.

Intrusione, is a Writ that lies against an *Intruder*, at the Suit of him that has the Fee, &c.

Invadiare, was a Word anciently used to denote to mortgage or pawn Lands.

Inventiones, was anciently used in some Charters for Goods or Treasure *found* by any Person, and not challenged by the right Owner; which by the Common Law becomes due to the King, who frequently grants that Privilege to another Person.

Inventory, is generally used to signify a Schedule, wherein is contained a full Description of all the Goods and Chattels of a deceased Person at the Time of his Death, together with the Value of the same as appraised by two indifferent Persons. Executors as well as Administrators are required to deliver in upon Oath to the Ordinary, indented *Inventories*, one Part whereof is to remain with the Ordinary, and the other Part with the Executor or Administrator. See 21 *Hen.* 8. *c.* 5. the Intention of which Statute was for the Benefit of the Creditors and Legatees, that the Executor or Administrator might not conceal any Part of the Personal Estate from them. Generally all the Personal Estate of the Deceased, of what Quality soever, ought to be put into the *Inventory*; but Goods given away in his Life-time, and actually in the Possession of the Party to whom they were given, and likewise the Goods to which a Husband is intitled as Administrator to his Wife, are not to be included in the *Inventory*. Tho' the above Statute requires the Inventory to be exhibited within three Months after the Person's Decease, yet it may be done afterwards, seeing that the Ordinary may dispense with the Time, and even whether it shall be exhibited or not; as in

Cases

Cases where the Creditors are paid off, and the Will performed, &c.

In ventre sa Mere, (*French,* signifying *In the Mother's Belly,*) is where a Woman is with Child at the Death of her Husband; the Infant, had it been then born, would have been Heir to the Husband's Lands: And on Account of the Expectation of the Birth of such a Child, the Law has a Regard for it, insomuch that a Devise to an Infant *in ventre sa Mere,* is good by Way of future executory Devise: He may likewise be vouched in the Mother's Belly; so that Action will lie for detaining Charters from him as Heir. It is here to be observed, that in all Cases where a Daughter comes into Lands by Discent, the Son born after may oust her, and enjoy the Land.

Invest, or **Investiture,** in general denotes a giving Livery of Seisin or Possession. There were anciently a Variety of Ceremonies used upon *Investitures*; as at first they were made by a certain Form of Words; and afterwards by such Things as had the greatest Resemblance to the Thing to be transferred; such as the Delivery of a Turf, &c. where Lands were intended to pass, which was performed by the Grantor to the Grantee.

Invoice, denotes a written Account of the Particulars of Merchandise, with its Value, Custom and Charges, &c. transmitted by a Merchant to his Factor or Correspondent in another Country.

Jobber, is generally taken for one who buys or sells Cattle for others: And *Stockjobbers,* are such as buy and sell Stocks for other Persons, &c.

Jocalia, in a special Sense, is said to signify such Things as are Ornaments to a Woman, and which in some Places abroad they call their own; as Diamonds, Ear-rings, Bracelets, &c. But within this Realm, a Wife on the Death of the Husband is not intitled to the Jewels, &c. unless they be suitable to her Quality, and the Husband leave sufficient Assets for the Payment of Debts, &c.

Jocus Partitus, denotes a Person who, when two Proposals are made to him, has Liberty to chuse which he pleases.

Joinder, signifies a Conjunction or joining of two Persons in the same Action. It is held, that in Personal Things, where two are chargeable to two, the one may satisfy it, and accept of Satisfaction, and thereby bind his Companion; but, at the same Time the one cannot have an Action without his Companion, nor can both only against one: It is likewise held, that in *joint Actions* against two Defendants, should they plead severally, and if the Plaintiff become Nonsuit by one before he recovers Judgment against the other, he will be barred against both: Yet where there is a Covenant to two Persons, not to do a Thing without their Consent, in this Case one of them may bring an Action for his particular Damages: But in case a Man, in Consideration of a certain Sum paid to him by *A.* and *B.* engages to procure them their Cattle, &c. distrained; if they are not, according to such Engagement, delivered, only one joint Action lies, for this Reason, that the Consideration cannot be divided. In an Action against the Owners of a Ship, on Account of Goods damaged, &c. the same must be brought against all of them. Where there are many Partners in Trade, but only one Partner that acts,

acts, Actions must be brought against all the Partners jointly, for the Acts of such acting Partner; so if two are Partners, and only one of them sells in Partnership, Action for the Value of the Goods sold must be brought in the Names of both the Partners. In personal Actions several Wrongs may be joined in one Writ.

Joint Executors, are where two or more are appointed such by Will, and in Law they are accounted but as one single Person; so that the Acts done by any one of them will be taken to be the Acts of all; seeing that all of them represent the Person of the Testator; as where two *joint Executors* are possessed of a Lease for Years in Right of their Testator, one of them may sell the Term without the other's *joining*, they being both possessed thereof as one Person in Right as aforesaid: And in like Manner it is, where one *joint Executor* gives a Release or Discharge, the other is bound by it, each of them having an Authority over the whole Estate. However, it is held that one *joint Executor* shall not be charged by the Acts of his Companion, further than such a one is actually possessed of the Goods of the Testator: Yet if *joint Executors* enter into Agreement among themselves, that each shall intermeddle with such a particular Part of the Testator's Estate; in this Case indeed each of them becomes chargeable for the Whole by the Agreement. It is held, that two *joint Executors* cannot plead separate Pleas, for this Reason, that their Testator, if living, on Action brought against him, could have been allowed but one Plea, he being only one Person. If all the Executors are not named in an Action brought by *joint Executors*, the Action must abate.

Joint Lives, is where any Thing is granted or given to two or more, during their Lives.

Joint Tenants, are such Persons as come to or hold Lands or Tenements jointly by one Title: And such Persons during their *joint Tenancy*, must jointly plead, as well as be jointly sued and impleaded. It will be proper to observe, that *joint Tenants* have a peculiar Quality of Survivorship vested in them, which Coparceners have not: As where there are two or more *joint Tenants*, and the one has Issue and dies, the other *joint Tenant*, or those other that survive, shall have the Whole. *Joint Tenants* are said to be called so, not only because Lands, &c. are granted or conveyed to them *jointly* by one and the same Title, but also for that they take by Purchase only; whilst an Estate in Coparcenery is always by Descent. If a Person seised of Lands or Tenements make a Feoffment to two or more, and their Heirs; or grant a Lease to them for Life, or a Term of Years; the Grantees in all these Cases hold a *joint Tenancy*, so that the Part of the *joint Tenant* who dieth, does not go to his Heir, Executor or Administrator, but only to the Survivor or Survivors of the *joint Tenants*: This Doctrine likewise holds, where two or more have a joint Estate in Possession, in a real or personal Chattel; or a joint Interest in a Debt, Duty, Covenant, Contract, &c. We are told, that the Stock and Debts which *joint* Merchants have in Partnership, go to the Executor, &c. of the Partner that dies, by the Law Merchant, and not to the Survivor. Where a Parent devises Lands, &c. to his eldest and other Sons, they become

come *joint Tenants*, and not Tenants in Common. If a Person that has only two Daughters, who are his Heirs apparent, devises his Lands to them and their Heirs, and afterwards dies, in this Case the Devisees, the two Daughters, are deemed *joint Tenants*, seeing that they take in another Manner than what the Law would have given them, which would have been as Copareners by Descent. Where Lands are devised to two equally, the Devisees become *joint Tenants*; but if the Devise had run to two, equally to be divided between them; that is not taken for a *joint Tenancy*, but generally for a Tenancy in Common: Tho' it has been held, that those Words *equally to be divided*, does not create a Tenancy in Common in a Deed, but a joint Tenancy. It has also been held, that a Devise to two equally to be divided, to hold to them and the Heirs of the Survivor, is a joint Tenancy. If Land be granted to a Man, and such Woman as he shall marry, upon his marrying there can be no *joint Tenancy*, so that the Husband will have the Whole. Where Lands are in the granting Part of a Deed given to three, to hold to one for Life, Remainder to another for Life, and the Remainder to the third for Life; in this Case the Grantees are not joint Tenants, but shall take successively. Joint Tenants, as well as Tenants in Common of Inheritance, are bound by Statute to make Partition as Coparceners are; and likewise joint Tenants, and Tenants in Common for Life or Years, by Writ of Partition, &c. may be compelled to do the same. The King can never be *joint Tenant* with any Person, for this Reason, *viz.* because none can be allowed to be equal with him.

Jointure, according to its general Signification, denotes a Settlement of Lands, &c. made on a Woman in Consideration of a Marriage; and it also denotes a Covenant, by which the Husband or some Friend of his assures Lands, &c. to his Wife for the Term of her Life: And this Word is said to be so called, either because it is granted by Reason, or on Account of the Joinder in Matrimony, or for that the Land in Frank-Marriage was jointly granted to Husband and Wife, and after them to the Heirs of their Bodies; by which Means the Husband and Wife were made as it were joint Tenants during the Coverture. A *Jointure* is further defined to be a Bargain and Contract of Livelihood, annexed to the Marriage-Contract; and which carries with it a competent Provision of Freehold Lands, &c. for the Benefit and Use of the Wife, to take Effect after the Husband's Decease, provided she herself is not the Cause of the Forfeiture of it. In order to make a perfect *Jointure* agreeable to the Statute 27 *Hen.* 8. *c.* 10. several Things ought to be observed: 1*st*, That it be made to take Effect for the Wife's Life, either in Possession or Profit, presently after the Decease of the Husband. 2*dly*, That it be for the Term of her own Life, or for a greater Estate; yet it may be limited to continue no longer than she remains a Widow, &c. 3*dly*, That it be expressed to be in Satisfaction of her whole Dower, and not a Part thereof. 4*thly*, That tho' it may be made either before or after Marriage; yet, if before, the Wife cannot wave it, and claim her Dower at Common Law; but if made afterwards, she may, at the Death of her Husband. It is
said

said, that all other Settlements in Lieu of *Jointures* that are not made according to the aforesaid Statute, are Jointures at Common Law, and no Bars to Claim of Dower. If a Father makes a Settlement of Lands, &c. to the Use of himself for Life, and afterwards to that of his Son and his Wife, for their Lives, for the Jointure of the Son's Wife, this has been held to be no Jointure, to bar the Wife of her Dower; for this Reason, that it might not commence immediately after the Death of the Husband, since the Husband might die before the Father's Decease. If a Husband devises Lands to his Wife for Life, as a Jointure, and in full Satisfaction of Dower, and she after his Death accepts of the same; she thereby becomes barred from claiming Dower at Common Law: And where a Man makes a Jointure on his Wife after Marriage, and afterwards by Will devises and ordains, that she shall have a third Part of all his Lands together with her Jointure; in this Case the Wife shall have the third Part of all his Lands, as a Legacy; and if she wave her Jointure, she may likewise have a third Part of the Residue for her Dower. It is said, that if Lands are conveyed to a Woman before Marriage, in Part of her Jointure only, and after Marriage other Lands are granted to her in full, she may in such Case refuse what was conveyed to her after the Coverture, and retain her first *Jointure*, as also her Dower: So likewise, if a Husband grant a Lease of Lands to Persons in Trust for his Wife and Children, in order that she may receive thereout at his Death 100 l. *per Annum*, or the like annual Sum; in this Case she may have the Provision settled, as also her Dower, the other being no *Jointure*. Upon the Death of the Husband, the Wife may enter upon her *Jointure*, and is not driven to a real Action; seeing that she is to recover Dower at Common Law; wherefore upon a lawful Eviction of her *Jointure*, she will be endowed according to the Rate of the Husband's Lands of which she was intitled to Dower at Common Law: And should she be evicted of Part of her *Jointure*, she shall have Dower for so much thereof. A Husband's Committing of Treason shall not occasion a Forfeiture of the Wife's *Jointure*; yet Feme Coverts committing the same or Felony, are liable to a Forfeiture of their *Jointures*; and by 3 *Jac.* 1. *c.* 4. upon Conviction of Recusancy, they incur the Forfeitures of two Parts in three of their *Jointures*, as well as *Dower.*

Jointress, or **Jointuress**, denotes the Person that has an Estate settled on her by her Husband, for her Life, in Case she survive him. Where an Estate settled is a *Jointure* by Law, if the *Jointress* alien the same by Fine, Feoffment, &c. with another Husband, such Alienation shall be a Forfeiture of the Estate settled as a *Jointure*: But a *Jointress* may by Lease demise an Estate for Forty Years, if she so long live, or for Life, without incurring a Forfeiture.

Journal, is a *Memorandum* or *Day-Book* of Transactions, used in sundry Cases; as in the daily Affairs of Merchants and other Tradesmen, &c. as also Mariners, in Regard to their Observations at Sea, &c.

Journals of Parliament, are Remembrances of Transactions done there;

there; but they are in no Respect held as Records.

Journeymen, formerly denoted such a one as wrought by the Day only, but it is now extended to those also who covenant to work with others in their Occupations by the Year.

Journeys Accounts, is a Term in our Law, which is taken to be where a Writ abates by the Death of the Plaintiff or Defendant, Want of Form, &c. in which Case the Plaintiff becomes intitled to have a new Writ by *Journeys Accounts,* that is to say, within as little Time as he possibly can after the Abatement of the first Writ; in which Case the second Writ shall be a Continuance of the Cause, as much as if the first Writ had never abated. This second Writ must be had within fifteen Days at least after the Abatement of the first Writ: But the Abatement of the first Writ must be without any Default of the Plaintiff, otherwise a second Writ may not be purchased by *Journeys Accounts;* yet if the Abatement be by the Default of the Clerk, for Want of Form, &c. in such Case the Plaintiff may have it.

Ipso facto, is where the same Clerk obtains two or more Preferments in the Church with Cure, who is not qualified by Dispensation, &c. the first Living, in that Case is said to be *ipso facto* void, that is to say, without any declaratory Sentence, and on that Account the Patron may present to it: There is likewise *Deprivation* for Crimes in striking a Person in a Church or Church-yard, for which Offence the Offenders are to be excommunicated *ipso facto;* so also an Estate or Lease may by Condition be rendered *ipso facto* void.

Ire ad largum, was formerly used to signify to escape, be set at Liberty or to go at large.

Irregularity, in our Law, denotes going out of Rule, or the common Road.

Irrepleviable, or Irreplevisable, denotes any Thing that neither may nor ought to be replevied: And it is said that it is against the Nature of a Distress for Rent to be *irrepleviable.*

Isle, denotes any Parcel of Land that is invironed in by the Sea, or fresh Water. The Isles of *Jersey* and *Guernsey,* tho' two Islands belonging to *England,* are not bound by any of our Acts of Parliament, unless specially named therein; nor do our original Writs run in either of those Islands: Nevertheless indeed, the King's Commission under the Great Seal runs there, for the Redressing of Injuries or Wrongs; but even in that Case the Commissioners are tied down to judge according to the Laws and Customs of those Islands: And if Controversies arise at Law among any of the King's Subjects in either of those Islands, the King and Privy Council are the proper Judges, without Appeal. For the Encouragement of the Inhabitants of *Jersey* and *Guernsey,* they, by 3 *Geo.* 1. *c.* 4. are allowed to import into any Part of this Kingdom, Goods of their own Growth, or Manufacture, Custom free. The *Isle of Man* also belongs to *England,* but is now a distinct Territory from it, it being intirely out of the Jurisdiction of our Court of *Chancery,* or of original Writs that issue from thence: And this Island has been formerly granted in Fee to divers Subjects, by *Letters Patent* under the Great Seal: And it has been adjudged, that no Person had any

Inheritance there, except the *Earl of Derby* and the Bishop of that Island; where the Inhabitants are intirely governed by their own Laws.

Issue, in our Law has sundry Significations, it being sometimes taken for the Children begotten between a Man and his Wife; sometimes for Profits accruing from Amercements and Fines; and sometimes for the Profits issuing out of Lands or Tenements: But this Word, according to the general Acceptation of it, denotes the *Point of Matter* which *issues* forth of the Allegations and Pleas of the Plaintiff and Defendant in a Cause that is to be tried by a Jury of Twelve Men. Of these Issues concerning Causes, there are two Kinds, viz. upon *Matter of Fact*, or *Matter of Law*: That of *Fact*, is where the Plaintiff and Defendant have fixed upon a Point to be tried by a Jury: But that of *Law* is where there is a Demurrer to a Declaration, Plea, &c. and a Joinder in Demurrer, which is termed an *Issue at Law*, only determinable by the Judges. *Issues of Fact* are either general or special: General, when it is left to the Jury to find whether the Defendant has acted any such Thing as the Plaintiff alledges against him: *Special*, is where some special Matter or material Point alledged by the Defendant in his Defence is to be tried. *General Issue* also denotes that Plea, wherein the Defendant is allowed to give the special Matter in Evidence, by Way of Excuse or Justification; and this is granted by several Statutes, in order to prevent the Prolixity of Pleading; wherefore upon *General Issues* in such Cases the Defendant may give any Thing in Evidence that may prove the Plaintiff to have no Cause of Action. It is to be observed, that where there is a *General Issue* upon *Not guilty*, and there are other Issues upon Justifications, the Trial of the *General Issue* in such Case is nothing but *Matter of Form*, the whole Point or Substance being upon the *special Matter*. In Actions where the Place is material, and made a Part of the *Issue*, the Jury in that Case cannot find the Fact in another Place, for that the Point in *Issue* is restrained to a certain Place, but is otherwise upon the *General Issue* pleaded, whereon the Jury may find all local Things in another County; for where the Substance of the *Issue* is found, it must be good, when the finding more may be reckoned Surplusage. All *Issues* must be joined in that Court which has Authority to try it, otherwise, as a certain Author observes, the *Issue* would be fruitless, seeing that if it was tried, the Trial would be *coram non judice*. Without Issue joined there can be no good Trial, nor indeed ought Judgment to pass. Issues ought to be so certain, and joined upon the most material Point in Question, so that the whole Matter in Dispute between the Parties may be tried. On a joint Action of Trespass by many Persons, there must be only one Issue joined; tho' in an Action for Damages, every Part according to the Loss the Plaintiff has sustained, ought to be put in Issue. In every Issue there ought to be an Affirmation on the one Part, as that the Defendant is indebted to the Plaintiff in a certain Sum, &c. and a Denial on the other Part, as that the Defendant does not owe the Money charged, &c. When once *Issue* is joined between Parties, if it be a good Issue, it cannot afterwards be waved

waved, without the Consent of both Parties: But in Case the Defendant pleads the *General Issue*, and does not enter the same, it is said he may within four Days of the Term wave that *Issue*, and plead specially; so if a Defendant plead in Abatement, he may at any Time after wave his special Plea, and plead the *General Issue*, provided there be not a Rule made for him to plead as he will stand by it; and in Case the Plaintiff omits to enter the *Issue* the Term it is joined, the Defendant may in the first five Days of the next Term, alter his Plea, and plead *de novo*: And where the Plaintiff will not try the *Issue* after it is joined, within such Time as he ought by the Course of the Law, the Defendant may give him a Rule to enter it; which if he do not, he shall become nonsuit, *&c.*

Issues on Sheriffs, are Amercements and Fines to the Crown, which are levied out of the *Issues* and Profits of the Lands of Sheriffs, for their Neglects and Defaults: But those *Issues* may, by Rule of Court be taken off before they are estreated into the *Exchequer*, good Cause being therefore shewn. *Issues* are also leviable upon *Jurors*, for Non-appearance; yet upon a reasonable Excuse proved by two Witnesses, the Justices may discharge the same.

Itinerant, denotes a Travelling or Taking a Journey: And such Persons as were anciently sent with Commission into divers Counties to hear Causes, were called *Justices Itinerant*.

Judaism, denotes the Custom, Religion or Rites of the *Jews*, and it likewise denoted the *Income* heretofore due to the King: And we are told that this Word was also used formerly for a Mortgage, and sometimes for Usury.

Judge, signifies any chief Magistrate in the Law, appointed to try Civil and Criminal Causes, and punish Offences: He is authorised with a certain Jurisdiction, and is particularly under the Nomination and Appointment of the King. A Judge upon his being created, takes an Oath of Office, *viz.* That he will serve the King, and indifferently minister Justice to all Men, without Respect of Persons; That he shall take no Bribe, give no Counsel where he is a Party, nor deny Right to any, even tho' the King by his Letters, or by express Words command the contrary, *&c.* and he is answerable in Body and Goods. The Lord *Coke* says, that Judges have not Power to judge according to that which they may think fit, but that which by Law they know to be right. *Plowden* says they are to give Judgment according to Law, and what is alledged and proved; and they have in themselves a private Knowledge, and a judicial one, tho' at the same Time they cannot judge of their own private Knowledge, but may use their Discretion: And yet where a *Judge* has a judicial Knowledge, he ought to give Judgment according to it. It is handed down to us, that King *Henry* IV. demanded of *Judge Gascoigne*, if he saw one killed in his Presence by *A. B.* and instead of him, *C. D.* who was in nowise culpable, should be indicted for this Murder, and convicted thereof before him, what he would do in such a Case? Whereto he answered, that his Duty was to respite the Judgment against him, and afterwards report the Matter to the King, in order to procure the Person under Conviction a Pardon; and for this Reason, that the

the *Judge* cannot acquit him, or give Judgment according to his own private Knowledge: And it is further said, that the same King *Henry*, when his eldest Son the Prince was committed to Prison, for a great Misdemeanor, blessed God that he had a Son of that Obedience, and a Judge of that Impartiality and Courage. It is held that our Judges cannot act by Deputy, nor transfer their Power to others, as those of the Spiritual Court may. Where there are several *Judges* in a Court of Record, the Act of any one of them is effectual, provided their Commission does not require more: So likewise what a Majority rules, when present, is the Act of the Court; and where a Majority is not had, as being divided in Opinion, two against two, the Cause shall be adjourned into the *Exchequer Chamber*; and for that Purpose a Rule is to be made, and the Record certified, &c. It is held, that to kill a Judge of any of the Superior Courts at *Westminster*, or of Assise, &c. on the Place of his administring Justice, is Treason; and the bare Drawing a Weapon on a Judge, in any of the Courts of Law, is such an Offence, as that the Offender shall lose his Right-Hand, forfeit his Lands and Goods, as likewise suffer perpetual Imprisonment. The Judges of the Courts of Record, are intirely exempted from all Prosecutions, except it be in the Parliament, where they doubtless may be punished, for any Thing done amiss in their own Courts as *Judges*; and this is said to be intended for the Support of their Dignity and Authority, and in order to draw Veneration to their Persons, as well as Submission to their Judgments: Yet we are told, that if a Judge shall so far forget his Dignity, as to turn Solicitor in a Cause which he is to judge, and extrajudicially tamper with Witnesses, or attempt to work upon Jurors, such Judge may be dealt with according to the same Capacity whereto he so basely degrades himself. *Judges*, who are guilty of Bribery, are punishable by Loss of Office, Fine, and Imprisonment. &c. If Justices of the Peace, on an Indictment of Trespass, arraign a Man of Felony, and condemn him to Death, on which he becomes executed, in such Case it is Felony in the Justices so acting.

Judger, has in *Cheshire* been used to denote a Person to serve on the Jury there.

Judgment, signifies the Determination or Sentence of the Judges upon a Suit, &c. and the Words anciently used for Judgments were, *Consideratum est per curiam*, &c. for this Reason, that *Judgment* is always given by the Court, upon Consideration had of the Record and Matter before them. Some *Judgments* are final, and some not; and *Judgments* may be given as well upon the Trial of the Issue, as by Default, *Nihil dicit*, Confession, or on Demurrer; to which may be added Outlawry, which is a Judgment in itself. *Judgment* is also to be had for *departing in Despight of the Court*; that is to say, without Leave in common Recoveries, &c. After Issue joined in a Cause, the Plaintiff may, if he thinks fit, without going to Trial, accept of a *Judgment* from the Defendant; but here it is to be observed, that on this *Judgment*, a Writ of Error may be brought without putting in of Bail, which cannot be done on a *Judgment* after Verdict. Judgment is sometimes had with *Cessat Executio*,

Executio, that is to say, a *Stay of Execution*, till a certain Day. It has been held, that if an Action of Debt be brought against an Executor upon the Testator's Bond, to which he pleads *Plene administravit*, this is no less than a Confession of the Debt, and the Plaintiff in that Case may have Judgment with a *Cessat Executio*, until the Defendant has Assets. *Judgment* upon a Demurrer to a Declaration, &c. is no Bar to any other Action, seeing that it does not pass upon the Merits of the Cause: Yet other Judgments may be pleaded in Bar to any other Action brought for the same Thing; so likewise Judgment in an inferior Court may be pleaded in Bar to an Action in a superior one. It is said, that a Judgment on *Nihil dicit*, in Case, Trespass, or Covenant, is not a perfect *Judgment* until Writ of Enquiry of Damages be taken out and executed thereon, whereof Notice must be given to the Defendant; but in Debt it is otherwise, for there it is a perfect Judgment the Moment it is signed. The Practice is where Damages are given upon *Judgment* without Trial, to issue out a Writ of Enquiry. Where a *Judgment* is unduly obtained, the Court will *vacate* it, and restore the Party damnified. If a Plaintiff does not take out Execution within a Year and a Day after *Judgment* obtained, the *Judgment* must be revived by a *Scire facias*. As to Judgments acknowledged for Debt, the Course is for the Person that acknowledges it, to give a general Warrant of Attorney to any Attorney, or to some particular Attorney of the Court wherein the *Judgment* is to be acknowledged, to appear for him at the Suit of the Party to whom the *Judgment* is to be acknowledged, and to file common Bail, and receive a Declaration, and then plead *Non sum informatus*, I am not informed; or to let it pass by *Nihil dicit*, he says nothing; and thereupon *Judgment* is entered for Want of a Plea. Where a Person grants a Warrant of Attorney to confess Judgment, and dies before it is confessed, the Warrant, by such his Death becomes countermanded; and in like Manner it is, if a *Feme* sole gives a Warrant to confess Judgment, and marries before it is confessed, the Warrant by the Marriage becomes countermanded. It is said, that if a Person under an Arrest grants a Warrant to confess *Judgment* in the *King's Bench*, in case no Attorney for the Defendant be then present, that Court, upon Supposition that the *Judgment* was obtained by Force or Fear, will set it aside: And it is likewise so where a Man under an Arrest is seemingly discharged, with Design that he should grant a Warrant to confess Judgment: Yet it has been held, that where one has continued in Prison for some Time, and he confesses *Judgment* to his Creditor voluntarily, that *Judgment* shall stand, even tho' no Attorney was present at the Signing of the Warrant. A Judgment may be confessed on Terms, which in Effect are conditional; in which Case the Court will see the Terms performed: But when a *Judgment* is acknowledged absolutely, and a subsequent Agreement made, as this does not affect the *Judgment*, the Court will take no Notice of it. It is reported in *Mod. Case* 49. that a Person gave Bond and *Judgment*, defeasanced on Payment of Money at a Day certain, and it was agreed that Execution should not be sued out before;

fore; yet a *Fieri facias* was sued but a Month before, and executed: And notwithstanding that this was a Breach of the Agreement, yet in Consideration that the Money levied for was a just Debt, the Court would not interfere, lest their so doing should frustrate the *Judgment*. If a Warrant of Attorney to confess *Judgment* be general, that is to say, authorises the Attorney to enter it of such a Term, or of any Term after, such Attorney may enter it at any Time during Life; but if it be not expressed in general as above, the Judgment must be entered of the Term particularly mentioned in the Warrant. If *Judgment* upon a Warrant of Attorney be not entered within the Year, it cannot afterwards be done without Leave of the Court, on Motion and Affidavit made of the Party's being living, and the Debt unsatisfied. By 4 & 5 *W. & M.* where a Person having acknowledged a Judgment for the Security of Money, and afterwards on borrowing more Money of another Person, mortgages his Lands, &c. without giving any Notice of the *Judgment* obtained to the Mortgagee; in such Case; unless the Mortgagor do within six Months pay off and discharge the Judgment, he shall intirely forfeit his Equity of Redemption. The Form of a Warrant of Attorney to confess *Judgment*, you may see in the *Young Clerk's Magazine*, and other Collections of Precedents in Conveyancing. It is not only usual, but really requisite to have a Release of Errors entered into at the Time of granting a Warrant of Attorney. If two *Judgments* are entered in one Term, and the last is first executed, in that Case the Creditor thereon has the best

Title. By 21 *Jac.* 1. c. 26. the Acknowledging a Judgment in the Name of another without his Privity or Consent, is made Felony. *Judgments* in Criminal Cases are divers Ways; as *Judgment* in High Treason is for the Offender to be drawn, hanged, his Entrails taken out and burnt, his Head cut off, and his Body quartered, &c. In Petit Treason the *Judgment* is to be drawn to the Place of Execution and hanged: But a Woman in all Cases of High and Petit Treason, is to be drawn and burnt. All Persons for Felony are to be hanged by the Neck till dead. Judgment in Misprision of Treason, is Imprisonment for Life: In *Præmunire* it is, that the Party offending forfeits the King's Protection, and the Body of the Offender is to remain in Prison during the King's Pleasure: And for the Offence of Misprision of Felony, the Offender is subject to Fine and Imprisonment. *Judgments* for Crimes and Misdemeanors of an infamous Nature, are discretionary, and lodged in the Breast of the Court. *Judgments arrested*, see **Arrest of Judgment.**

Judgment or Trial by the Holy Cross, was anciently a Trial in Use in Ecclesiastical Causes.

Judicatores Terrarum, denotes certain Persons in the County Palatine of *Chester*, who on a Writ of Error issuing out of the Court of *Chancery*, are to take into their Consideration the *Judgment* given in that County, and to reform it; for Neglect of which, or in case it be found erroneous, they forfeit 100 *l.* to the King by the Custom.

Judicial Proceedings. See **Process.**

Jura Regalia, denotes the Right of Kings. See **Regalia.**

Jurats, are Persons in Authority in the Nature of Aldermen, for the Government of Corporations; as *Romney Marsh*, &c. by *Chart.* 1 *Ed.* 4. is made incorporate of Bailiff, twenty-four *Jurats*, and the Commonalty thereof.

Juridical Days, denotes certain Days in Court, whereon the Law is administred. See **Day**.

Jurisdiction, denotes any Power or Authority which a Person has to exercise in Causes of Complaint, &c. The Courts and Judges at *Westminster* are not restrained to any particular County or Place, they having *Jurisdiction* throughout *England*: But all other Courts are confined to their particular *Jurisdictions*; which if they go beyond, all their Proceedings become erroneous. There are divers Sorts of inferior *Jurisdictions*; one of which is to *hold Pleas*, and the Plaintiff may either sue there or in the King's Courts: Another is the *Conusance of Plea*; whereby a Right is vested in the Lord of the Franchise to hold Pleas: A third Kind of inferior Jurisdiction is an *exempt Jurisdiction*; as where the King grants to a particular City or Corporation, that the Inhabitants shall only be sued within their own City, &c. yet at the same Time it is said, that there is no *Jurisdiction* whatever which can withstand a *Certiorari* to the Courts at *Westminster*. Where an Action is brought in a Town corporate, and in the Declaration it is not shewn, that the Matter arises within the Jurisdiction of the Court, it is not good, even tho' the Town be set down in the Margin; yet in superior Courts, the County wrote down in the Margin is sufficient.

Juris utrum, is a Writ that issues on Behalf of a Parson of a Church, whose Predecessor has aliened the Lands, &c. belonging thereto. This Writ is likewise grantable, in order to try whether free Alms belong to a Church, where they are transferred. A Successor to a deceased Parson may likewise have this Writ against a Man that intrudes into Lands, &c. So where a Parson is disseised of Lands, &c. the Successor may have this Writ.

Juror, denotes any Person that is sworn on a *Jury*.

Jury, denotes a certain Number of Men, who are sworn to make Inquiry of, and try the Matter of Fact in Dispute, and upon such Evidence as shall be given them in a Cause, to declare the Truth. The Privilege of Trial by a *Jury* is said to be of great Antiquity. Juries are not only used in Circuits of our Judges, but also in other Courts, &c. as where a Coroner by *Jury* makes Inquiry after the Death of a Person: So likewise the Justices of the Peace, at their Quarter-Sessions, the Sheriff at the County-Court, the Steward of a Court-Leet, Court-Baron, &c. where they make Inquiry of any Offence, &c. they do it by a *Jury*. These Juries are called *Petit Juries*, to distinguish them from what is termed the *Grand Jury*. We are told that anciently the Juries both in the *King's Bench* and *Common Pleas* were twelve Knights; and that to make a Jury on a Writ of Right, called the Grand Assise; there must be sixteen, thus made up, *viz.* four Knights and twelve others. The *Grand Jury* most commonly consists of twenty-four Men, of greater Note and Worth than those of a Petit Jury, who are indifferently chosen out of the whole County by the Sheriff. A *Petit Jury* consisting of twelve Men impanelled in Criminal Cases

Cafes, are called the *Jury of Life and Death*. In short, the *Grand Jury* finds the Indictments against Criminals; after which the *Petit Jury* convicts or acquits them by Verdict, in the giving of which the whole twelve must agree. *Jury-men* must be Freemen, indifferent, and not outlawed, or infamous; neither ought they to be Aliens, nor Men attainted of any Crime. Infants, Persons advanced in Years, *viz.* Seventy, or upwards, Clergymen, Apothecaries, &c. are exempted from serving upon Juries. By 28 *Ed.* 1. c. 9. Jurors impanelled are to be the next Neighbours, and such as are most sufficient and least suspicious; otherwise the Officer returning them is to forfeit double Damages. The Qualification of a Jury-man for a County is 10 *l. per Annum*, either in Freehold or Copyhold Estate within the same County. *Jury-men* that are summoned for not appearing, shall forfeit Issues, in case they have no reasonable Excuse for such their Defaults: And the Issues to be forfeited are these, *viz.* 5 *s.* on the first Writ, 10 *s.* upon the second, and upon the third 13 *s.*, 4 *d.* But by 18 *Eliz.* c. 5. no *Jury* is obliged to appear at *Westminster* upon a Trial, where the Offence was committed 30 Miles off, except it be required by the King's Attorney General. It is the Duty of Constables of Parishes, &c. yearly, at *Michaelmas* Quarter-Sessions, to return to the Justices of the Peace, Lists of the Names, and Places of Abode of Persons qualified to serve on *Juries*, who are between Twenty-one and Seventy Years of Age, attested upon Oath, upon Pain of forfeiting 5 *l.* A Duplicate of which Lists are to be delivered to the Sheriff by the Clerk of the Peace; and the Sheriff under the Penalty of 20 *l.* is to impanel no other Persons than are mentioned in those Lists. By 4 & 5 *W. & M.* No Sheriff, Bailiff, &c. under the Penalty of 10 *l.* shall return any Person to serve on a Jury, who has not been duly summoned six Days before the Day of Appearance; neither, under the like Penalty, shall he accept of Money, or other Gratuity, for excusing the Appearance of a *Juryman*. Where a Trial relates to any Thing that concerns a Sheriff or Under-Sheriff, the *Jury* must be returned by the Coroner. In the *King's Bench*, the Process to bring in a *Jury* is called *Distringas Juratores*; and in the *Common Pleas* it is called a *Venire facias*, & *Habeas Corpora Juratorum*. Upon the *Venire*, the Sheriff returns the Jury in a Panel, or small Piece of Parchment which is annexed to the Writ; after which the *Habeas Corpora* issues to bring in the Jury. In all Cases where, after Issue is joined, the Suit is continued on the Roll, the Process from Time to Time must be continued against the Jurors. According to Usage the Sheriff should return Twenty-four Jurors; but should he only return twelve, pursuant to the Writ, he is liable to be amerced. Lists of Jurors by 3 *Geo.* 2. c. 25. are now to be made from the Rates of each Parish, and fixed on the Doors of Churches, &c. twenty Days before *Michaelmas*, in order that publick Notice may be given of Persons omitted, that are qualified, or of Persons inserted that are not so: After which the Lists being settled by the Justices of the Peace at the Quarter-Sessions, Duplicates thereof are to be delivered to the Sheriffs by the Clerk of the Peace:

And the Names contained in these Lists must be entered Alphabetically by the Sheriffs in a Book to be kept for that Purpose, together with their Additions, and Places of Abode. Sheriffs are liable to be fined for returning Jurors, who have served two Years before. Sheriffs on Returns of Writs of *Venire facias*, are to annex a Panel of the Names of a competent Number of the Jurors mentioned in the Lists, not amounting to less in Number than Forty-eight in any County, nor more than Seventy-two, unless they are otherwise directed by the Judges at the Assizes. It is likewise by the said *Statute* enacted, that the Names of the Persons impanelled shall be wrote upon several distinct Pieces of Paper of equal Size, and be delivered by the Under-Sheriff to the Judges Marshal, who causes them to be rolled up, all in the same Manner, and put together in a Box; and when any Cause is brought on to Trial, some indifferent Person is to draw out Twelve of these Papers of Names, who, if not challenged, shall be the Jury to try the Cause: And in case any of them is challenged, and set aside, or does not appear, then a further Number is to be drawn till there is a full Jury: And Jurors neglecting to appear shall be fined in a Sum not exceeding 5 *l.* nor under 40 *s.* Jurors in *London* must not only be Housekeepers, but have Lands or Goods worth 100 *l.* and such Juror may be examined on Oath to that Point. Both the Plaintiff and Defendant are at Liberty to use their Endeavours for a Jury-man to appear; yet a Person who is not a Party to the Suit must not do so; where a Jury-man doth appear, but refuses to be sworn, or to give a Verdict, or in case he endeavours to impose upon the Court, or is guilty of any Misbehaviour after his Departure from the Bar, he may be fined, and also Attachment issue against him. When a Jury-man is once sworn, he must not depart from the Bar upon any Account whatsoever, until the Evidence is given, without the Leave of the Court; and if that be obtained, he must have a Keeper with him. Tho' Jurors are not to meddle with any Thing that is not in Issue, they may find a Thing of their own Knowledge, which has not been given in Evidence. The Jury, with the Leave of the Court, may eat or drink at the Bar, but not out of Court; for as soon as the whole Evidence given is summed up, the Jury are to be kept together till they bring in their Verdict, without being admitted to the Speech of any, and without either Meat, Drink, Fire or Candle. They are fineable, if they agree to cast Lots for their Verdict. It is reported to us, That a Jury has been permitted to recall their Verdict; as where a Person indicted of Felony, the Jury found him Not guilty; yet immediately before they went from the Bar, said they were mistaken, and found him Guilty, which last was recorded for their Verdict. See *Plowd.* A Jury is fineable for being tampered with, in Relation to the giving of their Verdict; but they are not so for giving a Verdict contrary to Evidence, or against the Court's Directions; for this Reason, that the Law presumes the Jury may have some other Evidence than what was given in Court. Nevertheless Attaint will lie against a Jury for giving contrary to Evidence, in case

case any Corruption appear. They are not punishable for giving their Verdicts unless by Attaint for a false Verdict; for which, if convicted, they are to lose their Lands and Goods, their Houses to be rased, and their Bodies thrown into Prison: But how far this Punishment is altered, you may see in 23 *Hen.* 8. *c.* 3. By 5 *Ed.* 3. *c.* 12. Where a Juror is guilty of Bribery, he becomes absolutely disabled to be of any Assises or Juries, and also to be imprisoned, and ransomed at the King's Pleasure. And by 38 *Ed.* 3. *c.* 12. in case a Juror takes any Thing, either of the Plaintiff or Defendant, to give his Verdict, he shall pay ten Times as much as he has taken, or suffer a Year's Imprisonment. It is most adviseable in all Cases of Difficulty, for the Jury to find the special Matter, and leave it to the Judges to determine how the Law stands upon the Fact. In Civil Cases a Jury may be discharged before they give a Verdict, as where Nonsuits are had, &c. There is also a Jury called a *Special Jury*, which, where it is conceived, that an indifferent and impartial Jury will not be returned between the Parties by the Sheriff, the Court, upon Motion, will order the Sheriff to attend the *Secondary* of the *King's Bench* with his Book of Freeholders of the County, when the *Secondary* in the Presence of the *Attornies* on both Sides, is to strike a Jury: And should there happen a Cause of Consequence to be tried at the Bar, the Court of *King's Bench*, on Motion upon Affidavit made, will make a Rule for the *Secondary* to name Forty-eight Freeholders, whereout each Party is to strike twelve, one at a Time, the *Plaintiff's Attorney* beginning first, and the Remainder of the Jurors struck shall be the Jury for the Trial. The Nomination of a *Special Jury* ought to be in the Presence of the *Attornies* on each Side; but if either of them neglect or refuse to attend, the *Secondary* may proceed *ex parte*, and then he strikes twelve for the *Attorney* that makes Default. By 3 *Geo.* 2. *c.* 37. in Trials of Issues on Indictments, &c. and in all Actions of what Kind soever, on the Motion of the Prosecutor, Plaintiff, or Defendant, &c. the Courts at *Westminster* are authorised to order a special Jury to be struck, in the like Manner as upon Trials at Bar. Where a special Jury is ordered by Rule of Court, in a Cause arising in a City, Corporation, &c. the Jury is to be made out of Lists or Books of Persons qualified, which are to be produced by Sheriffs, &c. before the proper Officer.

Jus, as it is defined in *Lit. Dict.* denotes Law or Right.

Jus accrescendi, in a legal Sense signifies the Right of Survivorship between Joint Tenants.

Jus Coronæ, in general denotes the Right of the *Crown*; and it is said to be a Part of the Law of *England*, tho' it differs in many Things from the general Law that relates to the Subjects.

Jus Duplicatum, hath a double Signification; that is to say, it denotes a Person's having a Thing in Possession, as well as a Right to it.

Jus Gentium, the Law of Nations, is that Law whereby Kingdoms, and Society in general, are governed.

Jus Habendi & Retinendi, is peculiarly applied to the Right one has, not only to have, but also to retain the Profits, Tithes, &c. of a Rectory or Parsonage.

Jus Patronatus, is defined to be a Kind of Commission granted by the Bishop to some Persons to inquire who is the rightful Patron of a Church; as if two *Patrons* present their respective Clerks, the Bishop in that Case is to determine who is to be admitted by Right of *Patronage*, on a Commission of Inquiry issued out for that Purpose, directed to six Clergymen, and six Laymen, residing near to the Church; which Commissioners are to inquire on Articles; 1*st*, Whether the Church is void? 2*dly*, Who last presented to it? 3*dly*, Who is the *Rightful Patron*? &c. It is said, that the Awarding a *Jus Patronatus* is not of Necessity, but at the Pleasure of the Ordinary, for his better Information, he having the Right of *Patronage*; seeing that, if he will at his Peril take Notice of the Right, he may admit the Clerk of either of the Patrons, without a *Jus Patronatus*.

Jus Possessionis, denotes a Right of Seisin or Possession.

Jus Præsentationis, in *Pars. Law* is defined to be the Right of the Patron of presenting his Clerk unto the Ordinary, to be admitted, instituted and inducted into a Church.

Jus Recuperandi, Intrandi, &c. signifies a Right of *Recovering* and *Entering* into Lands, &c.

Justice, denotes a Person deputed by the King to do Justice and Right by Way of Judgment; and is so called, because his Authority arises by Deputation, and not *Jure Magistratus*, by Right of Magistracy. In the Courts of *King's Bench* and *Common Pleas* there are two Judges called *Chief Justices*, each of whom retains the Title of *Lord* during the Time of his continuing in Office. The Lord *Chief Justice* of the *King's Bench* hears and determines all Pleas, in Civil Causes, brought before him in that Court; as also the King's Pleas, or Pleas of the Crown: Whilst, on the other Hand, the Lord *Chief Justice* of the *Common Pleas*, has the Hearing and Determining of all *Common Pleas*, in Civil Causes, as they may be distinguished from the Pleas of the Crown. There are many other Justices appointed by the King for the Execution of the Laws, besides the *Lords Chief Justices*, and the other Justices of the Courts at *Westminster*; as *Justices* of *Assise*, of the *Forest*, of *Nisi Prius*, *Oyer* and *Terminer*, &c. and *Justice of the Peace*, &c.

Justices of the Peace, are Persons appointed by the King's Commission to keep the Peace of the County where they reside; and of these some of a superior Rank or Quality are of the *Quorum*, for this Reason, that Business of Importance cannot be dispatched without their Presence, or at least the Presence of one of them. *Justices of the Peace* are created Conservators of the Peace, by Virtue of the King's Commission or *Letters Patent* under the Great Seal: But tho' the Power of appointing them is only in the King, they are generally created at the Discretion of the *Lord Chancellor* or *Lord Keeper*, by the King's Permission. The Number of *Justices of the Peace* in the several Counties of *England* and *Wales* are not limited; for the King may appoint as many of them as he shall think fit. *Lambard* very justly complains of the excessive Number of *Justices of the Peace*, they being now without any Limitation; and, as it is well observed, their prodigious Increase, together

together with the frequent unsuitable Appointment many Times made of Persons for this Trust, has rendered that Office contemptible in the Eyes of the better Sort, for whom it was originally intended. The Qualification to enable a Justice of the Peace to act, is his having an Estate of 100 *l. per Annum*, Freehold or Copyhold, in Possession, for Life, or for the Term of 21 Years certain, without Incumbrances: And if a Justice of the Peace, not thus qualified, shall presume to act in that Office, he is liable to the Penalty of 100 *l.* See 5 *Geo.* 2. By 2 *Hen.* 5. *Justices of the Peace* shall hold their Sessions four Times a Year, that is to say, the first Week after *Michaelmas*, the *Epiphany*, *Easter*, and St. *Thomas*, commonly called *Beckets*, which is the 7th of *July*. If a Justice of the Peace does not observe and pursue the Form of Proceeding laid down by *Statute*, his Act on such *Statute* is void, and is *coram non judice*: And indeed it is a *Query*, whether the Proceedings of some Justices of the Peace within the *Bills of Mortality* upon the late Act, vulgarly called the *Gin Act*, may not be reckoned *coram non judice*? See the *Perfect View of the Gin Act*. By 9 *Geo.* 1. *c.* 7. Justices of the Peace in any County, living in a City or Town Corporate without the County, may grant Warrants, take Informations, make Orders, &c. at their own Dwelling-Houses, tho' out of the County. Justices of the Peace are authorised to take Informations against Persons committing Treason, grant Warrants for their Apprehension, and commit them to Prison: They may also commit Felons, in order to the bringing them to Trial; and at the same Time bring over the Accusers to prosecute at the proper Place: And should they neglect to certify Examinations and Informations to the next Gaol-Delivery, or do not bind over the Prosecutors as above, they are liable to be fined. *Justices of the Peace*, at their Quarter-Sessions, may try Offenders for *Petit Larceny*, and other small Felonies; but Felonies of a higher Nature are to be tried elsewhere: Neither can they at their Sessions try a Cause of the same Sessions, without the Consent of Parties, &c. It is said that a *Justice of the Peace* may make a Warrant for bringing a Person before himself only; yet it is usual to make the Warrant to bring the Offender before him or any other *Justice* of the County, &c. It is likewise said, that where a *Justice* grants a Warrant above his Authority, the Officer notwithstanding must obey; but that if it be where the *Justice* has no Authority, the Officer may be punished if he executes it. Where a Person is a dangerous Person, and likely to break the Peace, a *Justice of the Peace* may require a Recognizance with a high Penalty of such Person for his keeping of the Peace: And for Want of Sureties for good Behaviour, the *Justice* may commit the Person to Prison: Yet a Person by giving Security in the *King's Bench* or *Chancery*, for keeping of the Peace, may have a *Supersedeas* to the Justices of the Peace in the Country, to discharge them from taking Security; so likewise where a Person hears of a Peace-Warrant out against him, he may go to another *Justice of the Peace*, and there give Surety of the Peace; by which Means he

KE

he prevents his being held upon the first Warrant.

Justice-Seat, is the highest Court held in a Forest, it being always held before the *Lord Chief Justice in Eyre of the Forest*, upon giving Forty Days Warning before.

Justicies, is a certain Writ or Process directed to the Sheriff, by Virtue whereof he may hold Plea of Debt in his County-Court for a Sum above 40 s. whereas by his ordinary Power he can only hold Cognizance of Sums under 40 s. The Form of the Writ follows, viz. *The King to the Sheriff of N. Greeting: We command you, that you Justice C. D. that justly, and without Delay, he render A. B. eight Pounds which to him he oweth, as is said, as reasonably shew he can, and which to render him he ought; that no more Clamour thereof we may hear, for Default of Justice*, &c.

Justification, in our Law denotes a Maintaining or Shewing a sufficient Reason in Court, why the Defendant did such a Thing which he is called to answer.

Justificators, has been used to signify a Kind of *Compurgators*, or such Persons as by Oath justify the Innocence or Oaths of others.

Justitias facere, is by *Selden* defined to hold Plea of any Thing.

K.

Kaiagium, anciently signified the Toll or Money paid for the Loading or Unloading Goods at a Key or Wharf.

Keelage, denotes Money payable for the Bottoms of Ships resting in a Port or Harbour.

Keeper of the Forest, is he that has the chief Government over all Officers belonging to the Forest; and warns them to appear at the Court of *Justice-Seat* on a Summons from the *Lord Chief Justice in Eyre*.

Keeper of the Great Seal, is one who by his Office is a Lord, and is stiled *Lord Keeper of the Great Seal of* Great Britain, and is always one of the Privy Council. All Grants, Commissions and Charters of the King, under the *Great Seal*, pass thro' the Hands of the *Lord Keeper*; for without that *Seal* many of those Grants, &c. would be of no Force in Law; the King being (as it is said) in the Interpretation of the Law a Corporation, and therefore passes nothing but by the *Great Seal*. By 5 *Eliz.* c. 18. The *Lord Keeper* is invested with the same Place, Authority, Preheminence, Jurisdiction and Execution of Laws, as the *Lord Chancellor* of *Great Britain* is invested with. The *Lord Keeper* is constituted by the Delivery of the *Great Seal*, &c.

Keeper of the Privy Seal, denotes a certain Officer through whose Hands all Grants, Pardons, &c. signed by the King, pass before they come to the *Great Seal*; and even some Things pass this Officer's Hands, which do not pass the *Great Seal* at all. This Officer is one of the Privy Council, yet was anciently only called *Clerk of the Privy Seal*; but now he is called *Lord Privy Seal*. The Duty of the *Lord Privy Seal* is to put the Seal to no Grant, &c. without a proper Warrant; nor with Warrant, where it is against Law, &c. but must first acquaint the King therewith.

Kerbere, is by *Cowel* defined to be a Custom to have a Cart-way; as also to be a Commutation for the customary Duty for *Carriage* of the Lord's Goods.

Kidders, is mentioned in the *Statute* 5 *Eliz. c.* 12. and denotes such as carry Corn, dead Victuals, or other Thing, up and down to sell, as a *Badger, &c.*

Kidnapping, denotes a Stealing or Conveying away of young or old Persons, and is a Crime punishable at Common Law. By 11 & 12 *W.* 3. *c.* 7. If a Master of a Ship, whilst abroad, shall force any of his Men ashore, and wilfully leave him behind, he shall for such Offence suffer three Months Imprisonment.

Kindred, denotes certain Persons that are related to each other. In our Law there are three Degrees of *Kindred*, one in the Right Line descending, another in the Right Line ascending, and the third in the Collateral Line. The right Line descending, in which the *Kindred* of the Male Line are called *Agnati*, and those of the Female *Cognati*, is from Father to Son, *&c.* to his Children in the Male and Female Line: And if there be no Son, then to the Daughter or Daughters; but if there be none of these, then to the Nephew or Niece, and so on *ad infinitum*, the Males in Descent in the right Line, being always to be preferred to the Females. The right Line ascending goes directly upwards; as from Son to Father or Mother; and if there be neither, then to the Grandfather or Grandmother; and for Want of these, then to the Great-Grandfather or Great-Grandmother, and so on upwards *ad infinitum*. The Collateral Line either descends by the Brother or Sister, and their Children downwards, or by the Uncle upwards. See *Nelson* on this Head.

King, denotes the Head of the Common-wealth. By 1 *W. & M.* the Coronation, or Obligatory Oath of the Kings of our Land is regulated, and is to this Effect, *viz.* that he is to govern the People of this Kingdom, according to the *Statutes* agreed on in Parliament, and the Laws and Customs thereof; to the utmost of his Power cause Law and Justice in Mercy to be executed in all his Judgments; to maintain as much as in him lies, the Laws of God, the true Profession of the Gospel, and the Protestant Reformed Religion by Law established; and also preserve to the Bishops and Clergy their Rights and Privileges that by Law appertain to them. It is the Opinion of Sir *Matt. Hale*, in his *Hist. Coronæ*, that there is a sacred Band between the King and his People, which cannot be dissolved without the free and mutual Consent of both in Parliament; and that by the Laws of this Kingdom the King cannot resign his Sovereignty without the Consent of his Parliament. *Hawkins* tells us, That our Kings have distributed their whole Power of Judicature to the Courts of Law; which Courts, by a long continued Usage, have gained a stated Jurisdiction, that no King can alter without Act of Parliament. As to the *King's* Prerogative, it extends further than what the *Statute* 17 *Ed.* 2. relating thereto contains. Among many other of the Prince's Royal Prerogative, it is his to make War or Peace: And, as Head of our State, he may at his Pleasure call, continue, prorogue and dissolve Parliaments; besides all *Statutes* must have his Consent, which it is in his Power to refuse to give to a Bill; and yet it is said, that his Denial to do it is no express Negative, but implies that he will advise upon it.

Altho' his Proclamation in calling or dissolving Parliaments, declaring War or Peace, &c. has doubtless the Effect of a Law; yet he cannot by Proclamation bring in new Laws; but may indeed inforce old ones that seem to have been discontinued. The *King* may dispense with any Penal Statute, which is not a Popular one. Tho' the *King* may determine Rewards as well as Punishments; mitigate the Rigour of the Law, and pardon Offenders, yet he cannot pardon Murder, in case Appeal is brought by the Subject. He likewise may lay an *Imbargo* on Shipping; but then it ought to be *pro bono Publico*, and not for the private Benefit of particular Traders. By 21 *Jac*. 1. *c*. 3. he has the Command of all Forts, and Places of Strength, &c. The King is also said to be the Fountain of Honour, he having the sole Power of conferring Dignities and Titles of Honour; as the creating of Dukes, Earls, Barons, Knights of the Garter, &c. He further at his Pleasure prefers and removes the great Officers of the Government. The King has also Power to incorporate a whole City, Town, &c., or a Part thereof, and to grant and annex sundry Franchises to such Corporations: But they must not, under Colour thereof, presume to set up a Monopoly. In him is lodged the supreme Right of Patronage throughout *England*, and he is the Founder, as well as Patron, of all Bishopricks, &c. and for that Reason none can be created Bishop without his Nomination. The Value can be put by him both upon Home and Foreign Coin. The *King*, in whatsoever Court he sues, cannot be nonsuit, he being supposed to be present in all his Courts.

King's Bench, denotes the Court where the King of *England* was sometimes wont to sit in Person; and on that Account was moveable with the Court or King's Houshold: And originally this Court was the only Court in *Westminster-Hall*; from whence it is thought the Courts of *Common Pleas* and *Exchequer* have been derived. The King in Person being still presumed in Law to sit in this Court, tho' only represented by his Judges, the Court is said to bear in it no less than Supreme Authority. It consists of a Lord Chief Justice (generally stiled *Lord Chief Justice of* England) and three other Justices. These are the Judges who are invested with a sovereign Jurisdiction over all Matters, whether of a Criminal or publick Nature, that are brought before them in a judicial Way, to give Remedy either by the Common Law, or by Statute-Law. All Crimes that are against the publick Good, tho' they do not injure any particular Person, are under the Cognizance of this Court; so that no private Subject can suffer any Kind of unlawful Violence or Injury against his Person, Liberties or Possessions, but that a proper Remedy is afforded him here, not only for Satisfaction of Damages sustained, but also for the Punishment of the Offender. Their Justices have it likewise in their Discretions to inflict Fine and Imprisonment, as well as an infamous Punishment on Offenders; and at the same Time may commit such to what Prison they think fit; from whence the Law does not allow any other Court to remove them. This Court frequently pro-

KI

proceeds on Indictments found before other Courts, and removed by *Certiorari* into this. *Hawkins* says, that this Court being the highest Court of Common Law, has Power to reform inferior Courts, reverse erroneous Judgments therein given, and punish the Magistrates and Officers for Corruption. Persons illegally committed, tho' even by the King and Counsel, or either of the Houses of Parliament, may be bailed in this Court; and in some Cases, even upon legal Commitments. Writs of *Mandamus* are issued by this Court for the restoring of Officers in Corporations, &c. unjustly turned out, as well as Freemen wrongfully disfranchised: And from hence likewise issues a Writ of *Quo Warranto* against Members of Corporations usurping Franchises or Liberties against the King, to seise the Liberties, &c. on a Misuser of Privileges proved: And the Authority of this Court still goes further, viz. that by a *Scire facias*, &c. issuing from thence, the King's *Letters Patent* may be repealed. The *King's Bench* is now divided into a *Crown Side* and a *Plea Side*; the one determining Criminal, and the other Civil Causes: As to the first of these it determines Criminal Matters of all Kinds, wherein the King is Plaintiff; such as Treasons, Felonies, Murders, Rapes, Robberies, Riots, Breaches of the Peace, and all other Causes that are prosecuted by Indictment, Information, &c. And into this Court not only Indictments from inferior Courts, but also Orders of Sessions, &c. may be removed: On the *Plea Side*, it holds Cognizance of all personal Actions commenced by Bill or Writ; among which may be ranked Actions of Debt, upon the Case, Detinue, Trover, and in short all other personal Actions, Ejectment, Trespass, &c. against any Person supposed to be, or really in the Custody of the Marshal of the Court. The Officers of this Court on the Crown Side, are the *Clerk of the Crown*, and the *Secondary of the Crown*: And on the Side of the Pleas, there are two chief Clerks of *Prothonotaries*, and their *Secondary* and *Deputy*, the *Custos Brevium*, two *Clerks of the Papers*, the *Clerk of the Declarations, Signer* and *Sealer of Bills*, the *Clerk of the Rules, Clerk of the Errors*, and *Clerk of the Bails*; to which may be added the *Filizers*, the *Marshal of the Court*, and the *Cryer*. The *Prothonotaries* are Masters of the *King's Bench* Office, and their Clerks are properly the *Attornies* of the Court, whose Business is to enter Declarations, Pleas, and all other Proceedings of the Court. The Office of their *Secondary* is constantly to attend the Sitting of the Court, to receive all Matters that are referred to him by the same, in order to be examined and reported by him to the Court: And his Duty further is, to sign Judgments, tax Costs, and give Rules to answer, &c. The Office of their *Deputy* is the Keeping of the Stamp, for signing Writs, &c. and also the Keeping of all Records. The *Custos Brevium*'s Duty is, to file Originals and other Writs on which Proceedings are had to Outlawry, and the several Clerks under him are for making up Records throughout *England*. The Business of the *Clerk of the Papers* is, to make up the Paper-Books of all special Pleadings and Demurrers. The Office of the *Clerk of the Declara-*

tions, is to file all Declarations, &c. The Office of the *Signer and Sealer* of Bills is to keep a Book of Entry of the Names of Plaintiff and Defendant in all Writs, &c. and Appearances are always entered with him. The Business of the *Clerk of the Rules*, is to take Notice of all Rules and Orders made in Court, and afterwards to draw them up, and enter them in a Book at large; and with this Officer are given all Rules of Course on a *Cepi Corpus*, *Habeas Corpus*, Writs of Inquiry, &c. and he, or the *Clerk of the Papers*, files all Affidavits made Use of in Court, and makes Copies of them. The *Clerk of the Errors* Business is to allow Writs of *Error*, and to make out *Supersedeas's* thereon, and likewise to transcribe and certify Records. The *Clerk of the Bails* Office, is to file the Bail-Pieces, and to mark the *Posteas*, &c. The *Filizers* of Counties, are those that make out the mesne Process, &c. The *Marshal* is he, who by himself or Deputy, is obliged constantly to attend the Court, in order to receive into his Custody such Prisoners as shall be committed by the Court. The *Cryer's* Business is to make Proclamations of the Meeting and Adjourning of the Court, to call Nonsuits, and to swear Jury-men, Witnesses, &c. *Jac. Law Dict.*

King's Silver, denotes that Money which is paid to the King in the Court of *Common Pleas*, on a Licence granted to levy a Fine of Lands, &c. which Money must be compounded in the Alienation Office, according to the Value of the Lands, &c. before the Fine can pass.

Kirby's Quest, is an ancient Record, which remains with the Remembrancer of the *Exchequer*, and it is so called from its being the Inquest of *John de Kirby*, Treasurer to King *Ed.* 1. *Jac. Law Dict.*

Kirkmote, properly denotes a Synod, and has some Times been taken for a Meeting in the Church or Vestry.

Knabe, (*Saxon*,) was anciently taken to denote Innocence, it having signified a Boy: But now this Word is greatly perverted, it being taken for a false and deceitful Fellow.

Knight's Fee, anciently denoted so much Inheritance as was sufficient to maintain a *Knight*.

Knight's Service, was an ancient Tenure, by which several Lands in this Realm were held of the King; so that it drew after it Homage, &c. But this Tenure, as well as all other Tenures of the like Kind, is now abolished. See 12 *Car.* 2. *c.* 24. See likewise **Chivalry**.

Knights of the Shire, by some called *Knights of Parliament*, are two *Knights* or Gentlemen of Estate, who are elected on the King's Writ, by the Freeholders of each County, to serve or represent them in Parliament. The necessary Qualification of a *Knight of the Shire*, is to have 600 *l.* per *Annum* in Freehold Estate.

Knighton Court, as we are told by *Butterfield*, was an Honour Court formerly held by the *Bishop* of *Hereford* at his Palace twice a Year; in which the Lords of Manors, and their Tenants holding by Knight's Service of the Honour of that Bishoprick were Suitors.

L.

Labarriſ, is a Writ that was anciently made Uſe of againſt Perſons who had no Way of Living, to oblige them to ſerve and do *Labour*; and it likewiſe lay againſt ſuch, as having ſerved in the *Winter*, refuſed to ſerve in the *Summer*.

Laches, in a legal Senſe denotes Negligence; as *Laches* of Entry, uſed by *Littleton*, ſignifies a Neglect in the Heir to enter.

Lagan, ſignifies Goods ſunk in the Sea upon a particular Occaſion; as where Mariners being in Danger of Shipwreck, in order to ſave themſelves and their Veſſel, caſt Goods into the Sea; and as they know they are heavy, and muſt of Courſe ſink to the Bottom, they generally faſten a Buoy or Cork to them, with an Intent they may have them again; and if the Ship be loſt, theſe Goods are called *Lagan*, and as long as they continue in the Sea, belong to the Lord Admiral; but in Caſe they be caſt away upon the Land, they are called a Wreck, and belong to the particular Lord intitled thereto.

Lagemen, were ſuch as we now call *Goodmen of the Jury*.

Lammas-Day, or **Lamb-mas-Day**, is the firſt Day of *Auguſt*, and in ſeveral Parts of the North, is one of the Quarter-Days for Payment of Rent in the Year: And on this Day formerly the Tenants that held Lands of the Cathedral Church of *York*, which is dedicated to St. *Peter ad Vincula*, were by their Tenure bound to bring a Lamb alive into the Church at High Maſs. To this very Day, in the North, in moſt Leaſes of Land, &c. where any of the Rent is reſerved to be paid on the firſt of *Auguſt*, the ſame is expreſſed to be made payable thus, *viz.* at the Feaſt-Day of St. *Peter ad Vincula*, commonly called *Lammas Day*.

Land, in our Law, is generally taken not only for arable Ground, Meadow, Paſture, Wood, Commons, Waters, &c. but likewiſe for Meſſuages or Tenements; ſeeing that, as *Coke* obſerves, in conveying the Land, Buildings paſs with it. In Law the Land of every Perſon is ſaid to be incloſed from that of another, yea tho' it lie in the open Field; and for this Reaſon, a Writ of *Quare clauſum fregit* will lie, in Caſe of any Treſpaſs therein.

Landcheap, was an ancient cuſtomary Fine, which was formerly paid upon every Alienation of Land within a Manor, or Liberty of a Borough.

Landefricus, did anciently denote the Lord of the Soil.

Landgable, formerly denoted a Tax or Rent payable out of Lands, and ſeems to be the ſame with what we call *Ground-Rent*.

Landlord, is the Perſon of whom Lands or Tenements are holden, and who may diſtrain on the Lands of common Right for Rent, Services, &c. See **Rent**.

Land-tenant, or **Ter-tenant**, is the Perſon who poſſeſſes Land let to him on Leaſe or otherwiſe.

Lanis de creſcentia Walliæ traducendis abſque Cuſtuma, &c. is an ancient Writ mentioned in *Reg. Orig.* which was directed to the Cuſtomer of a Port, requiring him to permit a Perſon to paſs Wool without paying Cuſtom, he having before paid it in *Wales*.

Lapſe, (from the *Latin*, ſignifying a *Ship*) denotes a Patron's Neglect or Omiſſion to preſent to a Church, within ſix Months after it becomes vacant;

vacant; in which Case the common Expression is, that Benefice is in *Lapse*, or is *lapsed*: And, according to *Wood*, *Lapse* is defined to be a Title given to the Ordinary to collate to a Benefice, on the Patron's Omission of presenting within due Time. Where after a Vacancy, the Patron does not present in six Months, the Ordinary has the next six Months to collate to the Benefice; and if he does not present within that Time, the Metropolitan then has further six Months to do it in; and if he should fail in doing it within his Time, *viz.* six Months, it then devolves to the Crown: Yet there is no *Lapse* against the King's Title; for the Maxim in Law in that Case is, *Nullum tempus occurrit Regi*.

Larceny, is a felonious Stealing, or Carrying away of another Person's Goods in his Absence; and in Regard to the Thing stolen, such felonious Taking is either great, as *Grand Larceny*; or small, as *Petit Larceny*. *Grand Larceny* denotes the felonious Taking and Carrying off the personal Goods or Effects of another, above the Value of 12 *d.* not in the Presence of the Person, or by Night in the House of the Owner: And on the other Hand *Petit Larceny* is where the Value of the Goods stolen does not exceed 12 *d.* The only Difference between *Grand* and *Petit Larceny*, is this, that *Grand Larceny* is for Goods stolen as already mentioned, above the Value of 12 *d.* whilst *Petit Larceny* is for Goods stolen of the Value of 12 *d.* or under. Should two Persons together steal Goods only to the Value of 13 *d.* it is *Grand Larceny* in both; but the Jury indeed, particularly at the *Old Bailey*, where the Theft appears to be the first Offence, frequently bring in their Verdict specially, *viz.* That the Things are not of above 10 *d.* Value; and by that Means they reduce the Offence to *Petit Larceny*, tho' the Offender is indicted perhaps for stealing to the Value of 30 or 40 *s.* and upwards. The Crime of *Grand Larceny* is punishable with Death, but that of *Petit Larceny*, only with some corporal Punishment, such as Whipping, &c. *Private Larceny*, that is to say, the Felonious Taking away from a Person above the Value of 12 *d.* is excluded the Benefit of the Clergy, provided it be laid in the Indictment, that it was done privately and secretly, &c. But *Open Larceny*, or such as is committed with the Party's Knowledge, as where a Thief does take off one's Hat or Periwig, and runs away with it, &c. is within the Benefit of the Clergy. The Thing stolen must be altogether personal, to make the Offence *Larceny*; so that if it be of any Thing in the Realty, or what is fixed to the Freehold, as Corn, Grain, or Fruit growing, &c. it cannot be *Larceny*. A Person may commit *Larceny*, by taking away his own Goods in the Hands of another; as where the Owner delivers Goods to a Carrier, &c. and afterwards secretly steals them away, with an Intent to charge him for them; because the Carrier, &c. had a special Property in the Goods, and a Possession thereof for a Time. *Dalton*, as well as others, observes, that in order to make good the Crime of *Larceny*, there must appear to be a felonious Taking, or at least a full Intent of stealing the Thing, at the Time it first comes to the Hands of the Offender, that is to say,

say, at the very Time of the Receiving. *Wood* tells that if a Person lend another a Horse to go to such a Place, and he goes there, but afterwards rides off with him; in this Case it is not *Larceny*; so that the only Remedy to be had is by Action for the Damage: Yet it is otherwise, where one comes under Pretence to buy a Horse, and the Owner gives the pretended Purchaser Leave to ride him; for in that Case, if the Stranger ride away with the Horse, it is Felony, there being an Intention implied. Where a Lodger has the Possession of the Landlord's Furniture, &c. by his Consent and Delivery, the Taking or carrying away thereof, with an Intent to steal them, is *Larceny*. See 3 & 4 *W. & M. c.* 9. Where a Servant, not being an Apprentice, goes away with any of his Master's Goods entrusted in his Care, or during his continuing in his Service, imbezils them, &c. with Intent to steal them, such Offence, provided the Value of the Goods imbeziled, &c. amounts to 40 *s.* or above, is Felony.

Lassarinus, denotes an Assassine or Murderer.

Last, signifies a certain Measure of Fish, &c. And in the Marshes of *Kent*, this Word is taken for a Court held there by the 24 *Jurats*, in which Orders are made for the Imposing and Levying of Taxes, &c. for the Preservation of the the said Marshes.

Lastage. This Word is defined by *Rastal* to be a Custom or Toll exacted in Fairs and Markets, to carry any Thing bought, where one will.

Latitat, is a Writ, that issues out of the *King's Bench*, and has its Name upon a Supposition that the Defendant does *lurk* and *lie hid*, and cannot be found in the County of *Middlesex*, so as to be taken by Bill, but is fled into some other County, to the Sheriff whereof this Writ is directed, commanding him to apprehend the Defendant there: So that a *Latitat* cannot issue into the County of *Middlesex*, unless the Court of *King's Bench* were to remove out of *Middlesex* into another County; seeing that the Process must be by Bill, in the County where the Court is. The *Teste* of all *Latitats* that are issued during Term-Time, are to be the first Day of the Term; and if issued in the Vacation, it must be the last Day of the preceding Term.

Law, in general, is defined to be a certain Rule for the good Government of Civil Society. Laws are either *Arbitrary*, or *Natural*: *Natural*, are such as in themselves are both just and good, and are binding in all Places where they are observed: *Arbitrary Laws* are founded on Convenience, and wholly depend upon the Authority of the Legislative Power that made them; and they are designed for maintaining of publick Order: In a Word, the *Natural* Laws are from God himself; whilst those that are *Arbitrary*, are nothing more than positive Institutions made by Men. The Laws of *England* at present are thus divided, viz. 1. The *Common Law*. 2. The *Statute Law*; which is made by the King, and both Houses of Parliament, for providing against new Mischiefs that may arise thro' the Corruption of the Times. 3. *Particular Customs* in divers Parts of the Realm: But our Laws are more largely divided, into the *Crown Law*; the Law and Custom of *Parliament*; the *Common Law*; the *Statute Law*;

Par-

Particular reasonable Customs; the Law of Arms; Ecclesiastical or Canon Laws; the Civil Law used in certain Cases; the Forest Law; the Law of Marque and Reprisal; the Law of Merchants, &c. It is by some in general well observed, that the Use of the Law is to secure the Property of what we enjoy; and that the Objects thereof concern Persons, their Estates, Crimes and Misdemeanors, &c.

Law-Day, otherwise called *View of Frankpledge*, is taken for any Day of open Court; and generally used for the County or Hundred Court.

Lawing of Dogs. See *Expeditate*.

Lawless Court. We are told by *Cowel*, that on *Kingshill* at *Rochford* in *Essex*, on *Wednesday* Morning, next after *Michaelmas-day*, at Cock-crowing, there is held a Court, vulgarly called, *The Lawless Court*, where they whisper, and have no Candle, nor any Pen and Ink, but a Coal; and he that owes Suit or Service, who does not appear, forfeits double his Rent every Hour he is missing. This Court, the same Author tells us, belongs to the Honour of *Raleigh*, and to the Earl of *Warwick*, and is called *Lawless*, because it is held at an unlawful Hour: And the Title of it in the Court-Rolls is said to run thus, *viz.*

Kingshill, in } ss.
Rochford, }

Curia de Domino Rege
Dicta sine lege,
Tenta est ibidem:
Per ejusdem Consuetudinem,
Ante Ortum Solis
Luceat nisi Polus,
Seneschallus solus
Nil scribit nisi Colle,
Toties voluerit,
Gallus ut cantaverit,
Per cujus soli sonitus
Curia est summonita:
Clamat clam pro Rege
In Curia sine lege,
Et nisi cito venerint
Citius pænituerint,
Et nisi clam accedant
Curia non attendat,
Qui venerit cum Lumine
Errat in Regimine,
Et dum sunt sine Lumine,
Capti sunt in Crimine,
Curia sine Cura.
Jurati de Injuria.

Tenta ibidem Die Mercurii (ante Diem) proximi post Festum Sancti Michaelis Archangeli, Anno Regni Regis, &c.

In *Cam. Britan.* we are told, that this servile Attendance was imposed on the Tenants, for conspiring at the like unseasonable Time to raise a Commotion.

Law of Marque, is that Law whereby Persons that are driven to it, do take the Shipping and Goods of that People of whom they have received Wrong, and cannot get ordinary Justice in another Nation, when they may take within their own Bounds or Precincts.

Law Merchant, is become a Part of the Laws of this Kingdom, and is proper to Merchants, it altogether differing from the Common Law.

Law Spiritual, denotes the *Ecclesiastical Law*, which is allowed by our Laws in all Cases where it is not repugnant to the Common Law, &c. This Law was anciently called *Law Christian*.

Lawyer, denotes a Counsellor, or one that is learned or skilled in the Law.

Lay-Fee, formerly was taken for Lands held in Fee from a *Lay-Lord*, by the usual Services, whereto Military Tenure was subject.

Lazzi, denoted Persons of a servile Condition.

Leakage, denotes a certain Allowance made out of the Customs to Merchants that import Wine, *viz.* twelve *per Cent.* and there is likewise a particular Allowance to be made to Brewers, &c. out of the Excise-Duty on Beer, &c.

Lease, or rather *Demise*, denotes a Parting with, or Letting of Lands for a Term of Years, Life, or at Will, under a Rent reserved. Leases may be either by Writing, or Word of Mouth, which last is called a *Lease Parol*. Upon a Lease for Life *Livery and Seisin* is required. A *Lease at Will*, denotes such a Lease as either the *Lessor* or *Lessee* may at their Pleasure or Will be free from. By 29 *Car.* 2. *c.* 3. all Estates or Terms for Years in Lands, &c. which are not reduced into Writing, and signed by the Parties, shall have no greater Effect than as Estates at Will; unless they be Leases of Terms not exceeding three Years from the making. In *Wood's Inst.* we read, That if the Substance of a Lease exceeding three Years be put in Writing, and signed by the Parties, tho' such Lease be not sealed, it shall have the Effect of a Lease for Years; and indeed Articles of Agreement, with a Covenant to make a Lease for a Term certain, under a particular Rent reserved, seems in itself to imply a Lease. One interested in Lands, &c. for a Term of Years may make a Lease of all the Years except one Day, or other short Part of the Term; for it must be granted for a less Term than the Lessor has in the Lands; otherwise it will be an Assignment. *Wood* says, That if a Lessee for Years grants a Lease for Life, the Lessee may enjoy it during the Lessor's Life, in case the Term of Years lasts so long: Yet if he gives Livery and Seisin upon it, this will occasion a Forfeiture of the Term: And further, that Joint-Tenants, Tenants in common, and Coparceners may make Leases for Life, Years, or at Will, of their own Parts, and thereby shall bind their Companions. If a Person make a *Lease* from three Years to three Years, it is good for six Years. It has been held, that if there be a Lease in Writing for a Year, and so from Year to Year, as long as both the Lessor and Lessee shall agree, this is only binding for a Year; yet if the Lessee enter upon the second Year, he thereby becomes bound for that Year. A *Lease* is frequently made for 21 Years; if the Lessee shall so long live, and is good, notwithstanding it contains a Certainty in an Uncertainty. If a *Lease* be made to *A. B.* for 99 Years, if *C. D.* and *E. F.* shall so long live; after which *C. D.* dies, by whose Death the *Lease* immediately becomes determined; and the Reason of this is, that the Words (*or either of them*) are omitted, which by being inserted would make the *Lease* good for both the Lives of the Lessees. It has been held, that if a Lessor accepts of Rent from an Assignee of the Lease, he cannot afterwards charge the Lessee with the Rent. Where there is a Lessee for Years, be the Term never so long, he has only a Chattel, whilst a Tenant for Life has a Freehold. The Person that grants the *Lease* is called the *Lessor*, and the Person to whom it is granted is called the *Lessee*. An Indenture of *Lease* usually

usually consists of the following Parts, viz. The Names and Additions of the Parties; the Thing demised or leased; the *Habendum* or explanatory Clause, to shew for what Time the Lease is to continue; *Reddendum*, or the certain Rent reserved; a *Proviso*, for Re-entry, in case of Nonpayment of Rent; a Covenant for Payment of Rent; another for the Repairing of Houses, (in case the Lease be of Messuages, &c.) and for delivering up the Premisses in good Repair at the End of the Term; and *lastly*, a Covenant from the Lessor for quiet Enjoyment. You may see divers Forms of Leases in the *Young Clerk's Magazine*, and in other Collections of Precedents in Conveyancing.

Lease and Release, denotes a certain Instrument in Writing used in our Law, for the Conveyance of a Right or Interest in Lands or Tenements in Fee to another. Anciently a Deed of Feoffment was the Conveyance chiefly used at Common Law; but since the *Statute* of Uses, 27 *Hen.* 8. *c.* 10. this Conveyance of *Lease and Release*, has taken Place; and by it *Livery* and *Seisin*, which is absolutely necessary on a Feoffment, is supplied without any actual Possession given, or Entry made. The Method of making this Conveyance is this, viz. A *Lease* or Bargain and Sale for a Year, bearing Date the Day next before the Date of the Release, and commencing the Day before the Date of the Lease, is first executed; to the Intent that by Virtue thereof, and of the Statute made for transferring of Uses into Possession, the Lessee may be in the actual Possession of the Lands, &c. intended to be granted by the Release, and be thereby enabled to take a Grant of the Reversion and Inheritance of the said Lands, &c. to him, his Heirs and Assigns for ever: After which the Release must be executed: And here it is to be observed, that it is proper in the Lease for a Year to reserve a Pepper-Corn Rent, which is held to be sufficient to raise a Use, so as to make the Lessee capable of a Release; and in this Lease, instead of the usual Words, *Demised, Leased*, &c. used in other Sorts of Leases, these Words must be made Use of, viz. *Bargain and Sell* in Consideration of a certain Sum of Money; and 5 s. tho' never paid, is a sufficient Consideration, whereby the Lessee for a Year becomes immediately in Possession on the Execution of the Deed, without any Entry: And it has been held, that if the Words, *Grant, Demise, Lease,* and to *Farm let* are used in a Bargain and Sale for a Year, the Bargainee cannot accept of a Release of the Inheritance, until he has actually entered and is in Possession. Unless a Person be in Possession of the Lands, &c. intended to be granted, he cannot make a Bargain and Sale. A *Lease* and *Release* being only in the Nature of one Deed, make but one Conveyance. The Form of a *Lease* and *Release* you may see in the *Young Clerk's Magazine*, and other Treatises on Conveyancing.

Lecherwite, anciently denoted a Fine on Fornicators and Adulterers.

Lecturer, denotes a Reader of Lectures, or one who usually is the Afternoon Preacher, who is chosen by a Vestry, or the chief Inhabitants of a Parish. A *Lecturer* must be licensed by the Bishop, as another Minister is: Yet the Bishop's Power does not extend to the Right of *Lectureship*, but only to to the Qualification and Fitness of the Person.

Leet, denotes a little Court held in a Manor, and is accounted the King's Court, on Account that its Authority to punish Offences originally belonged to the Crown.

Legabilis, denotes any Thing that is not intailed as hereditary; but may be bequeathed by a last Will and Testament.

Legacy, signifies any Thing that is given or bequeathed by a last Will or Testament. The Person to whom a *Legacy* is given is called the *Legatee*: And there is also a Residuary *Legatee*, that is to say, the Person to whom, after several Devises or Bequests made by Will, the Residue of the Testator's Estate and Effects are given. It is reported to us by *Salkeld*, That a Person devised 200 *l.* a-piece to the two Children of *A. B.* at the End of ten Years after the Testator's Death; that afterwards the Children dying within the ten Years, it was held to be a lapsed *Legacy*: But on a Devise of a Sum of Money, &c. to be paid such a one attaining the Age of twenty-one Years, or on the Day of Marriage, if the Legatee die before either of these happen, the Legatee's Administrator shall have the *Legacy*, for this Reason, that the Legatee had a present Interest therein, altho' the Time of Payment was not yet come. No Executor is obliged to pay a Legacy, without Security given him by the *Legatee*, to refund, in case there are Debts; seeing that the Legacy is not due till the Debts are paid: And in like Manner an Executor may be compelled to give Security to the Legatee for the Payment of his Legacy, by a Bill in Equity, setting forth, that he has wasted the Testator's Estate, and praying that he may give Security to pay the Legacy when it shall become due. Where a Legacy is bequeathed, and no certain Time of Payment mentioned, and the Legatee is an Infant, he shall be intitled to Interest for his Legacy, from the Expiration of a Year after the Testator's Death, which Time is allowed him to see whether there are any Debts: But it is otherwise where the Legatee is of full Age; for in that Case he shall not have any Interest but from the Time of the Demand of the Legacy; and if a Legacy is payable at a certain Day, it will carry Interest from that Day. It is held, that as Legacies are only Gratuities, Action will not lie at Common Law for the Recovery of the same; but Remedy may be had either in the Spiritual Court, or in *Chancery*: Yet if a Legacy be secured by Bond, in that Case the Legacy becomes a Debt, and there is no other Remedy for Recovery than an Action on the Bond. See **Executor**. See **Wills**.

Legalis Homo, is taken for a Person that is not outlawed, excommunicated, or infamous.

Legalis Moneta Magnæ Britanniæ, denotes Gold or Silver Money coined here by the Authority of the King.

Legatory or **Legatary**, has the same Signification with that of *Legatee*.

Legem facere, signifies to make Law or Oath.

Legem habere, denotes to be capable of giving Evidence upon Oath.

Legiosus, according to *Cowel*, denotes to be litigious.

Legitimation, signifies a making lawful; as Naturalization, which makes a Foreigner a lawful Subject of the State.

Leprosi amovendo, is a Writ which lay to remove a *Leper* or *Lazar*, who forced himself into the Company of his Neighbours, either in a Church or in some other publick Meeting, so as to annoy them.

Le Roy le veut, are Words used by the Clerk of the Parliament to signify the King's Assent to publick Bills, but to private Bills the King's Answer is, *Soit fait comme il est desire.*

Le Roy se avisera. By these Words, the King's Denial or Refusal of a Bill presented to him in Parliament is signified.

Lessa, was anciently used for a Legacy.

Lessor and **Lessee.** See **Lease.**

Letter of Attorney, is an Instrument in Writing, whereby a Person is authorised to do some lawful Act in the Place of another; as to give Livery and Seisin of Lands, &c. distrained for Rent due, receive Debts, or to sue a third Person, &c. The Drift of this Instrument is to give the Attorney authorised, the whole Power of the Maker, to accomplish the Act intended to be performed. This Writing is sometimes made *revocable,* which is when a bare Authority only is thereby given; and sometimes *irrevocable,* which is when Debts, &c. are assigned from one to another. In most Cases the Authority granted by a *Letter of Attorney,* determines upon the Death of the Person that gave it. The Form of this Instrument you may see in the *Young Clerk's Magazine,* and other Collections of Precedents in Conveyancing.

Letters Claus, or **Close Letters,** are opposed to *Letters Patent,* the first being commonly sealed up with the King's Signet or Privy Seal; whilst the *Letters Patent* are left open and sealed with the Broad Seal.

Letter of Credit, denotes a certain *Letter* which a Merchant or other Person writes to his Correspondent, requesting him to credit the Bearer with a particular Sum of Money therein mentioned.

Letter of Licence, is a Writing granted by Creditors to a Person that has failed in the World, allowing him a certain Time for Payment of his Debts, and protecting him from the Arrests of his Creditors, giving the Party Leave to go to and fro about his Business, without being subject to the Molestation of any of them. The Form of this Instrument you may see in the *Young Clerk's Magazine,* and other Treatises of Conveyancing.

Letters of Marque, is a Commission grantable by the *Secretaries of State,* with the Approbation of the King and Council, usually in Time of War, for making extraordinary Reprisals for Reparation to Merchants taken or depredated by Strangers at Sea. If Persons commissioned by *Letters of Marque* knowingly take a Ship or Vessel, &c. belonging to a different Nation, from that against whom the Commission is awarded, and which is in Amity with us, this is no less than *downright Piracy.*

Letters Patent, are certain Charters or Writings of the King, sealed with the Great Seal of *Great Britain,* and it is so called, on Account that they are open with the Seal affixed. See **Patents.**

Levant and Couchant, denotes Cattle that have been so long in another Person's Ground, that they have lain down, and are risen again to feed: The Space of Time of their having been there, so as
to

to make them be deemed *Levant and Couchant*, is supposed to be a Day and a Night.

Levari facias, is a Writ directed to the Sheriff, for levying a certain Sum of Money upon a Person's Lands, &c. upon his having forfeited his Recognizance. If a Year and a Day is past after the Forfeiture of the Recognizance, a *Scire facias* must issue. There is also a *Levari facias damna diffeisitoribus*, which is for the levying of Damages, wherein the Disseisor has before been condemned to the Disseisee. There is likewise a *Levari facias residuum debiti*, to levy the Remainder of a Debt upon the Lands, &c. of a Debtor, when Part thereof has been satisfied before: And to these may be added, the Writ of *Levari facias quando vicecomes returnavit quod non habuit emptores*, whereby the Sheriff is commanded to sell the Debtor's Goods, &c. which he has taken, and returned that he could not sell.

Levari foenum, denotes an ancient Service of one Day's Hay-making that was paid to the Lord by his inferior Tenants.

Levy, in a legal Sense denotes, to collect or exact; as to levy Money, &c. To levy a Fine of Land, &c. is the Term usually made Use of for to pass a Fine.

Ley gager, is the same as **Wager of Law**.

Libel, in our Law, denotes a scandalous Report of a Person spread abroad, or otherwise published, and thereupon called an *infamous Libel*: And a *Libel* may be either in Writing, or without: In Writing, is when any Thing is written and published to the Disgrace of another; and without Writing, is where a Person is painted out in a scandalous Manner, with Asses Ears, a Fool's Coat, &c. or where any ignominious Sign is fix'd at a Person's Door, such as a Gallows, &c. A *Libel* may in general be defined to be a malicious Aspersion of another, signified either in Printing or Writing; and which tends either to the Blackening the Memory of one that is dead, or the Reputation of one that is living, in order to expose him to publick Contempt, Hatred, or Ridicule. And a Libel may be extended to any Defamation whatsoever. Where a Libel is made against a private Man, it may be a Means to excite the libelled Person, or his Friends, to Revenge, and consequently to break the Peace; and should the *Libel* be against a Magistrate, it would be not only a Breach of the Peace, but also a Scandal to the Government. It is said, that tho' a private Person or Magistrate libelled be dead at the Time of publishing the *Libel*, yet the Offence is punishable, as it tends to the Breach of the Peace. It is no Justification of a Libel, that its Contents are true, or that the Person libelled had a bad Reputation; for this Reason, that the greater Appearance there is of Truth in a Libel, the more provoking it is. It is held, that, in a Prosecution on an Indictment or Information, it is not material whether the Matter *libelled* be true or not; yet in an Action upon the Case, the Defendant may justify that the Matter is true. Where one accidentally finds a Libel, he ought to burn it, or deliver it to a Magistrate. In case a *Printer* prints a Libel against a private Person, he may be indicted and punished for it. Where Persons write, print, or sell any Pamphlets or other Treatises reflecting on the Publick, or a private Person, such *libellous Treatises* may

may be seised, and the Persons concerned therein punished. Writers of false News are likewise indictable and punishable. It is reported by *Popham*, that a Person for libelling the *Lord Chancellor Bacon*, by affirming that his Lordship had done Injustice, &c. was fined 1000 *l*. and sentenced to ride on a Horse with his Face to the Tail, from the *Fleet* to *Westminster*, with his Fault writ on his Head, to acknowledge his Offence in all the King's Courts, and that one of his Ears should be cut off at *Westminster*, and the other in *Cheapside*; and further to be imprisoned during Life. The sending a scandalous Letter to the Party himself, without shewing or publishing it to a third Person, is no Libel; but if it be sent to a third, or otherwise dispersed, this is Publication of the Libel. The Writing or Publishing a *Libel* is an Offence against the King's Peace, and is punishable by Indictment. *Hawkins* tells us, that no Writing is esteemed a *Libel*, unless it reflect upon some particular Person; for where a Writing inveighs against Mankind in general, or against a particular Order of Men, it is no *Libel*, it not descending to Particulars. If a Person speaks scandalous Words, but does not put them in Writing, he is not guilty of a *Libel*; seeing that a *Libel* chiefly consists in reducing the infamous Matter into Writing. Printing or Writing has been held to be *libellous*, tho' the Scandal is not directly charged, but, on the contrary, in an oblique or ironical Manner; as where a Person by Writing pretends to recommend to the World the Character of some great Man for Imitation, in the Place of taking Notice of what he is famed for, pitches only upon such Qualities as his Antagonists charge him with the Want of; as for Instance, by proposing a certain Person to be imitated for his Learning, who is known to be a good Soldier or so, and at the same Time is noted for his being illiterate. In the *Modern Reports*, we are told, that in the Making of *Libels*, if one Person dictates, and another writes a *Libel*, both are culpable; since the Writing after another shews the Penman's or Transcriber's Approbation of what is contained in the *Libel*; and if one dictate, another write, and a third approve of what is written, they are all deemed Makers or Composers of the *Libel*; for this Reason, that all who concur or join in an unlawful Act, are in Law esteemed guilty. It is reported by *Salkeld*, That if a Person makes a Transcript of a *Libel*, and does not deliver it to others, the Copying of it is no Publication; yet he says, that it has been adjudged, that the bare Copying a Libel, without Authority, is writing a Libel, and the Writer thereof is looked upon as the Contriver; and further, that where a Person has a written Copy of a known Libel found in his Custody, it shall be looked upon as an Evidence of the Publication; but it is otherwise, in Case the Libel be not publickly known: And it is also said, that the Copying of a Libel is the same Thing as writing or composing the Libel itself, because it has the same pernicious Consequence. Where a Libel is found under a Person's Hand that is known, the Proof turns upon him, and in case he cannot produce the Composer, it will be difficult for him to be freed from being deemed the Man. The Composer, Procurer and Publisher of a Libel are punishable by Fine,

Imprisonment, Pillory, or the like Corporal Punishment, at the Discretion of the Court where the Trial is had. In all Law Proceedings there are two Ways of describing a Libel; the one by the Sense, in these Words, *viz. The Tenor of which follows*: And the other by an exact Description of the particular Words; and if there be any Variance in Respect to the Words charged, it will be fatal to the Cause.

Libera Chasea habenda, is a Writ granted to a Person for a *free Chase* appertaining to his Manor; after Proof upon an Inquiry of a Jury, that the same of Right belongs to him.

Liberate, carries with it different Significations: As first, it denotes a Writ that lies for the Payment of a yearly Pension, or annual Sum granted under the Great Seal, and which is for that Purpose directed to the Treasurers of the Exchequer: And in another Sense it is taken for a Writ directed to the Sheriff of a County, commanding him to deliver Possession of Lands, &c. extended upon the Forfeiture of a Recognizance; And it is likewise taken for a Writ issuing out of *Chancery*, directed to a Gaoler for Delivery of a Prisoner that has put in Bail for his Appearance.

Libertate probanda, is a Writ that anciently lay on Behalf of such as being demanded for Villeins, offered to prove themselves free.

Libertatibus allocandis, is a Writ which lies for a Citizen or Burgess, who is impleaded contrary to his *Liberty*, in order to have his Privilege allowed. There is likewise a special Writ *de libertatibus allocandis*, which is where a Person claims a special Liberty to be impleaded within some particular City or Borough, and not elsewhere, to suffer the Burgesses to use their Liberties, &c.

Libertatibus exigendis, is a Writ which was anciently in Use, whereby the King commanded the *Justices in Eyre* to admit of an Attorney for the Defence of another's Liberties.

Liberty, in a legal Sense, denotes some Privilege that is held by Charter or Prescription, whereby Persons enjoy a particular Benefit above the ordinary Subject. In a more general Sense it is taken to be a Power to act as one thinks fit; unless such Person be restrained by the Laws of the Land. *Lilly* observes, that the Laws of this Realm in general favour Liberty: And by *Magna Charta* it is ordained, That no Freeman shall be imprisoned or condemned without Trial by his Peers, or the Law.

Liberty to hold Pleas. See **Franchise**.

Librata Terræ, denotes a certain Quantity of Land, containing four *Oxgangs*. See **Fardingdeal**.

Licence, signifies an Authority given to a Person to do some lawful Act. If the Person licensed abuse the Power given him, he in that Case becomes a Trespasser. A *Licence to alien in Mortmain*, see **Mortmain**.

Licence to arise, denotes that Liberty of Time allowed by the Court to the Tenant to *arise* out of his Bed, who is essoined *de malo lecti* in an Action real.

Licence of the King, to go abroad. See **Ne exeat Regnum**.

Licentia concordandi, denotes the Licence for which the *King's Silver* is paid.

Licentia transfretandi, is a Process directed to the Keeper of *Dover Port*, &c. whereby he is commanded to suffer those to pass over Sea,

Li

Sea, who have obtained the King's Licence for it.

Lidford Law, is an old Proverbial Expression, by which is meant as much as to hang a Man first, and to judge him afterwards.

Liege, is sometimes taken for *Liege-Lord*, and sometimes for *Liege-Man*. *Liege-Lord* is he that acknowledges no Superior; whilst, on the other Hand, *Liege-Man* is the Person that owes Allegiance to the *Liege-Lord*. The Subjects of the King are called *Lieges*, or *Liege-People*.

Legiance, denotes a faithful Obedience of a Subject to his King.

Ligeancy. See **Allegiance**.

Lien, is a Word made Use of in our Law two different Ways; as *Personal Lien* denotes a Bond, Covenant or Contract; and *Real Lien* signifies a Judgment, Statute, or Recognizance which affects the Land.

Life-Rent, denotes a Rent payable for Term of Life, or for the Support of it.

Lignagium, generally is taken to signify the Right which a Person has to the Cutting of Fuel in *Woods*; but is sometimes taken for the Acknowledgment paid for such Right.

Ligula, is taken to be a Transcript of a Court-Roll.

Limitation, in our Law denotes a certain Space of Time assigned by Act of Parliament, for bringing Actions in; as by the *Statute* 21 *Jac.* 1. *c.* 16. it is enacted, That all Writs of *Formedon*, &c. for Title to Lands in Being, shall be sued out within 20 Years after the Title arose: But in this *Statute* there is a *Proviso* in Favour of Infants, Feme Coverts, Persons beyond Sea, or in Prison, and their Heirs, so as they, after their Impediment is removed, commence their Suits within the Time limited by the *Statutes*. By the same *Statute*, Actions of Debt, upon the Case (except for Words) Actions of Account (other than concerning Merchandise) of Detinue, Trover and Trespass, must be commenced within six Years after the Cause of Action; and not afterwards. Actions of Assault and Battery, Wounding and Imprisonment, must be brought within four Years after Cause of Action; and for Slander within two Years. It is to be observed, that this *Statute* is not pleadable to an Account current, but to an Account stated. Tho' an Action may be barred by this *Statute*, yet a fresh Promise shall revive it. According to *Carthew's Rep.* A bare Acknowledgment of the Debt within six Years of the Action will, tho' no Promise be made prevent this *Statute's* taking Place. A *Latitat*, taken out, filed and continued, is said to be an Avoidance of the *Statute*: And it is likewise said, that if after Proceedings in an inferior Court, the six Years expire, after which the Cause is removed into a superior Court, the Plaintiff in that Case may set forth the Suit below, and by that Means prevent his being barred by the *Statute*. Where the Plaintiff is abroad at the Time the Cause of Action accrued, he may upon his Return bring his Action; but should the Defendant be abroad, and the Plaintiff here, he must file an Original against the Defendant, and continue it till his Return. But this Part of the Law has been since altered; for now, in Case the Defendant be out of the Land, the Plaintiff may bring his Action against him after his Return, provided he does it within the Time limited.

Limi

Limitation of Estate, denotes the Length of Time an Estate shall continue; as where a Person grants Lands to another, to hold to him and his Heirs Males, and for Default of such Issue, then to his Heirs Females; in this Case the Daughters may not inherit so long as there is a Male Heir, for this Reason, that the Estate to the Heirs Male is first limited. Lands are frequently limited to one in Tail, Remainder to a second, and Remainder to a third in Fee, &c.

Limitation of the Crown, are Words which denote certain Acts of Parliament, made for the *Limitation of the Crown* of this Kingdom.

Litigator, denotes a Contender or Litigator of a Suit at Law.

Livery of Seisin, is a Term used in our Law, to signify the Delivery of Possession of Lands, &c. unto him that has Right thereto; and it is a certain Ceremony in Use with us, upon the Conveyance of Lands, &c. where a Fee or other Freehold is granted. A Livery of Seisin may be made of any Thing that is corporeal, as a House, Lands, &c. Where both a House and Lands are conveyed, the House is always looked upon as Principal, and on that Account the Livery must be made there, and not upon the Land. There are two Sorts of *Livery and Seisin*, viz. *Livery in Deed*, and *Livery in Law*: In *Deed* is where the Feoffor takes the Ring or Key of the Door, and delivers the same to the Feoffee in the Name of *Seisin*. *Livery in Law*, is where the Feoffor being in View of the House or Land granted, saith to the Feoffee, upon Delivery of the Deed, *I give to you yonder Land, &c. to hold to you and your Heirs; so go into the same, and take Possession thereof accordingly*. *Littleton* says, that if Lands lie in different Parts in one County, *Livery and Seisin* of one Parcel in one Place, in the Name of the whole granted in the Feoffment, is sufficient; yet if the Lands lie in several Counties, it is otherwise; for there *Livery and Seisin* must be in every County. It is likewise held, that no Person ought to be in the House, or upon the Land, at the Time Livery is made, except the Feoffor and Feoffee. A Person may make a Letter of Attorney to deliver Seisin by Virtue of the Feoffment, and the same may be either contained in such Deed, or in a Deed separate from it, viz. a special Letter of Attorney made for that Purpose: And a Letter of Attorney may be also made for Receiving of *Livery and Seisin*. The Method of giving *Livery and Seisin* is, the Parties to the Deed, the Feoffor and Feoffee, or the respective Attornies by them authorised, coming to the Door of the House, or upon some Part of the Land, do there, in the Presence of a Couple of Witnesses, declare the Occasion of their Meeting, or read the Deed, or Contents thereof; and in Case the *Livery and Seisin* be made by Attorney, the Letter of Attorney, or its Contents, is there read; after which, if the *Livery* be of a House, the Grantor takes the Ring, Key or Latch of the Door, (all Persons being thereout) or if Land, a Clod of Earth, and a Twig of one of the Trees thereon, and delivers the same Ring, &c. with the Deed to the Grantee, or his Attorney authorised to receive *Livery*, uttering these Words, viz. *I A. B. do hereby deliver to you C. D. Livery and Seisin of all this Messuage or Tenement, &c. to hold to you,* *your Heirs and Assigns, according to the Purport, true Intent and Meaning of this Indenture or Deed of Feoffment.* You may see the Form of making *Livery and Seisin,* in the *Young Clerk's Magazine,* and Books relating to Conveyancing.

Livery and Seisin, since the Making the *Statute* of *Uses,* is now seldom used, a Lease and Release being sufficient to vest the Grantee with Possession, without the Formality of *Livery.*

Livery and Ouster le Maine, was anciently where by Inquest before the *Escheator,* it was found, that nothing was held of the Crown, in which Case the Escheator was commanded to put out of his Hands the Lands taken into the King's Hands.

Local, in our Law, denotes something that is tied to a certain Place; as real Actions are *local,* they being to be brought in the County where the Lands lie; whereas personal Actions, such as Trespass, Battery, &c. are transitory, and not *local.*

Locus in quo, denotes the Place wherein any Thing is in Pleadings alledged to be done.

Locus partitus, is by *Fleta* defined to be a Division made between two Towns or Counties, in order to have it tried where the Land or Place in Question lies.

Loadsman, is the Person that undertakes to bring a Ship thro' the Haven, after she has been brought thither by the Pilot, to the Place of her Discharge.

Lodmanage, denotes the Hire of a Pilot, for the carrying of a Ship from one Port or Place to another.

Lot. See **Scot.**

Lunatick, is a Person that is sometimes of sound Memory and Understanding, and at other Times not so: And as long as he is without Understanding, he is said to be *non compos mentis.* A *Lunatick* without Memory, who does not understand what he does, his Acts in Criminal Cases shall not be charged to him, unless in Case of any Attempt upon the Person of the King: Yet where a Person incites a *Lunatick* to commit a Criminal Act, the Person so inciting is, in the Eye of the Law a principal Offender, and is punishable equally as if he had committed it himself. By 12 *Ann. Lunaticks,* or *Madmen,* that wander to and fro, may be apprehended by a Justice's Warrant, and locked up, and chained, if necessary; or be sent to their legal Settlement, and two Justices may charge their Estates for their Maintenance. Any Deed or Contract made by a Lunatick, who is *non compos* may be avoided; yet a *Lunatick* having purchased, if he recovers his Memory, he may agree to it, after which his Heirs cannot disagree thereto. The Deed of a *Lunatick* may not be avoided by himself. Commissions of *Lunacy* issue out of *Chancery,* impowering the Commissioners to examine whether a Person be a *Lunatick,* and also to make Inquest of his Lands, &c. In *Dyer* we are told, that tho' Lands be seised by the King, upon a Commission of *Lunacy,* and he grants the Custody of the *Lunatick sine computo reddendo,* without Account to be rendered, if the *Lunatick* afterwards becomes to be of sound Memory, he may have an Action of Account of the Profits. The Guardianship of the Lands of *Lunaticks* is the King's peculiar Right, yet he has not the sole Interest in granting, and the Custody of their Persons as he has of *Ideots:* And the Reason of this is, that a *Lunatick*

natick may recover his Memory, and by that Means have Discretion enough to dispose of and manage, so that the King in this Case may not have the Custody both of his Body and Lands; seeing that after he has recovered his Understanding he is to have his Estate entirely at his own Disposal. See **Ideot**.

Lupanatrix, was anciently used to denote a Bawd or Strumpet.

Lupinum caput gerere, was formerly used to signify to be outlawed; and it was so called, because it was customary for such Person to have his Head exposed like that of a Wolf's, with a Reward for bringing it in.

Lusburghs, or **Luxenburgs**, were an ancient base Sort of Coin of the Resemblance of the *English* Coin, brought into *England* from abroad.

Lyef-Silver, was a small Fine anciently paid by Customary Tenants to the Lord for Leave to plough and sow their Land.

M.

Mcegress anciently denoted such Persons as bought and sold stolen Flesh, knowing the same to be so.

Magbote, or **Megbote**, anciently denoted a certain Recompence for the slaying of one's Kinsman, when corporal Punishments for Murder were frequently changed into pecuniary Penalties, where the Friends of the slain Person were satisfied therewith.

Magick. See **Conjuration**.

Magistrate, is a Ruler or Minister of Justice, who is said to be the Keeper of both Tables of the Law; and if any such Person is slain in the Execution of his Office, &c. it is Murder, it being a Contempt both of the King and the Laws.

Magna assisa eligenda, is a Writ anciently used for summoning four lawful Knights before the Justices of *Assise*, there upon their Oaths to chuse twelve Knights of their Neighbourhood, &c. to pass upon the *Great Assise*, between such a one Plaintiff, and such a one Defendant.

Magna Charta. The great Charter of Liberties, which was granted 9 *Hen*. 3. is so called; and very likely took its Name on Account of the Excellency of the Laws it contains.

Maiden Assises, is a Term used, where at any *Assises* no Person is condemned to die.

Maiden-Rents, was a *Noble* that was anciently paid by the Tenant to his Lord, for his passing by the Custom of *Marcheta*, by which he was to have the first Night's Lodging with his Tenant's Wife, tho' it is thought to denote a certain Fine paid for a Licence to marry a Daughter.

Maihem or **Mayhem**, denotes a Wound or some corporal Hurt, whereby a Person loses the Use of a Member that might be of Defence to him; as where a Person has a Bone broken, a Foot, Hand, or other Member cut off; or where an Eye is put out, &c. Before 22 & 23 *Car*. 2. the Cutting of an Ear or Nose, the Breaking of the hinder Teeth, &c. was held to be no *Maihem*: But now it is enacted, that if any Person or Persons, on Purpose, of Malice forethought, and lying in Wait, shall cut off the Nose, put out the Eye, disable the Tongue, or cut off or disable any Limb or Member of any of the King's Subjects, with an Intent to *maihem* or disfigure him, the Offender, his Aiders,

ers, Abettors, &c. shall be deemed guilty of Felony without the Benefit of Clergy. It has been held, that if a Person of Malice forethought attack another, in order to murder him with a Bill, or the like Instrument, that cannot miss endangering the *maiming* of him; and if upon such Attack the Person does not happen to kill, but only to *maim* him, the Offender this Way is liable to be tried on this Statute, in which Case it shall be left to the Jury on the Evidence, whether there was a Design to murder by *Maiming*, and of Consequence a malicious Intent to maim as well as kill.

Mainpernable, denotes that a Person may be admitted to Bail.

Mainpernors, are those Persons to whom a Person in Custody or Prison is delivered, upon their becoming bound for the Defendant's Appearance, &c. which if the Defendant does not do, the *Manucaptors* forfeit their Recognizances.

Mainprise, in a legal Sense, signifies the Receiving of a Person into friendly Custody (when otherwise he might be committed to Prison) upon Security given that he shall be forthcoming at a certain Time and Place. There is a manifest Difference made between Bail and *Mainprise*; for the Person that is *mainprised*, is said to be at large from the Day of his being *mainprised*, until the Day of his Appearance; whilst, on the other Hand, where one is let to Bail by a Judge, &c. till a certain Day, in that Case he is in Law always accounted to be in the Ward of his Bail for that Time; and they may, if they are aminded, keep him in Prison; and therefore the Person that is so bailed, cannot be said to go at large, or be at his own Liberty. In short, *Mainprise* is an Engaging in a Sum certain; but Bail answers the Condemnation in Civil Cases. There is a Writ of *Mainprise* anciently in Use; whereby such Persons as are bailable, and have been refused the Benefit of being admitted to it, may be delivered out of Confinement.

Mainport, was a small Duty anciently paid to the Rector of the Parish, by the Parishioners, in Lieu of certain Tithes.

Mainswarn. In the Northern Parts of *England*, this Word is taken to be the same as forsworn.

Maintainors, are such as, not being interested in a Suit, maintain or second a Cause depending between others, either by disbursing Money for the Carrying of it on, or making Friends on Behalf either of the Plaintiff or Defendant.

Maintenance, denotes an unlawful maintaining or supporting a Suit. *Maintenance* may be either in the Country, as where a Person assisting another in his Pretension to Lands, takes or holds the Possession thereof for him; or it is where a Person is a Stirrer up of Quarrels or Suits in the Country: Or *Maintenance* may be in a Court of Justice; as where one in no Respect interested in a Suit depending interferes therein, and assists one of the Parties with Money or otherwise, in the Prosecution or Defence of the same. If a Person disinterested in a Cause shall officiously give Evidence, or open the Evidence in a Suit depending, without being called on for that Purpose; shall act the Part of Counsel with the Party, by speaking in the Cause; or shall retain an Attorney, &c. in the Cause; this is *Maintenance*: Yet it it is said that a Person cannot be guilty of *Maintenance*, for the Money he gives to another before any Suit is commenced; neither is it *Maintenance* for one to give another Advice, before the Commencement of a Suit, as to what Action is to be brought, or what other Method is to be taken, what Lawyer or Attorney shall be employed, or even for one to go along with another to his Counsel, provided he does give him Money. *Fitzherbert* tells us, That it is no *Maintenance* to give a poor Man Money out of Charity, to carry on a Suit: So likewise Attornies may lawfully disburse their Money for their Clients, in Expectation to be paid again; but they must not do it at their own Expence, on Condition of the common illegal Agreement of *no Purchase, no Pay*.

Majority, denotes the greater Part of any Thing; and there are sundry Acts that are to be determined by a *Majority*: As the *Majority* of Members of Parliament, by which our Laws are enacted; so also the Members themselves are chosen by a *Majority* of the Electors: And the Act of a *Majority* of any Corporation is in the Law accounted the Act of the whole.

Maisura, anciently denoted a House or Farm.

Majus jus, is a Writ or Method of Proceeding in some Customary Manors, for the Trial of the Right of Land.

Make Law. See **Wager of Law**.

Make Services and Customs, signifies to perform such.

Malandrinus, was formerly used to denote a Thief or Pirate.

Malecreditus, is taken for one of bad Credit, so as not to be trusted.

Malefeasance, signifies the acting of Evil.

Maletent, was anciently taken for a certain Toll payable for every Sack of Wool.

Malice, signifies a premeditated Design of doing some Mischief; as in Murder, it is Malice from whence that Crime proceeds: So where a Person has a malicious Intent to kill, and in the Execution of his malicious Design, by Chance slays a third Person, he shall on Account of his Malice be deemed guilty of Murder.

Malo grato, denotes an Unwillingness to do a Thing.

Malveilles, was anciently taken for Crimes and Misdemeanors.

Malveisin, (from the *French*) denotes a bad Neighbour.

Malveis Procurors, were formerly taken for such as pack Juries by the Direction of either the Plaintiff or Defendant in a Cause.

Malum in se, denotes any Thing that is evil in itself; and at Common Law all Offences are *mala in se*; yet the playing at unlawful Games, such as are prohibited by Statute, are *mala prohibita*, and at certain Seasons may not be *mala in se*.

Magnagium, was anciently used for a Mansion-house.

Manbote, denotes a Satisfaction due to the Lord for killing his Vassal.

Manciple, is a Name given in the Colleges of the Universities to the Clerk of the Kitchin or Caterer there.

Mandamus, is a Writ which issues out of the *King's Bench*, and lies on several Accounts; as against a Corporation, to command them to restore a Person to his Franchise, Office, &c. It lies for admitting him that has served his Apprenticeship to the Freedom of the City or Corporation. It likewise lies to restore a Mayor, or other Magistrate of a City, &c. into his Office.

Office. In this Writ the general Words are to this Effect, *We command you to admit or restore, or shew Cause why,* &c. Upon the Return of the first Writ, if not complied with, if the Court think it reasonable, they grant a second Writ, which we call a *peremptory Mandamus*. The Practice upon the Return of this Writ is, that the Person who sues out the Writ may plead to and traverse any of the material Facts contained in such Return, to which the Person making the Return must reply, take Issue, &c. after which the Parties proceed in the same Manner, as if Action had been brought upon a false Return. It is the Course, where a Person has a *Mandamus* to be admitted to any Office, &c. that he suggest every Thing that is necessary to intitle him to be admitted. A *Mandamus* can be directed to none but those that are to do the Thing thereby required in Obedience to the Writ. This Process is not by any Means to bear *Teste* before it is granted by the Court; and the Practice is, if the Corporation, &c. to which the *Mandamus* is directed, exceeds the Distance of 40 Miles from *London*, there must be 15 Days at least between the *Teste* and the Return of the first *Mandamus*; but if the Distance be only 40, or under, eight Days only are allowed: But it is here to be observed, that the *Alias* and *Pluries* may be made returnable *immediatè*, immediately, and likewise, that at the Return of the *Pluries*, in case none be made, after Affidavit has been made of the Service, *Attachment* issues for the Contempt, without so much as admitting a Hearing of Counsel by Way of Excuse. A *Mandamus* was also a Writ that formerly issued a Year and Day after the Omission of having the Writ called *Diem clausit extremum* issued, and sent to the Escheator on the Death of the King's Tenant in *Capite*, &c. And there was likewise another Writ of this Name, whereby the Sheriff was ordered to seize into the Hands of the King the Lands, &c. of the Widow of the King's Tenant, who, contrary to her Oath, married without his Consent.

Mandate, denotes a judicial Commandment of the King, or his Justices, to forward Dispatch of Justice.

Manentes, was anciently used to answer the same as *Tenentes*, or Tenants.

Mannire, is said to be in the Case where a Person is cited to appear in Court to answer.

Manor, (from the *French*) with us denotes an ancient Royalty, formerly called *Barony*, which consisted of Demesnes and Services, and of a Court Baron belonging thereto. It anciently was a noble Fee, being in Part granted to Tenants for particular Services to be performed, and partly reserved to the Use of the Lord's Family. As to the Original of Manors you may consult *Horn*'s *Mirr. Just. lib.* 1. A Manor cannot subsist without a Court-Baron; and not only so, but a Manor must have continued for Time out of Mind. There cannot be a Manor in Law where there want Freehold Tenants; neither can there be a *Customary Manor* without Copyhold Tenants, that Manor holding by Copy of Court Roll granted by other Manors.

Mansion, according to a legal Sense, commonly denotes the Lord's chief Dwelling-house within his Fee, which may be otherwise called the *Capital Messuage*, or *Manor-House*.

Manslaughter, which is generally termed *Homicide*, denotes the killing of a Person without Malice prepensed; as where two Persons upon a sudden Quarrel, and without any premeditated Intention of doing Harm, fight or engage together, and the one of them is killed; in this Case the surviving Party is guilty only of *Manslaughter*, and not of *Murder*, it not carrying with it any malicious Intention, which Murder does; and yet it carries with it a present Intent to kill, which *Chancemedley* does not. Tho' this Crime in our Law is made Felony, yet for the first Offence the Offender is allowed the Benefit of Clergy. *Crompt.* observes, that Manslaughter must be upon a sudden Quarrel, in which the Party may seem not to be Master of his Temper, by a serious or calm Manner of Talking on the Subject of the Quarrel, or otherwise, so that his Heat of Blood may be supposed to be cooled; as where two Persons meeting one another, and in striving for the Wall, the one kills the other; this is only Manslaughter: And it is likewise so, if upon a sudden Occasion they had gone directly into the Fields and fought, and one of them had been killed; for this Reason, that from the Beginning to the last it was one continued Act of Passion. *Hawkins* observes, that if two Persons who have formerly fought on Malice prepensed, are afterwards to all Appearance fully reconciled, but on a fresh Quarrel fight again, and the one kills the other, it shall not in this Case be construed that they were moved on their old Grudge, unless from the whole Circumstances of the Actions it should appear they were. The same Author observes, that if two suddenly fall out and fight, and the one breaks the other's Sword, whereon a Stander-by lends him another, wherewith the Adversary is killed, it is Manslaughter in both the Slayer and Stander-by: Also, if a Man's Relation or Friend be suddenly assaulted, and he in Vindication of such his Friend presently takes up an Instrument and kills the other, this is Manslaughter; yet if a Master go with Malice to kill another, and takes his Servant with him knowing of his Design, and the Master kills his Adversary, it is Murder both in Master and Servant. It is held that if a Person draws upon another in a sudden Quarrel, but makes no Pass at him, till his Sword is drawn, after which fighting with him, kills him, this is only *Manslaughter*, because, by giving the other Time to draw, shews the Intent of the Survivor was not to kill the other, but rather to combat with him. Where one stabs another, who has not a Weapon drawn, or struck first, so that the Person stabbed dies within six Months, notwithstanding there was not Malice forethought, it is Felony without the Benefit of Clergy. See 1 *Jac.* 1. *c.* 8. Where a Man is taken in Adultery with another's Wife, and the Husband presently draws and kills him, this is only Manslaughter, the Slayer having had a just Provocation for so doing.

Mansum Capitale, denotes the Manor-house, or the Lord's Court.

Mansus Presbyteri, denotes the Parsonage, or Vicarage-House.

Mantheof, was anciently used for a Horse-stealer.

Manucaptio, is a Writ which issues for a Person taken on Suspicion of Felony, &c. who is refused to be admitted to Bail by Persons

Manumission, anciently denoted the Discharging a Villein or Slave from Bondage.

Manutenentia, is a Writ used in a Case of *Maintenance*.

Manworth, is defined to be the Price of a Man's Life.

Marchet. See **Maiden-Rents**.

Marinarius, was anciently used for a *Mariner*. By the Law of Merchants, the *Mariners* of a Vessel are accountable to the Master or Commander; the Master, &c. to the Owners; and the Owners to the Merchant, for Damages sustained either by Negligence, or otherwise. By *Leg. Oleron*, as well as by the Common Law, if a Mariner be hired for a Voyage, and he deserts it before it is ended, he shall lose his Wages: And in case a Ship be lost by a Storm, &c. the Mariners likewise lose their Wages, as well as the Owners their Freight. By *Leg. Oleron*, in case a Mariner be wounded in the Ship's Service, he shall be provided for at the Ship's Charge; and should his Illness be very great, he is to be left ashore with necessary Accommodations; but the Vessel is not obliged to stay for him; and should he recover he may have his full Wages, only deducting therefrom what the Master laid out for him. By a *Geo. 2. c. 36.* no Master of a Ship is to retain a Mariner for a Voyage, without a signed Contract in Writing for his Wages, under the Penalty of 5 *l.* After the Contract is signed, if the Mariner refuse to proceed on the Voyage, he does not only forfeit his Wages, but also is liable, on Complaint to a Justice of the Peace, to be committed for 30 Days to hard Labour. Mariners that absent from their Ships are to forfeit two Day's Pay for each Day's Absence, to be applied to the Use of *Greenwich Hospital*: And if they leave the Ship before discharged in writing, they forfeit one Month's Wages. Within 30 Days after the Ship's Arrival at the End of her Voyage, or at the Time of the Discharge of the Mariners, the Master, on Pain of forfeiting 20 *s.* must pay the Men their Wages, he deducting thereout the Penalties imposed on the Mariners. *Ibid.* See more concerning *Mariners* in 39 *Eliz.* 17. & 43 *Eliz. c. 3.*

Maritime, denotes any Thing appertaining to Sea Affairs.

Maritima Angliæ, denotes an Emolument anciently accruing to the Crown from the Sea.

Market, takes its Name from a *Latin* Word that signifies Buying and Selling, and is a Privilege by Grant or Prescription, enabling a Town to erect and open Shops, &c. at a particular Place within the same, for the better providing and furnishing the Inhabitants thereof, together with their neighbouring People, and other Subjects with Victuals, &c. A *Market* is less than a Fair, and it is commonly held only once or twice a Week.

Marque, denotes the same as *Reprisals*, and *Reprisals* and it are used as synonymous Words; so likewise *Letters of Marque*, which see. *Marque* is said to be so called, on Acccount that the Wrongs, whereon *Letters of Marque* are granted, are usually about the Limits of every Country.

Marriage, properly denotes the Joining together of Man and Wife, in a constant Society and Contract of living together, which cannot be dissolved but by Death, or Breach of Faith, or other notorious Misbehaviour. The Requisites

sites in our Law to compleat a Marriage, is a free and mutual Consent between the Parties, provided they are not disabled to engage in Marriage, on Account of Nearness of Kin, Infancy, Precontract, or Impotency. By Marriage with a Woman, the Husband becomes intitled to all her real and personal Estate; and the Effects of this State are, the Husband and Wife are accounted but one Person; yet he has Power over her Person as well as her Estate: And they are so fast knit together, that the Husband cannot give any Thing to his Wife by Deed during the Coverture, tho' by Will he may. The Goods and personal Chattels of the Wife are by the Law, upon the Marriage, vested in the Husband, who may sell or keep them during his Life, and by Will give them away at his Death, even tho' she should happen to survive him: And the real Chattels the Wife has in her Possession in her own Right, by the Marriage the Husband shall enjoy; and these also he may dispose of in his Life-time by any Act or Deed of his; and in Case of Survivorship in him, he may retain them absolutely. On Promise of Marriage Damages are recoverable, if either Party refuse to marry, provided the Promise be mutual on both Sides, so as to ground the Action: But then no Action can be brought on a Contract of Marriage, unless it be in Writing, and signed by the Party chargeable. Upon Marriages, where Circumstances allow of it, Settlements are usually made of the Husband's real Estate to the Husband for Life, after his Decease to the Wife for her Life for her *Jointure*, and in Lieu of her Dower; and to the Issue of the Husband and Wife in Remainder, with Limitations to Trustees, to preserve contingent Remainders, and also Leases for Terms of Years to Trustees, to raise Daughters Portions. The Form of a Settlement or Jointure, you may see in the *Young Clerk's Magazine*, and other Books of *Conveyancing*. A Woman cannot be devested of her Jointure, but by her passing a Fine. By 3 *Hen.* 7. *c.* 2. if a Person take away any Woman that has an Estate in Lands or Goods, or who is Heir apparent, against her Will, and *marry* or defile her, the Offender herein is declared to be guilty of Felony. It is likewise Felony for a married Person to marry another Person, the former Husband or Wife being alive, yet it is otherwise where a Husband or Wife are beyond Sea, &c. seven Years, the one being ignorant of the other's being alive; or in case of a Divorce of the Husband and Wife. See 1 *Jac. c.* 11. It is held that if the first Marriage were abroad, and the latter here, the Offender may be prosecuted for it here; since it is the latter Marriage that makes the Crime.

Marshal of the King's Bench, is an Officer of that Court, who has the Custody of the *King's Bench* Prison in *Southwark*. This Officer is obliged to give his Attendance on the Court, and to take into Custody all Persons committed by the Court. There is likewise a *Marshal of the Exchequer*, into whose Custody that Court commits the King's Debtors, in order to secure the Debts.

Marshalsey, is the Court or Seat of the Marshal of the King's House. See **Court of Marshalsea.** This Word is likewise used for a certain Prison in *Southwark*, called by that Name.

Martial Law, is defined by *Smith de Repub. Angl.* to denote the Law of War, depending upon the just, tho' arbitrary Power of the Prince, or his Lieutenant; since, tho' the King cannot make any Laws without Consent of Parliament, yet in Time of War, he frequently uses absolute Power, out of the Necessity of guarding against Dangers, so that his Word in this Case becomes a Law.

Master of Chancery, is an Assistant to the *Lord Chancellor* or *Lord Keeper*, and *Master of the Rolls*: And of these Masters some are *ordinary*, and others *extraordinary*: Of the *Masters* in *ordinary* there are Twelve in Number, some whereof sit in Court every Day in Term-Time; and interlocutory Orders for stating Accounts, settling Damages, &c. are referred to them; as also, they administer Oaths, take Affidavits, Answers to Bills of Equity, and Acknowledgments of Recognizances and Deeds: The *extraordinary Masters* are purposely appointed to act in the several Counties of *England*, exceeding ten Miles Distance from *London*; and are to take Affidavits, &c. for the Ease and Benefit of the Suitors to the Court. A publick Office is by Authority fixed near the Rolls in *Chancery Lane*, for the *Masters* in ordinary to sit in for the Dispatch of Business, on which they are duly to attend.

Master of the Court of Wards and Liberties, was anciently the chief Officer of that Court.

Master of the Faculties, is an Officer of the Archbishop of *Canterbury*, whose Office is to grant Licences, Dispensations, &c.

Master of the Horse, is an Officer of high Account, who has the Government of the King's Stables, and of all Horses, &c. belonging to the King. He is the third great Officer of the King's Houshold.

Master of the Jewel Office, belongs to the King's Houshold, and has the Charge of the Plate made Use of at the King's Table, or by any great Officers of the Court.

Master of the Houshold, was an Officer anciently stiled *Grand Master* of the King's Houshold, and was the same with what we now call *Lord Steward of the Houshold*, under whom there is a chief Officer still called *Master of the Houshold*, whose Office is to survey the Accounts of the Houshold.

Master of the King's Musters, is an Officer in the King's Armies, and his Duty is, to see that the Forces are compleat, well armed and trained; and also to prevent Frauds that might tend to exhaust the King's Treasure, or weaken the King's Forces, &c.

Master of the Armory, is he that has the Care of the King's Arms.

Master of the Ceremonies, is an Officer of Court, who receives and conducts Ambassadors, &c. to the Audience of the King.

Master of the Mint, now called *Warden of the Mint*, has the Oversight of every Thing belonging to the Mint.

Master of the Ordnance, is a great Officer, to whom the Charge of the King's Ordnance and Artillery is committed.

Master of the Revels, is the Person who regulates the Diversions of Masking and Dancing in the King's Palace, &c.

Master of the Posts, is the same as is now stiled *Master of the General Post-Office*, who, with his Agents have the sending of all Letters, &c. throughout this Kingdom, at certain Rates; and his Duty is to keep constant Posts, and

MA

and on all Occasions to provide Persons with Post Horses. See 9 *Ann. c.* 10.

Master of the Rolls, is an Assistant to the Lord Chancellor or Lord Keeper in the Court of *Chancery*, in whose Absence he hears Causes there as well as in the Chapel of the Rolls. He has the Keeping of the Rolls of all Patents and Grants that pass the Great Seal, and also of the Records of the *Chancery*. He has the Disposal of the following Offices, *viz.* those of the six Clerks, the Clerks of the petty Bag, the Examiners of the Court of *Chancery*, and the Clerks of the Chapel.

Master of the Temple, was originally the Founder of the Order of Knights Templers, who, as well as his Successors, were so called.

Master of the Wardrobe, is a Person of high Station at Court, in whose Custody the Robes of all our former Kings and Queens, and likewise the Hangings, &c. of the Prince's Palaces anciently were.

Matricula, denotes an Entry or Register; as to be entered in the Register of the Universities, is said to be *matriculated* there.

Matter in Deed, in our Law, denotes nothing more than some particular *Matter of Fact* which is to be made out by some Specialty or Deed; as where a Man during his Absence abroad in the King's Service, is sued to an *Exigent*; in which Case, if the Person sued would take Advantage of this *Matter in Deed*, he must alledge it before a *Scire facias* for Execution be awarded; otherwise he can have no Recourse for Relief, but from *Matter of Record, viz.* some Error in the Proceedings appearing upon the Face of the Record. There is likewise, besides *Matter in Deed*, and *Matter of Record*,

MA

Nude Matter, that is to say, a naked *Allegation* of somewhat done, which can only be proved by Witnesses, and neither by *Record* nor *Specialty*.

Maugre, (from the *French*) according to the Acceptation of the Word with us, in general denotes an Unwillingness; as in the Case, where by *Littleton* it is said, that the Wife shall be remitted *maugre* the Husband, that is to say, whether the Husband is willing or not, or in Despight of him.

Maund, is mentioned in the Book of Rates, and is generally taken for a Quantity of eight Bales of Books in Sheets, each Bale containing 100 Pounds Weight.

Maxims in Law, are particular Rules laid down, which are the very Foundation of the Law, and therefore should never be impeached. The Judges can only determine what a Maxim is; and when they have done so, it bears in our Courts no less than the Strength of an Act of Parliament itself. The *Maxims* in our Books of Law are various, and many of them you may meet with in *Wood's Inst.* and elsewhere.

Mayor, denotes the Chief Magistrate of a City or Town, and in Corporations he is a Justice of the Peace for the Time. By the Corporation Act 13 *Car.* 2. *c.* 1. no Mayor, or other Magistrate is to bear any Office relating to the Government of any Corporation, who has not, within a Year before his Election to that Office, received the Sacrament according to the Rites of the Church of *England*, and likewise taken the Oaths of *Supremacy, &c.* And here it may not be improper to observe, that tho' this Statute absolutely deprives Persons, not qualified as above, from bearing any Office of Trust

in

in a Corporation, yet it does not in any Respect excuse a Nonconformist from bearing Offices of Burden there, such as that of Sheriff, &c. as has been determined in the Case of *Larwood*, reported in the *Modern Reports*. Altho' the Gown, Mace, or other Ensigns of Magistracy may not be worn or carried to Conventicles; yet by 5 *Geo.* 1. c. 6. the Magistrates themselves are not prohibited from frequenting such Places, which before, by 10 *Ann.* c. 2. they were restrained from, under the Penalty of 40 *l*. Where any Person intrudes into the Office of Mayor, a *Quo warranto* lies against him, upon which he shall not only be ousted, but fined, &c. No Mayor, or other Person holding an annual Office in a Corporation for one Year, is to be elected into the same Office the next. If the Mayor of a Corporation be not chosen on the Day by Charter appointed, the next in Place is the Day following to hold a Court and elect one: And in Case of Omission that Way, the Electors are liable to be compelled to chuse one, by Virtue of a Writ of *Mandamus* out of the *King's Bench*; and this Writ requires the Members that have a Right to elect, to assemble themselves upon a certain Day therein fixed, and proceed to Election, or to shew Cause to the contrary; which Kind of Writ is generally termed a *Mandamus nisi*, to distinguish it from what we call a *peremptory Mandamus*; that is to say, a *Mandamus* that positively requires a direct Obedience thereto. Mayors, or other Magistrates of a Corporation, who shall voluntarily absent on the Day of Election, are by 11 *Geo.* 1. c. 4. liable to be imprisoned for six Months, as also to be for ever afterwards disabled to hold any Office in the Corporation.

Mean or Mesne, denotes a *Medium* between two Extreams; and in Time it signifies the *Interim* betwixt one Act and another, and in that Case is applied to mean Profits of Lands between the Time of the *Disseisin*, and that of the Recovery. This Word is likewise applied to Honour or Dignity; as there is a Lord *Mean*, who holds of another Lord, and a *Mean Tenant*. This Word does likewise denote a Writ that lies when there being Lord *Mean* and *Tenant*, the Tenant is distrained by the superior Lord for the Rent or Service of his *Mean* Lord, whose Duty it is to acquit him to the superior Lord; in which Case the *Mean Tenant* has this Writ, to which should the *Mean Lord* not appear, he shall forfeit the Tenant's Service, and at the same Time be forejudged of his Seigniory; and, on the other Hand, the *Mean Tenant* shall immediately become Tenant to the Chief Lord. *Fitzherbert* says, That, in this Case the Tenant may recover Damages of the Mean Lord, who shall be compelled to pay the Rent, and perform the Services to the superior Lord.

Measure, denotes a particular Quantity or Proportion of a Thing sold, and differs in many Parts of this Kingdom; some Measures, particularly those of Corn, &c. in one Part being larger, and in others less; but the *Winchester* is by Statute the establish'd *Measure* throughout *England*, for the Sale of Beer, Ale, Salt, Corn, and other Grain. See 17 *Car.* 1. & 22 *Car.* 2.

Measurer or Meter, is an Officer deputed in the City of *London* and in other Ports of this Kingdom, for the

the Measuring of Cloth, Corn, Coals, &c.

Measuring Money, denotes Money that was formerly paid over and above *Alnage*.

Mediæ & Infimæ Manus Homines, are taken for Persons of the lower Rank or Condition.

Medietas Linguæ, is a Jury or Inquest impanelled, of which the one Half are Natives of this Land, and the other *Foreigners*; and is never used, except where one of the Parties in a Plea is a Stranger, and the other a Denizen. This Privilege to Foreigners is allowed in Petit Treason, Murder and Felony; but in High Treason it is not; for an Alien in that Case shall be tried according to the Rules of the Common Law, and not by a *Medietas Linguæ*, which was first granted by 27 *Ed*. 3. *c*. 8. According to *Wood*, a Grand Jury ought not in any Case to be of a *Medietas Linguæ*.

Medio acquietando, was a Writ formerly in Use for the Distraining a superior Lord on Account of his acquitting a mean Lord of a Rent, by him before owned in Court not to belong to him.

Medlefe, (from the *French*) denotes Quarreling or Brawling.

Meer, signifies a Mark of Land.

Melsceat, (from the *Saxons*) is the same with what we call an Informer's Fee; that is to say, the Reward allowed by Statute to the Discoverer of a Breach of any penal Law.

Melius Inquirendum, is a Writ which issues for a second Inquiry, where Partiality is suspected to have been shewn; particularly in the *Inquiry* of what Lands, &c. a Person died seised, on the finding an Office for the King.

Menials, denotes Domestick or Houshold Servants, who live under their Lord or Master's Roof.

Mensa, includes in it all Patrimony, and every other Thing necessary for Livelihood.

Mercenarius, is taken for a Hireling.

Merchant, was formerly taken for one that bought and sold any Thing: But now this Appellation is properly restricted only to such as traffick in Commerce by Way of Importation or Exportation, or trade in the Way of Buying, Selling, Barter, or Exchange, and who continually make it their Livelihood to buy and sell: To these we may add Bankers, as well as those that deal by Exchange, who are likewise termed *Merchants*. Such as buy Wares, &c. to change them by their own Art or Industry into other Forms, are not *Merchants*, but properly Artificers. As the Laws of *England*, or those of any other Nation are not sufficient for determining the Affairs of Commerce and Merchandize, Traffick being so universal, that it is next to an Impossibility to do it; therefore all Nations, as well as we, take particular Notice of, and shew Regard to the *Law Merchant*, which is a Law among themselves; and the Causes of Merchants are in most Cases left to their own Law, which you may see in *Lex Mercat*.

Mercimoniatus Angliæ. The Custom or Impost here upon Merchandize was anciently called so.

Mercuries. See **Hawkers**.

Mercy. See **Misericordia**.

Merger, is when the lesser Estate in Lands, &c. is drowned in the greater: As for Example, should the Fee come to Tenant for Years or Life, those two particular Estates are merged in the *Fee*, that is to say, are become extinct in the Fee. According to *Plowden*, where a Lessor, in whom the Fee is, intermarries with the Lessee for Years, this is no *Merger* of the Term of Years, for this Reason, that he has the Inheritance or Fee in his own Right, and the Lease in that of his Wife.

Mesne. See **Mean.**

Mesnalty, signifies the Condition of the *Mean* or *Mesne*.

Messarius, anciently denoted the chief Servant in Husbandry.

Messenger, is an Officer particularly imployed by Secretaries of State to convey Messages or Dispatches from them to different Parts: And to the Custody of these Officers State Prisoners are frequently committed, and by them detained, tho' regularly the Detention of a Person out of the common Gaol cannot be justified, unless a sufficient Reason can be given for such Detention; as in Case a Person be so dangerously ill, that it might in all Likelihood hazard his Life to carry him thither; but notwithstanding this is really the Law, yet it is notorious that Commitments to *Messengers* have been frequently made: And as *Skinn.* in his *Reports* observes, tho' these Commitments are irregular, yet the same are not void, for if the Person charged with Treason, escapes from the Messenger, he directly becomes guilty of Treason. There are likewise Messengers of the Exchequer, who attend that Court, of which there are four in Number.

Messuage, denotes a Dwelling-house with Lands adjoining.

Metegabel, denotes a certain Tribute anciently payable in Victuals, as well by the King's Tenants as others. *Jac. Law Dict.*

Meter. See **Measurer.**

Mettelhep, or **Mettenschep,** was anciently taken for an Acknowledgment paid in Corn, or a Fine imposed for Defaults in their customary Services of cutting the Lord's Corn.

Meum & tuum, in *English*, *Mine* and *Thine*, are Words that have occasioned many Controversies at Law; and yet, being rightly understood, are proper Guides of Right.

Militia, properly denotes such as are under the Direction of the King's Lieutenancy, and is applied to the Train'd Bands.

Mina, according to *Cowel*, anciently was taken for a Corn-Measure of a different Quantity, according to the Things to be measured by it; so *Minage* was the Duty paid for Liberty of selling by that Measure. But *Littleton* takes it to be a Measure of Ground of 120 Foot in Length, and as many in Breadth.

Mineral Courts, are Courts that take Cognizance of Affairs relating to Lead-Mines.

Mines, in a general Sense, are certain Places out of which Gold, Silver, Copper, and other Metals are digged: But Mines are said not properly to be called so, until such Time as the Ground is opened, it being before deemed nothing but a Vein or Seam; as of Tin, Iron, Coals, &c. There are also Mines that are dug under Ground, for the Undermining of Fortifications, &c.

Miniments, or **Muniments,** are used for the Evidences or Writings that relate to a Person's Estate, or other Thing he has a Right to, and whereby he is made able to maintain his Estate.

Ministri Regis. In these Words are comprehended both the Judges of the Land, and those that enjoy Ministerial Offices under the Government.

Minor. An Heir Male or Female, before they arrive at the Age of Twenty-one Years is called a *Minor*, and during the Minority of such, they are usually incapable to act for themselves.

Mint, is the Name of the Place wherein the King's Money is coined, viz. The *Tower of London*. The Officers that belong to the *Mint* are the following; viz. 1. *The Warden*, who receives of the Goldsmiths the Silver and Bullion, to be coined, and takes Charge of the same. 2. *The Master-Worker*, who takes the Silver from the *Warden*, and causes the same to be melted, after which he delivers it to the *Moniers*, and receives it from them again after made into Money. 3. *The Comptroller*, whose Business is to see, that the Money be made to the just Assise, &c. 4. *The Master of the Assay*, who not only weighs the Silver, but examines it whether it be according to Standard. 5. *The Auditor*, whose Business is to take Account of the Silver, &c. 6. *The Surveyor of the Melting*, before whom the Silver is to be cast out, in order that he may see that it is not altered after Trial made by the *Assay Master*, &c. 7. *The Clerk of the Irons*, who inspects the Irons, to see that they be clean and fit for working. 8. *The Graver*, who ingraves the Stamp. 9. *The Melters*, who melt down the Bullion, &c. 10. *The Blanchers*, who cleanse the Money. 11. *The Moniers*, some of whom shear the Money, others forge it, some round, and some stamp it. 12. *The Provost*, who provides for the *Moniers*, and has the Oversight of them, &c. There was likewise within these few Years a Place in *Southwark*, near the *King's Bench*, that was called the *Mint*, formerly a pretended Place of Privilege for insolvent Debtors; but it was intirely put down by *Stat.* 9 *Geo.* 1. whereby it is enacted, That if any Person within the Liberty of the Mint, shall obstruct an Officer, &c. within the Limits of the Mint, in the serving of any Writ, Process, &c. or assault any Person concerned therein, so that he receive any bodily Harm, the Offenders shall be guilty of Felony, and be transported, &c.

Minute Tithes, are those small Tithes as usually belong to the Vicar. See **Tithes.**

Misadventure, is diversly defined. By some it is defined to signify the Killing a Person, partly by Negligence, and partly by Chance: By others it is taken to be where a Person comes to his Death by some outward Violence, as the Running over of a Cart Wheel, Stroke of a Horse, Fall of a Tree or the like; And others again take it to be where a Man, without thinking any Harm, carelessly throws a Stone, by which another is killed: And it is termed *Homicide by Chance mixed*, when the Killer's Ignorance or Negligence is joined with the Chance.

Miscognizance, denotes Ignorance, or Want of Knowledge of a Thing.

Miscontinuance, is generally taken to be where a Continuance is made by undue Process, tho' some take it to be the same with *Discontinuance*, which see.

Mise, (from the *French*) in our Law denotes Costs, in which Sense it is generally used in the Entring up of Judgments in Actions personal; as where a Plaintiff recovers, it is entered, that he shall recover Damages to such a Value, and for Costs and Charges so much, &c. This Word has also

also another Signification, where it is taken for the Issue to be tried by Battail or Grand Assise, and so it is used in *Littleton*, Sect. 478, 482. and divers others, where Joining of the *Mise* upon the meer Right, is putting it in Issue who has the best or clearest Right. *Termes de la Ley*.

Misericordia, in our Law denotes an Amercement or Fine imposed on a Person for an Offence; as where the Plaintiff or Defendant in any Action is amerced, the Entry always is, *Ideo in Misericordia*, &c. as much as to say, he is in the Mercy of the Court, &c. and since the Proceedings at Law have been rendered into *English*, these Words have been used. And it is said, that it is called *Misericordia*, because the Amercement ought to be but small, and less than the Offence, according to *Magna Charta*; wherefore if a Person be outragiously amerced, in a Court that is not of Record, as in a Court Baron, &c. there is a Writ called *Moderata Misericordia*, to be directed to the Lord or his Bailiff, whereby they are commanded to take moderate Amercements, according to the Quantity of the Fault. *Termes de la Ley*.

Misfeasance, denotes a Trespass or other Misdeed.

Misfeasor, is a Misdoer or Trespasser.

Misnomer, denotes a Mistake of a Man's Name, or the using of one Name for another, which ought not to be done; for in all Cases a Distinction ought to be made between Person and Person, in order that the one may be certainly known from the other.

Misprision, in general denotes some Neglect or Oversight; as where one is privy to a Treason or Felony committed by another, and neglects the Revealing of it to the King or his Council, or to some Magistrate, but on the contrary intirely conceals the same. In all Cases of *Misprision* of Treason the Offender is to be imprisoned for Life, and forfeit his Goods and Chattels, together with the Profits of his Lands, &c. during Life: But in *Misprision* of Felony the Offender is to be punished by Fine and Imprisonment, and to remain in Prison till the Fine is paid. There is also *Misprison* at large, which is where a Person contemns the King's Prerogative, either by refusing to assist the King; by writing or speaking against his Person or Government; by receiving a Pension from a Foreign Prince, without Leave first had; by refusing to take the Oaths of Allegiance and Supremacy; by Contempts against the King's Palace, or against the Courts of Justice. Lastly, there is *Misprision* of Clerks.

Mistrial. See **Trial**.

Misuser, denotes some Abuse of any particular Liberty or Benefit. By *Misuser* the Charter of a Corporation, as well as that of an Office, may be forfeited.

Mittendo Manuscriptum Pedis Finis, in *Reg. Orig.* is defined to have been a judicial Writ directed to the Treasurer and Chamberlain of the *Exchequer*, requiring them to search for, and transmit the Foot of a Fine, acknowledged before the Justices in *Eyre* into the *Common Pleas*, &c.

Mittimus, hath two different Significations. 1st, It denotes a Writ for transferring of Records from one Court to another. 2dly, It denotes a Command in Writing, under the Hand and Seal of a Justice of the Peace, directed to the Gaoler or Keeper of some particular

MO

lar Prison, for the Receiving and safe Keeping of the Offender charged, until he be delivered by due Course of Law.

Mixt Tithes. See **Tithes.**

Moderata Misericordia. See **Misericordia.**

Modo & Forma, *in Manner and Form,* are Terms of Art frequently used in Law Pleadings, and particularly in a Defendant's Answer, wherein he denies to have done what is laid to his Charge in Manner and Form as charged by the Plaintiff.

Modus Decimandi, signifies Money, or other valuable Thing annually given in lieu of Tithes; the Trial whereof we are told belongs to the Common Law, and not to any Spiritual Court. *Termes de la Ley.*

Moiety, (from the *French*) denotes one Half of any Thing.

Monetagium, signified a Tribute anciently paid by Tenants to their Lord every third Year, in Consideration that he should not change the Money he had coined formerly, when it was lawful for great Men to coin.

Money, denotes Gold, Silver, Copper, or other Kind of Metal, that receives Authority by the King's Impression to be current; for it belongs to the King alone to put a Value, as well as the Impression on his Money, without which it could not be current. By 3 *Geo.* 2. *c.* 5. the King may by Proclamation at any Time prohibit his Subjects, for a Space not exceeding a Year, to lend or advance Money to a Foreign State, &c. without Licence under the Great or Privy Seal: And Persons transgressing herein are to forfeit treble the Value of the Money lent; yet Persons by this Statute are not prohibited to deal in Foreign Stocks, or be interested in any Bank abroad.

Moneyers, or **Moniers,** are particular Officers of the *Mint.* See **Mint.** Bankers, and others that make it their Business to turn and return Money, are likewise called *Moneyers.*

Monopoly, denotes a certain Allowance granted to one or more Persons for the sole Buying, Selling, Making, Working, or Using of any Thing, whereby others are distrained of the Freedom they had before that Way, or by which they are molested or hurt in their lawful Trade: And it may be briefly thus in general defined, *viz.* that it is where the Power of Selling is invested in one alone, or where a Man does ingross and get into his Hands a Parcel of Merchandizes, &c. as none may gain by them but himself. The evil Consequences attending a *Monopoly,* are apprehended at least to be these, *viz.* 1. The Raising of the Price of Merchandize. 2. The Commodity will not be so good. 3. The Impoverishment of poor Artificers. It is held, that the Making Use of, or procuring any unlawful Monopoly is punishable at Common Law. By 21 *Jac.* 1. *c.* 3. all Monopolies, Grants, &c. for the sole Buying, Selling and making of Goods and Manufactures, are void, except as in that Statute, are particularly excepted.

Monster, denotes one that is without human Shape, and yet born in lawful Wedlock; which Sort of Persons are not allowed in our Law to purchase or hold Lands; but still a Person that is deformed in Part of his Body may inherit his Ancestor's Lands.

Monstrans de Droit, is a Writ that issues out of the Court of *Chancery,* for the Restoring of a

MO

Person to Lands or Tenements that are his in Right, tho' by some Office found to be in the Possession of one lately dead, whereby the King would be intitled to the said Lands, &c.

Monstrans de Faits, in a legal Sense, is taken for the Producing of the Deeds in open Court, when an Action is brought upon a Deed. Here it is to be observed, that there is a Difference between *Monstrans de Faits*, and *Oyer de Faits*. One that pleads any Deed or Record, or counts upon it, ought to shew the same, which is termed *Monstrans de Faits*; and the other against whom the Deed or Record is pleaded, may demand *Oyer* thereof, a Sight of it; and this is called *Oyer de Faits*. If a Person plead a Deed, or declare upon one, making the same the Substance of his Plea or Declaration, and doth not plead it, or declare upon it, with a *Profert in Curia*; his Plea or Declaration upon a special Demurrer, shewing that Omission for Cause is naught: And in Case he does plead, or declare upon it, with a Profert, &c. yet if the other Party demand a Sight of it, he cannot proceed, until he has shewn it, and likewise granted a Copy, if required. See 4 & 5 Ann. c. 16.

Monstraverunt, is a Writ which issues on Behalf of Tenants *in Ancient Demesne*, holding by free Charter, when they are distrained to oblige them to perform to their Lords other Services, &c. than either they or their Ancestors used to do: And it also lies where such Tenants are distrained for the Payment of Toll, &c. contrary to that Liberty they do or ought to enjoy; in which Case the Sheriff is thereby required to charge the Lord that he do not distrain them for such unusual Services, &c. Whereupon should the Lord presume to persist in distraining his Tenants for other Services than of Right they ought to do, the Sheriff can command the Neighbours dwelling next the Manor, or else take the *Posse Comitatus*, the Power of the County, to resist the Lord, &c. This Writ of *Monstraverunt* may be sued out by many of the Tenants, without naming any of them by their proper Names, but only in general, that the Men of such a Place *sewed*, &c.

Moot, in the *Inns of Court* denotes that Exercise of arguing Cases, which young Barristers and Students at certain Times perform, in order to be the better enabled for Practice.

Mootmen, are taken for such as argue the Cases called *Moot-Cases*.

Moratur in Lege, signifies that one of the Parties in a Cause *demurs*, that is to say, *stays*, and does not proceed in Pleading, but rests upon the Judgment of the Court in some particular Point, either as to the Sufficiency of the Declaration, &c. or the Plea, &c. of the contrary Party; upon which the Court, after taking some Time to argue and advise, determine it. See **Demurrer**.

Morgangina, was anciently used to denote that Present which the Bridegroom gave his Bride on the Wedding Day; and this is now called *Dowry Money*.

Mortdancestor, is a Writ that is now seldom used. See **Assise of Mortdancestor**.

Mortgage, denotes a Pledge or Pawn of Lands, Tenements, &c. for Money borrowed: The Reason it is thus called, is because it is a *Dead-Pledge*, until the Money borrowed is repaid; or it is on Account

count that if the Money is not paid at the Day, the Land dies to the Debtor, and is forfeited to the Creditor. The common Method of making a Mortgage, is by Lease for a long Term of Years; and it may likewise be made by Assignment of a Term, or in Fee by Lease and Release. The Creditor in this Case is called the *Mortgagee*, or *Tenant in Mortgage*, who holds the Estate according to the Condition of the Deed, tho' usually the *Mortgagor*, or Debtor, holds the Land till Failure is made in Payment of the *Mortgage* Money: And even where Failure is made, and the *Mortgagee* enters for Non-payment, the *Mortgagor* hath a Right to the *Equity of Redemption* in the Court of *Chancery*, where he may call the Mortgagee to an Account for the Profits of the Lands, &c. *mortgaged*. Generally there is contained in a Mortgage, a Proviso or Covenant, that in Case the principal Money and Interest be paid at the Day limited for Payment thereof, the Deed of Mortgage shall be void: But where a Mortgage is made with a Proviso or Condition, that if the Mortgagor, &c. pay to the Mortgagee, &c. the Money borrowed at a certain Day, then the Mortgagor may re-enter; in which Case the Mortgagee comes immediately into the Possession, and holds till Payment, whilst in the other Case, the Mortgagor holds Possession till Failure. According to the Rules of the Court of Equity it is allowed, that in case Lands, &c. are thrice *mortgaged*, the third Mortgagee may buy in the first Mortgage to *protect* his own; and by that Means he shall hold against the second Mortgagee, in case such second Mortgagee do not satisfy him the Money paid on the first, as well as his own Money lent on the last. If a Purchaser on a valuable Consideration purchase a precedent Mortgage, or other Incumbrance, he shall thereby protect his Purchase against any that has a subsequent Mortgage: Also, if a Mortgagee, without having Notice of a former Incumbrance, buy in an Incumbrance precedent to that Incumbrance which precedes his Mortgage, he is not liable to be impeached in Equity, unless on Payment of all that is due to him on both Estates. By 7 *Geo.* 2. *c.* 20. where any Action of Ejectment is brought by a Mortgagee for the Recovery of the Possession of Lands, &c. mortgaged, and where there is no Suit depending in Equity for the Foreclosing or Redeeming the Equity of Redemption of those Lands, &c. in case the Person intitled to redeem, shall, *pendente lite*, pending the Action, bring all the Principal and Interest due, with Costs, into Court, it shall be taken as a full Satisfaction and Discharge of the Mortgage; and the Mortgagee shall thereon be obliged to reconvey the Land, &c. and deliver up all Deeds, &c. On a Bill of Foreclosure, that is to say, a Bill to compel the Mortgagor to pay the Mortgage-Money, or on Default thereof to be foreclosed, *viz.* to be deprived of the Benefit of Redeeming the Lands, &c. mortgaged, the Court, on being applied to by the Defendant, may make an Order therein, before the Cause is brought to a Hearing, provided the Right of Redemption is not in Dispute. A Deed of Mortgage usually consists of the following Parts, *viz.* The Parties Names, their Additions, and Places of Abode; the granting Part, and Thing granted; the *Habendum*

dum, or explanatory Clause, to shew what Estate the Grantee is to have; the Proviso or Condition for rendring the Mortgage void, on Payment of Principal and Interest; a Covenant for the Payment of the Money borrowed, with Interest; and all the other Covenants, are the same with what are generally used in other Conveyances, only that in a Deed of Mortgage it is the general Custom to add a Covenant from the Mortgagor, that the Mortgagee shall peaceably hold the Estate granted, until Default be made in Payment of the Mortgage-Money. In case the Mortgage be made by Lease for a Term of Years, &c. a Pepper-Corn Rent is usually reserved as is used in a Deed of Bargain and Sale. The Forms of Mortgages you may see in the *Young Clerk's Magazine*, and other Collections of Precedents of Conveyances.

Mortgagor. See **Mortgage**.

Mortmain, (from the *French* signifying a *Dead Hand*) is where Lands or Tenements are granted to any religious House or Corporation, sole or aggregate, which must not be done without the King's Licence. By 7 & 8 W. 3. c. 37, the King may grant any Person, Body Politick or Corporate, their Heirs and Successors, Licence to grant in *Mortmain*, and likewise to purchase and hold in *Mortmain*, in Perpetuity, &c. without their being liable to incur any Forfeiture.

Mortuary, is taken to be a Gift left by a Person at his Death to his Parish Church, in Recompence of Personal Tithes omitted to be paid in his Life-time; or, as defined in *Termes de la Ley*, it is that Beast, or other moveable Chattel, which after the Owner's Death, by the Custom of some Places, became due to the Parson, Vicar, or Priest of the Parish, in Lieu of Tithes or Offerings forgot, or not well and truly paid by the Deceased. We are told that the ancient Custom was to bring the *Mortuary* along with the Corpse, as it came to be buried, and to offer it to the Church, in Satisfaction of the supposed Negligence or Omission the Deceased had been guilty of, in not paying his Tithes; whence it was called a *Corpse Present*.

Moss Troopers, were a rebellious Pack, or Sort of People in the North of *England*, who lived by Robbery and Rapine.

Mote, in a legal Sense, denotes a Court or Convention.

Moteer, is a customary Service or Payment at the Lord's Mote or Court.

Motion in Court, is an Application in a petitionary Way in the several Courts of Law and Equity, by Barristers and Counsellors at Law, in Relation to Causes depending. Some Motions are of Course and some not. In the Court of *Chancery*, where a Motion is not of Course, but granted or refused as to the Court shall seem meet, generally an Affidavit of the Facts alledged must be read in Court, Notice having been first given in Writing to the Solicitor of the adverse Party, or to his Clerk in Court, wherein must be expressed every Thing intended to be moved for; which Notice must be served two Days at least before the Day on which the Motion is to be made. In the Court of *Chancery*, during Term-Time, *Tuesdays* and *Saturdays* are Days for *Motions*, so are likewise the first and last Days of every Term; and

M U

and in the Time of Vacation, only the Seal Days appointed by the *Lord Chancellor* are Days for *Motions*: But, in the Courts of Law, Motions may be made any Day, as the Business of the Court will permit.

Mulct, is a Fine of Money laid upon a Person who has committed some Misdemeanor: Also Fines imposed on Ships or Goods, by a Company of Trade, for raising Money for the Maintenance of Consuls, &c. are termed *Mulcts*.

Mulier, in our Law, denotes the legal Issue born in Wedlock, tho' begotten before, and is preferred before an elder Brother born out of Matrimony. If a Man has a Son by a Woman before Marriage, which Issue is a Bastard, and unlawful, and afterwards the Man marries the Mother of the Bastard, and they have another Son, this second Son is *mulier* and lawful, and shall be Heir of the Father, but the other can be Heir to no Man, for this Reason, that it is not known who was his Father, and on that Account he is said to be no Man's Son, or the *Son* of the *People*: And to such Sons you shall in our Law Books always find this Addition, *viz. Bastard eldest,* and *Mulier youngest*, whenever they are compared together. *Termes de la Ley.*

Muliery, denotes the Condition of a *Mulier*, which see.

Multa Episcopi, denotes a Satisfaction made to the King by the Bishops, in order that they might have Power to make their Wills, and have the *Probat* of the Wills of other Men, and also the granting of Administrations.

Muniments, are Evidences or Writings concerning a Person's Inheritance or Possession, by which he is enabled to defend his Estate; and in this Word are included all Manner of Evidences, such as Charters, Feoffments, Releases, &c.

Murage, denotes some reasonable Toll to be taken of every Cart and Horse that brings Lading thro' a City or Town, for the Building or Repairing the publick Walls thereof.

Murder, denotes a wilful Killing of a Person, upon Malice Forethought; provided the Party that is wounded, or otherwise hurt, die within a Year and a Day after the Fact was committed: And if in that Time the Person hurt die, thro' disorderly living, that will be no Excuse, seeing that the Wound, &c. will be judged the principal Cause of his Death; tho' where a Person dies after that Time, it will be presumed that he died a natural Death. This Crime of Murder may be committed several Ways; as by Weapon, Poison, Bruising, Smothering, Strangling, Starving, &c. If a Person bearing Malice to another strikes or shoots at him, but, instead of hitting him, kills another, this is *Murder*: Also, where Poison is laid in order to kill a particular Person, and another accidentally takes it and dies, this is Murder in the Person that laid the Poison. *Hawkins* observes, that anciently it was held, that the Causing an Abortion, either by giving a Potion to, or striking a Woman big with Child, was Murder; but that it is now said to be a great Misprision only, and not Murder, unless the Child be born alive, and die of the Bruise, &c. In Case the Death of a Bastard Child that is newly born be concealed, it shall be supposed to have been murdered, unless the Mother can prove it to have been born dead. A Person under the Age of Discretion,

cretion, or *non compos mentis*, cannot be guilty of Murder; yet if it do appear from strong Circumstances that the Infant hid the Body, &c. he is guilty of Felony. It is Malice, and not the bare Killing that makes the Crime of Murder, which is either expressed or implied; express, when it is evidently proved that there was some ill Will or old Grudge before the Killing, and the Fact was committed with a sedate Mind, and a formed Design of doing it: And implied is, where one kills another suddenly, having nothing to defend himself, in going along a Street, over a Field, or the like. The Person that voluntarily commits any violent or cruel Act, which is attended by Death, in the Eye of our Law is looked upon to do it of Malice forethought; as where a Man in cool Blood maliciously beats another in such a Manner, above any apparent Design of Chastisement, that he dies, this is Murder by express Malice, altho' he did not design to kill him. If a Person execute his Revenge, upon a sudden Provocation, in such a cruel Manner, as shews a malicious Intention of doing Mischief, and Death ensues thereon; this is express Malice and Murder from the very Nature of the Fact; as where a Person having chided his Servant upon some cross Answer given, directly runs a hot Iron that is in his Hand into the Servant's Belly, of which he dies: So likewise, where a Person trespasses upon another by breaking his Hedges, &c. upon which the Owner takes up a Hedge-Stake, wherewith he gives him a Stroke on the Head, of which he dies, this is Murder; for that it is a violent Act, beyond the Degree of the Provocation. Where two out of Malice forethought fight, and the Servant of one of them, ignorant of the Malice kills the other, this is Murder in the Master, and only Manslaughter in the Servant. Where two Persons fight in cool Blood, on a precedent Quarrel, and one of them is killed; or if a Person on a sudden Quarrel appear to be Master of his Passion, and kill another; this is Murder, for this Reason, that where two fight after a former Quarrel, it may be presumed to be out of Malice prepensed. It is also Murder, where a Person upon a Quarrel with another, tells the other, that he will not strike him, but will give him Money or Liquor to strike first, whereupon the Person, thus hired strikes him, and the Hirer kills him. Where a Person declares a Resolution to kill the first Person he meets, and does kill him; this is Murder, because in this Case Malice is implied against all Mankind. If a Bailiff or other Officer is killed in the Execution of his Office, it is Murder; for it is no Excuse that the Process was erroneous, or that the Arrest was in the Night-time, or that the Officer did not acquaint him with the Cause why he arrested him, or that he did not produce his Warrant, it being sufficient that he is a Bailiff or other Officer commonly known: Yet where the Warrant whereby he acts does not authorise him to arrest the Party; as where he arrests a wrong Person; or where a Warrant is executed in an illegal Manner; as in breaking open a Door or a Window to arrest a Person, or in Case the Arrest be on a *Sunday*, if upon any such Arrests the Officer be slain, it is only Manslaughter. If a Person stand by and encourage another to slay a Person; or in case he come with others

others on Purpose to kill him, and stand by till the Fact be committed, it is Murder in all present. Where two or more assemble together, in order to commit some unlawful Act, as to beat a Person, rob a Park, &c. and one of them by Chance kills another, this is Murder in all present, seeing that their meeting together was with the Intent of committing an unlawful Act. Offenders and Accessaries in Murder being indicted, may be arraigned at any Time within the Year at the King's Suit; and in case the Principal or Accessary be acquitted, the Justices are not to suffer them to go at large, but either send them back to Prison, or suffer them to be bailed out, until the Year and Day be out, which is the Time allowed for an Appeal. Where a Person is murdered in the Day-time, and the Murderer escapes, the Township that suffers him to escape, may be amerced. See *Manslaughter.* An Indictment for Murder runs thus, *viz.*

Middlesex,

THE *Jurors present for the Lord the King, upon their Oaths, that* A. B. *late of* —— *in the County aforesaid, not having God before his Eyes, but moved and seduced by the Instigation of the Devil, on the* —— *Day of* —— *at the Parish of* —— *in the County aforesaid, with Force and Arms, &c. in and upon one* C. D. *in the Peace of God, and of the Lord the King, then and there being, made an Assault, and the aforesaid* A. B. *with a Knife, &c. of the Value of* —— *which the said* A. B. *in his Right-Hand then and there had drawn, and held, feloniously, voluntarily, and of his Malice forethought, the aforesaid* C. D. *at* —— *aforesaid, in the County aforesaid, struck and wounded; and the said* C. D. *then and there feloniously, and of his Malice forethought, gave with the Knife aforesaid one mortal Wound in and upon the left Part of his Belly, of the Length of* —— *and Depth* —— *of which said mortal Wound the said* C. D. *instantly died; and so the Jurors aforesaid say, that the aforesaid* A. B. *the Day and Year abovesaid, at* —— *aforesaid, in the County aforesaid, the said* C. D. *in Manner and Form aforesaid, of Malice forethought, feloniously and voluntarily killed and murdered, against the Peace of the said Lord the King, his Crown and Dignity, &c.*

Muster, (from the *French*) denotes nothing more than to shew Men in Arms.

Mute, signifies one that is dumb, or who refuses to speak. A Prisoner may be said to stand mute two Ways, *viz.* 1. When he does not speak at all, in which Case it shall be inquired whether he stands mute out of Obstinacy, or by the Act of God? 2. When a Prisoner does not plead directly, or will not put himself upon the Inquest to be tried: or where the Prisoner feigns himself mad, and refuses to answer. A Prisoner is likewise said to stand *mute*, when on his Trial he peremptorily challenges above the Number of Jurors allowed by Law. In the Crime of High Treason, if the Prisoner stand *mute*, he shall forfeit Lands and Goods, in the same Manner as if he had been attainted: And in Felony and Petit Treason the Person that stands mute shall forfeit his Land and Goods, as on other Attainders: Yet it is said that when a Person standing *mute* is adjudged to his Penance for Felony, he thereby prevents

vents that Attainder, which otherwise might be incurred, and forfeits his Chattels only.

Mutual Promise, is where one Person promises to pay Money, or perform some other Act to another, which other, in Consideration thereof, promises to perform some other Act. See **Covenant**.

Mutuatus, *Borrowed.* Where a Person owes another a certain Sum, for which he has a Promissory Note, Action of Debt lies upon a *Mutuatus*.

Mutus & Surdus, denotes one that is both dumb and deaf, who being Tenant of a Manor, the Lord shall have the Wardship and Custody of him.

Mystery, denotes an Art, Trade or Occupation.

N.

Nam or **Naam,** signifies the Attaching or Distraining of another's moveable Goods. See *Horn's Mirror*.

Narr, is a Contraction of *Narratio*, which denotes a *Declaration* in a Cause.

Narrator, denotes a Pleader or Reporter.

Nativi de Stipite, anciently denoted Villeins or Bondmen by Birth, whilst *Nativi Conventionarii* denoted Persons made Villeins by Contract or Agreement.

Nativo habendo, was a Writ that lay for the Lord who claimed any Inheritance in any Villein, when he was run from him, for the Apprehending and Restoring him to the Lord. In short, this Writ was in the Nature of a Writ of Right to recover the Inheritance in the Villein.

Nativus, was anciently taken for a Servant: And formerly there were three Kinds of Servants, *Bondmen, Natives,* such as were born Servants, and *Villeins*.

Naturalization, is where an *Alien* is made the King's natural Subject by Act of Parliament, by which Means a Person becomes as much a Subject to all Intents and Purposes, as if he were actually born so; seeing that by *Naturalization* a Person's Issue, before the *Naturalization,* shall inherit. A Person that is *naturalized* may inherit Lands by Discent, as Heir at Law, as well as have them by Purchase. None is to be naturalized before he has received the Sacrament of the Church, and taken the Oaths of *Allegiance* and *Supremacy, &c.* And even when *naturalized,* they are disabled to be of the King's Privy Council, or to hold Offices, *&c.* All Children that are born out of the Dominions of the Crown, whose Fathers were or are natural-born Subjects of this Kingdom at the Time of their Birth, are to be adjudged natural-born Subjects of this Realm, except Children of Parents who are attainted of Treason, or who are in the actual Service of a Foreign Prince in Enmity with us. See **Denizen**.

Naufrage, signifies a Shipwreck.

Navy, denotes a Fleet of Ships of War. For the Regulation and Government of the *Royal Navy,* there are divers Articles and Orders established by 13 *Car.* 2. *c.* 9.

Ne admittas, is a Writ directed to the Bishop at the Suit of one that is Patron of a Church, where he is doubtful that the Bishop will collate one his Clerk, or admit another presented by another Person to the same Benefice. *Termes de la Ley*.

Ne exeat Regnum, or more properly **Ne exeat Regno,** is a Writ for

for the Restraining of a Person from going out of the Kingdom without the King's Licence; and it may be directed either to the Sheriff, to cause the Party to find Surety that he will not depart the Realm; or to the Party himself, in which last Case, if he goes, he is liable to be fined. Where a Suit is depending in the Court of *Chancery*, and the Plaintiff is afraid that the Defendant will fly abroad, upon a proper Application to the Court he may have this Writ; in which Case the Defendant must give Bond to the Master of the Rolls, in the Penalty of some large Sum, for submitting to the Writ; or else he must satisfy the Court by Answer, Affidavit, or otherwise, that he has no Design of leaving the Kingdom, and enter into Security accordingly.

Negative, is what cannot be testified by Witnesses.

Negative pregnant, is such a *Negative*, as implies an *Affirmative*; as where a Person brings an Action against another, and the Defendant pleads a *Negative* Plea in Bar of the Action, which is not so special an Answer to the Action, but that it includes also an Affirmative: As for Example, if a Writ of Entry *in casu proviso* be brought by one in Reversion, upon an Alienation made by Tenant for Life, supposing that he has aliened in Fee, which causes a Forfeiture of his Estate, and the Tenant pleads that he has not aliened in Fee; this is a Negative, wherein an Affirmative is included, because, tho' it may be true that he has not aliened in Fee, yet it may be he has made an Estate in Tail, which is also a Forfeiture. Where an Information was brought in the *Exchequer* against *J. S.* for that he bought Wool of *J. N.* between Shearing Time and the Assumption such a Year; to which the Defendant pleads, that he did not buy any of *J. N.* as is alledged, *&c.* this is a Negative Pregnant; seeing that if he bought it of any other, yet he is culpable for the Buying. *Termes de la Ley.*

Neif, or **Nief**, anciently denoted a Woman that was bound, or a She Villein; who, if she married a Free-Man, she thereby became free; and being once free, she could not be *Neif* after, without some particular Act of hers; such as Divorce, or Confession in Court of Record, *&c.* A Free-Woman was not bound by taking a Villein to her Husband, but their Issue were Villeins as their Father was; which is contrary to the Maxim of the Civil Law, *viz. Partus sequitur Ventrem. Termes de la Ley.*

Ne injuste vexes. See **Monstraverunt**.

Neifty, was a Writ anciently used, by which the Lord claimed such a Woman for his *Nief*.

Nemine Contradicente, are Words used in the House of Commons, to denote the *unanimous* Consent of the Members thereof to the Resolution of that House.

Ne Recipiatur, is a Rule entered against the Receiving and setting down of a Cause for Trial. See **Trial**.

Nient comprise, in the *New Book of Entries*, is defined to be an Exception to a Petition, on Account that the Thing desired is contained in the Deed, *&c.* on which the Petition is founded; as where a Person desires of the Court in which a Recovery is had of Lands, *&c.* to be put into Possession of a House, adjudged to him formerly among the Lands; whereto the other Party pleads, that the Petition ought

not to be granted; seeing that the House petitioned for is not comprised among the Lands and Houses, whereof he had Judgment.

Nient Dedire, denotes to suffer Judgment by Default of not opposing it.

Niger Liber, is the Name of a certain Register in the *Exchequer*, called the *Black Book*.

Night, is generally taken to be when it is so dark, that the Countenance of a Person cannot be discerned; tho' by some it is taken to be any Time after Sun-set, and before the Rising of the Sun.

Night-Walkers, are such as sleep in the Day-time, and *walk* by *Night*, and who, as well as other suspicious Persons may be taken up by the Constables and Watchmen, and may be detained by them till Morning. *Night-Walkers* are liable to be bound to the good Behaviour; and common Night-Walkers, as well as Frequenters of Bawdy-Houses, are indictable.

Nihil capiat per Breve, or per Billam, is defined to be the Judgment given against the Plaintiff in an Action, either in Bar thereof, or in Abatement of the Writ, &c.

Nihil dicit, or **Nil dicit**, is a Failure in the Defendant to put in an Answer to the Plaintiff's Declaration, &c. by the Day for that Purpose assigned; by which Omission, Judgment of Course passes against him.

Nihils, or **Nichils**, are Issues which a Sheriff who is apposed in the *Exchequer*, says are *Nothing worth*, and not to be levied, on Account of the Insufficiency of the Parties from whom the same are due.

Nil debet, is the ordinary Plea in an Action of Debt, but is no Plea in an Action of Covenant, on Breach assigned for Non-payment of Rent.

Nil habuit in Tenementis, is a Plea that can only be pleaded in an Action of Debt brought by a Lessor against a Lessee, without Deed; for if it be by Indenture of Lease it may not be pleaded, the Lease being an Estoppel; yet it is said, that if it be upon Deed Poll, it may be pleaded.

Nisi Prius, is a Commission directed to the Justices of *Nisi Prius*; and it takes its Name from a Writ of *Distringas*, wherein the Sheriff is commanded to distrain the Jury that are impanelled to appear at *Westminster* at a certain Day in the Term following, to try some Cause depending, *unless the Justices to take the Assises, before that Day come to such a Place*. A Writ of *Nisi Prius*, is when an Issue is joined, then there issues out a *Venire*, to summon the Jury to appear at a certain Day in Court; upon the Return of which Writ of *Venire*, with the Panel of the Jurors Names, the Record of *Nisi Prius* is made up and sealed; after which there issues a *Distringas*, to oblige the Jurors to come in Court, *unless the Justices, &c.* first come such a Day, to such a Place, in such a County. No Record of *Nisi Prius* for Trial at the Assises is to be sealed after three Weeks next following the End of the Term preceding. These Trials by *Nisi Prius* are purely intended for the Ease of the Country, by saving the Parties, Jurors and Witnesses, the Charge and Trouble of coming to *Westminster*, where, in Matters of great Consequence and Difficulty, the Judges, upon Motion, frequently retain Causes to be tried, even tho' the Facts be laid to be in the Country; in which Case the Jury, as well as Witnesses, must attend at *Westminster* for a Trial at Bar. The Chief Justice of the *King's Bench* or *Common Pleas*,

Pleas, and also the Chief Baron of the *Exchequer*, and in their Absence two other Judges, may in their respective Courts, as Justices of *Nisi Prius* for the County of *Middlesex*, try Causes on Writs of *Nisi Prius*.

Noctanter, is a Writ which issues out of the Court of *Chancery*, and returnable in the *King's Bench*: And this Writ lies where a Person having Right to improve waste Ground, erects a Ditch or Hedge, which is thrown down in the *Night-Time*, and it cannot be known by a Jury, by whom such Injury was committed; in this Case, if the neighbouring Vills do not find out and indict the Offenders, they shall be distrained to make good the same at their own Costs, &c. And the Sheriff by this Writ is commanded to make Inquiry who the Offenders are, &c. and upon the Return thereof, that the same is found by Inquisition, and that the Jury are ignorant who committed the Injury, there issues out of the Crown-Side of the *King's Bench* a *Distringas*, whereby the Sheriff is commanded to distrain the neighbouring Villages, Hedges, &c. in order to restore the Damages to the Party injured. This Word *Noctanter* was necessarily used in all Indictments for *Burglary*, and it is reported, that an Indictment of that Kind has been adjudged insufficient without it.

Nolle Prosequi, is a Term used in our Law, where a Plaintiff having commenced an Action will not proceed, and this frequently happens before a Verdict; in which Case it is stronger than a Nonsuit, which is only on the Plaintiff's making Default in Appearance, whilst this is a voluntary Acknowledgment, that the Plaintiff has no Cause of Action. The King's Attorney General, on Behalf of the King, may enter a *Nolle Prosequi* on an Information in the Crown-Office, which shall wholly stop the King's Proceedings, but not those of an Informer.

Nomination, denotes the Power a Person has of appointing a Clerk to a Patron of a Benefice, by him to be presented to the Ordinary. This Power or Right of Nomination a Person may have by Deed, in which Case should the Patron refuse to present the Person *nominated*, or instead thereof present another, the *Nominor* may bring a *Quare impedit*. If a *Nominator* do not appoint a Clerk within six Months after the Avoidance, but the Patron presents before the Bishop has taken Advantage of the Lapse, such Clerk is obliged to be admitted. It is said that Right of Nomination may be forfeited to the Crown as well as the Right of Presentation, in Case the *Nominator* makes any corrupt Agreement. See **Simony**.

Nomina Villarum. The Returns of the Sheriffs throughout *England*, all joined together, were formerly termed so.

Nomine Poenæ, denotes a certain Penalty incurred for Non-payment of Rent, &c. at the Day appointed for Payment thereof. Where Rent is reserved, and on the Non-payment thereof there is a *Nomine Pænæ*, if the Rent be behind, there must be an actual Demand of it made before the Person intitled to the Rent can distrain for it; seeing that the *Nomine Pænæ* is of the same Nature of the Rent itself, and issues out of the Lands, &c. whereout the Rent does issue. We are told, that where Money is to be forfeited *Nomine Pænæ* for Non-Payment of Rent at the Time appointed by the Lease, &c. the

Demand of the Rent ought to be made precisely on the Day, in Regard to the *Penalty*.

Non-Ability. See **Disability**.

Nonæ Decimæ, were Payments formerly made by Tenants of Church Farms; in which Case *Nonæ* denoted a Duty paid for Things appertaining to Husbandry, and *Decimæ* were particularly claimed in Right of the Church.

Non-Age, according to the general Acceptation of the Word, is all the Time that a Person continues under the Age of One and twenty; but in a special Sense it denotes all that Time a Person is under the Age of Fourteen, in Respect to Marriage, &c.

Non assumpsit, is a general Plea in personal Actions, whereby one denies any Promise made.

Non-Claim, denotes an Omission in a Person's not claiming within the Time limited by Law.

Non compos mentis, denotes that a Person is not of sound Memory and Understanding. There are four different Kinds of *Non compos mentis*, viz. an Ideot, or one born a natural Fool; a Madman, or one that has been of sound Memory, but by Sickness or the like has lost his Understanding; a Lunatick, that is to say, one sometimes of sound Memory, and sometimes not so; a Drunkard, who by Drinking deprives himself of his Reason for a Time; and tho' a Drunkard is at the Time *non compos mentis*, that can be no Benefit to him as to Acts done; for his Drunkenness does not extenuate, but on the contrary aggravates his Offence, either as to Life, Lands, &c. An Alienation made by a Person that is *non compos mentis* may be avoided by his Heir at Law, upon his shewing the Disability of his Ancestor; And it is likewise voidable by his Executors or Administrators, who, by setting forth the Infirmity of the Testator, or Intestate, may do the like. A Person that is *non compos mentis*, shall not, according to our Law, lose his Life for Felony or Murder; yet it is said, that where he does some corporal Hurt to, or commits a Trespass against another, he is compellable by Action to answer Damages.

Nonconformists, are such as do not conform or agree to the Uniformity of the Common Prayer, and Service of the Church of *England*.

Non damnificatus, is a Plea to an Action of Debt on Bond, conditioned for indemnifying or saving the Plaintiff harmless.

Non decimando, denotes a Custom to be discharged of all Tithes. See **Modus decimandi**.

Non distringendo, is a Writ denoting *not to distrain*, and is used in sundry Cases.

Non est culpabilis, or **Non Cul.** is a general Plea to an Indictment, or Action, by which the Defendant wholly denies the Fact charged; but it is otherwise in special Pleas, wherein the Defendant admits the Fact to be done, yet alledges some Reasons why he might legally do it. This is likewise the general Answer in all Criminal Prosecutions.

Non est Factum, is the general Plea where an Action is brought upon Bond, or other Deed, which the Defendant denies to be his Deed; as where a Bond or other Deed is rased in a material Part, whereby it becomes void. *Non est Factum* may be pleaded, and the special Matter of the Rasure may be given in Evidence, to shew that it was not the Defendant's Deed at the Time of the Plea.

Nonfeasance, signifies the Omission of what ought to be done.

Non implacitando aliquem de Libero Tenemento sine Brevi, is a Writ to prevent Bailiffs, &c. from distraining a Person concerning his Freehold without the King's Writ.

Non intromittendo, quando Breve Praecipe in Capite subdole impetratur, was a Writ anciently used and directed to the Justices of the *Bench*, or in *Eyre*, forbidding those that, under Colour of intitling the King to Land, &c. held of him *in Capite*, had indirectly obtained the Writ termed *Praecipe in Capite*, any Benefit thereof; but, instead thereof, to put him to his Writ of Right.

Nonjurors, denote such Persons who refuse to take the Oaths to the Government, who on that Account are subject to certain Penalties. See **Abjuration**. See **Oaths**.

Non Merchandizando Victualia, is a Writ directed to Justices of Assise, in order to inquire whether the Magistrates of such a Place sell victuals in Gross, or by Retail, whilst they are in Office; for which, if they do, they are punishable.

Non Molestando, is a Writ that issues where a Person is molested contrary to the King's Protection granted.

Non obstante, (in *English*, *Notwithstanding*,) is a particular Clause frequently to be met with in *Statutes* and *Letters Patent*, and is defined to be a Licence from the King to do a Thing, which at the Common Law might be lawfully done, were it not, that by being restrained by Act of Parliament, cannot be done, without the King's Licence. See **Dispensation**.

Non omittas, is a Writ that lies where the Sheriff returns upon a Writ directed to him, that he hath sent to the Bailiff of such a Franchise who has the Return of Writs, and that he neglects to serve the Writ sent him; wherefore the Sheriff is commanded to enter into the Franchise himself, and there to execute the King's Writ. The Sheriff is also to warn the Bailiff, that he be before the Justices at the Day mentioned in the Writ; and in Case he does not come and excuse himself, then all the judicial Writs, which shall issue out of the King's Court during that Plea, shall be Writs of *Non omittas*, and the Sheriff shall make Execution of them, during the Dependance of that Plea. *Termes de la Ley*. Tho' before a *Non omittas* issues, the Sheriff ought to make a Return, as above; yet, for the Sake of Dispatch, the Practice usually is to send a *Non omittas*, with a *Capias* or *Latitat*. It is said, that a *Capias utlegatum*, *Quo minus*, and all other Writs at the King's Suit, have the same Effect as this Writ of *Non omittas*.

Non-plevin, is where Land seised is not replevied in due Time.

Non ponendis in Assisis & Juratis, is a Writ that issues for freeing one from serving on Assises and Juries.

Non procedendo ad Assisam Rege inconsulto, is a Writ for stopping the Trial of a Cause belonging to a Person that is in the King's Service, until his Majesty's Pleasure be further known.

Non Pros. is where a Plaintiff in our Courts of Law does not declare in a reasonable Time; in which Case the Practice is for the Defendant's Attorney to enter a Rule for the Plaintiff to declare; and thereon afterwards a *Non Pros.* may be entered. See **Nolle Prosequi**. See **Nonsuit**.

Non-Residence, is particularly applied to Spiritual Persons who are not *Resident*, but wilfully absent themselves for the Space of a Month together, or two Months at different Times in the Year, from their Dignities or Benefices, for which they are punishable by the Statute of *Non-Residence*.

Non Residentia pro Clericis Regis, is a Writ which lies where a Clerk is imployed in the King's Service, whereby he is obliged to be *Non-Resident*; and it is directed to the Bishop, charging him not to molest such Clerk on Account of his *Non-Residence*.

Non sane Memory, or **Non sanæ Memoriæ**, in a legal Sense, is taken for an Exception to some Act, alledged to be done by another, on which the Plaintiff grounds his Action; as that the Party that performed it had not his right Senses at the Time of doing it. It is observed by some, that a Person of *sane* or sound Memory, at the Making of a Will, is not always where a Testator can answer *Yes*, or *No*, or perhaps in some Things sensibly; for in this Case he ought to have Judgment to discern, and at the same Time to be of perfect Understanding; otherwise the Will shall be void.

Nonsuit, denotes the Dropping or Desisting from a Suit or Action, or a Renouncing thereof by the Plaintiff or Demandant; which commonly happens upon the Discovery of some Error in the Plaintiff's Proceedings, when the Cause is so far proceeded in, that the Jury is ready at the Bar to deliver in their Verdict. It is also said, that where a Person brings a personal Action, and does not prosecute it with Effect, or in case upon the Trial, he refuses to stand a Verdict; then he directly becomes *Nonsuited*; so likewise where the Plaintiff is not ready for Trial at the Calling and Swearing of the Jury, it is in Law presumed he does not intend to proceed in the Cause, and on that Account the Court may call him *Nonsuit*: And in the like Manner it is on a Trial when the Jury comes in to deliver their Verdict, and the Plaintiff is called upon to hear the same; if he do not appear after being thrice called by the Crier of the Court, he becomes nonsuited; which *Nonsuit* is to be recorded by the Secondary, by the Direction of the Court: But should he afterwards appear before the *Nonsuit* is recorded, the Court may proceed to take the Verdict, for this Reason, that it is not a Verdict till it be recorded by the Secondary; upon Motion made by Counsel for that Purpose; because the Court will not order it to be recorded unless the Counsel pray it. The King, tho' the Attorney General may enter a *Nolle Prosequi* in his Name, cannot be nonsuit, seeing that by Judgment in Law he is always deemed present in Court: However, in a popular Action, notwithstanding the King cannot be nonsuited in an Information or Action wherein he himself is sole Plaintiff, an Informer *qui tam*, that is to say, a Plaintiff in a Popular Action, may be nonsuited, and by that Means wholly determine the Suit, both as to the King and himself. Where a Plaintiff becomes *Nonsuit*, he may begin his Proceedings afresh on a new Declaration; but may not proceed on that in which he became *Nonsuit*, that being absolutely void, and the Plaintiff having no Day in Court. On an Appearance entered at the Return of the Writ, should the Plaintiff neglect to give a Declaration in a Personal Action before the End of the next Term following, a *Nonsuit* may be entered, and the Plaintiff thereon becomes liable to pay Costs to the Defendant. See 13 *Car.* 2. *c.* 2.

Non sum Informatus, *I am not informed,* is a formal Answer of Course made by an Attorney, who is not instructed what to say in his Client's Behalf; on which Account he is deemed to leave the Cause undefended, and therefore Judgment passes against his Client.

Non-tenure, is defined to denote a Plea in Bar to a real Action, whereby the Defendant insists that he does not hold the Lands, &c. mentioned in the Plaintiff's Count, or some Part thereof. In Pleading there is *Non-tenure, General* and *Special: General,* is where one absolutely denies ever to have been Tenant of the Lands, &c. in Question: *Special,* is where the Defendant, by Way of Exception, pleads that he was not Tenant the Day whereon the Writ was purchased.

Non-Term, was formerly called the Days of the King's Peace; but it is now termed the Vacation between Term and Term.

Non-user. See **Office.**

Notary, usually denotes a Scrivener, or one who takes *Notes,* or frames Draughts of Contracts, Charter-Parties, or other Writings: But a Notary Publick is properly he that publickly attests Writings or Deeds, in order to make them authentick in another Nation; and he is principally in Business concerning Merchants; as to make Protests of Bills of Exchange, &c. on noting a Bill, which is to take Notice of a Merchant's Refusal to accept or pay the same.

Not guilty, denotes the general Issue of the Defendant in a Criminal Action, as also in Actions of Trespass, &c. See **Non est culpabilis.**

Notice, is defined to be the Making of somewhat known, which a Man might be ignorant of before. *Notice* is in several Respects by Law required to be given, in order to justify Proceedings, &c. Yet none is thereby bound to give Notice to another of what such other may inform himself. Upon Writs of Inquiry of Damages, either in real or personal Actions, Notice must be given to the other Party in the Suit; and Want of Notice upon divers Occasions, is often the Cause of Arrest of Judgment. *Notice* is likewise to be given of Trials and Motions, of a Robbery committed, in order to recover against the Hundred; of a prior Mortgage, on the Making of a second; of an Assignment of a Lease, in Cases of Distress, pursuant to the Statute; and of Avoidances of Churches by Resignation, &c. to the Patron, in order that he may present, &c.

Novel Assignment, is said to denote an Assignment of Time, Place, or the like, in an Action of Trespass, otherwise than as it was assigned before; as where a Person brings an Action of Trespass for breaking his Close; and the Defendant in his Plea justifies in a Place where no Trespass was committed; in which Case the Plaintiff assigns the Close where the Trespass was done; whereto the Defendant may plead Guilty, or justify by Title. *Termes de la Ley.*

Novel Disseisin. See **Assise of Novel Disseisin.**

Nuces Colligere, was anciently one of the Services imposed by Lords on their inferior Tenants, which was to gather Hazle Nuts.

Nude,

Nude, denotes somewhat that is naked or bare.

Nul tiel Record, is where the Plaintiff pleads that there is *no such Record*, upon the Defendant's pleading Matter of *Record* in Bar of the Action brought by the Plaintiff.

Nullum arbitrium, is the common Plea for the Defendant sued on an *Award*.

Nullity, denotes any Thing that is *null* or *void*.

Nuncupative Will, denotes a Declaration made by Word of Mouth by the Testator, before a sufficient Number of Witnesses, of his Will and Mind, which Declaration being reduced into Writing, either before, or after his Death, is good as to the Disposal of his personal. tho' not his real Estate. By 29 *Car.* 2. *c.* 3. no nuncupative Will shall be good, where the Estate bequeathed exceeds the Value of 30 *l.* unless such Will be proved by three Witnesses that are present at the Making of it, and desired by the Testator to bear Witness of his Will; or unless it be made in the last Sickness of the Testator, and in his own Habitation, or in such Place wherein he has been resident for ten Days at least before, excepting in the Case of a sudden Sickness abroad: And no Evidence is to be allowed on a *nuncupative Will*, after the Expiration of six Months after the Declaration or Speaking thereof, unless the Whole or Substance of it be reduced into Writing within six Days after the Making: Neither shall a Probate of such Will pass the Seals until fourteen Days after the Testator's Death, and until Process has issued to call in the Widow or next of Kin to the Testator.

Nuper obiit, is a Writ which lies for a Sister and Co-heir, who is deforced by her Coparcener of Lands, &c. of which their Ancestor died seised in Fee: But a Writ of *Rationabili Parte* lies where the Ancestor was once seised, yet died not seised of the Possession, but in Reversion.

Nusance, is where a Person raises a Wall, stops Water, or does any other Thing upon his own Ground to the Detriment or Annoyance of his Neighbour. *Termes de la Ley.* *Nusances* are either *publick*, or *private*: A *publick Nusance* is an Offence against the Publick in general, either by doing what tends to the Annoyance of all the King's Subjects, or by neglecting to do what the common Good requires: A *private Nusance* is, where only one particular Person is annoyed, or hurt by the Doing of any Thing; as where a Person stops up the Light of another's House, or builds so near it, and hanging over his Neighbour's House, that the Rain which falls from his falls upon the other's; as likewise, Turning or Diverting Water from running to a Man's House, Mill, Meadow, &c. or Stopping up a Way that leads from Houses to Lands; suffering a House to decay, to the Damage of the next House; setting up a Tan-house, Dye-house, &c. so near another Person's House, that the Smell of it annoys his Neighbour; or if they hurt one's Lands or Trees, corrupt his Water, &c. Indictment lies for a publick or common Nusance, at the King's Suit, whereon the Party offending shall be fined and imprisoned. Action on the Case, or Assise of *Nusance*, lies at the Suit of the Party grieved; and on an Action for *private Nusance*, Judgment follows that the *Nusance* shall be removed, and that the injured Party shall recover Damages. The
Difference

Difference between an Assise of *Nusance* and an *Action on the Case* is this, *viz.* That the first is to abate the *Nusance*, but the last, instead of abating it, is to recover Damages; in which Case, if the Action be removed, the Plaintiff becomes intitled to his Damages that accrued before; and supposing it be laid with a Continuance for a longer Time than the Plaintiff can prove, he becomes intitled to Damages for what he can make Proof to have sustained before the *Nusance* was abated. It is held, that both a common and private *Nusance* may be abated by such Persons as are prejudiced thereby: And it has been held, that any Person may remove a Nusance; so that even the Cutting of a Gate that crosses the Highway is legal. In Case two Houses, one of which is a *Nusance* to the adjoining House, that which is the *Nusance* may be pulled down, tho' none can justify more Damage than is necessary, &c. According to *Litt.* if a Ship be sunk in a Port or Haven, and is not removed by the Owner, he may be indicted for a common *Nusance*, on Account of its being prejudicial to the Common-wealth, in hindering Navigation and Trade. In *Ventris* it is reported, that one *Hall*, having begun to build a Booth near *Charing Cross*, for the Pastime of Rope-dancing, whereby a great Number of idle People were gathered together, the Lord Chief Justice ordered him not to proceed; but he proceeded notwithstanding, insisting that he had the King's Warrant as well as Promise to keep him harmless; whereupon being required to enter into Recognizance in 300 *l.* that he should not go on with the Work, and he refusing to comply, he was committed, and a *Nusance* was made by this Record, as upon the Judge's own View, and afterwards a Writ issued to the Sheriff of *Middlesex*, to order him to pull it down.

O

Oath, denotes a solemn Affirmation or Denial of any Thing before Persons that have Authority of administring the same, in order to discover and advance Truth and Right, the Persons sworn calling God to Witness that their Testimonies are true; and on this Account such Oath is termed *Sacramentum*, a Holy Band or Tie; and it is also called a *Corporal Oath*, for this Reason, that the Witness, when he swears, lays his Right-hand on the Book of the *Holy Evangelists*, or *New Testament*. *Nelson* reckons up four Sorts of Oaths, *viz. Juramentum Promissionis*, where an Oath is taken to do, or not to do such a Thing; *Juramentum Purgationis*, which is where a Person is charged with any Matter by Bill in Equity; *Juramentum Probationis*, where one is produced as a Witness to prove or disprove a Thing; and *Juramentum Triationis*, where one is sworn to try the Issue, such as a Juror. Where Oaths are administred by Persons not duly authorised, they are *Coram non Judice*, and consequently void; and, on that Account, the Person administring the Oath is guilty of a great Contempt, he doing it without Warrant of Law, and is therefore punishable both with Fine and Imprisonment. A Person who is to be Witness in a Cause may have two Oaths administred to him; the one to speak the Truth to what the Court shall think fit to ask him in Relation to himself,

himself, or any Thing else that is not Evidence in the Cause; and the other purely to give Evidence in the Cause wherein he is produced as a Witness: The former of which Oaths is called an Oath upon a *Voyer dire*. Where Oath is made against Oath, it is deemed a *Non liquet*, it is not clear to the Court which of the Oaths is true; wherefore the Court generally looks upon that Oath to be true, which tends to affirm the Verdict, &c. There are likewise Oaths required to be taken to the Government by Persons in Office, and others. By Statute, all that bear Offices of any Kind under the Government, Peers, and Members of the House of Commons, Ecclesiastical Persons, Members of Colleges, Schoolmasters, Preachers, Serjeants at Law, Counsellors, Attornies, Solicitors, Advocates, Proctors, &c. are required to take the *Oaths of Allegiance*, *Supremacy* and *Abjuration*; and Persons either neglecting or refusing to take those Oaths, are declared to be incapable to execute their Offices or Imployments, to be disabled to sue in Law or Equity, to be Guardians, Executors, &c. or to receive any Legacy, &c. and likewise to be liable to forfeit 500 *l*.

Objurgatrices were anciently taken for scolding Women.

Oblata, denotes Gifts or Offerings anciently made to the King; and in the *Exchequer* it denotes old Debts brought together from Years precedent, and charged to the Sheriff.

Oblations, denote certain Offerings or Gifts to the Church, and being in the Nature of Tithes, are recoverable in the Ecclesiastical Courts.

Obligation, denotes a Bond, wherein is contained a certain Penalty, conditioned for Payment of Money, or Performance of some other Act; and the Difference between it and a Bill is, that the latter is generally without a Penalty or Condition, tho' it may be made with a Penalty, and then is called a Penal Bill; otherwise it is termed a single Bill. The Forms of *Obligations*, and Bills, you may see in *the Young Clerk's Magazine*, and other Treatises on Conveyancing.

Obligee, is the Person to whom a Bond or *Obligation* is made.

Obligor, is the Person that enters into a Bond or *Obligation*.

Obventions. See **Oblations**.

Occupant, denotes the Person that first seises, or gets Possession of a Thing.

Occupation, in a legal Sense, is taken for Use or Tenure; as in Deeds it is frequently said, that such Lands, &c. are, or lately were, in the Tenure or Occupation of such and such.

Occupavit, is a Writ which issues on Behalf of the Person that is ejected out of an Estate of Inheritance in Time of Peace.

Octave, denotes the eighth Day after any Feast.

Odio & Atia, was a Writ anciently in Use, and directed to the Sheriff, to make Inquiry whether a Person committed to Prison on Suspicion of Murder were justly committed, or for Malice only; upon which Inquisition, if it were found that he was not guilty, then there issued another Writ to the Sheriff to bail him. *Termes de la Ley*.

Offence, denotes some Act committed either against, or omitted where the Law requires such Act. *Offences* are divided into *Capital* and not *Capital*: *Capital*, are such Offences, for which the Offender is liable to suffer Death; and not *Capital*, is where the Offender is
liable

OF

liable to the Forfeiture of his Lands and Goods, be fined, or suffer any corporal Punishment that does not extend to the Loss of Life. *Capital Offences* are either those of High Treason, Petit Treason, or Felony: And in such as are not *capital*, are included all other *Pleas of the Crown*, which bear the Name of Misdemeanors.

Offerings, are deemed to be of the like Nature of personal Tithes by Custom payable to the Parson of the Parish.

Office, does denote that Function by Virtue of which a Person has some particular Imployment in another's Affairs. The Officers that are under the King, who is the Chief or Supream for the Government of the Kingdom, are the *Ecclesiastical*, such as are concerned in Church Affairs; *Civil*, concerning Matters of Justice, &c. *Military*, relating to the Army. The Judges that sit at *Westminster*, are distinguished by the Name of *Judicial Officers*, and those that act under them are called *Ministerial*: There are also *Magisterial* Officers, such as the *Magistrates* of a City or Corporation, Justices of the Peace, &c. Offices are grantable in Fee, Tail, for Years, or for Life.

Office found, is where Inquisition is made to the King's Use of any Thing by Virtue of the Office of the Person that inquireth it, and such Thing is found by the Inquisition; so to return an Office denotes that which is found by Virtue of the *Office*. *Plowden* tells us, that if an *Office* be wrongfully found, the Person grieved may be relieved by a Traverse, or *Monstrans de droit*, either by Pleading or Petition; every Office being in the Nature of a Declaration, whereto any may plead, confess, or deny. See **Inquisition**.

ON

Official, is a Term anciently used in the *Civil Law*, and denotes one that is an Attendant upon a Magistrate. In the *Canon Law* it is defined to be the Person to whom the Bishop does generally commit the Charge of his *Spiritual Jurisdiction*; and in every Diocese there is one of these Officers, called *Officialis Principalis*, who with us, is generally termed *Chancellor*: And where there happen to be more, they are termed by the *Canonists Officiales Foranei*, whom we stile *Commissaries*.

Officiariis non faciendis, seu amovendis, is a Writ anciently used, whereby Magistrates were required not to create such a one an *Officer*, or to discharge him from his Office, until Inquiry be made of his Manners, &c.

Oleron Laws, are certain Laws made in Relation to *maritime Affairs*, by *Richard* I. when he was at *Oleron*, an Island in the Bay of *Acquitain*, which belongs to *France*.

Onerando pro rata portionis, is a Writ that issues on Behalf of a Jointenant, or Tenant in common, who is distrained for more Rent than his Proportion of the Land comes to.

O. Ni. is a *Latin* Contraction used in the *Exchequer* by the Sheriff, when he makes up his Accounts for Issues, Amercements, and mean Profits, at which Time he marks upon his Head O. Ni. whereby is denoted, *Oneretur, nisi habeat sufficientem exonerationem*, let him be charged, unless he have a sufficient Discharge; whereupon he forthwith becomes the King's Debtor, and a *Debet* or Debt is set upon his Head.

Onus Episcopale, were certain customary Dues paid to the Diocesan Bishop.

Onus Probandi, the Burden of Proof, which is by several of our penal Statutes laid upon the Claimer of Goods seised by the Officers of the Customs, &c.

Operarii, anciently denoted such Tenants as had some small Portions of Lands, on Account of the Duty of performing some servile Labours for the Lord.

Operatio, is defined to be a single Day's Work performed by a Tenant to his Lord.

Opposer. See **Exchequer**.

Orando pro Rege & Regno, was a Writ anciently in Use before there was any fixed Collect in the Church for a sitting Parliament, when both Houses of Parliament were assembled; and upon a Petition to the King this Writ issued in order to have the Prayers of the Bishops and Clergy, for the Peace and good Government of the Kingdom, &c.

Ordeal, (from the *Saxons*) denotes as much as *Not guilty*, and an ancient Kind of Trial made Use of in Criminal Cases; as when the Defendant, being arraigned, pleaded *Not guilty*, he had it in his Choice whether to put himself upon God and the Country; that is to say, upon the Verdict of twelve Men, as now used, or upon God only, on which Account it was called the Judgment of God, it being presumed that God would deliver the Innocent. This Trial was two Ways; the one by Fire, and the other by Water: That by Fire was, if the Person was of free Estate, he was to walk barefooted and blindfold over nine Plowshares Firehot, and in Case he escaped unhurt, he was acquitted, otherwise was condemned. If the Party was of servile Condition, he was to be tried by Water, which was divers Ways. *Term: de la Ley*.

Orders, are of different Kinds, and made by different Courts; as of the Court of *Chancery*, the *King's Bench*, *Common Pleas*, &c. Orders in the *Chancery* are either made of Course, or upon Motion of the Complainant or Defendant in a Cause, or of some interested therein. They are pronounced in open Court, and drawn up by the Register from the Notes thereof taken by him. After a Person has been once personally served with an *Order*, he may for Disobedience thereto be committed. *Orders* of the *King's Bench*, &c. are certain Rules from Time to Time made by the Court in Causes there depending, which, after they are drawn up and entered by the Clerk of the Rules, become Orders of the Court, wherein no Notice is taken of the *Orders* made in any other Court, they being only bound to proceed according to their own Rules. The Court of *King's Bench* has a peculiar Jurisdiction or Authority to quash Orders made at the publick or private Sessions of the Peace, or when they see Cause. The Justices of the Peace at their Sessions, the one being of the *Quorum*, may alter or revoke their Orders, and also make new ones.

Ordinance, denotes some Law, Statute, or Decree.

Ordinary, is a Term used in the *Civil Law*, and there denotes any Judge that is authorised to take Cognisance of Causes in his own Right, and not by Deputation; but in the *Common Law* it is said to be the Bishop of the Diocese, who is the true *Ordinary* to certify Excommunications, Marriages, and

O V   O U

and other Ecclesiastical Acts within his Diocese, to the Judges of the Common Law; and at the Common Law it is taken for every Commissary or Official of the Bishop, or other Spiritual Judge, having Authority within his Jurisdiction. There is likewise a Person stiled the *Ordinary of Newgate*, who is the Attendant in *ordinary* upon the Malefactors condemned there to prepare them for Death.

Orgild, was anciently taken to denote, that there was no Satisfaction to be made for the Death of a Person killed.

Originalia, according to *Jacob*, denotes the Transcripts, *&c.* sent into the Treasurer's Remembrancer's Office in the *Exchequer*, out of the Court of *Chancery*, to distinguish them from *Recorda*, the Judgments and Pleadings in Causes tried before the *Barons*.

Orphan, denotes a Fatherless Child; and the *Lord Mayor* and *Aldermen* of the City of *London* have the Custody of *Orphans*, who are under Age, and unmarried, of deceased Freemen; and also the Keeping of their Lands and Goods; and when they commit the Custody of an *Orphan* to a Person, he may have the Writ of *Ravishment of Ward*, in Case the *Orphan* be taken from him, or the *Ravisher* may be imprisoned, until the *Orphan* is produced.

Ostensio, was taken for the Tribute anciently paid by Merchants for Leave to sell their Wares in Markets.

Overcited, was a Term formerly used to denote a Person convicted of a Crime, where the Thing was found upon him.

Overseers of the Poor, are publick Officers appointed by Statute in every Parish to provide for the Poor therein.

Overt, is the same as open, *&c.* an *Overt-Act* denotes an open Act which in Law must be clearly proved. See **Treason**.

Ousted, denotes to be put out; as a Person that is put of Possession is said to be ousted out of Possession.

Ouster le main, is a Writ formerly in Use, and was directed to the *Escheator*, to deliver Seisin out of the King's Hands to the Party who sues out the Writ, for that the Lands seised are not held of the King, or that he ought not to have the Wardship of them, *&c.* It is also taken to denote the Judgment given in a *Monstrans de droit*, or upon a Traverse or Petition: But all *Ouster le mains*, Wardship, *&c.* are now taken away. See 12 *Car.* 2. *c.* 24.

Ouster le mer, (from the *French*) denotes a Cause of Excuse shewn to a Court on a Defendant's not appearing on Summons, by alledging that he was beyond the Seas.

Outfangthef, is taken for the Privilege anciently used by the Lord, when a Felon was taken out of his Fee; in which Case he could cause him to be brought back to Judgment in his own Court.

Outhouses, are Cottages or the like that are adjoining to Dwelling-houses.

Outlaw, denotes one that is deprived of the Benefit of the Law, and on that Account deprived of the King's Protection. Where an original Writ, and the Writs of *Capias*, *Alias* and *Pluries* have gone out against a Person, and returned by the Sheriff *non est inventus*, and after Proclamation made for him to appear, *&c.* which he omitting, he then becomes *outlawed*: But formerly a Person could not be outlawed except in the Case of Felony, when any Person was

allowed

allowed to flay the *Outlaw*; but now that is altered; seeing that none except the Sheriff is allowed to put the Person outlawed for Felony to Death.

Outlawry, is where a Person is *outlawed*, and on that Account loses the Benefit of a Subject. The Effect of an *Outlawry* in personal Actions is this, *viz.* That the Person outlawed, not only forfeits the Benefit of the Law, but also is liable to the Forfeiture of his Goods and Chattels to the King. The Method taken in suing to *Outlawry*, you may see in *Practis. Solic.*

Out-Riders, are certain Bailiffs generally stiled *Bailiffi errant*, such as are imployed by Sheriffs to *ride* to the furthermost Parts of Counties or Hundreds, in order more speedily to summon People into the County Courts, &c.

Ovelty, denotes Equality, as in the Case of the *Lord Mesne* and Tenant who holds of the Mesne, as he holds of the superior Lord.

Owlers, properly denotes Persons that carry Wool, &c. to the Sea-side in the Night-time, in order to be shipped off contrary to the Laws in Being.

Oxfild, is by *Lambert* defined to be a Restitution made by a County, &c. for any Wrong done within the same.

Oxgang or **Oxgate**, is taken for fifteen Acres of Land, or as much Ground as a single Ox can plough in a Year.

Oyer, was anciently taken for what we call the Assises.

Oyer of a Deed, is where Action being brought on a Bond or other Deed, the Defendant appears and craves that he may *hear* the Deed on which the Action is brought, which the Defendant of Course is allowed, as also a Copy thereof if he requires it; and he is not obliged to plead without it; and if he does plead without it, he cannot afterwards wave the Plea, and demand *Oyer*. It is said, that if there is a *Misnomer* in a Bond, the Defendant must plead that *Misnomer* with a *Non est factum*, without craving *Oyer*; for if he does, it will be taken that his Name there is right. It is likewise said, that where Executors bring an Action on a Deed, the Defendant may crave *Oyer* of the Will. There is also *Oyer de Record*, which is where the Plaintiff or Defendant moves the Court, that they will take *Oyer*, or look upon a Record. See **Monstrans de faits**.

Oyer and Terminer, is a Writ or Commission in *Latin, audiendo & terminando*, of *Hearing* and *Determining*; and it is either *general* or *special*: *General*, when it is directed to the Judges of Assise, and other Gentlemen of the Counties where their Circuits extend, in general to try all Offenders and Offences: But *Special* is only for the trying of particular Persons or Offences; and it usually issues directed to certain Justices on any sudden Insurrection or Trespass committed, wherein a speedy Reformation is required.

Oyes, is a Corruption of the *French* Word *Oyez*, hear ye, and is frequently used by the Cryers in our Courts, in making Proclamation, crying Silence, &c.

P.

Pin fort & dure, denotes a particular Punishment on a Person, who being arraigned for Felony refuses to put himself upon the common Trial of God and his Country,

Country, but, instead thereof, stands mute; and this *Pain fort and dure*, is by the vulgar called *Pressing to Death*. The Judgment of this Penance of *Pain fort and dure*, according as it is usually practised is thus, *viz.* The Prisoner is remanded back to Prison, and inclosed in some low dark Room, and there laid flat on his Back, without any other Covering than what is necessary to hide his Nakedness; after which his Legs and Arms are extended with Cords to the four Quarters of the Room, at which Time there is laid on his Body as much Weight or more than he can bear: And all the Time he is to have no other Support but the worst of Bread and Water, and is not to drink the same Day that he eats, nor to eat the Day he drinks; and in this low Course he is to be continued till his Death. The Court is generally so tender, that before they pass Judgment in *Pain fort and dure*, they cause him to have some Taste of the Pain he has to undergo, provided he will not comply to plead.

Pains and Penalties, are Words mentioned in an Act passed in the Reign of King *George* I. for inflicting Pains and Penalties on the late Bishop of *Rochester*, &c. on Account of a Conspiracy charged against them, when they were by Parliament found guilty, for Want of that Evidence required in our Common Law Courts.

Pais, (*French*) with us is restricted to denote the Country; as *Trial per Pais* signifies Trial by the Country.

Palace Court, is a Court of Record held in *Southwark*, and is now generally known by the Name of the *Marshalsea*.

Panel, denotes a Schedule or small Roll of Parchment which contains the Names of the Jurors returned by the Sheriff to pass upon a Trial; so that the *Impanelling of a Jury* is no more than the Sheriff's entering into his *Panel* or Roll. See **Jury**.

Paper-Books, in our Law are the Issues upon special Pleadings, which are made up by the *Clerk of the Papers*.

Papists, are such as profess the Religion of the Church of *Rome*, and generally distinguish themselves by the Name of *Catholicks*, concerning whom several Statutes have been made in this Kingdom.

Par, is defined to be a Term in *Exchange*, when one to whom a Bill is payable recovers of the Acceptor equal in Value to what was paid to the Drawer.

Parage, in our Law is usually taken to signify the Equality of Land in a Partition between Coheirs.

Paragium, was anciently taken for equal Condition of Parties that were to be contracted in Marriage. *Jacob's Law Dict.*

Paramount, (from the *French*) is taken for the highest Lord of the Fee.

Paraphernalia, are such Moveables as the Widow, after her Husband's Death, challenges over and above her Dower or Jointure; as Furniture for her Chamber, necessary wearing Apparel, and Jewels suitable to her Rank and Quality, which are not to be deemed Chattels of the Husband, and therefore need not be included in the Inventory after the Husband's Decease, neither can the Husband by Will bequeath them.

Paravail, denotes the lowest Tenant of the Fee, *viz.* him that is Tenant to one who holds over of another. See *Fitz. Nat. Brev.* 135.

Parceners, are of two Kinds; the

one according to the Course of the Common Law; and the other according to Custom. Those according to the Common Law are, where a Person is seised of an Estate of Inheritance in Lands, &c. and dies without any Issue, except Daughters, in which Case the Lands, &c. descend to the Daughters as *Parceners*, and they are but as one Heir to their deceased Ancestor. Where a Person dies seised without any Issue, or Male Heirs to inherit, the Lands will descend to the Sisters as *Parceners*; and for Want of Sisters, they descend to the Aunts or other Females of Kin in equal Degree, who are also *Parceners*: And they are so called, because by the Writ *de partitione facienda*, they may be obliged to make *Partition* of the Lands descended, in case they will not by Consent make it. Where there is an only Daughter, she is termed Daughter and Heir, not *Parcener*. Men may likewise be *Parceners* as well as Women; as where a Person leaves two Daughters, and the eldest of them has Issue both Sons and Daughters, and the youngest Issue only Daughters; in this Case the eldest Son of the eldest Daughter may not only inherit, but also all the Daughters of the youngest, and in this Case the eldest Son becomes *Parcener* with those Daughters, and shall have his Mother's Part; whence it is obvious, that Men descending from Daughters may be *Parceners* as well as Women. *Parceners* by Custom are, where a Person dies seised in Fee or Tail of Lands of the Tenure of *Gavelkind* in *Kent*, &c. and leaves Issue several Sons; in such Case those Lands by Custom will descend to all the Sons as *Parceners*, who shall inherit equally, and be compellable to make *Partition*, as Daughters are. The Form of a *Deed of Partition* you may see in the *Young Clerk's Magazine*, and other Treatises on Conveyancing.

Parcenary, is taken for the Holding of Lands jointly by *Parceners*; that is to say, when the common Inheritance remains undivided.

Parco fracto, is a Writ that lies against the Person that breaks any Pound, and takes out from thence Beasts there lawfully impounded. *Termes de la Ley*. See likewise *Fitz. Nat. Brev.*

Pardon, in a legal Sense denotes the Forgiving an Offence committed against the King: And this Pardon may be granted before Attainder or Conviction, or afterwards. General *Pardons* are either by Act of Parliament or the King's Charter; but a particular one is at the Coronation of a Prince, or at any other particular Time, when the Offence is committed: And a general Pardon not only discharges the Punishment which the Offender was liable to be inflicted with, but also the Guilt of the Crime itself; and it is said, to *pardon* the Crime so fully, that the Offender in the Eye of the Law is deemed as spotless and innocent, as if he had never committed it. It is said, that he that would reap Benefit from a general *Pardon*, must plead whereby it is granted, in order that the Court may judge whether his Offence be included in the Statute or not: Neither can the King's Charter of Pardon under the Great Seal be allowed, unless the same be pleaded, and produced in Court. In what Cases on the Discovery of Accomplices, *Pardons* are allowed by Statute, you may see in 4 & 5 *W.* & *M.* and 11 *W.* 3. in Relation to the Counterfeiting the Coin, 6 & 7 *W.* 3. in Respect of Burglary, &c. 5 *Ann.*

for the preventing the Molestation of Officers of the Customs in the Execution of their Office, 6 Geo. 1. *for the Discovery of Smuglers.*

Parent, is taken for either a Father or Mother; tho' more generally that Name is applied to the Father. Parents both by the Law of Nature and the Law of God are bound to educate, maintain and defend their Children, over whom by those Laws they have Power; and they likewise have Interest in the Profits of their Children's Labour, during their Nonage, in Case the Children live with, and are provided for by them.

Parish, denotes the Limits or Circuit of Ground, wherein the People belonging to one Church inhabit.

Park, denotes a large Quantity of inclosed Ground, wherein by Prescription, or the King's Grant, a Subject preserves his Game of wild Beasts, in our Law termed *Feræ Naturæ*.

Parkbote, denotes a being quit of inclosing a *Park*, or any Part of it.

Parliament, according to *Cowel*, is derived from the *French* Verb, *Parler*, to speak; and the Word *Ment* or *Mens*, the Mind: And it is a solemn Conference of all the States of the Kingdom summoned together by the King's Authority alone, to treat of the weighty Affairs of the Kingdom; and it may well be called the greatest Assembly of the Nation, as it consists of the King, and the three States of the Kingdom, *viz.* the Lords Spiritual, the Lords Temporal, and the Commons, for the debating of Matters concerning the Commonwealth, more especially the Making and Altering of Laws.

Parliament de la Bonde, was a *Parliament* in King *Edward* the Second's Time, that went by that Name; to which the Barons came armed against the two *Spencers*, with coloured Bands upon their Sleeves, for Distinction Sake. *Dug. Bar. 2 Part.*

Parliamentum Diabolicum. In 38 *Hen.* 6. there was a Parliament so termed, which was held at *Coventry*, in which *Edward* Earl of *March* (afterwards King) and several of the chief Nobility were attainted. See *Holt. Chron.*

Parliamentum Indoctorum, was a Parliament held at *Coventry* in the 6 *Hen.* 4. and was so termed, because by a special Precept to the Sheriffs in their respective Counties, no Person skilled in the Law was to come thereto.

Parliamentum insanum. We are told, was a Parliament that was held at *Oxford* in the 41 *Hen.* 3. and got this Name from the extraordinary Proceedings of the Lords, who came with great Retinues of armed Men to it, when many Things were acted contrary to the King's Pleasure, and his Royal Prerogative. *Cowel.*

Parochial, within or belonging to a Parish; whilst *Extraparochial* denotes quite the Reverse.

Parol, (*French*) is used by *Kitchin* for a Plea in Court: And this Word is sometimes joined with the Word *Lease*; as *Lease Parol* denotes a Lease by Word of Mouth, in order to make a Distinction between it and a Lease in Writing.

Parol Arrest, denotes an Arrest by Word of Mouth authorised to be made; as in the Case of a Breach of the Peace committed in a Justice of Peace's Presence, who thereon verbally orders the Offender to be arrested or seised.

Parol Demurrer, is said to be a peculiar Privilege allowed an Infant that is sued in Relation to

Lands which descended to him; when the Court will give Judgment that the Suit shall remain or continue till the Infant arrives at full Age, *viz.* twenty-one Years.

Parricide, properly denotes the heinous and unnatural Crime of one that kills either his Father or Mother.

Parson, denotes the Rector of a Church, and is so called, on Account of his Office, he being, by Virtue thereof, bound in proper Person to serve God.

Parson Imparsonee, denotes one that is in Possession of a Church, whether it be Impropriate or Presentative.

Parsonage, which is likewise termed a Rectory, denotes a Parish Church that is endowed with a House, Glebe, Lands, Tithes, *&c.*

Partes finis nihil habuerunt, according to *Co.* 3 *Rep.* denotes an Exception taken against a Fine levied.

Parties, in a legal Sense denotes the Persons that are named in a Deed or Fine; that is to say, those that made the Deed, or levied the Fine; and also those to whom such Deed was made or levied: And here it is to be observed, that if an Indenture be made between two Parties in the Beginning of the Deed particularly mentioned; and in that Deed one of them grants to another that is not named in the Beginning thereof, such Person is no Party to the Deed, nor can take any Thing thereby.

Partition, denotes a Dividing of Lands, *&c.* descended by the Common Law or by Custom among *Coheirs* or *Parceners*, where there are two at least: And this *Partition* or *Dividing* is made four Ways, whereof three are by the Consent or Agreement of the Parties, and the fourth is by Compulsion. The first *Partition* by Agreement is, where they themselves divide the Land equally into as many Parts as there are Coparceners of them, and each to chuse a Part in Order; as the eldest first, and so one after another, according to the Age they are of. The second is, when they chuse certain of their Friends to make *Partition* for them. The Third is, by drawing Lots after the following Manner, *viz.* Having first divided the Land into as many Lots as there are *Parceners*, they write every Part severally in a distinct Scroll, when wrapping it up close, each of them are thrown into a Hat, Cap, Bason, or other like Thing, whereout each *Parcener*, one after another, according to their Seniority, draws one; and the Lands, *&c.* accordingly become severally allotted. The fourth *Partition*, or that which is by Compulsion, is where one or more of the *Parceners*, on account of the Refusal of some other of them, sues out a Writ of *Partitione facienda*, by Virtue whereof they shall be compelled to part or divide their Land. In *Kent* where Land is of the Nature of *Gavelkind*, they call their *Partition Shifting*, from the *Saxon* Word *Shiftan*, denoting to divide. *Cowel*. *Partition* may be also made by Joint-tenants, or Tenants in common by Assent, Deed, or Writ. See 31 *Hen.* 8. *c.* 1. and 32 *Hen.* 8. *c.* 2. See also **Parceners**.

Partitione facienda, is a Writ that lies for such as hold Lands or Tenements in *Parcenary*, and would sever to every one his Part, against those of the *Parceners* that refuse to join in *Partition*; as Coparceners, Tenants in *Gavelkind*, Joint-

Joint-tenants, or Tenants in Common. See **Parcenary**.

Party Jury. See **Medietas Linguæ**.

Paschal Rents, are yearly Tributes paid by the inferior Clergy to the Bishop or Archdeacon, at their *Easter* Visitation. *Cowel.*

Pascua. See **Pasture**.

Pasturage, denotes the Grasing or Feeding of Cattle.

Passage, is used for the Hire a Person pays for being transported or carried over Sea, or over a River.

Passagio, is a Writ directed to the Keepers of the Ports in *England*, commanding them to permit a Person who has the King's Licence to pass over Sea.

Passator, was anciently taken for the Lord to whom a Duty was paid for Passage over a River.

Passport, denotes a Licence granted by one that has Authority, for the safe Passage of a Person or Ship from one Place or Country to another.

Pasture, in general denotes any Place where Cattle may feed; and it differs from *Pascua* in this, *viz.* that *Pascua* denotes a Place set apart on Purpose for Cattle to feed on; and therefore may properly be taken to be a Meadow, or what is usually termed *Pasture Ground*.

Patentee, denotes the Person to whom the King's *Letters Patent* are granted.

Patents. See **Letters Patent**.

Patria, which properly signifies a Country, in our Law is taken for a *Neighbourhood*; as when we say *Inquiratur per Patriam*, we thereby mean a Jury of the *Neighbourhood*.

Patrimony, denotes an hereditary Estate, or such a Right as descends from Ancestors.

Patron, in our Law is he that has the Advowson of a Parsonage, Vicarage, Free Chapel, or the like Spiritual Promotion appertaining to his Manor, or otherwise in gross, and on that Account may, or ought to give the same Benefice, or present thereto, whenever it becomes void. And this being *Patron* had Beginning for the most part by one of these three Ways, *viz.* either by Reason of the Foundation, on Account that the *Patron*, or his Ancestors, or others under whom he claims were Founders or Builders of the Church; or by Reason of Donation, in that they endowed or gave Lands to the same for the Maintenance thereof; or otherwise on Account of the Ground, for that the Church was built on their Soil, and frequently on Account of all three. *Termes de la Ley.* See **Advowson**, as also **Presentation**.

Patinge, denotes Money anciently paid towards the *Paving* of Streets or Highways.

Pauper. See **Forma Pauperis**.

Pawn, denotes a Pledge or Gage lodged for the Security of Payment of Money borrowed. It has been held, that if Goods be pawned for Money, and afterwards Judgment is obtained against the Pawner for Debt, the Goods in the Pawner's Hands are not liable to be taken into Execution on such Judgment, until such Time as the Money lent be paid to the Pawnee; for this Reason, *viz.* that he has a qualified Property in the Goods whilst the Judgment Creditor has only an Interest. In Case Goods are *pawned* for Money lent, and no Day fixed for their Redemption, they are said to be redeemable at any Time during the *Pawner's* Life; and tho' they may not be redeemed

redeemed after the *Pawner's* Death, they may be redeemed after the Death of the *Pawnee*: Yet it is the general Practice of the Brokers, where no Day is fixed for Redemption, not to stay longer than a Year for their Money, at the Expiration of which Time they usually sell the Goods.

Peace, in a legal Sense, particularly denotes a quiet and inoffensive Behaviour towards the King and his People. Where any Person goes in Danger of Harm or some bodily Prejudice from another, on Oath made thereof before a Justice of the Peace or other Magistrate, he may be secured by good Bond or Recognizance, which is commonly called Binding to the Peace.

Peace of the King, denotes that *Peace* or Security both of Life and Goods, which the King promises to all his Subjects, or others taken into his Protection. There is likewise the *Peace of the King's Highway*, which is to be free from all Annoyance and Molestation; to which may be added the Peace of the Plough, by which both the Plough and Plough-Cattle are secured from Distresses: And Fairs also may be said to have their *Peace*, seeing that no Person may be troubled therein for any Debt contracted elsewhere.

Peculiar, denotes a particular Parish or Church that has Jurisdiction within itself for granting Probate of Wills, Administrations, exempt from the Ordinary or Bishop's Courts. The King's Chapel is termed a *Royal Peculiar*, and is exempt from all Spiritual Jurisdiction, being reserved to the Visitation and immediate Government of the King himself, who there is supreme Ordinary. There is likewise the Archbishop's *Peculiar*; for it is an ancient Privilege of the See of *Canterbury*, that wherever any Manors or Advowsons belong to it, they forthwith become exempt from the Ordinary, and on that Account are accounted Peculiars.

Pecuniary, is applied to the Punishment of Offences by Mulct or Fine.

Pedis abscissio, donotes the Cutting off a Foot, which we are told was a Punishment anciently inflicted on Criminals instead of Death.

Peerage, denotes a Duty imposed for the Maintenance of a Sea *Pier* or Fortress against the Sea: And it is likewise used for the Dignity of the Peers of the Realm.

Peers, are those that are impannelled on an Inquest upon a Person, for the Convicting or Acquitting him of any Offence that he is charged with: And the Reason the Jury is so called, is because the Course and Custom of this Nation is, that every Person shall be tried by his Equals or *Peers*, so termed from the *Latin* Word *Pares*: But this Word is more frequently used for those of the Nobility of the Realm, and Lords of Parliament; and the Reason they are called so is, that tho' there be a Distinction of Degrees in our Nobility, yet in publick Actions they are equal; as in their Votes of Parliament, and also in passing Trial upon any Nobleman, &c. *Cowel*. Tho' a Peer of the Realm is to be tried by his Peers on Indictment for Treason, Murder or Felony; yet it is said that in Appeal of Felony he shall be tried by Freeholders, by whom also Indictments of *Peers* for Treason or Felony are to be found, after which they defend themselves before the Lord High Steward. By Statute, all the Peers that have a Right to sit and vote in Parliament,

ment, are to be summoned at least twenty Days before the Trials of Peers in Criminal Matters. The Method of proceeding to the Trial of a Peer that is indicted of Treason or Felony is, after the Indictment is found, the King by Commission under the Great Seal, appoints some *Peer*, (generally the Lord Chancellor, or Lord Keeper, or Lord High Steward) who sits Judge in these Cases; and the whole Peers of the Realm are commanded to be attendant on him, as also the Lieutenant of the Tower, with the Prisoner, &c. In Order to bring the Indictment before the *Lord High Steward*, a *Certiorari* is issued out of the Court of *Chancery*; and likewise another Writ issues for bringing up the Prisoner, a Precept being made for that Purpose by the *Lord High Steward*, assigning a Day and Place for Trial, and for summoning the Peers, who are to be above twelve at least present. The Day of Trial being come, and the Lord High Steward seated in his usual State, after the Commission is read, and the usual Ceremonies are over, his Lordship declares to the Prisoner at the Bar, the Cause of their Assembly, assures him of Justice, and at the same Time incourages him to answer without Fear: Then the Indictment is read over, and the Prisoner arraigned; and after the Hearing of all the Evidence produced for the King, and the Prisoner's Answer, the Prisoner is commanded to withdraw from the Bar, when the Lords that are *Triers* go to some Place by themselves to consider of the Evidence; and afterwards being returned in order to give in their Verdict, the *Lord High Steward* openly demands of the *Triers* one by one, whether the Prisoner be guilty of the Crime whereof he is arraigned; and if he be found guilty by a Majority of Votes more than Twelve, then he is brought to the Bar again, at which Time the *Lord High Steward* acquaints the Prisoner with the Verdict of his *Peers*, and passes Sentence and Judgment accordingly.

Penal, is generally applied to such Statutes as carry some Punishment along with them, either *Pecuniary*, *Corporal*, or that of *Banishment*. Where any Thing is by Law prohibited under a certain pecuniary Penalty, if that *Penalty*, or Part of it be not mentioned to go to the Informer or Prosecutor, it does of Course belong to the King. There is also a Penalty in Bonds, which the Obligor forfeits on the Breach of the Condition of the Obligation; for if an *Obligee* brings an Action of Debt upon a Bond for Performance of Covenants, he shall recover the whole Penalty of the Bond; and the Defendant can have no Relief in this Case but by Bill in Equity, praying an Injunction to stop Proceedings at Common Law, which the Court of Equity usually grants, till a Hearing of the Cause; and after that they frequently continue the Injunction further, and order a Trial at Law on a *Quantum damnificatus*, for a Jury to find what Damage the Plaintiff received by Means of the Breach of Covenant; and after the Verdict is given at the Common Law, both the Plaintiff and Defendant are obliged to go back to the Court of Equity for the Decree of that Court: But on a bare Action of Covenant it is otherwise, for without suing for the *Penalty* of the Bond, the Business will be at an End in a much less Time,

Penance, is a particular Punishment injoined by the Ecclesiastical Laws; and it is imposed with an Intent that the Offender shall make Acknowledgment of the Offence, by standing in some publick Place, to satisfy the Church for the Scandal thereto given by an evil Example; more especially in the Cases of Adultery, Fornication, &c. for which we are told the usual Punishment is, that the Offender stands in the Church Barefoot and Bareheaded, in a White Sheet, &c. Yet it is said, that for smaller Offences the *Penance* may be performed in Court, or before the Minister and Churchwardens, &c. as in the Case of Defamation, &c. There is likewise a *Penance* at Common Law, for which see **Pain Fort and Dure**.

Pension, properly denotes an annual Payment of Money to a Person in Recompence of some Services done. By 12 W. 3. and other Statutes, Persons having Pensions under the Crown are declared incapable of being elected Members of Parliament: An excellent Law indeed, were it but duly observed: The yearly Payment of each Member of the House to the Inns of Court are likewise called Pensions: And that which in the two *Temples* is stiled a *Parliament*, and in *Lincoln's Inn* a *Council*, is in *Gray's Inn* termed a *Pension*.

Pensioners, or rather **Gentlemen Pensioners**, to distinguish them from the Name of *Court Pensioners*, are a Band of Gentlemen, who attend as a private Guard to the King's Person.

Pension-Writ, is the Name of a certain peremptory Order that issues out against such of the Members of the Inns of Court as are in Arrear for *Pensions*; which Writ being once issued, none that are thereby sued shall be discharged, or permitted to come into Commons until all the Duties are paid.

Pentecostals, were certain pious Oblations formerly paid to the Parish Priest, &c. at the Feast of *Pentecost*, and they were also called *Whitsun Farthings*.

Perambulation, denotes a Walking thro', about or over, as in the Case of *Surveying*, *Perambulating*, or *Walking* about the Forest, or its Limits, by Justices or others for that Purpose constituted, in order to mark down the Metes and Bounds thereof. There is also *Perambulation of Parishes* to be made by the Minister, Church-Wardens and Parishioners, by going round their Parishes once a Year, at or about the Time of *Ascension-Week*.

Perambulatione facienda, is a Writ that lies where two Lordships lie adjoining the one to the other, and some Encroachments have been made; then by the Assent of both the Lords, the Sheriff shall take with him the Parties and Neighbours, and make *Perambulation*, and settle the Bounds as they were before. But if a Lord incroach upon another, and he will not assent to make Perambulation, then the Lord that is thus grieved, shall have a Writ of *de Rationalibus Divisis* against the other. *Termes de la Ley*.

Perch, according to *Cromp. Jurisd.* is taken for a Rod or Pole of six Foot and a Half in Length, whereof Forty in Length, and four in Breadth make an Acre of Ground: But by the Customs of divers Places this Measure differs.

PE

Per cui & post. See *Entry*.

Personalis Utlagariæ, denotes a Pardon to a Person outlawed for Contempt in disobeying the King's Process, and who afterwards surrenders himself.

Peremptory, when joined with a Substantive, denotes a final and determinate Act, without the least Hope of renewing or altering the same; as there is a *peremptory Day, Action, Mandamus*, &c.

Perinde valere, is a Term of the *Ecclesiastical Law*, denoting a Dispensation granted to a Clerk, who being deficient in Capacity, is *de facto* admitted to a Benefice or other Ecclesiastical Function: And it derives its Name from the Words which make the Faculty as effectual to the Party dispensed with, as if he were really capable for which he is dispensed with at the Time of his Admission. *Cowel.*

Perjury, in our Law denotes a Crime committed, where a lawful Oath is administred by one in Authority to a Person in any judicial Proceeding, who, after being sworn, swears positively and falsely in a Matter material to the Issue or Cause in Question, either by their own wilful Act, or by the Subornation of others. In Order to make an Offence *Perjury*, it must appear to be wilful and deliberate, and the Oath direct and positive, not where a Person swears as he thinks or believes, &c. and it must be likewise false in express Words or Intention, otherwise it is no Perjury: And should one swear what he is ignorant of, it is a false Oath in him, even tho' he should swear the Truth; as where the Plaintiff, in a Case handed down to us, caused two Persons to swear to the Value of Goods which they never saw, notwithstanding they swore what was true, yet because they were ignorant of what they swore, it was deemed Perjury in them, for which both the Procurer and Witnesses were sentenced in the Star-Chamber.

Per my & per tout, are used where a Joint-tenant is said to be seised of the Lands that he holds jointly, *by every Parcel, and by the Whole*.

Permutatione Archidiaconatus & Ecclesiæ eidem annexæ cum Ecclesia & Prebenda, is a Writ directed to the Ordinary, whereby he is commanded to admit a Clerk to a Benefice, upon an *Exchange* made with another.

Pernancy, denotes a Taking or Receiving, and is peculiarly applied to Tithes taken in Kind, usually termed Tithes taken in *Pernancy*.

Pernor of Profits, (from the *French*, signifying a Taker or Receiver) is he who takes the Profits of Lands, &c. *Pernor of Profits*, and *Cestui que use*, are said to be all one.

Perpetuity, in our Law, is used where an Estate is intended so to be settled in Tail, &c. that it cannot possibly be undone or made void, a Thing our Law will not bear, and on that Account all Perpetuities are avoided.

Per quæ Servitia, is a judicial Writ, which goes out upon the Note of a Fine, and lies for the Conusee of a Manor, Lands, Rents, or other Services, to compel the Tenant at the Time of the Fine levied to attorn to him.

Perquisite, by *Bracton*, is used to denote any Thing got by a Person's own Industry, or that is purchased by his own Money, different from what descends to him from his Father or other Ancestor.

Per-

PE   PL

Perquisites of Court, denote those Profits and Advantages that accrue to a Manor by Casualty, over and above the certain yearly Income of the Lands; as Escheats, Heriots, Waifs, Estrays, &c.

Personable, denotes as much as that a Person is enabled to maintain a Plea in Court. *Personable* is also defined to be capable to be of a Capacity to take any Thing granted.

Personal, when joined with Goods or Chattels, denotes any moveable Thing belonging to a Person, whether quick or dead.

Personal Action, denotes any Action that a Person may have against another on Account of a Contract for Money or Goods; and it is such an Action whereby a Debt, Goods or Chattels are demandable, or Damages for them, or for Wrong done to a Man's Person.

Personal Tithes, are *Tithes* payable out of the Profits that come by the Labour of a Man's Person, as by Buying and Selling, Gains of Merchandise, Handicrafts, &c. *Cowel.*

Personalty, bears the like Signification of *Personal*; when we say the Action is brought in the Personalty, we mean it is brought against the right Person, *viz.* the Person against whom in Law it lies.

Petition, in general denotes a Supplication made by an Inferior to a Superior, especially to one having Jurisdiction, for any Grace or Favour.

Petit Larceny. See **Larceny.**

Petit Serjeanty, was an ancient Tenure, intirely laid aside since 12 *Car.* 2. *c.* 24.

Petit Treason. See **Treason.**

Petty-Fogger, is by *Cowel* defined to be a Wooer, Suitor or Solicitor, a Silly Advocate, a Petty Attorney or Lawyer, or rather a Trouble-Town, having neither Law nor Conscience.

Piepowder Court. See **Court of Piepowder.**

Pillory, is a certain Engine made of Wood, and is so well known, that it requires no further Definition.

Pipe. There is a *Roll* in the *Exchequer* called so, otherwise the *Great Roll.* It is likewise taken for a Measure of Wine or Oil, containining the Quantity of Half a Ton, *viz.* Sixscore and six Gallons. See 1 *Ric.* 3. *c.* 3.

Pirates, are taken for those that maintain themselves by Pillage and Robbing at Sea. *Pirates* may well be said to be Enemies to all; and on that Account neither Faith nor Oath is to be kept with them; so that they are denied Succour by the Laws of Nations. The Admiral by Patent has the Goods of Pirates granted to him, that is to say their own Goods, but not *Piratical Goods,* such as are taken from others; yet the King shall have *Piratical Goods,* where the Owner is not known.

Piscary, denotes the Liberty of Fishing in the Waters belonging to another Man.

Placard, with us denotes a Licence whereby a Person is permitted to use unlawful Games, or to shoot with a Gun. *Termes de la Ley.*

Placita, comprehends Pleas, Pleadings, Debates and Trials at Law.

Plaint, is taken for the Exhibiting of an Action, real or personal; and the Person that makes such *Plaint,* is stiled the *Plaintiff.*

Plaintiff. See **Plaint.**

Plea, denotes what either Party in a Court alledges in a Cause depending there: And *Plea,* or *Pleading,* in a more extensive Sense, comprehends all the Points or Matters that succeed or follow the

the Declaration, both on the Defendnt's and Plaintiff's Side, till Issue be joined; tho' a Plea is most commonly taken to be only the Defendant's Answer to the Plaintiff's Declaration. Pleas in general are divided into the *Pleas of the Crown*, and *Common Pleas*: Those of the *Crown* are all Suits in the King's Name, or in the Name of his Attorney General on his Behalf, for Offences committed against his Crown and Dignity, and also against the Peace; such as Treasons, Murder, Felony, &c. Those termed *Common Pleas*, are such Suits as are carried on between common Persons in Civil Cases. To an Action there is either a *General Plea* or a *Special Plea*. A *General Plea* enters into the Merits of the Cause or Action, being a *General Answer* to the Declaration; as in Debt on Contract, the *General Plea* is, *He owes nothing*; in Debt on Bond, *It is not his Deed*, or, *He paid it at the Day*: In Action upon a Promise, the *General Plea* is, *He hath not promised*; in Trespass, *Not Guilty*: And in Covenant, the *General Plea* is *Performance of Covenants*. A *Special Plea* contains the Matter at large, and concludes to the Declaration: And these *Special Pleas* are of different Kinds, as, *that such a Thing was forced or extorted from him by Duress and Threats*; and in *Justification* of an Assault and Battery, *that the Plaintiff struck first*. See more on the Head of Pleas in *Practis. Attorn.*

Pledges, are either real or formal Sureties which a Plaintiff finds to prosecute his Suit.

Pledges of Goods. See **Pawns**.

Pledgery or **Pleggery**, is taken for Suretiship, an Undertaking or Answering for.

Plegiis acquietandis, according to *Fitz.* is a Writ which lies for a Surety against him for whom he stands Surety, in Case he does not pay the Money at the Day.

Plena Forisfactura. See **Forfeiture**.

Plenarty, is when a Benefice is full, and is directly contrary to Vacation, which is when a Benefice is void. Institution is held to be a good *Plenarty* against a common Person, but not against the King, without Induction.

Plene administravit, *fully administred*, is a Plea usually pleaded by an *Executor* or *Administrator*, where they have faithfully administred the Estate and Effects of the Deceased before an Action is brought against them. On this Plea, if it be proved that the Executor or Administrator has Goods in his Hands of the Testator or Intestate, he may be allowed to give in Evidence that he has paid to the Value out of his own Money, and need not plead it specially; seeing that when an Executor, before the Action brought, has paid the Money in equal Degree with what is demanded by the Plaintiff, he may plead *Plene administravit* generally, and give the special Matter in Evidence.

Plevin. See **Replevin**.

Plurality. This Word is generally applied to Clergymen who have more Benefices than one; in which Case the first becomes *ipso facto* void, and the Patron on that Account may present to it, provided the Clerk be not qualified by Dispensation, &c. to hold more Livings than one; seeing that the Law strictly enjoins Residence, and it is impossible that the same Person can reside in two Places at one and

Q q the

the same Time. See **Ipso Facto.**

Pluries, is a Writ which issues after two former Writs have gone out without Effect; for first an original Writ called a *Capias* goes out; which not being obeyed, then goes out an *Alias*, which also failing, then the *Pluries* issues.

Policy of Assurance, is defined to be a certain Instrument entered into by Insurers of Ships, Merchandise, &c. whereby they are bound to pay the Sum *insured*, in case of Loss: It being a Course taken by Merchants, who adventure Wares or Merchandises to Sea, on which Account, unwilling to run the Risque of losing the whole Adventure, they give to some other Person a certain Rate or Proportion, as 10 *l. per Cent.* or the like, to secure the safe Arrival of the Ship and Cargo at a Place agreed on; so that, should it happen that the Ship and Cargo should miscarry, the Assurer is obliged to make good to the Adventurer so much as by the Policy he engaged himself to secure; but should the Ship arrive safe, in that Case the *Insurer* clearly gains what the Merchant compounds or agrees to pay him. The Reason this Instrument is called *Policy* is, that in Order to prevent any Difference that might chance to arise between the *Insurer* and the Merchant, there is a particular Officer or Clerk appointed to set down in Writing the Sum of their Agreement. See **Insurance.**

Poll-Money, was a Tax formerly imposed upon the Heads of Men, according to their several Ranks and Degrees: But of late Years there was a general *Twelve-penny Poll-Tax* imposed.

Polygamy, denotes the Crime of a Man's being married to two or more Wives at the same Time, or that of a Woman's having two or more Husbands together; which Crime is made Felony, except in Case of Absence for seven Years.

Pone, is a Writ whereby a Cause depending in the County, or other inferior Court, may be removed into the *Common Pleas*.

Ponendis in Assisis, is a Writ that is mentioned in *Reg. Orig.* and *Fitz. Nat. Brev.* and is founded on the Statute of *Westm.* 2. c. 38. whereby is shewn what Persons ought to be impanelled on *Assises* and *Juries*, and what not.

Pone per Vadium, is a Writ directed to the Sheriff, whereby he is commanded to take Surety of a Person for his Appearance at a Day assigned. See *Reg. Jud.*

Ponendum in Ballium, is a Writ directed to the Sheriff, commanding him to allow a Prisoner to be bailed, in Causes that are bailable.

Pontage, is sometimes taken for a Contribution made towards the Maintenance or Repairing of a Bridge; and it is sometimes taken for the Toll paid by the Passengers for that Purpose.

Pontibus reparandis, is a Writ whereby the Sheriff is commanded to charge one or more, to whom a Bridge belongs, to repair it.

Poor, in general, denotes any Person who is in so low and mean a State, as that he is, or may become burdensome to a Parish. Under this Word *Poor*, may be included those that are so by Impotency; as the Aged, the Blind, the Lame, the Fatherless and Motherless: Persons may likewise be poor, by labouring under Sickness, by being Ideots, Lunaticks, &c. all of which the Overseers of the Poor are to provide for. There is also another Kind of *Poor*, such

such as decayed House-keepers, or those that have been ruined by *Fire*, Water, Robbery, Losses in Trade, &c. all of whom being able, are to be set to Work, otherwise they are to be relieved by the Parish; and in the like Manner it is in Respect to poor Persons overcharged with Children, disabled Labourers, &c. And, *lastly*, we may add a *Thriftless*, and indeed *Worthless* Sort of Poor, who thro' their Prodigality and Debauchery have reduced themselves to such a State; as slothful, loose, and idle Persons, Pilferers, Vagabonds, Strumpets, &c. all of whom are liable to be sent to the *House of Correction*. How poor Prisoners are to be provided for, you may see under *Tit.* **Prisoners.**

Popery. See **Papists.**

Popish Recusants. See **Recusants.**

Popular Action, denotes an Action that is in general given to any one that will sue for a Penalty incurred by the Breach of some Penal Law: And these Actions must be commenced within one Year after the Breach committed; whereas, where the Penalty only goes to the King, two Years are allowed for commencing the Prosecution in.

Portgreve, anciently denoted the chief Magistrate in certain Sea-Coast Towns.

Portion, by *Cowel*, is defined to be that Allowance which a Vicar usually has out of a Rectory or Impropriation, whether the same be certain or not.

Portioner, is where a Parsonage is served by two or more Clergymen alternately, in which Case the Ministers are called *Portioners*, because they have only their Proportion of the Tithes, or other Profits of the Living.

Portmote or **Portmoot**, is said to denote a Court held in a Haven-Town.

Posse Comitatus, that is to say, *The Power of the County*, comprehends in it the Attendance and Assistance of all Knights, Gentlemen, Yeomen, Labourers, Servants, Apprentices, and others, above the Age of Fifteen, that are within the County, except *Ecclesiasticks*, and such as are decrepit, and unable to travel: And this *Posse Comitatus* is used where a Riot is committed, a Possession upon a *Forcible Entry* is kept, or any Force or Rescue made, either in Opposition to the Command of the King's Writ, or the Execution of Justice. It is the indispensable Duty of all Sheriffs to be aiding and assisting to Justices of the Peace in the suppressing of Riots, &c. and to raise the *Posse Comitatus* for that Purpose, who may take with them what Weapons are necessary to enable them to do it; and it is said they may justify the Beating, Wounding, and even Killing of such Rioters as shall resist, or not submit to surrender themselves: And the Persons who shall refuse to assist the Sheriffs or Justices herein, are liable both to Fine and Imprisonment.

Posse, tho' an Infinitive Mood, is in our Law used Substantively, and denotes a Possibility; as where we say such a Thing is *in posse*, is meant there is a *Possibility* of such a Thing, or it may possibly be. See **Posse Comitatus**, where this Word is likewise used substantively. See also **Esse.**

Possessio Fratris, is where a Man seised in Fee has Issue a Son and a Daugh-

Daughter by one Woman or *Venter*, and a Son by a second *Venter*, and dies; and the first Son, as Heir to his Father, enters, and likewise dies, without Issue, in this Case the Daughter may enter as Heir to her Brother; yet if the eldest Son dies, not having made an actual Entry and Seisin, the Son by the second Wife may enter as Heir to his Father, and shall enjoy the Estate, and not the Sister.

Possession, is either actual, or in Law. *Actual Possession*, is where a Person actually enters into Lands, &c. that are descended or conveyed to him. *Possession in Law*, is where Lands, &c. are descended to a Person, and he has not as yet actually entered into them: And the Reason this is called Possession in Law is, because in the Eye of the Law he is deemed to be in Possession. *Termes de la Ley*. Until an Office is found of Lands escheated to the Crown by Attainder, the King has only Possession in Law. A *long Possession* is much favoured by the Law, as an Argument of Right, even tho' no Deed can be shewn, and it is more favoured than an ancient Deed without Possession; for he that is out of Possession must make an undeniable Title; and in Case one would recover any Thing from another, it will not be sufficient to destroy the Title of the Person in Possession, without you can prove your own better than his. A Person barely by Lease and Release is in Possession, without making any Entry upon the Lands, &c. yet it is said that is not such a Possession as will intitle him to bring Trespass.

Possibility, is said to denote any Thing that is altogether uncertain, or what may or may not be; and in our Law it is taken to be either near or remote; a near *Possibility* is, where an Estate is limited to one after another's Decease; whilst a remote *Possibility* is, to suppose something that is never likely to come to pass; as to suppose a Man to be married to such a Woman, and she shall die, and afterwards he shall marry another, &c.

Post Diem, is a small Fee by Way of Penalty upon a Sheriff, which is paid to the *Custos Brevium*, for the Sheriff's Neglect in returning a Writ after the Day assigned.

Post Disseisin, is a Writ which lies for the Person that has recovered Lands, &c. by *Præcipe quod reddat*, but on Default or Reddition is again disseised by the former Disseisor.

Postea, is the Record of the Proceedings upon a Trial by Writ of *Nisi prius*, which after the Trial is returned by the Judge, before whom the Cause was tried, into the Court where the Suit commenced; in order to have Judgment there given upon the Verdict.

Posteriority, denotes the Coming after, or Being behind, and is a Word that is opposed to Priority; as where one holds Lands, &c. of two Lords, he is said to hold of his ancienter Lord by *Priority*, and of his latter by *Posteriority*.

Post-Fine, is a certain Duty payable to the King for a Fine formerly acknowledged in his Court; which is paid by the Cognisee after the Fine is fully passed: And the Rate of this *Post-Fine* is so much, and Half so much as was paid for the *Præ-Fine*, and is collected by the Sheriff of the County where the Land lies whereof the Fine was levied, to be accounted for by him in the *Exchequer*.

Posthumous, is in our Law applied to a Child, or Children born after the

Postbumous the Father's Death: And in Settlements *Posthumous* Children are enabled to take Estates in Remainder, as if born in their Father's Life-time, even tho' no Estate be limited to Trustees for that Purpose.

Postnati, is properly applied to such Persons as were born in *Scotland* after the Discent of the Crown of *England* to King *James* I. who by the Judges were solemnly adjudged not to be Aliens here: But the *Antenati*, those born there before that Time, were adjudged to be Aliens here.

Postnatus, denotes the second Son.

Postponed denotes any Thing that is set or put after another.

Post-Term or **Post-Terminum**, is a Return of a Writ, not only after the Day assigned for its Return, but after the Term also for which the *Custos Brevium* has a Fee of 20 d. paid him: And this Word is likewise used for the Fee taken.

Postulation, denotes a Request or Petition.

Pound, denotes a Place of Strength to keep Cattle in that are distrained, or put in for Trespass committed, until they be replevied or redeemed: And this is called a *Pound Overt*, that is to say, an open *Pound*, which is usually built on the Lord's Waste, and is provided by the Lord for himself and Tenants; and it is also called the Lord's or Common Pound, to which the Owner of the Cattle impounded may resort to give them Meat. There is likewise a *Pound Covert*, which is a close Place, to which the Owner cannot come to feed his Cattle, without giving Offence; such as a House, Castle, &c. There is this Difference between the Effects of a common *Pound*, an open *Pound*, and a close *Pound*, viz. Where Cattle are kept in a common *Pound*, no Notice is necessary to be given to the Owner to feed them; but, if put in any other open Place, Notice must be given; and if Cattle are impounded in a close *Pound*, as in the Distrainer's Barn, &c. the Distrainer is to feed them at his Peril. A common *Pound* is kept in every Township, Lordship, or Village; and indeed there ought to be the like in every Parish.

Pound Breach, is where a Distress being taken and afterwards impounded, the Owner breaks the *Pound* and takes away the Distress, which if he does, whether the Cause of Distress were just or not, the Party distraining may not only have his Action, but retake the Distress wherever he can find it. *Hawkins* tells us, that *Pound-Breaches*, as they are common Grievances, may be inquired of in the Sheriff's Turn.

Poundage, is a certain Subsidy of 12 d. *per* Pound, granted to the Crown, on all Goods either exported, or imported.

Pound in Money, with us consists of Twenty Shillings, or Two hundred and forty Pence.

Pour fair proclaimer, que null injett Fimes ou Ordures en Fosses ou Rivers pres Cities, &c. is a Writ that was anciently directed to the Mayor, Sheriff, or Bailiff of a City or Town, whereby they were commanded to make Proclamation that none cast Filth into the Ditches or Places adjacent, and if any is already cast, to remove it.

Pourpresture, denotes a wrongful Inclosing or Incroaching upon another Person's Property.

Pour seisir terres la feme que tient en Dower, was a Writ anciently in Use, by which the King

King seised the Land which the Wife of his deceased Tenant, who held *in Capite* had for her Dowry; and this was in Case she married again without the King's Licence.

Power, according to the general Acceptation of the Word with us, denotes some particular Authority granted by one Person to another to represent him, or act in his Stead: And this Word is sometimes taken for a Reservation frequently made in Conveyances, &c. for the Grantor to do certain Acts; as to make Leases, &c.

Power of the County. See **Posse Comitatus**.

Poyning's Law, is a certain Act of Parliament that was made in *Ireland*, in King *Henry* the Seventh's Time; and it was so called, because Sir *Edward Poyning* was Lieutenant there, when that Law was made, whereby all Statutes then in Force in *England* were made to be in Force in *Ireland*, which before were not, nor are there any now in Force there that were made in *England* since that Time.

Præcipe in Capite, was a Writ that formerly issued out of the Court in *Chancery*, on Behalf of a Tenant holding of the King in Chief, as of his Crown, and not of him as of any Honour, Castle or Manor.

Præcipe quod reddat, is according to *Cowel*, the Form of a Writ of Right that extends as well to a Writ of Right, as to other Writs of Entry or Possession.

Præfectus Villæ, denotes the Mayor, or other chief Magistrate of a Town.

Præ-Fine, is that Fine which is paid upon the Suing out of the Writ of Covenant. See **Post-Fine**.

Præmunire, is taken two Ways, either for a Writ so called, or for the Offence whereon the same is granted. We are told that the Church of *Rome* did formerly carry Things to that Height, in Respect to her Supremacy, that King *Edward* the Third, in the Twenty-seventh Year of his Reign, made a Statute against such Persons as drew his Subjects out of the Realm to answer and sue for Things belonging to the King's Court: There were several other Statutes afterwards made, to snub the growing Power of the Pope, but that which is most express, is that of 16 *Rich.* 2. *c.* 5. commonly known by the Name of the Statute of *Præmunire*, which ordains the Punishment of Offenders on that Statute to be this, *viz. That they be out of the King's Protection, forfeit their Lands and Goods, and be attached by their Bodies, &c.* And there are several late Statutes which render a Person liable to the Penalty of a *Præmunire*; as, by 1 *W.* & *M. c.* 8. Persons that refuse upon Tender to take the Oaths thereby appointed, are subject to the Penalty of a *Præmunire*; and also, by 7 & 8 *W.* 3. *c.* 24. Counsellors, Attornies, Solicitors, or other Practitioners in the Law, practising as such, not taking the Oaths, &c. are subject to the same Penalty: And so in divers other Cases, an Offender may be liable to a *Præmunire*.

Præpositus Ecclesiæ, is taken for a Church-Warden.

Præpositus Villæ, is sometimes taken for the Constable of a Town, but more frequently for a Head or Chief Officer of the King in a Town, Manor, or Village.

Pragmaticus. See **Petty-Fogger**.

Preamble.

Preamble, denotes to walk before, or precede; as the Beginning or Preceding Part of an Act is termed the *Preamble*, which is as it were a Key to open the Minds or Intent of the Makers of the Law, and the Mischiefs intended to be thereby remedied.

Prebend, denotes that Portion which every *Prebendary* receives in Right of his Place for his Maintenance.

Prebendary, is he that enjoys a *Prebend*. See **Prebend**.

Precedents, denote certain Examples that are founded on good Authorities, which are to be followed both in Judgments and Determinations in the Courts of Law, and likewise in all other judicial Proceedings.

Prece partium, is when the Suit is continued by the Prayer, Assent, or Agreement of both Parties.

Precept, is taken divers Ways, tho' generally it is taken for a Commandment in Writing issued out by a Justice of the Peace, &c. for the Bringing of a Person or Records before him: And it is sometimes taken for the Provocation, whereby one Person incites another to commit a Felony, as Theft, Murder, &c.

Precontract, properly denotes any *Contract* made before another is, but, in a legal Sense, is generally applied to Marriage-Contracts.

Predial Tithes, are such as are paid of Things arising and growing from the Ground only, as Corn, Hay, Fruit of Trees, &c.

Preemption, denotes the first Buying of a Thing; as it was formerly the Privilege of the King's Purveyor to have the first Buying of Corn and other Provisions for the King's House.

Prelate, is generally taken for an Archbishop or Bishop.

Premisses, properly denotes the Thing granted in a Deed. See **Deed**.

Premium, is generally used for that Sum the *Insured* gives the *Insurer* for insuring of a Ship and Cargo.

Prender, denotes the Power or Right of taking a Thing before it is offered.

Prender de Baron, in a literal Signification, denotes to take a Husband; but in our Law is used as an Exception, to disable the Widow from pursuing an Appeal of Murder against the Slayer of her former Husband.

Prepensed, denotes Forethought; as Malice *prepensed* signifies a Malice forethought, which makes the Killing of a Person Murder. See **Murder**.

Prerogative, in general is taken for that Authority and Privilege which the King, in Right of his Crown, has and claims over and above other Persons, and beyond the ordinary Course of the Common Law.

Prerogative Court, is the Court wherein all Wills are proved, and Administrations granted, which belong to the Archbishop by his Prerogative, that is to say, where the Deceased had Goods of any considerable Value out of the Diocese wherein he died; which Value is usually 5 l. and upwards: And if any Dispute do arise between two or more in Relation to any such Will or Administration, the Cause is properly to be debated and decided in this Court before the Judge of the same, who is stiled *Judex Curiæ*.

Prerogativa Cantuariensis, the Judge of the *Prerogative Court of Canterbury*. An Appeal lies from this Court to the King, who appoints the Court of Delegates, &c.

&c. The Archbishop of *York* has also a Court of the like Nature of that of *Canterbury*, which is termed his *Exchequer*.

Presbyterian, denotes a Sectarist or Dissenter from the Church of *England*.

Prescription, is defined to be a Title that is acquired by Use, and Time, and allowed by Law; or it is when for a Continuance of Time, *ultra memoriam hominis*, beyond the Memory of Man, a particular Person has a particular Right against another; as where one claims any Thing on Account that he and his Ancestors, or they whose Estate he enjoys, have Time out of Mind had or used such a particular Privilege, &c. There is a wide Difference between a *Prescription*, Custom and Usage; for Prescription has Respect to some certain Person, who by Intendment may have Continuance for ever; as for Example, where it is said he and all they whose Estate he has in such a Thing, this is a *Prescription*; and a *Prescription* belongs to one or two only, but Custom is common to all, it being local and always applied to a certain Place; as where it is alledged that Time out of Mind there has been such a Custom in such a Place: But now as to Usage, it differs from them both, for that respects either Persons or Places; as for the Inhabitants of a Town to have the Privilege of such a Way, &c. Besides Prescription and Custom are in the Right, whilst Usage is in Possession. A Person may make Title by *Prescription* to an Office, a Fair, Market, Toll, Way, Water, Rent, Common, Park, Warren, Franchise, Court-Leet, Waifs, Estrays, &c. yet nothing can be prescribed, which is not grantable at this Day.

There is likewise a *Prescription* against Actions and Statutes; as by 7 *Hen.* 8. *c.* 3. it is ordained, that after the Expiration of four Years after the Offences therein mentioned have been committed, no Suit can be commenced. By 31 *Eliz. c.* 1. all Actions, &c. brought upon Statutes, the Penalty whereof belongs to the King, shall be brought within two Years after the Offence is committed, or otherwise shall be void. And by 23 *Eliz. c.* 1. all Offences therein comprised, are determinable by Justices of the Peace and Assise within a Year and a Day after the Offence committed. Wherefore, whosoever offends against any of these Statutes, and escapes unquestioned for four Years, two, or one Year and a Day, such Offender may prescribe against the Actions and Punishments respectively ordained by these Statutes. And there are several other Statutes that contain the like Limitations of Time. See **Action**. *Prescription*, as to Tithes. See **Modus Decimandi**.

Presentation, is properly taken for the Act of a Patron offering his Clerk to the Bishop to be instituted in a Benefice of his Gift, the same being void. See **Advowson, Patron, Simony**, &c.

Presentee, is the Clerk presented to a Benefice by the Patron.

Presentment, is defined to be a meer Denunciation of the Jurors themselves, a Justice of the Peace, Constable, or other Officer, without any Information, of an Offence inquirable by the Court to which it is presented: Or it may be said to be an Information made by the Jury in a Court before a Judge who has Authority to punish any Offence committed contrary to Law: And it is what a Grand Jury

Jury finds and presents to the Court without any Bill of Indictment delivered; yet it is afterwards reduced into the Form of an Indictment. *Presentments* are also made in Courts-Leet and Courts-Baron, before the Stewards of the same; and they are likewise made by Constables, Church-Wardens, Surveyors of the Highways, &c. of Matters relating to their respective Offices.

Prest, is taken for a Duty in Money payable by the Sheriff, upon his Account in the Exchequer, or for Money left in his Hands.

Presumption, in a legal Sense denotes an Opinion or Belief of a Thing. It is of three Kinds; 1. *Violent Presumption*, which is frequently taken as a full Proof; as where a Person is found killed in a House, and a Man is seen to come out with a bloody Sword or Knife, and no other Person was at that Time in the House; this is a *violent Presumption*, and amounts to a Proof, that that Man was the Murderer. 2. *Probable Presumption*, which may be of some Weight but of small Effect. 3. *Light Presumption*, which amounts to no Proof at all. In Case of a Feoffment or other Deed, if all the Witnesses thereto be dead, the *violent Presumption*, which stands for a Proof, is continual and quiet Possession. Where Rent is in Arrear for twenty Years or upwards, and the Landlord gives a Receipt for the last Year's Rent due, in that Case it is in Law presumed that all the rest is paid: And in the like Manner it is, where a Defendant pleads Payment to a Bond, which Debt by the Bond appears to have been of a long Standing, and no Demand can be proved to have been made, nor Interest paid for many Years; it shall be presumed the Bond is paid, notwithstanding the Plaintiff has it in his Custody.

Pretender. See **Abjuration.**

Pretensed Right, is where a Person is in Possession of Lands or Tenements, and another that is not in Possession claims and sues for it, in which Case the *pretensed Right or Title* is said to be in him who claims and sues for the same.

Prevaricate, is taken for one that falsly and deceitfully seems to undertake a Thing, or who may be said to shuffle and cut.

Pridegabel, is the Name of a certain Tribute paid in the Lordship of *Redley*, in the County of *Gloucester*, to the Lord by certain Tenants, by Way of Acknowledgment for their Liberty and Privilege of Fishing in the River *Severn* for Lamprays or *Lamprids*.

Primage, is taken for a Duty at the Water-side, due to the Master and Mariners of a Ship; to the Master for the Use of his Ropes, &c. to discharge the Merchant's Goods; and to the Mariners for loading or Unloading of the Vessel, in any Port or Haven.

Primier Seisin, was formerly a Branch of the King's Royal Prerogative, by which he had the first Possession, *viz.* The intire Profits for a Year of all the Lands, &c. whereof his Tenant, who held of him *in Capite*, died seised in his Demesne as of Fee, his Heir then being at full Age: And this we are told the King formerly took, until his Heir, in Case he were of Age, did his Homage; and if under Age, until he were so: But *Primier Seisins* were intirely taken away by 12 *Car.* 2. c. 24.

Primogeniture, is the Title of an elder Brother, in Right of his Birth.

Prince, is sometimes at large taken for the King himself; but generally for the King's eldest Son, who is stiled the *Prince of Wales*.

Principal, has divers Significations in our Law; as an Heir-lome, the best Beast, best Bed, Table, &c. which in some Parts of *England* go to the eldest Child. This Word is also applied to the original Debt, or Sum lent on Bond, Mortgage, &c. to distinguish the same from Interest; as the *Principal* with Interest of a Bond, &c.

Principal and Accessary, denote certain Persons concerned in the committing of any Crime: The *Principal* is he that commits it; and the *Accessary* is he that is aiding or assisting in the Doing thereof; as where a Person does wilfully hold a Man in his Arms until another kills him, the Person so holding the Party slain is a *Principal*; so likewise if one be present, and move a Person to kill another, which he accordingly does, the Mover here is a *Principal*, as well as the other. See **Accessary**.

Priority, denotes an Antiquity of Tenure, in Comparison of another not so ancient. See **Posteriority**.

Prisage, is that Part or Share that belongs to the King or Admiral, of such Merchandises as are taken at Sea by Way of lawful *Prize*.

Prisage of Wines, is a Word almost gone into Disuse, it being now termed *Butlerage*, because the King's Butler receives the Custom which before was challenged by the Prince out of every Ship or Vessel laden with Wines, containing less than Forty Tons, two Tons of Wine; the one before, and the other behind the Mast, at his own Price, *viz.* generally 20 *s*. a Ton; but this varies according to the Custom of the Port or Place.

Prison, is a Place of Restraint for the safe Custody of a Person to answer any Action personal or criminal: And it is observed by *Co. Lit. lib.* 3. *c.* 7. that this *salva Custodia*, this safe Custody, must only be *Custodia*, a Custody, not *Pœna*, not a Punishment; for this Reason, *viz. Carcer ad homines custodiendos, non ad puniendos dari debet*, a Prison ought to be given to keep Men, not to punish them.

Prisoner, denotes a Person that is restrained of his Liberty upon any Action civil or criminal, or upon Commandment: And one may be a Prisoner upon Matter of *Record*, or Matter of *Fact*. Prisoner upon Matter of *Record* is he who being present in Court, is by the Court committed to Prison; and the other is he that is carried there upon an Arrest, whether it be by the Sheriff, Constable, or other Officer. It has been held that the Court of *King's Bench* has Authority to send for a Prisoner out of the *Marshalsea* Prison by Rule of Court, and need not issue a *Habeas Corpus*, that Prison belonging to the Court of *King's Bench*, which cannot send for a Prisoner out of any other Prison, without a Writ of *Habeas Corpus*. Prisoners in the *King's Bench* and *Fleet* Prisons, on mesne Process, &c. are actually to be confined within these Prisons, or the respective Rules of the same, till they are discharged. By 1 *Ann. c.* 6. *Prisoners* in the said Prisons, who shall go out of the same, may be taken upon an Escape Warrant; yet on a Day-Rule of Court, they may go out about their Business, provided they do not go into the Country,

4

PR

Country, or to Plays, or other Diversions, &c.

Privation, denotes a Bereaving or Taking away, and is most commonly applied to a Bishop or Rector of a Church, when by Death or other Act they are deprived of their Bishoprick or Benefice.

Privement enseint, according to *Wood*, is where a Woman is with Child by her Husband, but not quick with Child.

Privies, in general, are such as are Partakers, or are interested in any Action or Thing, or have any Relation to another. There are *Privies in Blood*, as the Heir to the Ancestor; *Privies in Representation*, such as the Executor to the Testator, or the Administrator to the Intestate; *Privies in Estate*, as Donor and Donee, Lessor and Lessee, &c. and *Privies in Deed*, or *in Law*, that is to say, where the Deed makes the Relation, or the Law implies it, in Case of Escheats to the Lord, &c. And here it is to be observed, that only Parties and *Privies* shall take Advantage of Conditions of Entry on Lands, &c.

Privilege, denotes a particular Law, whereby a private Person or Corporation is exempted from the Rigour of the Common Law; or it may be defined to be some peculiar Benefit granted to Persons contrary to the due Course of Law. Privileges are said to be either *Personal* or *Real*. A *Personal Privilege* is such as is extended to Members of Parliament, and of the Convocation, and their menial Servants, who are not to be arrested in the Time of Parliament or Convocation, nor for certain Days before or after. Peers, Ambassadors, and their Servants are likewise exempted from Arrests. A *Real Privilege*, is that which is granted to some particular Place; as to the King's Palaces, the Courts at *Westminster*, the Universities, &c. whereby, 1. It is to be observed, that no Person is to be arrested in or near the King's Court, unless by Leave from the Board of *Green Cloth*. 2. That the Officers of the Courts at *Westminster*, such as Attornies, &c. and also the Members and Officers of the Universities must be sued within their own Courts or Precincts, and in no other Court. And there are divers other Places, as the Counties Palatine, Cinque Ports, &c. that have Privileges as to Pleas, &c.

Privy Council, is held to be a most honourable Assembly of the King and *Privy Counsellors*, in the King's Court or Palace on Matters of State: The King himself sits here in Council, and appoints *Privy Counsellors* without either Patent or Grant, by setting them down on the List, and on Removal striking them out, both which he may do at Pleasure.

Privy Seal, is a *Seal* which the King useth to such Things as pass the Great Seal; for first all Grants, &c. pass the *Privy Signet*; then the *Privy Seal*; and lastly the *Great Seal*: And the Grants, &c. that pass the King's *Sign Manual*, are wrote out by the Clerks of the *Privy Signet* Office, which being transcribed and sealed with the Signet, is a Warrant to the *Privy Seal*, as the *Privy Seal* is a Warrant to the *Great Seal*. The *Privy Seal* is sometimes in Matters of less Consequence, which never pass the *Great Seal*; as to discharge a Recognizance, Debt, &c.

Probate, anciently signified to claim a Thing as one's own.

Probate of Testaments, denotes the Exhibiting and Proving of last Wills

PR

Wills and Testaments before the Ecclesiastical Judge, delegated by the Bishop, who is Ordinary of the Place where the Party dies: And if all the Goods and Chattels of the Deceased, as well as Debts owing to him were in the same Diocese, then the Bishop of the Diocese is intitled to the *Probate of the Testament*; but if such personal Estate or Effects were dispersed in different Dioceses, so that any Part thereof were out of the Diocese where the Party lived, so as to make *Bona notabilia*, in that Case the Archbishop of *Canterbury* or *York* becomes Ordinary to make the Probate by his Prerogative. This *Probate* may be made two Ways, either in common Form, or *per Testes*, by Witnesses. *The Proof in common Form* is only by the Oath of the Executor, or Party that exhibits the Will, who swears upon his Belief that the Will by him exhibited is the last Will and Testament of the Deceased. *The Proof per Testes* is, when over and above his own Oath, he produces Witnesses, or other Proof to confirm the same, and that in the Presence of such as may pretend any Interest in the Deceased's Goods, or at least in their Absence, after they have been duly summoned to see the Will proved, if they think proper: And the latter Course is most commonly followed, where there is Fear of Contention about the Effects of the Deceased; for some hold that a Will proved in common Form only, may be called in Question any Time within Thirty Years after. Where a Freehold in Lands or Tenements is devised by a last Will and Testament, it is now frequently proved by *Witnesses in Chancery*. Cowel.

PR

Probator, is taken for an *Accuser* or *Approver*, viz. one who undertakes to prove a Crime charged upon another.

Procedendo, is a Writ that lies whereby an Action is removed out of an inferior Court into a superior, such as the Court of *Chancery*, *King's Bench*, or *Common Pleas*, by Writ of Privilege, *Habeas Corpus*, or *Certiorari*; to remit or send back the Cause to the Court from whence the same was removed, in order to proceed upon it there, it not appearing to the superior Court that the Suggestion of the Party that removed the Cause is sufficiently made out. This Writ likewise goes out, where the Person that sues out a *Habeas Corpus*, &c. does not put in good Bail in Time, (where such is required,) and the inferior is thereby allowed to proceed, *non obstante* the *Habeas Corpus*, &c.

Procedendo ad judicium, is a Writ which lies where the Judges of a Court delay either the Plaintiff or Defendant, and will not give Judgment, where they ought to do it.

Process, is in general taken for all the Proceedings, in any Action real or personal, civil or criminal, from the Beginning to the End of the Cause: And sometimes that is only called a Process, by which a Person is called into a Court, it being the Beginning or principal Part of the Proceedings whereby the rest is directed.

Processum continuando, is a Writ that lies for the *Continuance* of a Process, after the Death of the Chief Justice or other Justices in the Commission of *Oyer and Terminer*.

Prochein Amy, in our Law denotes the Person that is the next
Friend

Friend, or next of Kin to a Child in his Non-age, and on that Account is by Law allowed to act for the Infant in the Management of his Affairs; as to be his Guardian, if he hold any Land in *Socage*, and for the Redress of any Wrong done him. Tho' *Prochein Amy* is usually taken for a Guardian in Socage, yet it is sometimes taken for the Person that appears in Court for an Infant who sues out any Action, and aids or assists the Infant in the Pursuit of his Action; for an Infant cannot make an Attorney to sue, but instead thereof the Court will admit the next Friend of the Infant Plaintiff to do it; as they will also appoint a Guardian to defend on Behalf of an Infant that is Defendant in a Cause.

Prochein Avoidance, denotes an Authority to present a Minister to a Church, when the same shall become vacant.

Proclamation, in general denotes a publick Notice given of any Thing, whereof the King thinks proper to advertise his Subjects.

Proclamation of Courts, is what is particularly used at the Beginning or Calling of a Court, as well as the Discharge or adjourning of it; both for the Attendance of Persons, and Dispatch of Business there: And in *Courts-Baron*, Proclamation is made for Persons to come in and claim Copyholds that are vacant, whereof any Tenants died seised since the last Court; after which is done, the Lord may seise the Copyhold, if the Heir does not come in to be admitted upon Proclamation, &c.

Proclamation of Exigents, is a Writ of Proclamation, which on the Awarding of an *Exigent* issues out, directed to the Sheriff of the County where the Party dwells, to make three Proclamations for the Defendant to yield himself up, or be outlawed.

Proclamation of a Fine, denotes a Proclamation that is solemnly made in the Court of *Common Pleas*, when a *Fine* of Land, &c. is passed; Transcripts of which are also sent to the Justices of *Assise*, and Justices of the Peace of the County where the Lands lie, to be openly proclaimed there.

Proclamation of Rebellion, is a Writ whereby a Person, who does not appear upon a *Subpœna*, or an *Attachment* of Contempt, in the Court of *Equity*, is reputed and declared a *Rebel*, in Case he do not surrender himself by a Day assigned. See **Commission of Rebellion**.

Pro confesso, according to *Termes de la Ley*, is where a Bill is exhibited in the Court of *Chancery*, to which the Defendant appears, and becomes in Contempt for not answering, or makes an insufficient Answer; in this Case the whole Matter contained in the Bill shall be taken as if it were confessed by the Defendant. It has been held, that if a Defendant be in Custody for Contempt in not answering the Complainant's Bill, in which Case by Order of the Court, a *Habeas Corpus* issues, to bring him to the Bar, at which Time the Court assigns him a Day to answer; which being expired, and no Answer put in, a second *Habeas Corpus* issues, at which Time the Party being brought into Court, a further Day is assigned; and if he does not answer by that Day, then upon the Plaintiff's Motion the Bill shall be taken *pro confesso*, and the Substance of the Bill decreed to the Complainant.

Proctor, denotes a Person that undertakes to manage another Person's son's Cause in any Court of the Civil or Ecclesiastical Law, for his Fee.

Proctors of the Clergy, are Persons elected and appointed to appear for Cathedrals or other collegiate Churches; as also for the common Clergy of every Diocese, to sit in the House of Convocation in the Time of Parliament. The Manner of their Election, according to *Cowel*, is this, viz. *First,* The King directs his Writ to the Archbishop of each Province, for the summoning of all Bishops, Deans, Archdeacons, Cathedral and Collegiate Churches, and generally of all the Clergy of his Province, assigning them the Time and Place in the Writ; upon the Receipt of which the Archbishops proceed according to Custom; one Example whereof may serve for both: The Archbishop of *Canterbury* directs his Letters to the Bishop of *London,* as his Dean Provincial, first peremptorily citing himself, and then willing him in like Manner to cite all the Bishops, Deans, Archdeacons, Cathedral and Collegiate Churches, and in general all the Clergy of his Province to the Place, and against the Day assigned in the Writ; and withal directeth, that one Proctor be sent for every Cathedral or Collegiate Church, and two for the Body of the inferior Clergy of each Diocese: And by Virtue of these Letters authentically sealed, directs his like Letters severally to the Bishop of every Diocese of the Province, citing them in like Manner, and willing them not only to appear, but to admonish the said Deans and Archdeacons personally to appear, and the Cathedral and Collegiate Churches, and also the common Clergy of the Diocese to send their Proctors to the Place at the Day appointed; and also willeth them to certify to the Archbishop the Names of all and every the Persons so warned by them, in a Schedule annexed to their Letter certificatory. The Bishops proceed accordingly, and the Cathedral and Collegiate Churches, and likewise the Clergy make Choice of their Proctors; which being done, and certified to the Bishop, he returneth all at the Day.

Procurations, are certain Sums of Money which Parish-Priests pay annually to the Bishop or Archdeacon, on Account of *Visitation.*

Procurator, denotes a Person who has a Charge committed to him by another; as the Proxies of our Lords in Parliament are called *Procuratores, Procurators*: And this Word is said likewise to signify a Vicar or Lieutenant, who acts in the Place of another. There are also *Procuratores Cleri,* who are sent to the *Convocation;* and the Bishops are sometimes stiled *Procuratores Ecclesiarum.* And from this Word comes that of *Proctor;* and it is likewise used to denote the Person that gathers the Fruit of a Benefice for another Man.

Procuratores Ecclesiæ Parochialis, anciently denoted the Church-Wardens, who were to act as Proxies and Representatives of the Church.

Procuratorium, the Procuratory, was the Instrument whereby any Person or Community did delegate their Proctor or Proctors, to represent them in any judicial Court or Cause. *Cowel.*

Prodes Homines, is a Title frequently given in our old Books to the *Barons,* or other Military Tenants, who were called to the *King's* Council, and were no more than *Discreti & fideles homines,* who were to give their Counsel and Advice,

vice according to the best of their Skill and Knowledge.

Profaneness, denotes a disrespectful Regard shewn to the Name of God and his Laws; and Offences of this Kind are punishable by several Statutes.

Profer, (from the *French*) denotes the Time appointed for the Accounts of Sheriffs, and other Officers in the *Exchequer*, which is twice a Year.

Profert in Curia, is where the Plaintiff declares upon a Deed, or the Defendant pleads one; in either Case he must do it with a *Profert in Curia*, in order that the other Party may at his own Charges have a Copy thereof, until which Time he is not obliged to answer it: And in Case a Person plead an Indenture that is lost, on Affidavit thereof made, the Court will compel the other Party to produce his Part of the Indenture. If a Deed is pleaded and shewn in Court, the Deed in Judgment of the Law remains all the whole Term in which it is shewn; and where it is not denied, then at the End of the Term it is delivered to the Owner of it; but if it be denied it shall still remain in Court, in order that if it be found *Non est Factum*, it may be destroyed.

Prohibition, is a Writ which issues out of the *Chancery, King's Bench*, or *Common Pleas*, to *prohibit* or hinder the Ecclesiastical Court, Admiralty Court, &c. to proceed in a Cause depending there, upon a Suggestion, that the Cognisance thereof does not belong to those Courts, but to the Common Law Courts. It also lies for prohibiting a Judge of a Temporal Court from proceeding in any Cause that is not within the Jurisdiction of the Court. The Courts at *Westminster*, upon being informed by either Plaintiff or Defendant, or by a Stranger, that any Court, either Spiritual or Temporal, do hold Plea, in Cases where they have no Jurisdiction, may award a *Prohibition*, and thereby prohibit such Court, either before or after Judgment. This Writ is directed both to the Judge and the Party; and if either the Judge or he proceed notwithstanding the *Prohibition*, an Attachment or Action upon the Case lies against them: And this Writ is looked upon to be a proper Remedy in general, where an inferior Court exceeds its Jurisdiction. A Prohibition will lie in all Causes, wherein a *Habeas Corpus* lies, tho' it is most usually granted to the Spiritual Courts, when properly the Cause belongs to the Temporal Jurisdiction. After a Defendant has admitted the Jurisdiction of an inferiour Court, by pleading to the Action, he cannot have a Prohibition. Tho' a Prohibition may be granted to a spiritual Court, after Sentence given in that Court, yet the Court above, on being applied to will not grant it, until they have heard Counsel on both Sides; but before Sentence they will grant it upon a bare Suggestion of the Party, where the Matter will bear it; for that a Sentence of a Spiritual Court, is of the Nature of a Judgment at the Common Law, and it is presumed to have been given upon mature Deliberation. A Prohibition also lies, where a Person is sued in the County Court for a Debt of 40 s. or above.

Prohibitio de vasto directa parti, is a judicial Writ directed to the Tenant, prohibiting him from committing Waste upon the Land in Controversy, during the Continuance of the Suit.

Pro indiviso, is, in a legal Sense, taken for a Possession of Lands, &c. belonging to two or more, whereof none of them know their several Portion; as Parceners before Partition. See **Parceners**.

Proles, *Progeny*, are properly the Issue that proceed from a lawful Marriage; tho', largely taken, it may denote the Issue of an unlawful Bed.

Prolocutor of the Convocation, is an Officer elected by Ecclesiastical Persons publickly assembled in the *Convocation* by Virtue of the King's Writ, at the Time of Parliament. There are two of these *Prolocutors*, one of the higher House of *Convocation*, and the other of the lower. The *Prolocutor* of the lower House, immediately upon their first Assembly, being by the Motion of the Bishops chosen by the Members of the lower House, is presented to the Bishops for *Prolocutor*, that is to say, the Person by whom they intend to deliver their Resolutions to the higher House, and to have their own House especially ordered and governed: And his Office is to cause the Clerk to call the Names of such as are of that House, as he sees Cause, to read all Things propounded, gather Suffrages, &c.

Promise, is when upon any valuable Consideration one binds himself by Word of Mouth to another to perform a Thing agreed on: And upon such a Promise Action will lie for Breach; which it will not do, if the Promise be without Consideration, that being termed *Nudum Pactum*, a naked Bargain, from whence no Action can arise. It is held that where a verbal Promise is made to do a Thing, and there is no Breach thereof, the same may be discharged by Parol, or by Word of Mouth; but if Breach be once made, that cannot be discharged without some Receipt or Release, the Promise then being become a Debt.

Promoters, are taken to be such as in Popular and Penal Actions prosecute Offenders in their own Name and the King's; as Informers do, who have Part of the Forfeitures or Penalties for their Reward. These *Promoters* or Informers did formerly belong to the *Exchequer* and *King's Bench*; but of late we find they have chiefly lifted themselves under the Excise Banner; and are, as Sir *Edward Coke* very justly calls them, *Turbidum hominum genus*, the very Scum of Mankind.

Promulge, is generally applied to the Publication of a Law to the People; as to promulge a Law, denotes to publish or proclaim it; and so *Promulged* signifies published or proclaimed.

Pronotary. See **Prothonotary**.

Proof, denotes the Making of a Fact appear by Witnesses: And Proof is twofold, *viz. viva voce*, by living Witnesses; and *Probatio Mortua*, a dead Proof, such as that of Records, Deeds, or other Writings. It has been the Opinion of some, that the Law takes no Notice of any other Proof than that before a Jury, in a judicial Way, and that which is on Record.

Pro partibus liberandis, is a Writ for the Partition of Lands between Co-heirs. See **Partition**.

Property, is said to be the highest Right a Person either has, or can have to any Thing; seeing that it used to denote that Right which one has to Lands or Tenements, Goods or Chattels, in no Respect depending upon another's Courtesy: And this *Cowel* observes no Man can

can be said to have in Lands or Tenements, but only the King in Right of his Crown; for that all the Lands throughout the whole Realm are in the Nature of Fee, they being held either mediately or immediately of the Crown. However this Word is used for that Right in Lands or Tenements, which common Persons have therein. *Property* in Lands or Tenements are acquired either by Entry, Discent, by Law, or by Conveyance; but in Goods and Chattels, Property may be gained divers Ways; tho' usually by *Deed of Gift*, or Bargain and Sale. There is an absolute Property, which is where the Proprietor has an absolute Power vested in himself to dispose of his Estate as he pleases, subject only to the Laws of the Land; as also a qualified Property, as in the Case of Husband and Wife, wherein the Husband has only a qualified Property in the Wife's Lands, real Chattels, &c. but in her Personal Chattels he has an absolute *Property*. It has been held that he that has the Land which lies on both Sides of a Highway, has the Property of the Soil of the Highway in himself, notwithstanding the King has the Privilege for his People to pass thro' it at their Pleasures. Where a Person borrows or finds another Man's Goods, or should one even take them from another, none of these Acts will alter the Property: But should a Person take Corn from another, and convert it into Malt; or turn Timber into a House, &c. in both these Cases the Property is altered.

Prophecies, are taken for Foretellings of Things to come in ambiguous Speeches; which anciently occasioned great Commotions in this Kingdom.

Propounders. See **Monopolists.**

Proprietary, was formerly chiefly applied to him that had the Fruits of a Benefice to himself, and his Heirs or Successors.

Pro rata, is as much as to say in Proportion, as Joint-Tenants are to pay *pro rata*; in Proportion to their Estates.

Prorogue, denotes to prolong or put off to another Day; as the *Prorogation* of the Parliament, which anciently used to be confounded with the *Adjournment* of the Parliament; but of late a Distinction has been made between those Terms, a *Prorogation* making a Session, and an *Adjournment* only a Continuance.

Prosecutor, is he that follows a Cause in another's Name. See **Indictment, Information, Promoters.**

Protection, is used both in a general Signification and a special one. In the general it is taken for that Benefit and Safety which every Subject has secured to him by the King's Laws. In a special Signification, it is taken for an Exemption given by the King to a Person against Suits at Law for a certain Time, upon some reasonable Cause moving the King to grant such Immunity; and this is a Branch of the King's Royal Prerogative. Peers and Members of Parliament by their Privilege are protected from Arrests; and by Virtue of that Privilege they may protect their *Menial Servants*, and those that are actually imployed by them in their Service; but by a late Order this does not extend to others, on written Protections, which formerly were made too great a Handle of, to the Damage of many Creditors.

Protest. This Word is applied two different Ways; the one by Way of Caution, to call a Witness, as it were openly to affirm, that a Person does either in no Respect, or but conditionally, yield his Consent to any Act, that he may apprehend prejudicial to him, or unto the Proceeding of a Judge in a Court, in a Cause wherein his Jurisdiction is doubtful, &c. The other is by Way of Complaint to protest a Man's *Bill of Exchange*, on a refused Acceptance or Payment; which is absolutely necessary in order to recover Damages.

Protestando, is a certain Form of Pleading, where one will not directly affirm, nor deny any Thing that is alledged by another, or which he himself alledges: And it is two Ways, the one is when he pleads any Thing which he dare not directly affirm, or cannot plead for Fear of making his Plea double; as in conveying a Title to himself to any Land, he ought to plead divers Discents by different Persons, but dares not affirm that they were all seised at the Time of their Death, altho' he could do it, it would be a double Plea to plead two Discents; each of which by itself may be a good Bar: In this Case the Defendant ought to plead and alledge the Matter, intermingling this Word *Protestando*, as to say such a one died (*by Protestation*) seised, &c. And another Kind of *Protestation* is when one is to answer to two Matters, and yet by the Law he ought only to plead to one, in which Case, in the first Part of the Plea he shall say, *Protestando, That such a Matter is not true*, and then add to his Plea, *pro placito dicit*, for Plea faith, by which Means he may take Issue upon the other Part of the Matter.

Prothonotary, is a Chief Officer of the *King's Bench*, or *Common Pleas*, the first of which has only one of those Officers, and the other three. The Duty of those of the *Common Pleas* is to inroll all Declarations, Pleadings, Assises, Judgments and Actions, and also to make out all judicial Writs, except Writs of *Habeas Corpus* and *Distringas Juratores*, for which there is a particular Office, called the *Habeas Corpora Office*. The *Prothonotary* of the *King's Bench* records all civil Actions, in the like Manner as the *Clerk of the Crown Office* does all criminal Causes in that Court.

Proto-forestarius, was formerly taken for the Person whom our ancient Kings made Chief of *Windsor Forest*, whose Office was to hear all Causes, &c. he being a Kind of Lord Chief Justice in Eyre.

Province, is generally taken for the Circuit of an Archbishop's Jurisdiction; such as the *Province of Canterbury*, and that of *York*.

Provincial, denotes to be of or belonging to a Province.

Provision, is properly applied to the *Providing* of a Bishop, or any other Ecclesiastical Person with a Living by the *Pope* before the Incumbent is dead.

Proviso, in general, denotes a Condition inserted in a Deed, on the Performance of which the Validity of the whole Deed depends; yet it sometimes only amounts to a bare Covenant. A *Proviso* generally comes immediately next after the *Habendum* in a Deed. *Proviso* is likewise used in judicial Matters; as where a Plaintiff in an Action delays bringing his Suit to Trial in due Time; in which Case the Defendant may take out a *Venire facias* to the Sheriff, having in it these Words, *viz. Proviso quod*, &c. to the Intent, that if the Plaintiff take out any Writ to that Purpose the Sheriff shall summon only one Jury

Jury upon them both: And this is termed going to Trial by *Proviso*.

Probisor Victualium, was formerly taken for the King's Purveyor, he that provided for the Acccommodations of his Court. *Cowel*.

Provost Marshal, with us denotes an Officer of the Royal Navy, who has the Charge of the Prisoners taken at Sea: And this Word is said sometimes to be used for the like Purpose at Land.

Proxies, are Persons appointed in the Place of others, to represent them; as every Peer of the Land called to Parliament have the Privilege of constituting a *Proxy* to vote for him in his Absence. This Word is likewise taken for certain yearly Payments made by Parochial Clergy to the Bishop, &c. on Visitations.

Publication, in our Law is generally applied to Depositions of Witnesses in a Cause in *Chancery*, in Order to a Hearing thereof; for which End Rules may be given to pass Publication, whereby Authority is given to shew the Depositions openly, and to grant Copies of the same.

Publication of a Will, denotes a certain Solemnity requisite to the Making thereof, *viz.* That the Testator, in the Presence of two Witnesses at the least, do declare it to be his last Will and Testament.

Publick Faith, is by *Cowel* defined to be a certain rebellious Cheat to get Money from the seduced People, upon what they called the *Publick Faith* of the Nation, in Order to raise a Rebellion against King *Charles* the First, about the Year 1642.

Puis Darrein Continuance, denotes some new Matter that is pleaded, pending an Action, after the last Continuance.

Puisne, denotes younger, or born after. See **Mulier**.

Pulsator, signifies a Plaintiff or Actor; and the Verb *Pulsare*, denotes to accuse any one.

Punishment, denotes that Penalty which a Person incurs on the Breach or Transgression of any Law.

Pur auter Vie, is taken for Lands, &c. that are held for another's Life.

Purchase, denotes the Buying or Acquiring of Lands, &c. with Money, by Deed or Agreement; but not by Discent, or Right of Inheritance. A *joint Purchase* is where two or more Persons join together in a Purchase. Where a Person comes into Lands, &c. by Gift, Will, or any other legal Way, except it be by Discent as Heir at Law, that is a *Purchase*. All reasonable Creatures may purchase; and yet, tho' some have Capacity to purchase, they have not to hold; as Aliens, Felons, &c. Again, some have Capacity to hold or not to hold upon a *Purchase*, at their Election, as Infants, Feme Coverts, &c.

Purgation, signifies the Clearing a Person's Self of a Crime of which he is suspected and charged before a Judge; which formerly was much in Use in *England*: Purgation is either *Canonical* or *Vulgar*: Canonical Purgation is prescribed by the Canon Law, the Form of which is usually thus in the Spiritual Court, *viz.* The suspected Person takes his Oath, that he is innocent of the Crime he is accused of; and at the same Time brings some of his honest Neighbours to make Oath, that they believe he swears truly. Vulgar Purgation was anciently by Fire or Water, or else by Combat; and was practised both by Infidels and Christians, till the same was abolished by the Canon Law: But it is said, that *Purgation by Combat* may be still practised by our Laws in Causes which are doubtful; as where there is Want of Evidence, or other Proof, if the Defendant chuse the *Combat* rather than the other Trial.

Purgire Mulierem, denotes to defile a Woman. *Cowel.*

Purificatio beatæ Mariæ Virginis, is one of the Returns for Writs in *Hilary* Term, which is on the second Day of *February*, generally called *Candlemas Day*.

Purlieu, denotes all that Ground near any Forest, which being made Forest by *Henry* the Second, *Richard* the First, or King *John*, was, by Perambulations granted by *Henry* the Third, severed again from the same, and became Purlieu, that is to say, pure and free from the Laws of the Forest. See *Manwood*. A Person that has Ground within the *Purlieu*, and is able to expend Forty Shillings by the Year of Freehold, is on these two Accounts licensed to hunt in his own *Purlieu*, and is therefore stiled a *Purlieu Man*.

Purpars or **Purparty**, is taken for that Share of an Estate, that was first held in Common by Parceners, which afterwards by Partition is allotted to any of them.

Purpresture, denotes to take from another, and to appropriate to one's Self: And in a general Sense it is taken for any such Wrong acted by one Person to another. *Purpresture* in a Forest denotes any Incroachment in the King's Forest, whether it be by Building, Inclosing, or using of any Liberty without a legal Warrant for so doing. *Termes de la Ley.*

Purprisum, denotes a Close or Inclosure, also the whole Compass of a Manor. *Cowel.*

Purveyance, is properly applied to the Providing of Corn, Fuel, Victuals, &c. for the King's House, and *Purveyor* is the Officer appointed for providing the same.

Purview, (from the *French*, signifying a Patent or Grant) is often used by Sir *Edw. Coke* for that Part of an Act of Parliament which begins with *Be it enacted*, &c.

Putagium, or **Putage**, denotes a Female's Committing of Fornication, a Crime that was anciently so odious, that if a Female Heir under Guardianship were guilty of it, she forfeited her Part as Parcener, to the other Coheirs; and if she were a sole Heiress, she forfeited her Lands, &c. to the Lord of the Fee as an Escheat.

Putatibus, or **Putative**, is the same with reputed or generally esteemed; as the *Putative* Father of a Child, that is to say, the reputed Father of one.

Putura, denotes a certain Custom claimed by Keepers in Forests, and sometimes by Bailiffs of Hundreds, to take Man's Meat, Horse Meat, and Dog's Meat, of the Tenants *gratis*, within the Perambulation of the Forest, or Liberty of the Hundred.

Q.

Quadrantata Terræ, denotes the fourth Part of an Acre of Land.

Quadrugata Terræ, otherwise termed a *Team-Land*, is so much Ground as can be tilled with four Horses.

Quæ Servitia. See *Per quæ Servitia*.

Quæ est eadem, are Words used in Pleading, to supply a Traverse; as where a Defendant justifies a Trespass or an Assault, at another Day, or Place, than is specified in the Declaration, he ought to say, *Quæ est eadem Transgressio, &c.* which is the same Trespass, &c. But if he justifies, by saying at the same Time and Place the Plaintiff assaulted him, and that what Damages happened to him were of his own Wrong, this is sufficient, without saying *Quæ est eadem, &c.*

Quæ plura, is a Writ that formerly lay where an Inquisition had been taken by an Escheator, of such Lands, &c. whereof a Person died seised, where all the Lands, &c. were supposed not to be found by the Inquisition. By 12 *Car.* 2. *c.* 24. this Writ is intirely rendered useless.

Quære, or **Querie**, is where any particular Matter in Debate in Law is doubted.

Quærens non invenit Plegium, is a certain Return made by a Sheriff upon a Writ directed to him, having this Condition inserted, viz. *Si A. fecerit B. securum de Clamore suo prosequendo, &c.* See *Fitz. Nat. Brev.* 38.

Quæstus, denotes what a Person has by Purchase, as *Hæreditas* signifies that which a Person has by Discent, or *Hereditary Right*.

Quakers, are a Sort of Enthusiasts, who in the Exercise of their Religion, affect to tremble or *quake*; and formerly several Statutes were in Force to prevent private Assemblies of those People, who are now tolerated, and by 1 *W. & M. c.* 18. they are exempted from the Penalties of former Statutes. Where an Oath is required, *Quakers* are by Law permitted to make a Solemn *Affirmation*, declaring in the Presence of Almighty God the Evidence of the Truth, *&c.* yet they are not capable of being Witnesses in Criminal Causes, nor of serving on Juries; neither are they capable of enjoying Offices in the Government. By 1 *Geo.* 1. *c.* 6. and 8 *Geo.* 1. *c.* 6. the Form of the Affirmation is settled; in which the Words, *In the Presence of Almighty God*, are left out. On *Quakers* refusing to pay Tithes, or Church-Dues, the Justices of the Peace are impowered to determine all Complaints in that Respect, and order Costs, &c.

Quale jus, was a judicial Writ, which was formerly brought where a Person of Religion had Judgment to recover Land, before Execution was made of the Judgment: And this Writ went out to the Escheator, between Judgment and Execution, in order to inquire whether the Person had Right to recover, or whether the Judgment was obtained by Collusion between the Demandant and the Tenant, with an Intent to defraud the true Lord.

Quam diu se bene gesserit, is a Clause frequently to be found in Letters Patent of the Grant of Offices; as in those to the *Barons of Exchequer*, &c. which can be intended only to Matters concerning their Office.

Quantum meruit, that is to say, *How much he has deserved*, is a certain Action of the Case, which is grounded on a Promise to pay a Person for acting any Thing so much as he should deserve; as if a Person was to imploy a Carpenter to do a Piece of Work for him, without making any Agreement about the same; in this Case it is

by

by Law implied that he must pay for the Work, as much as it is worth, for which a *Quantum meruit* lies.

Quantum valebat, is an Action of the Case, which lies where Goods or other Things sold are delivered by one to another at no certain Price; in which Case the Plaintiff in his Declaration, is to aver them to be worth so much.

Quare ejecit infra Terminum, is a Writ which lies where a Lessee is thrown out of his Farm, before his Term in the Lease is expired, against the Person by whom the Lessee is ejected: And the Effect of this Writ is, to recover his Term again. It is at the Election of the Lessee, or of the Assignee, in Case the Term be granted over, to sue out a Writ of *Ejectione firmæ*, or a *Quare ejecit infra Terminum* against the Lessor or his Heir, if they eject the Termor.

Quare impedit, is a Writ which lies for the Person that has purchased an Advowson, against him that disturbs him in the Right of his Advowson, by presenting a Clerk thereto upon a Vacancy in the Church. This Writ differs from that which is called a *Darrein Presentment*, because that lies where a Person or his Ancestors did formerly present; but this lies for him that is the Purchaser himself.

Quare incumbravit, is a Writ which lies against a Bishop, who, whilst two others are contending at Law for the Right of Presentation, does, within six Months after the Vacation of the Benefice, confer it upon his Clerk.

Quare intrusit matrimonio non satisfacto, was a Writ which anciently lay for the Lord against his Tenant, where after convenable Marriage offered him by his Lord, marries another, and nevertheless enters upon his Land, without Agreement first made with his Lord and Guardian. This Writ since 12 *Car.* 2. *c.* 24. is altogether gone into Disuse.

Quare non admisit, is a Writ that lies where a Person has recovered an Advowson and sends his Clerk to the Bishop to be admitted, when the Bishop refuses to receive him; in which Case the Person that has the Advowson or Right of Presentation shall have this Writ against the Bishop.

Quare non permittit, is a Writ which lies for one who has a Right to present for a Turn against the *Proprietary*. *Cowel.*

Quarrel, is not only applied to Actions personal, but also to mixt; wherein the Plaintiff is called *Querens*, complaining: Whence it is, that if a Person release all Quarrels, it is taken to be as beneficial to the Releasee, as if it were a Release of all Actions; for thereby all Actions both real and personal are released, a Man's Deed being always most strongly taken against himself.

Quarentine, in our Law bears two or three different Significations. 1*st*, It is taken for a Benefit allowed to the Widow of a Man dying seised of Lands, &c. whereby she may challenge to continue in his Capital Messuage, or chief Mansion-House, (the same not being a Castle) for the Space of Forty Days after her Husband's Decease, in Order to have her Dower assigned: And if the Heir or other Person eject her, she may have the Writ *De Quarentina habenda*. 2*dly*, *Quarentine*, denotes a Furlong or Quantity of Ground containing Forty Perches. 3*dly*, It denotes the Space of Forty Days,

Quarentine, in which any Person coming here from foreign Parts infected with the Plague, is not permitted to land, until that Time be expired.

Quarentina habenda. See **Quarentine**.

Quare obstruxit, is a Writ that issues on Behalf of him, who having Liberty to pass through his Neighbour's Ground, cannot enjoy such his Right.

Quarterizatio, is taken for a Part of the Punishment of a Traitor, by dividing his Body into four Parts.

Quarter-Sessions, is a general Court held by the Justices of the Peace in each County, once every Quarter of a Year: This Court was originally erected for determining Matters concerning the Peace only; but now its Authority is much further extended. See **Justices of Peace**.

Quash, denotes to overthrow or make a Thing void; as where a Bailiff of a Liberty returns any out of his Franchise; the Array in such Case shall be quashed: And in like Manner it is, where an Array is returned by one that has no Franchise. The Court of *King's Bench* can quash Orders of Sessions, Indictments, &c. But they will not quash an Information; so that in Case it be insufficient, a Demurrer must be put in thereto.

Queen, is either she that holds the Crown by Right of Blood, who is termed *Queen Regnant*; or it is she that is married to the King generally stiled *Queen Consort*. The *Queen Regnant* is in all Construction the same with the King, and of like Power in all Respects: But a *Queen Consort* is inferior to the King, and is really his Subject; for she may sue and be sued in her own Name; yet according to *Staundf.* what she has is the King's, and what she loses the King loses.

Queen Dowager, is she that is the Widow of a deceased King, to whom no Person may be married without the Licence of the succeeding King, on Pain of the Man's forfeiting his Lands and Goods: Yet tho' she does marry any of the Nobility, or one that is under that Degree, she does not lose her Royal Dignity.

Queen-Gold, is a Royal Revenue that belongs to every *Queen of England*, during her Marriage to the King: and it is payable by divers Persons both in *England* and *Ireland*, upon sundry Grants of the King, by Way of Fine or Oblation, it being above one full tenth Part of the intire Fines on Pardons, Contracts or Agreements, which becomes a real Debt to the *Queen*, by the Name of *Aurum Reginae*, upon the Party's bare Agreement with the King for his Fine and recording it.

Que Estate, is the same as to say *which Estate*; and is a Plea used where a Person intitling another to Land, &c. saith that the same Estate he had, he has from him; as where in a *Quare impedit* brought, the Plaintiff alledges that two Persons were seised of Lands, whereto the Advowson in Question was appendant in Fee, and did present to the Church, after which the Church became void; *Que Estate*, that is to say, which Estate of the two Persons he has now, and by Virtue thereof he presented, &c.

Que est mesme, as much as to say, the same Thing, is a Term of Art used in Actions of Trespass, &c. for a positive Justification of the very Act complained of by the Plaintiff as a Wrong done; as where Tenants at Will bringing an Action against their Lord, say, that he threatned them in such a Manner, that he forced them to give up their Tenures; to which the Lord in his Defence pleads, that he said to them, that if they would not depart, he would sue them at Law; this being the *same Threatning* that he used, or to speak in a more artificial Way, *Que est le mesme*; which Defence is good.

Quem redditum reddit, is a Writ that lies for him to whom a Rent-seck or Rent-charge is granted, by Fine levied in the King's Court against the Tenant of the Land, who refuses to attorn to him, whereby to cause him to attorn.

Querela, denotes an Action or Complaint exhibited in any Court of Justice: And hence comes the Word *Querens*, Plaintiff or Complainant, or what is likewise termed *Qarrel* against a Person: As *Quietus esse a querelis* formerly denoted to be exempted from the customary Fees paid to the King, or Lord of a Court, for Liberty to prefer such an Action: But more commonly to be exempted from Fines and Amercements imposed for common Trespasses and Defaults.

Querela freſcæ fortiæ. See **Freſh Force**.

Querela coram Rege & Concilio diſcutienda & terminanda, is a Writ whereby a Person is called to justify a Complaint of a Trespass made to the King himself before the King and Council. See *Reg. Orig.* 124.

Questa or Queſt, signifies an Inquest or Inquiry upon the Oaths of an impanelled Jury.

Queſtus eſt nobis, is used in a Writ of *Nusance*, which lies against the Person to whom the House, or other Thing, that is the Cause of the *Nusance* is alienated. See 13 *Ed.* 1. *c.* 24.

Queſtus, or rather **Quæſtus**, from the *Latin* Verb *Quæro*, to seek, get, or acquire, is taken for that Land, &c. which does not descend to a Person by an hereditary Right, but is gained by one's own Labour and Industry.

Quia improvide, is taken to be a *Supersedeas* issued on the Behalf of a Clerk of the Court of *Chancery*, sued contrary to the Privilege of that Court in the *Common Pleas*, and pursued to the *Exigent*; and in divers other Cases where a Writ is erroneously sued.

Quid Juris clamat, is a Writ which issues out of the Record of the *Fine* that remains with the *Custos Brevium*, before the same is ingrossed; and it lies for the Grantee of a Reversion or Remainder, where the particular Tenant will not attorn. *Cowel.*

Quid pro quo, in a literal Sense, signifies what for what, and in Law it denotes a reciprocal Performance of both Parties to a Contract; as the Giving of one Thing of Value, for another of the like; and whatever Contract is contrary thereto is called *Nudum Pactum*.

Quietare, is a Word frequently to be met with in old Deeds; and signifies to acquit, release or discharge.

Quiete clamare, denotes to quitclaim all Pretension of Right and Title.

Quietus, is the same as to say freed or acquitted, and is used by the Clerk of the *Pipe*, and Auditors in the *Exchequer*, in their Discharges given to Accountants which usually conclude with these Words, *viz. Abinde recessit quietus*, generally termed a *Quietus eſt*.

Quietus Redditus. See **Quit Rent**.

Quinque

QU

Quinque Portus. See **Cinque Ports**.

Quinfleme, or **Quinzime**, (from the *French*, denoting a *Fifteenth*) in a legal Sense, is taken for a certain Tax, and takes this Name from its being raised after the Rate of the *fifteenth* Part of Mens Lands or Goods: The Manner of which Tax was by two Assessors appointed in every County by the King; and these Assessors appointed twelve in every Hundred, who made a true Valuation of every Person's Goods, and then caused the *fifteenth* Part to be levied. *Cowel.*

Quintal, is taken for one hundred Weight of Fish, &c.

Quint-extact, is taken for the last Call of a Defendant who is sued to *Outlawry*; at which Time, in Case he does not appear, he, by the Judgment of the Coroners, is returned *outlawed*.

Qui tam, is where an Action is brought, or an Information exhibited on a *Penal* Statute at the Suit of the King and the Informer, when the Penalty for Breach of the Statute is directed to be divided between them; in which Case the Informer prosecutes as well for the King as himself. See **Information**.

Quit-Claim, in our Law is taken for a Release of any Action that one Person may have against another; and it also denotes a *Quitting* of one's Claim or Title to Lands, &c.

Quit-Rent, is a certain small Rent that is annually payable by the Tenants of most Manors; whereby the Tenant goes quit and free from all other Services: And anciently this Payment was termed *White Rent*, on Account that it was paid in Silver Money.

Quoad hoc, is a Term frequently used in the Pleadings and Arguments in Law; and is as much as to say, *As to this Thing* the Law is so and so.

Quod Clerici beneficiati de Cancellaria, is a Writ to exempt a Clerk of the Court of *Chancery* from a Contribution towards the Proctors of the Clergy in Parliament.

Quod Clerici non eligantur in Officio Ballivi, is a Writ which lies for a Clerk, who, on Account of Lands he is possessed of, is created Bailiff, Beadle, or other such like Officer.

Quod ei deforceat, is a Writ that lies for a Tenant in Tail, Tenant in Dower, or Tenant for Life, having lost by Default, against the Person that recovered, or against his Heir.

Quod permittat, is a Writ which lies for the Heir of a Person that is disseised of his Common of Pasture against the Heir of the Disseisor, who is dead: And it is said that this Writ may be brought by one whose Ancestor died seised of Common of Pasture, or other such Thing annexed to his Inheritance, against the *Deforceor*. This Writ was formerly used in the Case of a *Nusance*; as where a Person erected a Building even upon his own Ground, so near to another's House, that it hung over, or became a Nusance to it: But now this Writ is seldom or never brought, seeing that an Action on the Case fully answers the End. See **Nusance**.

Quo Jure, is a Writ which lies where a Person has Land wherein another claims Common of Pasture Time out of Mind; and it is brought in Order to compel such Person to shew by what Title he challenges the same.

Quo minus, is a Writ that issues out of the Court of *Exchequer*, for

for the King's Farmer or Debtor, for Debt, Trespass, &c. And it takes its Name from the Plaintiff's alledging that by the Defendant's Detaining the Debt, &c. he is *less able* to pay the King. This Writ issues out of that Part of the *Exchequer* as is termed the *Office of Pleas*; and tho' formerly it was granted only to the King's Tenants or Debtors, the Practice is now become general for the Plaintiff to surmise that by the Wrong the Defendant does him, he is *less able* to satisfy his Debt to the King, by which Means Jurisdiction is given to the Court of *Exchequer* to hear and determine the Cause.

Quorum, is a Word frequently mentioned in our Statutes, and often used in Commissions, both of Justices of the Peace, and others; and it is so termed from the Words of the Commission, *Quorum A. B. unum esse volumus*: As when a Commission is directed to seven or more Persons, or to any three of them, whereof *A. B.* and *C. D.* to be two; in this Case *A. B.* and *C. D.* are said to be of the *Quorum*, because the others in the Commission cannot proceed without them. A Justice of the Peace and *Quorum*, is a Person without whom the rest of the Justices in sundry Cases cannot proceed.

Quorum Nomina, was a Writ in Use in the Reign of King *Henry* the Sixth, when the King's Collectors and other Accountants were much perplexed in passing their Accounts, by new extorted Fees; and on that Account were obliged to procure this Writ for their suing out their *Quietus* at their own Charge, without Allowance from the King.

Quota, denotes a Tax to be levied in an equal Manner.

Quo Warranto, is a Writ which lies against a Person or Corporation that usurps any Franchise or Liberty against the King; as to have *Waif, Stray, Fair, Market, Court-Baron, Leet*, or the like, without good Title to the same; and it is brought in order that the Usurper may shew by what Right and Title he holds or claims such Franchise or Liberty. This Writ likewise lies for Misuser or Nonuser of Privileges granted: And according to *Bracton*, it may be brought against him that intrudes himself as Heir into Land, &c. The Attorney General, by Virtue of his Office, may exhibit a *Quo Warranto* in the Crown-Office against any particular Person, Body Politick or Corporate, who use any Franchise or Privilege, without having a legal Grant or Prescription for the same; and compel them by Process to appear in that Office, and there shew Cause or set forth in Pleading what Title they have to the Privileges by them claimed; whereon Issue shall be joined, and a Trial thereon may be had by *Nisi Prius*, &c. as in other Cases. Upon an Affidavit made of a Person's having voted at the Election of a Mayor or other Magistrate of a Corporation, who according to the Deponent's Belief had no Right to do it, &c. an Information in the Nature of a *Quo Warranto* may be exhibited against the Person so voting. These Informations of *Quo Warranto* may be exhibited at the Relation of any Person that is desirous to prosecute, who is termed the Relator against the Usurper.

R. *Backeton*.

R.

Rachetum, or **Rachet**, is the same with **Theftbote**, viz. the Compensation or Redemption of a Thief.

Rack-Rent, denotes the full annual Value of Land let on Lease, and and is payable by Tenant for Life or Years, &c.

Rageman, is an ancient Word used in a Statute of Justices, assigned by *Edward* the First and his Counsel, to go a Circuit throughout *England*, for the Hearing and Determining of all Complaints of Injuries acted within five Years before *Michaelmas*, in the fourth Year of his Reign. *Cowel.*

Ran, according to *Lamb.* 125. denotes so open a Spoiling of a Man, that it cannot be denied.

Ranger, is a sworn Officer of the Forest, appointed every Day through the Forest, to see, hear and inquire as well of Trespasses as Trespassers within his Jurisdiction; to drive the Beasts of the Forest, &c. See *Manwood*'s Forest Laws.

Ransom, properly denotes the Sum paid for the Redeeming of a Person that is taken in War: And this Word is also used for Money paid for the Pardoning some great Offence committed. As *Ransom* being applied to a Redemption from a Corporal Punishment, it therefore differs from **Amercement**.

Rape, has two Significations: The *first* is when it is taken for a Part of a County; as *Sussex* is divided into six Parts, called *Rapes*. In another Sense it is taken for the violent Deflowering a Woman against her Will, whether she be young or old; which Offence by our Law is Felony without Benefit of Clergy. It is held, that if the Woman conceive, it is no *Rape*, because she cannot conceive, unless she consent. To make this Crime, there must be *Penetration* and *Emission*; tho' it is said *Emission* may *prima facie* be Evidence of *Penetration*, but no full Evidence. Where there is neither *Penetration* nor *Emission*, an Attempt to ravish, be it never so outragious, is deemed an Assault only. Aiders and Abettors in the Commitment of a *Rape*, are indictable as Principals; as in the Case of the Lord *Audley*, who was indicted and executed, for assisting a Servant in the Ravishing of his own Wife, who on the Trial was admitted as an Evidence against his Lordship.

Rape of the Forest, denotes some Violence committed in the Forest.

Rapine, is thus distinguished from *Theft*, viz. the Taking away a Thing against the Owner's Will, is Theft; but where it is taken away openly, or by Violence, the Crime is termed *Rapine*.

Raptu Hæredis, is an ancient Writ which lay for the Taking away of an Heir that held in *Socage*. See *Reg. Orig.*

Rate-Tithe, according to *Fitzherbert*, is where Sheep or other Cattle are kept in a Parish for less Time than a Year, the Owner must pay Tithe for them *pro rata*, according to the Custom of the Place.

Ratification, is taken for a Ratifying or Confirming, and is particularly applied for the Confirmation of a Clerk in a Prebend, &c. formerly granted him by the Bishop, &c. where the Right of Patronage is doubted to be in the King.

Ratio, in a legal Sense is taken two different Ways; it being sometimes taken for an Account, as *Reddere Rationem*,

RA

Rationem, to give an Account: It is also taken for a Cause or Judgment given therein; and *ponere ad rationem*, signifies to cite a Person to appear in Judgment.

Rationabilibus Divisis, is a Writ which lies where there are two Lords in different Towns, who have Seigniories joining together, and the one finds his Waste by little and little to have been incroached upon; then the Lord, on whose Ground the Incroachment was made, shall have this Writ against the other, to rectify the Bounds and Divisions. In the *Old Nat. Brev.* it is said that it is a Kind of *Justicies*, which may be removed by a *Pone* out of the County-Court, into the Common Pleas.

Rationabili Parte Bonorum, is a Writ that lies for the Widow against the Executors of her deceased Husband, who deny her the third Part of his Goods, after the Debts and Funeral Charges are discharged: But whether this Writ lies by the Common Law, or only by the Custom of some Countries, is a Question in our Books. *Termes de la Ley.*

Ravishment, denotes an unlawful Taking away either of a Woman, or an Heir that is in Ward; and it is also used in the same Sense with Rape; which see.

Ravishment de gard, was a Writ which formerly lay for the Guardian by Knight's Service, or in Socage against the Person that took from him the Body of his Ward. See more on this Head in the *New Nat. Brev.*

Ravisher, is he that by Violence deflowers a Woman. See Rape.

Razure, is peculiarly applied to the altering of a Deed without the Privity of the Party bound by it; in which Case, if the Alteration

RE

be in a material Part thereof, it will render the same void.

Reafforested, is where a Forest which had been *disafforested*, is created a Forest again.

Reasonable Aid, was a Duty that the Lord of the Fee claimed of his Tenants that held by Knight's Service or in Socage, to marry his Daughter, or to make his Son Knight: But this is taken away by 12 *Car.* 2. *c.* 24.

Reattachment, is a second *Attachment* of a Person that was formerly attached and dismissed the Court without Day, on Account of the not coming of the *Justices*, or other such Casualty, in which the Defendant, when reattached, must plead *de novo*.

Rebate, in *Mirch. Dict.* is defined to be an Abating what the Interest of a Sum comes to, in Consideration of Prompt Payment.

Rebellion, in general denotes a Taking up Arms traiterously against the Sovereign, whether it be by natural Subjects, or others once subdued. The Difference the Law makes between *Enemies* and *Rebels*, is this, *viz.* Enemies are such as are Foreigners, and out of the King's Allegiance, whereas those that are Subjects of the King whether in open War, or *Rebellion*, are not the King's Enemies, but *Rebels* or *Traitors*. The Word *Rebel* is also sometimes taken for him that wilfully breaks a Law; and likewise for a *Villein* disobeying his Lord.

Rebellious Assembly, is a Gathering or *Assembling* together of twelve Persons or more, with an Intent of unlawfully Making Use of their own Authority to change or alter any Laws or Statutes of this Kingdom, or to destroy the Inclosures of any Park or Ground, or Banks of a Fish-Pond, Pool or Conduit,

in

in Order that the same may lie waste and void; or to destroy the Deer in a Park, or any Cony-Warren, Dove-houses, Fish in Ponds; or any House, Barns, Mills or Bays; or to burn Stacks of Corn; or abate Rents or Prices of Victuals, &c.

Rebellum, was anciently taken for a Replication, Rejoinder, or an Answer in the Court of Equity. *Cowel*.

Rebinare, according to *Fleta*, was to plough the Ground a third Time.

Rebutter, (from the *French*, signifying to put back or bar,) is in *Termes de la Ley* defined to be, where one by Deed or Fine grants to warrant any Lands, &c. to another, and he that makes the Warranty, or his Heir, sues him to whom the Warranty is made, or his Heir or Assignee, for the same Thing; in which Case, if the Person sued plead the Deed or Fine with Warranty, and pray Judgment, whether the Plaintiff shall be received to demand the Thing which he ought to warrant against that Warranty in the Fine or Deed comprehending such Warranty, such a Pleading of the Warranty is called a *Rebutter*. This Word is likewise used for the Defendant's Answer to the Plaintiff's Surrejoinder in a Cause depending: And the Plaintiff's Answer to the Defendant's *Rebutter* is called a *Surrebutter*.

Recaption, denotes the Taking a second Distress of one formerly distrained for the same Cause during the Plea grounded upon the former Distress: It is also the Name of the Writ the Law gives to the Person that is thus distrained.

Receiver, in an evil Sense, is taken for a Person that receives stolen Goods, and conceals them, &c.

By 5 *Ann*. c. 31. any Person that receives or knowingly buys stolen Goods, or who conceals Felons, knowing of the Felony, shall be accessary to the Felony, and suffer Death as a Felon. See 4 *Geo*. 1. c. 11. which allows such Receivers to be transported. *Receiver* is likewise taken in a good Sense; as *Receiver of Rents*, signifies an Officer belonging to the King, or other great Person.

Receiver of the Fines, is an Officer appointed to receive the Money of such Persons as compound with the King upon original Writs sued out of the *Court of Chancery*.

Receiver General of the Dutchy of Lancaster, is an Officer belonging to the *Dutchy Court*, who collects all the Revenues, Fines, Forfeitures, and Assessments, within that Dutchy, or whatever else is to be received thence.

Receiver General of the Court of Wards and Liberties, was formerly an Officer belonging to that Court: But that Office is now intirely abolished. See 12 *Car*. 2. c. 24.

Recital, denotes a Rehearsal or making Mention in a Deed or other Writing, of something that has been acted before. A *Recital* is no direct Affirmation, and therefore is not conclusive; for if they were, Persons then might, by feigning Recitals in a true Deed, make what Titles they pleased; seeing that false *Recitals* are not punishable.

Recognisance, (from the *French*) is taken for a Bond or Obligation of Record, testifying the *Recognisor* to owe to the *Recognisee* a certain Sum of Money: And this is acknowledged in some Court of Record, or before some Judge, Master in *Chancery*, or Justice of the Peace. Those *Recognisances* that

that are acknowledged before a Justice of the Peace are by them to be returned to the Sessions, otherwise an Information lies against them. The Method of acknowledging a *Recognisance* before a Justice of the Peace is this, *viz.* The Condition of the *Recognisance* is to be read over to the Parties bound, calling them severally by their Names, thus, *You* A. B. *do acknowledge to owe to our Sovereign Lord the King*, &c. After which it is to be ingrossed on Parchment, and the Justice is to sign it. In those Recognisances before a Justice, the Principal is bound in double the Sum of the Sureties, the usual Number of whom are two, and the usual Penalty is 40 *l.* at least. Recognisances for Payment of Debts begin thus, *viz. Know all Men by these Presents, that we* A. B. *of, &c. and* C. D. *of, &c. and* E. F. *of, &c. are held and firmly bound unto* G. H. *of, &c. in Five hundred Pounds of lawful Money of* Great Britain, *&c.* The Execution upon a *Recognisance* is termed an *Extent*; and the Body of the *Cognisor*, in Case he be a Layman, and all his Lands, Tenements, Goods and Chattels are liable to that Writ. The Form of a *Recognisance* in *Chancery*, as likewise one of the Peace, you may see in the *Young Clerk's Magazine*, and other Collections of Instruments in Conveyancing.

Recognisor, is the Party bound in the *Recognisance*; and the *Recognisee* is he to whom it is made.

Recognizance. See **Recognisance.**

Recognition, denotes an Acknowledgment: And it is the Title of the first Chapter of the Statute 1 *Jac.* 1. wherein the Parliament acknowledged the Crown of *England*, on the Demise of Queen *Elizabeth*, to have rightfully descended to King *James*.

Recognitione annullanda per Vim & Duritiem facta, is a Writ directed to the Justices of the *Common Pleas*, for the Sending of a Record of a *Recognisance*, which the *Recognisor* suggests to have been acknowledged by *Force* and *Duress*, in Order that if it appear so, it may be *annulled*.

Recognitors, is a Word frequently used for the Jury impanelled upon an *Assise*; and they are so called, because by their Verdict they *acknowledge* a Disseisin.

Record, denotes an authentick Testimony in Writing, contained in Rolls of Parchment, and preserved in our Courts of *Record*, wherein are inrolled Pleas of Land, or Common Pleas, Deeds, or Criminal Proceedings: But in Courts not of *Record*, such as the Admiralty, Courts Christian, Courts Baron, *&c.* their Registry of Proceedings are not properly termed Records: Nevertheless, Courts held by the King's Grant, are Courts of Record. Where any judicial Act is done during the Term, the Record remains in the Breast of the Judges, and within their Remembrance, and on that Account the Roll is alterable during the Term, as the Court shall order; but after the Term is ended, the Record is in the Roll, and will not admit of any Alteration, Amendment, or Proof to the contrary. *Termes de la Ley.* There are reckoned three Sorts of *Records, viz.* A *Record Judicial*; as Attainder, *&c.* A *Record Ministerial* upon Oath; as an Office or Inquisition found; and a *Record* made by Conveyance and Consent; as a Fine or Deed inrolled, *&c.* It is held that a Matter of *Record* is to be proved by by the Record itself and not by Evidence, for this Reason, *viz.* that no Issue can be joined upon it, so as to be tried by a Jury as Matters of Fact; and a *Record* is of greater Credit than the Evidence of Witnesses: Yet when Matter of Record is mixed with Matter of Fact, it shall be tried by a Jury. Unless a *Record* be exemplified under Seal, the Judges cannot judge thereof, when given in Evidence; tho' a Jury may find a Record without its being exemplified, if they have a Copy thereof proved to them, or sufficient Matter given in Evidence to induce them to believe there was such a *Record*. See **Trial**.

Recordare facias, or rather **Recordari facias**, is a Writ directed to the Sheriff to remove a Cause out of an inferior Court, as a Court of Ancient Demesne, the Hundred-Court, or County-Court, into the *King's Bench* or *Common Pleas*. This Writ is called a *Recordare*, because the Sheriff is thereby commanded to make *Record* of the Proceedings in the County-Court; and then to send up the Cause. See **Certiorari**.

Recorder, denotes a Person, whom the Mayor and other Magistrates of a City or Corporation, having Jurisdiction and a Court of Record within their Precincts by the King's Grant, do associate to them for their better Direction in Matters of Justice, and Proceedings in Law: On which Account this Person is generally a Counsellor, or other Person well skilled in the Law.

Recovery, in a legal Sense denotes an Obtaining of any Thing by Judgment or Trial at Law. *Recovery* is divided into a *true Recovery* and a *feigned one*. A *true Recovery* is an actual *Recovery* of any Thing or the Value thereof by Judgment; as where a Person is sued for Lands or other Thing, real or Personal, and obtains a Verdict or Judgment in his Favour. A *feigned Recovery* is a formal Act by Consent, made Use of for the better Assurance of Lands, Tenements, *&c.* And the End and Effect of this *Recovery*, is to dock and destroy Estates-Tail, Remainders and Reversions, and to bar the Intails thereof. In Order to make a Common *Recovery* there must be three Parties at least, *viz.* The *Demandant, Tenant,* and *Vouchee*. The *Demandant*, is the Person that brings the Writ of Entry, and on that Account may be termed the *Recoverer*. The *Tenant* is he against whom the Writ is brought, and may be termed the *Recoveree*. The *Vouchee* is the Person whom the *Tenant* vouches, and calls to Warranty for the Land, *&c.* demanded. Where a Person is desirous to cut off an Estate-Tail in Lands, *&c.* in order to sell, give or devise the same to another, he causes, by the Contrivance of his Counsel or Attorney, a feigned Writ of Entry *sur disseisin en le post*, to be brought for these Lands, *&c.* and in a feigned Count or Declaration thereon made, pretends he was disseised by the Person who by a feigned Fine or Deed of Bargain and Sale is supposed to be the Tenant of the Land, *&c.* This feigned Tenant, in Case it be a single *Recovery*, is made to appear and vouch to Warranty the *Cryer* of the Court of *Common Pleas*, or the *Bag-bearer* of Writs for the *Custos Brevium* in that Court, who is termed the *Common Vouchee*, and is supposed to warrant the Title: And this Vouchee appears, as if he intended to defend the same; and for that End craves a Day for making his Defence,

but

but on the Day given he makes Default, and on that Account, the Demandant has Judgment to recover the Land against the Tenant or Defendant, and he to recover the Value against the common Vouchee; and thereupon goes out a Writ of *Seisin* for the Possession of the Lands, &c. But it is here to be observed, that this *Recovery* in Value is only imaginary; and yet is looked upon as a Bar to the Intail for ever. It is otherwise in Respect to a true Recovery, which is as well of the Value as of the Thing; as where a Person purchases Lands, &c. of another with Warranty, which a third Person afterwards by Law recovers against such Purchaser, the Vendee in this Case may have Remedy against the Vendor, to recover so much in Money as the Land is worth, or so much other Land, by Way of Exchange. A common *Recovery* is either with *single, double or treble Voucher*: In that with single Voucher, the Writ of Entry is to be brought against Tenant in Tail in Possession, who is to vouch the common Vouchee: But in a *Recovery* with double or treble Voucher, the Estate-tail must be discontinued by Fine, Feoffment, Lease and Release, &c. and a Tenant must be made Tenant to the Freehold of the Land granted; against which Tenant the Writ of Entry must be brought, who must vouch the Tenant in Tail, and he the common Vouchee. A *Recovery* with double Voucher is the most usual and safest Way of Proceeding: For a Recovery with single Voucher only bars the Tenant in Tail and his Heirs of the Estate-tail that is in his Possession, with the Remainder thereon depending, and the Reversion expectant, which others have; and of all Leases and Incumbrances derived out of such Remainder or Reversion; whilst a Recovery with double Voucher has the first Voucher and his Heirs of all such Estate as was at any Time vested in him, or any of his Ancestors, whose Heir he is; and all others having Right to Remainders, or Reversions dependant upon such Estate; and also all Leases and Incumbrances derived thereout. A Recovery with treble Voucher, is to make a perpetual Bar of the Estate of the Tenant, and of all such Estate of inheritance as had at any Time been in the first or second Vouchee, or their Ancestors, whose Heirs they are, &c.

Recoupe, (from the *French*) denotes to keep back or stop something; and with us it is used for to defalk or discount; as if a Person has ten Pounds issuing out of Lands, &c. and he disseises the Tenant of the Land in an Assise brought by the Disseisee, the Disseisor shall *recoupe* the Rent in the Damages. *Cowel*.

Rectare, denotes to cite a Criminal to Justice, or to accuse a Criminal. *Cowel*.

Rectatio, is defined to be a Claim of Right, or an Appeal to Law for the Recovery thereof.

Recto, is taken for a Writ of Right of so high a Nature, that whilst other Writs in real Actions are only for the Recovery of the Possession of the Lands, &c. in Question, this Writ tends to recover both the Seisin and the Property; by which Means both the Rights of Possession and Property become tied together: Wherefore if a Person lose his Cause upon this Writ, he is in that Case intirely remediless, and shall be excluded. This Writ is of two Kinds, *viz*. 1. A Writ of *Right Patent*, and a Writ of of *Right Close*. A Writ of *Right Patent* is so termed because it is sent open, and is the highest Writ of all others; it always lying for him that has the Fee-simple in the Lands, &c. sued for, and not for any other. 2. A Writ of *Right Close* lies where a Person holds Lands or Tenements by Charter in Ancient Demesne, in Fee-simple, Fee-tail, or for Term of Life, or in Dower, and is disseised: And this Writ is directed to the Bailiff of the King's Manors, or to the Lord of Ancient Demesne, in Case the Manor is in the Hands of a Subject, commanding him to do Right in his Court.

Recto de Dote, is a Writ of Right of Dower, that issues on Behalf of a Woman who has received Part of her Dower, and demands the Remainder against the Heir of her deceased Husband, or his Guardian, in Case the Heir be a Ward.

Recto de Dote unde nihil habet, is a Writ of Right, which lies, where a Husband having Lands or Tenements, has assigned no Dower to his Wife; on which Account she is driven to sue the Heir or his Guardian for her Thirds.

Recto de rationabili parte, is a Writ that lies between Privies in Blood; as Brothers in *Gavelkind*, Sisters, or other Coparceners; for Land in Fee-simple; as where there are two Sisters, whose Ancestor dies seised in Fee, and one of the Sisters enters into the whole Land of her deceased Ancestor, and deforces the other Sister, the deforced Sister shall have this Writ to recover Part.

Recto de advocatione Ecclesiae, is a Writ of Right which lies where a Person has Right of *Advowson*, and the Minister of the Church dying, a Stranger presents his Clerk to the Church, and he not having brought his Action of *Quare impedit*, nor *Darrein Presentment* within six Months, but instead thereof suffer'd the Stranger to usurp upon him: But this Writ only lies for him that claims the *Advowson* to himself, and his Heirs in Fee.

Recto de Custodia terrae & haeredis, was a Writ formerly in Use, and lay for him, whose Tenant holding in Chivalry died in Nonage, against a Stranger that entered upon the Land, and took the Body of the Heir.

Recto quando Dominus remisit, is a Writ of Right lying where Lands or Tenements which are in the Seigniory of any Lord, are demanded by a *Writ of Right*; in which Case, if the Lord hold no Court at the Prayer of the Plaintiff or Demandant, but sends his Writ to the King's Court, to put his Cause there for that Time, (saving to himself the Right of Seigniory) then this Writ issues out for the other Party.

Recto sur Disclaimer, is a Writ which lies where a Lord in the Court of *Common Pleas* avows upon his Tenant, and the Tenant *disclaims* to hold of him; whereupon the Lord may have this Writ, and in Case he prove that the Land is holden of him, he shall recover the Land for ever.

Rector, denotes a Governor; and *Rector Ecclesiae Parochialis*, is he that has the Charge and Cure of a Parish Church. It was formerly held, that *Rector Ecclesiae Parochialis* was he that had a *Parsonage* where a *Vicarage* was indowed; and he who held a *Parsonage* without a *Vicarage*, was stiled *Persona*.

Rectory, is taken for an intire Parish-Church, with all its Rights, Glebes, Tithes, and other Profits. The *Latin* Word *Rectoria* has been often applied to the *Rector's* Mansion or Parsonage-House.

Rectum, was anciently taken for a Trial or Accusation. This Word has been likewise used in another Sense; as *Esse ad* Rectum *in Curia Domini*, denotes to stand to or abide the Justice of the Court; and in the same Sense *Stare ad* Rectum is used.

Rectum rogare, is to petition the Judge to do Right.

Rectus in Curia, in a legal Sense is taken for him that stands at the Bar, against whom no Person objects any Thing. Where a Person that is outlawed reverses the Outlawry, so that he may partake of the Benefit of the Law, he is said to be *Rectus in Curia*.

Recusants, was formerly taken for such Persons as adhered to the Pope as Supream Head of the Church, and such as denied the King's Supremacy: A Recusant has been likewise described to be one that does not repair to some Church or Chapel, or usual Place of common Prayer to hear Divine Service. In the present Age, all Persons are deemed Popish Recusants convict, who refuse to take the Oaths of Allegiance, Supremacy and Abjuration, and in such Case are subject to suffer accordingly. See **Præmunire**.

Red Book of the Exchequer, is an ancient Manuscript Volume of several Miscellany Treatises in the Keeping of the *King's Remembrancer* in his Office in the *Exchequer*. This Book contains some Things (as the Number of Hides of Land in many of our Counties, &c.) relating to the Times before the Conquest; and therein are recorded divers other Matters of Antiquity.

Reddendum, in our Law is used substantively for the Clause in a Lease, whereby the Rent is reserved to the Lessor.

Redditarium, was anciently taken for a Rental or Roll, in which the Rents and Services of a Manor, or other Estate were set down.

Redditarius, was formerly used for a Renter or Tenant.

Reddidit se, is when a Person procures Bail to an Action in a Court of Law, and the Party that is bailed at any Time before the Return of the second *Scire facias*, *renders* himself in Discharge of his Bail; such Bail thereby becomes discharged.

Reddition, denotes a Surrendring or Restoring; and also signified a judicial Confession or Acknowledgment, that the Land or Thing in Demand belongs to the Demandant, or at least not to the Person so surrendring. See 34 & 35 *Hen.* 8. *c.* 24.

Redelivery, denotes a Yielding or Delivery back of a Thing.

Redemise, is a Granting back of Lands, &c. leased.

Redemptio, Redemption, denotes a Ransom, as by the Law of the old *Saxons*, a Person convicted of a Crime paid a certain Fine, according to the Estimation of his Head, *pro Redemptione sua*.

Redisseisin, is taken for a Disseisin made by one, who once before was found and adjudged to have disseised the same Person of his Lands or Tenements; in which Case there lies a special Writ, called a Writ of *Redisseisin*. See *Old Nat. Brev.* 106. See likewise *Reg. Orig.* 206, 207.

Redubbors, are such as buy stolen Cloth, knowing it to be such, and afterwards change it into some other Form or Colour to prevent its being known.

Re-entry, (from the *French*) signifies a Taking again of a *Possession before*

before had; as if a Perſon makes a Leaſe of Land, &c. the Leſſor thereby quits the Poſſeſſion; and if the Leſſee covenants, that upon Nonpayment of the Rent reſerved, the Leſſor may re-enter; this is as much as if it were conditioned for the Leſſor to take the Land, &c. again into his own Hands, and to recover the Poſſeſſion by his own Act, without the Aſſiſtance of the Law. It has been held that in Caſe of a Leaſe for Years, rendering Rent, with Condition, that if the Leſſee aſſign his Term, the Leſſor may *re-enter*; and the Leſſee does in Breach of the Condition aſſign, unknown to the Leſſor, who accepts of Rent from the Aſſignee, without having Notice of the Aſſignment, the Leſſor may re-enter, notwithſtanding the Acceptance of the Rent.

Re-exchange, denotes a like Sum of Money paid by the Drawer of a *Bill of Exchange* that is returned proteſted, for the Exchange of the Money mentioned in the Bill back again to the Place from whence it was drawn.

Re-extent, is a ſecond Extent upon Lands or Tenements, Complaint being made that the former *Extent* was partially performed.

Refare, was anciently taken for to take away or rob.

Reference, in a legal Senſe, is where a Matter is referred by a Court of Equity to a Maſter, and by the Common Law Courts to a *Prothonotary* or *Secondary*, in order to examine and report to the Court. In the Court of *Chancery* by Order of Court, Irregularities, Exceptions, Matters of Account, &c. are referred to the Examination of a Maſter of that Court: And in the Court of *King's Bench*, Matters that relate to the due or undue Proceedings in a Cauſe, by either the Plaintiff or Defendant, are proper Matters of Reference to the Secondary, and for him in ſome Caſes to compoſe the Differences between the contending Parties; and in other Caſes to make his Report how Matters do ſtand, ſo that the Court may have an Opportunity to ſettle the Differences according to the Rules and Orders of the ſame.

Referendary, was an ancient Officer here in the Time of the *Engliſh Saxons*, whoſe Office was to exhibit the Petitions of the People to the King, and acquaint the Judges with his Royal Commands.

Refuſal, is ſaid to be where a Perſon has in Law a Right and Power of having or doing ſomething of Advantage to himſelf, and he refuſeth it; as an Executor may refuſe an Executorſhip, and if he be ſummoned to accept or refuſe the Executorſhip, and he do not appear and prove the Will, the Court may grant Adminiſtration, which ſhall be good in Law until ſuch Time as the Executor has proved the Will; yet none can be compelled to take upon him the Executorſhip, unleſs he has intermedled with the Teſtator's Eſtate or Effects. In an Action of *Trover* and *Converſion*, a Demand of the Goods, and a Refuſal to deliver them muſt be proved.

Refutantia, denotes an Acquittance, or a Renouncing of all future Claim.

Regale Epiſcoporum, denotes the temporal Rights and Privileges of *Biſhops*.

Regal Fiſhes are taken for *Whales*, and *Sturgeon*; and, as ſome ſay, *Porpuſſes*. The King by his Prerogative has a Right to all Whales caſt on Shore in any Place within the Realm, (except the ſame be granted

granted to any of his Subjects) as a *Royal Fish*: And the King himself shall have the Head and Body to make Oil, &c. and the Queen shall have the Tail to make Whale Bones for her Royal Vestments.

Regalia, is taken for the Royal Rights of a King, which are by the *Civilians* reckoned to be six: 1. Power of Judicature. 2. Power of Life and Death. 3. All Kind of Arming. 4. Masterless Goods, such as Waifs, Estrays, &c. 5. Assessments. And, 6. The Minting of Money, &c. To these may be added the Crown, the Scepter, St. *Edward's* Staff, four several Swords, the Globe, and other the like Things, made Use of at the Coronation of our King's, which are likewise termed *Regalia*. This Word is also sometimes taken for the Dignity or Prerogative of the King, as likewise for those Rights and Privileges which the Church enjoys by the Grants of Kings: And sometimes this Word is taken to denote the Patrimony of the Church; and further it signifies those Lands, &c. that have been given by the Kings to the Church.

Regard, in a general Sense denotes any Care or diligent Respect shewn; but in a special Signification it is only made Use of in Matters of the Forest, and is there used two Ways, *viz.* the one for the Office of *Regarder*, and the other for the Compass of Ground belonging to the Regarder's Charge. See *Manwood's Forest Laws*.

Regarder, is defined to be an Officer of the Forest, who supervises all other Officers there, and was ordained in the Beginning of the Reign of King *Henry* the Second: And *Manwood* says he is an Officer of the King's Forest, who is sworn to make the Regard of the Forest, as the same has been anciently used; and also to view and inquire of all Offences or Defaults of the Foresters, and of all other Officers of the King's Forests, concerning the Execution of their Offices. See *Manwood*.

Rege inconsulto, is a Writ that issues from the King to the Judges, to prevent their proceeding in a Cause whereby the King may be prejudiced, until he is advised. It is said that a *Rege inconsulto* may be brought not only for the Party to the Plea, but upon the Suggestion of a Stranger, on Cause shewn that the King may be prejudiced by the Proceedings, &c.

Regio assensu, is in *Reg. Orig.* defined to be a Writ by which the King gives his Royal Assent to the Election of a Bishop or Abbot.

Register, is any Officer that keeps a *Registry*: And it is likewise the Name of a very ancient Book called the *Register of Writs*, wherein are contained most of the Forms of Writs used at the Common Law.

Register of the Parish Church, is that in which Baptisms, Marriages and Burials are yearly register'd in each Parish.

Registry, is properly taken to be the same with *Repositorium*, a Repository or Place where any Thing is laid up: Whence publick Books, wherein divers Things are inserted, are properly termed *Registers*; and in like Manner the Office Books and Rolls, in which the Proceedings of the Court of *Chancery* are recorded, are so termed.

Regrator, denotes the Person that buys and sells Wares or Victuals in the same Market or Fair; and by divers Statutes *Regrators* are described to be such as buy or get into

into their Hands in Fairs or Markets, any Grain, Fish, Butter, Cheese, Calves, Sheep, Lambs, Swine, Geese, Capons, Hens, Chickens, Pigeons, Conies, or other dead Victuals, brought to a Fair or Market to be sold there, and afterwards sell them again in the same Fair or Market, or in some other Place within four Miles of the same. *Regrators* are punishable as well as *Forestallers*. See **Forestallers**.

Reif, according to *Cowel*, was anciently taken for Robbery.

Rejoinder, is where the Defendant in any Action or Suit makes Answer to the Plaintiff's Replication. Every Rejoinder ought to be a sufficient Answer to the Replication and to follow and inforce the Matter of the Bar. *Termes de la Ley*.

Relation, is where, in Consideration of Law, two Times or other Things are considered as if they were one and the same; and by this the Thing subsequent is said to take its Effect by Relation at the Time preceding; as if one deliver a Writing to another, to be delivered to a third Person, as the Deed of him that delivered it, when the Person to whom it was designed to be delivered has paid a certain Sum of Money; in which Case, when the Money is paid, and the Deed delivered, this shall be taken as the Deed of the Person that delivered it, at the very Time it was first delivered, to which it has Relation. In like Manner it is in Respect to Bills of Parliament, whereto the King assents on the last Day of the Sitting of the Parliament; such Assent shall relate and be of Force from the first Day of the Beginning of the Parliament: And so it is in divers other the like Cases. *Termes de la Ley*.

Relator, is generally applied to an Informer. See **Quo Warranto**.

Relaxation, is the same as *Release*.

Release, is an Instrument in Writing whereby Estates, Rights, Titles, Entries, Actions, and other Things are extinguished or discharged; sometimes transferred, abridged or inlarged: But in general this Word denotes the Giving up or Discharging of the Right or Action which a Person has or claims against another, or his Lands, &c. and it is usually made by these Words, viz. *Have Remised, Released and Quitclaimed*, &c. The Person releasing is termed the *Releasor*, and he to whom the Release is made is called the *Releasee*. There are two Sorts of Releases, viz. A *Release* as to Lands, &c. (which is a Conveyance in our Law termed a *Lease and Release*,) as also to Goods and Chattels: And there is likewise a Release of Actions, whether real, personal or mix'd: And a Release may be either *in Fact expressed*, or *implied in Law*: A *Release in Fact*, is that which the very Words expresly declare: And a *Release in Law* is that which the Law makes, and does acquit by Way of Consequence or Intendment of Law; as where a Feme Debtor takes the Creditor to Husband; this is a Release in Law; but it is not so where a *Feme Executrix* takes the Testator's Debtor to Husband, because that would be a Wrong to the Deceased. The Form of a *Lease and Release*, as likewise that of a *General Release*, you may see in the *Young Clerk's Magazine*, and other Collections of Instruments in Conveyancing.

Relegation, denotes a Banishing or sending away for a limited Time only; whereas *Abjuration* signifies the Forswearing of the Realm for ever.

Relicta verificatione, is where a Defendant has pleaded, and Issue is entered of Record, and after that the Defendant *relicta verificatione*, forsaking his Plea, acknowledges the Action, and thereupon Judgment is entered for the Plaintiff. *Termes de la Ley*.

Relief, is defined to be a certain Sum of Money, which every Freehold Tenant, being of Age, formerly paid to his Lord at the Death of his Ancestor, on his Entrance upon the Inheritance of his Ancestor's Lands, &c. by Payment of which Money, the Heir was said to *relieve*, and as it were raise up again his Lands, after they were fallen down into his Superior's Hands. *Relief* is otherwise thus defined, viz. to be a feudatary or beneficiary Estate in Lands, which was at first granted only for Life, and after the Death of the Vassal or Tenant returned to the Chief Lord; and on that Account it was called *Feudum caducum*, that is to say, a *Feud* fallen to the Lord by the Death of the Tenant; afterwards these feudatory Estates being turned into an Inheritance by the Assent of the Chief Lord, when the Possessor of such an Estate died, it was called *Hæreditas caduca*, that is to say, fallen to the Lord, to whom after the Heir had paid a certain Sum, he was then said *relevare hæreditatem caducam* out of his Hands; and the Money so paid by the Heir was termed a *Relief*. This *Relief* is said to have been used only after the Conquest; because in the Time of the *Saxons* there were no *Reliefs*, but *Heriots* paid to the Lord at his Tenant's Death, and these were Horses, Arms, &c.

Religion, comprehends Piety, Devotion, and the Worship of God, to support which there are many good Temporal Laws in Force. *Hawkins* observes, that the Law has so tender a Regard to the King and Religion, that an Indictment will lie for acting any Thing that appears immoderately to tend to the Prejudice of either of them. All Offences tending to subvert Religion and Morality, are punishable by Fine and Imprisonment, and likewise a Corporal Punishment at the Discretion of our Temporal Judges.

Religious Houses, are such as are set apart for pious Uses, such as Monasteries, Churches, Hospitals, and other Places where Charity is extended.

Relinquishment, is taken to be a Forsaking, Abandoning, or Giving over of any Thing.

Reliques, are some Remains of Saints that are dead, preserved with great Veneration by Persons living: But these by several Statutes are prohibited to be used or brought into *England*.

Remainder, is an Estate that is limited in Lands, &c. to be enjoyed after the Expiration of another particular Estate; as where a Person grants Lands, &c. to another for the Term of his Life, the Remainder to a third Person for Life, a Term of Years, or in Fee. There is a Difference between a *Remainder* and a *Reversion*; for by a *Reversion* the Estate granted, after the limited Time, returns to the Grantor; whereas by a Remainder it goes to some third Person, or a Stranger. According to *Wood*, *Remainders* and *Reversions* are so termed, because they are Estates in Expectancy only; for they are, as that Author observes,

serves, a present Interest, and yet stand in a Degree removed from the Possession until the particular Estate is determined. *Contingent Remainders* are where the Estate is to take Place upon some uncertain Event, and these are preserved by making a Lease and Release, Feoffment, &c. to the Use of *A. B.* for Life, the Remainder to the Grantee, for the Life of such a one, and so on for the *Contingent Remainders*. A *Contingent Remainder* depends upon the Estate that precedes it, and may be destroyed by levying a Fine, suffering a Recovery, or otherwise defeating the particular Estate whereon the *contingent* Estate depends, before the Contingency happens.

Remembrancers, who were anciently called Clerks of the *Remembrance*, are certain Officers in the *Exchequer*, whereof there are three, who are distinguished by the Names of the *King's Remembrancer*, the *Lord Treasurer's Remembrancer*, and the *Remembrancer of the First Fruits*. The *King's Remembrancer's* Duty is, to enter all Recognizances taken before the Barons for any of the King's Debts, for Appearances, or for observing of Orders: He also takes all Bonds for any of the King's Debts, for Appearance, or observing of Orders; and he makes out Process for the Breach of them: He likewise issues Process against the Collectors of the Customs, Subsidies, Excise, and other publick Payments for their Accounts: And Informations upon penal Statutes are entered in his Office, where all Proceedings in Matters upon *English Bill* in the *Exchequer Chamber* remain: His Duty further is, to make out the Bills of Compositions upon Penal Laws, to take the Stalment of Debts: and into his Office is delivered all Kinds of Indentures and other Evidences, which may concern the Assuring of any Lands to the Crown: He yearly, *in Crastino Animarum*, reads in open Court the Statute for Election of Sheriffs, and gives them their Oath, and likewise openly reads in Court the Oath of all the Officers belonging to the same, when they are admitted: And there are divers other Things belonging to this Office. The *Lord Treasurer's Remembrancer* makes out Process against all Sheriffs, Escheators, Receivers, and Bailiffs for their Account: He also makes out Process of *Fieri facias* and *Extent*, for Debts due to the King, either in the Pipe, or with the Auditors: And this Officer also makes out Process for all such Revenue as is due to the King on Account of his Tenures: He also keeps a Record, by which it appears whether Sheriffs or other Accountants pay their Profers due at *Easter* and *Michaelmas*; and at the same Time keeps another Record, whether Sheriffs or other Accountants keep their prefixed Days: There are likewise brought into this Office all the Accounts of Customers, Controllers and Accountants, in Order to make Entry thereof on Record. The *Remembrancer of the First-Fruits*, is he that takes all Compositions and Bonds for First-Fruits and Tenths, and makes out Process against such as do not pay the same. *Cowel*.

Remitter, signifies to restore, and is where a Person has two Titles to Lands, &c. and he comes to such Lands by the last Title, which proving defective, he shall be adjudged in by Virtue of his former Title: As where Tenant in Tail discontinues the Tail, and afterwards disseises his Discontinuee, and

and dies seised of the Lands which descend to his Issue or other Person inheritable by Force of the Tail; in this Case he is said to be in by *Remitter*, that is to say, seised by Force of the Tail, whereby the Title of the Discontinuee becomes utterly defeated: And the Reason of such *Remitter* is, that such an Heir is Tenant of the Land, and there is no Tenant against whom he may bring his Writ of *Formedon*, to recover the Estate-Tail; seeing that he cannot bring an Action against himself. If a Tenant in Tail infeoff his Son or Heir apparent within Age, and afterwards dies; this is a *Remitter* to the Heir: But it would be otherwise were he of full Age, for this Reason, *viz.* because it was his Folly, that he being of full Age, would accept of such a Feoffment. If a Husband alien Lands which he has in Right of his Wife, and after that take an Estate again to him and his Wife for the Term of their Lives; this is a *Remitter* to the Wife, because the Alienation is the Act of the Husband, and not of the Wife: But in Case such Alienation be by Fine in a Court of Record, such a Taking again shall not make the Wife to be in her *Remitter*; seeing that on such Fine the Woman shall be examined, and by such Examination the Wife shall be for ever excluded. *Termes de la ley.*

Remittitur, is defined to be an Entry made in the *King's Bench*, on a Writ of Error's abating in the *Exchequer-Chamber.*

Remover. See **Habeas Corpus**.

Render, signifies to yield, or return; and it is a Word frequently made Use of in the Levying of a Fine, which is either single, by which nothing is given or rendered back again by the Cognisee to the Cognisor; or double, containing a Grant, or Render back again of Rent, &c. out of the Land itself to the Cognisor. *Cowel* observes that there are some Things in a Manor which lie in *Prender*, that is to say, which may be taken by the Lord or his Officer, when they happen, without any Offer made by the Tenant; such as Escheats, &c. And there are some that lie in *Render*, *viz.* such as must be rendered or answered by the Tenant, as Rents, Heriots, and other Services.

Rent, denotes a certain Sum or other Thing yearly payable out of Lands, &c. There are three Kinds of Rents, *viz. Rent-Service, Rent-Charge,* and *Rent-Seck. Rent-Service,* is where a Person holds his Land of his Lord by Fealty and certain Rent; in which Case if the Rent be behind, the Lord or Landlord may by the Common Law distrain for the same. *Rent-Charge,* is where a Person by Deed makes over his Estate in Fee, Tail, or for Term of Life, yet reserves to himself by the same Deed a Sum of Money to be paid him yearly, with a Clause impowering him to distrain in Case of Nonpayment: And this is called a *Rent-Charge,* because the Lands are charged with a Distress for Rent in Arrear, by Force of the Deed, and not by the Common Law, as in the Case of a *Rent-Service. Rent-Seck,* or a dry *Rent,* is what a Person making over his Estate by Deed, reserves yearly to be paid him, without any Clause of Distress mentioned in the Deed. An Action of Debt lies for Rent in Arrear upon a Lease for Life or Years. By 8 *Geo.* 2. *c.* 28. If Tenant for Life or Years hold over Lands after the Expiration of their Terms, they are to

pay

pay double the yearly Value, to be recovered by Action of Debt: And by the same Statute, when Half a Year's Rent is due from a Tenant, and no sufficient Distress can be found on the Lands, the Landlord may serve a Declaration in *Ejectment*, and recover Judgment, &c. against the Tenant, who within six Months may file his Bill in Equity to be relieved; yet he is not to have an *Injunction* to stop Proceedings at Law, until he bring the Rent due into Court. An Action of Debt may be brought for Part of *Rent* due, and a Distress taken for the other Part, and by that Means both the Person and Land become liable: If Tenant in Fee, or Tail die, his Executor may have Action of Debt for the Rent in Arrear, or he may distrain for the same. See 32 *Hen.* 8.

Rental, is taken for a Roll in which the Rents of Manors are set down, in Order for the Lord's Bailiff thereby to collect the same.

Rents of Assise, were certain Rents of ancient Tenants, paid in a set Quantity of Money or Provisions; and it was so called because it was *assised* or made certain, and was by that Means distinguished from *Redditus mobilis*, variable Rent, which arose and fell like the Corn-Rent at present reserved to Colleges. *Cowel.*

Rents resolute, are reckoned among the Fee-farm Rents to be sold by the Statute 22 *Car.* 2. *c.* 6. and were Rents anciently payable to the Crown, from the Lands of Abbies and Religious Houses; and after their Dissolution, notwithstanding the Lands were demised to others, yet the Rents were still reserved to the Crown. *Cowel.*

Reparationc facienda, is a Writ which lies in sundry Cases, one of which is where there are Tenants in Common, or Jointenants of a Mill or House which is fallen to Decay, and one of them is willing to repair the same, but the other will not; in which Case the Party that is willing to repair it shall have this Writ against the Persons refusing. This Writ does also lie where a Person has a Passage over a Bridge, and another ought to repair the same, but suffers it to decay, &c.

Repeal, (from the *French*) signifies a Revoking; as the *Repeal* of a Statute is the Revoking or Disanulling thereof.

Repleader, denotes to plead again that which was once pleaded before: And it is also defined to be, where the Plea of the Plaintiff or Defendant, or both, are ill, or an impertinent Issue is joined; in which Case the Court makes void all the Pleas that are ill, and awards the Parties to *replead*.

Replegiare, signifies to redeem a Thing taken or detained by another, by putting in legal Sureties. See **Replevin**.

Replegiare de Averiis, is a Writ that is brought by him whose Cattle are distrained or impounded by another Person, on Surety being given to the Sheriff to prosecute or answer the Action at Law.

Replevin, is a Writ which lies where a Person is distrained for Rent or other Thing, and it is directed to the Sheriff to deliver to him the Distress, the Owner thereof giving Surety to the Sheriff that he will pursue his Action against the Party distraining, and return the Distress again, if the Taking shall be adjudged lawful. The Person that is distrained becomes Plaintiff in the *Replevin*; and the Person distraining

ing is called the Defendant or Avowant, for this Reason, *viz.* That the Defendant's Justification is termed an *Avowry*. At the Common Law *Replevins* are by Writ, either out of the *King's Bench* or *Common Pleas*; but by Statute they are by Plaint in the Sheriff's Court, and Court-Baron; and it is said a Hundred Court may hold Plea of *Replevins*, but they are not to be granted out of Court. It is held that a Sheriff may act by Virtue of the Writ of *Replevin*, or *ex officio* by Precept to his Bailiff; and that he may take a Plaint on the Statutes, and make out a *Replevin* directly, and afterwards enter it in the County Court. By Statute the Sheriff at his first County-Court within two Months after he has his Patent, is to depute and proclaim in the County-Town, Deputies to make *Replevins*, &c. An Action of *Replevin* may be removed out of the County-Court; if it was sued out by Writ, may be removed out of the County-Court by *Pone*; but by *Recordari*, where the *Replevin* is upon Plaint, returnable into the *King's Bench* or *Common Pleas*, in order to be tried there. If a Plaint in *Replevin* be removed into the *King's Bench* or *Common Pleas*, and the Plaintiff makes Default or becomes nonsuit, or Judgment is given against him, the Defendant in *Replevin* shall have the Writ of *Retorno Habendo* of the Goods taken in Distress: And where a Plaint is removed, if the Plaintiff in *Replevin* becomes nonsuited before or after Avowry made, the Defendant may again distrain for the same Cause he at first distrained for: But even in this Case the Plaintiff may sue out a Writ of *second Deliverance* upon the same Record, by which the first Suit will be revived; after which second Deliverance, and Trial thereon had, in Case the Plaintiff becomes again nonsuit, there must be awarded a *Returnum irreplegiabile* to the Defendant, at which Time he may make his Avowry or Plea in Justification of his Distress, in order to ground a Writ to inquire of Damages; or else he may hold the Distress until he is satisfied. Where Cattle distrained are put into a Castle, the Sheriff must nevertheless make *Replevin* and Deliverance; in Case Occasion require, he may take the *Posse Comitatus*, the Power of the County, with him for that Purpose. See **Posse Comitatus**. See also **Withernam**. The general Issue in *Replevin* is *Non Cepit*; yet the Defendant may plead Property in himself, in Bar or Abatement to the Action. The Plaintiff in Replevin, according to *Lutwich*, is to lay it in the *Detinet* or *Detinuit*; if in the *Detinet*, the Plaintiff is to have his Goods again, with Damages for the Taking and Detaining them; but if in the *Detinuit*, he shall only recover for the wrongful Taking of them; because that Word being in the *Preterperfect Tense*, implies that the Plaintiff had his Goods again; and for this Reason it is, that if in the *Replevin* the Writ be in the *Detinet*, and the Plaintiff declare in the *Detinuit*, the Declaration will be deemed ill, on Account of there being a material Variance between the Writ and Declaration. A *Replevin* must be certain, in particularly setting forth the Number and Kind of Cattle, &c. distrained, otherwise it will not be good; seeing that the Sheriff cannot be supposed, on Account of the Uncertainty, to be able to tell how to make Deliverance of the Distress

dress complained of, when it is directed to him for that Purpose. Where a Person distrains Cattle in one County, and drives the same into another, the Person distrained upon may sue a *Replevin* in which of the Counties he pleases; tho' not in both.

Replebish, denotes to admit one to *Mainprise* upon Surety.

Replevy, is where a Tenant's Goods being taken by Distress for Rent, he brings a *Replevin* in five Days, in Order to have the same restored; without doing which, at the five Days End they may be appraised and sold. See 2 *W. & M. c.* 5. This Word is likewise used for the Bailing of a Man. See **Homine replegiando**.

Replication, denotes an Exception or Answer made by the Plaintiff to the Defendant's *Plea* in the Courts of Common Law; and it is also what the Complainant *replies* to the Defendant's Answer in the Court of *Chancery*, &c. A *Replication*, both in Law and Equity, is to contain Certainty, and not vary from the Declaration or Bill, but instead thereof must pursue and maintain the Cause of the Plaintiff's Action or Complaint; or else it will be deemed a Departure in Pleading, and a Running on to another Matter.

Report, according to *Co. on Lit.* is a publick Relation of Causes judicially argued, debated, resolved or adjudged in any of the King's Courts of Justice, with the Causes and Reasons of the same, as delivered by the Judges. Likewise when the Court of *Chancery*, or other Court, refers the Stating of a Case, or the Comparing of an Account to a Master of *Chancery*, &c. his Certificate thereon is called a *Report*. In *Chancery* the Practice upon Reports is this, viz.

The Master having an Order of Reference, issues his Summons for the Parties to attend him at a certain Time and Place; when and where they may come with their Counsel, Clerk or Solicitor, to defend themselves, and maintain or object against his *Report*. See **Reference**.

Reposition of the Forest, was a certain Act of Parliament, whereby certain Forest Grounds being made *Purlieu* upon View, were by a second View laid to the Forest again. See *Manwood's Forest Laws*.

Representation, denotes the Personating of another; as Executors are said to represent the Person of the Testator.

Representative, is generally taken for a Deputy or Member of Parliament.

Reprisal, denotes the Taking of one Thing in Satisfaction of the Loss of another. By a Statute made in the Reign of King *Henry* the Fourth, it was ordained, That upon Application being made to the Keeper of the Privy Seal, by Persons injured by Depredations at Sea contrary to Treaties, &c. subsisting, on Evidence produced, he may sign *Letters of Request* to demand Restitution; which not being granted in due Time, the *Lord Chancellor*, or *Lord Keeper* is to grant *Letters of Reprisal* to take Restitution by Force, and to indemnify the Persons interested. There are two Kinds of *Reprisals*, *Ordinary* and *Extraordinary*: The *Ordinary* Sort is to arrest and take the Goods of Merchant Strangers within the Kingdom; and the *Extraordinary*, is for recovering Satisfaction out of the Realm, and is under the Great Seal. In Case a Person be wounded, spoiled, or in any Respect damaged in a hostile

Manner,

Manner, within the Territories of any Prince or Potentate, to whom Letters of Request are transmitted, without any Satisfaction being made, *Letters of Reprisal* shall issue forth and thereupon the Prince against whom the same are granted, is obliged to make Satisfaction out of the Estates of the Persons who committed the Injuries; and for Want of Sufficiency that Way, it then becomes a common Debt on the Prince's Country. See Letters of Marque.

Reprises, is usually taken for Deductions or Payments that are yearly made out of a Manor or Lands; as *Rent-Charge*, *Rent-Seck*, *Pensions*, *Annuities*, &c. and on this Account it is, that when we speak of the clear yearly Value of a Manor or Estate in Land, &c. we say it is of so much *per Annum, ultrà Reprises*, besides *Reprises*.

Reprive, (from the *French*) properly denotes to take back, or suspend a Prisoner from the Execution of the Law for that Time. *Cowel*. Whatever Judge has Power to pass Sentence, has likewise Power to *reprive*. Where a Woman is condemned for Treason or Felony, and by a Jury of Matrons, upon pleading her Belly, is found quick with Child, Execution of Course is respited, and the Woman in that Case becomes reprived until her Delivery; but this Favour the Woman shall have granted only once.

Repugnant, denotes something that is contrary to what is said before; as *Repugnancy*, or a Contradiction in Deeds, Indictments, Verdicts, &c. which render the same void; yet it is held that the former Part of a Deed shall stand, where the latter Part is *repugnant* to it.

Reputation, in our Law is in general defined to be the same as a vulgar Opinion; and *Reputation* is not that which this or that Man says, but that which hath been commonly, and many have said or thought: And it is said, that a short Time is sufficient for the Gaining of a *Reputation*, whereof there need not be an ancient Pedigree to establish it; because general Acceptation will produce a *Reputation*. This Word is likewise taken for the same as Fame, which is ever under the Protection of the Law, seeing that all Persons have an Interest in their good Name, to which Scandal and Defamation are always injurious; but defamatory Words are not of themselves actionable, otherwise than as they appear to damage the Estate or Interest of the injured Party.

Request, is the same as to ask or demand. Where a Duty is incumbent or due, it is payable without *Request*; but it is otherwise where a Person by Contract agrees to perform some Collateral Thing, in which Case there ought to be a *Request* made to do it, before Action is brought; as where a Person promises to pay a *Stranger's* Debt upon *Request*, the Request in this Case is Part of the Agreement, and is traversable, for that there is no Duty before the Promise made; and therefore a *Request* must be specially alledged, seeing that the Bringing the Action is deemed not a sufficient *Request*.

Requests. There was a Court formerly held in the King's Palace before the Master of the *Requests*, that went by the Name of the *Court of Requests*, and it was anciently termed *Camera Alba*.

Rere County, has been taken for the full County.

Rescest, is an Admission of a third Person to plead his Right in a

Cause

Cause depending between two other Persons; as where an Action is brought against a Tenant for Life or Years, he in the Reversion comes in, and prays to be received to defend the Land, and plead with the Demandant: In the same Manner a Wife shall be received for the Default of her Husband in an Action brought against them both; so likewise a Tenant for Years shall be received to defend his Right, where in an Action brought against the Tenant of the Freehold he pleads faintly. *Termes de la Ley.*

Receit of Homage, is taken for the Lord's Receiving Homage of his Tenant at his Admission to the Land.

Rescous, denotes an illegal Taking away and Setting at Liberty of a Distress made, or of a Man that is arrested by Process or other Course of Law; as where a Bailiff or other such Officer arrests a Person upon a Writ, or the like, and others by Violence take the Prisoner away, or procure his Escape; this is a *Rescous in Fact*: And if a Man distrain Beasts for Damage-feasant in his Ground, and as he drives them in the Highway towards the Pound, they enter into the Owner's House, where he detains them, and will not upon Demand deliver them, this Detainer is deemed a *Rescous in Law.* This Word is also used for a Writ that lies for this Fact, which is termed *Breve de Rescussu.* In Case a Distress be taken without Cause, as where no Rent is due; or if a Person distrain out of his Fee, or on the Highway; or distrain *Averia Carucæ,* where there is sufficient Distress otherwise; or in Case the Landlord distrain any Thing that is not distrainable, the Person whose Goods are distrained may make a *Rescous,* as they are going to the Pound; but even tho' the Distress be without Cause, when once impounded, the Owner may not break into the Pound to rescue the Distress: And where the Owner of the Cattle, before Distress, tenders his Rent, after which a Distress is taken for the same, the Distress in that Case is wrongful, and the Tenant may *rescous;* but he cannot do so, where he tenders the Rent after the Distress, the Taking being lawful. In a *Rescous* of one arrested it has been held, that the Plaintiff at the Suit of whom the Arrest was made upon mesne Process, may have his Action against the Rescuer, but cannot bring it against the Sheriff: Yet where a Person is rescued, that has been taken upon a *Capias ad satisficiendum,* an Action lies for the Plaintiff both against the Rescuer and the Sheriff. *Rescous* in some Cases, such as Matters relating to Treason, is Treason, and in Matters touching Felony, is Felony. It is held that on Action for an Escape on mesne Process, if the Sheriff plead a *Rescous,* it is good; but it is otherwise upon an Execution, because the Sheriff may raise the *Posse Comitatus* to secure the Prisoner. The Return of a Rescous must be, that the Prisoner was rescued out of the Custody of the Sheriff, and not of the Bailiff, tho' in Fact he was rescued out of the Bailiff's Custody; because the Sheriff is properly the Officer, and the Bailiff only his Servant. *Rescuers* are liable to be indicted or sued by an Action at Law; but if the Process whereon the Defendant was arrested be naught, and a *Rescous* of the Prisoner is made, there is no Remedy to be had against the *Rescuer.* In Case a Bailiff has a Warrant to arrest

arrest a Person, but is hindered in the Execution of his Office by another Person; here for Want of an actual Arrest, such Hindrance is no *Rescous*, tho' it is deemed a great Contempt of Court. Where a *Rescous* is made, the same must be returned on the Writ; at which Time it is proper to move the Court for an Attachment against the *Rescuers*, and not to ground such Motion on Affidavits. Where a *Rescous* is returned, the *Rescuers* are to answer thereto upon Interrogatories; and if the *Rescous* be found against them, they may be fined for the same, or the Party grieved may have a Writ of *Rescous* against them.

Rescussor, is the Person who commits a *Rescous*, which see.

Reseiser, denotes the Taking of Lands into the King's Hands, of which a general Livery, or *Ouster le main*, was before misused, contrary to the due Form of Law.

Reservation, denotes a Keeping to one's Self; as where a Person lets his Lands, &c. but *reserves* or *provides* for himself, &c. a Rent thereout; and sometimes this Word is taken for a Saving or Exception; as where one lets a House, reserving to himself one Room; in this Case the Room reserved is excepted out of the Lease.

Reset, or **Resetter**, is defined to be the Receiving or Receiver of an outlawed Person. See *Skene*.

Resiance, is taken for a Man's Abode or Continuance in a Place; and hence comes the Participle *Resiant*, that is to say, continually dwelling or abiding in a Place: And *Resiance* is indeed the same with *Residence*; but only that Custom ties this last to Ecclesiastical Persons.

Residence, both in the *Common* and *Canon Law*, is peculiarly applied to the Continuance of a Parson or Vicar upon his Benefice; the Default whereof (except the Party be duly qualified and dispensed with) is the Forfeiture of 10 *l*. for every Month. It is an incumbent Duty on Clergymen, that they be resident upon their Livings; and by 21 *Hen.* 8. *c.* 13. the Parson is to abide upon his Rectory in the Parsonage-House, because that Statute is not only intended for serving the Cure, and for Hospitality; but likewise for maintaining the House in Repair, so as to prevent *Dilapidations*: But lawful Imprisonment, Sickness, &c. being Things of Necessity, are good Causes of Excuse of Absence; and in like Manner it is where a Parson is imployed in some important Business for the Church or King, or is entertained in the King's Service. Leases made by Parsons, who are Non-Resident for the Space of Eighty Days in one Year are void.

Residens, is a Tenant that is bound to reside on his Lord's Land, and not to depart from thence.

Residuary Legatee, is the Person to whom the remaining Part of an Estate is given or devised by Will; which *Legatee* being made Executor with others, shall hold against the rest. In Case there be two *Residuary Legatees*, and one dies intestate, his Administrator shall have a Moiety of the Surplus of the Testator's Personal Estate, contrary to joint Executors, who are not intitled to Moieties; for this Reason, *viz.* that by making them *Residuary Legatees*, it is to be presumed the Testator intended an equal Share to both. In Case a *Residuary Legatee* die before the Will is proved, his Executor may have Administration. See **Executor**.

Resignation,

Resignation, is peculiarly applied to the Giving up of a Benefice into the Hands of the Ordinary, which by us is called a *Renunciation*. Tho' the general Signification of this Word is all one in Nature with that of *Surrender*, yet by Custom it is restrained to the Yielding up a Spiritual Living to the Bishop, whilst Surrender denotes the Giving up of Temporal Lands into the Hands of the Lord: And it is said that a *Resignation* may be now made into the Hands of the King, as well as the Diocesan, the King having the *Supreme Ecclesiastical Authority*, as the *Pope* had anciently here. It is held, that every Person who resigns a Benefice, must make his *Resignation* to his Superior; as an Incumbent to the Bishop, a Bishop to the Archbishop, and an Archbishop to the King, who is Supreme Ordinary; and that a Donation must be resigned to the Patron, and not to the Ordinary.

Resort, denotes the Authority or Jurisdiction of a Court.

Respectu Computi Vicecomitis habendo, is a Writ for the Respiting of a Sheriff's Account; and it is directed to the Treasurer and Barons of the *Exchequer*.

Respite, signifies a Delay, Forbearance, or a Continuance of Time.

Respite of Homage, was used for the *Forbearing of Homage*, which was first of all to be performed by the Tenant that held by *Homage*, but was most frequently used for such as held by *Knight's Service* and *in Capite*, who anciently paid into the *Exchequer* every fifth Term some small Sum of Money to be respited the Performing of their *Homage*. See 12 Car. 2. c. 24. by which this is taken away.

Respondeat Ouster, denotes to answer over in an Action to the Merits of the Cause, &c. As where a Demurrer is joined upon a Plea, which is adjudged against the Defendant; and this is termed a *Respondeat Ouster*.

Respondeat Superior, is applied to a Superior's Answering for the Insufficiency of an Inferior; as where Sheriffs of *London* are insufficient, the *Lord Mayor* and Commonalty must answer for them, as their Superior: So if a Coroner of a County be insufficient, the County, as his Superior must answer for him. *Superior Officers* must also answer for their Deputies in Civil Actions, in Case they be insufficient to answer Damages; as where a Gaoler deputes another under him, and the Person deputed suffers an Escape; in that Case the Gaoler must answer for the Insufficiency of his Deputy.

Responsalis, is used for the Person that answers for another in Court at a Day assigned. A Difference is made by *Fleta* between *Essoniatorem, Responsalem*, and *Attornatum*, and says that *Essoniator* was the Person who came only to declare the Cause of the Party's Absence, whether such Party were Demandant or Tenant; but *Responsalis* was for the Tenant not only to excuse his Absence, but also to signify what Trial he intended to undergo, viz. the Combat or the Country. See **Attorney**.

Responsions, we are told is a Word anciently applied by the Knights of *Saint John of Jerusalem*, to certain Accounts made by such of them as held their Lands, &c.

Restitution, denotes a Restoring back of any Thing unjustly taken from another. And this Word is frequently used for the Putting a Per-

Person into Possession of Lands, &c. who has been unlawfully disseised of them: It is likewise defined to be a Writ that lies, where Judgment is reversed, to restore and make good to the Defendant, what he has lost by the Judgment; and the Court, on the Reversal of the Judgment, gives a Judgment for *Restitution*, and thereon a *Scire facias quare Restitutionem habere non debet* must issue: But yet the Law frequently restores Possession to a Person without a Writ of *Restitution*, *viz.* by a Writ of *Habere facias Possessionem*, in the common Proceedings at Common Law upon a Trial at Law. It has been held, that if a Lease be taken in Execution upon a *Fieri facias*, and sold by the Sheriff, after which the Judgment is reversed; the Restitution must be of the Money for which such Lease was sold, and not of the Term. Where Money is levied and paid on an Execution, and the Judgment is afterwards reversed, there the Defendant shall have *Restitution* without a *Scire facias*, because it appears on the Record what the Party had lost and paid; but it is otherwise, if the Money were only levied, and not paid, then in that Case there must issue a *Scire facias*, setting forth the Sum levied, &c. Justices of the Peace, before whom an Indictment for *forcible Entry* is found, must give the Party grieved by such *forcible Entry*, Restitution of his Lands, &c. Yet where a Man is indicted for a *forcible Entry*, and the Defendant traverses the Indictment, in that Case there cannot be *Restitution* before Trial and Verdict, and Judgment thereon given for the Party injured, even tho' the Indictment were actually erroneous; because it is too late to move to quash the Indictment after the Traverse is entered, because that puts the whole Matter upon Trial. A Person who is attainted of *Treason*, or his Heirs, may have Restitution of his Lands by the King's Pardon: But it is otherwise in Respect to *Restitution* of Blood, for that can only be by Act of Parliament; some whereof are of Blood only, and some both of Blood, Honour, and Inheritance. Where a Felon is tried on Indictment, after the Attainder of the Felon, there shall issue a Writ of Restitution granted to the Owner of the Goods stolen.

Re-restitution, is where a Writ of Restitution has been before granted; as *Restitution* is generally Matter of Duty, so *Re-restitution* is Matter of Grace and Favour.

Restitutione extracti ab Ecclesia, was a Writ in Use to restore a Person to the Church, which he had recovered, being suspected of Felony. *Cowel*.

Restitutione Temporalium, is a Writ which lies where one is elected and confirmed *Bishop* of any Diocese, and has the King's Assent thereto, for the Recovery of the *Temporalities* or Barony of the said Bishoprick. See *Fitz. Nat. Brev.* 169.

Resummons, is taken for a second Summons or the Calling of a Person to answer an Action, where the first Summons, on any Account is defeated; by the Death of the Party, &c. See **Reattachment**.

Resumption, is particularly applied to the Taking again into the King's Hands such Lands, &c. as before, upon false Suggestion, had been granted by his Letters Patent.

Retainer, in a legal Sense denotes a Keeping or Maintaining of a Servant, who is not menial or continually dwelling with the Master, but

but only attends sometimes upon special Occasions. Counsellors and Attornies are frequently retained to attend and manage Causes of their Clients, in the several Courts. See **Retaining Fee**.

Retaining Fee, denotes the first Fee given to a Serjeant or Counsellor at Law, in order to make him sure, that he shall not be on the contrary Side.

Reteiner. See **Retainer**.

Retenementum, is by *Cowel* defined to be a Restraint, Detaining or With-holding; by whom it is also said to be a full and absolute Conveyance that was anciently made in this Phrase; *Sine ullo Retenemento*.

Rete-penny, was anciently used for a Rate-penny, or customary Due of one Penny for each Person to the Parish-Priest.

Retinentia, denotes a Retinue, or Persons retained to a Prince or Nobleman.

Retraxit, is taken to be where a Plaintiff comes in Person into the Court where his Action is brought, and declares he will not proceed therein; in which Case the Action is for ever barred: And it is so called from its being the most effectual Word in the Entry; and it was till of late entred thus, *viz. Et præd. Quer. in propria Persona sua venit & dicit, quod ipse placit. suum præd. Defenden. ulterius prosequi non vult, sed abinde omnino se retraxit, &c.* which briefly signifies that the Plaintiff will proceed no further. The Difference between a *Retraxit* and a *Nonsuit* is this, *viz.* it is always where the Plaintiff or Demandant is personally present in Court; whilst a *Nonsuit* is, when upon a Demand made he does not appear, but instead thereof makes Default; besides, as already observed, a *Retraxit* is for ever a Bar, which a *Nonsuit* is not; for in that the Plaintiff is at Liberty to commence an Action of the like Nature again.

Return, in our Law has divers Significations; the one is the *Return of Writs* by Sheriffs and Bailiffs, which is only a Certificate made by them to the Court, of what they have done concerning the Execution of any Writ that is directed to them; as where a Writ is executed, or the Defendant cannot be found, &c. this Matter is indorsed on the Back of the Writ by the Officer, and returned or sent back to the Court from whence the Writ issued, at the Day of the *Return* of the same, in order that it may be filed. Where the Sheriff does not make a Return of a Writ, the Court will amerce him; and in like Manner it is, in Case the Sheriff makes an insufficient Return; and should he make a false Return, he is liable to an Action upon the Case by the Party grieved. The Sheriff's Name must be to the Return of all Writs directed to him, otherwise it will not appear how they came into Court; and if a Writ be returned by a Person to whom it was not directed, the Return will not be good, it being held to be the same as if there were no Return at all upon it. After a Return is once filed, it cannot be amended. There are some Returns that are in the Nature of a Declaration of an Accusation; as that of a *Rescous, &c.* which must be certain and perfect, or otherwise they will be ill. There is also Return of a Commission, which is a Certificate or Answer to the Court whence the Commission issued, of what is done by the Commissioners. This Word is likewise in the Case of *Replevin*, where a Person distrains Cattle,

Cattle, &c. for Rent, &c. and he afterwards justifies or avows such his Act, which being found unlawful, the Cattle before delivered to him that was distrained, upon Security given to follow the Action, shall be *returned* to the Person that distrained them. To these we may add a Return of Juries by the Sheriff, as also certain Days in every Term, called *Return-Days*, or Days in Bank. See *Term*.

Returno habendo, is a Writ that lies for the Person that has avowed a Distress by him made, and proved the same to be lawfully taken, for returning to him the Cattle distrained, which before were replevied by the Party distrained, upon Surety given to prosecute the Distrainer for such Distress: This Writ does also lie where the Plaint in *Replevin* is removed by *Recordari*, or *Accedas ad Curiam* into the Court of *King's Bench* or *Common Pleas*, and the Person whose Cattle were distrained makes, and does not prosecute his Suit.

Returnum Aberiorum. See **Returno habendo**.

Returnum irreplegiabile, is a judicial Writ directed to the Sheriff for the Return of Cattle to the Owner when unjustly taken or distrained by another, and so found by Verdict.

Reve, more especially in the West of *England*, denotes the Bailiff of a Franchise or Manor: And hence comes the Word *Shire-reve*, for Sheriff.

Reveland, which is said to have been anciently *Thaneland*, is taken for such Land as being formerly reverted to the King upon the Death of his *Thane*, who had it for Life, was not since granted out to any by the King, but rested in Charge upon the Account of the *Reve*, or Bailiff of the Manor.

Revels, is with us taken for Sports of Dancing, Masking, &c. used in the King's Court, the Inns of Court, or Noblemens Houses; and there is a proper Officer appointed to supervise the same.

Revenue, is properly taken for the yearly Rent or Income that accrues to a Person from his Lands or other Possessions; and it is generally applied to the *Revenues* or Profits of the *Crown*.

Reversal, is generally applied to the Making of a Judgment void on Account of Error. The ancientest Judge of the Court, and in his Absence, the next in Seniority to him, does always pronounce the *Reversal* of an erroneous Judgment in open Court upon the Prayer of the Party. A *Reversal* of a Judgment may be pronounced conditionally, *viz*. That the Judgment is reversed, in Case the Defendant in the Writ of Error does not shew Cause to the contrary at a certain Time fixed; and this is termed a *Revocatur nisi*, a Reversal unless: At the Expiration of which Time limited, if no Cause be shewn, the Judgment stands *reversed* without further Motion.

Reversion, denotes a Returning again, and in our Law has two Significations; the one of which is an Estate left, which continues during a particular Estate in Being; and the other is the Returning of the Land after the particular Estate is ended: But according to the usual Definition of a Reversion, it is the Residue of an Estate left in the Grantor, after a particular Estate granted away ceases, continuing in the Grantor of such particular Estate; and where the particular Estate is derived out of his Estate;

as in Gift in Tail, the *Reverſion* of the Fee-ſimple is in the Donor; as in a Leaſe for Life, or Years, the Reverſion is in the Leſſor. The Difference between a *Reverſion* and a *Remainder* is this, *viz.* a *Remainder* is general, and may be to any Perſon except him that granted the Land, &c. for Life only, or otherwiſe; but a Reverſion is to the Grantor himſelf, by whom the Conveyance of the Land was made, and it is commonly perpetual, as to his Heirs alſo: Alſo a Reverſion takes Place after a Remainder, when a Perſon makes a Conveyance of a leſs Eſtate, than that whereof he was ſeiſed at the Time of making the Diſpoſition. A Reverſion of an Eſtate in Fee may be granted by Will, Deed of Bargain and Sale inrolled, a Leaſe and Releaſe, Fine, &c. And tho' by the Grant of Lands a Reverſion will paſs, yet by the Grant of a Reverſion, Land in Poſſeſſion will not paſs. See *Bridgm. Conveyan.* Reverſions expectant upon an Eſtate-Tail, are held not to be deemed Aſſets, nor of any Account in Law, for that they may be cut off by Fine and Recovery; yet it is otherwiſe of a Reverſion on an Eſtate for Life or Years. See *Wood's Inſt.* See alſo **Remainder**.

Review. There is a Bill of *Review* in the Court of *Chancery*, which is where a Cauſe has been heard, and a Decree thereon ſigned and inrolled; and ſome Error in Law appears upon the *Decree*, or ſome new Matter is diſcovered in Time after the Decree made: But this Bill muſt be exhibited by Leave of the Court, which is uſually obtained on Oath made of the Diſcovery of the new Matter, which could not be had or uſed at the Time of paſſing the Decree; beſides the Sum of 20 *l.* muſt be paid into Court on the Bringing this Bill, by Way of Security for Coſts and Delay, in Caſe the Matter ſhould be found againſt the Party. If one Part of a Decree in *Chancery* be repugnant to another, the Decree may be reverſed by a Bill of Review.

Revivor, is a Term uſed in *Chancery*; and is where a Bill has been exhibited in that Court againſt one who anſwers, and before the Cauſe is heard, or if heard, before the Decree is inrolled, either of the Parties thereto dies; in which Caſe a Bill of Revivor muſt be brought, praying that the former Proceedings may ſtand revived, and be put upon the ſame Footing as at the Time of the Abatement. In Caſe one of the Parties to a Bill dies, a Female Plaintiff marries, or there have not been any Proceedings upon a Decree for the Space of a Year, there the Decree and Proceedings muſt be revived by a *Subpœna Scire facias*, or, if the Decree be inrolled, by a Bill of Revivor; yet where the Parties are neither Heirs nor Executors, &c. to the deceaſed Party; the Decree or Cauſe muſt be revived by original Bill, and not by *Subpœna Scire facias*, or Bill of *Revivor*.

Reviving, denotes a Renewing of Actions, Rents, &c. that were before extinguiſhed.

Revocation, ſignifies the Recalling of a Thing granted, or the Annulling and Making void of ſome Deed that had Exiſtence until the Act of Revocation thereof took Place. Revocation may be either *general* or *ſpecial*: General, is of all Acts and Things before done; Special is only to revoke ſuch a particular Thing. It is common in voluntary Deeds or Conveyances to insert a Proviso containing Power of Revocation, which being coupled with a Use, and tending to pass by raising of Uses, are allowed to be good, and not repugnant in Law. A Will is *revocable*; and the last Will revokes all former Wills made: Yet it is said that where there are two Wills, a new Publication of the first Will will revoke the last; and Wills must be revoked by some other Will in Writing, signed in the Presence of three Witnesses, or by Cancelling; and the Testator must be of a good disposing Mind, at the Time he revokes his Will, as well as when he makes it. A Warrant of Attorney from a Defendant to appear and accept of a Declaration, and to plead for him cannot be revoked, with an Intent to stay the Plaintiff's Proceedings; but nevertheless he may, on good Cause shewn to the Court, change his Attorney, provided he plead by another in due Time.

Ribaud, is defined to be a Vagrant, Luxurious Spend-thrift, a Rogue, Whoremonger, or a Person addicted to all Kinds of Wickedness.

Rider-Roll, is taken for a Schedule or small Piece of Parchment, usually added to some Part of a Roll or Record.

Riding-Clerk, is one of the six Clerks in *Chancery* who in his Turn for one Year, keeps the Controlment-Books of all Grants which pass the Great Seal during that Time.

Ridings, is used for the Names of the Parts or Divisions of the County of *York*, which are three, *viz.* The *East-Riding*, *West-Riding*, and the *North-Riding*.

Riens arrear, is a Plea used in an Action of Debt, for Arrearages of Account, by which the Defendant alledges there is nothing in Arrear.

Riens passe per le fait, which is as much as to say, *Nothing passes by the Deed*, is the Form of an Exception in some Cases taken to an Action.

Riens deins le gard, is by *Coke* defined to have been a Challenge to a Jury or Inquest of *London*, for that four sufficient Men were not impanelled.

Riens per Descent, that is to say, *Nothing by Descent*, is the Plea of an Heir sued for his Ancestor's Debt, who has no Lands, &c. from his Ancestor by *Descent*, nor Assets in his Hands.

Rier-County, (from the *French*) is a Word that is opposed to full and open County, and is taken to be some publick Place appointed by the Sheriff for the Receipt of the King's Money after the End of his County-Court.

Rifflare, has been used to denote the Taking away of any Thing by Force; and hence comes our *English* Word *Rifle*.

Right, is in general taken to include not only a *Right*, for which a Writ of *Right* lies; but also any Title or Claim, either by Virtue of Condition, Mortgage, &c. for which no Action is by Law given, but an Entry only. There is a *Right of Entry*, and of *Action*, where a Person is put out of his Lands; of *Property* and *Possession*, where one is disseised, &c. As for Example, in this last, if a Person be disseised of his Lands, the Disseisee has a *Right of Property*, and the Disseisor a *Right of Possession*; and in Case the Disseisee release to the Disseisor, he has both the Right of Property and Possession in him. There is likewise a *present*, as well as a *future Right*;

Right; *Jus in Re*, which is grantable to a Stranger; and a *Jus ad Rem*, or naked Right, where an Estate is turned to a Right, on a Discontinuance, &c. Tho' it is said that a Right may sometimes sleep, but never dies, yet it is held a long Possession, exceeding the Memory of Man, will create a Right.

Rights and Liberties. There was a Declaration so termed, against the Conduct of a late unfortunate Prince, who was thereby charged to have by the Assistance of evil Counsellors endeavoured to subvert the Laws and Liberties of this Realm, by exercising a Power of dispensing with, and suspending of Laws; by levying of Money for the Crown's Use by Pretence of Prerogative, without Consent of Parliament; by raising and keeping a standing Army in Time of Peace; by violating the Freedom of Elections of Members to serve in Parliament; by violent Prosecutions in the Court of *King's Bench*; and by causing partial and corrupt Jurors to be returned on Trials, excessive Bail to be taken, excessive Fines imposed, as well as cruel Punishments inflicted, &c. all which by 1 *W. & M. c.* 2. were declared to be illegal, and contrary to the ancient *Rights and Liberties* of the People.

Ringildor, has been used for a Kind of Bailiff or Serjeant.

Riot, (from the *French*) is taken to be where three or more Persons assembled together, commit some unlawful Act, with Force and Violence, to the Disturbance of the Peace; as by beating some Person, forcibly entring upon the Possession of the Lands, Houses, &c. of another; breaking down Inclosures, &c. It is held, that in every *Riot* there must be some Intention of Force or Violence; and on that Account it is, that Assemblies for Wrestling, Playing at Cudgels, Dancing, &c. are not deemed *riotous*. This Violence must relate to some private Quarrel only, otherwise it is no *Riot*; for if the Intention of the Assembling be to redress Grievances of a publick Nature, and such Intention be put in Execution, it is deemed no less a Crime than that of levying of War against the Sovereign, and consequently Treason. There must be three at least to make a *Riot*, for two alone cannot be guilty of it, tho' two Persons may make a Conspiracy, &c. When three or more assemble together, tho' at first in a peaceable Manner, and after assembled commit some deliberate *riotous Act*, this is deemed a *riotous Assembly*; for the riotous Act has Relation to their Assembling together, and the Intentions of Persons are best interpreted by their Actions; yet if Persons on an unlawful Meeting should quarrel, in this Case there being no Intention of an unlawful Act, it is no *Riot*, but only a sudden Affray, seeing that the Meeting together was lawful, and the subsequent Breach of the Peace happened unexpectedly: But still it is said, that if Persons do innocently assemble together, and afterwards upon a Quarrel happening among them, form themselves into Bodies or Parties, and then make an Affray, this shall amount to a *Riot*, for this Reason, *viz.* because upon their confederating together, with an Intent to break the Peace, they may as properly be looked upon to have been assembled for that Purpose, from the Time of such Confederacy, as if the first Coming had actually been with that Intent: And in like Manner
it

it is, where Persons assembled on any lawful Occasion shall on a sudden Proposal go in a Body to pull down a House, break an Inclosure, or commit any other Act of Violence to the Disturbance of the Peace, and shall execute such their Purpose, the Persons concerned shall be deemed *Rioters*; because their Associating themselves together for such new Purpose, is in no Respect extenuated by their having at first met upon another Design: And, according to *Hawkins*, if a Man, seeing others engaged in a *Riot*, shall join and assist them therein, he then becomes in the Eye of the Law as much a *Rioter*, as if he had at first assembled with them for that Intent; neither shall his Alledging that he came there innocently any Way avail him; because it is impossible to discover whether every particular Person that is ingaged in a *Riot* was really one of the first Assembly, or had been made privy to the Design of the Tumult. It is said, that any one may assemble a Number of Persons together to defend his House or Habitation against Injury or Violence offered; but yet if a Person be threatned, that in Case he comes to such a Place, he shall be beaten, or otherwise maletreated, and he thereupon assembles a Company to go with him thither, yea tho' for the Safety of his Person, this may be deemed a *Riot*, on Account of the Danger the Government may be in from such Assemblies; and besides the Law affords him another Remedy, *viz.* the Demanding the Surety for the Peace. It has been held, that Persons assembled together to commit any Thing prohibited by Statute, if they peaceably perform the same, shall not be deemed *Rioters*; and *Rioters* by the Common Law are punishable by Fine and Imprisonment, and if great and enormous, by *Pillory*: And *Riots* are cognisable by the Justices of the Peace, who, together with the Sheriff or Under-Sheriff, may, if Occasion require, raise the *Posse Comitatus*, the Power of the County, to suppress *Riots, Routs, &c.* arrest and secure the Offenders, and record what is acted in their Presence, by which Record the Offenders shall stand convicted: And in Case the Rioters be departed, the said Justices, *&c.* shall within a Month after the *Riot* committed make Enquiry thereof, and hear and determine the same, in which Time if the Truth cannot be discovered, the Justices of the Peace and Sheriff within another Month shall certify to the King and Council, on Default of which they forfeit 100 *l.* By 1 *Geo.* 1. *c.* 5. it is enacted, that if any Persons, to the Number of twelve or more, unlawfully and riotously assemble against the Peace, who being required by a Justice of the Peace, Sheriff, under-Sheriff, Mayor, or other Head-Officer of a City or Town, by Proclamation in the King's Name to disperse themselves, do notwithstanding continue together for the Space of an Hour afterwards, they shall be deemed guilty of Felony without Benefit of Clergy; and the Offenders are to be apprehended and carried before a Justice of the Peace, *&c.* And if in Resistance any of the *Rioters* be killed, the Persons concerned in such Killing shall be indemnified: And it is likewise by this Statute made Felony in Persons by Force hindering the Proclamation to be read; and the *Rioters* are nevertheless guilty, in Case they do not disperse; And

And further, that *Rioters*, who demolish any Church, Chapel, or Dwelling-House are guilty of Felony; and moreover, the Inhabitants of Towns or Hundreds are to yield Damages for the Rebuilding or Reparation of such Church, &c. to be levied and paid in such Manner as Money recovered against the Hundred by Persons robbed on the Highway may be. But Prosecutions on this Statute are to be prosecuted within one Year after the Offence is committed. It is here to be observed, that this Law, severe as it is, does not take away any Authority in the Suppressing of a Riot, either by Common Law, or by other Statutes.

Rivagium, Rivage, or **Riverage,** is a certain Toll or Duty paid to the King in some Rivers, for the Passage of Boats or Vessels. *Cowel.*

Riveare, denotes to have the Liberty of Fishing or Fowling in a River.

Robbery, is defined to be a Felonious and Violent Assault made upon a Man's Person, by putting him in Fear, and taking from him his Goods or Money on the Highway: And it is thought this Offence takes the Name of *Robbery,* either on Account that the Offenders bereaved the Person robbed of some of his Robes or Garments, or because his Money or Goods were taken from his Person out of some Part of his Garment or *Robe:* But *Robbery,* in a large Sense is taken for any wrongful Taking away of Goods, &c. *Robbery* on the Highway is Felony without Benefit of Clergy, tho' the Sum or Value taken be under Twelve Pence, or even be no more than a single Penny; but in other Thefts Judgment of Death is only where the Thing stolen is above the Value of 12 *d.* In a *Robbery* on the Highway there must be something taken to make it Felony without Clergy; for if any Thing be taken from the Person of another, without putting the Owner thereof in Fear, this properly is no *Robbery,* but Felony wherein Clergy is allowed, the Putting in Fear being the chief Article that distinguishes the *Robbery* from other Stealing from a Man's Person. The bare Attempt to *rob,* tho' not Felony, is a Misdemeanor, and punishable by Fine and Imprisonment. In *Robberies,* there is a Taking in Deed, and a Taking in Law: As where a *Robber* compels a Man out of Fear of Death, to swear he will bring him a certain Sum of Money, which the sworn Person delivers to the other; this is a Taking at Law, and adjudged a *Robbery.* It is held that if a Robbery be committed by several in a Gang, and one of them only takes the Money or Goods of the Person robbed, in this Case every one of the Company shall be said to take it, on Account of that Encouragement which they gave to one another through the Hopes of mutual Assistance; and should they even miss of their first intended Prize, and one of them afterwards rides off from the rest, and robs another Person in the same Highway without their Knowledge or Consent, out of their View, and then returns to them, all of them are guilty of the Robbery, because they came together with an Intent to *rob,* and to assist each other in the Doing of it. By 6 *Geo* 1. Streets in Cities are made Highways, in Respect to Robberies; and by 7 *Geo.* 6. *c.* 21. Persons that assault, or in a forcible Manner demand Money, &c. of another,

with

with an Intent to commit a Robbery, shall be guilty of Felony, and be transported for seven Years. Where Robberies are committed on the Highway in the Day-time of any Day, except *Sunday*; the Hundred wherein the Robbery was committed becomes liable to answer it, in Case the Robbers be not taken in Forty Days, &c. Hue and Cry being made after the Robbers. Whoever apprehends and prosecutes a Robber on the Highway, so as to convict him, is intitled to receive of the Sheriff of the County, where the Robbery was committed, 40 *l*. upon such Person's producing a proper Certificate of the Judge before whom the Robber was convicted; with the Horse, Furniture and Arms, &c. of the convicted Person: And if a Person out of Prison, having committed a Robbery, will discover two or more of his Accomplices or Robbers, he shall be intitled to a Pardon. See 4 *W. & M. c.* 8. See also **Hue and Cry**, and **Hundred**.

Robbers, according to *Lamb.* are nightly Thieves.

Robersmen, or **Roberdsmen**, were a Pack of great Thieves, who are said to have taken their Names from *Robin Hood*, a noted Robber that lived on the Borders of *England* and *Scotland* in the Reign of King *Richard* the First.

Rod, which is otherwise called a *Perch*, is a Measure of sixteen Foot and a Half long.

Rodknights, otherwise **Radknights** were certain Servitors who held their Lands by serving their Lords on Horseback.

Rogue, is taken for an idle, sturdy Beggar, who wanders from Place to Place without License, after he has by the Justices of the County been settled, or offered to be settled on some certain Place of Abode; for the first Offence whereof he was called a *Rogue of the first Degree*, and punished by Whipping, and Boring thro' the Gristle of the Right-Ear with a hot Iron; and for the second Offence he was termed a *Rogue of the second Degree*, and executed as a Felon, in case he were above eighteen Years of Age. *Cowel.* By 12 *Ann. c.* 23. In Case Justices of the Peace at their Sessions adjudge a Person to be a dangerous and *incorrigible Rogue*, they are directed to cause him to be whipped three Market-Days successively, and to be kept at hard Labour in the House of Correction, from whence if he escapes he becomes guilty of Felony. See **Vagrants**.

Roll, denotes a Shedule of Parchment, which may be wound or rolled up with the Hand in the Form of a Pipe: And *Rolls* are Schedules of Parchment, whereon all the Pleadings, Memorials and Acts of Court are entered and filed with the proper Officer, which being done, these *Rolls* become Records of the Court.

Rolls Office, is an Office in *Chancery-Lane*, which was anciently called *Domus Conversorum*, wherein is contained all the *Rolls* and Records of the Court of *Chancery*, the Master whereof, who is stiled the *Master of the Rolls*, is the second Person in that Court.

Rolls of Parliament, are the Manuscript Registers or Rolls of the Proceedings of some ancient Parliaments, which, before *Printing* came in Use, were all ingrossed on Parchment, and proclaimed openly in every County. In these Rolls are said to be contained many difficult Points in Law, which were often formerly referred to the Determination of this Supreme Court

Court of Judicature by the Judges of both Benches.

Rolls of the Exchequer, are divided into the *Wardrobe Roll*, the *Cofferer's Roll*, the *Subsidy Roll*, &c.

Rolls of the Temple. In the two *Temples* there is a Roll called the *Calves-Head Roll*, in which every Bencher, Barrister and Student is annually taxed, at such a Rate to the Cook, and other Officers of the House, in Consideration of a Dinner of *Calves-Heads* provided in *Easter* Term.

Romescot, was the Tribute of a Penny anciently paid yearly by every Family to *Rome*. It was also called *Romepenny*.

Rood of Land, is with us the fourth Part of an Acre.

Rosland, denotes Heathy Land, or Land full of Ling; and it is also taken for Watery or Moorish Land.

Rother-Beasts, comprehends Oxen, Cows, Steers, Heifers, Sheep, and other like horned Beasts.

Rout, in our Law is applied to an Assembly of Persons going forcibly to commit some unlawful Act, whether they execute it or not: And *Rout* is looked upon to be the same as what the *Germans* call *Rot*, meaning a Band or large Company of Men gathered together, and going to execute, or actually executing any *Riot* or other unlawful Act. The Difference between a *Rout* and *Riot* seems to be this, *viz.* That a *Rout* is an unlawful Assembly, whereas *Riot* is taken for the disorderly Fact committed by such unlawful Assembly. Two Things however are common both to *Riot*, *Rout* and *unlawful Assembly*, the one is, that three Persons at least be gathered together; the other, that being together they disturb the Peace, either by Words, Shew of Arms, turbulent Gesture, or actual Violence.

Royal Assent, denotes that Assent which the King gives to any Thing formerly done by others; as to the Election of a Bishop by Dean and Chapter; and it is likewise which he gives to a Bill passed in both Houses of Parliament; and when this Assent in Parliament is once given, the Bill is indorsed with these Words, *Le Roy le veult*, it pleases the King; but if he refuse to give such Assent, then it is indorsed thus, *Le Roy le avisera*, the King will advise. *Cowel.*

Royalties. See **Prerogative**, and **Regalia**.

Rubricks, are the Constitutions of our Church founded upon the Statutes of Uniformity and publick Prayer, which were anciently wrote down in *red* Letters, and thence are called *Rubricks*.

Rules of Court, are certain Orders from Time to Time made in our Courts of Law, which the Attornies are bound to observe, to avoid Confusion; and both the Plaintiff and Defendant are at their Peril also bound to pay Obedience to Rules made in Court in Relation to the Cause depending between them. In Case a Rule of Court is made, and is not drawn up and entered before the Continuance-Day of the same Term, the Clerk of the Rules will not draw it up afterwards, until such Time as the Court be moved, and it be again ordered to be entered up. An Attachment lies for the Breach and Contempt of a Rule of Court; and it does likewise so, where a Rule of Court is made betwixt two Parties by both their Consents, and one of the Parties disobeys the same. Yet usually an Attachment is not grantable for

Disobedience to a Rule, where the Party has not been personally served; nor for Disobedience to a Rule made by a Judge in his Chamber, in Case the same be not entered, a Rule which is not entered being of no Force to ground a Motion upon. A Rule of Court is granted every Day the Courts at *Westminster* sit, to Prisoners of the *King's Bench* or *Fleet* Prisons, to go at large about their private Business.

Runlet, is a certain Measure of Wine, *&c.* which contains eighteen Gallons and a Half; but by some it is said to be an uncertain Quantity of Liquor, from three to twenty Gallons.

Ruptarii, were Robbers that likewise went by the Name *Rutarii*; and *Rutta* denoted a Company of such: From whence we derive the Word *Rout* and *Bankrupt*.

Ruptura, is a Word found in ancient Charters, and denotes arable Land, or Ground broke up.

Rural Deans, are said to have been certain Persons who had Ecclesiastical Jurisdiction over other Ministers and Parishes near adjoining, assigned by the Bishop and Archdeacon, being placed and displaced by them.

Rustici, were the Clowns, Churls, or inferior Country Tenants, who held Cottages and Lands by the Services of Ploughing, and other the like Labours for the Lord; and Land of this ignoble Tenure was sometimes distinguished by the Name of *Terra rusticorum*.

S.

SAC, is said to be an ancient Privilege that a Lord of a Manor claims of holding of Plea in his Court, in Causes of Trespass that arise among his Tenants, and of imposing Fines and Amercements concerning the same; yet by some Writers it is taken for the Forfeiture itself.

Sacaburgh, is taken for the Person that is robbed, or by Theft deprived of his Money or Goods, and puts in Surety to prosecute the Thief with fresh Suit.

Saccus cum Brochia, was an ancient Service or Tenure of finding a *Sack*, and a Breach to the King for his Army's Use.

Sack of Wool, with us denotes a certain Quantity of Wool, containing twenty-six Stone, and every Stone fourteen Pounds.

Sacrament, is the most solemn Act of Worship in our Religion, it being instituted by our Saviour himself; and by the Rubrick there must be three at least to communicate, and no Minister can without lawful Cause deny it, to such as decently and humbly desire it. The Parson, who refuses to administer the Sacrament without just Cause, may be sued in an Action upon the Case; because a Man may receive some temporal Loss by Means of such Refusal; for by 13, 14, & 25 *Car.* 1. no Person shall be chosen into any Office of Magistracy or Place of Trust, *&c.* unless he receive the Sacrament according to the Rites of the Church of *England*, and deliver a Certificate to the Court of *King's Bench*, or Quarter-Sessions, under the Hand of the Minister, and prove it by Witnesses. Persons that revile the Sacrament of the Lord's Supper are punishable by Fine and Imprisonment.

Sacramento recipiendo, quod Vidua Regis se non maritabit sine Licentia Regis, is an ancient Writ of Commission to a Person,

Person for the Taking of an Oath of the King's Widow, that she shall not marry without the King's Licence.

Sacramentum, in a legal Sense, is used for an Oath; and the common Form of all Inquisitions made by a Jury, whilst the Proceedings in our Law were in *Latin*, did run thus, *viz. Qui dicunt super Sacramentum suum, &c.* And hence it is thought probably the Proverbial Offering to take the *Sacrament* of the Truth of a Thing, was first meant, by attesting upon Oath.

Sacramentum altaris, denotes the Sacrifice of the Mass, or what in our Church is called the *Sacrament of the Lord's Supper*.

Sacrilege, is used for a *Church-Robbery*, or an unlawful Taking of any Thing out of a Place of Worship; as where one steals any Vessels, Ornaments or Goods belonging to the Church; which Act is said to be a Robbery of God, or at least of what is dedicated to his Service. Persons who commit this Crime are guilty of Felony without Clergy: Yet it is said, that no *Sacrilege* is within the Statutes that exclude the Offenders from the Benefit of Clergy, unless such *Sacrilege* be accompanied with the actual Breaking of a Church. This Word was anciently taken to denote an Alienation to Laymen, and to profane or common Purposes, of what was given to religious Persons, and pious Uses, a Crime our Forefathers were very tender of incurring the Guilt or Scandal of.

Safe Conduct, is a certain Security given by the King, under the Great Seal, to a Foreigner; for his quiet and safe Coming into and passing out of the Kingdom.

Safe-Guard, formerly termed *Salva Garda*, or *Gardia*, is a Protection given by the King to a Stranger, who is in Fear of Violence from some of his Subjects, for the Seeking of his Right by Course of Law.

Safe-Pledge, is used for a Surety given for a Person's Appearance against a Day assigned.

Sageman, is said to denote a Tale-teller, or secret Accuser.

Sagibaro, or **Sachbaro**, is said to be the same as we now call *Justitiarius*, a Judge.

Saio & Saiones, was formerly used for a Tipstaff or Serjeant at Arms.

Salary, denotes a Recompence made to a Person for his Pains or Industry about another's Business; and it is generally taken for any Wages, Stipend, or Allowance.

Sale, does in general denote the Transferring of the Property of Goods from one to another, upon some valuable Consideration; as where in a Bargain for Goods, one agrees to give the other 5 *l.* for them, and thereupon gives the Seller *Earnest*, which he accepts; this is a perfect Sale, and shall bind both Buyer and Seller; yet if Earnest be given to the Seller, and Part of the Goods are taken away by the Buyer, he must pay the Residue of the Money upon fetching away the rest of the Goods; for that no other Time is appointed for the Doing thereof. The Buyer indeed upon *Earnest* given has a Right to demand the Goods; yet such Demand without Payment of the Money is void. After *Earnest* is once accepted, the Seller cannot dispose of the Goods to any except the Buyer, unless there be some Default in him; and therefore if the Buyer does not take away the

Goods and pay the Money, the Seller ought to require him to do it; after which, if he does not in a reasonable Time pay the same, the Bargain is said to be dissolved, and then the Seller may dispose of them to any other Person: And tho' the Seller is bound to keep the Thing sold a convenient Time for Delivery, yet where no Time for Delivery is appointed, or for Payment of the Money, it is commonly implied that the Delivery be made immediately, and that thereon the Money be directly paid.

Salique Law, is a Law peculiar to *France*, whereby none but Males are to inherit.

Salt-Silver, was a Tribute of one Penny anciently paid on the Feast of St. *Martin*, by Servile or Customary Tenants to their Lord, as a Commutation for the Service of carrying their Lord's Salt from the Market to his Larder. *Cowel*.

Salvage, is a Reward or Recompence allowed by the Civil Law for saving of Ships or Goods from the Dangers of the Seas, Pirates or Enemies: And by 12 *Ann. c.* 18. where any Ship or Vessel shall be in Danger of being stranded or driven on Shore, Justices of the Peace are directed to command the Constables to assemble as many Persons as are necessary to save the same; which being by their Means preserved, the Persons that were assisting shall within thirty Days after be paid a reasonable Reward for the *Salvage*, either by the Master of the Ship, or the Merchant concerned; otherwise the Ship or Goods shall remain in the Custody of the Officers of the Customs, as a Security for such Recompence.

Sanctuary, is defined to have been a Place privileged by the Prince, for the Safe-guard of the Lives of Offenders, being founded upon the Law of Mercy, and upon the great Reverence, Honour and Devotion which the Prince bore to the Place whereto he granted such Privilege; which was formerly so great, that such Privileges have been granted even in Cases of Treason committed against the Prince himself, Murders, Rapes, or other capital Crimes of what Nature soever. *Termes de la Ley*.

Sane Memory, denotes a Person to be of sound and perfect Mind and Memory, as *Non sane* denotes one to be quite the Reverse.

Sanguinem emere, was where Villeins were anciently bound to buy or redeem their Villein Blood or Tenure, and to make themselves Freemen. *Cowel*.

Sanguinem redimere, is by *Cowel* said to denote the accustomed Fine for Leave given to servile Tenants to dispose of their Daughters in Marriage.

Sanguis, was anciently taken for the Right or Power the Lord of the Fee had to determine Cases of Bloodshed.

Satisfaction, in a legal Sense denotes the Payment of Money due on Bond, Judgment, *&c.* in which last such Satisfaction must be entered on Record: It likewise is taken for the Rendring a Recompence for an Injury done, or Damage sustained.

Saver-Default, is the same as to say to excuse a Fault; as where a Person has made Default in Appearance in Court, he comes afterwards and alledges a good Cause for such his Default; as Imprisonment at the same Time, or the like.

Scandalum Magnatum, is particularly applied to any *Scandal* or other Wrong committed against a Person of Dignity; for which a
Writ

Writ that bears that Name is granted for the Recovery of Damages. Persons who, by either Writing or Speaking, shall report any false or scandalous News concerning great Personages, whereby Discord may arise between the Prince and his Subjects, are to be imprisoned until they produce the Author. See *Westm.* 1. *c.* 34. See also 2 *Ric.* 2. *c.* 5. upon which last Statute, an Action of *Scandalum magnatum* is usually brought for the Slander of Peers, &*c.* yet if the same be published in a Libel, the Publisher is indictable, and may be fined and imprisoned: Where an Action of *Scandalum magnatum* is brought, the same must be made a *qui tam*; that is to say, sued in the Name of the King and the Party.

Scavage, was a Toll or Custom anciently exacted by Mayors, Sheriffs, and Bailiffs of Cities and Towns corporate, of Merchant-Strangers, for Wares exposed and offered to Sale within their Liberties; which Exaction by 22 *Hen.* 8. *c.* 8. was prohibited.

Scavenger, is an Office into which two of every Parish within *London* and its Suburbs, are annually chosen; and their Office is to hire Persons stiled Rakers, and Carts to cleanse the Streets, and carry away the Dirt and Filth: And these *Scavengers* are obliged every Day, except *Sundays* or *Holidays*, to have their Carts brought into the Streets, and by Bell, or the like, give Notice of the Carrying away of the Dirt thereof, and must stay a convenient Time for the same, or otherwise are liable to the Forfeiture of 40 *s.* Where *Scavengers* are duly elected, and do not within seven Days after such Election take upon them the Office, they forfeit 10 *l.* See 2 *W.* &*M. c.* 2. and also 1 *Geo.* 1. *c.* 48.

Scharpenny. It is thought by *Cowel*, that formerly some customary Tenants were obliged to pen up their Cattle at Night in the Pound or Yard of the Lord for the Benefit of their Dung, or for Want of doing so, they paid a small Compensation, called *Scharpenny* or *Scharnpenny*, that is to say *Dung-penny*, or Money paid instead of Dung.

Schavaldus, was the Officer that collected the *Scavage-Money*. See *Scavage*.

Schedule. See *Lease*.

Schetes, was a Term anciently used for Usury.

Schirrens-geld, is said to have been an ancient Tax paid to the Sheriff for keeping the Shire or County-Court.

Schism, denotes a Division in the Church.

Scilicet, is a Word formerly often used in our Law Proceedings, and signifies, *that is to say*.

Scire facias, is a judicial Writ which is most usually issued to call a Person to shew Cause to the Court whence it goes out, why Execution of a Judgment passed should not issue; as where one has recovered Debt or Damages in a Court of Record, and does not take out Execution within a Year and a Day after Judgment recovered; in that Case he shall have this Writ to summon the Defendant to shew Cause why Execution should not go out against him upon the said Judgment; which if he do not, Judgment goes, that the Plaintiff shall have Execution: But where Judgment is obtained against a Testator, a *Scire facias* must issue against the Executor, even tho' within a Year after the Judgment had; so in like Manner against an Administrator to an Intestate: A

Scire

Scire facias must likewise issue, where Judgment is recovered against a Feme Sole, who marries within the Year and Day, to summon the Husband to shew Cause why Execution should not be awarded against him. It has been held, that if any of the Writs of Execution, either in personal or real Actions, are not executed within the Year and Day after Judgment, a *Scire facias* must issue; yet in Case the Plaintiff sues out any of these Executions within the Year and Day, he may continue them after that Time till Execution can be had, without suing out a *Scire facias*. This Writ also lies against the Bail to an Action; as where upon a Judgment recovered against the Principal, a *Capias ad satisfaciendum* is issued, and returned *Non est inventus*, and the Writ afterwards filed; a *Scire facias* in that Case may be brought against the Bail, in order to have Execution against them: And if in the *King's Bench*, upon the *Scire facias*, and two *Nihils* returned, the Bail do not appear, Judgment will be entered against them. There are divers other Writs of *Scire facias* which you may see in the Table of the *Register, Judicial* and *Original*.

Scite or **Site**, is generally taken for the Situation of any Capital Messuage or Mansion-House.

Scolds, according to our Law are taken for all such troublesome and turbulent Women, as by their Wrangling and Bawling disturb the publick Peace, who according to *Kitchin*, are indictable and punishable at the Sheriff's Turn, and may be punished by the *Cucking-Stool*.

Scot, denotes a certain Custom or common Tollage made to the Use of the Sheriff or his Bailiff.

Scot and Lot, is taken for a customary Contribution imposed upon all Subjects according to their Abilities.

Scotal or **Scotale**, is where any Officer of the Forest keeps an Alehouse in the Forest, to the Intent he may oblige Persons to come to his House and spend their Money there; for Fear of his Displeasure, or in order that he may wink at their Offences in the Forest.

Scotate, is taken for such Tenants as have their Lands subject to pay *Scot*.

Scutage, was an ancient Tax imposed on such as held Lands, &c. by Knight's Service, towards furnishing the King's Army.

Scutagio habendo, was an ancient Writ which lay for the King or other Lord against such as held by *Knight's Service* to serve in Person, or to send a sufficient Man in his Room, or to pay, &c.

Sea-Laws. See *Oleron*.

Sea-Robers. See *Pirates*.

Seal, denotes some small Figure graven or molten, and which is used as a Signet in the Sealing of Deeds. A Seal is absolutely necessary in Respect to Deeds; because the Sealing of them makes Persons Parties thereto, and without being sealed, they become void in Law. It is held, that if a Seal be broken off, it will render the Deed void, as also, where several are bound in a Bond, the Pulling off the Seal of one will vacate it as to the others.

Sealer, is an Officer in *Chancery* appointed by the Lord Chancellor, or Lord Keeper of the Great Seal, to seal the Writs and Instruments there made in his Presence.

Secondary, is an Officer that is next to the Chief Officer, as the *Secondaries* to the *Prothonotaries* of the Courts of *King's Bench* and *Common Pleas*; the *Secondary* of the Fine-Office, the *Secondary* of the *Compters*, the *Secondary* of the Office of *Privy Seal*, *Secondary* of the *Pipe*, and *Secondary* of the *Remembrancer* in the *Exchequer*. *Cowel*.

Second Deliverance, is a Writ which lies after a Plaintiff in *Replevin* has been nonsuited, and a Return of the Cattle, &c. replevied is adjudged to the Party distrained, whereby the Sheriff is commanded to replevy the same Cattle again, upon Surety given by the Plaintiff in *Replevin* to redeliver them, in Case the Distress be justified: And this may well be called a *Second* Writ of *Replevin*.

Second Marriage, which in our Law is termed *Bigamy*, is where a Man, after the Decease of his Wife, marries a second one.

Secretary, according to *Cowel*, did formerly signify any Confident, or Favourite; but it is now applied to the two *Secretaries of State*, who have an extraordinary and considerable Trust reposed in them, and in whose Hands the Petitions of the Subjects are for the most part lodged, in order to be represented to the King; after which is done, they make Dispatches thereon, according to his Majesty's Pleasure and Directions. They are also Members of the Privy Council, which is seldom or never held without one of them being present; and by Turns one of these *Secretaries* are daily attendant on the Court, and by Virtue of the King's Warrant, prepare all Bills or Letters for his Majesty to sign, wherein Matter of Law is not contained: They also keep the *Signet* or King's Seal, wherewith the King's Letters are sealed. The Power of these Principal *Secretaries* of State is great, they having, as incident to their Office, Authority to commit Persons for Treasons and other Offences against the State, as Conservators of the Peace at Common Law, or as Justices of the Peace throughout this Kingdom.

Secta ad Curiam, is a Writ which lies against the Person that refuses to perform his Suit either at the County-Court or Court-Baron.

Secta ad justitiam faciendam, is a Service that a Person is by his Fee bound to perform. *Bract*.

Secta Curiæ, was taken for the Suit and Service done by Tenants at their Lord's Court.

Secta facienda per illam quæ habet æniciam partem. There is a Writ so called to compel the Heir, who has the Elder's Part of the Coheirs, to perform Service for all the *Coparceners*.

Secta Molendini, is a Writ that lies for the Lord against his Franktenant, who held of him by making Suit to his Mill; and it also lies against the Person that was wont to grind at a certain Mill, and afterwards goes to another with his Corn.

Secta Regalis, was a Suit whereby all Persons were obliged twice a Year to attend the Sheriff's Tourn, in order to be informed of Things that relate to the Peace of the Publick; and this Suit got this Name, on Account that the Sheriff's Tourn was the King's Leet, and was held for the People to be bound by Oath to bear true Allegiance to the King; and all Persons above the Age of Twelve were obliged to take the Oath of Allegiance in this Court. *Cowel*.

Secta unica tantum facienda pro pluribus hæreditatibus, is a Writ lying for an Heir distrained by by the Lord for more Suits than one in Respect of the Lands of divers Heirs descended to him. See *Reg. Orig.* 177.

Sectis non faciendis, is, according to *Reg. Orig.* brought by a Woman, who for her Dower ought not to perform Suit of Court: And this we are told also lay for one in Wardship, to be freed of all Courts during his Wardship.

Secunda superoneratione pasturæ, according to *Old Nat. Brev.* is a Writ which lies where Admeasurement of *Pasture* has been made; and he that first surcharged the Common does again surcharge it, notwithstanding the Admeasurement.

Securitatem inveniendi quod se non divertat ad partes exteras sine Licentia Regis, is an ancient Writ of the like Nature with that of a *Ne exeat Regnum*, which lies for the King against any of his Subjects, to stay them from going out of his Kingdom: And the Ground of this Writ is said to be, that every Man is bound to serve the Common-wealth as the King shall think meet.

Securitate pacis, is a Writ that lies for a Person who is threatned Danger from another, against him that threatens; and issues out of the Court of *Chancery*, and is directed to the Sheriff.

Se defendendo, is a Plea used for him that is charged with the Death of another, by alledging he was under a Necessity, *in his own Defence*, of doing what he did; which is as much as to say, the other assaulted him in such a Manner, that if he had not done as he did, he must have been in Hazard of his own Life: But according to *Staundf.* this Danger ought to be so great, as that it may appear otherwise to have been inevitable; as where a Person is on a sudden falling out attacked, and before a mortal Wound is given, he flies to the Wall, or other like unpassable Place, in order to save his Life, but being still pursued kills the Person that attacked him; this Killing, as well as others in the like Cases, is *se defendendo*. In *se defendendo*, tho' the Offender justify the Killing to have been in his own Defence, yet he is driven to sue out his Pardon from the Lord Chancellor, which is of Course granted; but notwithstanding thereof his Goods and Chattels become forfeited to the King.

Seignior, (from the *French*) in general is taken for a Lord; but is particularly applied to the Lord of the Fee or Manor.

Seigniorage, according to *Cowel*, is taken for a Royalty or Prerogative of the King, whereby he challenges Allowance of Gold and Silver brought in the Mass in Exchange for Coin.

Seigniory, seems to signify the same as a Manor or Lordship.

Seisin, in our Common Law is taken for Possession, in the like Manner as the Verb to *seise* denotes to take Possession of any Thing; so likewise *primier Seisin*, signifies the first Possession. *Seisin* is divided into that in Deed or in Fact, and that in Law: A *Seisin* in Deed is where a Possession is actually taken; but a *Seisin* in Law is where Lands descend, and the Party has not entered on them, or in other Words, where a Person has a Right to Lands, &c. but is by Wrong disseised of them. A Person that has had but one Hour's actual Possession taken in a peaceable Manner, is said to have *Seisin de droit, & de claime*, whereof a Person may disseise

seise him, without being forced to his Action.

Seisina habenda, quia Rex habuit Annum, Diem & Vastum, is in *Reg. Orig.* defined to be a Writ which lies for Delivery of *Seisin* to the Lord of his Lands or Tenements, after the King in the Right of his Prerogative has had the Year, Day and Waste, on a Felony committed.

Self Preservation. See **Se defendendo.**

Senators, are with us at this Time taken for the Members of Parliament.

Seneschal, in a legal Sense is taken for a Steward, and in some Cases it is applied to one that has the Authority of dispensing of Justice; as the High *Seneschal*, or Steward *of England: Seneschal de le Hotel de Roy*, Steward of the King's Houshold.

Senescallo & Mareshallo quod non teneant Placita de libero tenemento, is a Writ directed to the Steward and Marshal of *England*, forbidding them to take Cognisance of an Action in their Court, which concerns Freehold.

Senencia, was anciently used for *Widowhood*, and according to *Cowel*, if a *Widow* having Dower, after the Death of her Husband, married, or brought forth a Son or a Daughter in her Widowhood, she forfeited and lost her Dower in what Place soever in *Kent*.

Separation, is properly applied to a Man and Wife's living asunder. See **Divorce.**

Septum, is taken for a Close, or other Inclosure, and is so called, because it is inclosed with a Hedge or Ditch, at least with a Hedge. *Cowel.*

Sequatur sub suo Periculo, is a Writ that lies where a Summons *ad warrantizandum* is awarded, and the Sheriff returns that the Defendant has nothing whereby he may be summoned; in which Case issues an *Alias* and a *Pluries*; upon which last Writ, if he does not come in, this Writ of *Sequatur, &c.* shall go out.

Sequela causæ, denotes the Process and depending Issue of a Cause or Trial. *Cowel.*

Sequela curiæ, is taken for a Suit of Court.

Sequela molendini, is taken for the Owning Suit to a particular Mill, or being bound to grind Corn in that Place only, which was a Duty and Service anciently imposed upon many Tenants. *Cowel.*

Sequela Villanorum, is taken for all the Retinue and Appurtenances to the Goods and Chattels of Villains or servile Tenants, which were at the arbitrary and absolute Disposal of the Lord.

Sequester, is a Term used among the Civilians for renouncing of a Right; as when a Widow comes into Court, and there or otherwise disclaims to have any Thing to do, or to intermedle with the Estate of her deceased Husband, who died intestate.

Sequestration, denotes the Setting aside of a Thing in Controversy from the Possession of both the Parties that contend for it: And *Sequestration* is of two Kinds, *Voluntary* and *Necessary: Voluntary* is that which is done by the Consent of both Parties; but *Necessary* is what the Judge of his own Authority does, whether the Parties will consent or not. This Word is also used for the Act of the Ordinary in disposing of the Goods of a deceased Person, whose Goods no Body will intermeddle with: And further, there is a *Sequestration* on a Person's standing out all the

Proceſſes of Contempt for Non-appearance in the *Chancery* or Exchequer upon a Bill exhibited; and in like Manner it is where Obedience is not yielded to a Decree; in which the Court will grant a Sequeſtration of the Party's Lands. To theſe may be added a *Sequeſtration* in *London*, made on Account of Debt, the Courſe of Proceeding in which Caſe, according to *Practic. Solic.* is this, *viz.* the Action being entered, the Officer goes to the Defendant's Shop or Warehouſe, when no Perſon is there, and takes a Padlock, and hangs it on the Door of ſuch Shop or Warehouſe, uttering theſe Words, *viz. I do ſequeſter this Warehouſe, and the Goods and Merchandiſes therein, of the Defendant in this Action, to the Uſe of the Plaintiff, &c.* after which he puts on his Seal, and makes a Return of the Sequeſtration in the *Compter*: This being done, and four Days paſt after the Return made, the next Court after the Plaintiff may have Judgment to open the Doors of the Shop or Warehouſe, and to appraiſe the Goods contained therein by a Serjeant, who takes a Bill of Appraiſement, with two Freemen to appraiſe them, which Appraiſers are to be ſworn at the next Court holden for that *Compter*; after which the Serjeant puts his Hand to the Bill of Appraiſement, and the Court grants Judgment: But yet the Defendant may put in Bail before Satisfaction, and by that Means diſſolve the *Sequeſtration*, and after Satisfaction may put in Bail to diſprove the Debt, &c.

Sequeſtro habendo, is a judicial Writ for the Diſſolving of a *Sequeſtration* of the Fruits of a Benefice granted by a Biſhop at the Royal Command of the King, in order to compel the Parſon to appear at the Suit of another; which Parſon upon his Appearance, may have this Writ, and thereby diſcharge the Sequeſtration.

Sequitur, is in our Law applied to the Preferring of an Action, and proſecuting of a Suit or Cauſe, as Attorney or Proctor in a Court of Juſtice. *Qui ſequitur pro Rege*, is where the King's Attorney General proſecutes for the King.

Serjeant or Sergeant. This Word with us is applied to divers Offices, and Callings. *Firſt*, a Serjeant at Law, or of the *Coif*, is the higheſt Degree to be taken at the Common Law, as that of a Doctor is in the Civil: And to theſe Gentlemen, as Perſons beſt learned and moſt experienced in the Law and Practice of the Court, one Court, *viz.* the *Common Pleas*, is ſet apart for them to plead in by themſelves, and yet they are not reſtrained from pleading in any other Court, where the Judges (who cannot have that Honour till they have taken the Degree of *Serjeant at Law*) call them *Brothers*, and hear them with great Reſpect, next to the Regard always ſhewn to his Majeſty's Attorney, and Solicitor General. Theſe *Serjeants* are created by the King's Mandate or Writ, commanding them upon a great Penalty to take upon them that Degree by a certain Day therein aſſigned: And one or more of the Serjeants at Law is ſtiled the King's Serjeant, who is choſen out of the reſt, in Reſpect of his great Learning, to plead for him in all Cauſes, eſpecially in thoſe of Treaſon. See *Dyer*. See alſo *Staundf. Pl. Coron.* The next is a *Serjeant at Arms*, or *Mace*, whoſe Office is to attend the King's Perſon, to arreſt Traitors or Perſons of Condition, and to attend the Lord

Lord High Steward, when sitting in Judgment upon a Traitor, and the like. The Number of these Officers are by 13 *Ric.* 2. *c.* 6. limited to that of thirty; two of which by the King's Allowance attend on the two Houses of Parliament: And the Office of him that attends the House of Commons is the Keeping of the Doors, and the Execution of such Commands relating to the Apprehension of any Offender, as that Honourable House shall injoin him. Another of these Officers attends on the Lord *Chancellor* or Lord *Keeper* in the *Chancery*; another on the Lord *Treasurer*; and also another attends upon the Lord Mayor of *London* upon extraordinary Solemnities. See *Crompt. Jur.* There is likewise a more inferiour Kind of *Serjeants of the Mace*, of which there is a Band or Troop in the City of *London*, and other Corporations, who attend the Mayor or other Head Officer, chiefly for Matters of Justice: And *lastly*, there are Serjeants of the King's Houshold, who execute several Functions or Offices in the *King's Houshold*.

Serjeanty, in a legal Sense is taken for a Service that cannot be due from a Tenant to any Lord, except the King only: And this is either Grand or Petit Serjeanty; the first of which is where a Person holds Land of the King by Service, which he ought to perform in his own Person; as to bear the King's Banner, Spear, &c. The other, which is termed *Petit Serjeanty*, is where one holds of the King, to yield yearly some small Thing towards his Wars; as a Sword, Dagger, Bow, &c. *Cowel.* By 12 *Car.* 2. *c.* 24. these Services, excepting the Honourary ones, in *Grand Serjeanty*, are entirely taken away. See **Chivalry**.

Servants, are properly those whom Men of Trades or Professions imploy under them in their particular Callings; or they are such Persons as are retained by others to do the Work, or transact the Affairs of their Families. Some Servants are *Menial*, and some are not: Those that are *Menial*, are properly termed *Domesticks*, they living within the Walls of their Master's House or Habitation. By 7 *Jac.* 1. *c.* 4. If any *Servant* who is hired for a Year, depart before the End of his Term, without reasonable Cause to be allowed by a Justice of the Peace; or after his Term is expired, without giving a Quarter's Warning, he is liable to be committed to Prison by two Justices, until he give Security to serve out the Time; or he may by one Justice be sent to the House of Correction, to be punished there as a disorderly Person. On the other Hand, by 5 *Eliz.* a Master cannot put away his Servant before the End of the Term, he was hired for, without some reasonable Cause allowed by a Justice of the Peace, nor after the Expiration of the Term without a Quarter's Warning given; if he does otherwise he forfeits 40 *s.* According to *Dalt.* if a Servant that is hired for a Year fall sick, &c. such Servant ought not to be discharged, nor his Wages abated on that Account: And if a Master discharge his Servant, he must pay him his Wages to the very Time he served; but if the Servant depart from his Service before the End of his Term, he shall in that Case forfeit all his Wages. According to *Wood*, where a Master always gives his

Aaa 2 Servant

Servant Money, he is not liable to answer what the Servant buys on Trust for him; but if he send sometime on Trust, he becomes liable to answer to his usual Tradesmen what is taken by his Servant in his Name upon Trust. By 21 *Hen.* 8. and 12 *Ann. c.* 7. Servants running off with, imbezling or purloining their Master's Goods to the Value of 40 *s.* are guilty of Felony.

Servi, was anciently used for Bondmen, or *Servile Tenants*. The proper *Servi* were of four Sorts; the *first*, such as sold themselves for a Livelihood; the *second*, Debtors that were sold for Payment of their Debts; the *third* Captives in War, who were kept and imployed as perfect Slaves; the *fourth*, *Nativi*, such as were born Servants, and by Discent were the sole Property of the Lord; the Persons of all whom, as well as their Children and Goods, were absolutely at the Disposal of their Lord, and incapable of making a Will, or giving away any Thing.

Service, is properly that Duty which the Tenant on Account of his Fee owes to his Lord. There were anciently many Divisions of *Services*, which at this Time it is needless to give a particular Account of, because by 12 *Car.* 2. *c.* 24. which has turned all Tenures into common Socage, all *Services* are utterly abolished.

Service secular, which denotes worldly Service, is opposed to that which is termed Spiritual or Ecclesiastical Service.

Servitium Forinsecum, was a Service that only belonged to the King.

Servitium intrinsecum, was a Service that was due to the Chief Lord alone from his Vassal.

Servitium liberum, was a Service anciently due from the feudatory Tenants, who were distinguished from Vassals by the Name of *Liberi homines*, as well as the Nature of their *Services*, which were not base, as those of the Vassals were.

Servitium ferrandi, according to *Cowel*, denotes the Service of Shoeing Horses.

Servitium Regale, or **Royal Service**, denotes the Rights and Prerogatives which within certain Manors belong to the King as Lord of the same; and of these there were generally reckoned to be the six following, *viz.* 1. The Power of Judicature in Matters of Property. 2. Power of Life and Death in Felonies and Murders. 3. A Right to Waifs and Strays. 4. Assessments. 5. Minting of Money. 6. Assise of Bread, Beer, Weights and Measures; all which are said to be intire Privileges annexed to some Manors by the King's Grant.

Servitiis acquietandis, is a judicial Writ which lies for a Person that is distrained for Service due to one, who owes and performs the same to another, for the Acquittal of those Services.

Servitors of Bills, is taken for such Servants or Messengers of the Marshal of the *King's Bench*, as were sent out with Writs or Bills, to summon Persons to that Court.

Sesscur, is taken for the Assessing or Rating of Wages.

Sessions, in general, denotes a Sitting of Justices in Court upon Commission; as the *Sessions* of *Oyer and Terminer*, the *Quarter-Sessions*, otherwise termed the *General* or *Open Sessions*, in Opposition to what is called an *Especial* or *Privy Sessions*, which are

held

held upon some particular Occasion, for the speedier Dispatch of Justice: And this *Quarter-Sessions* is a Court of Record held before two or more Justices of the Peace (one being of the *Quorum*) for the Execution of the Authority granted them by their Commission and particular Statutes, whereby they are authorised to hear and determine Trespasses against the publick Peace, &c. and likewise divers Offences declared so by Statute. This Court of Sessions is held four Times in the Year, in one Place or other in every County.

Sessions of Parliament, denotes the Sitting or Meeting together of the House of Lords and Commons in Parliament, which is always continued until it be prorogued or dissolved; and it never breaks off by Adjournment.

Several Action, is by *Jacob* said to be where two or more are severally charged in any Action.

Several Inheritance, is where an *Inheritance* is so conveyed, as to go to two Persons severally, by Moieties, &c. *Jacob.*

Several Tail, denotes that Land which is intailed severally on two; as where Lands are given to two Men and their Wives, and to the Heirs of their Bodies to be lawfully begotten; in which Case the Donees have a joint Estate for their two Lives, and at the same Time have a several or separate Inheritance; for the Issue of the one shall have his Moiety, and the Issue of the other his. *Cowel.*

Several Tenancy, is a Plea or Exception taken to a Writ which is taken out against two Persons as Jointenants, who in Fact are not so, but *several*.

Severance, is the Singling or Separating of two or more joined in one Writ; as where two join in a Writ *de libertate probanda,* and the one of the Plaintiffs afterwards becomes nonsuit, in this Case *Severance* is allowed; so that after the Nonsuit of the one, the other may proceed severally. There is likewise *Severance* of the Tenants in Assise, which is where one, two or more Disseisors appear upon the Writ, and not the other. There is also *Severance* in Debt, as where two or more Executors are Plaintiffs in a Suit, and the one of them refuses to proceed therein. According to *Hale,* there are two Kinds of *Severances,* one where a Plaintiff will not appear, and the other where several Plaintiffs appear, but some of them will not proceed in the Suit. To these may be added the *Severance of Corn,* which denotes the Cutting or Carrying the same off the Ground; and sometimes it is taken for the Setting out the Tithe from the rest of the Corn.

Steward, (from the *Saxons*) denotes a Person that guards the Sea-Coasts.

Sewer, according to *Cowel,* is a Passage or Gutter made to carry Water into the Sea or a River. The Commissioners of *Sewers* are those who by Authority under the Great Seal, were appointed to see Drains and Ditches well kept and maintained in marshy and fenny Countries, for the better Conveyance of Water into the Sea, and the Preserving of Grass upon the Land for feeding of Cattle. In a Word, the Business or Office of the Commissioners of *Sewers* is to repair Sea-Banks, and Walls, survey Rivers, publick Streams, Ditches, &c. and to make Orders for that Purpose; and they also have Authority to make Inquiry

quiry of all Nusances and Offences committed by the Stopping of Rivers, erecting Mills not repairing Banks, Bridges, &c. and to tax and assess Persons chargeable, for the amending of Defaults that tend to the Obstruction or Hindrance of the free Passage of the Water thro' its ancient Courses.

Sextary, was an ancient Measure, that contained about an usual Pint and a Half.

Sextery Lands, denotes Lands formerly given to a Church or religious House for the Maintenance of the *Sexton*.

Shack, is a Name peculiarly applied to a Custom in the County of *Norfolk*, to have Common for Hogs from the End of Harvest till Seed-time, in all Persons Grounds without Exception: And according to *Cowel, to go at Shack*, is as much as to say, to go at large.

Sharping Corn, is a customary Gift of *Corn*, which the Farmers pay in sundry Parts of *England* to their Smith, for sharping their Plough-Irons, Harrow-tines, &c. which does not exceed Half a Bushel for a Plough-Land.

Sheading, by *Cowel* is said to be a Riding, Tithing or Division in the *Isle of Man*, where the whole Island is divided into six *Sheadings*, in each whereof there is a *Coroner* or Chief Constable, who is appointed by the Delivery of a Rod at the *Tinewald* Court or annual Convention. *Cowel*.

Sheriff or **Shire-reve**, signifies the chief Officer under the King, in every County or Shire, and according to *Cambd. Brit.* is so called from the first Division of this Kingdom into Counties. *Sheriffs*, tho' anciently elected in the County-Court by the People, are now appointed by the King, and the Lord Chancellor, and also the Treasurer, and Barons of the Exchequer, &c. who annually nominate three Persons for each County, out of whom the King pitches upon one, who is accordingly created Sheriff by Letters Patent. A Sheriff is said to be a Royal Officer, and one that takes Place of every Nobleman in the County, during the Time of his continuing Sheriff. A *Sheriff* at the Time of his Entrance upon his Office must attend on the Remembrancer's Office in the Exchequer, and there enter into Recognizance, with Sureties, conditioned for Payment of his Proffers on Accounts; whereupon his Attorney, or other proper Person that acts for him, must write him a Note, thereby declaring that such Person is chosen Sheriff of the County, and has entered into Recognisance; and this he must deliver to one of the six Clerks in *Chancery*, in Order to make his Patent by; after which is done, the new Sheriff, if in *London*, is to go to a Master in *Chancery*, or, if in the Country, to one of the Judges of Assise, or before two Justices of the Peace of the same County, for that Purpose commissioned, before whom he must take the Oaths of Allegiance Supremacy, &c. and also an Oath for the due Execution of his Office. Notwithstanding a new Sheriff is appointed, the old one remains Sheriff till the new one is sworn, as soon as which is done the old Sheriff's Office ends. According to *Wood*, as soon as the new Sheriff is elected, he is to deliver the Writ of Discharge to the old Sheriff, who thereupon delivers over all the Prisoners in the Gaol, with all Writs, &c. by Indenture of Assignment to the new Sheriff; before which is done, the Prisoners are deemed to be in the Custody of the old Sheriff. It has been held, that

that if a Person be in Execution in the Custody of the old Sheriff, and has not been turned over to the new Sheriff, if he escape, the old Sheriff in that Case is chargeable, and not the new one. A Sheriff is invested with a *judicial* and *ministerial* Power: His judicial consists in Hearing, and Determining Causes in his *Tourn*, and County-Court; and also in keeping the Peace of the County, he being by the Common Law the principal Conservator of the Peace there, and on that Account is to assist the Justices, and raise the *Posse Comitatus*, to keep the Peace, when Occasion requires: The Ministerial Authority of the Sheriff consists in the Execution of Writs and Processes out of the King's Courts. Tho' a Sheriff is not by Law allowed to break open the Door, if shut, to execute a Writ, yet it is held, that if he do so, and arrest the Party, it is good. Another Part of a Sheriff's *ministerial* Office is, to return Juries for Trials, as well in Civil as in Criminal Cases, except where there is Cause of Challenge against him; in which Case the *Coroners* are to return Juries: Their Office is likewise to proclaim Statutes, and make Return of Writs for electing Knights of the Shire, &c. and they also collect the King's Rents, seise the Profits of Lands forfeited, and Goods of Felons, levy the King's Debts, Fines, Amerciaments, &c. and they are accountable to the King for the Profits of their Counties; for which they are to account in the *Exchequer*, &c. And, *lastly*, their Duty is to see that Criminals be executed, and the Order of Law observed in putting them to Death. A Sheriff has usually under him an *Under-Sheriff*, Bailiffs, and a Gaoler for all whom he is answerable; but if he thinks fit, he may execute his Office himself without an Under-Sheriff. Tho' the Office of Sheriff is generally executed by the Under-Sheriff, yet in some particular Cases the High Sheriff is to execute his Office in Person; as in Case of a Writ of Partition, Waste, Redisseisin, &c. The High Sheriff is amerceable in the *Exchequer* for every Default in the Execution of his Office. No Under-Sheriff is to act as an Attorney, during the Time he bears that Office; yet such of them as are Attornies may practise in another Person's Name.

Sheriffalty, denotes the Time of a Person's being Sheriff, as *Sheriffwick* denotes the Extent of a Sheriff's Authority.

Sheriffwick. See **Sheriffalty.**

Sheriffgeld, is taken for a Rent that was anciently paid by the *Sheriff*.

Sheriff-tooth, according to *Cowel*, is taken for a Tenure by the Service or Duty of providing Entertainment for the Sheriff at his County-Tourns or Courts.

Ship-money. In the Reign of King *Charles* the First, there was a certain Imposition that went under that Name, which was charged upon the Ports, Cities, Towns, Boroughs and Counties of *England*, by Writs under the Great Seal, termed *Ship-writs*, or the providing certain Ships for the King's Service, &c.

Shire. See **County.**

Shiremote, is taken for an Assembly of the County or *Shire* at the Assises.

Shoplifters, are such Persons as privately steal Goods out of *Shops*; which amounting to the Value of 5 s. is by 10 & 11 W. 3. c. 23. made

made Felony without the Benefit of Clergy.

Shorling and Morling, are Words used to distinguish Fells of Sheep; the first denoting the Fells after the Fleeces are first *shorn off* on the Sheep's Back; and the other signifying the Fells *flead off* after the Sheep are killed, or die alone.

Sicut alias, is a second Writ issued out where the first was not executed.

Sidemen, otherwise **Questmen**, are such as are annually elected, according to the Custom of every Parish, to assist the Church-wardens in the Inquiry and Presenting of such Offenders to the Ordinary as are punishable in the Spiritual Court. *Cowel.*

Sign Manual, is used to denote any Bill or Writing signed by the King's own Hand.

Signet, is one of the King's Seals made Use of in sealing his private Letters, &c.

Significavit, is a Writ that issues out of the Court of *Chancery*, upon a Certificate granted by the Ordinary of a Person's standing *Excommunicate* for Forty Days, in Order to have him laid up in Prison, until he submit to the Authority of the Church. According to *Reg. Orig.* there is another Writ of this Name, directed to the Justices of the *Bench*, enjoining them to stay a Suit that is depending between such and such Parties, on Account of an Excommunication alledged against the Plaintiff, &c. There are other Writs that bear this Name, which you may see in *Fitz. Nat. Brev.* But the common one is the same with the Writ *De excommunicato capiendo.*

Signum. See **Seal.**

Simony, is an unlawful Contract made to have a Person presented to a Rectory or Vicarage, which is prohibited by 31 *Eliz. c.* 6. whereby it is enacted, that if any Person for any Sum of Money, Reward, Gift, Profit or Benefit, or by Reason of any Promise, Agreement, Grant, Bond, Covenant, or other Assurance for any Sum of Money, Reward, &c. shall present or collate any Person to any Benefice with Cure, Dignity or Living Ecclesiastical; or give or bestow the same, in Respect of any such corrupt Cause or Consideration, every such Presentation, Collation, Gift, and Bestowing, and every Admission and Induction thereupon shall be utterly void; and the Crown in such Case may present for that Turn: And the Person or Persons that shall give or take any Sum of Money, or shall take or make such Promise, &c. shall forfeit double the Value of one Year's Profit of every such Benefice; and the Person so corruptly taking such Benefice shall from thenceforth be disabled to have and enjoy the same. See 12 *Ann. c.* 12. which, according to *Wood*, only restrains those that are to be presented to the Living on the next Avoidance upon Purchase, &c. but not Laymen, or such Clergymen, as are not to be presented to the Church.

Simplex, which signifies simple, is generally applied to a *Deed-Poll*, or single Deed.

Simplex Beneficium, denotes an inferior Dignity in a Cathedral or Collegiate Church, a Sine-Cure, a Pension out of a Parochial Church, or any other Ecclesiastical Benefice opposed to a Cure of Souls, and which on that Account is inconsistent with any Parochial Cure, without coming under the Denomination of Pluralities. *Cowel.*

Simplex

Simplex Justitiarius, was a Stile anciently used for any puisne Judge, that was not Chief in any Court; and *Cowel* tells us, that there is a Writ registred, which begins thus, *viz. I* John Wood, *a simple Judge of the Common Pleas,* &c.

Simul cum, are Words that were formerly made Use of in Indictments, and Declarations of Trespass, where there were several Defendants, whereof some are known, and others not.

Sine Assensu Capitali, is a Writ lying where a Bishop, Dean, Prebendary, or Master of an Hospital aliens the Lands holden in Right of his Bishoprick, &c. without the *Consent* of the *Chapter, Convent and Fraternity*; in which Case his Successor shall have this Writ. See *Fitz. Nat. Brev.*

Sine Cure, is defined to be where a Rector of a Parish has a Vicar under him endowed and charged with the Cure, insomuch that the Rector is obliged neither to Duty nor Residence: And according to *Wood*, when a Church is fallen down, and the Parish becomes destitute of Parishioners, it is said to be a *Sine Cure*.

Sine Die, that is to say, without Day, is a Term frequently made Use of in our Proceedings at Common Law: As when Judgment is given against the Plaintiff, he is said to be *in misericordia pro falso Clamore suo*; so when Judgment passes for the Defendant, it is said, *Eat inde sine Die*, which is as much as to say, he is dismissed the Court.

Si non omnes, is a Writ of Association, whereby, in Case all in Commission cannot meet at the Day assigned, it is allowed, that two or more of them may finish the Business. *Cowel.*

Si Recognoscunt, is a Writ which anciently lay for a Creditor against his Debtor, who before the Sheriff in the County-Court acknowledged to owe his Creditor a certain Sum received of him.

Site. See **Scite**.

Sithesoca, otherwise **Sipesoca**, is taken for a Franchise or Liberty of a Company of Men, or a Hundred.

Sithindi, is by *Cowel* defined to be Servants of the same Nature with *Rod-Knights, viz.* such as were bound to attend their Lord wheresoever he went; notwithstanding which, it seems such Servant was among the *English Saxons* accounted as *Liber Homo*, a Freeman, for that he held Lands in Fee, subject only to such Tenure.

Slander, denotes a Defaming of a Person's Character, Profession, or Imployment; for which an Action of the Case lies.

Sloug-silver, is said to be a Rent payable to the Castle of *Wigmore*, and is instead of certain Days Work in Harvest, formerly reserved to the Lord from his Tenants.

Smoak-silver, is taken to be a certain Payment made to the Ministers of several Parishes; and the same is so done in lieu of Tithe *Wood*. This is also called *Smoakpenny*.

Smuglers, is properly taken for such Persons as conceal or run prohibited Goods, or Goods that have not answered his Majesty's Customs; against which Offence there is a very severe Statute in Force, *viz.* 8 *Geo.* 1. *c.* 18.

Soc, is taken for a Power or Liberty of Jurisdiction; and hence it is that our *Latin* Word, *Soca*, has been used for a Seigniory or Lordship, enfranchised by the King, with the Liberty of holding or keeping a Court of his Sockmen, or *Socagers*, viz. his Tenants, whose Tenure is there called *Socage*.

Socage, in *Termes de la Ley*, is defined to be a certain Tenure, whereby one holds of a Lord Lands or Tenements, under a certain Rent in Lieu of all Manner of Services: And to hold by *Socage*, is not to hold by Knight's Service; neither does Ward, Marriage, or Relief belong thereto; but the Tenant was upon the Death of his Ancestor to pay double the Rent. *Socage* is said to be three Ways, viz. *Socage* in free Tenure, *Socage* in ancient Tenure, and *Socage* in base Tenure. *Socage* in free Tenure, is where one holds of another by Fealty and certain Rent in Lieu of all Services as already observed: And of all Lands held in *Socage*, the next of Kin shall have the Ward, because the Heritage may not descend, till the Heir be of the Age of Fourteen. If a Guardian in *Socage* commit Waste, he may not be impeached thereof, but must yield an Account to the Heir when he attains to the full Age of Twenty-one Years. *Socage* in ancient Tenure was where People held in Ancient Demesne, who were used to have no other Writ than the Writ of *Right-Close*, which was determined according to the Custom of the Manor; and the *Monstraverunt* to discharge them, when the Lord distrained them to oblige them to perform other Services than they ought. *Socage* in base Tenure is where a Person holds in ancient Demesne, who may not have the *Monstraverunt*; and for that Reason it is called *Base Tenure*. Since the Statute 12 *Car.* 2. *c.* 24. all Tenures have been adjudged to be turned into free and common *Socage*.

Socagers. See **Socmen**.

Socmen, is taken for such Tenants in Ancient Demesne as held their Lands by *Socage*; but according to *Fitzherbert*, the Tenants in Ancient Demesne were properly called *Sockmans*.

Socna, according to *Cowel* denotes a Privilege, Liberty or Franchise.

Socome, is taken for a Custom of grinding at the Lord's Mill; and hence came the Name or Term of *Bond-Socome*, by which the Tenants were bound to it, and also *Love-Socome*, where they did it voluntarily out of Love to their Lord. *Cowel.*

Sodomy. See **Buggery**.

Soka, Soc, Sok, Soke, are Words that are generally taken for the Liberty of Tenants excused from customary Burdens and Impositions.

Solarium, is frequently to be found in old Charters or Deeds, and in *English* is called a *Sollar*, which is taken for an upper Room or Garret.

Solet & Debet. See **Debet**.

Sole Tenant, denotes one that holds Lands, &c. in his own Right only, without any other joined; as where a Man and his Wife hold Land for their Lives, the Remainders to their Son; in this Case, if the Man dies, the Lord shall not have an Heriot, because he does not die *Sole Tenant*. See *Kitchin* 134.

Solicitor, denotes a Person that is imployed to take Care of and manage Suits depending in the Courts of Law or Equity; and according to *Cowel*, such Persons were only allowed to Nobility, whose menial Servants they were; but now are too often made Use of by others, to the Damage of the People, and the Increase of Champerty and Maintenance. There is likewise a great Officer of the Law next to the *Attorney General*, who is ftiled the King's *Solicitor General*.

Solidata Terræ, is said to have been as much Land as was annually worth one Shilling.

Solidatum, taken fubftantively is faid to denote that abfolute Right or Property which a Perfon has in any Thing.

Solinus Terræ, in *Kent*, is faid to denote 160 Acres.

Sollar, or **Soller**. See **Sollarium**.

Solvendo effe, is a Term ufed in our Law to denote, that a Perfon is in a Capacity to pay, or in other Words, is *folvent*.

Solvere Pœnas, denotes to undergo the Punifhment inflicted for an Offence.

Solvit ad Diem, is a Plea to an Action of Debt upon a Bond, Penal Bill, &c. wherein it is alledged that the Money was paid at the Day limited in fuch Bond, &c.

Solutione Feodi Militis & Burgenf. Parliamenti, are Writs by which Knights of the Shire and Burgeffes may recover their ancient Allowance, if it were denied them.

Son Affault, is a Juftification in an Action of Affault and Battery, whereby the Defendant alledges that the Plaintiff made the firft *Affault*, and that what the Defendant did in Return was in his own Defence; yet it is held that this cannot be pleaded by a Defendant who commits a violent Battery.

Sontage, according to *Stow*, was a Tax of 40 s. impofed on every Knight's Fee.

Sorcery, is taken for a Kind of Witchcraft, or a Divination by Lots.

Sors is a Term anciently ufed in Sums of Money lent upon Ufury, denoting the Principal, as diftinguifhed from the Intereft.

Sovereign, denotes a Chief Perfon, one that is in Dignity higheft of all; as a King, &c.

Sowne, (from the *French*) fignifying remembred, is a Term ufed in the *Exchequer*, where Eftreats that *fowne* not, are fuch as the Sheriff by his Care and Diligence cannot levy, and *Eftreats that fowne*, are fuch as he may levy.

Spatæ Placitum, is taken for a Court Martial, for the fpeedy Execution of Juftice on military Delinquents.

Speaker of the Parliament, is the Chief Officer in that high Court; and is, as one may fay, the Mouth of the reft: And, according to *Cowel*, as that Honourable Affembly confifts of two Houfes, the upper and the lower Houfe, viz. the *Lords* and *Commons*; fo there are two *Speakers*, the one called the *Lord Speaker of the Houfe of Peers*, who is ufually the *Lord Chancellor*, or *Lord Keeper of the Great Seal*: And the other being a Member of the *Houfe of Commons*, is termed the *Speaker* of that Houfe, the refpective Duties of which two *Speakers* chiefly confift in managing Debates putting Queftions, and by that Means collecting the Senfe of each Houfe, the Paffing of Bills, and feeing the Orders of each Houfe duly obferved.

Special Matter in Evidence. See **General Iffue**.

Specialty, is ufed for a Bond, Bill, or other Deed executed under the Hand and Seal of the Parties thereto.

Spigurnel, denotes the Sealer of the King's Writs; and it is faid took this Name from one *Galfridus Spigurnel*, whom King *Henry* the Third first appointed in that Office.

Spinster, is an Addition in our Law usually given to all unmarried or single Women; but it is the Opinion of Sir *Edward Coke*, that *Generosa* is a good Addition for a Gentlewoman, and if such be named *Spinster* in an original Writ or Indictment, they may abate and quash the same.

Spiritual or Ecclesiastical Courts, are such as have Jurisdiction in matrimonial Causes, and for Probate of Wills, and granting Administration of Goods: It likewise has Jurisdiction in Regard to Tithes, and also in Cases of Defamation, &c.

Spiritualties of a Bishop, are taken for those Profits that he receives as a Bishop, and not as a Baron of Parliament: As for Example the Duties of his Visitation, Prestation-Money, his Benefit arising from Ordinations and Institutions of Priests. &c.

Spoliation, is a Writ lying for one Incumbent against another, where the Right of Patronage does not come in Debate; as where a Parson is created a Bishop, and obtains a Dispensation to keep his Rectory, after which the Patron presents another to the Church, who is instituted and inducted; in which Case the Bishop may have this Writ in the Ecclesiastical Court against the new Incumbent, seeing that they both claim under one Patron, and for that Reason the Right of Patronage does not come in Question, and because the other Incumbent came to the Possession of the Benefice by Course of the Spiritual Law, that is to say, by Institution and Induction, otherwise a Writ of *Spoliation* would not lie, but instead thereof a Writ of Trespass, or Assise of *Novel Disseisin*. In like Manner it is where a Clergyman having a Plurality of Livings, accepts of another Benefice, on which Account the Patron presents another Clerk, who becomes instituted and inducted; the one in this Case may have a *Spoliation* against the other, whereupon it will come in Question whether he has a sufficient Plurality, or not. *Termes de la Ley*.

Spouse-breach, is taken for *Adultery*, as opposed to simple Fornication.

Stabilia, was a Writ founded on a Custom in *Normandy*, which was where a Person in Power claimed Lands in the Possession of an inferior Person, he petitioned the Prince that they might be put into his Hands until the Right was decided; whereupon he had this Writ.

Stablestand, according to *Manwood*, is taken for one of the four Evidences or Presumptions, whereby a Person is convicted of an Intention to steal the King's Deer in the Forest; as where a Person is found at his *Standing* in the Forest, with a Cross-Bow or Long-Bow bent, ready to shoot at Deer, or standing close by a Tree with Grey-Hounds in a Leash, ready to slip.

Stadium, is taken to be a Furlong of Ground, *viz.* the eighth Part of a Mile.

Staff-hording, is used to denote a Right to follow Cattle in a Forest.

Stagiarius, is taken for a Canon Residentiary in a Cathedral Church. *Cowel* observes, that this Distinction is generally made betwixt *Residentiarius*, and *Stagiarius*, *viz.* every Canon installed to the Privileges and Profits of Residence was termed *Residentiarius*; and when he actually kept such stated Residence

ST

Residence, he was said to be *Stagiarius*, or *Stagionarius*.

Stalkers, are a Sort of Fishing Nets mentioned in 13 *Ric.* 2. *c.* 20.

Stallage, is taken for the Liberty of pitching Tents or erecting Stalls in Fairs or Markets; or for the Money paid for such Liberty.

Stallarius, was anciently the Appellation of the Officer we now stile *Master of the Horse*.

Stamp-Duties, are certain Impositions laid on all Vellum, Parchment and Paper, on which Deeds, Grants, or other Instruments, or any Process in Law or Equity are written or engrossed. See 5 & 6 *W. & M. c.* 21. and 9 & 10 *W.* 3. See also 12 *Ann.*

Standard, in a legal Sense is taken for the King's Standing Measure; according to which all Measures ought to be framed by Clerks of Markets, Aulnagers, and other the like Officers. The *Standard of Money*, is that whereby the Quantity of Silver and Gold, and how much Allay are ordained to be contained in old *Sterling* Coin, Standard of Plate and Silver Manufactures.

Standardus, is taken for true *Standard*, or legal Weight or Measure.

Staple, (from the *French*) denotes certain Towns or Cities, whereto the Merchants of *England* were by Statute obliged to carry their Wool, Cloth, Lead, and other the like Staple Commodities of this Realm, in order to utter the same by Wholesale. The *Staple* Commodities of this Kingdom are by some said to be these, *viz. Wool, Leather, Wool-fels, Lead, Tin, Butter, Cheese, Cloth, &c.* but others allow only the five first to be so.

Star, is a Name that was anciently given to a Deed, Contract, or other Obligation of the *Jews*.

ST

Star-Chamber, was a High Court at *Westminster*, wherein the Chancellor, assisted by others for that Purpose appointed, had Authority to punish *Routs, Riots, Forgeries, Perjuries*, and other the like Misdemeanors as were not by the Common Law provided against: But now this Court, with all its former Power and Jurisdiction, is absolutely dissolved.

Stationarius. See **Stagiarius**.

Statute, in our Law has divers Significations, it being sometimes taken for an Act of Parliament made by the King, the three Estates of the Realm: At other Times it is used for a short Instrument in Writing termed a *Statute Merchant*, or a *Statute Staple*, which are in the Nature of Bonds, and according to *Cowel*, they are called *Statutes*, on Account of their being made pursuant to the Forms prescribed by Statutes, whereby it is directed before what Persons, and how they are to be made. A *Statute-Merchant* is by *West* defined thus, *viz.* that it is a Bond acknowledged before one of the Clerks of the Statutes Merchant, and Lord Mayor of the City of *London*, or two Merchants thereof for that Purpose; or before the Mayor, chief Warden, or Master of other Cities or Corporations, or other sufficient Persons for that End appointed, sealed with the Seal of the Debtor and the King, upon Condition that if the Obligor pay not the Debt at the Day, Execution may be awarded against his Body, Lands and Goods; in which Case the Recognisee or Obligee shall hold the Lands to him his Heirs and Assigns until such Time as the Debt is levied. Where a Debtor has not Goods within the Jurisdiction of the Mayor, the Recognisance may be sent to the Lord Chan-

Chancellor under the King's Seal; who shall thereupon direct a Writ to the Sheriff of the County wherein any of the Debtor's Goods are, and the Sheriff is to proceed thereon as the Mayor could have done, had the Goods been within his Jurisdiction; and in Case the Debtor has not Goods to be levied upon, he may be imprisoned, and shall continue there until Satisfaction or an Agreement be made with the Creditor: And in like Manner, the Debtor's Sureties, in Case he have any, may be proceeded against, provided the Debt cannot be levied on the Debtor's Goods, otherwise the Sureties shall not be liable. *Statute-Staple* particularly concern Merchants of the *Staple*, and are of the same Nature with *Statutes-Merchant*, and are for Debt acknowledged before the Mayor of the *Staple* in our chief Cities, &c. in the Presence of one or more of the Constables of the *Staple*; by Virtue of which the Creditor, on Nonpayment of his Money, when due, has the same Remedy against his Debtor, as is to be had upon a *Statute-Merchant*. A *Tenant* by *Statute-Merchant* or *Statute-Staple*, denotes the Person that is in Possession of Lands on a *Statute-Merchant* or *Staple*.

Statutes-Merchant. See *Statutes*.

Statutes-Staple. See *Statutes*.

Statuto Mercatorio, is a Writ lying for the imprisoning of a Debtor, on the Forfeiture of his Bond, termed *Statute-Merchant*, until such Time as the Debt be satisfied.

Statuto Stapulæ, is a Writ which lies for taking the Body of a Debtor on a *Statute-Staple* Bond; and for seising the Lands and Goods of him that has forfeited such Bond.

Statutum de Laborariis, is an old Writ for the apprehending of those Labourers that refuse to work pursuant to the Statute.

Statute-Sessions, is taken for a Meeting of Constables and Housholders, by Custom, for the Debating of Differences between Masters and Servants, the Rating of Servants Wages, and bestowing such Persons in Service as are fit to serve, &c.

Staurum, is taken for any Store or standing Stock of Cattle, Provision, &c. And *Cowel* tells us, that when formerly the Bishops stocked their own demesne Lands, at their Diocese they were obliged to leave such a fixed Number of Cattle for a Stock to their Successor; and this Stock upon the Ground was called *staurum, de stauro,* and *de instauro*.

Stealing, denotes a fraudulent Taking away of another Man's Goods, with an Intent to convert the same to his own Use, without the Privity or Consent of the Owner.

Sterling, was an Epithet for Silver Money current within this Realm. This Word with us is now almost wholly disused, for instead thereof we commonly say, lawful Money of *Great Britain*; yet in the Mint they still say *Sterling* Money.

Steward, (from the *Saxons*) denotes a Person appointed in another's Place or Stead, and is always taken for a principal Officer within his Jurisdiction. The greatest of such Officers is the *Lord High Steward of England*, an Office that was anciently the Inheritance of the Earls of *Leicester*, till forfeited to King *Henry* the Third by *Simon de Mountfort*: But as *Cowel* well observes, the Power of this Officer being very great, he has not been appointed for any long Time, but only for some special Business, as the Arraignment of some Nobleman in

Cafe

Case of Treason or the like, which once being over his Commission ceases. There is also the *Lord Steward of the King's Houshold,* who is now called the *Great Master of the Houshold,* who is chief Officer of the King's Court, and has the Care of the King's House; and has Authority over all the Officers and Servants of the Houshold, except such as belong to the Chapel, Chamber, and Stable. There is likewise a *Steward of the Marshalsea,* of whose ancient Authority you may read in *Fleta.* In short, there is in most Corporations, and in all Houses of Honour throughout the Kingdom, an Officer of this Name and Authority of *Steward* to be found. See *Fleta,* to know what a Steward of a Manor or Houshold is, or at least ought to be.

Stewes, or **Stues,** were certain Places formerly permitted in *England* to Women of professed Incontinency, and who for Hire would prostitute their Bodies to all Comers; and they were so called, because dissolute Persons are wont to prepare themselves for venereal Acts by Bathing. And *Homer,* in the eighth Book of his *Odyss.* reckons *Hot Baths* among the effeminate Sorts of Pleasures.

Stocks, is a certain Wooden Engine, for confining the Legs of Offenders in, by Way of Punishment of disorderly Persons in divers Cases.

Stone, is generally taken for a Weight of 14 Pounds, generally used for the weighing of Wool, &c. but in *London* a *Stone* of Beef is no more than 8 Pounds, nor is a *Stone* of Wax any more.

Stranded, is where a Ship by Tempest, or the ill Management of the Mariners, is run on Ground, and by that Means perishes. Where a Ship or Vessel is stranded, the Justices of the Peace are impowered to command the Constables near the Sea-Coasts to call Assistance, in order, if possible, to preserve the same. See 12 *Ann.* c. 18.

Stranger, (from the *French*) according to the general Acceptation of the Word, denotes a Person that is born out of the Kingdom, or one that is unknown; but in our Law it is used in a quite different Sense, and is taken for him that is not *privy* to some particular Act; as a *Stranger* to a Deed denotes a Person who has nothing to do therewith, in which Sense it is directly opposed to the Term *Party* or *Privy.*

Stray. See **Estray.**

Strumpet, which was formerly used for an Addition, denotes a Whore, Harlot, or one that will prostitute her Body for Hire.

Stryk, signifies an eighth Part of a Seam or Quarter of Corn; a *Strik* or *Bushel.*

Subdeacon, was an ancient Officer in the Church, who was made by the Delivery of an empty Platter and Cup by the Bishop, and of a Pitcher, Bason and Towel by the Archdeacon. His Office was to wait on the Deacon, with the Linen, whereon the Body, &c. was consecrated, and to receive and carry away the Plate with the Offerings, and the Cup with the Wine and Water in it, &c. *Cowel.*

Subligerius, is taken for one that is guilty of Incest.

Sub-Marshal, or **Under-Marshal,** is an Officer that is Deputy to the *Chief Marshal* of the King's House, who is commonly called the *Knight-Marshal,* and has the Custody of the Prisoners there.

Subornation, with us denotes a secret or underhand preparing, instructing or bringing in a false Witness: And from hence comes

Subornation

Subornation of Perjury, which is a corrupting or enticing a Person to Perjury. By 6 *Eliz. c.* 9. Persons suborning of a Witness to give false Evidence in a Court of Record, in Relation to Lands or Goods, forfeit 40 *l.* or are to be imprisoned for Half a Year, stand on the Pillory, &c.

Sub-pœna, is a Writ whereby all Persons under the Degree of Peerage may be called into *Chancery*, in any Case where the Common Law cannot afford a Remedy. There are divers Sorts of these Writs in the Court of *Chancery*; as the *Sub-pœna ad respondendum*, to answer, *Sub-pœna ad replicandum*, to reply, *Sub-pœna ad rejungendum*, to rejoin, *Sub-pœna ad testificandum*, to give Evidence, and the *Sub-pœna ad audiendum judicium*, &c. Where a Defendant, after having been duly served with a *Sub-pœna ad Respondendum*, does not appear and answer, an Attachment shall issue out against him. A *Sub-pœna ad testificandum*, lies for the bringing in of Witnesses to give their Testimonies in a Cause, not only in the Court of *Chancery*, but in all other Courts. A Writ of *Sub-pœna* takes its Name from the Words thereof, whereby the Party is summoned to appear at a certain Day and Place assigned, *sub pœna Centum librarum*, under the Penalty of 100 *l.* which Sum is therein inserted *in terrorem*, it being never levied.

Subsidy, denotes an Aid or Tax granted to the King by Parliament for the necessary Occasions of the Kingdom, and is to be levied on every Subject, according to the Rate of his Lands or Goods: But this Word is in some of our Statutes frequently confounded with that of *Customs*.

Substitute. See **Attorney.**

Successor, is he that succeeds or comes in another's Place. It has been held that a *sole Corporation* may take an Estate in Fee to them and their *Successors*; yet not without the Word *Successors*; neither can such a Corporation in Succession take Goods or Chattels: Nevertheless an *Aggregate* Corporation may take a Fee in Succession, without expressing the Word *Successors*, and likewise may have Goods and Chattels in Succession, which shall accordingly go to the Successors.

Sufferance, is applied to that Tenant that holds over his Term at first lawfully granted, in which Case he so holding over is termed *Tenant at Sufferance*.

Suffragan, is said to be a titular Bishop appointed to aid and assist the Bishop of the Diocese in the Discharge of his spiritual Function. *Suffragans*, by some are called subsidiary Bishops, the Number of whom are limited by the Statute 26 *Hen.* 8. *c.* 14. whereby it is ordained, that it shall and may be lawful for every Bishop at his Pleasure, to elect two honest and discreet spiritual Persons within his Diocese, and to present them to the King, in order that he might give the one of them such Title, Stile, and Dignity of such of the Sees in the said Statute as he should think fit: And that every such Person should be called *Bishop Suffragan* of the same See.

Suggestion, in a legal Sense denotes a Representing of a Thing by Surmise; and it is frequently used as a Ground to move for *Prohibitions* to Suits depending in a Spiritual Court.

Suit, denotes a Following of another, but in different Senses; as, *First*, a *Suit in Law*, which is divided into *Real* and *Personal*, and

is

is all one and the same with Action *Real and Personal*. Secondly, *Suit of Court*, or *Suit-Service*, which is an Attendance the Tenant owes to his Lord's Court. Thirdly, *Suit-Covenant*, where a Person has covenanted to do Service in the Court of his Lord. Fourthly, *Suit-Custom*, which is where one and his Ancestors have owen *Suit* Time out of Mind. Fifthly, *Suit Real or Regal*, where Persons come to a Sheriff's Turn or Leet. Sixthly, *Suit* signifies the following one in Chase; as *fresh Suit*. And, lastly, it signifies a Petition to the King, or any Person of Dignity. *Suits at Law* are by 21 *Jac*. 2. *c*. 16. to be commenced and prosecuted within a certain limited Time.

Suit of the King's Peace, denotes a Pursuing of a Person for Breach of the *King's Peace*, such as Treasons, Insurrections, or Trespasses.

Suit-Silver, according to *Jacob*, is some small Sum paid in some Manors, to excuse the Appearance of Freeholders at their Lord's Courts.

Summoneas, is a judicial Writ mentioned in *Register Judicial*, of which there is great Diversity, according to the different Cases wherein it is used.

Summoner, is said to be some inferior Officer that cites or warns Persons to appear in any Court. And we are told that *Summonitores, Summoners*, were properly the *Apparitors* who cited in Delinquents to appear at a certain Time and Place, to answer any Charge or Complaint exhibited against them. In Citations from a superior Court the Summoners were to be Peers or Equals of the cited Party; at least the Barons were to be summoned by none under the Degree of Knights.

Summonitores Scaccarii, were certain Officers that assisted in collecting the King's Revenues, by citing the Defaulters into the Court of *Exchequer*.

Summons, in our Law is as much as *Vocatio in jus*, or *Citatio* among the *Civilians*.

Summons in Terra petita, is taken for that *Summons* which is made upon the Land, which the Party, at whose Suit the Summons issues, seeks to have.

Summons ad warrantizandum, is the Process whereby the Vouchee is called.

Sumptuary Laws, were such as were formerly made to restrain Excess in Apparel, by prohibiting costly Cloaths, but they are all repealed.

Sunday, with us denotes the Lord's Day set apart for the Service and Worship of God. By 29 *C*. 2. *c*. 7. no Person under the Penalty of 5 *s*. is to do any worldly Labour on a *Sunday*, except Works of Necessity and Charity: And if any Person cry or expose to Sale any Wares or Goods on that Day, the same become forfeited to the Poor, &c. on the Offenders being convicted thereof before a Justice of the Peace, who is authorised to cause the Penalties and Forfeitures to be levied by Distress: Yet this extends not to Dressing of Meat, either in private, or publick Families, such as Inns, Cook-Shops, &c. nor to the Crying or Selling of Milk in the Morning and Evening of a *Sunday*, nor to the Crying or Selling of Mackarel on that Day: No Process in Law on that Day lies; except in the case of Treason, Felony, or on an Escape, by 5 *Ann*, for the Maxim is, *Dies Dominicus* *non est Dies Juridicus*, the Lord's Day is not a Day in Law.

Supercargo, denotes one that is imployed by Merchants on a Voyage, to oversee their Cargo, and dispose thereof to the best Advantage.

Super-Institution, signifies one *Institution* upon another; as where *A. B.* is *instituted* to a Benefice upon one Title, and *C. D.* is instituted upon that of another. See **Institution**.

Super-jurare, anciently in Use in our Law, and was where a Criminal endeavoured to excuse himself by his own Oath, or by the Oath of one or two Witnesses, and the Crime was so notorious, that he was convicted upon the Oaths of many more Witnesses; and this was called *Super jurare*.

Superoneratione Pasturæ, is a judicial Writ that lies against the Person that is impleaded in the County-Court, for the Overburdening or *Surcharging* a Common with his Cattle, in a Case where he was formerly impleaded for it in the same Court, and the Cause is removed into one of the Courts at *Westminster*. *Cowel.*

Super Prærogativa Regis, is a Writ which formerly lay against the King's Widow for marrying without his Licence.

Supersedeas, according to *Fitzherbert*, is a Writ that lies in divers Cases, and in general signifies a Command to stay some of the ordinary Proceedings in Law, which, on good Cause shewn, ought not to proceed. It is likewise used for the Staying of an Execution after a Writ of Error is allowed, and Bail put in; but not before Bail is given, in Case there be Judgment upon Verdict, or by Default in Debt, &c. yet according to 2 *Lill. Abr.* 543. in an Action of Case and Trespass, where Damages are only recovered, on the bringing and allowing of the Writ, the Clerk of the Errors will make out a *Supersedeas* without Bail. It has been held, that if before Execution the Defendant bring a Writ of Error, and the Sheriff executes a *Fieri facias*, and levies the Money, the Court may award a *Supersedeas quia erronicè emanavit*, and to have Restitution of the Sum levied. *Hawkins* observes, that after a *Certiorari* is once delivered, it is of the same Nature of a *Supersedeas* to an inferior Court; which being allowed, all the Proceedings there afterwards in the Cause will be erroneous; and they are punishable. It is held to be false Imprisonment to detain a Prisoner after a *Supersedeas* delivered, because that Writ must be obeyed; and therefore Detention of the Prisoner is deemed a new Caption without any Cause. A Person of Course ought to have Surety of the Peace against him of whom he will swear he is afraid, and the Justice of the Peace thereunto required cannot deny him; but nevertheless, if the Party sworn against be already bound to the Peace, either in *Chancery*, or elsewhere, a *Supersedeas* will lie to stay the Justice from doing that which he ought not to deny. *Reg. Orig.* and *Judic.*

Supersedere, was a Writ anciently used, and signifies to neglect to appear in Court and plead.

Super statuto 1 *Ed.* 3. *c.* 12, 13. is by *Fitzherbert* said to be a Writ that lay against the King's Tenant holding in Chief, that aliened the King's Land without his Licence.

Super Statuto de Pois, *quo null ferra Uiteller*, is a Writ that lies against a Person Victualling, either in Gross, or by Retail in a City

Super Statuto facto pour Seneschal & Marshal de Roy, &c. is a Writ lying against the *Steward* or *Marshal*, for holding Plea in his Court, or for Trespass or Contracts not made within the King's Houshold. See *Fitz. Nat. Brev.*

Super Statuto de articulis Cleri, is a Writ that issues against the Sheriff or other Officer who distrains in the King's Highway, or in the Glebe Lands anciently given to Rectories. *Cowel*.

Super Statutum Edwardi 3. versus Servantes & Laboratores, is a Writ that lies against the Person that keeps another's Servants departed from their Service contrary to Law.

Supervisor, denotes a Surveyor or Overseer: And as *Cowel* observes, it anciently was, and still is, a Custom among some, especially those of the better Sort of People, to appoint a Supervisor of a Will, to see that the Executors thereof do punctually observe and perform the same; but indeed this Office of late Years has been so indifferently and negligently executed, that such an Officer seems to be to little or no Purpose. Supervisor formerly was taken for the same as Surveyor of the Highway. There are likewise certain Officers of the Excise who are called *Supervisors*, on Account of their having the Supervising and inspecting of the Books, &c. of the inferior Officers belonging to that Branch of the Revenue.

Supplicavit, is a Writ which issues out of the Court of *Chancery*, for taking Surety of the Peace, where a Person is apprehensive of receiving some Bodily Hurt from another; and it is founded on 1 *Ed.* 3. *c.* 16. and directed to the Justices of Peace and Sheriff of the County. The Manner of suing out this Writ is this, *viz.* The Party requiring it goes before one of the Masters in *Chancery*, and makes Oath that he does not desire it out of any Malice, but purely for his own Safety, and the Security of his Person; upon which the Master makes out a Warrant, by which the Writ is made by one of the Clerks of the six Clerks Office; after which the Writ is to be delivered to the Sheriff for his Warrant thereon, in Order to have the Party arrested, &c. Afterwards, according to *Practif. Soliciter*, they having sued out a *Certiorari*, it is to be delivered to the Persons that took Bail thereon, in order that they may certify it, which they are required to do. Here it is to be observed, that after a *Supplicavit* has issued directed to the Justices of the Peace, against a Person, the Defendant may come into the Court of *Chancery*, and there find Sureties that he will not do any Hurt or Damage to him that sues out the Writ; whereupon of Course he shall have a Writ of *Supersedeas*, directed to the Justices of the Peace, &c. commanding them that they cease to arrest him, or compel him to find Sureties, &c. And, according to *New Nat. Brev.* if the Person that ought to find Sureties, cannot appear in *Chancery* to find the same, another Person may sue out a *Supersedeas* for him, therein reciting the Writ of *Supplicavit*, and that such and such are bound for him in that Court, in such a particular Sum, for his keeping the Peace, according thereto. And the Justices, &c. by the said *Supersedeas*, shall be commanded to take Surety from the Party himself pursuant to the Writ, to keep the Peace, &c. and further that they do not arrest him, or in Case he be arrested on that Account, that they deliver him.

Supremacy, is taken for a Sovereign Dominion or Authority, which our Kings have held, ever since King *Henry* the Eighth's Time, who was the first that shook off the Yoke of *Rome* in this Kingdom, and settled the *Supremacy* on himself, after it had been long enjoyed by the *Pope*.

Surcharge, in *Merch. Dict.* is defined to be an Over-charge, and that which is above what is just and right. There is likewise a *Surcharge* of a Forest, which is where a Commoner puts more Beasts on the Forest than he has a Right to do.

Sur cui in vita, is a Writ that lies for the Heir of that Woman, whose Husband has aliened her Land in Fee, and she neglected to bring her Writ of *Cui in vita* for the Recovery of her own Land; in which Case the Heir may, after her Decease, have this Writ against the Tenant.

Surety, in general denotes a Bail, or Persons that engage and undertake for another in a Criminal Case, or Action of Trespass, &c. There is also another Kind of Surety, termed a *Surety of the Peace*, which is so called for that the Party that was in Fear is thereby secured by Bond or Recognisance of the offending Party and his Sureties entered into to the King, taken by a competent Judge of Record, for the *Keeping of the Peace*. This Peace a Justice of the Peace may command, either as a Minister, when commanded thereto; or as a Magistrate or Judge, as when he does it of his own Authority, founded on his Commission. *Cowel* mentions another Sort of Surety, which is terms *Securitas de bono Gestu*, Surety for the good Abearing or good Behaviour; and he makes this Difference between *Surety of the Peace*, and that of *de bono Gestu*, that the first is not broken without some Affray, &c. whereas the other may be broken by the Number of a Man's Company, or by his other Weapons, &c.

Surplusage, in the Common Law denotes a Superfluity, or a needless Addition, which is sometimes the Reason that a Writ abates; nevertheless in Pleading it is frequently void, and the Residue of the Plea shall stand good. *Termes de la Ley*. This Word is likewise applied to Matter of Account, and denotes a greater Disbursement than the Charge of the Accountant amounts to.

Surrebutter, is used for a second Rebutter, or a Rebutting more than once. See **Rebutter**.

Surrejoinder, is a second Defence of the Plaintiff's Declaration or Charge, and answers the Defendant's *Rejoinder*.

Surrender, is a certain Instrument in Writing, whereby it is testified that the particular Tenant of Lands, &c. for Life, or Years, does yield and give up his Estate or Term, to the Person who has the immediate Estate in Remainder or Reversion, so that he may have the present Possession of the same. As there may also be a *Surrender* without Writing; on that Account there is said to be a *Surrender in Deed*, and a *Surrender in Law*: That in *Deed* is that which is actually and sensibly performed; but a *Surrender in Law* is according to the Intendment of the Law by Way of Consequent, and not actual; as where a Person has a Lease of a Term, and

and during the Term of his Leafe accepts of a new Leafe of the fame Lands, &c. this Act in Law is deemed a Surrender of the former Leafe. There is likewife a *Cuftomary Surrender* of Copyhold Land, for which fee *Co. Lit.* There is likewife a *Surrender* of Letters Patent to the King, in Order that he may grant the Eftate to whom he thinks meet.

Surrogate, denotes a Perfon that is deputed or fubftituted in the Room of another, moft commonly of a Bifhop, or Bifhop's Chancellor.

Surfife, is taken to be a Name efpecially ufed in the Caftle of *Dover*, for fuch Penalties and Forfeitures as are impofed on thofe that do not duly pay their Duties or Rent for *Caftleward*.

Survey, fignifies to meafure or particularly lay out a Manor or Eftate in Lands; and to fet out not only the Bounds and Royalties thereof, but alfo the Tenure of the refpective Tenants thereof, and the Rent and Value of the fame: And in this laft Signification *Jacob* tells us, it is taken for a *Court*; becaufe on the Falling of an Eftate, confifting of Manors, to a new Lord, where there are Tenants by Leafe, and Copyholders, a *Court of Survey* is generally held, &c.

Surveyor, is taken for a Perfon that has the Overfeeing or Care of fome great Perfon's Lands or Works; as the Surveyor General of the King's Manors, &c.

Survivor, in our Law denotes the longer Liver of the Jointenants, or of any two jointly interefted in a Thing; in which Cafe if there be only two Jointenants, the Whole, upon the Death of the other, goes to the Survivor; but if there be more than two, the Part of the Deceafed goes among all the *Survivors*.

Sufpence, or **Sufpenfion**, is a Temporal Stop of a Perfon's Right, and is where a Rent or other Profit iffuing out of Land, on Account of the Unity of Poffeffion of the Rent, &c. and of the Land whereout it iffues, is not *in effe*, for a Time, *& tunc dormiunt*, then fleep, but may be awaked or revived, and therefore differs from *Extinguifhment*, which dies for ever. *Sufpenfion* is likewife taken for a Cenfure whereby *Ecclefiaftical Perfons*, are forbidden to exercife their Office or to take the Profits of their Benefices, or when they are prohibited in both of them for a certain Time, either in Whole or in Part; whence, according to *Wood*, is *Sufpenfio ab Officio*, or *Sufpenfio a Beneficio*, and *ab Officio & Beneficio*. *Sufpenfio ab Officio*, is where a Minifter for a Time is *fufpended* or declared unfit to execute his Office, *Sufpenfio a Beneficio*, is where a Minifter is for a Time deprived of the Profits of his Benefice. *Sufpenfio ab Officio & Beneficio*, is where a Minifter is deprived both of his Office and Benefice.

Swainmote, or **Swanimote**, is a Court touching Matters of the Foreft; and is held thrice a Year before the Verderors as Judges.

Synod, denotes a Meeting or Affembly of Ecclefiaftical Perfons concerning Matters of Religion: And there are four Kinds of Synods: 1*ft*, A *General*, or *Univerfal Synod*, which is where Bifhops of all Nations meet. 2*dly*, A *National Synod*, where thofe of one Nation only affemble. 3*dly*, A *Provincial Synod*, where they of one Province only meet. 4*thly*, A *Diocefan Synod*, is an Affembly of of Ecclesiasticks of one Diocese. See **Convocation**.

Synodal, denotes a Tribute in Money paid to the Bishop, or Archdeacon by the inferior Clergy, at *Easter* Visitation.

Synodales Testes, was an Appellation given to the Urban and Rural Deans, the Office of whom was to inform of, and attest the Disorders of the Clergy and People in the Episcopal *Synod*: But afterwards when they sunk in their Authority, the Synodical Witnesses were a Sort of a Grand Jury impanelled, or made up of a Priest or two or three Laymen of every Parish, for the Presenting of Offenders: And at last two principal Persons for each Diocese were yearly chosen, until by Degrees this Office of Inquest devolved upon the Church-wardens.

T.

Tabellion, is taken for a Notary Publick, or Scrivener than is allowed by Authority to ingross and register private Contracts and Obligations. Table-Rents, according to *Cowel*, were Rents paid to Bishops or Religious Prelates, reserved or appropriated to their Table or House-keeping: And such Rents paid in *Specie*, or in Provision of Meat and Drink were sometimes called *Bord-land Rents*.

Table of Fines, is the Making of a Table for every County where the King's Writ runs, wherein is contained the Contents of every *Fine* passed in each Term, with the Name of the County, Towns and Places, wherein the Lands or Tenements lie, the Name of the Demandant and Deforceant, and of the particular Lands, &c. mentioned in the Fine. This properly is to be done by the *Chirographers of Fines* of the Court of *Common Pleas*, whose Duty is every Day of the next Term, after the Ingrossing of such Fine, to fix those Tables in some open Place of the said Court during the Time of its Sitting; and his Duty further is, to deliver to the Sheriff of every County, his Under-Sheriff or Deputy, fairly wrote in Parchment, a perfect Content of the *Table* so made for that County, in the Term next before the Assises, or between the Term and the Assises, to be set up at the Assises in an open Place of that Court, where the Justices of Assise shall then sit, and to continue there during their Sitting: And by 23 *Eliz. c.* 3. if either the Chirographer or Sheriff fail herein, he is liable to the Penalty of 5 *l.*

Tail or **Fee-Tail**, is a limited Estate or Fee opposed to that of *Fee-simple*; that is to say, it is an Inheritance, whereof a Person is seised to him and the Heirs of his Body begotten or to be begotten, which is called *General Tail*, because how many Wives soever the Tenant that holds by his Title shall have one after another in lawful Marriage, his Issue by them severally have all a Possibility of inheriting in their Turns: But *Tail special* is quite the Reverse, it being where Lands, &c. are limited to a Man and his Wife, and the Heirs of their two Bodies begotten; and it is so called, because if the Husband bury his Wife before Issue, and takes another, the Issue by the second Wife cannot inherit the Land, &c. In like Manner it is where Lands, &c. are granted to a Man and his Wife, and to their Son *A.* for ever. *Co. Lit.* observes that before the Statute

tute of *Westm.* 2. 13 *Ed.* 1. if Lands were given to a Man and the Heirs of his Body, it was deemed to be a Fee-simple directly by the Gift, upon Condition that he had Issue; and even if he had Issue, the Condition was supposed to be performed for three Purposes, *viz.* to alien and disinherit the Issue, and thereby to bar the Donor and his Heirs of all Possibility of the Reversion; to forfeit the Estate for Treason or Felony, and to charge the same with Rent, &c. Nevertheless by the beforementioned Statute, the Intention and Will of the Donor is to be observed, *viz.* that the Tenant in Tail shall not alien either before or after Issue had, or forfeit or charge the Lands longer than for his own Life; and such Estate shall remain to the Issue of the Donee and his Heirs, or, in Case of no Issue, then to the Donor and his Heirs. As daily Experience shewed that great Mischiefs had crept into the Law by Inheritances being intailed, such as Frauds to Creditors, &c. and the Disobedience of Sons when they knew they could not be disinherited; on which Account the Judges, laying their Heads together, found out a Way to bar an intailed Estate with Remainders over, by a feigned Recovery, and since by a Fine to bar the Issue. See 12 *Ed.* 4. and 32 *Hen.* 8. *c.* 36. By 32 *Hen.* 8. *c.* 18. Power is given to Tenants in Tail to make Leases for twenty-one Years, or three Lives, &c. And *Wood* observes, that notwithstanding the many Inconveniences that arise from intailed Estates, there are Methods to be taken in Settlements to limit Estates, so that no Law or Statute can reach them. It is held that a Lease for Years to a Person and the Heirs of his Body is void; but an Assignment of such Lease may be made in Trust, to permit the Issue in Tail to receive the Profits; and that in Effect is an *intailed* Estate. Where Lands, &c. are given to a Husband and Wife, and to the Heirs of the Body of the Husband, he in that Case has an Estate in general *Tail*, and the Wife an Estate only for Life, because the Word *Heirs* has Relation in general to the Body of the Husband; and if an Estate be limited to a Man's Heirs that he shall beget on the Body of his Wife, it creates a special *Tail* in the Husband; yet the Wife will in that Case be intitled to Nothing. Where Lands, &c. are given to a Man and his Heirs Male or Female of his Body begotten, the Male or Female Issue shall only inherit according to the Limitation; for whosoever makes Claim as Heir to an Estate-tail *per formam doni*, must take his Discent by such Heirs to whom the same is limited, that is to say, if it be to Heirs Male of the Body, the Pedigree in that Respect must descend by Heirs Male; and on the other Hand, if it be to Heirs Female, his Title must be derived by Heirs Female one after another: As where a Grant is to one, and the Heirs Male of his Body begotten, and he has Issue a Daughter, who has a Son, and dies, the Son cannot inherit the Estate; seeing that he cannot make his Discent by Heirs Male. In an Estate-Tail, if there be no Heir to take in Pursuance of the Limitations; as where Issue fails, the Lands, &c, shall revert to the Donor, or descend to such Person as is limited to have it after the Estate-tail is spent.

Tail

Tail after Possibility of Issue extinct, is when Lands, &c. are given to a Husband and Wife, and the Heirs of their two Bodies begotten, and one of them dies without Issue had between them; in such Case the Survivor shall hold the Land for the Term of his own Life, as *Tenant in Tail after Possibility of Issue extinct*. Tenants in Tail after Possibility of Issue extinct, are not punishable for Waste, as Tenants for Life are; yet neither they, nor Tenants for Life may suffer a Recovery.

Taint. See *Attaint*.

Tales, is a Word used in our Law for a Supply of Men impanelled on a Jury, who not appearing, or upon Appearance being challenged for the Plaintiff or Defendant as not indifferent; in which Case the Judge, upon Motion, of Course grants a Supply to be made by the Sheriff of some Persons there present, equal in Reputation to those that are impanelled: And hence it is, that this Act of Supplying is termed a *Tales de Circumstantibus*. Nevertheless the Person that has had but one *Tales*, either upon Default or Challenge, tho' he may have another, may not have the latter to contain so many as the former, because the first *Tales* must be under the Number of the principal Panel, except in the Cause of Appeal; and in like Manner, every *Tales* less than other, until the whole Number be made up of Persons present in Court, and such as are without Exception. *Termes de la Ley*. There are two Kinds of *Tales*; the one *de circumstantibus*, and the other a *Decem Tales*: That of *Circumstantibus*, is where a full Jury does not appear at the *Nisi Prius*, or so many are challenged, as not to have a full Jury, in which Case, on Motion, the Judge will grant this *Tales*, which is immediately returned by the Sheriff into Court: And a *Decem Tales* is when a full Jury does not appear at a Trial at Bar, in which Case this Writ goes out to the Sheriff, commanding him to *apponere Decem Tales*; and it is made returnable in some convenient Time in the said Term, in order to try the Cause.

Tallage, is taken to denote a Share of a Person's Substance paid by Way of Tribute, Toll, or Tax.

Tallagium facere, signifies to give up Accounts into the *Exchequer*, where the Method of Accounting is by *Tallies*. *Talley* is a Stick cut in two Parts, on each whereof was mark'd with Notches what was due between Debtor and Creditor, which was the ancient Method of keeping Accounts; one Part of this *Talley* being kept by the Debtor, and the other by the Creditor. There are two Sorts of *Tallies* mentioned to have been long in Use in the *Exchequer*; the one whereof is termed *Tallies* of Debt, that is to say, a Kind of Acquittance for Debt paid to the King; upon Payment of which each Debtor receives one of these *Tallies*, who upon carrying them to the Clerk of the Pipe-Office, has an Acquittance there given him in Parchment for his full Discharge. The other Kind of *Tallies*, are *Tallies of Reward*, which are taken to be an Allowance or Recompence made to Sheriffs for such Matters as they have performed to their Charge, or for such Sums as they of Course have cast upon them in their Accounts, but cannot levy, &c. *Cowel*.

Tam quam, in our Law is used in the same Manner as *Qui tam*; and is where a Person prosecutes as well for the King as himself upon

an

an Information for Breach of any Penal Law or Statute, by which a Penalty is given to the Party that sues. See *Information*.

Tare and Tret. The first of these denotes the Weight of a Box, Cloths, &c. wherein Goods are packed; and the other signifies a Consideration allowed in the Weight for Waste, in emptying and reselling of Goods. *Cowel*.

Tath. According to *Spelman*, in *Norfolk* and *Suffolk*, the Lord of each Manner had the Privilege of having their Tenants Flocks of Sheep brought at Night upon their own Demeine Grounds, there to be folded for the Benefit of their Dung; which Liberty of improving their Land was called *Tath*.

Tauri liberi Libertas, was anciently used for a common Bull; and was so termed, on account that he was common to all the Tenants of such a Manor or Liberty.

Tawers. By 9 *Ann. c.* 11. *Collar-makers*, Glovers, Bridle-cutters, and others who dress *Skins* in Allom, &c. and cut the same into Wares are to be deemed *Tawers*.

Tax, according to *Cowel* was such a Tribute as being certainly rated upon every Town, was wont to be paid annually, but now not without Consent of Parliament, as Subsidies are; and it differs from a *Subsidy* in this, that it is always certain, as it is set down in the Exchequer Book, and in general levied of every Town, and not particularly of every Man.

Taxers are Officers yearly chosen in *Cambridge* to see the true Gage of all Weights and Measures; tho' it took its Name from taxing or rating the Rents of Houses, which anciently was the Duty of their Office. *Cowel*.

Teding-penny, Tething-penny. Tithing-penny or **Thirding-penny**, was a small Tax paid to the Sheriff from each *Tithing* towards the Charges of keeping his Court, &c.

Teller, is an Officer of the *Exchequer*; and there are four of these Officers in Number, whose Duty is to receive all Sums due to the King, and to give the Clerk of the Pell a Bill to charge him therewith: And they also pay all Money payable by the King, by Warrant from the *Auditor of the Receipt*, and make weekly and yearly Books, both of their Receipts and Payments, which they deliver to the *Lord Treasurer*. *Cowel*.

Telligraphiæ, is taken for written Evidences of Things past.

Telwore is said to be certain Labour which the Tenant was bound to do for his Lord for a certain Number of Days.

Templers or Knights of the Temple, we are told was a certain religious Order of Knighthood, instituted about the Year 1119. and was so called because they dwelt in Part of the Buildings belonging to the *Temple* at *Jerusalem*, and not far from the Sepulchre of our Lord.

Temporalties of Bishops, is taken for such Revenues, Lands, &c. and Lay-Fees, as have been laid to Bishops Sees by Kings and other great Personages of this Land; as they are Barons and Lords of Parliament.

Tenant denotes one that holds or occupies Lands or Tenements of some Lord or Landlord, by Rent, Fealty, &c. And this Word is used with different Additions; as *Tenant* in Fee, Tail, for Life, Years, or at Will; *Tenant* in Dower, by the Curtesy, by Copy of Court-Roll; *Tenant* in Mortgage, by Statute Merchant, and Statute Staple,

Staple, *Elegit*, &c. There are likewise *Tenants* in common; and they are such as hold Lands, &c. for Life or Years by several Titles, or by one Title and several Rights; and they have several Freeholds, whilst *Jointenants* have only one joint Freehold. A *Tenant* in common by a Conveyance is thus made, viz. if the Deed be made to two Persons; *Habendum* the one Moiety to one and his Heirs; and the other Moiety to the other and his Heirs; this is a *Tenancy in Common*; and the Heirs and Executors of *Tenants* in Common shall respectively have their Parts or Shares, and not the Survivors, as in the Case of *Jointenants*. See *Jointenants*. Tenant to the *Præcipe* is the Person against whom the Writ of *Præcipe* is to be brought in suing out a common *Recovery*.

Tender, in our Law denotes as much as carefully to offer, or circumspectly endeavour the Performance of a Thing; as to *tender Rent* is to offer it at the Time and Place where and when it ought to be paid: And a *Tender* of Rent on any Part of the Land occupied, or at any Time of the last Day of Payment, will save the Proviso or Condition for that Time, whether the Landlord accepts of it or not; yet tho' the Rent be duely tendered, the Landlord may afterwards bring Action of Debt; but he cannot thereon recover Damages; for that the *Tenant's* Tender excuses the Damages, but does not debar the Landlord of his Rent: But it is here to be observed that a *Tender* of Rent made in order to save the Forfeiture must be of the whole Rent due without any Deduction on Account of Taxes, &c. unless it be particularly so agreed between the Landlord and Tenant; for Stoppage is no Payment in Law. It is held that where one pleads a Tender of a Debt at the Day, he need not plead *semper paratus*, that he was always ready, but *Uncore prist*, still ready, and then bring the Money into Court.

Tenement, according to its proper Signification denotes a House or Homestall; but more largely it is taken for a House or Land which a Person holds of another.

Tenementalis, is Land that was possessed by the Tenant, and distinguished by that Name from the Demesne Land of the Lord, called *Inland*.

Tenementary Land was divided into two Sorts, viz. *Inland* and *Outland*. The *Inland* is said to have been the Demains which the Lord kept in his own Hands. The *Outland* was granted out to Tenants under arbitrary Rents and Services.

Tenementis Legatis, was an ancient Writ that lay to the City of *London*, or any other Corporation (where the old Custom was that Men might devise *Tenements* as well as Goods and Chattels, by their last Will) for the determining of any Controversy relating thereto, and for rectifying the wrong *Tenant*. See *Tenant*.

Tenentibus in Assisa non onerandis, is a Writ lying for the Person to whom a Disseisor has alienated the Land, whereof he disseised another; that he be not arrested for the Damages awarded, in Case the Disseisor has wherewith to satisfy them himself.

Tenor, in our Law denotes the Substance or Purport of Writs, Records, Deeds, &c.

Tenore Indictamenti mittendo, is a Writ for the Removing of a Record of an *Indictment*, and the

the whole Process thereon out of another Court into that of the *King's Bench*.

Tenor Præsentium, by the *Tenor of these Presents*, is taken for the Substance, true Intent, or Meaning of a Deed or other Writing.

Tenths, in Latin *Decimæ*, are that Portion or Tribute which every spiritual Living annually pays to the King.

Tenure, denotes the Manner whereby Lands, &c. are held of the Lord; or it is the Service the Tenant owes to his Lord. Tenures were anciently divided thus, *viz. Escuage*, that is to say, Land held by the Service of the Shield; and thereby the Tenant was at his own Expence bound to follow his Lord into the Wars. The next Tenure was *Knight's Service* and *Chivalry*, which was where Lands were held of the King or mesne Lord, to perform Service in War. The next was *Burgage*, Land holden of the Lord of the Borough at a certain Rent. A fourth was *Villenage*, which is otherwise termed a base *Tenure*, whereby the Tenant was bound to perform all inferior villeinous Services commanded by the Lord. A fifth is *Grand Serjeanty*, Lands held by honorary Services at the King's Coronation, &c. And *Petit Serjeanty*, which is, where held of the King to contribute yearly some small Thing towards his Wars. *Frankalmoine* was a *Tenure* by which Lands were held of Ecclesiasticks in free and perpetual Alms. *Socage* is where Lands are holden by Tenants to plough their Lord's Land, and perform other Services of Husbandry at their own Expence. But all these ancient Services are by 12 *Car. c.* 24. intirely taken away and reduced into Common and Free-Socage. *Curtesy* Tenure, is where a Man having married a Woman seised in Fee, &c. has Issue born alive by her; in which Case after her Death, the Husband is Tenant by the Curtesy of *England*. *Dower* Tenure is where a Widow holds for her Life a third Part of her Husband's Land, whereof he was seised in Fee at any Time during the Coverture. As to Copyhold Tenure, it is a Holding for Lives or in Fee, at the Will of the Lord, according to the Custom of the Manor, &c. And lastly there is a Tenure for Life or Years, which is when Lands are held for those Terms, on reserved Rents.

Term, is generally taken for the Bounds and Limitation of Time; as a Lease for Term of Life or Years: And a Lease for a Term of Years is a Chattel real, whereas Goods and other Things that are moveable, are termed Chattels personal.

Termini censuales, are said to be Rent Terms, *viz.* the four quarterly Feasts, whereon Rent was usually paid.

Termor, is taken for the Person that holds for a Term of Years or Life.

Terms, is particularly applied to that Time wherein our Courts of Justice are open; in Opposition to which the rest of the Year is called *Vacation*. There are four of these Terms in a Year, *viz.* The one called *Hillary-Term*, which begins the 23d of *January*, (but if that happen to be on a *Sunday*, then the next Day after,) and ends the 12th of *February* following. The next is *Easter-Term*, which begins the *Wednesday* Fortnight after *Easter* Day, and ends the *Monday* next after *Ascension-Day*. The third is *Trinity-*

TE

Trinity-Term, which begins the *Friday* next after *Trinity-Sunday*, and ends the *Wednesday* Fortnight after. And the fourth is *Michaelmas-Term*, which begins the 23d of *October*, unless it fall on a *Sunday*, then the Day after; and it ends the 28th of *November* following.

A TABLE of *the respective Returns of Writs in the* King's Bench *and* Common Pleas.

Hillary-Term, contains three Weeks and has four Returns.

In the King's Bench.
1. On ——— Day next after eight Days of *Hillary*,
2. On ——— next after the fifteenth of *Hillary*.
3. On ——— next after the Purification of the Blessed Virgin *Mary*.
4. On ——— next after the eighth of the Purification of the Blessed *Mary*.

In the Common Pleas.
1. In eight Days of *Hillary*.
2. From the Day of *Hillary* in fifteen Days.
3. In the Morrow of the Purification of the Blessed *Mary*.
4. In eight Days of the Purification of the Blessed *Mary*.

Easter-Term contains three Weeks, and six Days, and has five Returns.

In the King's Bench.
1. On ——— Day next after the fifteenth of *Easter*.
2. On ——— next after three Weeks of *Easter*.
3. On ——— next after one Month of *Easter*.
4. On ——— next after five Weeks of *Easter*.
5. On ——— next after the Morrow of the *Lord's Ascension*.

In the Common Pleas.
1. From the Day of *Easter* in fifteen Days.
2. From the Day of *Easter* in three Weeks.
3. From the Day of *Easter* in one Month.
4. From the Day of *Easter* in five Weeks.
5. On the Morrow of the Lord's Ascension.

Trinity-Term wants one Day of three Weeks, and has four Returns.

In the King's Bench.
1. On ——— Day next after the Morrow of the *Holy Trinity*.
2. On ——— next after eight Days of the *Holy Trinity*.
3. On ——— next after fifteen Days of the *Holy Trinity*.
4. On ——— next after three Weeks of the *Holy Trinity*.

In the Common Pleas.
1. In the Morrow of the *Holy Trinity*.
2. In eight Days of the *Holy Trinity*.
3. From the Day of the *Holy Trinity* in fifteen Days.
4. From the Day of *Holy Trinity* in three Weeks.

Michaelmas Term contains five Weeks and two Days, and has six Returns.

In the King's Bench.
1. On ——— Day next after three Weeks of St. *Michael*.
2. On ——— next after one Month of St. *Michael*.
3. On ——— next after the Morrow of *All Souls*.
4. On ——— next after the Morrow of St. *Martin*.
5. ——— next after the Octave (eighth Day) of St. *Martin*.

In the Common Pleas.
1. From the Day of St. *Michael* in three Weeks,
2. From the Day of St. *Michael* in one Month.
3. On the Morrow of *All Souls.*
4. On the Morrow of St. *Martin.*
5. On the *Octaves* (eighth Day) of St. *Martin.*
6. From the Day of St. *Martin* in fifteen Days.

It is here to be observed, that, as in the *King's Bench* all Returns are to be made on some particular Day of the Week in each Term, Care must be taken not to make the Writs out of that Court returnable on a Non-judicial Day, a Day not of the Law; such as a *Sunday, All Saints* and *All Souls* in *Michaelmas* Term, the Purification in *Hillary,* the Ascension in *Easter,* and *Midsummer-Day,* unless it should fall on the first Day of *Trinity-Term.*

Terms of the Law, are, according to *Hawkins,* certain technical Words and *Terms of Art,* peculiarly adapted to the Profession of the Law.

Terms for Payment of Rent, are the four quarterly Feasts whereon Rent is usually paid, *viz.* in the South of *England,* on *Lady-Day, Midsummer-day, Michaelmas-Day,* and *Christmas-Day.* But in the North, on *Candlemas-Day, May-Day, Lammas-Day,* and *Martinmas-Day.*

Terra, is generally in a legal Sense taken to denote arable Land.

Terra affirmata, is defined to be Land let to Farm.

Terra Boscalis, was formerly taken for woody Land.

Terra culta, denotes Land that is tilled or manured; as *Terra inculta* is taken for quite the reverse.

Terra dominica, vel indominicata, was used for the Demain Land of a Manor. *Cowel.*

Terra excultabilis, is taken for Land that may be tilled or ploughed.

Terra extendenda, is a Writ that is directed to the Escheator, &c. commanding him to make Enquiry after the true yearly Value of any Land, &c. by the Oath of 12 Men, and to certify the *Extent* into the Court of *Chancery,* &c. See *Reg. of Writs.*

Terra frusca or **frisca,** is taken for Land not lately ploughed, or what is generally called Fresh-Land.

Terra Hydata, was anciently used for Land subject to the Payment of *Hydage.*

Terra lucrabilis, is taken for such Land as may be gained from the Sea, or inclosed out of a Waste to some particular Use.

Terra sabulosa, has been used for gravelly or sandy Ground.

Terra vestita is used in old Charters for Land sown with Corn. *Cowel.*

Terra Wainabilis, is taken for tillable Land.

Terra Waretta, according to *Cowel* denotes Fallow Land.

Terra Warennata, has been used for Land that has the Liberty of Free Warren.

Terrage, is by *Cowel* thought to be an Exemption *a Precariis,* from Boons of Ploughing, Reaping, &c.

Terrar, is a Book or Survey containing the several Lands with their Bounds and Limits of any particular Person, or of a Town or Manor, together with the Quantity of Acres, the Names of the Tenants, &c. And in the *Exchequer* we are told there is a *Terrar of*

TE

of all the Glebe Lands in *England*, which was made about 11 *Ed.* 3.

Ter-Tenant, is one that has the actual Possession or Occupation of the Land; as where a Lord of a Manor has a Freehold, or who lets out his Freehold to another to be occupied; this Occupier having the actual Possession, is called the *Terre-tenant*.

Terris, Bonis, & Catallis rehabendis post Purgationem, is a Writ that lies for a Clerk to recover his Lands, Goods and Chattels formerly seised, after he has cleared himself of the Felony wherewith he was charged, and delivered to his Ordinary to be purged.

Terris Liberandis, is a Writ which lies for a Person convicted by Attaint, to bring the Record and Process before the King, and to take a Fine for his Imprisonment, to deliver him his Lands and Tenements again, and to release him of the Strip and Waste. It was also formerly a Writ for the Delivery of Lands to the Heir after Homage and Relief performed, or upon Security given to perform them. See *Reg. Orig.* 232. *&* 293.

Terris & Catallis tentis ultra Debitum levatum, according to *Reg. Judic.* is an original Writ, for the restoring of Lands or Goods to a Debtor that is distrained above the Amount of the Debt.

Test. To bring one to the *Test*, is the same as to bring him to Trial and Examination, *&c.* There is likewise a Statute of King *Charles the Second*, which goes by the Name of the *Test-Act*, which requires all Officers both Civil and Military to take the Oaths, and *Test, viz.* the Sacrament according to the Rites and Ceremonies of the Church of *England*; for the Neglect of which, the Person executing any Office mentioned in that Statute, forfeits the Sum of 500 *l.* See 25 *Car.* 2. *c.* 2.

Testa de Nevil, is said to be an ancient Record composed by *Jollan de Nevil*, a Justice *Itinerant*, in the 18 and 24 of *Hen.* 3. wherein is contained an Account of all Lands held in grand or petty Serjeanty, *&c.* And this Record remains in the Custody of the King's Remembrancer.

Testament, is defined to be a Witness of the Mind; or it may rather be taken for the true Declaration of our last Will in that which we would desire to be done after our Death. There are two Sorts of *Testaments, viz.* a *Testament* in Writing, and a *Testament* in Words, which last is termed a Nuncupative *Testament* or Will; that is to say, where a Person being sick, for Fear lest Death, Want of Memory, or Speech should so suddenly come upon him, that he should be prevented, in Case he staid the Writing of his Testament, desires his Neighbours or Friends to bear Witness of his last Will, and then presently declares the same in Words before them: which being done, after the Decease of the Party, is proved by Witnesses, and put in Writing by the Ordinary, and then stands as valid, as if it had at first in the Testator's Life-time been reduced into Writing; except it be in the Case of Lands, which are only deviseable by a Testament in Writing executed in the Life-time of the Testator; for by 29 *Car.* 2. *c.* 3. it is ordained that all Devises of Lands or Tenements shall be made in Writing, and signed by the Devisor, in the

Presence

Presence of three Witnesses at least: And that such Will shall not be revoked unless by Writing, or by cancelling of the same by the Testator himself, or by some other in his Presence, by his Consent or Direction: In like Manner a Will in Writing concerning a personal Estate, shall not be revoked by Words only, except that in the Life-time of the Testator it be put in Writing and read to him, and he assent thereto. A *Parol* or *Nuncupative* Will of above 30 *l.* shall not be good unless such Will be proved by the Oath of three Witnesses. *Termes de la Ley.*

Testator, is the Person that makes a *Testament* or Will. See **Wills**.

Testatum, is a Writ in personal Actions, and lies where a Defendant cannot be arrested upon a *Capias* in the County where the Action is laid, and thereupon the *Capias* is returned *Non est inventus* by the Sheriff; in which Case this Writ may be sent out into any other County where the Defendant is supposed to be, or to have wherewith to satisfy. The Reason that this Writ is called a *Testatum* is that the Sheriff *testified* that the Defendant was not to be found in his Bailiwick.

Teste, is a Word usually to be met with in the Conclusion of every Writ, wherein the Date is contained, and beginning with these Words, *Teste Meipso, &c.* in Case it be an original Writ; or if Judicial, then *Teste*, naming the Chief Justice of the *Bench* whence the Writ issues. See **Writs**.

Testimonial, is a Certificate under the Hand of a Justice of Peace, *certifying* the Place and Time, when and where a Mariner or Soldier landed, and the Place of his Dwelling and Birth, whereto he is to pass, &c. There are likewise *Testimonials* of Clergy, which according to *Countr. Parf. Compan.* are necessary to be made by Persons present, that a Clergyman inducted to a Benefice has in every Respect complied with the *Act of Uniformity*; and to evidence that the Clerk has complied with what the Law requires on his Institution and Induction.

Thanage is the same with *Thane-Lands*, which see.

Thane, according to *Skene* was a Name of Dignity, and appears to have been equal with the Son of an Earl: But this Word is sometimes taken for a Nobleman; sometimes a Freeman, and sometimes a Magistrate, or an Officer or Minister of the King. After the Conquest these Men were called *Barones Regis*; and there were likewise *Thani minores*, who were also called Barons: They were Lords of Manors, and had a particular Jurisdiction within their Limits, and over their own Tenants in their Courts, which to this Day are called *Court-Barons*.

Thane-Lands, were such Lands as were granted by Charters of the *Saxon* Kings to their *Thanes* with all Immunities, except the threefold Necessity of Expedition, Repair of Castles, and Mending of Bridges. *Cowel.*

Theft, is an unlawful and felonious taking away of another's moveable and personal Goods, against the Owner's Will, with an Intent to steal the same. *Theft* is divided into *Theft* simply so called, and *Petit Theft*, the one of which is of Goods above the Value of Twelve-pence, and is Felony; the other under that Value, and is no *Felony*, but termed *Petit Larceny*. Theft from the Person, or in the owner's Presence, is

properly

properly called *Robbery*. See **Felony** and **Larceny**.

Theft-bote, is defined to be the Receiving of a Persons Goods again from a Thief, after stolen, or the Receiving of some other Amends in order not to prosecute the Felon, and with a Design to let the Thief escape. This Offense is punishable with Fine and Imprisonment.

Thelonium, has the Signification of *Toll*; and in order to be free therefrom, there is a Writ termed *Breve essendi quieti de Thelonio*.

Thelonmannus, from *Thelonium*, *Toll*, is the Toll-man or Officer, that received Toll.

Themmagium, was a Duty anciently paid by inferior Tenants in Respect of *Theme* or *Team*.

Theoden, is said to have been a Husbandman or inferior Tenant, or *Under-Thane*. See **Thane**.

Theowe or **Thew**, is taken for a Slave or Bondman; and among the *Saxons* Bondmen were called *Theowes* and *Esnes*, which Sort of Persons were not reckoned Members of the Commonwealth, but Parcels of their Master's Goods and Substance.

Thingus, is the same as *Thane*, which see.

Thirdborow, is taken for a Constable.

Thirdings, is said to be the third Part of the Corn or Grain growing on the Ground at the Tenant's Death, which is due to the Lord for a Heriot within the Manor of *Turfat* in the County of *Hereford*.

Third Night Awn-hinde, is a Term used in King *Edward the Confessor's* Time, by whose Laws if any Guest lay a *third Night* in an Inn, he was deemed a Domestick, and the Inn-keeper was answerable for any Offence he should commit. *Bract.* saith *Forman-Night* or Uncuth, was he that lay at an Inn the first Night, and therefore reckoned only a Stranger; and that he that lay there a second Night was called *Twa-night*, and accounted a Guest; but that *Awn-hinde* was a Domestick.

Tidesmen, are certain inferior Officers belonging to the Custom-house, whose Office is to watch or attend upon Ships, until the Customs be paid. These Officers take that Name upon their going on board of Ships, on their Arrival in the Mouth of the *Thames* or other Port, and come up with the Tide.

Tigh or **Teage**, is used in *Kent* for a Close or Inclosure.

Timberlode, is said to be a Service, whereby the Tenant was to carry felled *Timber* from the Woods to the Lord's House.

Tinel le Roy, was used for the King's Hall, where his Servants used to dine and sup.

Tineman or **Tienman**, was anciently taken for a Petty Officer in the Forest, who had the nocturnal Care of Vert and Venison, and was subject to other servile Offices.

Tinkermen, according to *Stow*, were those Fishermen that destroyed the young Fry on the River *Thames* by Nets and unlawful Engines, till suppressed by the Mayor and Citizens of *London*.

Tinpenny, in Contradiction to *Du Fresne*, is by *Cowel* said to be a customary Tribute formerly paid to the *Tithing-man*, to support the Charge and Trouble of his Office.

Tipstaff, is an Officer that attends the Judges with a kind of *Staff* tipt with Silver, and takes into his Charge all Prisoners that are
either

either committed or turned over at the Judge's Chambers.

Tithes, denotes the tenth Part of the Increase that annually arises from the Profits of Lands, and the Industry of the Parishioners, which is payable for the Maintenance of the Parson of the Parish. By Statute it is enacted, that all Persons shall duly set forth and pay *Tithes*, on Neglect whereof, the Party grieved may summon those that detain them before the spiritual Judge, who is authorised to hear and determine, &c. and such Persons as after Sentence refuse Payment, are to be committed to Prison by two Justices of Peace, on Certificate from the Ecclesiastical Judge; and if Persons are disseised of a Parsonage or *Tithes* that are made temporal, they are allowed the like Remedy in the temporal Courts as for other Lands. See 32 *Hen.* 8. *c.* 7. None are to carry away their Corn before they have justly set forth the tenth Part, or agreed for the *Tithes* with the Parson or other Proprietor intitled to the same, on Pain of forfeiting treble the Value of the *Tithes* taken away; and the Owner who claims those *Tithes* may depute his Servant to view the same, and to see that they are truly set out and severed from the nine Parts; and to take away the same: And in Case any one shall load or carry his Corn or Hay before the Tithe thereon is set forth, or withdraw his *Tithes*, or stop the Owner or his deputed Servant from viewing or carrying the same away; in such Case upon due Proof before a spiritual Judge, the Party offending shall pay double the Value of the *Tithes* besides Costs of Suit; and moreover in Suits for substracting of *Tithes*, the Judge of the spiritual Court may excommunicate Persons that disobey his Sentence, &c. See 2 & 3 *Ed.* c. 13. *Note*; the treble Damages above allowed are recoverable in the temporal Courts by Action of Debt, those Damages not being limited where to be recovered: And it is the Opinion of some, that the double Damages above-mentioned may be recovered in the spiritual Court; and that the same is equivalent to the treble Forfeiture recoverable in the temporal Courts, seeing that the Person grieved may sue in the Ecclesiastical Court for the *Tithes* themselves, or a Recompence in lieu of the same; and at the same Time may also have the double Value. It has been held that where a Person sows his Land, and before Severance the Minister of the Parish dies, the *Tithes* of such Land shall go to the Successor; but in Case the Corn be cut down before the Decease of such Minister, his Executors shall have the *Tithes*. Both Executors and Administrators are liable to be sued for *Tithes*; and in Case of Assets, in their Hands, must pay the same. *Small-Tithes* that are under the Value of 40 *s.* are recoverable before two Justices of Peace, who are in no Respect interested in the Tithes, within 20 Days after Demand made, and two Years after due: And the Justices may by Distress levy the Money by them adjudged, upon the Party's Refusal to pay, ten Days after Notice, &c. See 7 & 8 *W.* 3. *c.* 6. Where a *Quaker* refuses either to pay or compound for great or small *Tithes*, the two next Justices of the Peace, may on Complaint thereof made summon such *Quaker* before them, and after examining the Matter of Complaint on Oath, may by Order

der under their Hands and Seals, direct the Payment in all Cases under 10 l. And in Case, after such Order, the *Quaker* refuses to comply therewith, any one of the Justices may by Warrant order the same to be levied by Distress, &c. See 7 & 8 W. 3. c. 34. which by 1 Geo. 1. c. 6. is made perpetual. Nevertheless *Tithes*, if of any considerable Value, are usually sued for in the *Exchequer* by *English Bill*, except where the Suit is founded on the before-mentioned Statute of 2 & 3 Ed. 6. for double or treble Value, &c. *Tithes* are of three Kinds, Predial, Personal and mixt: *Predial* are such as immediately arise from the Land, whether it be by manuring, or its own Nature; as Corn, Grain, Hay, Wood, Fruit, and Herbs, which are said to be due without deducting the Costs: Personal are such as only arise from a Person's Labour and Industry, they being a tenth Part of his Gains in Trade, &c. after Charges deducted: Yet this is seldom paid in *England*, and when it is, it is only due by Custom, and is payable where the Party dwells, hears divine Service, &c. *Mix'd Tithes* are such as arise not directly from the Ground, but from Cattle and other Things that receive their Nourishment from and are maintained thereout; as Calves, Colts, Pigs, Wool, Lambs, &c. *Tithes* are further divided into *Great* and *Small: Great* are Corn, Hay, and Wood; *Small* comprehend all other *Predial* Tithes besides Corn, &c. as likewise such Tithes as are *Personal*, and *Mix'd Tithes* which are *extraparochial*, not lying in any Parish, and belong to the King.

Tithing, according to *Lamb.* was a Company of ten Men with their Families, who were all bound to the King for the peaceable Behaviour of each other: And of these Societies or Companies there was one chief or principal Person, who from his Office was stiled *Teothing-man*, at present in some Places Tithing-man, but in Fact a Constable, the old Way of *Tithing* being long since left off. *Tithing-men* at this Day are taken for a kind of Petty Constables, who are elected by Parishes, and sworn in their Offices at the Court-Leet, and sometimes by Justices of Peace, &c.

Title, is where a Person hath just Cause of Entry into Lands, &c. of which another is seised; as also the Means by which a Person comes to Lands, &c. As by Fine, Feoffment, Will, Descent, &c. Every Right is a *Title*, but every *Title* is not such a Right for which an Action lies; wherefore it is held that *Titulus est Justa Causa possidendi quod nostrum est*, and denotes the Means whereby one holds Lands, &c. According to *Hob.* Where a Person would recover any thing from another, he must make out a better Title thereto than that other has; otherwise it will not be sufficient to destroy his Title; for it is not allowed for the Party to forsake his own Title and fly upon another's; because he must recover by his own Strength, and not by the other's Weakness.

Titles of the Clergy, denotes the Church to which a Clergyman was ordained, and where he was constantly to reside. There are several Reasons why a Church is called *Titulus*: But that which *Cowel* takes to be the best, is because anciently the Name of the Saint to whom the Church was dedicated, was ingraved on the Porch, as a Sign that the Saint had

had a *Title* to that Church; and from thence the Church itself was afterwards called *Titulus*. According to some Writers none shall be ordained without a *Title*; and this is in order to keep out such from the Ministry, who for Want of Maintenance, might otherwise bring a Disgrace upon the Church. In short, a *Title* is an Assurance of being preferred to some Ecclesiastical Benefice, that is to say, a Certificate that the Clerk is provided of some Church or Place, or where the Bishop that ordains him, intends shortly to admit him to a Benefice or Curacy when void.

Tod of Wool, according to 12 *Car.* 2. *c.* 32. contains twenty-eight Pounds or two Stone.

Toft, is taken for a Messuage, but rather for the Place where a Messuage has stood; and it has been frequently used in *Fines*, wherein you may frequently read *Toftum & Croftum*.

Toftman, is used for the Owner or Occupier of a *Toft*.

Tol, in a legal Sense denotes to bar, defeat, or take away; as to *Tol* an Entry is to take away the Right of Entry.

Toll, according to its proper Signification is a Payment in Towns, Fairs and Markets, for Goods bought and sold there; and it is also taken for a Liberty as well to take as to be free from *Toll*.

Toll-booth, denotes the Place where Goods are weighed.

Tolcestrum, is taken for an Excise or Tribute formerly paid by the servile Tenant for Liberty to brew and sell Ale.

Toll-corn, is that Corn that is taken for Toll ground at a Mill.

Toll-hop, is the Dish or Measure wherein they take *Toll* for Corn sold in an overt Market.

Tolt, is a Writ whereby a Cause depending in a Court-Baron is removed to the County-Court.

Tolta, denotes Extortion, or any thing that is exacted or imposed contrary to Right and Justice.

Tonnage, is a Custom or Impost paid to the Crown for Merchandize or Wares carried out or brought in Ships or Vessels, according to a certain Rate imposed on every Tun. See **Tunnage**.

Tort, (*French*) denotes Injury or Wrong. See **De son Tort**.

Tortfeasor, is taken for a Wrong-doer or Trespasser.

Toties quoties, is often used in Deeds and Conveyances, and signifies *as often as*.

Totted, is used to denote that a Debt is good to the King; and a Debt is noted for such by the *foreign Appofers* or other Officers in the *Exchequer*, by writing the Word *Tot* to it.

Tourn. See **Turn**.

Tout temps prist & uncore est, that is to say always was, and is at present ready, is a Kind of Plea by way of Defence or Excuse for a Person sued for any Debt or Duty.

Towage, is particularly used for that Money which is given by Bargemen to the Owner of the Ground next a River, where they tow a Barge or other Vessel.

Town denotes a Place or Borough that is walled.

Trade, in general denotes Traffick or Merchandize, as also a private Way of Living. The Law does so far favour Trade, that if a Person by Bond or Contract restrains himself from the Exercise of any Trade, tho' such Restraint extends to a particular Place only, if there was no Consideration made for that Promise, it is void; yet it is said, that in case of a Con-

Confideration it may be good. But if the Reftraint be throughout the Kingdom, even tho' there be a Confideration, the Reftraint will be void.

Tranfcript, fignifies a Copy of any Record, Deed or Writing; that is to fay, when the Record is written over again or exemplified.

Tranfcripto pedis finis levati mittendo in Cancellarium, is a Writ for certifying the Foot of a Fine levied before Juftices in Eyre, &c. into the Court of Chancery.

Tranfcripto Recognitionis factæ coram Jufticiariis itinerantibus, is a Writ directed to Juftices in Eyre, for certifying a Recognifance by them taken.

Tranfgreffione, is a Writ commonly termed an Action of Trefpafs, of which two Sorts are reckoned; the one *Vicountiel*, fo termed on Account of its being directed to the Sheriff, and is not returnable, but to be determined in the County: And the Form of this differs from the other, becaufe according to *Fitzherbert*, it has thefe Words, viz. *Quare Vi & Armis*, &c. The other is termed a Writ of *Trefpafs* upon the Cafe fued in the *King's Bench* or *Common Pleas*, and then always thefe Words *Vi & Armis*.

Tranfire, fignifies a Warrant from the Cuftom-houfe, to let pafs.

Tranfitory, denotes a paffing away and is oppofed to *Local*; as *tranfitory* Actions are fuch as may be laid in any County, or Place. See **Local**.

Tranflation, according to the Acceptation of the Word is particularly confined to denote the Setting from one Place to another; as to remove a Bifhop from one Diocefe to another; and this is called 'Tranflating; and fuch Bifhop does not write *Anno Confecrationis*, but *Anno Tranflationis noftræ*.

Traverfe, (from the *French*) fometimes denotes to deny, and fometimes to overthrow or undo a Thing, or to put one upon the Proof of the Matter; and it is much ufed in Anfwers to Bills in *Equity*; and it is likewife defined to be that which the Defendant pleads or fays in Bar to avoid the Plaintiff's Bill, either by confeffing and avoiding, or by denying and *traverfing* the material Parts thereof; the formal Words of which are, *Without that*, in *Latin*, *Abfque hoc*, and in our *French*, *Sans ceo*. It is held that a Plea is ill, wherein the Plaintiff's Title, &c. is neither traverfed nor confeffed. Though each Matter of Fact alledged by the Plaintiff may be *traverfed*; yet no Matter of Law, or where it confifts of Part Matter of Fact, and Matter of Law, may be fo; neither may a Record be traverfed, which is not to be tried by a Jury. Thefe Rules are laid down by fome Writers as neceffary to be obferved in *Traverfes*, viz. 1. That the *Traverfing* of a Thing immediately alledged, will vitiate a good Bar. 2. That nothing muft be traverfed but what is exprefly alledged. 3. That Surplufage does enforce a Traverfe. 4. That it muft be made to the fubftantial Part of the Title. 5. That where an Act may be indifferently intended to be at one Day or another, there the Day is not *traverfable*. 6. That in an Action of Trefpafs the Day is not generally material; yet if a Matter be to be done upon fome particular Day, in that Cafe the Day is material and *traverfable*. To *traverfe an Indictment or Prefentment*, is to take Iffue thereon, contradict or deny fome chief Point

Point thereof: As in *Lamb. Eren.* 522. *&c.* If a Person be presented for a Highway overflowed with Water, by Default of scouring a Ditch, *&c.* the Defendant may traverse either the Matter, that there is no Highway there, or that the Ditch is sufficiently scoured; or otherwise he may *traverse* the Cause, *viz.* that he has not the Land, or that he, and they whose Estate, *&c.* have not used to scour the Ditch. To *traverse* an Office is nothing more than to prove that an Inquisition made of Land or Goods by the Escheator is defective and untruly made.

Traytor, denotes a State Offender, or one that is a Betrayer, *&c.* See **Treason**.

Trayterous Position, is applied to the taking *Arms* by the *King's Authority against his Person*, and those that are commissioned by him, condemned by 14 *Car.* 2. *c.* 3.

Treason, in general signifies a Betraying, and it is divided into *High Treason* and *Petty Treason*. The first of these is defined to be an Offence committed against the Security of the King or Kingdom, whether it be by Imagination, Word or Deed; as to compass or imagine the Death of the King, Queen, or their eldest Son and Heir; or in Case he violate or deflower the King's Wife, or his eldest Daughter unmarried, or the Wife of the King's eldest Son; or if he levy War against the King within his Kingdom, or adhere to his Enemies, give them Aid or Comfort within the Realm, or elsewhere; or if he counterfeit the King's Great or Privy Seal, or his Money, or bring false Money into the Kingdom, like to what we have here, and utter the same; if he kill the Chancellor, Treasurer, Justices of either *Bench*, Justices of Assise, or of *Oyer* and *Terminer*, sitting in Judgment or in the Execution of their Office. See 25 of *Ed.* 3. *c.* 2. The Offender in *High Treason* is to be hanged, drawn, and quartered, and also forfeit his Lands and Goods to the King. *Petty Treason*, is where a Servant kills his Master, a Wife her Husband; or where a secular or religious Person kills his Prelate or Superior, to whom he owes Faith and Obedience: And Aiders and Abettors, as well as Procurors, are within the Act 25 *Ed.* 3. *c.* 2. But if the Killing be upon a sudden falling out, or upon *se defendendo*, *&c.* this is not *Petty Treason*; because, according to *Hawk.* Persons accused shall be adjudged Not guilty, or Principal or Accessary, according to the Rules of Law in other Cases: So strict a Construction is put upon the Words of this Statute, that no Case that cannot be brought within the Meaning of the Words thereof, are liable to be punished by it; wherefore if a Son kill his Father, he shall not be tried for *Petty Treason*, except he served his Father for Wages, *&c.* and in that Case he must be indicted by the Name of a Servant; tho' the Offence is doubtless much more heinous in a Son than in a Servant. *Petty Treason* in short, is that which is committed against the Head, tho' not against the supream Head. All *Petty Treason* implies the highest Degree of Murder, and occasions the Forfeiture of the Lands by Escheat to the Lord of the Fee, *&c.* and the further Punishment of the Man is to be drawn, hanged, and quartered for it; and a Woman burnt.

Treasurer

Treasurer, is defined to be an Officer, to whom the Treasure of another is committed to be kept and truly disposed of: And the chief of these in this Kingdom is the *Treasurer of England*, who by his Office bears the Title of Lord, and is one of the greatest Men in the Land, having under his Charge and Government all the King's Wealth that is contained in the *Exchequer*. This Officer holds his Place *durante Beneplacito*, during Pleasure; and has the Check of all the Officers employed in collecting the Customs and other royal Revenues; and in his Gift and Disposition are all the Officers of the Customs in the several Ports of the Kingdom; and Escheators in every County are nominated by him. There is likewise a *Treasurer of the King's Houshold*, who is of the Privy Council, and in the Absence of the *Steward of the King's Houshold*, has with the *Comptroller* and *Steward of the Marshalsea*, great Power. To these may be added the *Treasurer of the County* for poor Soldiers. And most Corporations throughout the Kingdom have an Officer of this Name, whose Office is to receive their Rents, and disburse their common Expences, and is of great Credit among them.

Treasurer of the County, is an Officer that keeps the *County Stock*, in which Office there are two in every County, who are chosen by the major Part of the Justices of the Peace at *Easter-Sessions*. They are to continue in their Office only for a Year, and account at the Year's End, or at least within ten Days after the Expiration of the Year to their Successors, under certain Penalties. The County Stock, whereof this Officer has the keeping, is raised by rating every Parish annually; and the same is from Time to Time disposed of to charitable Uses, towards the Relief of maimed Soldiers, and Mariners, Prisoners in the County Gaols, paying the Salaries of Governours of Houses of Correction, and relieving poor Almshouses, &c. See 43 *Eliz.* c. 2. 7 *Jac.* 1. c. 4. 11 & 12 *W.* 3. c. 18. 5 *Ann.* c. 32. and 6 *Ga.* 1. c. 23.

Treasure-trove, according to *Bract.* is where any Treasure is found hid in the Earth, but not lying upon the Ground, and no Person knows to whom it belongs; in which Case the Property thereof belongs to the King, or the Lord of the Manor, which last has it by special Grant or Prescription. By some Writers it is said, that nothing is to be deemed *Treasure-trove*, but Gold and Silver; and that it is the Duty of every Subject, as soon as he has found any such Treasure in the Earth, to make it known to the Coroners of the County, &c. and that the Concealing thereof is punishable by Fine and Imprisonment.

Treasury, is sometimes taken for the Place where the King's Treasure is reposited; and sometimes for the Office of *Lord Treasurer*: And there are Commissioners to act in this Office, when it is not committed to one single Person; which Commissioners are titled *Lords of the Treasury*.

Trespass, denotes any Transgression of the Law under Treason, Felony, or Misprision of either: But it is most commonly used for any Wrong or Damage, either to the King in his Forest, or by one private Person to another; and in this Signification it is of two Sorts,

Sorts, *Trespass general*, which is otherwise termed *Trespass Vi & Armis*; and *Trespass special*, or *Trespass upon the Case*. Trespasses against a Man's Person are these, viz. a Threatning to hurt him; an Assaulting or Setting on one to beat him; a Battery, which is an actual Beating; Maiming of a Man, so that he loses the Use of his Limbs; an unlawful Imprisonment of another, or illegally Restraining him of his Liberty, &c. Trespasses against a Man's Property may be committed several Ways; as against his Wife, Children, or Servants, or his House and Goods, &c. or against his Land, by carrying away the Deeds or other Evidences concerning the same, cutting the Trees, or damaging the Grass therein. See *Fitz. Nat. Brev.* The Difference between an Action of *Trespass Vi & Armis*, and *Trespass upon the Case*, is this, viz. the one lies where the original Act was a Wrong in itself; and the other where it is consequential to a lawful Act: At *Common Law*, in *Trespass Vi & Armis*, in Case the Defendant be convicted, he is liable to be fined and imprisoned.

Trespasser, denotes a Person that commits a *Trespass*, or Wrong, against another.

Trial, is taken for the Examination of a Cause, Civil, or Criminal, according to the Laws of the Land, before a proper Judge. There are sundry Kinds of *Trials*; as those of Matters of Fact, which must be *tried* by a Jury; Matters of Law which are only *triable* by the Court; and Matters of Record, which are to be *tried* by the Records themselves. In all criminal Cases, the Custom is to ask the Prisoner how he will be *tried*; which, as *Blount* observes, was formerly a very significant Question, tho' not so now, because anciently there were *Trials by Battle*, by *Ordeal*, and by Jury; and when the Prisoner answered, *By God and his Country*, it appeared he made Choice to be *tried* by a Jury; which last is the only Way now used for the *Trial* of Criminals. The Method of proceeding to Trial in Criminal Cases is this, first the Bill of Indictment against the Offender is prepared, and the Prosecutor and his Witnesses attend on the grand Jury therewith, and there give in their Evidence, which being done, the Grand Inquest, either find the Bill of Indictment, or bring it in *Ignoramus*: And if the Bill be found, the Prisoner is brought to the Bar of the Court, and the Clerk of the Arraignment says to him, *A. B. (calling him by his Name)* hold up thy Hand. Thou standest indicted by the Name of *A. B.* for such a Felony, &c. *(setting forth the Crime laid in the Indictment)* How sayest thou, art thou guilty of this Felony whereof thou standest indicted or not guilty? To which the Prisoner answering Not guilty, the Clerk says *Culprit*. How wilt thou be tried? Whereupon the Defendant answers, *By God and my Country*; which Plea of the Prisoner the Clerk records, and then the Panel of the Petty Jury is called over; all or most of whom appearing, the Prisoner is told that they are to pass upon his Life and Death, and that he may challenge any of them before they are sworn, for Partiality or other Defect: After the Jury is sworn, and the Indictment is read over to them, and they are charged, the Evidences both for and against the

Prisoner

Prisoner, are called, sworn and examined in open Court; after which is done, and the Jury have laid their Heads together, they bring in their Verdict, and if they bring in the Prisoner guilty, such their Verdict is recorded, and the Prisoner is taken from the Bar; but if they bring him in Not Guilty, the Prisoner is bid to fall down upon his Knees, &c.

Trinity-House, is a College or House at *Deptford*, belonging to the Company or Corporation of Seamen, who by the King's Charter have Power to take Knowledge of such Persons as destroy Sea-marks, and to redress those Doings; as also to correct the Faults of Sailors, &c. and to take Care of other Things that relate to Navigation. *Cowel.*

Trinoda Necessitas, is taken for a necessary Tax or Imposition whereto all Lands were subjected at the Time of the *Saxons*, towards the Repairing of Bridges, &c.

Triours, according to *Broke*, are such Persons as are chosen by the Court to examine whether a Challenge made to the whole Panel or to any Part thereof, be just or not.

Triroda Terræ, is said to be a Quantity of Land containing three Rods or Perches.

Tristis, is taken for an Immunity, by which a Man is freed from his Attendance on the Lord of a Forest, when he thinks fit to chase therein; and he shall not be compelled to hold a Dog, follow the Chase, or stand at any fixed Place, which otherwise he might be obliged to do, under Pain of Amercement.

Tronage, according to *Cowel*, is a Custom or Toll taken for weighing of Wool: And hence comes the Word *Tronator*, an Officer in the City of *London*, whose Office is to weigh the Wool that is brought thither.

Tronator. See **Tronage**.

Trover, (from the *French*) is an Action that lies against one, who having found his Goods, refuses to deliver them upon Demand; or it lies where a Man has in his Possession another's Goods, by Delivery to him, or otherwise; and the Person so possessed, sells or otherwise makes use of them without the Owner's Consent. This Action is called *Trover and Conversion*, and is a special Action on the Case, lying for the Recovery of Damages to the Value of the Goods, &c. And it is called *Trover and Conversion* because the Plaintiff in his Declaration surmises, that he lost such and such Goods, and that the Defendant found them, and at such a Place converted them to his own Use: And here it is to be observed, that the Losing is nothing but a mere Suggestion, and in no Respect material; for if the Plaintiff delivered the Goods to the Defendant; or if the Defendant took them in his Presence, &c. this Action will lie, provided a Conversion can be proved, which is the main Point of the Action, and therefore must be particularly set forth; as where a Person finds Goods, and refuses to deliver them to the Owner upon Demand, this is a *Conversion* in Law; yet if he should answer, that he does not know whether the Person demanding is the right Owner or not, this is held to be no Conversion, should he on that Account keep them from the Owner. It is held that where an actual Conversion cannot be proved, then Proof is to be had of a Demand

having

having been made, before the Action brought, of the Goods for which the Action is commenced, and that the Things demanded were not delivered; in which Case tho' an actual *Conversion* is not proved, a Demand, and Refusal to deliver what is demanded, is a sufficient Evidence to the Jury, that he converted the same, until the contrary appears; for a Denial of Goods to him that has a Right to demand them, is in Law a Conversion; and after a Demand and Refusal made, should the Defendant tender the Goods demanded, and the Plaintiff refuse them, that will avail nothing, further than go in Mitigation of Damages, but not to the Right of the Action of *Trover*; for that the Plaintiff is still intitled to that. According to *Bulst.* if Goods be delivered over to one Person to be delivered to another, and he to whom they were first delivered, refuses to deliver them over accordingly, and converts them to his own Use; he is liable to an Action of *Trover*, not only at the Suit of the Person that first delivered them, but also of him to whom they were to be delivered; and the Owner may chuse to have this Action against the first Finder of Goods, or any other who gets them afterwards by Sale, &c. This Action also lies for an Executor for the Testator's Goods; seeing that the Law gives him a Property therein, which draws the Possession to it, tho' there be not an actual Possession. In this Action a Right or Property in the Goods, or a lawful Possession thereof, is absolutely necessary to be proved by the Plaintiff in *Trover*, before the Goods came to the Defendant's Hands; but then it is here to be observed that in case he does find his Goods in the Hands of another, if the Person, on whom they are found, bought them in an open Fair or Market, the Property is altered, and the Owner cannot recover them. *Action of Trover* frequently takes Place of *Detinue*, because in *Trover* the Defendant cannot wage his Law, which in *Detinue* he may.

Trop-weight. See **Weight**.

Trust, denotes that Confidence which one Person reposes in another; and where any Breach or Nonperformance is of the same, the Remedy is by Bill in *Equity*. Servants going away with their Masters Goods are guilty of a *Breach of Trust*.

Tun, is a Vessel of Oil or Wine, that contains Twelve-score and Twelve Gallons, or four Hogsheads.

Tunnage, is used for a Custom or Impost payable to the Crown for Merchandize imported or exported, and is to be paid after a certain Rate for every Tun thereof.

Turbary, denotes a Right to dig Turfs on the Ground of another; and according to the Opinion of some ancient Writers it denotes the Ground where Turfs are digged.

Turn, is applied to a Court held twice a Year, *viz.* within a Month after *Easter* and *Michaelmas* respectively, by the Sheriff of the County. It is the King's Leet throughout the County, and the Sheriff sits Judge there, whence the Court, which is incident to his Office, is called the Sheriff's *Turn* or *Tourn*, which Appellation it is thought it originally got from the Sheriff's taking a *Turn* or Circuit about his Shire, and holding a Court in several Parts thereof. The Sheriff is a

Judge

VA

Judge of Record, and in his *Turn* may make Inquiry of all Treasons and Felonies by the common Law, as well as the lowest Offences against the King; common Nusances, Annoyances, &c. and amerce for Offences, &c.

Turnetum, is said to be a Tax anciently paid to the Sheriff, as an Acknowledgment for holding his *Turn*.

Turno Vicecomitum, is a Writ that lies for those that are called to the Sheriff's *Turn* out of their own Hundred. See *Reg. Orig.*

Twa-night-Geste, was a Guest that staid at an Inn a *second Night*, for whom the Host was not answerable for any Injury he did, as he was in the Case of a *Third Night Awn-hinde*, which see.

Twelfhinous, is the same with *Thanus*, or *Thane*, among the English *Saxons*, where every Person was valued at a certain Price: And if an Injury was done either to the Person or Goods, a pecuniary Mulct was imposed, and paid in Satisfaction of that Injury, according to the Worth and Quality of the Person to whom it was done: Those that were worth 1200 Shillings were called *Twelfhindi*; and if an Injury was done to such Persons, Satisfaction was to be made according to their Worth. *Cowel.*

Twelfhindi. See **Twelfhinous.**

Twelve-Men, otherwise *Jury* or *Inquest.* See **Jury.**

Tythes. See **Tithes.**

V.

Vacation, is the whole Time betwixt the End of one Term and the Beginning of another. This Word is also applied to the Death of a Bishop or other spiritual Person, till the Bishoprick or Dignity is supplied with another; and this is called *Vacation*.

Vacatura, denotes a Vacancy of an Ecclesiastical Benefice.

Vadiare Duellum, to wage a Combat; that is to say, to give and take as it were a mutual Pledge of fighting; as where a Person challenged another to decide a Controversy by Camp-fight or Duel, and the one threw down a Gauntlet or the like Sign of Defiance, which the other took up. *Cowel.*

Vagabond, is one that wanders about, and has no certain Dwelling; an idle Fellow. See **Vagrants.**

Vagrants, by 12 *Ann.* c. 23. are described to be Persons pretending to be Patent-gatherers, or Collectors for Prisons, and wander about for that End: Among which are included all Fencers, Bearwards, common Players of Interludes, Minstrels, Jugglers; all Persons pretending to be Gypsies, or wandering in the Habits of such, or pretending Skill in *Physiognomy*, Palmestry, or the like, or to tell Fortunes; all such as use any subtle Craft, unlawful Games or Plays, or being able in Body run away leaving their Wives or Children to the Parish; all Persons who cannot otherwise maintain themselves, loiter about and refuse to work for the usual Wages.

Value, is a known Word; and yet there is a nice Distinction made by *West* in his *Symbol* between Value and Price, *viz.* The Value of those Things in which Offences are committed, is usually comprised in Indictments, which seems necessary in *Theft* to make a Difference from *Petit Larceny*, and in Trespass to aggravate the Fault, and increase the Fine: But no Price of Things that are *feræ Naturæ*, may be expressed, such as Deer, Hares, &c. if they be not in Parks or Warrens, which is a Liberty; nor of Charters of Land. Where the Number of the Things taken are to be expressed in the Indictment, as young Doves in a Dove-house, young Hawks in a Wood, there may be said either *Pretii*, of such a Price, or *ad Valenciam*, to such a Value; but of sundry dead Things, *ad Valenciam*, and not *Pretii*, must be used; and of current Coin, neither *Pretii* nor *ad Valenciam* shall be used, the Value and Price thereof being certain.

Value of Marriage, was a Writ that formerly lay for the Lord, having proffered convenable *Marriage* to the Infant, without Disparagement, if he refused to take the Lord's Offer, to recover the *Value of the Marriage*.

Vargi or **Wargi**, is taken for Persons outlawed, that live by Robbery.

Variance, denotes an Alteration, or Change of a Thing, and in a legal Sense is applied to that Change of a Thing formerly laid in a Plea; or it is where the Declaration in a Cause differs from the Writ or Deed, on which the same is grounded; as where there appears to be a material *Variance* between the Matter pleaded and the Manner of Pleading it, which makes it not a good Plea, because the Manner and Matter of pleading ought to agree in Substance, otherwise there will be no Certainty in it; tho' indeed it is held, that when a Plea is good in Substance, a small Variance shall not hurt it.

Vassal, according to *Skene* is he that holds Land in Fee of his Lord, and is more usually called *Tenant in Fee*, of whom some owe Fidelity and Service, and are called *Vassalli Jurati*: And *Vassallus* is *quasi Bassallus*, i. e. inferior *Socius*, because the Vassal is inferior to his Master, and must serve and reverence him; and yet he is in a Manner his Companion, because each of them is obliged to the other.

Vasselleria, denotes *Vasselage* or the Tenure of *Vassals*.

Vasto, is a Writ which lies for the Heir against the Tenant for Term of Life, or Years, for committing Waste; or it lies for him in the Reversion or Remainder.

Vastum, denotes a Waste or Common lying open to the Cattle of all Tenants that have a Right of Commoning. *Cowel*.

Vastum Forestæ vel Bosci, is taken for that Part of a Forest or Wood wherein the Trees and Under Wood were so destroyed, that it lay in a Manner *Waste* and Barren.

Veal-Money. We are told by *Cowel*, that the Tenants of one of the Tithings within the Manor of *Bradford* in *Wiltshire*, paid an annual Rent by this Name to their Lord, the Marquis of *Winchester*, in Lieu of *Veal* formerly paid in Kind.

Vejours, is supposed to come from the *French*, and is taken for those that are sent by the Court to take View of any Place in Question, for the better Decision of the Right to the same: And it is also taken to signify such as are sent to view such Persons as essoin themselves *de Malo Lecti*, whether in Fact they be so sick, as that they cannot appear, or whether they counterfeit it. And further it is taken for those that are appointed to view an Offence; such as a Man

VE

Man that is murdered, or a Virgin ravished.

Venditioni exponas, is a judicial Writ directed to the Sheriff, commanding him to sell Goods already taken into his Hands, for the satisfying a Judgment given in the King's Court; as where the Sheriff upon a *Fieri facias* has taken Goods in Execution, and returns that he has so done, and cannot find Buyers; or in Case he delay to deliver them to the Plaintiff, then this Writ shall issue to the Sheriff, to make Sale of the Goods, and bring in the Money.

Venditor Regis, the King's Seller or Salesman, was formerly an Officer of the King, that exposed to Sale those Goods and Chattels which were seised or distrained to answer any Debt due to the King: But *Anno 2 Ed. 2.* this Office was seised into the King's Hands on Account of the Abuse thereof.

Venire facias, is a judicial Writ directed to the Sheriff, commanding him to cause a Jury to appear upon a Cause brought to Issue, in order to try the same; upon which Writ if the Jury do not appear at the Day of the Return of this Writ, then a *Habeas Corpus* shall go out, and afterwards a Distress until they do appear. A *Venire facias* is also the common Process upon any Presentment, not being for Felony, it being in the Nature of a Summons for the Defendant to appear; and it is likewise the proper Process to be awarded on an Indictment for any Crime that is under the Degree of Treason, Felony or *Maihem*, except in Cases wherein other Processes are directed by Statute: And if on the Return of this Process it appear that the Defendant has Lands, &c. whereby he may be destrain-

VE

ed, a Distress infinite shall go out till he do appear; and in such Case he shall forfeit on every Default so much as the Sheriff returns upon him in Issues: Yet if a *Nihil* be returned, a *Capias, Alias* and *Pluries* shall issue. It is said, that this Writ of *Venire facias ad respondendum*, may be made out without a certain Day, because by the Appearance of the Defendant the Fault is cured; tho' *Venire facias ad triandum Exitum* must be returnable at a Day certain.

Venire facias tot Matronas. See **Ventre inspiciendo.**

Venter, is taken for the Belly or Child a Woman goes with; and in Law there is a first and second *Venter*, &c. See **Descent.**

Ventre inspiciendo, is a Writ that issues for the Search of a Woman that alledges she is with Child, and by that Means with-holds Lands from the next Heir: And this Fact must be tried by a *Jury of Women*: And Women condemned for Felony, &c. who plead their Bellies, that is to say, pretend they are with Child, are likewise to be searched and tried by a *Jury of Matrons*.

Venue, is taken for a neighbouring Place, whence a Jury are to come. In all Actions of Trespass and Ejectment the *Venue* must be laid in the Town, County, &c. where the Trespass was committed, or where the Lands in Question lie: And in like Manner it must be in respect to all real Actions: Yet the Judges may in all transitory Actions alter the *Venue* from the Place, where otherwise it should be, in Case they have Reason to believe, there cannot be an indifferent Trial had in that Place or County. If one would move to have the *Venue* altered, he must make Affidavit that

that the Cause of Action (if any) did arise in the County in which he would have the *Venue* to be laid, and not in the County where the Action is laid; upon which Motion if the Court order the *Venue* to be altered, the Plaintiff must in that Case alter his Declaration, by laying his Action in the County the *Venue* is ordered to be in. There is a Rule in the *King's Bench*, that a Motion to alter a *Venue* must be in eight Days after the Declaration is delivered; but that is said not to be strictly observed: However, this Motion is never granted after the Rules for pleading are out.

Verderor, is a judicial Officer of the King's Forest, and is chosen by the King's Writ, in the full County of the same Shire, within the Forest where he lives; and he is sworn to maintain and keep the Assises of the Forest, and to view, receive and inrol the Attachments and Presentments of all Manner of Trespasses of Vert and Venison in the Forest. See *Manwood*.

Verdict is the Answer that is given to the Court by the Jury, concerning the Matter of Fact in any Cause committed to their Trial: And in this Answer every one of the Jurors must agree, otherwise it can be no Verdict: And the Duty of the Jury is to try the Fact, whilst that of the Judges is to adjudge thereon according to the Law. A *general Verdict* is that which is brought into Court in like general Terms to the general Issue; as where a Defendant pleads Not guilty, or that he has done no Wrong, in that Case the Issue is *general*, and is to be tried whether he is guilty, or the Fact charged be wrong or not; which being committed to the Jury charged with the Trial thereof, they either bring in their Verdict for the Plaintiff by saying the Defendant is Guilty; or for the Defendant, by saying he is Not guilty. A *special Verdict* is where the Jury find the Matter at large, according to the Evidence given, *viz.* that such a Thing is done by the Defendant; and at the same Time declare the Course of the Fact, as in their Opinions it is proved; and pray the Judgment of the Court as to what the Law is in that Point. *Verdicts* are likewise publick and private: *Publick*, when the same is given in open Court; and *Private*, when given out of Court, before any of the Judges of the same; and the Reason it is called *Private*, is, that such Verdict is to be kept secret till it is confirmed in Court: But a private *Verdict* in Strictness is looked upon to be no *Verdict*, it being only a Favour that is allowed by the Court to the Jury for their Ease; and according to some Writers, the Jury may vary from it, and when come into Court give a contrary Verdict; yet this must be before the private Verdict is recorded. A private Verdict cannot be given in criminal Causes, such as concern Life, as Felony, &c. because the Jury are commanded to look upon the Prisoner at the Bar when they give in their *Verdict*, and on that Account the Prisoner must be then present. Where the Court directs the Jury to bring in a special Verdict in a Civil Cause, one of the Counsel on each Side agrees upon Notes for it, which they draw up, and set their Hands to; which afterwards are to be delivered to the Jury in a convenient Time, otherwise the Court will take like a general *Verdict*. Where at the Prayer of either Plaintiff or Defendant, a special *Verdict* is directed, the Party praying it is to prosecute the special *Verdict*, in order that the Matter in Law may be determined; and in case either of the Parties to the Suit delay to join in drawing it up, and pay his Part of the Charges, or if the Counsel for the Defendant refuse to subscribe the special *Verdict*, the Person praying it may draw it up and enter it *Ex Parte*. See more of this in 2 *Lill. Abr.* 645, &c. It is held that in Capital Cases a Verdict must be actually given; and if a Jury cannot all agree thereon, they are liable to be carried in Carts, after the Judges, round the Circuit, until such Time as they do agree; and in every such Case when agreed they may give in their *Verdict* in another County. According to *Wood*, the Court may set aside a *Verdict* that contrary to Evidence convicts a Man in a criminal Case; but cannot set aside a *Verdict* that acquits him: But in a Civil Action, where a *Verdict* is given against Evidence, either as to Plaintiff or Defendant, the same may be set aside, and a new Trial had, &c.

Verge, with us is taken for the Compass of the King's Court, wherewith the Jurisdiction of the *Lord Steward of the Houshold* is bounded, which is thought to have been twelve Miles round. This Word has also another Signification, and is taken for a Stick or Rod, by which one is admitted Tenant to a Copyhold Estate, by holding it in his Hand, and swearing Fealty to the Lord of the Manor. *Verge land*. See **Vardland**.

Vergers, according to *Fleta*, are such as carry White Wands before the Justices of either *Bench*.

Vert, in the Forest Laws is taken for every thing that grows and bears a green Leaf within a Forest, which may cover a Deer. See *Manwood* on this Head.

Very Lord and very Tenant, are taken for those that are immediate Lord and Tenant one to another.

Vested, seems to denote settled or fixed; as if an Estate in *Remainder* is limited to a Child before born; when such Child is born, the Estate in Remainder is said to be vested in him.

Vestry, not only denotes a Place adjoining to a Church, where the Vestments of the Minister are kept, but also a Meeting at such Place, consisting of the Minister, Churchwardens and chief Men of most Parishes, who make a Parish Vestry or Meeting. By Custom there are *select Vestries*, being a certain Number of Persons chosen to have the Government of the Parish, make Rates, and take the Accounts of Churchwardens, &c. And according to *Wood*, when Rates are made, the Parishioners must have Notice of a *Vestry* held for that Purpose; in which Case all that are absent shall be concluded by a Majority of the Parishioners present, who in Construction of Law are the whole Parish.

Vestry-men, are a select Number of the chief Parishioners in every Parish within the City of *London* and Suburbs, and elsewhere, who annually chuse Officers for the Parish, and take Care of its Concernments; and they are so called, because they usually meet in the Vestry of the Church. *Cowel*.

Vetitum Namium, is where a Lord's Bailiff distrains Beasts or Goods, and the Lord forbids his Bailiff to deliver them, when the Sheriff comes to replevy the same, and for that Intent drives them to Places unknown.

Via Regia, is the Highway or common Road, or what is generally termed the King's Way, it being authorised by him and under his Protection.

Vicar. The Priest of every Parish is called *Rector*, unless the Predial Tithes be impropriated, in which Case he is stiled *Vicar*, *Vicario deliberando occasione cujusdam Recognitionis, &c.* is a Writ which anciently lay for a spiritual Person, imprisoned upon Forfeiture of a Recognisance. See *Reg. of Writs* 147.

Vice-admiral, An Under-*Admiral* at Sea is so called.

Vice-Chamberlain, is a great Officer in Court, and is next under the *Lord Chamberlain*, having in his Absence the Controul of all Officers that appertain to that Part of the King's Houshold, which is stiled the Chamber above Stairs.

Vicecomes, denotes a *Sheriff*, which see.

Vice-Dominus, is the same with *Vice-comes*.

Vice-Dominus Episcopi, is the Official, Commissary, or Vicar General of a Bishop. *Cowel.*

Vicegerent, is taken for a Deputy or Lieutenant.

Vicinage. See **Venue**.

Vicinetum. See **Visne**.

Vicis & Venellis mundandis, is a Writ which lies against a Mayor or Bailiff of a Town, for the clean keeping of their Streets.

Vicount or **Viscount**, denotes the same as Sheriff, and also is taken for a Degree of Nobility.

Vicountiel or **Viscountiel**, is taken to signify as much as belonging to the Sheriff; as Writs *Vicontiel* are such Writs as are triable in the Sheriff's Court. Vicountiels are taken for certain Farms, for which the Sheriff pays a certain Rent to the King, and makes what Profit he can of them.

Vicontiel Jurisdiction, denotes that Power or Jurisdiction which belongs to the Officers of a County, as Sheriff, Coroner, Escheator, &c. *Cowel.*

Victuallers, are properly those that sell Victuals: And with us all common Alehouse-keepers go by the Name of *Victuallers*.

Viduitatis professio, is taken for the making of a solemn Profession to live a sole and chaste Widow, which was an ancient Custom in *England*.

Vidimus. See **Innotescimus**.

Vi & armis are Words made use of in Indictments and Actions of Trespass, to shew the violent Commission of any Trespass or Crime.

View, signifies the Act of Viewers; for when a real Action is brought, and the Tenant does not certainly know what Land it is the Demandant requires; then may he pray that the Jury may *view* the same, that is to say, see the Land that is claimed. Formerly there could not have been a *View* in a personal Action, unless upon withdrawing of a Juror after they were sworn, and Consent of the Parties by Rule of Court; but now by 4 & 5 *Ann. c.* 16. it may be granted in any *Action*, depending in the Courts at *Westminster*, where thought necessary, in order for the better Understanding the Evidence, when the Cause comes to be tried; in which Case the Practice is for the Courts to order special Writs

Writs of *Distringas*, or *Habeas Corpora* directed to the Sheriff, commanding him to have six of the Jury, or a greater Number of them, at the Place in Question, some convenient Time before the Trial, who shall have the whole Thing in Dispute shewn to them by two Persons named in the said Writ, and by the Court for that Purpose appointed; upon the Execution of which Writ of *Distringas*, the Sheriff is specially to return the *View* made accordingly, &c.

View of Frank-pledge, is the Office which the Sheriff in his County-court, or the Bailiff in his Hundred, performs in looking to the King's Peace, and seeing that every Man be in some Pledge. See the new *Book of Entries*.

Vi Laica amovenda, according to *Cowel*, is a Writ that lies, where the Bishop of the Diocese has certified into the Court of *Chancery*, that the Rector or Vicar of any Church within his Jurisdiction, is kept out of his Manse, Glebe or Church by any Lay Force or intruding Power; in which Case this Writ shall go out to the Sheriff, to remove all such Violence and Usurpation.

Vi Laica removenda, is a Writ which lies where a Debate is between two Parsons or Provisors for a Church, in which one of them enters with a great Number of Laymen, and holds the other out *Vi & Armis*; in which Case he that is holden out shall have this Writ directed to the Sheriff, that he remove the Force that is within the Church: And the Sheriff shall be commanded, that if he find any Man withstand or resist him, he take with him the *Posse Comitatus*, the Power of his County, in case Need so require, and arrest the Bodies of all that resist, and put them in Prison, so that he have their Bodies before the King at a certain Day to answer the Contempt. This Writ is returnable, and shall not be granted, before the Bishop of the Place, where such Church is, has certified into the *Chancery* such Resistance and Force. *Termes de la Ley*.

Vill, is sometimes taken for a Manor, and sometimes for a Parish, or a Part of one. *Fortescue* tells us, that the Boundaries of *Villages*, are not by Houses, Streets or Walls, but by a large Circuit of Ground, wherein may be several Hamlets, Waters, Woods, and Waste-ground. By *Fleta*, the Difference made between a Mansion, a *Village*, and a Manor, are these, *viz.* a Mansion may consist of one or more Houses, but must be of one Dwelling-place, and none near it; because if other Houses are contiguous, it is a Village; and Manor may consist of several *Villages*, or of one alone.

Villa Regia, is taken for a Title formerly given to those Country Villages where the Kings of *England* had a *Royal* Seat or Palace, and held the Manor in their own Demesne, and there commonly had a free Chapel, not subjected to Ecclesiastical Jurisdiction.

Villein, denotes a Man of servile or base Condition, *viz.* a Bondman or Servant: Of which Bondmen or *Villeins*, there were anciently two Sorts in *England*; the one termed a *Villein in Gross*, who was immediately bound to the Person of his Lord and his Heirs; and the other a *Villein regardant* to a Manor, he being bound to his Lord as a Member belonging and annexed to a Manor, of
which

which the Lord was Owner; and he was properly a pure *Villein*, of whom the Lord took Redemption to marry his Daughter, and to make him free; and whom the Lord might put out of his Lands and Tenements, Goods and Chattels at his Will, and beat and chastise, but not maim him.

Villanis Regis subtractis reducendis, is a Writ that anciently lay for the Bringing back of the King's Bondmen, who had been carried away by others out of his Manors, whereto they belonged. See *Reg. Orig.*

Villeinous Judgment, according to *Stamf.* is that which casts the Reproach of *Villany* and Shame upon the Person against whom it is given; as a Conspirator, &c. and he calls it villeinous, because the Judgment in such Cases shall be like the ancient Judgment in *Attaint*, viz. that the Offender shall not be of any Credit afterwards; nor shall it be lawful for him to approach the King's Court; and his Lands and Goods shall be seised into the King's Hands, his Trees rooted up, and his Body imprisoned, &c. And at this Day, as *Cowel* observes, the Punishment ordained for Perjury (having somewhat more in it than corporal or pecuniary Pain, that is to say, the Discrediting of the Offender for ever) may partake of this Name of *Villeinous Judgment*. See **Pillory**.

Villenage, takes its Name from Villein, and signifies a kind of Tenure anciently belonging to Lands or Tenements, whereby the Tenant was bound to do all such Services as the Lord commanded, or such as were fit for a Villein or Bondman to do.

Vinagium, is said to have been an ancient Tribute or Payment of a certain Quantity of Wine instead of Rent to the chief Lord for a Vineyard.

Virgata Terræ. See **Yard-land**.

Viridario eligendo, is a Writ that lies for the Choice of a *Verderor* in the Forest.

Vis, denotes any kind of Force or Violence, relating to the Person of a Man, or his Goods or Chattels, &c.

Viscount, is taken to be a Degree of Nobility next to that of an Earl; and he is created by Patent, as an Earl.

Visitation, is that Office, that is performed by the Bishop in every Diocese, once in every three Years, or by the Archdeacon, by visiting the Churches and their Rectors, &c.

Visne, denotes a neighbouring Place, or a Place near at Hand.

Visus, denotes a View, or Inspection.

Vita Justiciæ & Legis. *The Life of Justice and the Law*. The Sheriff of a County is said to be *the Life of Justice*; for no Suit begins, nor any Process is served, but by him; and he is said to be *the Life of the Law*, because after Suits are ended, he has the making of Execution.

Viva Pecunia, according to *Cowel* was anciently used for Live Cattle.

Vivary, in general denotes a Place of Land or Water, where living Creatures are kept; but in Law it is most commonly taken for a Park, Warren, Fish-pond or Piscary.

Viva Voce. See **Deposition**.

Ulnage. See **Alnage**.

Ulna ferrea, is the Name of the Standard *Ell of Iron*, that is kept in the *Exchequer* for the Rule of Measure.

G g g   Umpire,

Umpire, denotes a single Person chosen by contesting Parties for determining the Matter in Controversy according to the Compromise and Submission.

Umpirage, is where there is but one Person chosen by Parties at Variance, for determining the Matters in Dispute; and it is usually where two or more Arbitrators are chosen by the contending Parties, to whose Arbitrament they submit their Differences; and if those Arbitrators cannot agree, or are not ready to deliver their Award in Writing before a certain Time limited, then the whole Matter in Dispute is referred to the final Judgment of another, who is usually termed Umpire. The Form of an *Umpirage*, you may see in *the Young Clerk's Magazine*, and other Books of Conveyancing.

Uncore prist, is a Plea for a Defendant that is sued for a Debt due at a Day past, wherein he says, that he tendered the Debt or Sum of Money due, at the Time and Place, and that there was none there to receive it; and that he is ready to pay the same.

Uncuth, (from the *Saxons*) signifies the same with *Incognitus*, unknown, and was anciently used for a Person that came into an Inn Guestwise, and lay there but one Night, in which Case his Host was not bound to answer for any Offence that he committed.

Unde nihil habet. See **Dote unde nihil habet**.

Under-Chamberlain of the Exchequer, is an Officer in that Court, who clears the Tallies, written by the Clerk of the Tallies, and reads the same, in order that the Clerk of the Pell, and the Comptrollers thereof, may see their Entries to be true; he also makes Searches for all Records in the Treasury, and has the Custody of *Domesday* Book. *Cowel*.

Under-Sheriff. See **Sheriff**.

Under-Treasurer of England, was an Officer, as some think, first created in the Reign of King *Henry the Seventh*; whose Duty was to chest up the King's Treasure at the End of every Term; to note the Content of Money in each Chest, and to see it carried into the King's Treasury, for the Ease of the *Lord Treasurer*, as being a Thing too mean for him to be troubled with, and yet at the same Time fit to be performed by a Person of great Secrecy and Trust: But this Officer did not get the Name of *Under-Treasurer*, till the Reign of Queen *Elizabeth*. See 39 *Eliz.* c. 7.

Undres, according to *Fleta*, was used for Miners, or Persons under Age.

Ungeld, is a Word anciently used to denote a Person so far out of the Protection of the Law, that if he were murdered, no *Geld* or Fine should be paid, or Composition made by the Person that killed him.

Uniformity, denotes one Form of publick Prayers and Administration of Sacraments, and other Ceremonies of the Church of *England*; whereto all by 1 *Eliz.* c. 2. & 14 *Car.* 2. c. 4. must submit: But see **Dissenter**.

Union, in general is defined to be a combining or Consolidating of two Churches into one, which is done by the Consent of the Bishop, the Patron, and the Incumbent: And there are two other Sorts of this Kind of *Union*, as where one Church is made subject to another, and one Parson is made Rector of both; and where a Cona Conventual Church is made a Cathedral.

Union of England and Scotland, denotes that grand and glorious Work of bringing about an intire *Union* between those two Kingdoms; the Completion of which Blessing we find was reserved to the fifth Year of the Reign of Queen *Anne*, when this *Union* happily took Effect. It is not unknown to us, as a certain Writer observes, that a compleat *Union* betwixt those two Kingdoms had long earnestly been endeavoured, both before and after those two Nations came to be united under one Sovereign, viz. King *James the First*, on his Accession to the Crown of *England*, but without the desired Success; and the principal Causes assigned for retarding the Blessing sought for, were the indefatigable Pains of the *French* Court, on the one Side, and the secret Cabals of the popish Clergy, on the other, who equally dreaded such a Conjunction; to which may be added the ill-grounded Jealousies about Trade in *one Nation*, meaning *England*; the unreasonable Fondness of *Independency*, in the other, viz. *Scotland*; together with the inveterate Prejudices on both Sides about *religious Worship*, and Church Discipline, &c. However, as already mentioned, it has at last been compleated, and now subsists; the Articles whereof, as ratified at *Edinburgh* the 16th of *January* 1707. and afterwards confirmed by 5 *Ann. c.* 8. follow.

The Articles of Union between *England* and *Scotland*.

1. That the two Kingdoms of Scotland and England, shall upon the first Day of May next ensuing the Date hereof, and for ever after, be united into one Kingdom, by the Name of *Great Britain*, and that the Ensigns Armorial of the said united Kingdom, be such as her Majesty shall appoint; and the Crosses of St. Andrew and St. George be conjoin'd, in such Manner as her Majesty shall think fit, and used in all Flags, Banners, Standards and Ensigns, both at Sea and Land.

2. That the Succession to the Monarchy of the United Kingdom of Great Britain, and of the Dominions thereunto belonging, after her most Sacred Majesty, and in Default of Issue of her Majesty, be, remain and continue to the most Excellent Princess Sophia, Electress and Dutchess Dowager of Hanover, and the Heirs of her Body, being Protestants, upon whom the Crown of England is settled by an Act of Parliament, made in England in the Twelfth Year of the Reign of his late Majesty King William the Third, entituled, An Act for the further Limitation of the Crown, and better securing the Rights and Liberties of the Subject. And that all Papists, and Persons marrying Papists, shall be excluded from, and for ever incapable to inherit, possess, or enjoy the Imperial Crown of Great Britain, and the Dominions thereunto belonging, or any Part thereof. And in every such Case, the Crown and Government shall from Time to Time descend to, and be enjoyed by such Person, being a Protestant, as should have inherited and enjoyed the same, in case such Papist, or Person marrying a Papist, was naturally dead, according to the Provision for the Descent of the Crown of England, made by another Act of Parliament in England, in the First Year of the Reign of their late

Majesties King William *and Queen* Mary, *entituled*, An Act declaring the Rights and Liberties of the Subjects, and settling the Succession of the Crown.

3. *That the United Kingdom of* Great Britain *be represented by one and the same Parliament, to be stiled the Parliament of* Great Britain.

4. *That all the Subjects of the United Kingdom, shall from and after the* Union *have full Freedom and Intercourse of Trade, and Navigation, to, and from any Port or Place within the said United Kingdom, and the Dominions and Plantations thereunto belonging; and that there be a Communication of all other Rights, Privileges and Advantages which do, or may belong to the Subjects of either Kingdom, except where it is otherwise expresly agreed in these Articles.*

5. *That all Ships or Vessels, belonging to her Majesty's Subjects of* Scotland, *at the Time of* ratifying the Treaty of Union of the two Kingdoms in the Parliament of Scotland, *though foreign built, be deem'd, and pass as Ships of the Build of* Great Britain; *the Owner, or where there are more Owners, one or more of the Owners, within Twelve Months after the first of* May *next, making Oath that at the Time of* ratifying the Treaty of Union in the Parliament of Scotland, *the same did,* in whole or in part, *belong to him or them; or to some other Subject or Subjects of* Scotland, *to be particularly named, with the Place of their respective Abodes; and that the same doth then,* at the Time of the said Deposition, *wholly belong to him or them, and that no Foreigner directly or indirectly hath any Share, Part or Interest therein: Which Oath shall be made before the chief Officer or Officers of the Customs, in the Port next to the Abode of the said Owner or Owners: And the said Officer or Officers shall be impowered to administrate the said Oath: And the Oath being so administred, shall be attested by the Officer or Officers, who administred the same. And being registred by the said Officer or Officers, shall be delivered to the Master of the Ship for Security of her Navigation; and a Duplicate thereof shall be transmitted by the said Officer or Officers, to the chief Officer or Officers of the Customs in the Port of* Edinburgh, *to be there enter'd in a Register, and from thence to be sent to the Port of* London, *to be there entered in the general Register of all trading Ships, belonging to* Great Britain.

6. *That all Parts of the United Kingdom, for ever, from and after the* Union, *shall have the same Allowances, Encouragements and* Drawbacks, *and be under the same Prohibitions, Restrictions, and Regulations of Trade, and liable to the same Customs and Duties on Import and Export. And that the Allowances, Encouragements,* and Drawbacks, *Prohibitions, Restrictions, and Regulations of Trade, and the Customs and Duties on Import and Export, settled in* England, *when the* Union *commences, shall from and after the* Union *take Place throughout the whole United Kingdom: Excepting and reserving the Duties upon Export and Import, of such particular Commodities, from which any Persons, the Subjects of either Kingdom, are specially liberated and exempted by their private Rights, which after the Union are to remain safe and entire to them in all respects, as before the same. And that from and after the* Union, *no* Scots *Cattle carried into*

into England, shall be liable to any other Duties, either on the Publick or Private Accounts, than those Duties, to which the Cattle of England are, or shall be liable within the said Kingdom. And seeing by the Laws of England, there are Rewards granted upon the Exportation of certain kinds of Grain, wherein Oats grinded or ungrinded are not expressed, that from and after the Union, when Oats shall be sold at Fifteen Shillings Sterling per Quarter, or under, there shall be paid Two Shillings and six Pence Sterling for every Quarter of the Oatmeal exported, in the Terms of the Law, whereby, and so long as Rewards are granted for the Exportation of other Grains; and that the Beer of Scotland have the same Rewards as Barley: And in Respect the Importation of Victual into Scotland, from any Place beyond Sea, would prove a Discouragement to Tillage, therefore that the Prohibition, as now in force by the Law of Scotland, against the Importation of Victual from Ireland, or any other Place beyond Sea into Scotland, do, after the Union, remain in the same Force as now it is, until more proper and effectual Ways be provided by the Parliament of Great Britain, for discouraging the Importation of the said Victual from beyond Sea.

That all Parts of the United Kingdom be for ever, from and after the Union, liable to the same Excises upon all Exciseable Liquors, excepting only that the thirty four Gallons, English Barrel of Beer or Ale, amounting to twelve Gallons Scots present Measure, sold in Scotland by the Brewer at nine Shillings and six Pence Sterling, excluding all Duties, and retailed including Duties, and the Retailer's Profit at two Pence the Scots Pint, or eighth Part of the Scots Gallon, be not, after the Union, liable, on Account of the present Excise upon Exciseable Liquors in England, to any higher Imposition than two Shillings Sterling upon the aforesaid thirty four Gallons, English Barrel being twelve Gallons, the present Scots Measure. And that the Excise settled in England on all other Liquors, when the Union commences, take Place throughout the whole United Kingdom.

8. That from and after the Union, all Foreign Salt, which shall be imported into Scotland, shall be charged at the Importation there, with the same Duties as the like Salt is now charged with, being imported into England; and to be levied and secured in the same manner. But in regard the Duties of great Quantities of Foreign Salt imported may be very heavy upon the Merchants, Importers; That therefore all Foreign Salt imported into Scotland, shall be cellar'd and lock'd up under the Custody of the Merchant Importer and the Officers employed for levying the Duties upon Salt; and that the Merchant may have what Quantities thereof his Occasions may require, not under a Weigh, or forty Bushels at a time, giving Security for the Duty of what Quantities he receives, payable in six Months. But Scotland shall, for the Space of seven Years, from the said Union, be exempted from paying in Scotland for Salt made there, the Duty or Excise now payable for Salt made in England; but from the Expiration of the said seven Years, shall be subject and liable to the same Duties for Salt made in England, to be levied and secured in the same manner, and with proportional Drawbacks and Allowances as in England, with this Exception, that Scotland shall, after the said seven Years, remain exempted from the Duty of two Shillings and
four

four Pence the Bushel on Home Salt, imposed by an Act made in England in the ninth *and tenth Years of King* William *the Third of* England; *and if the Parliament of Great Britain shall, at or before the expiring of the said seven Years, substitute any other Fund in place of the said Two Shillings and Four Pence of Excise upon the Bushel of Home Salt,* Scotland *shall, after the said seven Years, bear a Proportion of the said Fund, and have an Equivalent in the Terms of this* Treaty. *And that during the said seven Years, there shall be paid in* England *for all Salt made in* Scotland, *and imported from thence into* England, *the same Duties upon the Importation as shall be paid for Salt made in* England, *to be levied and secured in the same manner, as the Duties on Foreign Salt are to be levied and secured in* England. *And that after the said seven Years, how long the said Duty of Two Shillings and Four Pence a Bushel upon Salt is continued in* England, *the said Two Shillings and Four Pence a Bushel shall be payable for Salt made in* Scotland, *and imported into* England, *to be levied and secured in the same manner; and that during the Continuance of the Duty of Two Shillings and Four Pence a Bushel upon Salt made in* England, *no Salt whatsoever be brought from* Scotland *into* England *by Land in any manner, under the Penalty of Forfeiting the Salt and the Cattle and Carriages made Use of in bringing the same, and paying Twenty Shillings for every Bushel of such Salt, and proportionably for a greater or lesser Quantity, for which the Carrier, as well as the Owner, shall be liable, jointly and severally, and the Persons bringing or carrying the same to be imprisoned by any one Justice of the Peace, by the space of six Months without Bail, and until the Penalty be paid. And for establishing an equality in Trade, that all Flesh exported from* Scotland *to* England, *and put on board in* Scotland, *to be exported to Ports beyond the Sea, and Provisions for Ships in* Scotland, *and for Foreign Voyages, may be salted with Scots Salt, paying the same Duty for what Salt is so employed, as the like Quantity of such Salt pays in* England; *and under the same Penalties, Forfeitures and Provisions, for preventing of Frauds, as are mentioned in the Laws of* England. *And that from and after the* Union, *the Laws and Acts of Parliament in* Scotland *for Pineing, Curing and Packing of Herrings, white Fish and Salmon, for Exportation, with Foreign Salt only, without any Mixture of* British *or* Irish *Salt; and for preventing of Frauds of Curing and Packing of Fish, be continued in force in* Scotland, *subject to such Alterations as shall be made by the Parliament of Great Britain; and that all Fish exported from* Scotland *to parts beyond Seas, which shall be cured with Foreign Salt only, and without Mixture of* British *or* Irish *Salt, shall have the same Eases, Premiums and Drawbacks, as are or shall be allowed to such Persons as export the like Fish from* England; *and that for Encouragement of the Hering-Fishing, there shall be allowed and paid to the Subjects, Inhabitants of Great Britain, during the present Allowances for other Fishes, Ten Shillings, and Five Pence Sterling for every Barrel of white Herrings which shall be exported from* Scotland; *and that they shall be allowed Five Shillings Sterling for every Barrel of Beef or Pork, salted with Foreign Salt, without Mixture of* British *or* Irish *Salt, and exported for Sale from* Scotland *to*

Parts

Parts beyond Sea, alterable by the Parliament of Great Britain. And if any Matters of Frauds, relating to the said Duties on Salt, shall hereafter appear, which are not sufficiently provided against by this Article, the same shall be subject to such further Provisions as shall be thought fit by the Parliament of Great Britain.

9. That whenever the Sum of one Million, nine Hundred, ninety seven Thousand, seven Hundred and sixty three Pounds, eight Shillings, four Pence half Penny, shall be enacted by the Parliament of Great Britain, to be raised in that Part of the United Kingdom, now called England, on Land and other Things usually charged in Acts of Parliament there, for granting an Aid to the Crown, by a Land-Tax; that Part of the United Kingdom, now called Scotland, shall be charged by the same Act, with a further Sum of Forty-eight Thousand Pounds, free of all Charges, as the Quota of Scotland to such Tax, and so proportionably for any greater or lesser Sum raised in England, by any Tax on Land, and other Things usually charged together with the Land; and that such Quota for Scotland, in the Cases aforesaid, be raised and collected in the same manner as the Cess now is in Scotland, but subject to such Regulations in the manner of collecting, as shall be made by the Parliament of Great Britain.

10. That during the Continuance of the respective Duties on Stamp-Paper, Vellum and Parchment, by the several Acts now in force in England, Scotland shall not be charged with the same respective Duties.

11. That during the respective Duties payable in England on Windows and Lights, which determines on the First Day of August, One Thousand, Seven Hundred and Ten, Scotland shall not be charged with the same Duties.

12. That during the Continuance of the Duties payable in England on Coals, Culm and Cynders, which determines the Thirtieth Day of September, One Thousand, Seven Hundred and Ten, Scotland shall not be charged therewith for Coals, Culm and Cynders consumed there; but shall be charged with the same Duties, as in England, for all Coals, Culm and Cynders not consumed in Scotland.

13. That during the Continuance of the Duty payable in England on Malt, which determines the Twenty-Fourth Day of June, One Thousand, Seven Hundred and Seven, Scotland shall not be charged with that Duty.

14. That the Kingdom of Scotland be not charged with any other Duties laid on by the Parliament of England, before the Union, except those consented to in this Treaty; in regard it is agreed, that all the necessary Provision shall be made by the Parliament of Scotland, for the publick Charge and Service of that Kingdom, for the Year One Thousand, Seven Hundred and Seven, providing nevertheless, that if the Parliament of England shall think fit to lay any further Impositions, by way of Custom, or such Excises, with which, by virtue of this Treaty, Scotland is to be charged equally with England; in such Case, Scotland shall be liable to the same Customs and Excises, and have an Equivalent to be settled by the Parliament of Great Britain, with this further Provision, that any Malt to be made and consumed in that Part of the United Kingdom, now called Scotland, shall not be charged with any Imposition on Malt during

during this War. And seeing it cannot be supposed that the Parliament of Great Britain will ever lay any sort of Burdens upon the United Kingdom, but what they shall find of Necessity, at that time, for the Preservation and Good of the whole; and with due Regard to the Circumstances and Abilities of every Part of the United Kingdom; therefore, it is agreed, that there be no further Exemption insisted on for any Part of the United Kingdom, but that the Consideration of any Exemptions beyond what is already agreed on in this Treaty, shall be left to the Determination of the Parliament of Great Britain.

15. That by the Terms of this Treaty, the Subjects of Scotland, for preserving an Equality of Trade throughout the United Kingdom, will be liable to several Customs and Excises now payable in England, which will be applicable towards Payment of the Debts of England, contracted before the Union; it is agreed that Scotland shall have an Equivalent for what the Subjects thereof shall be so charged, towards Payment of the said Debts of England, in all particulars whatsoever, in manner following, viz. that before the Union of the said Kingdoms, the Sum of Three Hundred Ninety-Eight Thousand Eighty-Five Pounds Ten Shillings be granted to her Majesty by the Parliament of England, for the Uses after mentioned, being the Equivalent to be answered to Scotland, for such Parts of the said Customs, and Excises upon all Exciseable Liquors, with which that Kingdom is to be charged upon the Union, as will be applicable to the Payment of the said Debts of England, according to the Proportions, which the present Customs in Scotland, being Thirty Thousand Pounds per Annum, do bear to Customs in England, computed at One Million, Three Hundred Forty-One Thousand, Five Hundred and Fifty-Nine Pounds per Annum: And which the present Excises on Exciseable Liquors in Scotland, being Thirty-Three Thousand and Five Hundred Pounds per Ann. do bear to the Excises on Exciseable Liquors in England, computed at Nine Hundred, Forty-Seven Thousand, Six Hundred and Two Pounds per Annum; which Sum of Three Hundred, Ninety-Eight Thousand and Eighty-Five Pounds Ten Shillings, shall be due and payable from the Time of the Union: And in regard, that after the Union, Scotland becoming liable to the same Customs and Duties payable on Import and Export, and to the same Excises on all Exciseable Liquors, as in England, as well upon that Account, as upon the Account of the Increase of Trade and People (which will be the happy Consequence of the Union) the said Revenues will much improve beyond the before mentioned Annual Values thereof, of which no present Estimate can be made; yet nevertheless, for the Reasons aforesaid, there ought to be a proportional Equivalent answered to Scotland; it is agreed, that after the Union, there shall be an Account kept of the said Duties arising in Scotland, to the end it may appear what ought to be answered to Scotland, as an Equivalent for such Proportion of the said Increase, as shall be applicable to the Payment of the Debts of England. And for the further and more effectual answering the several Ends hereafter mentioned, it is agreed, that from and after the Union, the whole Increase of the Revenues of Customs, and Duties on Import and Export, and Excises upon Exciseable Liquors in Scotland, over and above the Annual Product

of the said respective Duties, as above stated, shall go, and be apply'd, for the Term of Seven Years, to the Uses hereafter mentioned; and that upon the said Account there shall be answered to Scotland annually, from the End of Seven Years after the Union, an Equivalent in Proportion to such Part of the said Increase, as shall be applicable to the Debts of England: And generally, that an Equivalent shall be answered to Scotland for such Parts of the English Debts, as Scotland may hereafter become liable to pay by Reason of the Union, other than such for which Appropriations have been made by Parliament in England, of the Customs or other Duties on Export and Import, Excises on all Exciseable Liquors, in Respect of which Debts, Equivalents are herein before provided. And as for the Uses to which the said Sum of Three Hundred Eight Thousand and Eighty-Five Pounds, Ten Shillings, to be granted as aforesaid, and all other Monies which are to be answered or allowed to Scotland, as said is, are to be apply'd, it is agreed, that in the first Place out of the aforesaid Sum, what Consideration shall be found necessary to be had for any Losses which private Persons may sustain, by reducing the Coin of Scotland to the Standard and Value of the Coin of England, may be made good. In the next Place, that the Capital Stock, or Fund of the African and Indian Company of Scotland, advanced together with the Interest for the said Capital Stock, after the Rate of Five per Cent. per Ann. from the respective times of the Payment thereof, shall be paid; upon Payment of which Capital Stock and Interest, it is agreed the said Company be dissolved and cease; and also, that from the time of passing the Act of Parliament in England, for raising the said Sum of Three Hundred, Ninety-Eight Thousand and Eighty-Five Pounds, Ten Shillings, the said Company shall neither trade, nor grant Licence to trade; providing, that if the said Stock and Interest shall not be paid in Twelve Months after the Commencement of the Union, that then the said Company may from thence-forward trade, or give Licence to trade, until the said whole Capital-Stock and Interest shall be paid. And as to the Overplus of the said Sum of Three Hundred, Ninety-Eight Thousand and Eighty-Five Pounds, Ten Shillings, after Payment of what Consideration shall be had for Losses, in repairing the Coin, and paying the said Capital Stock and Interest; and also the whole Increase of the said Revenues of Customs, Duties and Excises, above the present Value, which shall arise in Scotland, during the said Term of Seven Years, together with the Equivalent which shall become due, upon the Improvement thereof in Scotland, after the said Term of Seven Years: And also, as to all other Sums, which, according to the Agreements aforesaid, may become payable to Scotland, by way of Equivalent, for what that Kingdom shall hereafter become liable, towards the Payment of the Debts of England; it is agreed, that the same may be applied in the manner following, viz. That all the Publick Debts of the Kingdom of Scotland, as shall be adjusted by this present Parliament, shall be paid: And that Two Thousand Pounds per Annum for the space of Seven Years shall be applied towards encouraging and promoting the Manufacture of Coarse-Wool, within those Shires which produce the Wool; and that the first Two Thousand Pounds Sterling be paid at Michaelmas next, and so Yearly at Michaelmas, during the space aforesaid. And afterwards the same shall be wholly applied towards the encouraging and promoting the Fisheries, and such other Manufactories and Improvements in Scotland, as may most conduce to the General Good of the United Kingdom: And it is agreed, that her Majesty be empowered to appoint Commissioners, who shall be accountable to the Parliament of Great Britain, for disposing the said Sum of Three Hundred, Ninety-Eight Thousand and Eighty-Five Pounds, Ten Shillings, and all other Monies which shall arise to Scotland, upon the Agreements aforesaid, to the Purposes before mentioned; Which Commissioners shall be empowered to Call for, Receive and Dispose of the said Monies in manner aforesaid; and to inspect the Books of the several Collectors of the said Revenues, and of all other Duties, from whence an Equivalent may arise, and that the Collectors and Managers of the said Revenues and Duties, be obliged to give to the said Commissioners, subscrib'd authentick Abbreviates of the Produce of such Revenues and Duties arising in their respective Districts; and that the said Commissioners shall have their Office within the Limits of Scotland, and shall in such Office keep Books, containing Accounts of the Amount of the Equivalents, and how the same shall have been disposed of from time to time; which may be inspected by any of the Subjects, who shall desire the same.

16. That from and after the Union, the Coin shall be of the same Standard and value throughout the United Kingdom, as now in England, and a Mint shall be continued in Scotland, under the same Rules as the Mint in England, and the present Officers of the Mint continued, subject to such Regulations and Alterations, as her Majesty, her Heirs, or Successors, or the Parliament of Great Britain shall think fit.

17. That from and after the Union, the same Weights and Measures shall be used throughout the united Kingdom, as are now established in England; and Standards of Weights and Measures shall be kept by those Burghs in Scotland, to whom the keeping the Standards of Weights and Measures now in use there, does of special Right belong; all which Standards shall be sent down to such respective Burghs from the Standards kept in the Exchequer at Westminster, subject nevertheless to such Regulations as the Parliament of Great Britain shall think fit.

18. That the Laws concerning regulation of Trade, Customs, and such Excises, to which Scotland is, by by Virtue of this Treaty, to be liable, be the same in Scotland, from and after the Union, as in England; and that all other Laws in use, within the Kingdom of Scotland, do after the Union, and notwithstanding thereof, remain in the same force as before (except such as are contrary to and inconsistent with this Treaty) but alterable by the Parliament of Great Britain, with this difference betwixt the Laws concerning publick Right, Policy and Civil Government, and those which concern private Right; that the Laws which concern publick Right, Policy and Civil Government, may be made the same throughout the whole United Kingdom; but that no Alteration be made in Laws which concern private Right, except for evident Utility of the Subjects within Scotland.

19. That the Court of Sessions, or College of Justice, do after the Union, and notwithstanding thereof, remain in all time coming within Scotland,

as it is now constituted by the Laws of that Kingdom, and with the same Authority and Privileges as before the Union, subject neverthelefs to such Regulations for the better Administration of Justice, as shall be made by the Parliament of Great Britain; and that hereafter none shall be named by her Majesty and her Royal Successors, to be ordinary Lords of Session, but such who have served in the College of Justice as Advocates, or principal Clerks of Session for the space of five Years, or as Writers to the Signet, for the space of ten Years; with this Provision, that no Writer to the Signet be capable to be admitted a Lord of the Session, unless he undergo a private and publick Trial on the Civil Law before the Faculty of Advocates, and be found by them qualified for the said Office, two Years before he be named to be a Lord of the Session: Yet so, as the Qualification made, or to be made, for capacitating Persons to be named ordinary Lords of Session, may be altered by the Parliament of Great Britain. And that the Court of Justiciary do also, after the Union, and notwithstanding thereof, remain in all time coming within Scotland, as it is now constituted by the Laws of that Kingdom, and with the same Authority and Privileges as before the Union, subject neverthelefs to such Regulations as shall be made by the Parliament of Great Britain, and without Prejudice of other Rights of Justiciary; and that all Admiralty Jurisdictions be under the Lord High Admiral or Commissioner for the Admiralty of Great Britain, for the time being; and that the Court of Admiralty now established in Scotland, be continued; and that all Reviews, Reductions, or Suspensions of the Sentences in Maritime Cases, competent to the Jurisdiction of that Court, remain in the same manner after the Union, as now in Scotland, until the Parliament of Great Britain shall make such Regulations and Alterations, as shall be judg'd expedient for the whole United Kingdom, so as there be always continued in Scotland, a Court of Admiralty such as in England, for Determination of all Maritime Cases relating to private Rights in Scotland, competent to the Jurisdiction of the Admiralty Court; subject neverthelefs to such Regulations and Alterations, as shall be thought proper to be made by the Parliament of Great Britain; and that the heritable Rights of Admirals and Vice-Admirals in Scotland, be reserved to the respective Proprietors as Rights of Property; subject neverthelefs, as to the manner of exercising such heritable Rights, to such Regulations and Alterations, as shall be thought proper to be made by the Parliament of Great Britain; and that all other Courts now in Being, within the Kingdom of Scotland, do remain, but subject to Alterations by the Parliament of Great Britain; and that all inferior Courts within the said Limits do remain subordinate, as they are now to the Supream Courts of Justice within the same in all time coming; and that no Causes in Scotland be cognoscible by the Courts of Chancery, Queen's Bench, Common Pleas, or any Court in Westminster-Hall; and that the said Courts, or any other of the like Nature, after the Union, shall have no Power to cognosce, review or alter the Acts or Sentences of the Judicatures within Scotland, or stop the Execution of the same. And that there be a Court of Exchequer in Scotland, after the Union, for deciding Questions

con-

concerning the *Revenues of Customs and Excises* there, having the same Power and Authority in such Cases, as the *Court of* Exchequer *has in* England; and that the said *Court of* Exchequer *in* Scotland *have Power of passing Signatures, Gifts, Tutories, and in other Things as the Court of* Exchequer *at present in* Scotland *hath*; and that the *Court of* Exchequer *that now is in* Scotland, *do remain, until a new Court of* Exchequer *be settled by the Parliament of* Great Britain, *in* Scotland, *after the* Union; and that after the Union, the Queen's Majesty and her Royal Successors may continue a Privy Council in Scotland, for preserving the Publick Peace and Order, until the Parliament of Great Britain shall think fit to alter it, or establish any other effectual Method for that End.

20. That all heritable Offices, Superiorities, heritable Jurisdictions, Offices for Life, Jurisdictions for Life, be reserved to the Owners thereof, as Rights of Property, in the same manner as they are now enjoyed by the Laws of Scotland, notwithstanding this Treaty.

21. That the Rights and Privileges of the Royal Burroughs in Scotland as they now are, do remain intire after the Union, and notwithstanding thereof.

22. That by Virtue of this Treaty of the Peers of Scotland, at the Time of the Union, Sixteen shall be the Number to sit and vote in the House of Lords, and Forty-five the Number of the Representatives of Scotland in the House of Commons of the Parliament of Great Britain; and that when her Majesty, her Heirs or Successors, shall declare her or their Pleasure, for holding the first, or any subsequent Parliament of Great Britain, until the Parliament of Great Britain shall make further Provision therein, a Writ do issue under the Great Seal of the United Kingdom, directed to the Privy Council of Scotland, commanding them to cause sixteen Peers, who are to sit in the House of Lords, to be summoned to Parliament, and forty-five Members to be elected to sit in the House of Commons of the Parliament of Great Britain, according to the Agreement in this Treaty, in such manner as by an Act of this present Session of the Parliament of Scotland is or shall be settled; which Act is hereby declared to be as valid as if it were a Part of, and engrossed in this Treaty: And that the Names of the Persons so summoned and elected shall be returned by the Privy Council of Scotland into the Court from whence the said Writ did issue. And that if her Majesty, on or before the first Day of May next, on which Day the Union is to take Place, shall declare under the Great Seal of England, that it is expedient that the Lords of Parliament of England, and Commons of the present Parliament of England, should be the Members of the respective Houses of the first Parliament of Great Britain, for and on the Part of England, then the said Lords of Parliament of England, and Commons of the present Parliament of England, shall be the Members of the respective Houses of the first Parliament of Great Britain, for and on the Part of England. And her Majesty may by her royal Proclamation, under the Great Seal of Great Britain, appoint the said first Parliament of Great Britain to meet at such Time and Place as her Majesty shall think fit, which Time shall not be less than fifty Days after the Date of such Proclamation, and the Time and Place

of meeting of such Parliament being so appointed, a Writ shall be immediately issued under the Great Seal of Great Britain, directed to the Privy Council of Scotland, for the summoning the sixteen Peers, and for electing forty-five Members by whom Scotland is to be represented in the Parliament of Great Britain: And the Lords of Parliament of England, and the sixteen Peers of Scotland, such sixteen Peers being summoned and returned in the Manner agreed in this Treaty; and the Members of the House of Commons of the said Parliament of England, and the forty-five Members for Scotland, such forty-five Members being elected and returned in the Manner agreed in this Treaty, shall assemble and meet respectively in their respective Houses of the Parliament of Great Britain, at such Time and Place as shall be so appointed by her Majesty; and shall be the two Houses of the first Parliament of Great Britain, and that Parliament may continue for such Time only as the present Parliament of England might have continued, if the Union of the two Kingdoms had not been made, unless sooner dissolved by her Majesty; and that every one of the Lords of Parliament of Great Britain, and every Member of the House of Commons of the Parliament of Great Britain in the first, and all succeeding Parliaments of Great Britain, until the Parliament of Great Britain shall otherwise direct, shall take the respective Oaths appointed to be taken, instead of the Oaths of Allegiance and Supremacy, by an Act of Parliament made in England in the first Year of the Reign of the late King William and Queen Mary, intituled, An Act for the Abrogating of the Oaths of Supremacy and Allegiance, and appointing other Oaths; and make, subscribe, and audibly repeat the Declaration mentioned in an Act of Parliament made in England in the thirtieth Year of the Reign of King Charles the Second, intituled, An Act for the more effectual preserving the King's Person and Government, by disabling Papists from sitting in either House of Parliament, and shall take and subscribe the Oath mentioned in an Act of Parliament made in England in the first Year of her Majesty's Reign, intituled, An Act to declare the Alteration, in the Oath appointed to be taken by the Act intituled, An Act for the further Security of his Majesty's Person, and the Succession of the Crown in the Protestant Line; and for extinguishing the Hopes of the pretended Prince of Wales and all other Pretenders, and their open and secret Abettors; and for the declaring the Association to be determined at such Time and in such Manner as the Members of both Houses of Parliament of England are by the said respective Acts, directed to take, make, and subscribe the same, upon the Penalties and Disabilities in the said respective Acts contained. And it is declared and agreed, that these Words, This Realm, the Crown of this Realm, and the Queen of this Realm, mentioned in the Oaths and Declarations contained in the aforesaid Acts, which were intended to signify the Crown and Realm of England, shall be understood of the Crown and Realm of Great Britain; and that in that Sense, the said Oaths and Declaration be taken and subscribed by the Members of both Houses of the Parliament of Great Britain.

§3. That

23. That the aforesaid sixteen Peers of Scotland, mentioned in the last preceding Article, who are to sit in the House of Lords of the Parliament of Great Britain, shall have all the Privileges of Parliament which the Peers of England now have, and which they, or any Peers of Great Britain, shall have after the Union; and particularly the Right of sitting upon the Trials of Peers: And in Case of the Trial of any Peer, in Time of Adjournment or Prorogation of Parliament, the said sixteen Peers shall be summoned in the same Manner, and have the same Powers and Privileges at such Trials, as any other Peers of Great Britain: And that, in Case any Trials of Peers shall hereafter happen, when there is no Parliament in Being, the sixteen Peers of Scotland, who sat in the last Parliament, shall be summoned in the same Manner, and have the same Powers and Privileges at such Trials, as any other Peers of Great Britain: And that all Peers of Scotland, and their Successors to their Honours and Dignities, shall from and after the Union, be Peers of Great Britain, and have Rank and Precedency next and immediately after the Peers of the like Orders and Degrees in England at the Time of the Union, and before all Peers of Great Britain, of the like Orders and Degrees, who may be created after the Union; and shall be tried as Peers of Great Britain; and shall enjoy all Privileges of Peers, as fully as the Peers of England do now, or as they or any other Peers of Great Britain may hereafter enjoy the same, except the Right and Privilege of sitting in the House of Lords, and the Privileges depending thereon, and particularly the Right of sitting upon the Trials of Peers.

24. That from and after the Union, there be one Great Seal for the United Kingdom of Great Britain, which shall be different from the Great Seal now used in either Kingdom; and that the Quartering the Arms, and the Rank and Precedency of the Lyon King at Arms of the Kingdom of Scotland, as may best suit the Union, be left to her Majesty: And that in the mean Time, the Great Seal of England be used as the Great Seal of the United Kingdom; and that the Great Seal of the United Kingdom be used for sealing Writs to elect and summon the Parliament of Great Britain, and for sealing all Treaties with Foreign Princes and States, and all publick Acts, Instruments, and Orders of State, which concern the whole United Kingdom, and in all other Matters relating to England, as the Great Seal of England is now used; and that a Seal in Scotland, after the Union, be always kept, and made use of in all things relating to private Rights or Grants, which have usually passed the Great Seal of Scotland, and which only concern Officers, Grants, Commissioners, and private Rights within that Kingdom: And that until such Seal shall be appointed by her Majesty, the present Great Seal of Scotland shall be used for such Purposes: And that the Privy Seal, Signet Casset, Signet of the Justiciary Court, Quarter Seal, and Seals of Courts, now used in Scotland, be continued: But that the said Seals be altered and adapted to the State of the Union, as her Majesty shall think fit; and the said Seals and all of them, and the Keepers of them, shall be subject to such Regulations as the Parliament of Great Britain shall hereafter make; And that the Crown, Scepter, and Sword of State, the Records

tords of Parliament, and all other Records, Rolls and Registers whatsoever, both Publick and Private, General and Particular, and Warrants thereof, continue to be kept as they are within that Part of the United Kingdom now called Scotland; and that they shall so remain in all Time coming, notwithstanding of the Union.

25. *That all Laws and Statutes in either Kingdom, so far as they are contrary to, or inconsistent with the Terms of these Articles, or any of them, shall from and after the Union cease and become void, and shall be so declared to be, by the respective Parliaments of the said Kingdoms.*

Notwithstanding the above written Articles, it is by 6 *Annæ, cap.* 14. enacted, That a Peer committing High Treason, or Felony in *Scotland*, may be tried by Commission under the Great Seal, constituting Justices, *&c.* to make Enquiry thereof, *&c.* in *Scotland*; and Commissions of *Oyer* and *Terminer* in *Scotland*, to determine such Treasons, *&c.* are grantable by the King. By another Statute, *viz.* 7 *Annæ, cap.* 21. Persons having Lands in *Scotland*, and being guilty of High Treason, by corresponding with, assisting, or remitting Money, *&c.* to the Person called the Pretender, on Conviction, are liable to the Pains of Treason; and in case their Vassals continue in dutiful Allegiance, they shall hold the said Lands of her Majesty in Fee and Heritage for ever, in case those Lands were so held of the Crown by the Offender; and Tenants that continue peaceable and occupy the Lands forfeited, may hold the same two Years rent-free. See 1 *Geo.* 1. *cap.* 20.

Unity of Possession, denotes a joint Possession of two Rights, by several Titles; as where a Person takes a Lease of Land, *&c.* from one upon a certain Rent, and afterwards buys the Fee-simple; this is a *Unity of Possession*, whereby the Lease is extinguished, by Reason that the Person who before had the Occupation only for his Rent, is become Lord of the same, and is to pay his Rent to none but himself. *Cowel.*

University, is taken for a Place where all Kinds of Literature are usually taught. The Universities in this Kingdom are taken for those two Bodies that are the Nurseries of Learning and liberal Sciences, *viz.* Oxford and *Cambridge*; which two Places are endowed with great Privileges.

Unlage, is taken for an unjust Law; and in that Sense it is used in *Leg. Hen.* 1. *cap.* 34.

Unlawful Assembly, denotes the Meeting of three or more Persons together, by Force, in order to commit some *unlawful* Act, and continuing together, tho' nor endeavouring the Execution thereof; as to assault or beat a Person, to enter his House and Land, *&c.* See **Assembly**.

Unques prist, That is to say, *always ready* to perform that which the Demandant or Plaintiff requires; and it is used in pleading to an Action, which if the Plaintiff cannot prove to the contrary, according to *Kitch.* he shall recover no Damages.

Vociferatio, signifies an Outcry, or Hue and Cry.

Voidance, denotes a want of an Incumbent upon an Ecclesiastical Benefice; and this is twofold, either *in Law*, as where a Man has more Benefices incompatible; or *in Deed*, as when the Incumbent is dead, or actually deprived.

Void and **Voidable**, are Terms frequently used in our Law. A thing may be said to be *void*, that is done contrary to Law at the time of the doing of it, and no Person shall be bound thereby: But where a thing is only *voidable*, and not *void*, altho' it be what the Person that did it ought not to have done; yet, when it is done, the Doer cannot avoid the same; notwithstanding by some Act in Law it may be made *void* by his Heir, &c.

Voire dire is a Term used, when it is prayed upon a Trial at Law, that the Witness may on Oath speak the *Truth*, whether he shall get or lose by the Matter in Controversy; and according to *Blount*, in case it appear that he is unconcerned or disinterested, his Testimony is allowed, otherwise not. In *Termes de la Ley*, a Witness is said to be examined upon a *Voire dire*, where he is sworn and examined, Whether he be not a Party interested in the Cause, as well as the Party for whom he is an Evidence, *viz.* the Plaintiff or Defendant?

Volumus, Is the first Word used in a Clause of the King's Writs of Protection and Letters Patent.

Voluntas, is where a Tenant on Lease holds Lands, &c. at the Will of the Lessor, or Lord; and that is in two Manners; that is to say, where a Person makes a Lease to another of Lands, &c. to hold at the Will of the Lessor, in which Case he may put him out at his Pleasure: But if the Tenant sow the Ground, and the Landlord puts him out, then the Tenant shall have his Corn with free Egress and Regress, till it be ripe to cut, and afterwards carry it out of the Ground. The other *Tenant at Will of the Lord*, is by Copy of Court-Roll, according to the Custom of the Manor; which Tenant may surrender the Land into the hands of the Lord, in pursuance of that Custom, to the Use of another for Life, in Fee, or in Tail; and in that Case he shall take the Land of the Lord, or his Steward, by Copy, and shall make Fine to the Lord. *Cowel.*

Vouch, in a Legal Sense is taken to call one to warrant Lands, &c.

Voucher, is a Term in Law, and is when a Tennant calls another into Court, who is bound to him to Warranty; and is either to defend the Right against the Demandant, or yield him other Lands to the Value, &c. And it extends to Lands or Tenements of Freehold or Inheritance, but not to any thing Personal or Mixt. He that *voucheth* is called the *Voucher*, and the Person that is *vouched*, is called the *Vouchee*. The Process by which the *Vouchee*, is called, is a *Summoneas ad Warrantizandum*, on which Writ, in case the Sheriff return that the Party has nothing whereby he may be summoned, there issues another Writ called *Sequatur sub suo periculo*, &c. A Recovery with *single Voucher* is, when there is but *one Voucher*; and with *Double Voucher*, when the *Vouchee voucheth over*; and so a *treble Voucher*. There is likewise a *Foreign Voucher*, which is where the Tenant being impleaded within a particular Jurisdiction, as in *London*, or the like, *voucheth* one to warranty, and prays that he may be summoned in some other County, out of the Jurisdiction of that Court, and this may more aptly be called a *Voucher* of a Foreigner.

Vox, is a Word used by *Bracton*, to signify an infamous Person, *viz.* such

US

such a one as is not admitted to be a Witness.

Upland, is taken for high Ground, or, according to some Writers, *Terra firma*, in Opposition to Marshy or Low Ground.

Usage. See **Prescription**.

Use, is taken for the Profit or Benefit of Lands or Tenements; or for a Trust and Confidence reposed in a Person for the Holding of Lands, &c. That he, to whose use the Trust is made, may take the Profits of the same. According to *Nelson's Abridgment*, an Use is only a Trust or Confidence which one puts in another; and on that Account it is not a Thing issuing out of the Land, but collateral to it, and annexed to the Privity of the Estate between them; that is to say, That he to whom the Use is made shall have the Profits; and that the Tenant of the Land shall make an Estate as he shall direct: But the *Cestui que use* has neither *jus in Re* or *ad Rem*; because his only Remedy is in *Chancery* to compel the *Cestui que Trust* to execute the Use. By *Cowel* it is said that every Deed consists of two principal Parts, *viz. The Premisses*, and *the Consequents*: The *Premisses* is the former Part of the Deed, and that which precedes the *Habendum* or Limitation of the Estate; that is to say, the Persons contracting and the Things contracted: The Consequent is what follows the *Premisses*, *viz.* the *Habendum*, wherein are two Limitations; the one of the Estate or Property, which the Party passive shall receive by the Deed; the other of *the Use*, which is to express in the *Habendum* to or for what Use or Benefit, the Party shall have the same Estate.

User de Action, denotes the pursuing or bringing of an Action in the proper Place or County.

Usher, which denotes a Door-keeper of a Court, is an Officer in the *Exchequer*, of which kind there are four who attend the Barons and Chief Officers of that Court at *Westminster*, as also Juries, Sheriffs, and all other Accountants, at the Pleasure of the Court. There are also *Ushers* in the King's House, such as those of the Privy Chamber, &c.

Usucaption, according to *Cowel*, signifies the enjoying of a Thing by Continuance of Time, or receiving the Profits, long Possession or Prescription.

Usufructuary, is taken for the Person that has or reaps the Profit of any thing.

Usurpation, is most commonly used, where any one presents a Rector or Vicar to a Church without a good Title. There is likewise an *Usurpation of Franchises and Liberties*, which is, where a Person unjustly makes use of any Royal Franchises, &c. And by some Writers it is said to be an *Usurpation* upon the *King*, who in that Case shall have a Writ of *Quo Warranto* against the *Usurpers*.

Usury, is defined to be the Gain of any thing by Contract above the Principal, of that which was lent, and exacted in Consideration only of the Loan thereof, whether it be of Money or any other Thing. By 12 *Ann. cap.* 16. which is called the Statute against excessive Usury, no Person shall directly or indirectly take for Loan of any Money or other Thing, above the Value of 5 *l.* for the Forbearance of 100 *l.* for a Year, and so in Proportion for a greater or less Sum; and by that Act, it is declared, that all Bonds, Contracts and Assurances made for Payment of any principal Sum to be lent on

Usury,

UT

Usury, above the Rate of 5 *l. per Cent*. shall be void; and that whosoever shall take, accept or receive by way of corrupt Bargain, Loan, &c. a greater Interest than that just mentioned, shall forfeit treble the Value of the Money lent; and also, that Scriveners, Sollicitors, and Drivers of Bargains shall not take or receive above 5 *s*. for the procuring the Loan of 100 *l*. for one Year, on Pain of forfeiting 20 *l*. &c. On this Statute it has been adjudged, that a Contract for 6 *l. per Cent*. made before the Commencement of that Law, is not within the Meaning thereof, and on that Account it is still lawful to receive such Interest, in respect of any such prior Contract. According to *Hawkins*, in pleading an *usurious* Contract, by way of Bar to an Action, the whole Matter is to be set forth specially, because it lies within the Party's own Privity; yet on an Information on the Statute for making such Contract, it is sufficient to mention the Corrupt Bargain Generally, because Matters of this Kind are supposed to be privily transacted; and such Information may be brought by a Stranger.

Utas, is taken for the eighth Day following any Term or Feast; as the *Utas* of *Saint Michael*, &c. and any Day between the Feast and the *Octave*, is said to be within the *Utas*.

Utensil, according to *Cowel*, is taken for any thing necessary for one's Use and Occupation; as Houshold-stuff.

Utfangthef, is taken for an ancient Privilege or Royalty granted to a Lord of a Manor, by the King, whereby Power is given him to punish a *Thief* dwelling out of his Liberty, and committing *Theft*

UT

without the same, in case he be taken within his Fee.

Utlagh, signifies an *Outlaw*.

Utlagato Capiendo quando utlagatur in uno comitatu et postea fugit in alium, is a Writ, the Form and Nature of which you may see in *Reg. Orig.* 133.

Utlawry or **Utlary**. See *Outlawry*.

Utlepe, according to *Fleta*, denotes an Escape of a Felon out of Prison.

Utrum, is a Writ which lies where the Right of any Church is aliened and holden in Lay-Fee, or translated into the Possession of any other Church, and the Alienor dies; then his Successor shall have this Writ, whereof an Inquest shall be charged to try whether it be free Alms of the Church or Lay-Fee. *Termes de la Ley*.

Utter Barristers, according to *Cowel*, are those who for their long Study and great Industry bestowed upon the Knowledge of the Common Law, are called from their Contemplation to practise, and openly take upon them the Protection and Defence of Clients: And according to the same Author, the Time before any ought to be called to the Bar, by the ancient Orders, was Eight Years, but now reduced to Seven; and the Exercises done by the Person called, provided he was not called *Ex Gratia*, out of Favour, were 12 *Grand Moots*, performed in the Inns of *Chancery* in the Time of the Grand Readings, and 24 *Petty Moots* at the Inns of Chancery in the Term-times, before the Readers of the respective Inns of *Chancery*.

W.

W.

Wage, denotes the giving Security for the Performance of any Thing; as to *Wage Law*, *Wage Deliverance*, &c. *Wager of Law* is used where an Action of Debt is brought against a Person, upon a simple Contract between the Parties, without Deed or Record, and the Defendant in the Presence of his Compurgators swears in Court, that he owes the Plaintiff nothing in Manner and Form as he has declared; and it is said, that the Reason of *Waging of Law* is, because the Defendant may have paid to the Plaintiff his Debt in private, or before Witnesses who may be all dead, and therefore the Law allows him to *wage* his Law in his Discharge: And in that Case his Oath shall rather be accepted to discharge himself, than the Law will suffer him to be charged upon the bare Allegation of the Plaintiff. *Wager of Law*, is practised in Actions of Debt without Specialty, as also in Actions of Detinue, for Goods or Chattels lent to, or left with the Defendant, who may swear on a Book, together with certain Persons with him, that he does not detain the Goods in manner as the Plaintiff has declared. The Method used in *Waging of Law* is this, viz. The Defendant brings Six Compurgators with him into Court, and stands at the end of the Bar towards the Right Hand of the Chief Justice; on which Time the Secondary asks him, Whether he will *wage his Law*? Whereto if he answers that he will, the Judges admonish him to be well advised, telling him the Danger of taking a false Oath; and if he still persist, the Secondary says, and the Defendant, who *wages his Law*, repeats after him, *Hear this ye Justices, that I A. B. do not owe to C. D. the Sum of nor any Penny thereof, in Manner and Form as the said C. D. has declared against me. So help me God.* After the Defendant has thus sworn, and the Compurgators given in upon Oath, that they believe he swears true, the Plaintiff is for ever barred.

Wages, is defined to be that which is agreed upon by a Master or Mistress to be paid to a Servant, or other Person hired or retained to do Business for him or her.

Waifs, are such Goods as a Thief having feloniously stolen, on his being closely pursued, are left by the Felon; in which Case the same become forfeited to the King or the Lord of the Manor; as where a Felon being pursued *waves* the Goods, or having them in his Custody, and apprehending that Pursuit is made, he for his own Ease and more speedy Flight flies away and leaves the Goods behind him. Though *Waif* is properly applied to Goods that are stolen; yet it may also be of Goods not stolen; as where a Person is pursued with *Hue and Cry* as a Felon, and he flies and leaves his own Goods; in this Case these shall be forfeited as stolen Goods, or what are properly called *Fugitives Goods*, which are not forfeited till it be found before the Coroner, or otherwise of Record, that he fled for Felony.

Waive, according to the general Acceptation of the Word, signifies to forsake; but is especially applied to a Woman, who for any Crime, for which a Man may be outlawed, is termed *Waive*. See *Reg. Orig.*

WA

Waiver, denotes the paſſing by of a Thing, or a Refuſal to accept thereof.

Walkers, are thoſe that are otherwiſe called *Foreſters*. See *Crompt. Juriſd.*

Waltham Blacks, were a Set of deſperate Villains that ſtarted up in the Reign of King *George* the firſt, and were headed by one whom they ſtiled *King John*; who by Blacking, or otherwiſe diſguiſing themſelves, robbed ſeveral Foreſts, Parks, &c. deſtroyed Cattle, levied Money on their Neighbours, by threatning to fire their Houſes; and committed divers other Outrages. See *Stat.* 9 *Geo.* 1. *cap.* 22. whereby thoſe Villains were declared *Felons*.

Wapentake, is all one with that which we call a Hundred; and it is more eſpecially uſed in theſe Days, in the Counties beyond the River *Trent*. *Termes de la Ley*.

War, is uſed for a fighting between two Kings or Nations, in Vindication of their juſt Rights.

Ward, in our Law is taken divers ways; as a Ward in *London* denotes a Diſtrict or Diviſion of the City committed to the Charge of one particular Alderman: And in that City there are 26 *Wards*, anſwering to the Number of the Lord Mayor and Aldermen, of which every one has his Ward for his proper Guard and Juriſdiction. According to *Manwood* a Foreſt is divided into *Wards*. A Priſon is likewiſe called a *Ward*. And laſtly, before 12 *Car.* 2. *cap.* 24. The Heir of the King's Tenant that held in *Capite*, was called a *Ward*, during his Nonage.

Warden, denotes the Perſon that has the Cuſtody or Charge of any Thing by Office; as *Wardens* of the Fellowſhips in *London*; *Wardens* of the Marches of *Wales*; *Wardens* of the Peace; *Wardens* of the Tables of the King's Exchange; *Warden* of the Armour of the *Tower*; *Wardens* of the Rolls of the *Chancery*; *Warden* of the King's Writs and Records of his Court of *Common Pleas*; *Warden* of the Lands for repairing *Rocheſter* Bridge; *Warden* of the Stannaries; *Warden* and Minor Canons of *St. Paul's* Church; and *Warden* of the Fleet-Priſon, &c.

Wardmote, is a Word mentioned in the Statute of 32 *Hen.* 8. *cap.* 17. and ſignifies a Court held in every Ward of *London*, which is uſually called the *Wardmote* Court, or the *Wardmote* Inqueſt, who have Power to inquire into and preſent all Defaults, &c.

Wardpeny, is taken for Money formerly paid and contributed to Watch and *Ward*.

Wards, according to *Jacob*, was a Court at firſt erected by King *Henry* 8. and afterwards augmented by him with the Office of *Liveries*; and on that Account it was ſtiled the *Court of Wards and Liveries*, which by 12 *Car.* 2. *cap.* 24. is now utterly aboliſhed.

Warnoth, is applied to an ancient Cuſtom, where any Tenant holding of the Caſtle of *Dover*, failed in paying his Rent at the Day, that he ſhould forfeit double, and for the ſecond Failure treble.

Warrant, is uſed for a Precept under Hand and Seal, directed to ſome Officer, commanding him to bring an Offender before the Perſon granting the ſame. *Warrants* of Commitment are either iſſued by the *Privy Council*, a *Secretary of State*, or a Juſtice of the Peace, &c. upon a private Information given in, or where a Witneſs has depoſed againſt an Offender. According to *Dalt*. any one under the Degree of Nobility, may be arrested for a Misdemeanor, or any thing done against the Peace of the Kingdom, by Warrant from a Justice of the Peace; yet if the Person be a Peer of the Realm, he must be apprehended for a Breach of the Peace by Process out of the *King's Bench*, &c. It is held that a Constable ought not to execute a Justice's *Warrant*, where the Warrant is unlawful, or the Justice has no Jurisdiction; and if he does, he is punishable: But that if any Person abuse it by throwing it in the Dirt, &c. or refusing to execute a legal Warrant, it is a Contempt of the King's Process, for which the Offender may be indicted and fined. There is likewise a *Warrant of Attorney*, which is an Authority given by a Client to his *Attorney*, to appear and plead for him; or to suffer Judgment to pass against him by confessing the Action by *Nil dicit*, He says nothing, *Non sum informatus*, &c. I am not informed, &c. A *Warrant* of Attorney that warrants the Action, is of Course put in by the Attornies for the Plaintiff and the Defendant; and on that Account it differs from a *Letter of Attorney*, which passes ordinarily under the Hand and Seal of the Person that makes it, and is executed before Witnesses, &c.

Warranty, according to *West*, is a Covenant or Promise made by Deed by the Grantor, who for himself and his Heirs engages to *Warrant* or secure the Grantee and his Heirs, against all Men for the enjoying of the Thing granted; and *Warranty is real or personal*; real, as when it concerns Lands or Tenements granted in Fee, for Life, &c. And these *Warranties* are either in Deed, as by the Word *Warrantizo*, I warrant; or in *Law*, which is implied by the Word *Dedi*, &c. I have given; and according to *Litt.* a Deed of Gift and Exchange have a *Warranty* in Law implied; and *Warranty* is said to be of three Kinds, viz. *Warranty Lineal*, *Warranty Collateral*, and *Warranty* that commences by Disseisin: *Warranty Lineal* is where a Person seised in Fee makes a Feoffment, whereby he binds himself and his Heirs to *Warranty*, and has Issue a Son, and dies, and the *Warranty* descends to his Son and Heir; for this Reason, that if no Deed with *Warranty* had been made, the Right of the Lands should have descended to the Son as Heir to his Father, and by that Means he would have conveyed the Descent from Father to Son; *Collateral Warranty*, is where the Party, to whom the *Warranty* descends, cannot convey the Title which he has in the Land from him that made the *Warranty*, or shew that he is his Heir, &c. As when Tenant in Tail discontinues, or aliens the Lands, and then dies, leaving Issue, and the Uncle of the Issue, releases to the Discontinuee with *Warranty*, and dies without Issue; this is a *collateral Warranty* to the Issue in Tail and binds his Right without Assets, it descending upon him, and he can't make a Title to the Intail from his Uncle. See *Litt.* 703. and 704.

Warranty by Disseisin, is where a Person having no Right to the Freehold of another, enters and conveys it away with *Warranty*; which shall not bind or bar the Person disseised. For *Warranty of Goods* sold, see Action on the *Case* and *Seal*.

Warrantia

WA

Warrantia Chartæ, is a Writ which lies for a Person that is infeoft with *Warranty*, and is afterwards sued or impleaded in an Assise or other Action wherein he cannot vouch; in which Case he may have this Writ against the Feoffor or his Heir; to compel them to warrant the Land to him; and if the Land be recovered from him, he shall recover as much Lands against the *Warrantor*, &c.

Warrantia Diei, is an old Writ that lies where one has a Day assigned personally to appear in Court to any Action, is in the mean Time imployed in the King's Service, so that he cannot appear in Court at the Day appointed; then he may have this Writ directed to the Justices, in order that they may not record him to be in Default for his not appearing.

Warren, is taken for a Place privileged by Prescription or Grant from the King, for the Preservation of Hares, Conies, Partridges, Pheasants, &c. It is held that where Conies are on the Soil of the Party, he has a Property in them, on Account of the Possession. So that Action lies for killing them; but if they run out of the *Warren*, into another Man's Ground and eat up his Corn, the Owner of the Land in that Case may lawfully kill them.

Waste, is where a Tenant for Life or for Term of another Life, Tenant for Years, Tenant in Dower, or Tenant by the Courtesy, does make *Waste* or Destruction upon the Land he holds, That is to say, pulls down the House, cuts down Timber, or willingly suffers the House to fall, or digs the Ground; in this Case he in Reversion shall have a Writ for that *Waste*, and shall recover the Place where the *Waste* is committed with treble Damages: But if a Person cut down Timber without Licence and therewith repairs old Houses, that shall be deemed no *Waste*; tho' if with that Timber he build a new House, the Cutting down of such Timber is *Waste*. Also the Cutting down of Under-wood, or Willows, which is no Timber, shall not be said to be *Waste*, unless they grow in the Sight or Shadow of the House. *Waste* by the Civil Law is called Dilapidation, and for that the Executor of a Rector or Vicar are answerable in the Ecclesiastical Court. This Word has likewise another Signification, and is taken for those Lands that are not in any particular Person's Occupation, but lie in Common; and they are so called, because the Lord cannot make such Profit of them as of other Lands, on Account of that Use which others have thereof, in passing to and fro, &c. yet according to *Co. Litt.* none may build upon such Lands, cut down Trees, or dig there, without the Lord's Licence. It is here to be observed that a *Lease without Impeachment of Waste*, takes off all Restraint from the Tenant of committing the same; and in such Case he may pull up, or cut down Wood or Timber, dig Mines, &c. at his Pleasure, without being liable to any Action.

Watch, is a Word that denotes a Standing of Centry or attending as a Guard, &c. which is properly intended for the apprehending of Rogues in the Night-time, as *Warding* is for the Day; and for Default to *Watch* and *Ward*, the Township, &c. is punishable.

Water-

WE

Water-Bailiff, is an Officer in Seaport-Towns, appointed for the Searching of Ships, and in *London* the *Water-Bailiff* hath the Supervising and Search of Fish brought thither; and the gathering of the Toll arising from the *Thames*: His Office is likewise to arrest Men for Debt, &c. or other personal or criminal Matters committed upon the River *Thames*.

Water-Gavel, is said to be a Rent paid for fishing in, or other Benefit received from some River.

Water-Ordeal. See *Ordeal*.

Wabeson. See *Jetson*.

Way. See *Highway*.

Wealreaf, (from the *Saxons*) is taken for the Robbing of a Deadman in his Grave.

Wed, according to *Cowel* denotes a Covenant or Agreement; whence comes the Word to *Wedd*, as a *wedded* Husband, a wedded Bondslave.

Week, comprehends seven Days of Time, four whereof make a Month.

Weigh, denotes the Weight of 256 Pounds of Cheese or Wool.

Weights and Measures, are what are used between a Buyer and Seller of Goods, &c. for reducing the Quantity and Price to a Certainty, to prevent Room being given for Deceit and Imposition, and there are two Sorts of Weights in Use in this Kingdom, *viz. Troy-weight* and *Averdupois*: Troy-weight is that which contains 12 Ounces to the Pound, and no more; and thereby Gold, Silver, Pearl, Jewels, Medicines, Silk, &c. are weighed. *Averdupois* contains 16 Ounces in the Pound, by which Weight Grocery Wares, Copper, Iron, Lead, Flesh, Cheese, Butter, Hemp, Wool, &c. are weighed; and by this Weight 12

WH

Pounds over are allowed to every Hundred; so that 112 Pounds make the 100 *Weight*. See *Dalt*. By 8 *Hen*. 6. c. 5. every City, Borough and Town shall have a Common Ballance, with Common Weights sealed, on Pain of 10 *l*. to the City, 5 *l*. the Borough, and 40 *l*. the Town; yet by 11 *Hen*. 7. c. 4. only Cities and Market-Towns are enjoined to to have common Ballances, *Weights* and *Measures*, by which Statute *Weights* are to be marked by the chief Officers of Places, and sealed, &c. And by 17 *Car*. 1. c. 19. Mayors and such Officers once a Year are to take a View of all *Weights* and *Measures*, and burn and destroy such as are defective; and at the same Time are to fine the Offenders, &c. See also 22 *Car*. 2. c. 8. See likewise *Measure*.

Were, antiently denoted a Sum paid for killing a Man, when such Crimes were punishable with pecuniary Mulcts, not Death.

Werelada, is said to have been used where a Person was slain, and the Price whereat he was valued, not paid to his Relations, but the Party denied the Fact; in which Case he was to purge himself by the Oaths of several Persons, according to his Degree; and this was called *Werelada*.

Wergild, is an antient Word which used to denote the Price of *Homicide*, and was paid partly to the King for the Loss of his Subject, partly to the Lord whose Vassal he was, and partly to the next of Kin of the Person slain.

Westminster, is the Place where our High Court of Parliament, and Courts of Judicature sit.

Whales. See *Regal Fishes*.

Wharf, is a broad Place, near some Creek or River, whereon Goods and

and Wares are laid, in order to be shipp'd and transported from Place to Place.

Wharfage, is used for Money that is paid for Landing of Goods at a *Wharf*, or for shipping and taking Goods into a Boat or Barge from thence.

Wharfinger, is taken for the Person that owns or keeps a *Wharf*; and they commonly keep Boats or Lighters of their own, for the carrying out and bringing in of Goods, in doing of which, if any Loss or Damage happen thereto, according to *Lex Mercat.* they are in some Cases liable to answer.

Whitehart-Silver, by some Writers is said to be a Mulct on certain Lands in or near the Forest of *White-hart* which is paid yearly into the *Exchequer*, and was imposed by King *Hen.* 3. upon *Thomas de la Linde* for killing a beautiful *White-Hart*, which that Prince had before spared in Hunting.

Widow, denotes the Relict or one that is bereft of her Husband. In *London* a Freeman's *Widow* may exercise her Husband's Trade, so long as she continues such.

Widow of the King, was she who after her Husband's Death, being the King's Tenant in *Capite*, could not marry again without the King's Consent.

Widowhood, denotes the State of a *Widow*.

Wife, denotes a Woman that is married; whose Will after Marriage, in Judgment of Law is subject to the Will of the Husband; and a Wife cannot contract nor bring Actions, &c. without her Husband.

Will, otherwise termed a *Last Will and Testament*, signifies the Declaration of a Man's Mind and Intention, relating to the Disposition of his Lands, Goods, or other Estate, or of what he would have done after his Death. In the Common Law there is a Distinction made between a *Will* and a *Testament*; for that is called a Will, where Lands or Tenements are given; but where the Disposition concerns Goods and Chattels alone, that is termed a *Testament*: Besides, in a *Will* of Goods there must be an Executor appointed; but not of Lands without Goods, an Executor having nothing to do with the Freehold; and where Lands are given by *Will*, such Gift is called a *Devise*; but where Goods and Chattels are given, they are termed a *Legacy*. It is the Opinion of some that if Lands are devised by *Will*, the *Will* ought to be proved *in Chancery*; but if it be of Goods it must be proved in the *Spiritual Court*; and a *Will* consisting both of Lands and Goods may be proved in the *Spiritual Court*. In the making of a *Will*, there are these several essential Rules to be observed, *viz.* 1. That it be done whilst the *Testator* is of sound Mind and Memory. 2. That there be two Parts thereof, the one to remain in the Hands of the Party that made it; and the other in the Custody of some Friend, in order to render it less liable to be suppressed after the *Testator*'s Death. 3. That the whole be written in one Handwriting, and if possible in one Sheet of Paper or Parchment. 4. In Case there be more Sheets than one, That the *Testator* sign and seal every Sheet thereof, before the Witnesses present at the Execution. The Form of a Will you may see in the *Young Clerk's Magazine*, and other Treatises on Conveyancing.

Window-Tax, is a certain Duty that is charged on the Occupiers or Inhabitants of Houses, and not Landlords; which is 6 s. for such Houses as have ten *Windows* and under twenty; 10 s. for those that have twenty Windows and under thirty; and 20 s. for such as have thirty *Windows*, or more. See 7 & 8 *Wil.* 3. 9 *Anne, cap.* 4. 6 *Geo.* 1. *cap.* 21.

Witam, anciently was used for a Person's purging himself by the Oaths of so many Witnesses according as the Nature of his Offence was.

Wite, was anciently taken for a Punishment, Pain, Penalty, Mulct, &c.

Witena-Gemot, according to *Jacob* was a Convention or Assembly of great Men to advise and assist the King, which in the Time of the *Saxons* was answerable to our Parliament.

Withernam, is a Writ that lies where a Distress is driven out of the County, and the Sheriff cannot make Deliverance to the Party destrained; in which Case this Writ is directed to the Sheriff, commanding him to take as many of the Beasts and Goods of the Party that did thus unlawfully destrain, into his Keeping, until the Party make Deliverance of the first Distress, &c. See *Replevin*.

Withersake, is taken for an Apostate or perfidious *Renegade*.

Witness, is the Person that gives Evidence in any Cause, who being indifferent to each Party, is sworn to speak the Truth, the whole Truth, and nothing but the Truth.

Wolfeshead or **Wolfesheod**, was anciently used to denote the Condition of such Persons as were outlawed in the Time of the *Saxons*, who, if they could not be taken alive, in order to be brought to Justice, might be slain, and their Heads brought to the King; they being no more accounted of than a *Wolf's Head*.

Women. See *Baron and Feme*.

Woodgeld, is taken for the Gathering or Cutting of Wood within the Forest, or Money paid for the same to the Foresters; and this Word is likewise taken to be free from such Payment. *Termes de la Ley*.

Woodmote, was anciently the Name of that Court of the Forest, which is now stiled the *Court of Attachments*.

Wool-Buyers, are taken for such as buy Wool of the Sheep Owners, and carry the same on Horseback to the Clothiers, or to Market-Towns, in order to sell again.

Wreck, is where a Ship is perished on the Sea, and no Person escapes alive out of her, and the Ship or Part thereof so perished, or the Goods of the Ship come to the Land of any Lord; in which Case the Lord shall have the same as a *Wreck* of the Sea: But if a Man or a Dog, or other living Creature escape alive out of the Ship, so that the Party, to whom the Goods belong, come within a Year and a Day, and prove the Goods to be his, he shall have them again. See the Statute of *Westm.* 1. 3 *Ed.* 1. *cap.* 4. But they are no *Wrecks* so long as they remain at Sea, within the Jurisdiction of the Admiralty. The Year and Day that shall subject the Right to be forfeited, must be accounted from the Time of Seizure, in which Time if the Owner of the Goods die, his Executors or Administrators may make Proof: And when the Goods are *Bona peritura*, the Sheriff may sell them within the Year;

provided he disposes of the same to the best Advantage, and accounts for them, &c. See *Wood's Inst.* 214. It is held, where a Ship is ready to sink, and all the Men therein, for the Preservation of their Lives, quit the same, and afterwards she perishes; in that Case if any of the Men are saved, and come to Land, the Goods are not forfeited. By 12 *Anna*, c. 18. If any *Wreck* happen by any Fault or Negligence of Master or Mariners, the Master must make good the Loss; but if the same was occasioned by Tempest, Enemies, &c. he shall be excused: And making Holes in Ships, or doing any thing wilfully tending to the Loss thereof, is by that Statute declared Felony; and by this Act Justices of the Peace are required to command Assistance for preserving Ships in Danger of *Wreck* on the Coasts; and under the Penalty of 100 *l.* Officers of Men of War, and other Ships are to be aiding and assisting in the preserving such Vessels; and further no Person shall enter such Vessel without Leave of her Commander, or a Constable, &c. And Persons carrying away Goods from such Ships, shall pay treble Value: But then the Persons affording such Assistance, shall be paid by the Master a reasonable Reward for *Salvage*, &c.

Wreckfree, was anciently taken to be exempt from the Forfeiture of Ship-wreck'd Goods and Vessels.

Writ, in general, denotes the *King's Precept* in Writing under Seal, and issuing out of some Court, directed to the Sheriff or other proper Officer, and commanding something to be done in relation to a Suit or Action, or giving Commission to have it done, and according to old *Nat. Br.* a Writ is said to be a formal Letter of the King in Parchment, sealed with his Seal, and directed to some Judge, Officer, or Minister, &c. at the Suit of a Subject, for the Cause briefly expressed, which is to be determined in the proper Court according to Law; the Writs in *Civil Actions* are either *Original* or *Judicial*: *Original*, are such as are issued out of the Court of *Chancery*, for the summoning of a Defendant to appear, and are granted before the Suit is commenced, in order to begin the same; and *Judicial Writs* issue out of the Court where the Original is returned, after the Suit is begun. The *Originals* bear Date in the Name of the King; but *Judicials* bear *Teste* in the Name of the Chief *Justice* or Chief *Baron*: And here it is to be observed, that there must be fifteen Days, at least, between the *Teste* and *Return* of all *Writs*, where the Suit is by Original; yet by 13 *Car.* 2. c. 2. delays in Actions by Reason of fifteen Days between the *Teste* and Return of *Writs* in personal Actions and Ejectments are remedied. The most common Writs in daily Use are in Debt, Detinue, Trespass, Action upon the Case, Account, and Covenant, &c.

Writ of Assistance, is a *Writ* that issues out of the Court of *Exchequer* to authorize Persons to take a Constable, or other publick Officer, to seize Goods or Merchandizes prohibited and uncustomed, &c. and it is grounded on the 14 *Car.* 2. *cap.* 1. whereby it is enacted that any Person authorized by a *Writ of Assistance*, may in the Day-time, and in the Presence of a Constable or other publick Officer, break open Doors, Chests, Warehouses and other Places to search

WR

search for and seize prohibited and uncustomed Goods.

Writ of Enquiry of Damages, is a *judicial Writ*, which issues out to the Sheriff upon a Judgment by Default, in Action on the Case, Covenant, Trespass, Trover, &c. whereby he is commanded to summon a Jury to inquire what Damages the Plaintiff has sustained *occasione præmissorum*, on Account of the Premisses; which being returned with the Inquisition, the Rule for Judgment is given upon it; and if nothing be said to the contrary, Judgment is thereupon of Course entred, and this *Writ* likewise lies upon a Judgment obtained on a *Nihil dicit*, *Non sum informatus*, or a Demurrer; but not upon a Verdict: And the Execution thereof is before the Sheriff or his Deputy, at the doing of which both Parties have the Liberty of being heard by their Counsel or Attornies, and Evidence may be given on both Sides. According to *Lill.* where an *Indebitatus Assumpsit* is brought for 100 *l.* for Goods sold, &c. and the Defendant lets this go by Default, if the Plaintiff at the Execution of the Writ of Enquiry, give no Evidence to the Jury of any Goods sold or delivered to the Defendant; in such Case the Jury must find some Damages; because the Defendant has confessed the Action, and thereby admitted that there is Damage; yet as there is not any proved, they ought to find only a Peny, or some such small Matter. A *Writ of Enquiry* may be quashed, if executed without giving due Notice thereof to the Defendant.

Writ of Rebellion, is a Writ issuing out of the Court of *Chancery* or *Exchequer*, against a Person who is in Contempt for not appearing

YE

in one of those Courts. See *Commission of Rebellion*.

Wrong. See *Tort.*

X.

Xenodochium, is taken to denote an Inn, allowed by publick Licence for the Entertainment of Strangers and other Guests.

Y.

Yard-Land, is taken for a certain Quantity of Land, in some Counties 15 Acres; and in others 20; in some 24, and in others 30 and 40 Acres.

Year and Day, denotes a certain Time that by Law determines a Right, or Works of Prescription in many Cases; as in the Case of an *Estray*, if the Owner do not challenge it within that Time, it becomes forfeited to the Lord; so of a *Wreck*, &c. The like Time is given to prosecute Appeals in; and where a Person wounded dies in a *Year and Day* after the Wound received, it makes the Offender guilty of Murder. There is also *Year and Day* and Waste, which is taken to be a Part of the King's Prerogative, by which he has the Profits of the Lands and Tenements *for a Year and a Day* of those that are attainted of Petty Treason or Felony; and the King may cause *Waste* to be made on the Lands, &c. by destroying the Houses, plowing up the Meadows and Pastures, rooting up the Woods, &c. unless the Lord of the Fee agree with him for the Redemption of such Waste.

Yeoman, is a certain Degree of Commoners, by some placed next in Order to Gentlemen; and chiefly Freeholders and Farmers are *Yeomen*; yet this Word, in general, comprehends all under the Rank of Gentlemen, and is a proper Addition to a Name. *Yeoman* is also taken for an Officer of the King's House, between the Serjeant and the Groom; as the *Yeoman of the Stirrup*; to which may be added the *Yeomen* of the Guard, &c.

Yeoven, (from the *Saxons*) is the same with *Given*; and it was formerly used at the End of Indentures and other Instruments, instead of the Day and Year above written. *Jacob.*

Yielding and Paying, are Words made use of in Leases for Terms of Years, &c. and is that Part thereof which is generally termed the *Reddendum*, whereby a Rent or some other Acknowledgment is reserved to the Lessor.

Z.

Zealot, is a Word generally taken in the worst Sense; and on that Account we term one that is a Separatist or *Schismatick* from the Church of *England*, a *Zealot* or *Fanatick*.

FINIS

An **Alphabetical Table** of the most usual Contractions that are to be found in our antient Latin Records and Evidences.

𝔄.	A.	*A.*
Ab̃ïa	Abbatia	*An Abbey*
Acc̃o	Actio	*An Action*
Accõem	Actionem	*Idem*
Accões	Actiones	*Actions*
Ads	Ad Sectam	*At the Suit*
Aiar̃	Animarum	*Souls*
Als	Alias	*Otherwise*
Appõsr̃	Appositus	*Put to*
Archus	Archangelus	*Archangel*
Archi	Archangeli	*Idem*
Archo	Archangelo	*Idem*
Archum	Archangelum	*Idem*
Archiepus	Archiepiscopus	*An Arch-bishop*
Archiepi	Archiepiscopi	*Idem*
Archiepum	Archiepiscopum	*Idem*
Ar̃ or Armr̃	Armiger	*Esquire*
Assess	Assessatus	*Assessed*
Assignd	Assignatus	*An Assign*
Assia	Assisa	*An Assise*
Assias	Assisas	*Assises*
Attorñ	Attornatus	*An Attorney.*

𝔅.	B.	*B.*
Ballia	Balliva	*A Bailiwick*
Ballius	Ballivus	*A Bailiff*
Ballium	Ballivum	*Bail*
Bar̃	Baronettus	*A Baronet*

An Alphabetical Table of the

Bill	Billa	*A Bill*
Bon	Bona	*Goods*
Btus	Beatus	*Blessed*
Bta	Beata	*Idem*
Bti	Beati	*Idem*
Bte	Beatæ	*Idem*
Bto	Beato	*Idem*
Btum	Beatum	*Idem*
Bre	Breve	*A Writ*
Bris	Brevis	*Idem*
Bri	Brevi	*Idem*
Bria	Brevia	*Writs*
Brium	Brevium	*Idem*
Bribs	Brevibus	*Idem.*

C.   C.   C.

Clicus	Clericus	*A Clerk*
Clici	Clerici	*Idem*
Clico	Clerico	*Idem*
Clicu	Clericum	*Idem*
Clicor	Clericorum	*Clerks*
Clm	Clausum	*A Close*
Cli	Clausi	*Idem*
Clo	Clauso	*Idem*
Clis	Clausis	*Closes*
Cõis	Communis	*Common.*
Cõi	Communi	*Idem*
Cõem	Communem	*Idem*
Cões	Communes	*Idem*
Cõibs	Communibus	*Idem*
Compum	Computum	*An Account*
Compi	Computi	*Idem*
Compa	Computa	*Accounts*
Comis	Computis	*Idem*
Cons	Consideratum	*Considered*

Cĩm

most usual Contractions, &c.

Crm	Crastinum	*The morrow*
Cri	Crastini	*Idem*
Cro	Crastino	*Idem*
Cur	Curia	*A Court.*

D. D. D.

Dñus	Dominus	*A Lord*
Dñi	Domini	*Idem*
Dño	Domino	*Idem*
Dñum	Dominum	*Idem*
Dñor	Dominorum	*Lords*
Dcus	Dictus	*said*
Dci	Dicti	*Idem*
Dce	Dictæ	*Idem*
Dco	Dicto	*Idem*
Dcum	Dictum	*Idem*
Dca	Dicta	*Idem*
Dcor	Dictorum	*Idem*
Dcos	Dictos	*Idem*
Dcas	Dictas	*Idem*
Dcis	Dictis	*Idem*
Debium	Debitum	*A Debt*
Debi	Debiti	*Idem*
Debo	Debito	*Idem*
Deba	Debita	*Debts*
Debor	Debitorum	*Idem*
Debis	Debitis	*Idem*
Des	Defendens	*A Defendant*
Defcus	Defectus	*A Defect*
Defcum	Defectum	*Idem*
Dilcus	Dilectus	*Beloved*
Dilci	Dilecti	*Idem*
Dilco	Dilecto	*Idem*
Dilcum	Dilectum	*Idem*
Dnico	Dominico	*Demesne*

An Alphabetical Table of the

Dnicum	Dominicum	Idem
Dnica	Dominica	Idem *Demesnes.*

E.   E.   E.

Ecclia	Ecclesia	*A Church*
Ecclie	Ecclesiæ	*Idem*
Eccliam	Ecclesiam	*Idem*
Eccliarum	Ecclesiarum	*Churches*
Eccliis	Ecclesiis	*Idem*
Ecclias	Ecclesias	*Idem*
Effcus	Effectus	*Effect*
Effcum	Effectum	*Idem*
Eidm	Eidem	*The same*
Exaiatr	Examinatur	*Is examined*
Exatat	Examinatus	*Examined*
Extrapose	Extrapositus	*Put out*
Exex	Executor	*Executor.*

F.   F.   F.

Fcus	Factus	*Made*
Fci	Facti	*Idem*
Fco	Facto	*Idem*
Fcum	Factum	*Idem*
Fca	Facta	*Deeds*
Fcor	Factorum	*Idem*
Fcis	Factis	*Idem*
Flus	Falsus	*False*
Fli	Falsi	*Idem*
Flo	Falso	*Idem*
Flum	Falsum	*Idem*
Flis	Falsis	*Idem*
Feod	Feodum, &c.	*A Fee*
Ftis	Fratris	*Brother*
Fti	Fratri	*Idem*
Ftem	Fratrem	*Idem*

Fte

most usual Contractions, &c.

Frē	Fratre	Idem
Frēs	Fratres	Brethren
Frum	Fratrum	Idem
Frībus	Fratribus	Idem.

G.

Gavis	Gavisus, &c.	Glad
Genr̄	Generosus, &c.	A Gentleman
Geñal	Generalis, &c.	A General
Gtis	Gratis	Free
Gra	Gratia	Favour
G've	Grave	Heavy.

H.

Hēas	Habeas	May have
Hēt	Habet	He has
Hēns	Habens	Having
Hēnt	Habent	They have
Hēnd	Habendum	To have
Hēre	Habere	Idem
Hūit	Habuit	He had
Hūerunt	Habuerunt	They had
Hōis	Hominis	Man
Hōies	Homines	Men
Hoibs	Hominibus	Idem
Humōi	Hujusmodi	The like.

I.

Ido	Ideo	Therefore
Ibm̄	Ibidem	There
Ipe	Ipse	He
Ipúm	Ipsum	Idem
Ipós	Ipsos	Them
Ipis	Ipsis	Idem
Incrum	Incrementum	Increase

Ingtus

An Alphabetical Table of the

Ingrūs	Ingreſſus	*An Entry*
Impþum	Imperpetuum	*For ever*
Inſtanc	Inſtantia	*Inſtance*
Jur	Jurator	*A Jury-man*
Juſtic	Juſticiarius	*A Juſtice.*

L.   L.   L.

Lat	Latitat	*He lies hid*
Leglis	Legalis	*Lawful*
Legle	Legale	*Idem*
Leglia	Legalia	*Idem*
Libe	Libere	*Freely*
Libtas	Libertas	*Liberty*
Libtem	Libertatem	*Idem*
Licet	Liceret	*It might be lawful*
Litime	Legitime	*Lawfully*
Lra	Litera	*A Letter*
Lre	Literæ	*Idem*
Lram	Literam	*Idem*
Lras	Literas	*Letters*
Lris	Literis	*Idem.*

M.   M.   M.

Mia	Miſericordia	*Mercy*
Min	Minime	*Leſs*
Milimo	Milleſimo	*One Thouſand*
Magr	Magiſter	*A Maſter*
Mar	} Mareſchallus {	*Marſhal*
Marelc		*Marſhalſea*
Midx	Middleſex	*Middleſex*
Mis	Miſis	*Coſts.*

N.   N.   N.

Narr	Narratio	*A Declaration*
Natlis	Natalis	*A Birth-day.*

Not

most usual Contractions, &c.

Nob	Nobis	*To us*
Nr	Noster	*Our*
Nra	Nostra	*Idem*
Nri	Nostri	*Idem*
Nro	Nostro	*Idem*
Nrum	Nostrum	*Idem*
Nror	Nostrorum	*Idem*
Nris	Nostris	*Idem*
Noen	Nomen	*A Name*
Nois	Nominis	*Idem*
Noi	Nomini	*Idem*
Noie	Nomine	*Idem*
Noiatr	Nominatur	*Is named*
Nup	Nuper	*Lately*
Nunqm	Nunquam	*Never.*

O.   O.   O.

Occoe	Occasione	*Occasion*
Oēs or Omes	Omnes	*All*
Ois	Omnis	*Idem*
Oi or Omi	Omni	*Idem*
Oem	Omnem	*Idem*
Oia	Omnia	*Idem*
Oium	Omnium	*Idem*
Oib or Oib9	Omnibus	*Idem*
Oio or Omio	Omnino	*Altogether*
Omiod	Omnimodum	*Idem*
Omitr	Omittas	*Omitt.*

P.   P.   P.

ppum	Perpetuum	*Perpetual*
ptin	Pertinentiis, &c.	*Appurtenances*
Ptris	Patris	*Father*
Ptri	Patri	*Idem*
Ptrem	Patrem	*Idem*

ptia

An Alphabetical Table of the

Ptia	Patria	*A Country*
p̄	Prædictus, &c.	*Aforesaid*
p̄dcum	Prædictum	*Idem*
p̄dco	Prædicto	*Idem*
p̄dci	Prædicti	*Idem*
p̄dce	Prædictæ	*Idem*
p̄dcos	Prædictos	*Idem*
p̄dcas	Prædictas	*Idem*
p̄dca	Prædicta	*Idem*
p̄dcis	Prædictis	*Idem*
Pt'r	Præteritus, &c.	*Passed*
Plitum	Placitum	*A Plea*
Pliti	Placiti	*Idem*
Plito	Placito	*Idem*
Plita	Placita	*Idem*
Plitor	Placitorum	*Idem*
Plitis	Placitis	*Idem*
pr'	Proximus	*Next*
Poste	Postea	*Afterwards*
Pt	Post	*After*
ppr	Proprius	*Proper*
ppria	Propria	*Idem*
pprium	Proprium	*Idem*
ppt	Propter	*For*
Pleg de ps	Plegii de pro-sequendo	*Pledges of pro-secuting*
Pō lō	Ponit loco	*He puts in Place*
Parl	Parliamentum	*A Parliament*
Parli	Parliamenti	*Idem*
Parlo	Parliamento	*Idem*
Parla	Parliamenta	*Idem*
Parlis	Parliamentis.	*Idem.*

most usual Contractions, &c.

Q.	Q.	Q.
Qm̃	Quam	*Than*
Quer̃	Querens	*A Plaintiff*
Quereł	Querela	*A Complaint*
Qd̊	Quod	*That or which*
Quibzcunqz	Quibuscunque	*Whatsoever.*

R.	R.	R.
Recogñ	Recognoscendum	*To acknowledge*
Respc̃us	Respectus	*Respect*
Respc̃um	Respectum	*Idem*
Respons̃	Responsum	*Answer*
R̃oria	Rectoria	*A Rectory*
R̃orie	Rectoriæ	*Idem*
R̃oriam	Rectoriam	*Idem*
R̃oriar̃	Rectoriarum	*Idem*
R̃orias	Rectorias	*Rectories*
R̃oriis	Rectoriis	*Idem*
Rñi	Regni	*Reign*
Rõne	Ratione	*Reason*
Rõnabłis	Rationabilis	*Reasonable*
Rõnabłr̃	Rationabiliter	*Reasonably*
Rotło	Rotulo	*Roll.*

S.	S.	S.
Sabti	Sabbathi	*Saturday*
Sac̃rum	Sacramentum	*An Oath*
Sac̃ri	Sacramenti	*Idem*
Sac̃ro	Sacramento	*Idem*
Sac̃ra	Sacramenta	*Oaths*
Sac̃ris	Sacramentis	*Idem*
Sałtm	Salutem	*Greeting*
Sc̃us	Sanctus	*Holy*
Sc̃i	Sancti	*Idem*

An Alphabetical Table of the

Sčo	Sancto	Idem
Sča	Sancta	Idem
Sčor	Sanctorum	Idem
Sčis	Sanctis	Idem
Sčdus	Secundus	*Second*
Sčdi	Secundi	Idem
Sčdo	Secundo	Idem
Sčdum	Secundum	Idem
Sčcium	Scaccarium	*The Exchequer*
Sčci	Scaccarii	Idem
Sčcio	Scaccario	Idem
Scot	Scotia	*Scotland*
Sile	Simile	*The like*
Silis	Similis	Idem
Sili	Simili	Idem
Silem	Similem	Idem
Silr	Similiter	Idem
Silia	Similia	Idem
Silium	Similium	Idem
Silibz	Similibus	Idem
Scilt	Scilicet	*To wit*
Spec or Specificat	} Specificatus, &c.	*Specified*
Sum	Summonitus	*Summoned*
Supdctus	Supradictus	*Above mentioned*
Supdcta	Supradicta	Idem
Supdctum	Supradictum	Idem
Supdctam	Supradictam	Idem
Supdcto	Supradicto	Idem
Supdctæ	Supradictæ	Idem
Supdctor	Supradictorum	Idem
Supdctar	Supradictarum	Idem
Supdctis	Supradictis	Idem
Spialis	Specialis	*Special*
Spiali	Speciali	Idem
Spialem	Specialem	Idem

z   Spiale

most usual Contractions, &c.

Spĩale	Speciale	Idem
Spĩalia	Specialia	Idem
Spĩalium	Specialium	Idem
Spĩalibʒ	Specialibus	Idem
Spĩaliͨ	Specialiter	*Specially*
Spũalis	Spiritualis	*Spiritual*
Spũale	Spirituale	Idem
Spũalem	Spiritualem	Idem
Spũali	Spirituali	Idem
Spũalia	Spiritualia	Idem
Spũalium	Spirtualium	Idem
Spũalibʒ	Spiritualibus	Idem.

T.

Tlis	Talis	*Such*
Tle	Tale	Idem
Tlem	Talem	Idem
Tli	Tali	Idem
Tlia	Talia	Idem
Tlium	Talium	Idem
Tlibʒ	Talibus	Idem
Titlus	Titulus	*A Title*
Titli	Tituli	Idem
Titlo	Titulo	Idem
Titlum	Titulum	Idem
Titlor	Titulorum	*Titles*
Titlos	Titulos	Idem
Titlis	Titulis	Idem
Tent	Tentus, &c.	*Held*
Teñtum	Tenementum	*Tenement*
Teñti	Tenementi	Idem
Teñto	Tenemento	Idem
Teñta	Tenementa	*Tenements*
Teñtor	Tenementorum	Idem
Teñtis	Tenementis	Idem

An Alphabetical Table of the

T'	Teste	*Witness*
Tmīnus	Terminus	*Term*
Tmīni	Termini	*Idem*
Tmīno	Termino	*Idem*
Tmīnis	Terminis	*Idem*
Testm̄	Testamentum	*A Testament*
Testī	Testamenti	*Idem*
Testo	Testamento	*Idem*
Testa	Testamenta	*Testaments*
Testis	Testamentis	*Idem*
Tñsgr̄	Transgressio, &c.	*Trespass*
Trīn	Trinitas, &c.	*Trinity.*

V.   V.   V.

Ven̄	Venit, &c.	*Comes*
Vener̄	Venerunt	*Came*
Vic̄	Vicecomes, &c.	*A Sheriff*
Vid	Vidua	*A Widow*
Vicīn or Vicīn̄	Vicinitas	*Neighbourhood*
Vizt or Videlt	Videlicet	*That is to say,*
Volunt	Voluntas, &c.	*Will.*

V.   U.   U.

Ul̄c	Ultimus	*Last*
Ul̄ca	Ultima	*Idem*
Ul̄cum	Ultimum	*Idem*
Ul̄ci	Ultimi	*Idem*
Ul̄co	Ultimo	*Idem*
Ul̄ca	Ultima	*Idem*
Ul̄cor̄	Ultimorum	*Idem*
Ul̄cis	Ultimis	*Idem*
Uxr̄	Uxor	*A Wife*
Uxis	Uxoris	*Idem*
Uxi	Uxori	*Idem*
Uxēm	Uxorem	*Idem*
Uxē	Uxore	*Idem*

Uxes

most usual Contractions, &c.

Ures	Uxores	*Wives*
Uxor	Uxorum	*Idem.*

W.	**W.**	***W.***
Westm	Westmonasterium	*Westminster.*

X.	**X**	***X.***
Xicm	Duodecim	*Twelve*
Xa	Quindena	*The Fifteenth*
Xam	Quindenam	*Idem, &c.*

Here follow the *Contractions* of *Christian* NAMES.

A.	**A.**	***A.***
Abrus	Abrahamus	*Abraham*
Abri	Abrahami	*Idem*
Abro	Abrahamo	*Idem*
Abrum	Abrahamum	*Idem*
Alex	Alexander	*Alexander*
Alexi	Alexandri	*Idem*
Alexo	Alexandro	*Idem*
Alexum	Alexandrum	*Idem*
Andr	Andreas, &c.	*Andrew*
Anthus	Anthonius	*Anthony*
Anthi	Anthonii	*Idem*
Antho	Anthonio	*Idem*
Anthum	Anthonium	*Idem.*

B	**B.**	***B.***
Bapta	Baptista	*Baptist*
Bapte	Baptistæ	*Idem*
Baptam	Baptistam	*Idem*
Barthus	Bartholomæus	*Bartholomew*

Barthi

An Alphabetical Table of the

Bartͪi	Bartholomæi	Idem
Bartͪo	Bartholomæo	Idem
Bartͪum	Bartholomæum	Idem
Benjamiͬ	Benjaminus, &c.	*Benjamin*
Benedͨus	Benedictus	*Bennet*
Benedͨi	Benedicti	Idem
Benedͨo	Benedicto	Idem
Benedͨum	Benedictum	Idem.

C.   C.   *C.*

X'toforus	Christophorus	*Christopher*
X'tofori	Christophori	Idem
X'toforo	Christophoro	Idem
X'toforum	Christophorum	Idem.

E.   E.   *E.*

Edus	Edmundus	*Edmund*
Edi	Edmundi	Idem
Edo	Edmundo	Idem
Edum	Edmundum	Idem
Edͮus	Edvardus	*Edward*
Edͮi	Edvardi	Idem
Edͮo	Edvardo	Idem
Edͮum	Edvardum	Idem
Eliz'a	Elizabetha	*Elizabeth*
Eliz'e	Elizabethæ	Idem
Eliz'am	Elizabetham	Idem.

F.   F.   *F.*

Francus	Franciscus	*Francis*
Franci	Francisci	Idem
Franco	Francisco	Idem
Francum	Franciscum	Idem.

Galfrus

most usual Contractions, &c.

G.	G.	G.
Galfrus	Galfridus	*Geffrey*
Galfri	Galfridi	Idem
Galfro	Galfrido	Idem
Galfrum	Galfridum	Idem
Gilbtus	Gilbertus	*Gilbert*
Gilbti	Gilberti	Idem
Gilbto	Gilberto	Idem
Gilbtum	Gilbertum	Idem
Godfrus	Godfridus	*Godfrey*
Godfri	Godfridi	Idem
Godfro	Godfrido	Idem
Godfrum	Godfridum	Idem.

H.	H.	H.
Humphus or Humfrus	Humfridus	*Humfrey*
Humfri	Humfridi	Idem
Humfro	Humfrido	Idem
Humfrum	Humfridum	Idem.

I.	J.	J.
Johes	Johannes	*John*
Johis	Johannis	Idem
Johi	Johanni	Idem
Johem	Johannem	Idem.

M.	M.	M.
Michis	Michaelis	Michael
Michi	Michaeli	Idem
Michem	Michaelem	Idem.

N.	N.	N.
Nichus	Nicholaus	Nicholas
Nichi	Nicholai	Idem

Nicho

An Alphabetical Table, &c.

Nicho	Nicholao	Idem
Nichum	Nicholaum	Idem.

P.   P.   P.

Phus	Philippus	*Philip*
Phi	Philippi	Idem
Pho	Philippo	Idem
Phum	Philippum	Idem.

R.   R.   R.

Rcus	Ricardus	*Richard*
Rci	Ricardi	Idem
Rco	Ricardo	Idem
Rcum	Ricardum	Idem.

S.   S.   S.

Stephus	Stephanus	*Stephen*
Stephi	Stephani	Idem
Stepho	Stephano	Idem
Stephum	Stephanum	Idem.

W.   W.   W.

Walkus	Walterus	*Walter*
Walki	Walteri	Idem
Walko	Waltero	Idem
Walkum	Walterum	Idem
Willus	Willielmus	*William*
Willi	Willielmi	Idem
Willo	Willielmo	Idem
Willum	Willielmum	Idem
Wilfrus	Wilfridus	*Wilfred*
Wilfri	Wilfridi	Idem
Wilfro	Wilfrido	Idem
Wilfrum	Wilfridum	Idem.

F I N I S.